From **Today**
of the Old Te
American Bi

THE SHATTERING
OF
SILENCE

The Book of Job

The Bible Study Textbook Series

NEW TESTAMENT

The Bible Study New Testament Ed. By Rhoderick Ice	**The Gospel of Matthew** In Four Volumes By Harold Fowler (Vol. IV not yet available)	**The Gospel of Mark** By B. W. Johnson and Don DeWelt
The Gospel of Luke By T. R. Applebury	**The Gospel of John** By Paul T. Butler	**Acts Made Actual** By Don DeWelt
Romans Realized By Don DeWelt	**Studies in Corinthians** By T. R. Applebury	**Guidance From Galatians** By Don Earl Boatman
The Glorious Church (Ephesians) By Wilbur Fields	**Philippians · Colossians Philemon** By Wilbur Fields	**Thinking Through Thessalonians** By Wilbur Fields
Paul's Letters To Timothy & Titus By Don DeWelt	**Helps From Hebrews** By Don Earl Boatman	**James & Jude** By Don Fream
Letters From Peter By Bruce Oberst	**Hereby We Know (I-II-III John)** By Clinton Gill	**The Seer, The Saviour, and The Saved (Revelation)** By James Strauss

OLD TESTAMENT

O.T. History By William Smith and Wilbur Fields	**Genesis** In Four Volumes By C. C. Crawford	**Exploring Exodus** By Wilbur Fields	**Leviticus** By Don DeWelt
Numbers By Brant Lee Doty	**Deuteronomy** By Bruce Oberst	**Joshua · Judges Ruth** By W. W. Winter	**I & II Samuel** By W. W. Winter
I & II Kings By James E. Smith	**I & II Chronicles** By Robert E. Black	**Ezra, Nehemiah & Esther** By Ruben Ratzlaff & Paul T. Butler	**The Shattering of Silence (Job)** By James Strauss
Psalms In Two Volumes By J. B. Rotherham		**Proverbs** By Donald Hunt	**Ecclesiastes and Song of Solomon** — By R. J. Kidwell and Don DeWelt
Isaiah In Three Volumes By Paul T. Butler		**Jeremiah and Lamentations** By James E. Smith	**Ezekiel** By James E. Smith
Daniel By Paul T. Butler		**Hosea · Joel · Amos Obadiah · Jonah** By Paul T. Butler	**Micah · Nahum · Habakkuk Zephaniah · Haggai · Zechariah Malachi** — By Clinton Gill

SPECIAL STUDIES

The Church In The Bible By Don DeWelt	**The Eternal Spirit** By C. C. Crawford	**World & Literature of the Old Testament** Ed. By John Willis	**Survey Course In Christian Doctrine** Two Bks. of Four Vols. By C. C. Crawford
New Testament History — Acts By Gareth Reese		**Learning From Jesus** By Seth Wilson	**You Can Understand The Bible** By Grayson H. Ensign

BIBLE STUDY TEXTBOOK SERIES

THE SHATTERING

OF

SILENCE

Job, Our Contemporary

by
James D. Strauss

———

Questions for Discussion
by Don DeWelt

———

Today's English Version

College Press, Joplin, Missouri

Library of Congress Catalog Card Number: 77-155412
International Standard Book Number: 0-89900-015-0

DEDICATION

To Three Deans
Whom God is Using
To Break His Silence
In the Contemporary World

Dr. Wayne Shaw, Dean
Lincoln Christian Seminary

Dr. Rondal Smith, Dean
Lincoln Christian College

Prof. Thomas Ewald, Dean of Students
Lincoln Christian College

Colleagues at Lincoln Christian College and Seminary

and

To My Three J's
Jewel, Joye, and Jeaneen

and

To One Christian Rabbi

To our late brother, colleage, and contemporary of Job
John Ralls, Rabbi par-excellence in Job's native tongue,
who more than any among us knew the wealth to be mined
from the rich ore of the Old Testament.

67167

v

vi

TABLE OF CONTENTS

JOB, OUR CONTEMPORARY [1]

MYSTERY OF SILENCE
Chapters 1—2

MEANING OF SILENCE
Chapters 3—14

---

[1] Basic structure of outline provided by my colleague, S. Edward Tesh, professor of Old Testament in Lincoln Christian Seminary.

---

[2] V. Frankl's theory of therapy which maintains that healing can take place only in a context of honest, full communication.

(These discourses of Elihu, "at this point of the book . . . constitute at once a negative and a positive preparation for the hearing of the voice from the whirlwind (38:1—42:6). Rhetorically, they produce dramatic suspense between the hero's oath of clearance and the intervention of the Lord. Psychologically, they show man's inability to cope with the depth of human suffering and isolation. Theologically, they condition the hero for the immediate confrontation of God. Elihu does not succeed in making Job realize the theological dimensions of sinfulness: only the voice from the whirlwind can achieve this purpose. But Elihu does succeed in raising Job's thinking from the level of egocentricity to a region at whose center God reigns in glory. In this respect the discourses of Elihu are comparable to a vestibule of the holy of holies" (Samuel Terrien, in *Interpreters Bible*).

THE SHATTERING OF SILENCE

(At last an audience with God, as Job had desired [9:3, 14-20; 9:28-35; 13:22; 31:25-37]. But, no charges are brought, and nothing is explained. Job is questioned in such a way as to reveal that man is in no position to judge God. Man is finite, God infinite. God's wisdom is beyond the grasp of man.)

PREFACE

Every believer in Jesus Christ, Job's vindicator, who is old enough to be aware of international crises of cataclysmic proportions which are visible in our western civilization, as well as the Third and Fourth Worlds, must become sensitive to the intensification of evil in all our personal and social structures. Population explosions, famine, wars and rumors of wars, inflation, radically destructive revolutions, diseases, and general deterioration of our social institutions are everywhere self-evident.

The Book of Job is a highly relevant resource for Christians who are asking, as did Job, "Why me, God?" Our commentary could be used effectively for both personal, devotional, and group studies of a central concern of our era—Why so much human hurt, hunger, and hopelessness if God has spoken once and for all in His Son, Jesus Christ? If God has actually shattered his silence in Christ, then the cult of evil and the astronomical number of those participating in the syndrome of insecurity must be banished from the world by the "new man" in Christ. This volume is set forth to the whole body of believers who are called of God to proclaim His triumph over tragedy in that Christ was raised from the dead. Christ, our hope, has redeemed us from sin and evil and has given to us the ministry of reconciliation; therefore, we must "always be prepared to make a reasoned defense for the hope" that orients our daily participation in the fallen universe (I Peter 3:15). This is especially true in that ours is the time in which the presence of evil keeps millions from giving heed to God's silence shattering and final word—Jesus Christ. To all believers, He is the only reorderer of the disordered world (Col. 1:10; Eph. 1:10).

INTRODUCTION TO THE BOOK OF JOB[1]

Milieu of Misery

Theme: The fundamental problem with which we are confronted in the Book of Job is why do the righteous suffer? Basically, the theme is not why does suffering exist in a world which was created by an *all-powerful* and *holy* Creator-redeemer God, but why do "good" people suffer? Two issues must be faced by all Christians as we witness to a world where evil intensifies daily: (1) What is the *cause* of evil? Is it caused by rebellion against the will of God? or economic and social injustice? or genetic and environmental factors? etc. and (2) What is the explanation of evil?[2]

Name of Major Participant in the Drama:[3] The work receives its title from the dominant character 'Iyyov. The name

---

[1] See especially the studies of E. J. Young, *An Introduction to the Old Testament* (Grand Rapids: Eerdmans, 1949), pp. 309-321; and R. K. Harrison, *Introduction to the Old Testament* (Grand Rapids: Eerdmans, 1969), pp. 1022-1046; for more mature students of the Word, see A. Bentzen, *Introduction to the Old Testament* (Copenhagen: G. E. C. Gad Pub., 6th ed., 1961), Vol. II, 174-179; E. Sellin and G. Fohrer, *Introduction to the Old Testament* (Nashville: Abingdon, E. T. by David Green, 1968), pp. 323-334; Eissfeldt, *The Old Testament—An Introduction* (New York: Harper & Row, E. T. by P. R. Acbroyd, 1966 printing), pp. 454-470; and H. H. Rowley, *From Moses to Qumran* (New York, 1963), pp. 141-83.

[2] See my essay, "Silence, Suffering, and Sin: Present Evil in the Presence of a loving, holy, creator-redeemer God." The Christian view of the origin and solution to the problems precipitated by the fact of sin and evil have been challenged by the genetic and behavioral sciences since the 18th century. Biblically sin and its solution have both *vertical* (God) and *horizontal* (social) dimensions. Presently the WCC and its Neo-Marxian interpretation of Salvation contains only the horizontal category, i.e., economic, social, and political factors which preclude the production of the "good society" full of "good individuals." The Gospel has imperative social ramifications, and when these two dimensions are in harmony in the concrete world of human injustice, contemporary man might once more believe, as did Job, that our hope is based only in resurrection possibilities. Resurrection and hope are inseparable. The resurrection of Christ (Job's Vindicator and our Suffering Servant—Ps. 22; 69; 73; Isa. 53:1ff; the books of Habakkuk and Jeremiah) is a history-making event and not only an historical event.

[3] The Hebrew of the word for Job probably comes from the root system meaning "come back" or "repent." The name Job appears in Akkadian inscriptions, in the Mari documents of the eighteenth century B.C., and in the Tel el Amarna Letters. See Koehler-Baumgartner, *Lexicon*, for suggestion that root comes from word "to hate, be at enmity," and Brown-Driver-Briggs, *Lexicon*, for suggestion that the root means "object of enmity."

is transcribed as *Iob* in the Septuagint (Greek translation or LXX of the Hebrew Bible); and also *Iob* in the Latin Vulgate. It is only one further step in deriving the English name Job, which is the Latinized form of the Greek *Iob*. The book carries the name of its main character and that he was an historical person is strongly supported by Ezekiel 14:14 and James 5:11. There is no positive evidence which justifies the widely held view that the book is anonymous.

Place in the Bible: Canon: The LXX and our English Bibles place Job in the historical books. In the Syriac versions, the book is located after the five books of Moses, because according to the Baba Bathra 14b, Moses was the author of Job.[4] At least this suggestion fits the patriarchal description in chapter one. The description plus the fact that not one Israelite institution is mentioned could indicate the antiquity of the events related in the book. There is not one positive bit of evidence against the probability that Job was a contemporary of Abraham, Isaac, and Jacob. But some of the grammar of the prologue (latter sections) suggests a later linguistic revision. Yet the critical arguments which attack the unity of the book are at best unnecessary. All available information can fit the period between the time of the Patriarchs and the Solomonic age without doing violence to the evidence or the intellectual integrity of the student. The exact date is impossible to determine, but the biblical text does not provide a specific date, so we are in no way jeopardizing God's activity in the production of The Book of Job.

Possible Dates for Authorship: The Prologue-Epilogue reflect an authentic patriarchal background. Job's wealth consists of cattle and slaves, like Abraham (Job 1:3; 42:12; compare

---

[4] For Jewish opinions concerning the person of Job, see full discussion in H. Torczyner (Tor-Sinai), *Commentary on Job,* 1957 ed., pp. 391-94; Baba Bathra, 14b-15a. Rabbinic opinions range from ca. 2100-1550 B.C. The strongest reason for this suggestion is the presence of some words in both the Pentateuch, i.e., Patriarchal to Persian period, and Job such as 'ulam, tnu'ah, netz, yeret, and qshitah. On the critical issues concerning The Canon see reprint of W. H. Green, *General Introduction to the Old Testament* (Joplin: College Press, 1972) with my annotated bibliography "The Canon Revisited," pp. 1-14.

with Gen. 12:16 and 32:5). Job appears as priest for the family
(Job 1:5; 42:8). There is neither central place of worship nor
priesthood mentioned in the text of Job. Both the Chaldeans
and Sabeans are pictured as nomadic raiders which antedates
their later more developed political and economic order (Job
1:15, 17). The money unit mentioned in 42:11 is found elsewhere in the Old Testament only in Gen. 33:19 and Jos. 24:32.
Literary features and motifs found in Job are found also in
both Akkadian and Ugaritic literature. This fact would also
suggest a date sometime during the patriarchal period. The
antiquity of Job is already assumed in Ezekiel 14:14, 20 (see
also James 5:11) where he is identified along with Noah and
Daniel. Mesopotamian parallels[5] to Job also reinforce the
strong probability of a patriarchal date for Job.[6]

Literary Influence of Job: Job's influence persists to this
very hour in the last quarter of the 20th century. "The play's
the thing," declares Hamlet, "wherein I'll catch the conscience
of the king." *Catch* is the emphatic word. Job is our contemporary, and he "catch"es every invader of his domain of
despair. Is Job Camus' absurd man? Well, then, how about
Dostoevsky's "Underground Man," who eloquently says
"Shower upon [man] every earthly blessing . . . even then out
of sheer ingratitude, sheer spite, man would play you some
nasty trick . . . simply to introduce into all this positive good
sense his fatal fantastic element."[7] This fatal contradiction
on the side of evil is also posited by both C. S. Lewis and
Tolkien. These two weavers of words powerfully reveal that the
mystery of evil is its rejection of joy. The same type of joy was
experienced by Job when he knew the *who* (came to the knowledge that his redeemer lives) even when he did not understand

---

[5] For full citation of this literature, see *Babylonian Wisdom Literature* by W. G.
Lambert (Oxford, 1960), pp. 27ff; see also J. Nougayrol, "une version ancienne du
'juste souffrant." *Revue Biblique*, 1952, pp. 239-50.

[6] For complete survey on opinions on date for Job, see R. Pfeiffer, *Introduction
to Old Testament* (New York: Harper, 1948), pp. 675-78.

[7] F. Dostoyevsky, *Notes From the Underground* (New York: The Dial Press, 1945),
p. 149.

the *why*.

The consummate art of "the matterhorn of the Old Testament" surely fulfills the three criteria of literary greatness which are set forth by Rabbi Reichert: (1) "It must have the dimension of height—that upreaching unto the sublime that brings one nearer to the eternal stars . . . (2) It must possess the dimension of breadth—that spacious universal quality that can leap barriers of creed, color, rank, and race . . . and (3) It must know the dimension of depth—that drive into the soul of man where as in a well of living water surge the profoundest tensions of the heart. . . ."[8]

Martin Luther as theologian, Tennyson as poet, Dostoevsky as novelist, each proclaims that Job is indeed a literary work of the most sublime order. Job is indeed every man's contemporary because he is infinitely provocative. Job has sent both messages of hope and despair into the human orbit. Job's God is not the solution to the haunting penetration of the dark spaces of a lonely universe. Dostoevsky exclaims "How much that is great, mysterious, and unfathomable there is in it!" From Aeschylus' *Prometheus Bound* to Pascal's *Pensées* we detect a cycle of suffering, doubt, and acceptance by faith of that most disturbing dimension of existence: Why do the righteous often suffer and the unrighteous often prosper? The French unbeliever, Voltaire, projects the problem of evil and innocent suffering in his *Candide*. The persistence of modern man's preoccupation is startlingly expressed in Camus' *La Peste*. Here we wrestle all night to no avail with the horror of meaningless suffering and death. This emphasis has a long history of classic expression. It is widely conceded that Dante's *Divine Comedy* and Milton's *Paradise Lost* have penetratedly looked long into the Jobian pool reflecting on our cosmic hurt. The paradox of the *Fortunate Fall* appears in the first book of *Paradise Lost*. Why is Satan permitted to roam freely among men?

---

[8] Victor E. Reichert, *Job*, The Soncino Press, 1946, p. XIII.

That reiterated crimes he might
Heap on himself damnation, while he sought
Evil to others and enraged might see
How all his malice served but to bring forth
Infinite goodness, grace and mercy shown
On man by him seduced. . . .[9]

Only in the resurrection is hope assured that we will not be
eternally deaf to the voice of God.

During the great intellectual, spiritual, and cultural revolutions, between Milton and Goethe, the influences of radical
individualism and deism began to capture the modern mind.
Faust is placed in a Jobian situation. The "Prologue in Heaven"
is heavily saturated with the presence of Mephistopheles. He
extracts from Faust the promise of his soul in exchange for
youth and pleasures "no man yet has seen."[10] Faust's radical
naturalistic individualism becomes crystal clear as he seeks
meaning through his own will and action, not in the will and
purpose of Job's creator-redeemer God. Faust's anti-God
diatribe reveals his intentions:

My bosom of its thirst for knowledge sated,
Shall not, henceforth, from any pang be wrested,
And all of life, for all mankind created
Shall be within mine inmost being tested:
The highest, lowest forms my soul shall borrow,
Shall heap upon itself their bliss and sorrow,
And thus, my own sole self to all their selves expanded,
I, too, at last shall with them all be stranded![11]

Faust's ultimate salvation is through sheer human effort

---

[9] John Milton, "Paradise Lost," *The Complete Poetical Works of John Milton*,
ed. by H. F. Fletcher (Cambridge: Houghton Mifflin, 1941), Bk I, lls pp. 214-219;
compare also his Samson Agonistes, patterned after Sophocles and Euripides.

[10] J. W. von Goethe, *Faust*, Parts I & II, *Great Books of the Western World* (Chicago: Encyclopedia Britannica, Inc., 1952), 1.1674.

[11] J. W. von Goethe, *Faust*, Part I. Tr. by B. Taylor (New York: Three Sirens Press),
p. 94.

"who e'er aspiring, struggles on, For him there is salvation."[12] (Sounds strangely similar to the contemporary Neo-Marxian Liberation by Revolution thesis.) Another Jobian figure appears in Melville's *Moby Dick.* Melville's Ahab is embittered by the blows of fate and knowing no way to challenge it except at the origin of his own plight. Ahab responds to Starbuck's questioning that

> All visible objects, man, are but as pasteboard masks.
> But in each event—in the living act, the undoubted deed—
> There, some unknown but still reasoning thing
> Put forth the mouldings of its features from behind
> The unreasoning mask. If man will strike, strike through
> the mask![13]

One of the most penetrating of all modern[14] literary efforts to employ the Job theme is Archibald MacLeish in his *J.B.* While the drama recreates the tale of the trial of Job, the character of J.B. is completely at variance with the biblical Job. J.B. is caught in a vortex of violence. We enter the drama as two has-beens, Nickles and Mr. Zuss, decide to perform the story of Job late at night after the roar of the crowd is gone, silenced by the night. Mr. Zuss, after finding the proper masks, takes the role of God, while Nickles plays Satan. Satan's mask represents the nihilism[15] that tempted Job. The God-Mask represents absence or indifference. MacLeish's God is not the source of *Shattered Silence,* which is necessary for solution. We

---

[12] Goethe, *Faust*, Part II, v. lls, 11936-37.

[13] H. Melville, *Moby Dick* (New York: The American Library of World Literature, 1963), p. 167. Here we can note Melville's rebellion against his classic Calvinistic background.

[14] Of all modern authors, only Robert Frost approaches our theme in a light vain. In his *Masque of Reason*, an epilogue or "Forty-Third Chapter" to the Book of Job, is a verbal caricature of a scientific-technological world-life viewpoint. See his *Selected Poems of Robert Frost* (New York: Holt, Rinehart and Winston, 1962); and Elizabeth S. Sergeant, *Robert Frost: The Trial by Existence* (New York: Holt, Rinehart and Winston, 1960).

[15] See my essay on nihilism in *The Baker Dictionary of Christian Ethics,* ed. by C. F. H. Henry, p. 461ff.

are left with the Father of Lies who is the rebel and accuser of God, not J.B. J.B. loves life and expresses a buoyant faith in the God who has blessed him. The misfortune strikes a series of paralyzing blows. Into this arena of suffering come three callous scavengers who "smell the . . . human smell of heartsick misery . . ." After J.B. cries out "My God! My God! What have I done?!"[16] he is trounced with Marxian critique, behavioral psychology, and a Freudian view of culturally caused guilt. Bildad expounds that "guilt is a sociological accident."[17] Eliphaz rhapsodizes on the naturalistic philosophy of Skinnerian behaviorism, while denying the reality of such concepts as guilt and justice. Zophar, the ecumenically open-minded cleric, declares that "Guilt is illusion? Guilt is reality! The one reality there is!"[18] J.B. defends God's integrity, while Zophar, collapsing, repeats, "without the Fall, we're Madmen all, . . ."[19] MacLeish concludes that only humanism, i.e., the "light within" can honestly respond to the enigma of suffering.

As we plunge deeper into the century toward 2000, we have been blessed in the western world with a brilliant and powerful spokesman for a Christian view of suffering. Such a one is Alexander I. Solzhenitsyn. We have been both warned and blessed by this voice in the wilderness from his *One Day in the Life of Ivan Denisovich* to the multiple volumed *The Gulag Archipelago*. Solzhenitsyn is a fellow sufferer with Job, our contemporary. With splendid elaboration he declares that only the resurrection can ultimately give meaning to suffering and death. In part four of Gulag, entitled "The Soul and Barbed Wire," he uses as epigraph I Cor. 15:51: "Behold, I show you a mystery; we shall not all sleep, but we shall all be changed." Here he identifies with Job and our contemporary need for God to continually Shatter His Silence during our suffering.

---

[16] A. MacLeish, *J.B.*, p. 117.

[17] *Ibid.*, p. 121.

[18] *Ibid.*, p. 122.

[19] *Ibid.*, p. 127. (Esp. for Job theme analysis *The Voice out of the Whirlwind*, ed. by R. E. Hone (San Francisco: Chandler Pub., 1960); and Jean Steinmann, *La Livre De Job* (Paris: Cerf., 1954), pp. 323-379.

STRUCTURAL ANALYSIS OF JOB

Simplified Outline

Job 1-2: Facing the Issues, A Look at the Whole Book, Prologue of Job

Job 3-5: A Surprising Lament, Enter Eliphaz, "The Speeches of Job's Friends," "Eliphaz's First Speech"

Job 6-8: Enter Eliphaz, "Job's Responses to Eliphaz," "First Response to Eliphaz," Bilious Bildad, "The Speeches of Bildad," "Bildad's First Speech"

Job 9-11: Bilious Bildad, "Job's Responses to Bildad," "First Response to Bildad," Zealous Zophar, "The Speeches of Zophar," "Zophar's First Speech"

Job 12-15: Zealous Zophar, "Job's Responses to Zophar," "First Response to Zophar," Enter Eliphaz, "Eliphaz's Second Speech"

Job 16-18: Enter Eliphaz, "Second Response to Eliphaz," Bilious Bildad, "Bildad's Second Speech"

Job 19-21: Bilious Bildad, "Second Response to Bildad," Zealous Zophar, "Zophar's Second Speech," "Second Response to Zophar"

Job 22-25: Enter Eliphaz, "Eliphaz's Third Speech," "Third Response to Eliphaz," Bilious Bildad, "Bildad's Third Speech"

Job 26-31: Bilious Bildad, "Third Response to Bildad," Hymn to Wisdom, Summation for the Defense

Job 32-34: Enterprising Elihu, "The Fourth Friend," "Elihu's First Speech," "Elihu's Second Speech"

Job 35-37: Enterprising Elihu, "Elihu's Third Speech," "Elihu's Fourth Speech"

Job 38:1—40:5 Voice from the Whirlwind, "God's First Speech," "First Reply to God"

Job 40:6—42:17 Voice from the Whirlwind, "God's Second Speech," "Second Reply to God," Epilogue of Job, Summary

xxviii

A PRE-PROLOGUE OVERVIEW

The Meaning of the Book of Job
For A Broken World

Concerning the Book of Job, M. Buttenweiser, an American Jewish scholar, says: "Of the masterpieces which time has handed down, of the Biblical books especially, it is the one which in every age is felt to be modern."[1] Job is indeed our contemporary. The significance of this great work of art for the weary pilgrim who walks in a world filled with injustice and violence cannot be over-estimated. Mankind's experiences over the past three decades have brought him face to face with the horrors of the concentration camps and the haunting loneliness of Bangladesh's hungry and homeless. As alienation, exploitation, and human tragedy continue to fragment humanity, we turn once more into the full face of Job to gaze deeply into his wounded soul and ask once more—Why?

Suffering—A Common Near Eastern Theme

The precise literary form of Job has received extended but often futile treatment. The same fundamental question raised by Job, i.e., Why do the righteous suffer? is also discussed by the Greek philosophical tragedies and Babylonian wisdom poetry. Prometheus, though not innocent, responds to his excessive punishment with bitterness and despair. Oedipus Rex undergoes an accumulation of destructive misfortunes; and the sadistic cruelties of the gods crush Heracleus. But does the Book of Job fit the exact framework of the Near Eastern writings? The Accadian "Suffering Just Man" reveals that the Babylonian tradition was also vitally concerned with the theme of the suffering of the just.[2] Though the theme is in common with the Book of Job, H. H. Rowley is correct in asserting that "in truth it is

---

[1] M. Buttenweiser, *The Book of Job* (New York, 1922), p. 3.

[2] For excellent survey of the principal extrabiblical texts relating to the problem, see Jean Steinmann, *Le Livre de Job* (Paris: Les Editions du Cerf, 1955), pp. 17-55; see also H. H. Rowley, *From Moses to Qumran* (New York: Association Press, 1963), pp. 141ff.

not to be classed with any of these."[3]

Before the message of Job can be appreciated and assimilated, it will first be necessary to examine the contents of the book as a whole. The Prologue 1:1—2:13 relates to us that Job is both a pious and prosperous man. Job lives east of Palestine in the Arabian desert.[4] Two factors in the prologue suggest a pre-Mosaic age: (1) Job is priest for the household, and (2) he presents a burnt offering ('olah). The Prologue suggests a parallel with the results of the fall narrative in Genesis. In Genesis the first sin has disorganizing power, to such an extent that the relationship between (1) *God and man* is fractured; e.g. especially since first scientific revolution to the Death of God, Political Theology and Politico-Revolutionary Theology have replaced salvation by grace revealed in Jesus; (2) *Man and self;* i.e., man is internally fragmented, e.g. the pathology scrutinized by both psychologists and psychiatrists; (3) *Man and others* reflect the disordering power of sin, egs. social, economic, political anomalies; and (4) *Man and creation* are at variance, e.g. ecological crisis. Each of these factors also appears in the structure of the Jobian drama.

Drama Begins—First Series in Dialogue

The patience of Job exhibited in the Prologue is short lived as patience metamorphisizes into complaint—3:1-26. It next appears in the drama of the three friends who enter the world of Job's hurt by way of *Discourses*—4:1—31:40. Eliphaz's first speech—4:1—5:27—begins by showing apparent sympathy for our uninhibited sufferer. But sympathy soon turns into an assertion of Job's guilt. Job's first response in 6:1—7:21

---

[3] *Ibid.*, p. 142.

[4] The appendix of the LXX rightly places the land of Uz on the border of Idumea and Arabia. Some details of the book suggest some relation to the Egyptian world, egs. 28:1-11—mines of Sinai; 40:15—41:26; Behemoth and Leviathon; 9:26—boats made of reeds; 8:11—papyrus; 40:11-12—lotus, compare evidence in Father Tournay's reply (*Revue Biblique*, Paris, 1956, p. 134) to Fr. Humbert's claims in *Recherches sur les sources egyptiennes de la litterature sapientiale d' Israil* (Paris), pp. 75-106.

is a bitter outcry to God, either pardon him, or he will perish. Bildad's first discourse—8:1-22—asserts that Job's plight is the result of God's judgment. Job's second response in 9:1— 10:22 begins by admitting the basic principle set forth in Bildad's speech, and then enters upon a verbal tirade against God for His irresponsible use of power both in bringing Job into existence and permitting evil to elicit more than its just share of Job's happy and prosperous life. Next, impetuous Zophar enters the discussion—11:1-20. He first condemns what has been going on in the form of the "multitude of words," then sets forth God's incomprehensibility as balm for Job's woes. Job reveals that he is unimpressed by Zophar's wisdom—12:1—14:22. Intensification of Job's suffering causes him to bitterly complain about God's injustice. Job's discourse on the weakness and frailty of man (chp. 14) ends the first round of discourses.

Cycle Two of Dramatic Debate

In the second cycle of speeches, Eliphaz appeals to ancient tradition for his words of wisdom—15:1-35. Nevertheless, ancient authorities cannot heal the gaping wound in Job's existence. Despondency and despair fill his cross-shaped emptiness. Realizing the futility of his friend's council, Job responds for the fourth time—16:1—17:16. Sinking more deeply into his sickness unto death, Job still hopes in ultimate vindication as he confesses that the "righteous shall hold on his way and he that has clean hands shall grow stronger and stronger," 17:9. Bildad's second speech—18:1-21—describes the fate of the wicked, but he has not modified his basic assumptions which appear in the first cycle of discourses. Next appears Job's fifth response—19:1-29. His complaint is now lodged against his friends. His hope is grounded in his *Living Vindicator* (go'el—one who defends, see Book of Ruth).[5] In Zophar's

---

[5] In light of Resurrection hope, Job can now reflect on his existential situation without being destroyed by suicidal despair. Contemporary man is preoccupied with *Death*

second speech—20:1-29—he describes the punishment of the unrighteous. Job's sixth response in 21:1-34 manifests his new confidence and boldly exposes the fallacies of his former attitudes.

Third Cycle in the Dramatic Dialogue

Eliphaz's third discourse initiates the third cycle of this dramatic dialogue—22:1—31:40. Eliphaz's defective theology appears in his assertion that God has no interest in human suffering, except as an instrument for vindicating His justice. Job's former bitterness is absent from his seventh reply—23:1—24:25. Bildad's third speech in 25:1-6 is a brief protest against Job's former response. But Job immediately asserts that Bildad's counsel is irrelevant pedantry—26:1-14. The silence of God has been shattered, and thus Job can set forth in mashal or proverb his final and mature conclusion regarding the relationship of a just sovereign creator-redeemer God to human suffering—27:1—31:40.

The Speeches of Elihu: 32:2—37:24

Though the poetical accents are retained throughout the section of the text, there is a change indicated by an introduction in prose—32:1-5. The Aramaic flavor and other grammatical peculiarities do not necessarily imply different authorship as many contemporary commentators would imply.

Yahweh's Speech and The Final Shattering of Silence
38:1—42:6

Only if God is sovereign Lord of heaven and earth is there

---

in the face of despair. See my essay, "Death Be Not Proud," in *The Seer, The Saviour, and The Saved* (Joplin, Mo.: College Press, 1972 ed.), pp. 366-381; and E. Becker, *The Denial of Death* (New York: Free Press, pb); and J. Choron, *Death and Western Thought* (New York: Collier, MacMillan, 1975 printing, pb.)

grounds for human hope in the midst of a tragedy-filled world where malignant forces perpetrate injustice in millions of lives. Human suffering is a problem fit for God![6]

QUESTIONS FOR DISCUSSION

1. What is the basic problem in the book?
2. How is righteousness defined? Was Job a sinless man?
3. Is all suffering permitted by God or is some of it sent by God?
4. What can we learn about Satan from the book of Job?
5. Show the contemporary value of the book of Job.
6. What is the response of Greek philosophical thought to suffering?
7. Job is a very ancient book—how do we know of its antiquity?
8. How can we compare Job with the fall of man in Genesis?
9. Job is patient—but he is also full of complaint—why? Is this a contradiction of terms?
10. Of what does Eliphaz accuse Job? Why does he do it?
11. Job does have hope—what is it?

---

[6] For the critical problems involved in a study of The Book of Job, see especially H. H. Rowley's brilliant survey, "The Book of Job and Its Meaning," in his *From Moses to Qumran* (New York: Association Press, 1963), pp. 141-183; E. F. Sutcliffe, *Providence and Suffering in the Old and New Testaments* (London, 1955); N. H. Torczyner (Tur-Sinai), *Job,* reprinted in 1957; M. Dahood, "Some Northwest-Semitic Words in Job," *Biblica* XXXVIII, 1957, 306-20; Charles L. Feinberg, "The Poetic Structure of the Book of Job and the Ugaritic Literature," *Bibliotheca Sacra,* CIII, 1946, 283-92; W. A. Irwin, "Job's Redeemer," *Journal of Biblical Literature,* LXXXI, 1962, 217-29; C. Kuhl, "Neure Literarkritik des Buches Hiob," *Theologische Rundschau* NF, XXI, 1953, 163-205—indispensable survey; P. W. Skehan, "Strophic Patterns in the Book of Job," *Catholic Biblical Quarterly* XXIII, 1961, 125-43; M. A. Regnier, "La distribution des chps. 25-28 du livre de Job," *Revue Biblique* XXXIII, 1924, 186-200; R. J. Tournay, "L'ordre primitif des chapitres XXIV-XVIII du Livre de Job," *Revue Biblique* LXIV, 1957, 321-34; R. A. F. MacKenzie, "The Purpose of the Yahweh Speeches in the Book of Job," *Biblica,* XL, 1959, 435-44; W. G. Lambert, *Babylonian Wisdom Literature,* Oxford, 1960; and Sellin-Fohrer, *Introduction to the Old Testament* (Nashville: Abingdon, E. T., 1968), pp. 304ff, esp. pp. 323-334.

INTRODUCTORY BIBLIOGRAPHY

A. GENERAL:

Hulme, W. E. *Dialogue in Despair.* Abingdon, 1968.
Kent, H. H. *Job—Our Contemporary.* Eerdmans, pb., 1967.
Kierkegaard, S. *The Sickness unto Death,* pb.
_____. *The Gospel of Suffering,* pb., English Translation, 1955, (many paperback editions).
Lewis, C. S. *The Problem of Pain,* pb.
Morgan, G. C. *The Answers of Jesus to Job,* 1950.
Unamuno, M. de. *The Tragic Sense of Life,* pb.
Wenham, J. W. *The Goodness of God.* InterVarsity Press, 1974, pb.

B. EVIL:

Hick, John. *Evil and the God of Love.* pb., 1966.
Hopkins, H. A. E. *The Mystery of Suffering.* London, 1959.
Journet, C. *The Meaning of Evil.* New York, 1963.
Sutcliffe, E. F. *Providence and Suffering in the Old and New Testament.* Edinburgh, 1953.

C. COMMENTARIES:

Basic but often contain technical discussion:

Andersen, F. I. *Job.* InterVarsity Press, 1976.
Delitzsch, F. *Job.* 2 vols. Eerdmans reprint.
Dhorme, E. *A Commentary on the Book of Job.* New York: Nelson E.T., 1967—The paradigm of a technical commentary—for advanced students only.
Driver, S. R. and Gray, G. B. *A Critical and Exegetical Commentary on the Book of Job.* ICC, T. & T. Clark, 1950.
Pope, M. H. *Job, Introduction;* translation and notes—New York: Doubleday, Anchor Bible, 1973.

Rowley, H. H. *The Book of Job.* New York: Nelson, 1970.

D. SPECIALIZED WORKS PERTAINING TO THE BOOK OF JOB:

Blommerde, C. M. *Northwest Semitic Grammar and Job.* (Biblica et Orientalia, 1969).

Calvin, John. *Sermons from Job.* English Translation, L. Nixon, 1952.

Candale, G. S. *Animals of the Bible,* 1970.

Coleman, E. D. *The Bible in English Drama,* 1931.

Fisher, L. R., ed. *Ras Shamra Parallels I.* (Analecta Orientalia, No. 49, 1973) The Job parallels are given on pp. 472-74 of the index. They number over 250. Parallels are found throughout Job and are an impressive mark of literary unity.

Kidner, D. *Psalms* 1-72. InterVarsity Press, 1973—for felicitous introduction to Hebrew Poetry, pp. 1-4.

Reymond, P. "L'eau, sa vie et sa signification dans l'ancien Testament," supplement, *Vestus Testamentum,* VI, 1958.

Siggens, L. D. "Mourning: A Critical Survey of the Literature," *International Journal of Psycho-Analysis,* 1966, pp. 14-25.

Ploeg, J. P. M. van der, and Woude, A. S. van der, eds. *Le Targum de la Job de Grotte XI de Qumran,* Leiden, Brill, 1972.

MAJOR JOURNAL ABBREVIATIONS
USED IN THIS COMMENTARY

AASOR	*The Annual of the American Schools of Oriental Research,* New Haven
AnBibl	*Analecta Biblica,* Rome
ANEP	*The Ancient Near Eastern Texts relating to the Old Testament* edited by J. B. Pritchard, Princeton, 2nd ed., 1955
AOS	*American Oriental Series,* New Haven
BA	*The Biblical Archeologist,* New Haven
BASOR	*The Bulletin of the American Schools of Oriental Research,* New Haven, Baltimore
BDB	F. Brown, S. R. Driver, C. A. Briggs, eds. of W. Gesenius' *Hebrew and English Lexicon of the Old Testament,* 2nd ed. Oxford, 1952
BH	*Biblia Hebraica,* edited by R. Kutel, 9th ed., 1954
BHEAT	*Bulletin d'Histoire et d'Exegese de l'Ancien Testament,* Louvain
Bibl	*Biblica,* Rome
BJRL	*The Bulletin of the John Rylands Library,* Manchester
BS	*Bibliotheca Sacra,* Dallas, Texas
BWL	*Babylonian Wisdom Literature* by W. G. Lambert, Oxford, 1960
BZAW	*Beihefte Zür Zeitschrift für die alttestamentliche Wissenschaft,* Berlin
CAH	*The Cambridge Ancient History,* Cambridge
CBQ	*The Catholic Biblical Quarterly,* Washington
ET	*The Expository Times,* Edinburgh, Aberdeen
HAT	*Handbuch zum Alten Testament,* edited by Otto Eissfeldt, Tübingen, J. C. B. Mohr (Paul Siebeck)
HThR	*The Harvard Theological Review,* Cambridge, Mass.
HUCA	*Hebrew Union College Annual,* Cincinnati, Ohio

ICC	*The International Critical Commentary of the Holy Scripture of the Old and New Testaments,* Edinburgh
INT	*Interpretation,* Richmond, Virginia
INTB	*The Interpreter's Bible,* Nashville, Tennessee
IDB	*The Interpreter's Dictionary of the Bible,* Nashville, 1962
JBL	*Journal of Biblical Literature,* Philadelphia
JewEnc	*The Jewish Encyclopedia,* New York
JNES	*Journal of Near Eastern Studies*
JQR	*The Jewish Quarterly Review,* Philadelphia
JThS	*The Journal of Theological Studies,* Oxford
KBL	Ludwig Kohler, Walter Baumgartner, *Lexicon in Veteris Testamenti libros,* Leiden, 1953
LThK	*Lexikon für Theologie und Kirche, Bd 1-10,* Freiburg, 1957ss
QT	Qumran Targum (11Qtg Job) *Le Targum de Job de la Grotte XI de Qumran,* edited by J. P. M. van der Ploeg and A. S. van der Woude, Leiden: Brill, 1972
RB	*Revue Biblique*
RE	*Review and Expositor,* Louisville, Kentucky
VT	*Vetus Testamentum,* Leiden
VTS	*Supplements to Vetus Testamentum,* Leiden
ZATW	*Zeitschrift für die alttestamentliche Wissenschaft*

MAJOR REFERENCE WORKS

Dhorme, *Job*	E. Dhorme, *A Commentary on the Book of Job.* New York: Nelson, E.T., 1967
Leveque, *Job*	Jean Leveque, *Job et Son Dieu* Tomes I-II, Paris: Librairie Lecoffre J. Gabalda, 1970
Pope, *Job*	M. H. Pope, *Job.* The Anchor Bible. New York: Doubleday, 1965
Rowley, *Job*	H. H. Rowley, *Job,* New Century Bible. Ontario, Canada: T. Nelson & Sons Ltd., 1970
Steinmann, *Job*	Jean Steinmann, *Le Livre de Job.* Paris: Cerf., 1955

PROLOGUE TO THE GREAT TESTING
MYSTERY OF SILENCE
JOB: MIRROR OF MODERN MAN—1:1—2:13

1. Job's wealth and piety (1:1-5)

TEXT 1:1-5

1 There was a man in the land of Uz, whose name was Job; and that man was perfect and upright, and one that feared God, and turned away from evil. (2) And there were born unto him seven sons and three daughters. (3) His substance also was seven thousand sheep, and three thousand camels, and five hundred yoke of oxen, and five hundred she-asses, and a very great household; so that this man was the greatest of all the children of the east. (4) And his sons went and held a feast in the house of each one upon his day; and they sent and called for their three sisters to eat and to drink with them. (5) And it was so, when the days of their feasting were gone about, that Job sent and sanctified them, and rose up early in the morning, and offered burnt-offerings according to the number of them all: for Job said, It may be that my sons have sinned, and renounced God in their hearts. Thus did Job continually.

COMMENT 1:1-5

Job: Whose Face in the Mirror?
"He who knows the *why* can bear with any *how*."[1] Nietzsche

The prose narrative of The Prologue (i.e., 1:1—2:13) is divided into six scenes that unfold the dramatic events leading to the dialogue. The drama contains sparse yet powerful simplicity. Charges and countercharges are always delivered with an economy of words. Each dialogue is between two

---

[1] Viktor Frankl, the Viennese psychiatrist, powerfully uses Nietzsche's insight in the development of his Theory of Logotherapy. Dr. Frankl is surely psychologically correct in his assertion that man's search for meaning is our most fundamental project. See his *Man's Search for Meaning.*

1

individuals only. Though these dialogues do not engender optimism for the "miracle of dialogue" (cf. R. Howe, *The Miracle of Dialogue*), as is often suggested in contemporary encounter literature, we do see the fundamental issues in sharpest focus. But only when Yahweh speaks (chapters 38:1— 41:26) do we experience *The Shattering of Silence.* Only the word from outside[2] can break the solitude of man enslaved in a world of sin and evil.[3]

Verse 1—The verse does not begin with the standard Hebrew formula for a historical narrative "there was a man"—*wayehi 'is* but rather with the expression "a man there was (*'is hayah*). This phrase indicates a new beginning without any reference to preceding events (e.g. II Sam. 12:1 and Es. 2:5).[4]

There is strong evidence for two different locations for Job's homeland—Uz. Technically the location is feasible in either one of the two options: (1) One suggests Hauran, and (2) the other to Edom. As Job is identified with "the people of the east," (1:3) Hauran, i.e., a location northeast of Palestine, is more in harmony with the claim in verse 3. Job is not described as a Jew but rather as a foreigner. This claim suggests that we should not connect Uz with any specific contact in Palestine. Lamentations 4:21 says that the daughter of Edom dwells in Uz. Yet in Jeremiah 25:20 Uz is described separately from Edom, but related to the Philistines. Uz is said to be a son of Dishan and related to the area of Seir in Genesis 36:28. Uz is the name of a son of Aram in Genesis 10:23 (see Josephus, *Antiquities,* 1.6.4) and of Nahor's oldest son in Genesis 22:21. In a special appendix to Job in the LXX (42:17), Job's homeland

---

[2] My forthcoming exegetical-theological commentary on The Johannine Epistles will be entitled *The Word from Outside.* How vital John's message is to the church in a world which is continuing to experience a crisis in *knowledge* and *community.*

[3] For analysis of this literary structure, See G. Fohrer's "Zur Vorgeschichte und Komposition des Buches Hiob," *Vetus Testamentum,* 6 (1956), 249-67; H. Rongy, "Le prologue du livre de Job," *Revue ecclessiastique de Liege* 25 (1934), 168-71; and N. M. Sarua, "Epic Substratum in the Prose of Job," *Journal of Biblical Literature* 76 (1957), 13-25.

[4] For exhaustive discussion, see E. Dhorme, *Job* (New York: Nelson, E. T., 1967, pp. 1ff.

is located near Idumea and Arabia. The above possibilities place Job in both the north and the south, but in all probability the suggestions that Hauran or a northern location is closest to the data found in the verse is to be accepted.

The root meaning of the name Job also presents a difficulty. In Hebrew the name is spelled *'Iyyob* (possible root *'yb*—meaning the hated one or aggressor). Job the person is pictured as a great near eastern potentate, who was in all probability a comparatively young man (15:10). His character is analyzed in four virtues: (1) *Blameless* (Hebrew *-tam* is similar in import to the Latin word *integer,* perfect or well rounded). His character is without flaw or inconsistency. The Hebrew word does not mean sinless; perhaps our English word "integrity" adequately expresses the connotation. (2) *Upright* (Heb. *Yasar*—life and behavior measured up to a standard; one who is upright in relations to others—see Ps. 25:21 for parallel between perfection and uprightness). (3) *Fearing God* means a relationship based on *obedient* reverences, cf. Prov. 3:7; 14:16; 16:6. (4) *Avoiding evil*—or turned away from evil means that Job deliberately and persistently chooses the good. Right living before God always means obedience to the will of the Lord; and reverence is the very foundation of obedience.

Verse 2—Directly following the analysis of Job's character, our text reveals the close connection between Job's uprightness and the Lord's reward (Ps. 127:3; 128:6) of many children. The grammar contains a consecutive *waw* which could be translated "and so there were born to him" as a result of his righteousness (compare with I Sam. 2:5; Ruth 4:15; and Job 42:13).

Verse 3—Job's blessings include such property as a seminomadic potentate might possess (Gen. 12:16; 24:35). The collective term *miqneh* is translated by substance in our A. V. text. The term usually designates cattle and sheep and does not include the main sign of the nomad's wealth, camels and asses. The female asses were valued for both their milk and their foals. They were also easier to ride than the male asses. Job's wealth was so enormous that he was the greatest (Heb.

3

verb be, become great—Gen. 26:13) of all the easterners (Hebrew *qedem*). In Genesis 29:1 the term describes the Arameans near the Euphrates. In Isaiah 11:14 the word refers to Israel's enemies to the east, i.e., Ammonites, Moabites, and Edomites in contrast to the Philistines on the west. (See also Judges 6:3, 33; 7:12; Jeremiah 49:8; Ezekiel 25:4).

Verse 4—Though it is not clear from our text whether or not the sons were married, they had their own homes, like David's two sons (II Sam. 13:7; 14:28). Like David's daughters, Job's unmarried daughters stayed in their father's house (II Sam. 13:7, 8, 20). It is not to be assumed that we are being confronted with incessant celebration, though the verb forms are in the perfect tense of habit. Probably, the feast was a yearly affair, such as found in Exodus 34:22; Leviticus 23:26; Numbers 29:35; and II Chronicles 7:9. This much is certain from our text—each of the seven sons had his celebration in his own house, and that their sisters were present at each meeting. Those commenters who suggest impropriety, rather than deep affection, have the disadvantage of being at variance with the entire spirit of the drama. Misfortune came upon Job's household when there was no rational explanation for the calamity. We must also remember that not one of Job's three friends suggested any impropriety within Job's family.

Verse 5—Apparently Job did not visit any of the festive celebrations. As soon as sons and daughters had completed the days of their feast, Job sends a summons to his sons. The purpose of the summons is to invite them to the sacrifices which he would offer, as in the case of Balaam, Numbers 23:1, 14, 29. The prescribed sacrifices in Job 42:8 are seven bulls and seven rams, as in the Balaam account. The term translated "burnt offerings" is not the term used for "sin offering," but it is clear that the sacrifice is for the propitiation of sins which they might have committed during the heat of wine. Job rose up early (Heb. verb *hsem* means to rise early and also connotes quickly, urgently—Jer. 7:13; Hos. 6:4; Zeph. 3:7) and offered the sacrifice. The Hebrew word translated "renounced" *Elohim* in our text literally means blessed. It is a

4

euphemism for *cursed* and is so used in Job 1:11; 2:5, 9; I Kings 21:10, 13; Ps. 10:3.[5] The Hebrew word translated "heart" means even in the inner thoughts and attitudes. The Hebrew *lev* or *levav* means seat of the intellect and will more than of the affections and emotions.[6]

2. Satan's insinuation (1:6-10)

TEXT 1:6-10

(6) Now it came to pass on the day when the sons of God came to present themselves before Jehovah, that Satan also came among them. (7) And Jehovah said unto Satan, Whence comest thou? Then Satan answered Jehovah, and said, From going to and fro in the earth, and from walking up and down in it. (8) And Jehovah said unto Satan, Hast thou considered my servant Job? for there is none like him in the earth, a perfect and upright man, one that feareth God, and turneth away from evil. (9) Then Satan answered Jehovah, and said, Doth Job fear God for nought? (10) Hast not thou made a hedge about him, and about his house, and about all that he hath, on every side: thou hast blessed the work of his hands, and his substance is increased in the land.

COMMENT 1:6-10

Verse 6—Here we encounter the first scene in heaven—1:6-12: Yahweh is represented as an oriental king seated on His throne. Here Satan is challenged to find a single flaw in

---

[5] Much that is found in S. H. Blank, *Hebrew Union College Annual*, XXIII, Part I, 1950-1, 83ff, is unnecessary for adequate understanding of this euphemism.

[6] For thorough analysis of the biblical vocabulary translated "heart," see J. Behm, "Kardia," *TWNT* 2, 609-616; and R. Jewett, *Paul's Anthropological Terms* (Leiden: Brill, 1971), esp. pp. 305ff.

Job's character. Satan first responds by impugning the motives of Job. The name of the game is that every man has his price! The Hebrew text means "there came a day when" with the succeeding phrase introduced by *waw* consecutive and the imperfect verb form.[7] The "sons of Elohim" are identified in the LXX as angels or messengers (compare Gen. 6:1-4; 11:5ff; Job 38:7; and I Kings 22:19ff). The phrase "to station themselves" (Heb. *lehityasseb*) implies the attitude of the servant before his master (see also Zec. 6:5). The same term describes how David stood before Saul in I Sam. 16:21 and Jer. 52:12. The definite article stands before the word Satan, i.e., The Satan. Satan is the adversary at law, the accuser (see Ps. 109:6; and compare I Chron. 21:1 with its parallel passage II Sam. 24:1). The character of Satan is clearly defined: He will challenge the uprightness of Job, and inflict calamities on Job.[8]

Verse 7—Yahweh asks Satan to give an account of his doings. God's question does not imply ignorance, rather it becomes a point of encounter (see Exodus 4:2). Satan responds that he has been roaming throughout the earth (see I Peter 5:8). The Hebrew is the common verb—to walk or stroll (Numbers 11:8; II Sam. 24:2; and Zechariah 1:10-11). The image does not suggest that of vigilantes but rather of prosecutors. We are now at the boundary of the action of the drama.

Verse 8—Job is God's paradigm of a righteous man. Yahweh asks Satan, Have you turned your attention to my servant Job? The Hebrew grammar presents a marvelous image—"to

---

[7] For the evidence regarding the specific "day" which the text might have in mind, see R. de Vaux, *Ancient Israel* (New York: McGraw Hill, 1961), pp. 502-4. The day clearly depicts two councils in which Job's fate is at stake. Compare Job's vindication with Kafka's *The Trial* in which cosmic justice is unavailable.

[8] The origin and nature of most technical discussions of Satan contain naturalistic comparative religion assumptions. In our age when people have difficulty believing in God, surely we should not be surprised regarding their hesitancy to accept the ontological existence of Satan. See appropriate Kittel articles and especially R. S. Kluger, *Satan in the Old Testament* (Evanston: Northwestern University Press, 1967); H. Torczyner suggests the idea that the origin of Satan is to be found in the concept of Persian secret police. See his commentary on Job.

give one's heart" or focus strong attention on an object of vital concern. The locution of "my servant Job"⁹ is a characteristic of both the Prologue (2:3) and Epilogue (42:7, 8). But why all the concern for Job's integrity? Yahweh sets forth Job as an example of perfect human loyalty to Himself. Satan sceptically interprets Job's characteristics as mere self-interest. Satan vows Job is a kind of Machiavellian prince. At the heart of this confrontation between Yahweh and Satan is—who is the organizing center for life and all reality—man or God? The issue is a central factor in our twentieth century malaise. What is the value of such a victory—that is of locating a single righteous man in all the earth? (Ezekiel 14:14, 20 appeals to the examples of Noah, Daniel, and Job; see also Jeremiah 31:29; Job 22:27-30; Isaiah 52:13—53:12).

Verse 9—"Is it for nothing (Heb. *Hinnam*—without justification, irrationally, or arbitrarily) that Job fears Elohim?" Satan's irony is expressed in this rhetorical question. Here we meet Job our contemporary. The question is addressed to every man. Do God's good gifts come to those whose motives are self-interest? If we do good, good fortune follows as a reward; if we do evil, punishment follows. The American Dream syndrome runs dangerously parallel to the assumption that success implies the blessings of God; and failure entails God's disfavor. What is the relationship of piety to prosperity? Are there no poor righteous? (Note the poor in America and the Third and Fourth Worlds). The Bible consistently warns about the snares of riches (Deut. 32:15; Prov. 30:8ff; Ps. 73:3-9; Mark 10:23).

Verse 10—Satan now declares—No wonder Job is loyal. *You* (Hebrew is emphatic) have built a protective hedge (Hebrew—surround with thorns for purposes of protection) about him. The thorn hedge is Job's prosperity! Everything Job does, he prospers. Little wonder that he is God's man. Job's possessions are literally "breaking out" (Hebrew verb means to overflow—

---

⁹ See C. Lindhagen's exhaustive study, *The Servant Motif in the Old Testament,* 1950; also Jeremias' excellent study.

Gen. 38:29; Mic. 2:13) in uncontrolled prosperity. "While his prosperity is a barrier against attack, it is without barrier against its own increase" (Rowley, *Job,* p. 32).

3. Satan asks and receives permission to test Job. (1:11, 12)

TEXT 1:11, 12

(11) **But put forth thy hand now, and touch all that he hath, and he will renounce thee to thy face. (12) And Jehovah said unto Satan, Behold, all that he hath is in thy power; only upon himself put not forth thy hand. So Satan went forth from the presence of Jehovah.**

COMMENT 1:11, 12

Verse 11—Satan suggests to Yahweh that if you remove the security of his wealth, he will curse you to your face (see 6:28; 13:15; 16:8). The form of the Hebrew sentence is that of an *oath* meaning "I swear that he will curse you." (Is Marx correct, too—is *alienation* caused by things, or the absence of things?)

Verse 12—Yahweh accepts Satan's challenge. What is the real motive of Job's piety? Will Job love God when his physical security is removed? Real piety must be based in disinterestedness with respect to reward or punishment. How relevant this issue is for contemporary man! Job immediately is confronted with Satan's attack. The speed with which God allows Satan to afflict Job is surely evidence of God's complete trust in Job's integrity and piety.

4. The first trial—loss of possessions and loved ones (1:13-19)

TEXT 1:13-19

(13) And it fell on a day when his sons and his daughters were eating and drinking wine in their eldest brother's house, (14) that there came a messenger unto Job, and said, The oxen were plowing, and the asses feeding beside them; (15) and the Sabeans fell *upon them*, and took them away: yea, they have slain the servants with the edge of the sword; and I only am escaped alone to tell thee. (16) While he was yet speaking, there came also another, and said, The fire of God is fallen from heaven, and hath burned up the sheep and the servants, and consumed them; and I only am escaped alone to tell thee. (17) While he was yet speaking, there came also another, and said, The Chaldeans made three bands, and fell upon the camels, and have taken them away, yea, and slain the servants with the edge of the sword; and I only am escaped alone to tell thee. (18) While he was yet speaking, there came also another, and said, Thy sons and thy daughters were eating and drinking wine in their eldest brother's house; (19) and, behold, there came a great wind from the wilderness, and smote the four corners of the house, and it fell upon the young men, and they are dead; and I only am escaped alone to tell thee.

COMMENT 1:13-19

Verse 13—With telling efficiency Satan proceeds to carry out the permitted testing. Swift disasters strike at the household of Job. In rapid succession the entire life style of Yahweh's servant has been violently removed. Violence[10] is basic to

---

[10] As violence is a fundamental sign of contemporary social, economic, and political disorder, how must Christians respond? See Jacques Ellul, *Violence*, NY: Seabury, E. T., 1969; also his *Hope in Time of Abandonment*, NY: Seabury, E. T., 1973, and G. Sorel's classic *Reflections on Violence*. This theme is a fundamental issue and must be faced if we are to encounter the contemporary world in Christ's name.

9

Satan's method in every age. The formula "now there was a day" suggests a lapse of time between the scene in heaven and the initiation of the trial. This suggests that the family disasters are not involved in either his or his family's misconduct. The unexpectedness of each event leaves no time interval for Job to rationalize any explanation of the ensuing crises. How will Job respond to misfortune? How will he analyze his new condition—in view of his explicit trust in Yahweh?

Verse 14—Life is progressing as usual; then the disorganizing phenomena occur. How will Job cope with his new situations? We are told that men must always either "cope" or "adjust" to the factors about us. Is this the only option for contemporary believers in Job's vindicator? (See Toffler's *Future Shock* and discuss.)

The messenger emphasizes the calm before the raid. Just the right conditions for surprise. "The oxen were ploughing" describes that the plans for the fall work were being fulfilled. The season for ploughing is winter and everything is perfectly normal; then disaster strikes. Job will have passed from wealth to destitution in four "moments."

Verse 15—"The Sabeans fell upon them." But who are the Sabeans?[11] (Hebrew *seba*—Genesis 10:7; I Chronicles 1:9; Genesis 25:3; I Kings 10; Isaiah 40:6; Jeremiah 6:20; Job 6:19; and Joel 3:8) The specific identification is contingent upon the location of Uz. There are Sabeans related to distant South Arabians. These people are located ca. 1000 miles south of Jerusalem from which the Queen of Sheba came to visit Solomon (I Kings 10:1-10). The distance seems highly improbable for a raid to Job's homeland. The Sabeans meant here are perhaps those from the region now known as Yemen (see W. Phillips, *Qataban and Sheba*, NY, 1955). In Job 6:19, Sheba is parallel to Tema. In Isaiah 21:13 and Jeremiah 25:23 Tema is in the geographical area of Dedan. This would imply

---

[11] The specific identification is quite complex and unnecessary for our purposes, but see R. L. Bowen, *Archeological Discoveries in South Arabia*, 1958, pp. 215-86; and G. W. van Beek, *"South Arabian History and Archeology,"* in the Bible and the Ancient Near East (in honor of W. F. Albright, NY, 1961). There are three groups.

a North Arabian identification.

The lone surviving witness to the disaster bears the sad tidings—"I alone" escaped the sword. This feature is found a number of times in the Old Testament (egs., I Kings 18:22; Genesis 44:20; Josiah 13:12; II Samuel 13:32; and Ezekiel 9:8.) The Hebrew is very vivid in its description of death by the sword. Literally the text says "and the servants (boys) were killed by the mouth of the sword" (Hebrew idiom expressing the fact that the sword ate its victims).[12]

Verse 16—Even "while he was still speaking" disaster intensified. The first calamity came from the hands of man; the second from nature. The Hebrew grammar indicates the simultaneity of the two disasters. The "fire of God" is probably lightning. In the great Elijah encounter in I Kings 18:38, the lightning is called the "fire of Yahweh" to emphasize that the source was not Baal, the Canaanite weather god. The fire was so devastating that it literally "ate" all before it (see Job 15:34; 20:26; 22:20; and Numbers 16:35; 26:10).

Verse 17—First the Sabeans fell on them; then the Chaldeans. The mention of the Chaldeans here suggests an early origin for Job, i.e., from a marauding tribe. From the ninth century B.C., when they first appear in the Assyrian records of Ashurnasirpal II (884-859) to the period when they provided the rulers of the neo-Babylonian empire of Nebuchadrezzar the Old Testament is aware of the presence of the Chaldeans. They finally gained control of Babylon in the late eighth century B.C. before Nabopolassar, in 626 B.C., founding the Neo-Babylonian Empire. The description of the Chaldeans here in Job is from a much earlier period than the neo-Babylonian era. The idiom translated "formed three bands" literally means "put three heads," i.e., they made a three-pronged attack. This strategy is mentioned in Judges 7:16, 20; 9:34, 43-45; and I Samuel 11:11; 13:17.

---

[12] For the archeological data on these ancient swords see T. J. Meek, *Bulletin of the American Schools of Oriental Research*, 122, 1951, pp. 31-33. Note further use of imagery in Revelation 1:16; 2:16; 19:15 where sword proceeds from the mouth of the Messiah.

Verses 18, 19—Now disaster will strike deep into the very heart of Job's household. Before, property was the object of destruction, now persons. The scene now reverts to that sketched in vs. 13. All the children are gathered in the house for the final hour of doom. Only a whirlwind could have struck the four corners of the house. The first and third calamities were brought about by human agency, and the second and fourth were the results of nature's violence. Satan has power over both men and nature. He has the greatest power in the universe, second only to our creator-redeemer God. The word translated "young men" is the same one rendered as "servants" in the previous accounts.

5. Job maintains his integrity. (1:20-22)

TEXT 1:20-22

(20) Then Job arose, and rent his robe, and shaved his head, and fell down upon the ground, and worshipped; (21) and he said, Naked came I out of my mother's womb, and naked shall I return thither: Jehovah gave, and Jehovah hath taken away; blessed be the name of Jehovah. (22) In all this Job sinned not, nor charged God foolishly.

COMMENT 1:20-22

Verse 20—Job had received the agonizing news while seated. Then according to Near Eastern custom, he "arose" and "rent his robe" as a sign of grief (Genesis 37:29; II Samuel 13:31). The robe (*me'il*) was the mantle worn over the tunic by men of high social rank (I Samuel 15:27), or by the high priest (Exodus 28:31). Then follows the rite of mourning, i.e., shaving his head (Isaiah 15:2; 22:12; Jer. 7:29; Amos 8:10; Micah 1:16). Now Job falls to the ground in reverential awe, not in despair (II Samuel 1:2; II Chronicles 20:18). Job has defeated

12

Satan in the first series of catastrophes and now bows himself submissively to Yahweh's merciful grace.

Verse 21—Job now reveals his complete resignation to his tragedy. Satan's oath to God has thus far been completely broken. God's faith in his servant Job has been vindicated. Job's triumphant shout of victory "blessed be the name of the Lord" contains the tetragrammaton, i.e., the only name for God in the Old Testament. In the dialogue sections, Yahweh is avoided and El, Eloah, and Shaddai appear. Whereas the prologue and epilogue freely employ the name Yahweh. Job's friends never use the name Yahweh. Though Job is not a Jew, he is always presented as a worshipper of Yahweh (1:1), and Job 1:8 plainly declares that God accepts him as such. Job employs the name Yahweh in the prologue only in his expression of resignation 1:21. Only once in the dialogue does the name Yahweh appear (12:9), and here it is uttered by Job. In the rubrics introducing the speeches of Yahweh and Job's replies (38:1; 40:3, 4) the name Yahweh appears.

Verse 22—In all these threatening circumstances, Job did not sin, either mentally or by some overt act like charging God with foolish (*tiplah*—makes perfectly good sense in spite of efforts to amend the word. The Hebrew term means reproach or blame) behavior. The entire universe is intrinsically interrelated. Systems, analysis, the ecological crisis, etc. suggest a staggering interdependence exemplified by both nature and all social systems. This should provide a fundamental insight into the cause, responsibility, and explanation of misfortune. Neither classical fatalism nor contemporary radical determinism, both genetic and environmental, can explain that evil as well as good is intentional. Dostoevsky asks the more penetrating question—"Why is there any good?," not "why is there evil?" in the world. Job has pronounced Yahweh's name three times, which otherwise he avoids. Now we turn to Satan's more drastic measures. Will Job betray Yahweh?

TODAY'S ENGLISH VERSION

Satan Tests Job

1 There was a man named Job, who lived in the land of Uz. He worshipped God and was faithful to him. He was a good man, careful not to do anything evil. ² He had seven sons and three daughters, ³ and owned 7,000 sheep, 3,000 camels, 1,000 head of cattle, and 500 donkeys. He also had a large number of servants and was by far the richest man in the East.

⁴ His sons used to take turns giving a feast, to which all the others would come, and they always invited their three sisters to join them. ⁵ After each feast was over, Job would get up early the next morning and offer sacrifices in order to purify his children. He always did this because he thought that one of them might have sinned by insulting God unintentionally.

⁶ When the day came for the heavenly beings to appear before the Lord, Satan was there among them. ⁷ The Lord asked him, "What have you been doing?"

Satan answered, "I have been walking here and there, roaming around the earth."

⁸ The Lord said, "Did you notice my servant Job? There is no one on earth as faithful and good as he is. He worships me and is careful not to do anything evil."

⁹ Satan replied, "Would Job worship you if he got nothing out of it? ¹⁰ You have protected him and his family and everything he owns. You bless everything he does, and you have given him enough cattle to fill the whole country. ¹¹ But now suppose you take away everything he has—he will curse you to your face."

¹² The Lord said to Satan, "All right, everything he has in your power, but you must not hurt Job himself." So Satan left.

Job's Children and Wealth Are Destroyed

¹³ One day when Job's children were having a feast at the home of their oldest brother, ¹⁴ a messenger came running to Job. "We were plowing the fields with the cattle," he said, "and the donkeys were in a nearby pasture. ¹⁵ Suddenly the Sabeans attacked and stole them all. They killed every one of your servants except me. I am the only one who escaped to tell you."

¹⁶ Before he finished speaking, another servant came and said, "Lightning struck the sheep and the shepherds and killed them all. I am the only one who escaped to tell you."

¹⁷ Before he finished speaking, another servant came and said, "Three bands of Chaldean raiders attacked us, took away the camels, and killed all your servants except me. I am the only one who escaped to tell you."

¹⁸ Before he finished speaking, another servant came and said, "Your children were having a feast at the home of your oldest son, ¹⁹ when a storm swept in from the desert. It blew the house down and killed them all. I am the only one who escaped to tell you."

²⁰ Then Job got up and tore his clothes in grief. He shaved his head and threw himself face downward on the ground. ²¹ He said, "I was born with nothing and I will die with nothing. The Lord gave, and now he has taken away. May his name be praised!" ²² In spite of everything that had happened, Job did not sin by blaming God.

QUESTIONS FOR DISCUSSION 1:1-22

12. There is only one act that can break the solitude of man enslaved in a world of sin and evil. What is it?
13. Just where was Uz? Give two possibilities.

14. What is the meaning of the name Job?
15. Discuss the four virtues of the man Job. How do these virtues relate to us?
16. Does God indeed always reward uprightness? Cf. Psalms 127:3; 128:6.
17. Just how wealthy was Job, i.e., compared to others?
18. Are we to conclude there was something wrong with the feasting mentioned in 1:4? Discuss.
19. Show a possible connection between the sacrifices and the feasting.
20. According to Satan the name of the game is what? Is it true? Prove your answer.
21. Who are "the sons of God"?
22. The character of Satan is clearly indicated. Give two qualities.
23. Why does God ask Satan where he has been; doesn't God already know? Discuss.
24. What does Satan do in this earth?
25. Why all the concern for Job's integrity?
26. Does Satan admit Job is righteous?
27. Satan and God are both interested in motives. Why?
28. The "American Dream" syndrome runs dangerously close to a false assumption. What is it?
29. Why does Job serve God? Does prosperity have anything to do with service? Discuss.
30. Prosperity and piety alway go together—true or false? Do we really believe our answer?
31. Prosperity is a hedge—how? Discuss.
32. Satan takes an oath before God. What is Satan's promise by an oath?
33. God does not hesitate a moment to take up Satan's challenge—why so soon?
34. Does this example of Job suggest to us that God is in every circumstance of our life? Discuss.
35. How does violence and Satan relate?
36. What other option does man have besides coping or adjusting?

6. The second trial—bodily suffering (2:1-8)

TEXT 2:1-8

2 Again it came to pass on the day when the sons of God came to present themselves before Jehovah, that Satan came also among them to present himself before Jehovah. (2) And Jehovah said unto Satan, From whence comest thou? And Satan answereth Jehovah, and said, From going to and fro in the earth, and from walking up and down in it. (3) And Jehovah said unto Satan, Hast thou considered my servant Job? for there is none like him in the earth, a perfect and an upright man, one that feareth God, and turneth away from evil: and he still holdeth fast his integrity, although thou movedst me against him, to destroy him without cause. (4) And Satan answered Jehovah, and said, Skin for skin, yea, all that a man hath will he give for his life. (5) But put forth thy hand now, and touch his bone and his flesh, and he will renounce thee to thy face. (6) And Jehovah said unto Satan, Behold, he is in thy hand; only spare his life.

(7) So Satan, went forth from the presence of Jehovah, and smote Job with sore boils from the sole of his foot unto his crown. (8) And he took him a potsherd to scrape himself therewith; and he sat among the ashes.

COMMENT 2:1-8

Verses 1-3—Verses 1-3a repeat 1:6-8 almost verbally. In verse 3b "without cause" is the very same adverb as appears in 1:9 translated as "for nothing." It is Satan's cynicism, not Job's integrity, that goes for nothing. Now Satan begins his sustained attack on the "individual" as against the corporate. Job's ultimate concern is neither things nor family, but his integrity before Yahweh. Strip him of all his values and security symbols and he will still reverence God. The verb translated "holds

17

fast" literally means to hold firmly or tenaciously to something. One may also hold firmly to anger (Micah 7:18; or to deceit—Jeremiah 8:5). In Job 27:6 we are told that he holds firmly to his innocence. The verb translated "movedst" or incited me against him generally is used in a negative sense—36:18; Deuteronomy 13:7; Joshua 15:18. Yahweh even gives Satan his due for instigating the experiment.

Verse 4—The proverbial saying "skin after skin" is meaningful only because of the following phrase—"all that a man has he will give for his life." Then the Lord gives Satan permission to get under Job's skin, anything short of his death. The Hebrew word translated "his life" (*napso*) means himself as a person.[1] Satan does not want Job dead because then he could never prove that Job's piety rested in self-interest. A martyr for a cause is hardly an appropriate example of radical self-interest.

Verse 5—God has permitted Satan to only lightly touch Job, i.e., externally and superficially. Now, from "skin to skin" into the depths of Job's being—flesh and bone. Surely now Job will revolt against Yahweh when He afflicts his bones and flesh. Such is Satan's shrewd strategy. But stripped of honor and health, Job still fears God.

Verse 7—Job is afflicted with some unnamed but disfiguring disease which causes continual pain and sleeplessness. The first disease has been identified with leprosy, because the ancients considered elephantiasis as a disease peculiar to Egypt.[2] The Hebrew word means 'to be inflamed, hot' Thus the disease which afflicts Job is an inflammation of the skin which causes sores and boils. We do not seek to minimize Job's agony and alienation, but it seems idle to seek a precise identification of his disease. The symptoms of his despicable disease are presented throughout the Jobian drama: (1) inflamed

---

[1] See the indispensable comparative study of Hebrew psychological terms used metaphorically in Edouard Dhorme, *L'Emploi metaphorique des noms de parties du corps en hebreu et in akkadian* (Paris, 1923).

[2] Pliny, *Natural History,* XXVI, 7ff; and Lucretius, VI, 1105ff.

eruptions—2:7; (2) intolerable itching—2:8; (3) disfigured appearance—2:12; (4) maggots in his ulcers—7:5; (5) terrifying dreams—7:14; (6) running tears which blind his eyes—16:16; (7) fetid breath—19:17; (8) emaciated body—19:20; (9) erosion of the bones—30:17; (10) blackening and peeling off of his skin—30:30.[3]

Verse 8—Because of the intolerable itching, Job takes a broken piece of pottery "to scrape himself." How much Lord? He sat among the ashes. This describes the dunghill (*mazbaleh*) outside of town. Here the rubbish was thrown. Children, outcasts, and dogs came here. When tragedy came, men came here to sit (Isaiah 47:1; Jonah 3:6), or roll in the ashes (Jeremiah 6:26; Micah 1:10); or to throw ashes on their heads (Ezekiel 72:30).[4]

7. Job refuses to curse God. (2:9, 10)

TEXT 2:9, 10

(9) Then said his wife unto him, Dost thou still hold fast thine integrity? renounce God, and die. (10) But he said unto her, Thou speakest as one of the foolish women speaketh. What: shall we receive good at the hand of God, and shall we not receive evil? In all this did not Job sin with his lips.

COMMENT 2:9, 10

Verse 9—Not Job, but his wife reacts as Satan intended. Here the Septuagint inserts a long speech from Job's wife. (The Qoran also refers to Job's rebuke of his wife in 38:43.) But the lean and spare simplicity of our text proceeds to set the stage for the dramatic dialogue. This situation must not be

---

[3] A document from the Dead Sea Scrolls, *The Prayer of Nabonidus* reveals that he is afflicted with the same disease as is Job. See R. Meyer, *Das Gebet des Nabonid,* 1962, p. 16, A 2f.

[4] See Dhorme, *Job*, p. 19 for description.

psychoanalyzed, especially now that we are deeply involved in women's liberation mentality. Psychoanalysis of dead people is a most precarious scientific pastime. We accept it as a matter of fact. "Curse Elohim and die." Resignation is not the chief attribute of Job's wife. She, like many of us, are only prepared for "good" not "evil" in God's universe.

Verse 10—The sufferer responds to his wife's mindless suggestion. He calls her "foolish." This is not a reflection on her intelligence, but rather on her moral character. Nabal (I Samuel 25:25—masculine form) is the masculine form of the same word and means one who is both morally and intellectually obtuse. David describes a fool (same word) as one "who says there is no God"—Psalm 14:1. This fool is one who wants to live as though there is no God before whom we will give an account of every thought and action. Job has accepted the loss of property and family. He here accepts his illness, in hope of resurrection. Death is not our greatest enemy as the Buddhist mentality of the 20th century seeks to say; live it up, for today may be all that you have.

8. Three friends come, and a further great trial begins (their insinuations). (2:11-13)

TEXT 2:11-13

(11) Now when Job's three friends heard of all this evil that was come upon him, they came every one from his own place: Eliphaz the Temanite, and Bildad the Shuhite, and Zophar the Naamathite; and they made an appointment together to come to bemoan him and to comfort him. (12) And when they lifted up their eyes afar off, and knew him not, they lifted up their voice, and wept; and they rent every one his robe, and sprinkled dust upon their heads toward heaven. (13) So they sat down with him upon the ground seven days and seven nights and no one spake a word unto him: for they saw that his grief was very great.

20

COMMENT 2:11-13

Verse 11—The passage in verses 11 to 13 prepares for the coming dialogue. Job's three comforters are professional wise men from Edom (the proverbial home of wise men, Obadiah 8; Jeremiah 49:7). Their concern is both genuine and charitable. They find Job's condition worse than they had expected and begin expressing the ritual gestures for mourning for the dead by a week long silence.[5] They wait for Job to break his silence before attempting to comfort him. Silence is often the deepest comfort. Our mere presence is frequently the most powerful therapy for broken hearts. Three concerned wise men come to console Job: (1) Eliphaz, (probably means "God is fine gold"— Genesis 36:11, 15, 42; I Chronicles 1:36, 53) the Temanite. Teman is from a root meaning the right hand of "southland," because when one faces the rising sun his right hand is to the south. Teman is probably located in Nabatean territory about 15 miles from Petra (Jeremiah 49:7; Ezekiel 25:13; Amos 1:12f; Obadiah 9—Teman is always a principal location of Edom). (2) Bildad, (meaning uncertain[6]) the Shuhite. Shuah is mentioned as a son of Abraham and Qeturah—Genesis 25:2; I Chronicles 1:32. The geographical location is, in all probability, also to be found in Edom or Arabia. (3) Zophar, (means "young dove,"—the name appears only in Job) the Naamathite. The most likely location is that of Jebel el Na'ameh, approximately 40 miles east of Tebuk.[7] The three made an appointment with Job for the purpose of consoling him. The verb means "to move to and fro," i.e., to move the body as a sign of mutual grief.

Verse 12—Job was so disfigured by the disease that they did not recognize him. To this extent Job is similar to the Suffering

---

[5] N. Lohfink, *Vetus Testamentum* 12 (1962), pp. 260-77.

[6] See suggestions of Speiser and Albright. Speiser, *Archiv für Orientalforschung*, 6 (1930), p. 23; and W. F. Albright, *Journal of Biblical Literature*, 54 (1935), p. 174, N. 3.

[7] For major possibilities see F. M. Abel, *Geographie de la Palestine* Tome I, Paris, 1933, p. 287, N. 4.

Servant of Isaiah 53:3, Job's vindicator, and our Saviour. Each of the three sheikhs wore a robe as a badge of nobility, like Job—1:20. As a sign of torturous grief one tore his robe and sprinkled dust upon his head (Joshua 7:6; Ezekiel 27:30).

Verse 13—The three wise men "sat down" with him on the ground. This was the Near Eastern custom for mourners (Lamentations 2:10). The seven days and nights was also the custom for mourning the dead. Surely they thought Job would die, so aggravated was his condition. Sympathy and grief comingled between the sufferer and the mourners. (Ezekiel sat seven days and nights among the exiles—3:15.)

TODAY'S ENGLISH VERSION

Satan Tests Job Again

2 When the day came for the heavenly beings to appear before the Lord again, Satan was there among them. [2] The Lord asked him, "Where have you been?"

Satan answered, "I have been walking here and there, roaming around the earth."

[3] The Lord asked, "Did you notice my servant Job? There is no one on earth as faithful and good as he is. He worships me and is careful not to do anything evil. You persuaded me to let you attack him for no reason at all, but Job is still as faithful as ever."

[4] Satan replied, "A man will give up everything in order to stay alive. [5] But now suppose you hurt his body —he will curse you to your face."

[6] So the Lord said to Satan, "All right, he is in your power, but you are not to kill him."

[7] Then Satan left the Lord's presence and made sores break out all over Job's body. [8] Job went and sat by the garbage dump and took a piece of broken pottery to scrape his sores. [9] His wife said to him, "You are still as faithful as ever, aren't you? Why don't you curse God

and die?"

¹⁰ Job answered, "You are talking nonsense! When God sends us something good we welcome it. How can we complain when he sends us trouble?" Even in all this suffering Job did not say anything against God.

Job's Friends Come
¹¹ Three of Job's friends were Eliphaz, from the city of Teman, Bildad, from the land of Shuah, and Zophar, from the land of Namah. When they heard how much Job had been suffering, they decided to go visit him and comfort him. ¹² While they were still a long way off they saw Job, but did not recognize him. When they did, they began to weep and wail. They tore their clothes in grief and threw dust into the air and on their heads. ¹³ Then they sat there on the ground with him for seven days and nights without saying a word, because they saw how much he was suffering.

QUESTIONS FOR DISCUSSION 2:1-13

37. What is cynicism? Who is the father of it?
38. How well would we do stripped of all our security symbols? Discuss.
39. Read verse three and discuss how it is that Satan is able to move God.
40. What is meant by the phrase "skin for skin"?
41. Describe the disease sent by Satan. Discuss its ten characteristics.
42. Why sit in the ashes?
43. Someone reacted like Satan expected, who was it? Why?
44. In what sense did Job call his wife foolish?
45. Who is our greatest enemy?
46. Who are Job's friends? What was their job? From where?

THE MEANING OF SILENCE
Chapters 3 — 14

I. NO EXIT: HELL IS OTHER PEOPLE—Sartre
SPEECHES FULL OF SOUND AND FURY 3:1—14:22

A. WHY ME, LORD? (3:1-26)

1. He curses his day. (3:1-10)

TEXT 3:1-10

3 After this opened Job his mouth, and cursed his day.
2 And Job answered and said:
3 Let the day perish wherein I was born,
And the night which said, There is a man-child conceived.
4 Let that day be darkness;
Let not God from above seek for it,
Neither let the light shine upon it.
5 Let darkness and the shadow of death claim it for their own;
Let a cloud dwell upon it;
Let all that maketh black the day terrify it.
6 As for that night, let thick darkness seize upon it:
Let it not rejoice among the days of the year;
Let it not come into the number of the months.
7 Lo, let that night be barren;
Let no joyful voice come therein.
8 Let them curse it that curse the day,
Who are ready to rouse up leviathan.
9 Let the stars of the twilight thereof be dark:
Let it look for light, but have none;
Neither let it behold the eyelids of the morning:
10 Because it shut not up the doors of my *mother's* womb,
Nor hid trouble from mine eyes.

COMMENT 3:1-10

Job on *Dover Beach?*
The Sea of Faith
Was once, too, at the full, and round earth's shore
Lay like the folds of a bright girdle furl'd.
But now I only hear
Its melancholy, long, withdrawing roar
Retreating to the breath
Of the night-wind down the vast edges drear
And naked shingles of the world.

M. Arnold, *Dover Beach*

Verses 1-2—Why Me, Lord? Except for 3:1-2, the entire section from 3:1—31:40 is in poetic form. This is important for understanding the text, as poetry is parallel in literary form, which means that each line is not necessarily a new thought. In between Job's initial (chp. 3) and concluding (chps. 29-31) soliloquies, we encounter a series of alternate speeches by the three friends with Job's response.[1] Eliphaz speaks first (chps. 4-5), after chp. 3, Zophar perhaps speaks last, before chps. 29-31. Thus, we are presented with nine speeches by Job's friends alternating with eight responses from Job. The literary form is that of a lament, i.e., a prayer of petition in which Job appeals to God for a hearing, describes his destitution, anxieties, and attacks from his enemies, and asks God to break His silence and heal or explain his suffering. The three wise men attempt to console Job by entering in the lamentation. Each of the three consolers conveys his doctrine on retribution. Because of their concept of retribution, they come prepared to participate in a psalm of penitence, whereas Job cries out from the depth of his anguish in a psalm of innocence. Does suffering always imply guilt? Does a successful

---

[1] The textual problems in chps. 25-27 confront us with dilemmas regarding the last few speeches; note commentary regarding these matters. The conventional grouping of the speeches into three cycles might not represent the author's style.

life always imply innocence?[2] Job's consolers only manage to intensify his anguish. Here we are faced with the paradox— consolers that are not consolers. One of the results of this fact is that two subordinate themes enter Job's lament: (1) denunciation of enemies, and (2) his oath of exultation. As Job's condition worsens, the consolers persist in claiming that they are merely pronouncing God's judgment on Job. As a result, he includes God as one of his enemies, i.e., the nature of God as presented by his calamitous comforters. The central issue in Job's trial is the nature of God, not the nature of suffering and evil. If God loves him, why all the suffering? The ultimate answer is available only in the resurrected "Suffering Servant."[3] "After this" means after the seven days of silence (Gen. 15:14; 25:26). Job now breaks his silence as he "opened his mouth" and cursed the day of his birth. When he prospered, he perhaps never thought of such a response. Though Jeremiah (chp. 20:14-18) too cursed the day of his birth, he was mindful of the futility of cursing a past event. What will he do with the present? As with Job, he must face the present, but how and why? Many people in the twentieth century can identify with him. These verses are clearly the introduction to Job's ensuing soliloquy.

Verse 3—Job is so embittered that he wishes that life had never begun. Like Schopenhauer and Camus, Job is suggesting that suicide is the answer to unrelenting suffering. There is not one word suggesting this response as solution to Job's plight. But why not? Only if there is a God to whom we will give account because neither suffering nor death is our ultimate concern. Job telescopes the night of conception and day of birth.

---

[2] As America enters its third century, it is a most appropriate matter to consider. The *American Dream* has turned into a *nightmare* because most Americans share the doctrine of Job's three friends, i.e., if we're "successful," this means God is blessing our existence; if we are failures, we are not pleasing God, thus the presence of suffering. Biblically, much of the Bi-centennial emphasis is heretical. We are Christians by *vocation* and Americans by *avocation*.

[3] A. Feuillet, "L'enigme de la souffrance et al response de Dieu," *Dieu vivant*, 17 (1950), 77-91; and D. Barthelemy, "Dieu meconnu par le vieil homme, Job," *Vie spirituelle*, 105 (1961), 445-63.

The night is personified with power to know the sex of the child conceived. In the Near East, the news of the birth of a son is a momentous event. Job even curses the man who brought the news of his birth to his father. Note that Job does not include direct petition for relief but begins his soliloquy with the most radical assertion of his misery, utterly rejecting life itself. Other parallels, such as Jeremiah 20:14-18; I Kings 19:4; Jonah 4:3-8, reveal the realism of the biblical record.[4] Each in his own way denies that the life that God has given him is good, and would have preferred not to have received it from him. Even in this rejection, there is affirmation of belief in God as creative source of life.[5] *Affirmation in the Midst of Resentment!* The imagery conceives God as summoning the days to take their place as their turn comes. Even in Job's denial, God is indispensable. If He can control the days, why not evil? Job, like others, wants darkness at noon. The good things in his life prior to his suffering did not produce such a response. "All sunshine makes the desert."

Verse 4—Our limited English vocabulary for darkness makes translation difficult in verses 4-6. Different words for darkness express everything that is mysterious and evil (Job 12:25; Exodus 20:21; Isaiah 5:20; Psalm 82:5; and see also Matthew 5:23).

Verse 5—Our text (A.V.) translates *salmawet* as the "shadow of death." If the older view is correct, i.e., that the word is a compound word from "shadow" and "death," then the translation is sound; but more recent lexicography prefers *salmut* as the reading, thus the root for dark. May the day be eclipsed (M.T. *kimrire yom*) meaning "like bitterness of the day." The word is used in the context where there is no thought

---

[4] The differences between the LXX and M.T. are examined by Dhorme, *Job,* pp. 24ff; Pope, *Job,* p. 28; and W. B. Stevenson, *Critical Notes on the Hebrew Text of the Poem of Job,* 1951.

[5] After western man moves into the 19th and 20th scientific revolutions and is less committed to Christian theism, we are confronted with "The Death of God" from Nietzsche's *Thus Spoke Zarathustra* to Rubenstein's *After Auschwitz.*

of death—Amos 5:9; Job 28:3.[6]

Verse 6—"Let thick darkness seize it" in the sense of claim[7] it for its own.

Verse 7—Job asks that the night be "barren," (Hebrew *galmud*), stony or unproductive. The word is used in Isaiah 49:21 for childlessness, i.e., barren. May the night never again see offspring, so that no one else experiences the misery known by Job. May the night be sterile, then surely suffering will cease.[8]

Verse 8—Out of his resentful heart comes only cursing. Curse—Curse! Here we have two different Hebrew words, both different from the one used in verse 1. Speiser has demonstrated that the word means to "cast a spell on."[9] Job calls for a professional curser, i.e., those "who are skilled to rouse up Leviathan," (Hebrew *liwyah*, wreath, meaning something coiled). There has been much discussion concerning the supposed mythological allusion since Günkel published his *Schöpfung und Chaos*, 1895 (see esp. pp. 59-61), but the text makes perfectly good sense without any such origin for its imagery.[10]

Verse 9—The word *nesep* means twilight, either the morning as here and 7:4 or evening twilight as in 24:15 and Proverbs 7:9. The reference here is surely to the morning stars Mercury and Venus. If they had remained dark, Job's day would not have come. Without the "light" of the dawn, he would not be able to see[11] the new day.

---

[6] See discussion by Dhorme, *Job*, pp. 26ff; D. W. Thomas, *Journal of Semitic Studies*, VII, 1962, 191ff, who argues for the *salmawet* reading.

[7] See N. H. Snaith's discussion of this root in *Annual of Leeds University Oriental Society*, III, 1963, 60ff.

[8] For the magnificent witness of a contemporary sufferer, read Corrie Ten Boom, *Tramp for The Lord* and *The Hiding Place* (New Jersey: Spire, Revell, pbs., 1976 printing.)

[9] E. H. Speiser, *Journal of American Oriental Society*, LXXX, 1960, 198ff; see also the Balaam account in Numbers 22-24 for expert in cursing or blessing.

[10] See W. F. Albright, *Journal of Biblical Literature*, LVII, 1938, 227, and his arguments for repointing *yom-day*, *toyam-sea*. But this is unnecessary; the text makes perfectly good sense without it.

[11] For the discussion concerning the Hebrew *'ap appayim*, see Mitchell Dahood, *Psalms*, Vol. III, note on Ps. 132:4 where he cites a Qumran text 4Q184:13 in support

Verse 10—The A. V. correctly sees reference to Job's mother's womb from the literal Hebrew which says "my womb," i.e., the womb from which I came. The night did not prevent the womb from conceiving, "nor hid trouble," i.e., toil, sorrow and suffering from Job. Now the sufferer turns from God to himself, and a new factor enters Job's complaint. The query "why" in verses 11-12, and again in verse 20, is a crucial new development.

2. Asks why he was born (3:11-19)

TEXT 3:11-19

11 Why died I not from the womb?
   Why did I not give up the ghost when my mother bare me?
12 Why did the knees receive me?
   Or why the breasts, that I should suck?
13 For now should I have lain down and been quiet;
   I should have slept; then had I been at rest,
14 With kings and counsellors of the earth,
   Who built up waste places for themselves;
15 Or with princes that had gold,
   Who filled their houses with silver:
16 Or as a hidden untimely birth I had not been,
   As infants that never saw light.
17 There the wicked cease from troubling;
   And there the weary are at rest.
18 There the prisoners are at ease together;
   They hear not the voice of the taskmaster.
19 The small and the great are there:
   And the servant is free from his master.

COMMENT 3:11-19

Verse 11—A.V. is a literal rendering of the Hebrew and

---

of "eyes" instead of "eyelids" in the above verse; also Dhorme's *Job*, pp. 29ff modification of the text is unnecessary.

means "at birth," Job 10:18-19.[12]

Verse 12—Perhaps "the knees" refers to the father receiving the child as his own—Genesis 50:23 and Eccl. 15:2a. But both Dhorme and Buttenwieser interpret the phrase to mean the mother's knees as receiving the child to nurse it.

Verse 13—Job is now preoccupied with death, as is contemporary man. His measure of misery is that death would be better. Since Elizabeth K. Ross published her *Death and Dying*, there has been an epidemic of literature on the phenomenon of death. Note that throughout this Jobian soliloquy there has been no intimation of Job taking his own life. Hebrew eschatology maintained that Sheol is not necessarily a place of victory over death. Only when Job knows that his vindicator lives does he resolve his existential crisis. His sickness is then— not unto death. For references to Sheol in Job read 3:19; 7:9; 10:12ff; 14:10ff; 14:21-22; 17:16.

Verse 14—Though the Hebrew could mean "rebuilt ruins," (A.V. build up, i.e., rebuild), it makes little sense in this passage. Kings do not build among ruins. Efforts at repointing the text fare no better. Perhaps the meaning is that suggested by Rowley "who build for themselves the ruins." Nothing lasts forever.

Verse 15—Great kings were prosperous, but they, too, died. Rich and poor alike are leveled in death. If equality is unavailable in life, it is a virtue shared by all in death.

Verse 16—Job's present misery blots out all the happy memories of the good years. We could not bear to carry every hurt (or joy) forever, so God's grace is involved in our forgetfulness.

Verse 17—In Sheol we are not troubled, or as the text says, we "cease from agitating" ourselves. The same word is rendered "rage" of horses in 39:24 and rumbling of thunder in 37:2.

---

[12] M. Dahood, *Biblica*, 1963, p. 205. Verses 11-16 present a problem of chronology. Some of the verses do not seem to follow, egs. 16 does not follow naturally from 15. See Dhorme, *Job*, pp. 31ff.

Verse 18—Even slaves suffer less than does Job. Captives who are in forced labor and are brutally treated are more at ease than Job. Job in Auschwitz? The hard Egyptian taskmaster (used in Exodus 3:7; 5:6 of the Egyptian taskmasters over the Hebrew slaves) left a lasting effect on Israel's memory; as a result both Old and New Testaments employ in vital theological sections, *The Exodus Motif.*

Verse 19—In Sheol everyone is equal. The slave (servant) is free.[13]

3. And why he should go on living (3:20-26)

TEXT 3:20-26

20 Wherefore is light given to him that is in misery,
   And life unto the bitter in soul;
21 Who long for death, but it cometh not,
   And dig for it more than for hid treasures;
22 Who rejoice exceedingly,
   And are glad, when they can find the grave?
23 *Why is light given* to a man whose way is hid,
   And whom God hath hedged in?
24 For my sighing cometh before I eat,
   And my groanings are poured out like water.
25 For the thing which I fear cometh upon me,
   And that which I am afraid of cometh unto me.
26 I am not at ease, neither am I quiet, neither have I rest;
   But trouble cometh.

COMMENT 3:20-26

Verse 20—Though the verb in the Hebrew text should be translated actively, i.e., "gives," the versions construe the verb

---

[13] I. Mendelsohn, *Bulletin of American Society Oriental Research*, 83 (1941), 36-9, has shown that the root significance of this important word—*hopsi*—is "free proletarian" or "tenant farmer"; and E. R. Lacheman, ibid, 86, 1942, shows that in the Nuzi tablets this word means a "semi-free man."

to be passive. The omission of the subject may be due to the reluctance to charge God directly (verse 23 provides an implied subject). But under the attack of his three consolers, Job later charges God directly. Here light is life. The bitter in soul is plural, thus Job has reference to all those who suffer, not only himself. So, he clearly identifies himself with the fellowship of suffering (I Samuel 1:10; II Samuel 17:8).

Verse 21—In Hosea 6:9 the same verb used here means "lying in ambush." The term "who long for death" expresses Job's eagerness for death. Buried treasure creates its own fever to dominate all searchers. Even the rumor of treasure creates almost uncontrolled excitement. This is the kind of frenzied search for death which is enslaving Job.

Verse 22—Job searches "beyond measure," literally "to the point of exultation" for the place to house his body racked with excruciating pain. The grave would also free his agonizing soul. Spiritual hurt is always more painful than physical malady.

Verse 23—Why is life (light) given when the way of fulfillment is hidden?[14] Bewilderment intensifies because he cannot see any way out. "Whom God has hedged in" in a restrictive sense. The same verb "hedge" appears in 1:10 in the conversation of Satan, when he said that God has put a protective hedge about Job.

Verse 24—The first clause makes little sense. The phrase "before I eat" in the A.V. is literally in Hebrew "as or like my bread"[15] (see I Samuel 1:16 and Ps. 42:3). The word

---

[14] This is the thesis of Kafka's *The Castle:* "There is no way, what appears to be the way is only wavering." The theme is that of a man who has been invited to the castle of the prince-king, but he can only look from afar; he can never arrive. Deep despair is inevitable.

[15] For examination of the meaning of this rare word, see G. R. Driver, *Jewish Quarterly Review*, XXVIII, 1937-8, 121ff. Some needlessly omit the verse because of difficulty in attaining the meaning of this word.

32

translated "my groanings" is used of the roaring of the lion, and here emphasizes Job's loud cries.

Verse 25—The torturous power of fear is actively controlling Job's imagination. What new evil will befall him next? "Why make a gift that is a painful burden to the recipient?" (*The Jerome Biblical Commentary, Job,* p. 515).[16]

Verse 26—Continual agony (same word as in verses 10 and 20). The patient submissiveness of the Prologue has turned to bitter complaint throughout this soliloquy. But still Job has not cursed God! Surrounded by trouble, drowned by trouble, agitation keeps coming. Will it ever stop? What does it all mean? Why me, Lord? Note that Job does not merely ask why? He asks Why me?

TODAY'S ENGLISH VERSION

Job's Complaint to God

3 Finally Job broke the silence and called down a curse on the day on which he had been born.

Job
²⁻³ God, put a curse on the day I was born;
    put a curse on the night when I was conceived.
⁴ Turn that day into darkness, God;
    never again remember that day;
    never again let light shine on it.
⁵ Make it a day of gloom and thick darkness;
    cover it with clouds and blot out the sun.
⁶ Blot that night out of the year,
    and never let it be counted again;
⁷   make it a barren, joyless night.
⁸ Tell the sorcerers to curse that day,

---

[16] Jesus said of Judas, "It would have been better for that man if he had not been born," Matt. 26:24. See my essay, *The Nature of Gifts,* in *The Christian Standard;* and P. Tournier's *Gifts.* Many gifts are given for the purpose of domination, or to get something in return. Is that what God has done with His gift of life?

those who know how to command Leviathan.
⁹ Keep the morning star from shining;
    give that night no hope of dawn.
¹⁰ Curse that night for letting me be born,
    for exposing me to grief and trouble.

¹¹ I wish I had died in my mother's womb,
    or died the moment I was born.
¹² Why did my mother hold me on her knees?
    Why did she feed me at her breast?
¹³ If I had died then, I would be at rest now,
¹⁴   sleeping like the kings and rulers
    who rebuilt ancient palaces.
¹⁵ Then I would be sleeping like princes
    who filled their houses with gold and silver,
¹⁶   or sleeping like children born dead.
¹⁷ In the grave wicked men stop their evil,
    and tired workmen rest at last.
¹⁸ Even prisoners enjoy peace,
    free from shouts and harsh commands.
¹⁹ Everyone is there, great and small alike,
    and slaves at last are free.

²⁰ Why let men go on living in misery?
    Why give light to men in grief?
²¹ They wait for death, but it never comes;
    they prefer a grave to any treasure.
²² They are not happy till they are dead and buried;
²³   God keeps their future hidden
    and hems them in on every side.
²⁴ Instead of eating, I mourn,
    and I can never stop groaning;
²⁵   everything I fear and dread comes true.
²⁶ I have no peace, no rest,
    and my trouble never ends.

QUESTIONS FOR DISCUSSION 3:1-26

47. Why is it important that we understand the literary form in which Job is written?
48. Who speaks the most in this book—Job or his friends? What could this suggest as to the problem of suffering?
49. What is a "lament"?
50. Why are the three friends all prepared for a psalm of pentitence?
51. Job's consolers only manage to intensify his anguish. Why?
52. What are the two subordinate themes that enter Job's lament? Why?
53. There is only one ultimate answer to the question, "If God loves me, why all this suffering and evil?" What is it?
54. Job seems to have a short memory. Why curse the day of his birth? He had lived much longer in prosperity than pain.
55. Does Job consider suicide as an escape? Is suicide ever justified?
56. Even in Job's selection there is an affirmation of God. Explain.
57. The word "darkness" is important in these verses. How is it used?
58. What is meant by asking that "the night be barren"? (vs. 7)
59. Cursing is used in at least two ways. What are they?
60. What is "Leviathan" as used in verse eight?
61. What are "the eyelids of the morning"?
62. Why blame the night? Discuss.
63. Whose "knees" are involved in verse 12?
64. Why has man been preoccupied with the subject of death?
65. What is Sheol?
66. To what does the expression "waste places" in verse 14 refer?
67. Death is a great equalizer. Explain.
68. Show how God's grace is seen in our forgetfulness.
69. Death offers welcome relief. Explain. Is this a present day attitude?
70. There is an indirect charge against God in verse 20. Why?

B. CALAMITOUS COMFORTER—ELIPHAZ (4:1—5:27)

1. Job should not complain; the righteous will not be cut off (mild rebuke; 4:1-11).

TEXT 4:1-11

4 Then answered Eliphaz the Temanite, and said,
  2 If one assay to commune with thee, wilt thou be grieved?
But who can withhold himself from speaking?
3 Behold, thou hast instructed many,
And thou hast strengthened the weak hands.
4 Thy words have upholden him that was falling,
And thou hast made firm the feeble knees.
5 But now it is come unto thee, and thou faintest;
It toucheth thee, and thou art troubled.
6 Is not thy fear *of* God thy confidence,
And the integrity of thy ways thy hope?
7 Remember, I pray thee, who *ever* perished, being innocent?
Or where were the upright cut off?
8 According as I have seen, they that plow iniquity,
And sow trouble, reap the same.
9 By the breath of God they perish,
And by the blast of his anger are they consumed.
10 The roaring of the lion, and the voice of the fierce lion,
And the teeth of the young lions, are broken.
11 The old lion perisheth for lack of prey,
And the whelps of the lioness are scattered abroad.

COMMENT 4:1-11

Verse 1—Enters Eliphaz! Since Job has broken his silence, Eliphaz is now free to speak. He is presumably the oldest, thus the wisest, thus first speaker. He is also the most gracious and most eloquent. His deep esteem and profound sorrow for Job leaps from each phrase he utters. Eliphaz has been shocked at the fact that Job had wished death and has uttered no prayer for the recovery of prosperity and joi de vie (joy of life). Eliphaz asks Job, "Could you bear it?" (literally "would you be weary?"), i.e., Are you physically and psychologically able to hear my analysis of your condition? To Job, his misfortune was an enigmatic mystery; to Eliphaz the calamities have been sent to punish Job for some sin or sins (see John 9 and Jesus' rejection of this standard Jewish, but not Old Testament, concept). Eliphaz has come to help Job examine his conscience.[1]

Verse 2—Eliphaz declares that if only Job would repent of his sins he could regain God's favor.[2] The speech regularly starts with a question and reference to Job's words. Eliphaz introduces the *Doctrine of Retribution,* i.e., Retributive Justice.

Verse 3—First he gently appeals to Job's own good advice to others in the past. But this type of counseling was already beside the point, because Job had already accepted the standard doctrine of retribution (29:18-20), but now is beginning to challenge its adequacy simply because it does not explain his present existential situation. "With great delicacy and consideration" Eliphaz has now opened the first cycle of speeches.[3] The root of the word translated "instructed" (*ysr*) means discipline and in 5:17 the noun from this root means "discipline by suffering" (see Hebrews 12:3ff). Job has instructed many. His instruction has strengthened them, i.e., from "weak hands" which hang down in helpless despair (Isaiah 35:3; Hebrews 12:12).[4]

Verse 4—His words have also strengthened "feeble knees" (see same scriptures as above for imagery).

Verse 5—It is easy for a well man to give sound advice. Some commentators see sarcasm in Eliphaz's word; but the

---

[1] Note this powerful insight into the relationship of truth, integrity, guilt, and healing, long before Freud's theory of repression was ever conceived. The scriptures sit in judgment on Freud's theory that all guilt is socially caused.

[2] See K. Fullerton, *Journal Biblical Literature* 49, 1930, 320-74; Pss. 32 and 51 and see Chamberlain's, *Repentance* (Joplin, MO: College Press reprint, 1972) with my bibliographical essay on repentance.

[3] For relationship of Job and Wisdom Literature, see H. Ranston, *The Old Testament Wisdom Books and Their Teaching,* 1930, p. 139; S. Rankin, *Israel's Wisdom Literature* (T & T Clark, 1936); and G. van Rad's *Wisdom in Israel* (Nashville: Abingdon E. T., 1972).

[4] See the penetrating analysis by M. Dahood, *Biblica,* 48, 1967, 425.

psychoanalysis of a dead author should capture only the absolute minimum of everyone's time, both authors and readers.

Verse 6—Literally, "your fear" of God should sustain you. He should have confidence in his past faithfulness to God. After all, Job's piety and integrity are not being questioned—yet. Job is blameless—1:1—has confidence (*kesel*—confidence, here the form is *kislah*—8:4; Eccl. 7:25. This root has polarized meaning, i.e., opposite, eg. confidence—folly), and thus has integrity or consistency.

Verse 7—Is Job an exception to the rule? It is only casuistry to reply that Job is not in the category with the wicked because God has spared his life (Ps. 37:25; Prov. 12:21; Eccl. 2:10). Yet each of us can appreciate the dilemma of Job's comforters. Each comforter, in his own way, sought recovery for Job. There is still hope, since he is alive. If Job will only confess his guilt and seek God's grace, recovery would follow. Many of the modern specialists in healing are not radically different in their method than Job's friends. The power of confession (e.g. Jung, *Modern Man in Search of a Soul*) has long since been clinically proved. But the problem of theodicy is not thereby overcome. Why are some individuals signaled out for unbearably severe physical and spiritual torture? Suffering Servant—we turn to you! Help us to participate in the suffering of your fallen creation. Is suffering for discipline or destruction?[5]

Verse 8—"Those who plough iniquity" are those persons who are wicked. They who cultivate sin and perform it with intentional glee, also reap the results—Hosea 10:13 and Gal. 6:7.

Verse 9—The wicked perish. This doctrine says that misfortune is divine retribution. This teaching is at the heart of America's "Success Syndrome," i.e., if you are prospering, you are being blessed; if you are in destitute circumstances, it is God's way of expressing retributive justice. God's justice

---

[5] Concerning the problem of evil: For those philosophically inclined see the indispensable, though technical work, Alvin Plantinga, *God and Other Minds* (New York: Cornell University Press); C. S. Lewis, *Problem of Pain* for beginners; for those hostile to Christian theism, see E. H. Madden and P. H. Hare, *Evil and the Concept of God* (Springfield, IL: Charles C. Thomas, Publ.; for best single survey see John Hick, *Evil and the God of Love* (New York: Harper & Row), now also in paperback.

is likened to a scorching hot wind. Thanks be to God Jesus repudiates this blasphemous and heretical instruction, Luke 13:1-5. The cross, the ten official Roman persecutions, the martyrdom of thousands of the faithful, if not millions, both in the classical church history and in the twentieth century, all speak against this doctrine.

Verse 10-11—The image of the lion is common in Near Eastern Wisdom Literature—Pss. 17:12; 22:14; Prov. 28:15; and Isa. 30:6. When the roar dies down and the teeth of the lion are broken, it is powerless and can no longer hold the prey.

2. The Vision—no mortal can question God's just acts. (4:12-21)

TEXT 4:12-21

12 Now a thing was secretly brought to me,
And mine ear received a whisper thereof.
13 In thoughts from the visions of the night,
When deep sleep falleth on men,
14 Fear came upon me, and trembling,
Which made all my bones to shake.
15 Then a spirit passed before my face;
The hair of my flesh stood up.
16 It stood still, but I could not discern the appearance thereof;
A form was before mine eyes:
There was silence, and I heard a *voice, saying,*
17 Shall mortal man be more just than God?
Shall a man be more pure than his Maker?
18 Behold, he putteth no trust in his servants;
And his angels he chargeth with folly:
19 How much more them that dwell in houses of clay,
Whose foundation is in the dust,
Who are crushed before the moth!
20 Betwixt morning and evening they are destroyed:
They perish for ever without any regarding it.
21 Is not their tent-cord plucked up within them?
They die, and that without wisdom.

COMMENT 4:12-21

Verse 12—Eliphaz now relates the content of a night's vision to Job (33:15). The description is of the terrifying psychological effects of a nightmare.[6]

Verse 13—The Hebrew word *seippim* occurs only here and 20:2. Its root meaning is probably "be disquieted" or deeply troubled. The deep sleep is the same that fell on Adam in Gen. 2:21.

Verse 14—The extreme form of pathological behavior manifested here reveals the terrible consequences of the nightmare long after the experience.

Verse 15—Besides experience (4:8; 5:3), Eliphaz brings a proof from a private revelation (head—4:16). He powerfully describes a mysterious audition. In verse 12 he calls it a *dabar* or word and *semes* or a whisper which produced dread. He may be claiming supernatural authority for the wisdom that he is dispensing to Job. The word translated spirit can mean mind or breath. Nowhere else does the Old Testament use this word of disembodied spirits. The shades in Sheol are called *repa-im.* When the witch of Endor raised Samuel, he is called *elohim.* The word translated in A.V. is "passed" literally means "glided," and is in the imperfect form, which means that he is still passing through the experience, or is again passing through it. The hair (*sa-a-rat* means a single hair) of my flesh creeped.[7]

Verse 16—It stood still! The object is unnamed. The Hebrew consists of but a single word. It is as though Eliphaz is attempting to catch his breath "as the horror of that moment returns to Eliphaz" (Rowley, *Job,* p. 55). The awe-inspiring voice of

---

[6] E. Robertson, *Bulletin of John Rylands Library*, 42, (1960), 417. Note the powerful therapeutic effect of expression—long before Freud developed his theory of dream analysis. Elihu regards dreams as warnings—33:15.

[7] M. Dahood, *Biblica*, XLVIII, 1967, 544ff, repoints the text to read "tempest or storm." This is not necessary, and "stood up" is used only here (in intensive form) and Ps. 119:120, and means that the flesh creeped. Experience effected his whole body. See also Dhorme, *Job,* p. 50.

silence is now contrasted with the voice of thunder.

Verse 17—the A.V. translates "more just than God," and this is grammatically possible, but Job has never suggested that he was. Better, I think, is the translation "righteous before God." Eliphaz has received this vision sometime in the past and is not connected with Job's soliloquy, and Job had not yet attacked God's holiness and righteousness. The meaning is that no man can be considered just and pure in comparison with God. No one is blameless or innocent before our holy God. Eliphaz is emphasizing that Job should accept God's verdict.

Verse 18—The servants are the angels in the next line. Old Testament angelology does not make a distinction between good and evil angels. Satan appears among the angels in 1:6.[8] The angels are charged with (*toh-o-lah*) error. The word is used only here and the A.V. is probably correct in rendering it "folly."

Verse 19—If angels are impure, "how much more" (the Hebrew can also mean "how much less," i.e., verse 18a) is man whose body is dust. The "houses" are figures for bodies (II Cor. 5:1; II Pet. 1:14). The same argument is repeated in 15:15-16. Paul argues in I Cor. 15:42-54 that resurrection is necessary to ultimately modify man's corruptible body, though the corruption is death and not unrighteousness as here. Man is compared to the moth. Man is crushed by God like man crushes a moth. "The moth is one of the easiest insects to catch and crush" (Pope, *Job,* p. 38).

Verse 20—Man's life is quickly over "between morning and evening."[9]

Verse 21—Some commentators object to the Hebrew texts—

---

[8] See Paul Heinisch, *Theology of the Old Testament* (The Liturgical Press, 1955), pp. 138ff; L. Kohler, *Old Testament Theology* (Philadelphia: Westminster, E. T., 1957), pp. 166ff; see entire range of Kittel articles on vocabulary discussed above.

[9] M. Dahood, *The Bible in Current Catholic Thought,* ed. by J. L. McKenzie, 1962, esp. p. 55 regarding the phrase "without regarding it." Dahood repoints the Hebrew to mean "without name" or unimportant. The extra "m" he regards as an enclitic ending and gives Ugaritic grammar evidence in support.

"tent cord," but this makes perfectly good sense. The verb (*ns'*) used in three passages in Isaiah (40:24; 33:20; and 38:12), and is a technical term for pulling stakes and ropes and moving on. The context of Eliphaz's speech is the contrast between men and angels, vis-a-vis God, and not the fate of the wicked. In essence, he says that man does not live long enough to acquire adequate wisdom to understand.

TODAY'S ENGLISH VERSION

The First Dialogue
(4.1—14.22)

4

Eliphaz

¹⁻² Job, will you be upset if I speak?
    I can't keep quiet any longer.
³ You have taught many people
    and given strength to feeble hands.
⁴ When someone stumbled, weak and tired,
    your words encouraged him to stand.
⁵ Now your turn has come for trouble,
    and you are too stunned to face it.
⁶ You worshipped God, and your life was blameless;
    you should have confidence and hope.
⁷ Think back now. Name a single case
    when a righteous man met with disaster.
⁸ I have seen people plow fields of evil
    and plant wickedness like seed;
    now they harvest wickedness and evil.
⁹ In his anger, God destroys them like a storm.
¹⁰ The wicked roar and growl like lions,
    but God silences them and breaks their teeth.
¹¹ Like lions with nothing to kill and eat,
    they die and their children are all scattered.

¹² Once a message came quietly,
    so quietly I could hardly hear it.
¹³ It was like a nightmare which disturbed my sleep.
¹⁴   I trembled and shuddered;
    my whole body shook with fear.
¹⁵ A light breeze touched my face,
    and my skin crawled with fright.
¹⁶ I could see something standing there;
    I stared, but couldn't tell what it was.
    Then I heard a voice out of the silence,
¹⁷ "Can a man be right in the sight of God?
    Can anyone be pure before his Creator?
¹⁸ God does not trust his heavenly servants;
    he finds fault with his angels.
¹⁹ Do you think he will trust a creature of clay,
    a thing of dust that can be crushed like a moth?
²⁰ A man may be alive in the morning,
    but die unnoticed before evening comes.
²¹ All that he has is taken away;
    he dies, still lacking wisdom."

QUESTIONS FOR DISCUSSION 4:1-21

71. Give the facts about Eliphaz. He is shocked. Why?
72. John the ninth chapter relates Eliphaz's attitude. How?
73. The scriptures sit in judgment upon Freud's theory. Show how.
74. Why remind Job of his counsel to others?
75. Read 29:18-20 and show how these verses relate here.
76. Job was very helpful to others in trouble. Why remember this?
77. Is Eliphaz sarcastic in verse 5? Discuss.
78. Job has confidence. From what source?
79. Is Job an exception to the rule stated in verse 7? Discuss.
80. There is a strong principle of truth stated in verse 8. How does it apply to Job?

81. What teaching is at the heart of America's "Success Syndrome"?
82. Jesus repudiates a blasphemous and heretical instruction. How? Cf. Luke 13:1-5.
83. Why are some people separated to be the objects of much suffering?
84. Eliphaz is going to tell Job of a night vision. Why?
85. Under what special condition did he receive his vision?
86. Verse 15 discusses another communication from God. What was it?
87. Why this ghost story? What was the message?
88. What is Eliphaz suggesting by these stories? or testimonies?
89. Even angels sin. Cf. verse 18. Who are "his servants"?
90. The temporary nature of man's body is well described in verse 19. Discuss.
91. Man lives but one day. What is the meaning of verse 20?
92. How is the expression "tent-cord" used in verse 21?

From **Today's English Version** of the Old Testament, Copyright, American Bible Society, 1971

3. The fate of the wicked (the foolish) is certain destruction. (5:1-7)

TEXT 5:1-7

5 **Call now; is there any that will answer thee?
And to which of the holy ones wilt thou turn?**
**2 For vexation killeth the foolish man,
And jealousy slayeth the silly one.**
**3 I have seen the foolish taking root:
But suddenly I cursed his habitation.**
**4 His children are far from safety,
And they are crushed in the gate,
Neither is there any to deliver them:**
**5 Whose harvest the hungry eateth up,
And taketh it even out of the thorns;
And the snare gapeth for their substance.**
**6 For affliction cometh not forth from the dust,
Neither doth trouble spring out of the ground;**
**7 But man is born unto trouble,
As the sparks fly upward.**

COMMENT 5:1-7

Verses 1-2—None of the holy ones (*qedosim*) can save man (Hos. 11:12; Dan. 4:10, 14; Zech. 14:5; Ps. 89:7). Eliphaz warns Job against any form of lament. A sinner who refuses to repent cannot be forgiven, thus healed. This verse may be an apologetic against the Mesapotamian idea of a finite but personal god whom a man could rely on to make intercession to the greater gods (9:33; 16:19, 21; 33:23-4). Perhaps verse 2 is a proverbial saying (Prov. 14:30) which suggests that one should not get excited about that over which he has no control. Only the fool will die of indignation (A. V., jealousy).

Verses 3-5—On center stage Eliphaz says that he himself has seen the fool take root. The unrighteous often strike deep into the earth their strange roots. Prosperity is thus effectively

45

presented by an analogy with a vigorously growing tree. The effect of this experience of Eliphaz was that he immediately cursed (same verb as 3:8) the dwelling of the prosperous fool. In so doing, Eliphaz was merely expressing the prejudices of his cultural ethics. When misfortune visits the head of the family, the entire family suffers. They cannot receive justice at the city gate, which was the administrative center where justice was dispersed and other legal issues were considered (Gen. 23:10; Deut. 21:19-21; Ruth 4:1-11; Amos 5:15). A helpless unfortunate person was not likely to receive much consideration in the gate (31:21). The two lines in verse 5 are grammatically impossible,[1] as they stand in the text, but their general sense is clear. Unfortunates, perhaps Bedouins, who function at the edge of cities and lands and seize what they can, are represented in the imagery.

Verse 6—This verse refers to 4:8. Eliphaz commits a logical fallacy by asserting that because a fool meets disaster, all who meet disaster must be fools. He declares that Job is responsible for all of his misery. Sympathy will not be a major preoccupation of anyone who believes that prosperity is proof of God's blessings.

Verse 7—A contradiction appears once more in Eliphaz's speech. If trouble comes naturally and inevitably to man, then this claim is in conflict with verse 6, which says just the opposite. Perhaps Dahood correctly renders the text—"it is man who engenders mischief itself."[2] The phrase "as the sparks fly upward" has generated endless and fruitless discussion. Perhaps the phrase—*bene resep*—might refer to the Resheph the Phoenician god of the lightning,[3] which would be possible if the book is from the patriarchal period. The R. S. V. translation is superior to that of the A. V. As surely as sparks fly upward, man falls into sin, and he is responsible for his own decisions.

---

[1] See Dhorme, *Job,* pp. 59-60; and Rowley, *Job,* p. 58.

[2] M. Dahood, *Biblica,* XLVI, 1965, p. 318.

[3] A. Caquot, *Semitica,* VI, 1956, pp. 53ff.

4. My advice—a) Return to God who rewards the righteous.
(5:8-16)

TEXT 5:8-16

8 But as for me, I would seek unto God,
  And unto God would I commit my cause;
9 Who doeth great things and unsearchable,
  Marvellous things without number:
10 Who giveth rain upon the earth,
  And sendeth waters upon the fields;
11 So that he setteth up on high those that are low,
  And those that mourn are exalted to safety.
12 He frustrateth the devices of the crafty,
  So that their hands cannot perform their enterprise.
13 He taketh the wise in their own craftiness;
  And the counsel of the cunning is carried headlong.
14 They meet with darkness in the day-time,
  And grope at noonday as in the night.
15 But he saveth from the sword of their mouth,
  Even the needy from the hand of the mighty.
16 So the poor hath hope,
  And iniquity stoppeth her mouth.

COMMENT 5:8-16

Verse 8—Job is not prepared to agree that his misfortunes are God's judgments on his sins. The strong Hebrew adversative "But" contrasts what is being said with what precedes. In verse one, Eliphaz had warned Job against appealing to angels for help. He should go directly to God. "Seeking God" (*daras*) is a vital theme in the prophets—Amos 5:4-6. The two lines contain two different words for God—*el* and *elohim* (see parallel *Shaddai, el* and *eloah*, verse 17; 6:4; 8:3; 13:3; 22:2, 3; 27:10; and 31:2). Elohim is rare in the Dialogue (here and

47

28:23 and once in the Elihu speeches in 34:9).

Verse 9—Repeated by Job in 9:10 (Pss. 136:4; 145:3; and Eccl. 43:32), Eliphaz reveals a very perceptive mind but often draws erroneous conclusions from his own analysis.

Verse 10—God is lord of nature. He sends rain upon the fields, which is an example of God's power and benevolence (Pss. 65:10; 68:10; 104:13). He who makes the barren places fruitful can also change suffering into joy. To his "power in nature corresponds His power among men."[4]

Verse 11—Verses 11-16 are echoed in the magnificat—Luke 1:51-53. The high, steep almost inaccessible place is God's reward to the lowly. Mourners wear dirty black clothes or have dirty bodies, because they sprinkle ashes on their heads as a sign of grief. These very mourners shall be set on high (word rendered "stronghold" in Ps. 9:9 is from this root) in prosperity.

Verse 12—God frustrates the malicious devices of the crafty who scheme to gain from the poor and innocent (Mic. 3:1-3, 7:3; Isa. 32:7). The translation "cannot perform their enterprise" is a technical term employed in Wisdom Literature, two exceptions Isa. 28:29 and Mic. 6:9, found only in Job and Proverbs. It means true wisdom or true prosperity. Those who trust God are truly pious.

Verse 13—This verse is the only directly quoted Jobian text in the New Testament—I Cor. 3:19 (cf. allusion to Job 41:11 in Rom. 11:35). Theologically, the same point is at issue in both Job and Paul. "The counsel of the cunning," or tortuous men who pursue any means to attain their ends. The word translated "cunning" connotes success or victory without regard to moral quality. This type of person is "brought to a quick end."[5]

Verse 14—The image of total confusion which ensnares the crafty (Deut. 28:29; Isa. 19:14; and 59:10). They are like blind people groping at mid-day.

---

[4] F. Delitzsch, *Job,* Vol. I, Eerdmans, p. 99.
[5] Driver & Gray, *Job, ICC,* p. 54; Pope, *Job,* p. 43.

Verse 15—God frustrates the designs of the crafty, the poor He saves—from their craftiness. The major problem in this text is whether deliverance is from the *mouth* or the *sword*.[6] The technical issue is that poetic parallel demands a companion word to "the poor," which our present text lacks. What does all this mean to Job?

Verse 16—The social customs of the Near East are clearly set before us. Men of power and wealth aggrandize themselves at the expense of the poor and defenseless. But there is hope in the time of abandonment—8:13; 17:18; 14:7; Jeremiah 31:17; Ezekiel 37:11; Proverbs 19:18; Ruth 1:2; and Lamentations 3:29. This verse sums up the results of God's intervention in human affairs according to Eliphaz's theological assumptions—that justice always triumphs (Ps. 107:42; Isa. 52:15).

b) Accept his chastening and enjoy his blessings. (5:17-27)

TEXT 5:17-27

17 Behold, happy is the man whom God correcteth:
   Therefore despise not thou the chastening of the Almighty.
18 For he maketh sore, and bindeth up;
   He woundeth, and his hands make whole.
19 He will deliver thee in six troubles;
   Yea, in seven there shall no evil touch thee.
20 In famine he will redeem thee from death;
   And in war from the power of the sword.
21 Thou shalt be hid from the scourge of the tongue;
   Neither shalt thou be afraid of destruction when it cometh.
22 At destruction and dearth thou shalt laugh;
   Neither shalt thou be afraid of the beasts of the earth.
23 For thou shalt be in league with the stones of the field;
   And the beasts of the field shall be at peace with thee.

---

[6] Dhorme, *Job*, p. 63, for the technical discussion. His solution is to be preferred over the other suggestions, as it involves no change of the Hebrew text.

24 And thou shalt know that thy tent is in peace;
  And thou shalt visit thy fold, and shalt miss nothing.
25 Thou shalt know also that thy seed shall be great,
  And thine offspring as the grass of the earth.
26 Thou shalt come to thy grave in a full age,
  Like as a shock of grain cometh in its season.
27 Lo this, we have searched it, so it is;
  Hear it, and know thou it for thy good.

COMMENT 5:17-27

Verse 17—According to Eliphaz, suffering is always a form of divine discipline. This is also a thesis set forth in Elihu's speeches—32:19ff, Proverb 3:11-12, which is quoted in Hebrews 12:5ff. The emphasis is beautiful and moving in its attempt to bring Job to repentance. The thesis is only marred by its inapplicability to Job. He has not sinned; and Eliphaz's argument makes no impression on him. "Thus the words which were meant for healing make his wounds smart the more" (V. E. Reichert, *Job,* Soncino, p. 20). The word for God (Almighty) is *Shaddai.*[7] It occurs in the Old Testament approximately 48 times, mostly in Job. The word is present in other literature from the patriarchal period—Gen. 17:1; Ex. 6:3.

Verse 18—God almighty makes sore and also heals—Deut. 32:39; Hos. 6:1; and Isa. 30:26.

Verse 19—Eliphaz enumerates the blessings which Job can expect if he follows his advice. The numerical idiom is common

---

[7] The Book of Job uses *Elohim* 40 times, 31 times *Shaddai,* which only occurs 17 times more in the entire Old Testament, within poetic structure of Job proper; 55 times it uses *El, Elohim* (only once 12:8), and Jahweh (in chps. 1, 2, 38:1, 40, 42)—31 times. See O. Grether, *Name und Wort Gottes im Alten Testament,* 1934; and G. R. Driver, "The Original Form of the Name Jahweh," *Zeitschrift für die alttestamentliche Wissenschaft,* 46, 1928, 7-25; Jean Leveque, *Job et Son Dieu,* Tome I, Paris: Gabalda, pp. 146-179; O. Eissfeldt, *El im ugaritischen Pantheon,* 1941; M. Pope, *El in the Ugaritic Texts,* V. T. S., II, 1955; D. N. Freedman, "The Name of the God of Moses," *JBL,* 79 (1960), 151-6.

in Hebrew poetry (also in Ugaritic myths and epics), cf. Amos 1:3-13; 2:1-16; Mic. 5:4; Prov. 6:16, 30:15, 18, 29; and Eccl. 11:2, 25:7. The related use of the multiple of seven and eleven occurs in the Song of Lamech—Gen. 4:24; and in Jesus' answer to Peter's question in Matt. 18:22.[8]

Verse 20—The almighty is able (Job) to deliver from famine, death, war, etc., those scourges of the ancient Near East.

Verse 21—For the tongue (*lason*) as a powerful weapon, see Isa. 54:17; Jer. 18:18; Pss. 12:3-5, 31:21; and James 3:5-6. The destruction (*sod*—devastation) of the tongue might refer to efforts at incantations and use of black magic. Hence, some commentators read—*sed*—demon for M. T. *sod*—devastation. (The Hebrew *sod* occurs in the next verse in relationship to famine.)

Verse 22—The beasts of the field were feared in Palestine. One of Ezekiel's "four sore judgment" is the beasts—14:21.

Verse 23—Stones will not accumulate to mar the fields, nor beasts attack his flock. The word translated "league" is *berith* or covenant. It is as though they have a covenant with the rocks and beasts—Isa. 11:6-9.

Verse 24—Job describes the prosperity of the wicked in similar fashion in 21:7ff. The A. V. renders the Hebrew pastoral term "tent" as "fold" and means dwelling as in verse 3. The word translated "miss" is one of the Hebrew terms for sin (*ht-*) which means to miss the mark or fail to attain a goal.[9] All of Job's property will be safe if he follows Eliphaz's suggestions.

Verse 25—Eliphaz's orthodox theology is consistently untouched by human feeling. Eliphaz apparently has forgotten that Job's children were all destroyed. But he declares that his "offspring" will be great—Isa. 34:1; 42:5; 53:10. This will come to pass, but how does Eliphaz know?

---

[8] Regarding the Old Testament use of numerical proverbs, see W. M. W. Roth, "Numerical Sayings in the Old Testament," *Vetus Testamentum,* Supplement XIII, 1965; and A. Bea, *Biblica,* 21 (1940), 196-8.

[9] F. D. Coggan, *Journal of the Manchester University Egyptian and Oriental Society,* XVII, 1932, 53-6.

Verse 26—Eliphaz knows nothing of resurrection, only a full age (Hebrew *kelah*[10]—full vigor). This is a quality here assured to the righteous. Eliphaz's pontifical announcements, which were meant to heal, only irritated Job's sore soul.

Verse 27—As Job's counselor, Eliphaz offered "empty chaff well meant for grain." Though it is no comfort to Job, Eliphaz's discourse is one of the masterpieces of the book. With only partial vision, Eliphaz identified his words with exhaustive truth. This weakness vitiated his genuine concern for Job's condition. "To Job all these fine words must have seemed bitterly inappropriate."[11]

TODAY'S ENGLISH VERSION

5 Call out, Job. See if anyone answers.
   Is there any angel to whom you can turn?
² To worry yourself to death with resentment
   would be a foolish, senseless thing to do.
³ I have seen fools who looked secure,
   but I called down a sudden curse on their homes.
⁴ Their sons can never find safety;
   in court no one stands up to defend them.
⁵ Hungry people will eat the fool's crops—
   even the grain growing among thorns—
   and thirsty people will envy his wealth.
⁶ Evil does not grow in the soil,
   nor does trouble grow out of the ground.
⁷ No! Man brings trouble on himself,
   as surely as sparks fly up from a fire.

---

[10] See W. F. Albright, "The Natural Force of Moses in the Light of Ugaritic," *Bulletin American Society Oriental Research,* 94, 1944, 32-5; and M. Dahood, *Gregorianum* 43, 1962, 66.

[11] Much significant insight into Job from a counseling perspective is found in Wm. E. Hulme's *Dialogue in Despair* (Abingdon, 1968).

⁸ If I were you, I would turn to God
   and present my case to him.
⁹ We cannot understand the great things he does,
   and there is no end to his miracles.
¹⁰ He sends rain on the land and waters the fields.
¹¹ Yes, it is God who raises the humble
   and gives joy to all who mourn.
¹²⁻¹³ He upsets the plans of tricky men,
   and traps wise men in their own schemes,
   so that nothing they do succeeds;
¹⁴   even at noon they grope in darkness.
¹⁵ But God saves the poor from death;
   he saves the needy from oppression.
¹⁶ He gives hope to the poor and silences the wicked.
¹⁷ Happy is the person whom God corrects!
   Do not resent it when he reprimands you.
¹⁸ God bandages the wounds he makes;
   his hand hurts you, and his hand heals.
¹⁹ Time after time he will keep you from harm;
²⁰   when famine comes, he will keep you alive,
   and in war protect you from death.
²¹ God rescues you from lies and slander;
   he saves you when destruction comes.
²² You will laugh at violence and hunger
   and not be afraid of wild animals.
²³ The fields you plow will be free of rocks;
   wild animals will never attack you.
²⁴ Then you wil live at peace in your tent;
   when you look at your sheep, you will find
      them safe.
²⁵ You will have as many children
   as there are blades of grass in a pasture.
²⁶ Like wheat that ripens till harvest time,
   you will live to a ripe old age.
²⁷ Job, we have learned this by long study.
   It is true, so now accept it.

QUESTIONS FOR DISCUSSION 5:1-27

93. What is the purpose of verse one? i.e., in the speech of Eliphaz?
94. Verse one may be an apologetic. How so?
95. Read Proverbs 14:30 and show how it relates to verse two.
96. The prosperity of the wicked causes a reaction from Eliphaz. What is it? Why?
97. Why do the children of the foolish suffer?
98. How is the term "gate" used here?
99. What is the meaning of verse five?
100. Eliphaz commits a logical fallacy. What is it: Show how this cancels out sympathy.
101. If man is born to trouble "as the sparks fly upward" how is it that only fools suffer—i.e., according to previous logic?
102. How is it that the little phrase "as the sparks fly upward" has caused so much discussion?
103. There are two different words for God in verse 8. What does this suggest?
104. Eliphaz is right and wrong at the same time. About what subjects?
105. How does the thought of "mother nature" relate to verse 10?
106. In what other passage in the N.T. are verses 11 through 16 echoed? Discuss.
107. Explain the phrase "cannot perform their enterprise."
108. The only direct N.T. quotation from Job is found in these verses. Where?
109. Does the description of verse 14 always describe the end of the crafty? Discuss.
110. What does all this speech mean to Job?
111. The principle of verse 17 is stated in Prov. 3:11, 12 and is quoted in Heb. 12:5ff—To whom does it apply?
112. All these words to Job are to make his wound hurt more. Why?
113. There is a strange covenant promised in verse 23. What is it?

C. SEARCH FOR COMFORT AND JOB'S CONFRONTATION WITH GOD (6:1—7:21)

1. There is adequate reason for his complaint. (6:1-7)

TEXT 6:1-7

6 Then Job answered and said,
2 Oh that my vexation were but weighed,
And all my calamity laid in the balances!
3 For now it would be heavier than the sand of the seas:
Therefore have my words been rash.
4 For the arrows of the Almighty are within me,
The poison whereof my spirit drinketh up:
The terrors of God do set themselves in array against me.
5 Doth the wild ass bray when he hath grass?
Or loweth the ox over his fodder?
6 Can that which hath no savor be eaten without salt?
Or is there any taste in the white of an egg?
7 My soul refuseth to touch *them;*
They are as loathsome food to me.

COMMENT 6:1-7

Dachau: Eine Welt-Ohne Gnade
(Dachau—a world without grace)

Verse 1—Job now replies to Eliphaz's first speech. Job is responding to the three friends (6:2-30; plurals in 6:24-29) rather than Eliphaz alone. First Job defends his first soliloquy (chp. 3), for which Eliphaz had rebuked him. Because of his suffering (vss. 2-7) he desires to die (vss. 8-10). Being without hope and sympathy from his friends, Job seeks the friendship of death. Why is life so difficult (7:1ff), especially since he is innocent? Receiving no comfort from the three wise men, Job turns to God (probably from 7:1, certainly from 7:7—as remember is second singular). After an appeal to God's compassion (vss. 7-10), without restraint (vs. 11) he asks why He

55

plagues Job with impossible suffering (vss. 12-21).[1] Job's three friends are bound to him by a covenant of friendship (*hesed*).[2] Thus, they should not assume that Job is guilty of sin because of his suffering. Since they fail to express covenant concern and sympathy, Job turns to God. The speech falls into three parts: (1) Affirmation of his bitterness, (2) Disappointment in his friends (6:14-30); and (3) Intensification of his complaint at his lot, and more open appeal against God's treatment of him (7:1-21).

Verse 2—Job's anguish (*ha-as*—A. V. as vexation—translated as impatience in 5:2 and displeasure in 10:17. The basic sense of the root is "happen," hence "accident," "misfortune") is heavier than the "sands of the seas." Job's theme is not God's indignation but his own undeserved suffering.

Verse 3—Job's anguish and calamity correspond in parallelism; either of them would outweigh the sand. Job admits (therefore) that his words have been wild but not unjustified. His speech has been "rash."[3]

Verse 4—Job now names God (Shaddai—the Almighty, used by Eliphaz 5:17) as the author of his misery. Job, no less than Eliphaz, believes the suffering comes from God; but rejects Eliphaz's claim that Job is unrighteous, thus deserving of his plight. Why is the pain harder to bear merely because he believes in God? The imagery of God as an archer appears frequently in the Old Testament—Deut. 32:23; Ezek. 5:16; Pss. 7:13, 38:2, 64:7. The poisoned arrows mentioned here are not referred to elsewhere in the Old Testament. The word translated "poison"—venom—is the same word as that used of the deaf adder in Ps. 58:4. Oil-soaked materials covering

---

[1] See the excellent exposition of three kinds of suffering which the scriptures carefully distinguish in Delitzsch, *Job*, Vol. I, 105ff. (1) Suffering of the godless; (2) Suffering of the righteous to intensify trust as fidelity; and (3) Suffering for witness. Compare this with the experience of a recent Job, C. S. Lewis, *A Grief Observed* (Seabury, 1963).

[2] See Nelson Glueck's exhaustive study, *The Word "hesed" in Old Testament Usage*, 1927, reprinted.

[3] E. F. Sutcliffe, *Biblica*, XXI, 1950, 367ff, renders the Hebrew "charged with grief."

arrowheads were used in war. The "terrors" of God assault Job's very existence; they "wear me down" (A. V. array against me),[4] he boldly asserts. Paul uses the imagery of the flaming darts of Satan in Eph. 6:16.

Verse 5—Using powerful distress imagery (wild ass in distress for a lack of food—Jer. 14:6). Job suggests that it would be better to identify the cause of his suffering rather than explain it. The wild ass "brays" is used only here and 30:7, where it describes the agonizing cries of social outcasts. The second descriptive word is the verb translated "loweth" in A. V. It is used only here and in I Sam. 6:12, where it is used of cows deprived of their calves. Even the animals understand what Eliphaz fails to comprehend.

Verses 6-7—Though the text is difficult in these uncertain verses, something nauseating is implied. Eliphaz's counsel is tasteless; it lacks the salt of sympathy. The A. V.'s phrase "the white of an egg" might better be understood as "the slime of purslane" (so R. S. V., Rowley, Driver and Gray). The purslane is a leguminous plant which secreets mucilaginous jelly. Job rejects Eliphaz's explanation as he (*nephesh*—soul) would reject tasteless food. In Hebrew psychology, "nephesh" (soul) is the seat of desire—Deut. 24:15; Hos. 4:8; and, in particular—of appetite—Deut. 14:26; 23:25; Isa. 29:8; Mic. 7:1; and Prov. 23:2. The condition of Job's flesh[5] (*lehem*—literally bread but here is flesh or meat), like Eliphaz's comfort, is sickening—7:5; 18:13; 30:30.

2. In his wasted condition, death is desirable. (6:8-13)

TEXT 6:8-13

8 Oh that I might have my request;
And that God would grant *me* the thing that I long for!

---

[4] G. R. Driver, *Vetus Testamentum* Supplement III, 1955, 73; also Saydon, *Catholic Biblical Quarterly*, XXIII, 1961, 252.

[5] There is no need to emend the text as does Kissane *et al.* The "they" refers to Eliphaz's arguments. Words and *lehem* in its present parallel structure means Job's flesh or body.

9 Even that it would please God to crush me;
   That he would let loose his hand, and cut me off!
10 And be, it still my consolation,
   Yea, let me exult in pain that spareth not,
   That I have not denied the words of the Holy One.
11 What is my strength, that I should wait?
   And what is mine end, that I should be patient?
12 Is my strength the strength of stones?
   Or is my flesh of brass?
13 Is it not that I have no help in me,
   And that wisdom is driven quite from me?

COMMENT 6:8-13

Verse 8—Job's entreaty is that he be allowed to die—3:11. No facile repentance can remove Job's sickness unto death. All that he desires is the healing of a hurried death—chp. 3.

Verse 9—Oh that God, "would be willing" to free this prisoner of pain (cf. Isa. 53:10). The Hebrew which is translated "let loose his hand" is a verb used of setting prisoners free—Ps. 105:20; 146:7.[6]

Verse 10—Job has one consolation that is that he has not betrayed God's trust; that is, even though called on to endure such severe punishment. "No accusing conscience would impair his comfort in death" (Driver). Job has been and still is an obedient servant to the Holy One of Israel—Isa. 40:25; Heb. 3:3.

Verse 11—Job can endure no more. Wait? For what? Eliphaz's promised blessings. What does the future hold for Job?

Verse 12—Men of stone and bronze feel nothing. Job is

---

[6] Job has no awareness of guilt—compare with Lady MacBeth. The haunting, enslaving power of guilt is absent from Job's existential "angst." Note also this powerful imagery in C. Fry's *The Sleep of Prisoners*. An enslaved spirit is more torturously imprisoned than a shackled body. See Solzhenitsyn's *One Day in the Life of Ivan Denisovich; The Gulag Archipelago;* and compare with Paul's imprisonments and Bonhoeffer's.

58

flesh and blood whose power to resist pain is all but exhausted.

Verse 13—This verse contains an emphatic interrogative particle as in Numbers 17:28, and the question form is to express strong avowal, which means that it is a fact that I do not have within me the power to help myself. Naturalistic humanism would not care for Job's pessimism. All human power to alleviate Job's suffering is already banished from him.[7] Job is not thinking of rescue from suffering but of the strength to bear the pain.

3. Bitter disappointment from his friends, who are
   unreasonably hard (6:14-23)

TEXT 6:14-23

14 To him that is ready to faint kindness *should be showed*
      from his friend;
   Even to him that forsaketh the fear of the Almighty.
15 My brethren have dealt deceitfully as a brook,
   As the channel of brooks that pass away;
16 Which are black by reason of the ice,
   And wherein the snow hideth itself:
17 What time they wax warm, they vanish;
   When it is hot, they are consumed out of their place.
18 The caravans *that travel* by the way of them turn aside;
   They go up into the waste, and perish.
19 The caravans of Tema looked,
   The companies of Sheba waited for them.
20 They were put to shame because they had hoped;
   They came thither, and were confounded.
21 For now ye are nothing;
   Ye see a terror, and are afraid.
22 Did I say, Give unto me?
   Or, Offer a present for me of your substance?
23 Or, Deliver me from the adversary's hand?
   Or, Redeem me from the hand of the oppressors?

---

[7] For analysis of this question form, see M. Dahood, *Biblica et Orientalia* XVII, 1965, 13; and E. F. Sutcliffe, *Biblica,* XXXI, 1950, 368ff.

COMMENT 6:14-23

Verse 14—The text of only three words literally says "For the fainting—from his friend—loyalty." Job attacks his would-be sympathizers with this charge—your lack of sympathy reveals your lack of true covenant concern, i.e., righteousness. Kindness (*hesed*—covenant love) is due to a friend. If his friends really cared, they would treat Job with kindness, not groundless insinuations of his guilt.

Verse 15—Note that Job still calls the three friends brethren, not foes. But he describes them as a brook (*nachal*), a stream which is a raging torrent during the rainy season, but dried up during the summer, when one really needs help. The streams of sympathy have dried up—Her. 15:18.

Verse 16—This verse describes a thaw which breaks the ice and sends the waters raging downward. The phrase "hideth itself" means to melt.[8]

Verse 17—The A. V. contains a very obtuse translation—"wax warm" (wax from old German waxen—to grow, the root *zarab* is found only here and means seared or scorched). When the snow and ice melt, they (the torrents) disappear,"[9] or "are extinguished," 18:5-6; the friends are as unreliable as a *wadi* which is empty.

Verse 18—The travelers (A. V. caravans) expect to find water in the desert, but coming to them they find none; they soon perish under the scorching sun. This is Job's blistering attack on his friends. This disappointment describes Job's despair.

Verse 19—Tema is an oasis Southeast of the head of the Gulf of Aqaba—Isa. 21:14; Jer. 25:23. Sheba is South Arabia, which is the home of the Sabean raiders (chp. 1:15), but here they are merchants.[10]

---

[8] See M. Dahood, *Biblical*, 33, 1952, 206; also *Biblica*, 43, 1962, 65.

[9] G. R. Driver, *Zeitschrift für die alttestamentliche Wissenschaft*, N. S., XXIV, 1953, 216ff.

[10] W. F. Albright, *Bulletin the American Society of Oriental Research*, 163, 1961, 41, n. 24.

Verse 20—The caravans from the south sift us to dry oases. Job's friends have been compared to "dry wadi" and now "dry oases." There is no possibility that they can be of help to him.

Verse 21—There is a play on words here—"you see" (tir'u) and "you fear" (tire'u) II Sam. 10:19. The sight of Job in his desperate and horrible condition has frightened his friends out of their wits and caused them to forget their covenant (*hesed*) of loyalty to him. His oppressors are tyrants who would sell him, but not redeem him.

Verses 22-23—Job has not asked for money (which their covenant would have obliged), only friendship. Jeremiah cries, "I have not lent or borrowed, yet everyone curses me," Jer. 15:10. Job responds here with strong sarcasm. He has not asked for charity, though he has lost everything; he asks only for concern.

4. Their words are academic. Where is his sin?
(6:24-30)

TEXT 6:24-30

24 Teach me, and I will hold my peace;
   And cause me to understand wherein I have erred.
25 How forcible are words of uprightness!
   But your reproof, what doth it reprove?
26 Do ye think to reprove words,
   Seeing that the speeches of one that is desperate are as wind?
27 Yea, ye would cast *lots* upon the fatherless,
   And make merchandise of your friend.
28 Now therefore be pleased to look upon me;
   For surely I shall not lie to your face.
29 Return, I pray you, let there be no injustice;
   Yea, return again, my cause is righteous.
30 Is there injustice on my tongue?
   Cannot my taste discern mischievous things?

COMMENT 6:24-30

Verse 24—If his friends can help him, he will listen in silence

61

for their sympathetic words. He only asks for proof, not mere assertions, concerning his guilt. For discussions of inadvertent and presumptuous sins, see Lev. 4; Num. 15:22-9; Ps. 19:13.

Verse 25—The A. V. translates *nimras* as "how forcible." It is used here and occurs again only in Job 16:3.[11] Job asks once more for what specific sin do you accuse me? Your arrogant generalities are meaningless, and only provoke me to more pain.

Verse 26—Are Job's words but "wind"? His friends have only been concerned to rebuke Job for his expression of his grief, instead of comforting him by identifying the cause of his words. "You think that your words are correct and hold the words of him who is in anguish to be vanity." "One that is desperate"[12] is one that is as hopeless (Hebrew "a despairing man—Isa. 57:10; Jer. 2:25; and Jer. 18:12) as wind, meaning that they will soon be blown away; then we can forget them.

Verse 27—Eliphaz's complacent lecturing is inhumane. As a healer, he is more interested in the disease than the patient. Though the general sense is evident, the phrase "cast lots" is a problem, as the Hebrew contains no word "lots," but see verses 14-23. They bargain over—"make merchandise" of—their friends. "Make merchandise," barter, is used in 40:30 where the same verb is used of fish dealers (wholesalers) haggling over Leviathan. The same verb is used in Hos. 3:2 concerning Hosea's purchase of a prostitute on the slave market—Deut. 2:6. Job is suffering, while they are haggling with him as an object in a consumer trainee program.

Verse 28—The verse is in the form of an oath—"I swear I will not lie." But his friends have turned from him, unable to bear either his physical appearance or his violent words.

Verse 29—Return (Heb. *subu*—return you) does not mean that his friends are departing from him, but rather that he is asking them to change their attitude toward him. The A. V. translation "my cause is right" is possible but unclear. Dhorme

---

[11] G. R. Driver, *Journal of Theological Studies*, XXIX, 1927-8, 394ff, argues for "be bitter."

[12] Reichert, *Job*, Soncino, p. 28.

reveals the meaning in his translation—"my righteousness is still in tact."[13] Job still maintains his innocence, even in his "furnace of affliction."

Verse 30—Job says if there was poison on my tongue, would I not know it? Cannot my palate (Hebrew) discern mischievous things, i.e., am I not able to discern the flavor of my own suffering? Neither his palate nor his moral integrity have lost their powers of discernment.

TODAY'S ENGLISH VERSION

6
Job

1-2 If my troubles and griefs were weighed on scales,
3   they would weigh more than the sands of the sea.
    My wild words should not surprise you—
4   Almighty God has shot me with arrows,
        and their poison spreads through my body.
    God has lined up his terrors against me.
5   A donkey is content when eating grass,
        and a cow is quiet when eating hay.
6   But who can eat flat, unsalted food?
        What taste is there in the white of an egg?
7   I have no appetite for food like that,
        and everything I eat makes me sick."
8   Why won't God give me what I ask?
        Why won't he answer my prayer?
9   I wish he would go ahead and kill me.
10 If I knew he would, I would leap for joy,
        no matter how great my pain.
    I know that God is holy;

---

[13] Dhorme, *Job,* p. 94.

I have never opposed what he commands.
¹¹ What strength do I have to keep on living?
Why go on living when I have no hope?
¹² Am I made of stone? Is my body bronze?
¹³ I have no strength left to save myself;
there is nowhere I can turn for help.

¹⁴ In trouble like this I need loyal friends—
whether I've forsaken God or not.
¹⁵ But you, my friends, you deceive me like a stream
that goes dry when no rain comes.
¹⁶⁻¹⁷ The stream is full of snow and ice,
but in the heat they disappear,
and the stream bed lies bare and dry.
¹⁸ Caravans get lost looking for water;
they wander and die in the desert.
¹⁹ Caravans from Sheba and Tema search,
²⁰   but their hope dies beside dry streams.
²¹ You are like those streams to me;
you see my fate and are shocked.
²² Have I asked you to give me a gift,
or to bribe someone on my behalf,
²³   or to save me from some enemy or tyrant?

²⁴ All right, teach me; tell me my faults.
I will be quiet and listen to you.
²⁵ An intelligent argument might convince me,
but you are talking nonsense.
²⁶ You think I am talking nothing but wind;
then why do you answer my words of despair?
²⁷ You would even roll dice for orphan slaves,
and make yourselves rich off your closest friends!
²⁸ Look me in the face. I won't lie.
²⁹ You have gone far enough. Stop being unjust.
Don't condemn me. I'm in the right.
³⁰ But still you think I am lying—
you think I can't tell right from wrong.

QUESTIONS FOR DISCUSSION 6:1-30

114. Job responds to Eliphaz, but also to more than Eliphaz. Show how so.
115. Job finds no comfort from his friends so he turns to whom?
116. There are three kinds of suffering carefully distinguised in the scriptures. What are they? Discuss.
117. Name the three parts into which Job's speech falls.
118. Job's theme is not God's indignation but something else. What?
119. Job admits he has been "rash." How so? Why?
120. Why is the pain harder to bear merely because he believes in God?
121. Is God an archer? Does He aim arrows at us? Discuss.
122. Powerful distress imagery is used by Job. Cite two examples.
123. Something nauseating is implied in verses six and seven. What does the imagery say about the speech of Eliphaz?
124. Job's strong and often request was for one thing. What was it?
125. What is meant by the expression "let loose His hand" in verse 9?
126. Job has one consolation in the midst of his suffering. What was it?
127. Job has lost hope. Of what? Why?
128. What is meant by the question of verse 13?
129. Job's friends did not really care. What indicated this fact?
130. In what way were Job's brethren like a brook?
131. How can we relate verse 16 to Job's friends?
132. These friends are very unreliable. To what are they compared?
133. Job is very disappointed. To what is his disappointment compared?
134. Job has a real capacity for creating the metaphor. List the ones used in verses 15-23.
135. Job's friends have been frightened and have forgotten. How so?

5. God decrees what man receives. (7:1-10)

TEXT 7:1-10

7   Is there not a warfare to man upon earth?
   And are not his days like the days of a hireling?
2 As a servant that earnestly desireth the shadow,
   And as a hireling that looketh for his wages:
3 So am I made to possess months of misery,
   And wearisome nights are appointed to me.
4 When I lie down, I say,
   When shall I arise, and the night be gone?
   And I am full of tossings to and fro unto the dawning of
   the day.
5 My flesh is clothed with worms and clods of dust;
   My skin closeth up, and breaketh out afresh.
6 My days are swifter than a weaver's shuttle.
   And are spent without hope.
7 Oh remember that my life is a breath:
   Mine eye shall no more see good.
8 The eye of him that seeth me shall behold me no more;
   Thine eyes shall be upon me, but I shall not be.
9 As the cloud is consumed and vanisheth away,
   So he that goeth down to Sheol shall come up no more.
10 He shall return no more to his house,
   Neither shall his place know him any more.

COMMENT 7:1-10

"Having done such a thing there is loneliness which cannot be borne," Pablo—*For Whom The Bell Tolls*

Verse 1—Job's friends reject his appeal. He then ceases to address them, as he returns to his lament. He compares life in general to forced military service, to the work of a day laborer,

and to simple slavery, three wretched states of existence.[1]
Job vehemently retorts to Eliphaz's easy optimism—5:17ff. Job
believes in the validity of Nietzsche's remark: "Great problems
are in the streets." Does the "human condition" consistently
reveal a basic absurdity as well as an implacable nobility?
Job's condition is always the stuff of human revolt, not only
against social institutions but ultimately against God. In
western thought, men have long talked of "human nature,"
but after the revolutions of the 18th-19th centuries in the
physical, biological, and behavioral sciences, men began to
talk of the "human condition,"[2] which could be modified
through the application of the scientific method. Here lies
the challenge of our contemporary Job—Is a life of happiness
through peace, prosperity, and progress possible, or is life
really absurd? Twentieth century men will not take lightly
to any naive suggestions which are grounded in the heresy
of utopia. We live, like Job, in a world which experiences the
inveteracy of evil—Mark 7:21-3. We know that Dostoevsky
is speaking of all of us in his *Notes from Underground*. A man
will often, without rhyme or reason, do things which are irrational and absurd. Man has a passion to destroy. This
passion, Dostoevsky exposes in his reflections on the Crystal
Palace which was erected in London in 1851 to celebrate the

---

[1] See M. David, *Revue philosophique,* 147, 1957, 341-49. It is a striking parallel
to existentialist visions of life, Job comes to see that acceptance of his world must be
based on other than normal grounds based in empirical justice. Nahum N. Glatzer,
The Dimensions of Job (New York: Schocken Books, 1969); and C. G. Jung, *Answer
to Job* (New York: Meridian Books, 1960), speaks of the "dark face of God." Glatzer
distinguishes between Judaic, Christian, and Humanist traditions in Job interpretation;
much current interest in the Book of Job comes from the Existentialist, both theistic
and atheistic, tradition.

[2] See Hanna Arendt, *The Human Condition* (Chicago: paperback); and Social
Theory from Hegel and Marx to the Frankfort School of Social Research (Frankfort,
Germany) which is the origin of much Neo-Marxist theory of revolution—liberation.
Is man the captain of his own fate? or is Camus correct in asserting that man is an
eternal rock-pusher (*Myth of Sisyphus*), and that analysis of our contemporary intellectual malady requires the recognition of the absurdity of human life? The secret
complicity that joins the logical and the everyday to the tragic is a fundamental theme
of Kafka, *Metamorphasis.*

Great Exhibition of Science. He foresees the coming clouds of totalitarian tyrannies (cf. America's 1876 centennial and 1976 Bi-Centennial celebrations).[3] Job understands that his experience, while exceptional in the intensity of his suffering, is typical in the fact of suffering. The word translated "hireling" is used of a laborer, and a mercenary soldier—Jer. 46:21. The imagery of warfare (Num. 1:3; I Sam. 28:1) and hard work of one trapped in ceaseless toil are fused in Job's lament.

Verse 2—In Mesopotamia it was assumed that everyone (not in high political lineage) was a slave and servant of the gods. Every slave was compelled to work the long and hot days without respite—Matt. 20:12. They longed for the decline of the sun and the cooling breezes of the evening. The slave[4] received wages every day—Deut. 24:15, which was his endurance motive. To withhold his pay was prohibited—Lev. 19:13; Mal. 3:5; Rom. 4:4; I Cor. 3:8; I Tim. 5:18; Jas. 5:4.

Verse 3—Job now turns from contemplating man's universal condition to his own affliction. Months[5] of vanity (Hebrew *shaw* may mean emptiness, vanity, or moral evil—11:11; 31:5) and nights of wearisome anguish. When will the months pass away?

Verse 4—The night, like the months, are long (*middah*—to measure—be extended, cf. Einstein's relativity thesis and

---

[3] The contemporary preoccupation with evil and pervasive meaninglessness stems from the developments in 19th century thought. Hegel reflects on God's "wisdom and righteousness." The question of God's justice is bound up with the question of his purposefulness. Only if nature-history will ultimately realize God's purposefulness (Eschatology) can we speak of God as righteous. In contrast, Gilbert Murray claims not that God is righteous but that He is "Beyond Good and Evil." Nietzsche criticized a believer's acceptance of God as being a relinquishment of personal freedom. Thus the freedom thesis enters through the door of atheism, a la Sartre, *et al.* R. Otto also denies that the final chapters in Job "intend . . . to suggest . . . teleological reflections or solutions (Glatzer, *The Dimensions of Job*, p. 277).

[4] For exhaustive analysis of slavery in the ancient Near East, see R. deVaux, *Ancient Israel* (New York, pp. 80-90) with excellent bibliography; the excellent studies of Lindhagen, *The Servant Motif in Old Testament;* and Scott Bartchy on Slavery in the Graeco-Roman milieu of the New Testament. Bartchy's work was originally a Harvard Ph.D. thesis.

[5] From this allusion to months, Rabbi Aqiba assumed that Job's suffering lasted a year (*Mishnah,* 'Eduyot 2:10; *The Testament of Job* says that he suffered seven years.

contemporary man's preoccupation with time.) Killing time before time kills us, e.g. leisure, play, vacations, etc., and the quality of our lived time (Dilthey's Erlebnis).[6] Job tosses and turns all night—his *Long Day's Journey Into Night*. There is no relief even from the dawning (*nasheph*) of the day. *Nasheph* means morning light in contrast to *ereb*, evening twilight. Acute discomfort enslaves this vain searcher for peace. Even his dozing invites diabolic nightmares (verse 14). Unabating misery—*Oh, come sweet Death!* The grave is no darker than his nights of loneliness and despair.

Verse 5—Job's ulcers are repulsive to the sight and smell. His skin is covered with dirty scabs filled with worms. The scabs break open and run with pus.[7]

Verse 6—Is Job contradicting himself when first he claims that life passes so slowly (of course, in his condition the psychology of suffering is imperative for our understanding his statements), and now complains that it is too brief? Here we note a play on the words for hope (*tiqwah*) and thread. The same word is used in Joshua 2:18, 21 for the scarlet thread which identified Rahab's house. As the weaver's shuttle runs out of thread, so now Job's existence is running out of hope. "Swift as a weaver's shuttle fleet our days," Browning.

Verse 7—The pathos of this pitiful cry penetrates into the depths of every sensitive person. But will God hear? He has turned once more from his tormenting counselors directly to God. Life is at best transient (Ps. 78:39; Isa. 51:29; Jer. 5:13; Eccl. 1:14; Jas. 5:13ff), and he will never again see prosperity and happiness. Until Tolkien's eucatastrophe in the form of our Lord's resurrection, neither Job nor any of his contemporaries

---

[6] Note the significance of time—and reality in the physical and biological sciences in contrast to the humanities and behavioral sciences, cf. quality of daily existence and our existential-phenomenological response to time. See the late M. Heidegger's *Being and Time;* S. M. Cahn. *Fate, Logic, and Time* (Yale University Press); Caponigri, *Time and Ideas* (University of Notre Dame Press; Jiri Zeman, ed., *Time in Science and Philosophy* (New York: Am. Elsevier Pub.); and O. Cullinann, *Christ and Time* (Westminster Press).

[7] This verse is omitted by the LXX and others. This is unnecessary at best. See Dhorme, *Job*, p. 102; and J. Weingreen, *Vetus Testamentum*, IV, 1954, 56ff.

could hope beyond suffering and the grave. Rashi observes that here Job denies the resurrection. But in 19:24-7 he reaches beyond the despair-creating view of man's finitude and of the finality of death to something better than Sheol. Note contemporary man's concern with *death* and his multiplication of his futile efforts to generate new men and new societies, where all are happy and prosperous.

Verse 8—Time is too short to expect (hope for) his restoration. God alone will prevail.

Verse 9—"Vanish away" translates Hebrew which means "comes to an end." Sheol (see Kittel article) is described as a place from which no traveler has returned—10:21; a land of darkness and despair—10:21ff; as deep—11:8; place where the dead are hidden—14:13; place for everyone—3:19 and 30:23. Only resurrection can break the spell of this despair.

Verse 10—The theme of the finality of death reoccurs several times—7:21; 10:21; 14:10, 12, 18-22; 17:13;16; 19:25-27; also Ps. 103:16b for the second line.

6. He finds no mercy, neither from God or from his friends.
(7:11-15)

TEXT 7:11-15

11 Therefore I will not refrain my mouth;
I will speak in the anguish of my spirit;
I will complain in the bitterness of my soul.
12 Am I a sea, or a sea-monster,
That thou settest a watch over me?
13 When I say, My bed shall comfort me,
My couch shall ease my complaint;
14 Then thou scarest me with dreams,
And terrifiest me through visions:
15 So that my soul chooseth strangling,
And death rather than *these* my bones.

COMMENT 7:11-15

Verse 11—For the first time, Job charges God with being his tormentor. Bitterness oozes out of the disease of soul sickness.

Verse 12—God has set limits to the sea—Gen. 1:10 and watches that it does not violate its appointed boundary. Do I, cries Job, need to be watched like that great inanimate ocean?[8] God is creator of the universe and, thus, Lord of the waters.[9] Job reminds God that he cannot threaten Him. The word translated A. V. "set a watch" means guard, or perhaps with Dahood, a muzzle—Pss. 39:2; 68:23; and 141:3. God, you are trying to put a muzzle on me, so I will be silent.

Verse 13—See Eliphaz's description of his nightmare— 4:12-16, and Job's discussion of his restless tossing—verse 4.

Verse 14—Job accuses God of causing his nightmares. Terrify is a major word in Job's theology, where it occurs in intensive form eight, out of the total of thirteen, times in the entire Old Testament.

Verse 15—This verse means that "my soul prefers choking, my bones prefer death."[10]

7. To God he addresses some difficult questions. (7:16-21)

TEXT 7:16-21

16 I loathe *my life;* I would not live alway:
   Let me alone; for my days are vanity.
17 What is man, that thou shouldest magnify him,
   And that thou shouldest set thy mind upon him,
18 And that thou shouldest visit him every morning,
   And try him every moment?
19 How long wilt thou not look away from me,

---

[8] Buttenweiser's (*The Book of Job*) claim that this verse refers to the Babylonian creation myth is unsubstantiated and unnecessary in order to understand this verse, neither is it necessary to compare this verse with the West Semitic Ugaritic myths; but see for both J. B. Pritchard, ed., *Ancient Near Eastern Texts Relating to the Old Testament* (Princeton, 1955).

[9] For discussion of the claim of the influence of the Ugaritic creation myth, see M. Dahood, *Journal of Biblical Literature*, LXXX, 1961, 270ff; O. Kaiser, "Die mythische Bedeutung des Meeres in Agypten, Ugarit und Israel," *Beihefte zur Zeitschrift für die alttestamentliche Wissenschaft,* 78, 1959.

[10] N. M. Sarna, *Journal of Jewish Studies,* 6, 1955, 109.

Nor let me alone till I swallow down my spittle?
20 If I have sinned, what do I unto thee, O thou watcher of
    men?
    Why hast thou set me as a mark for thee,
    So that I am a burden to myself?
21 And why dost thou not pardon my transgression, and take
    away mine iniquity?
    For now shall I lie down in the dust;
    And thou wilt seek me diligently, but I shall not be.

COMMENT 7:16-21

Verse 16—"I loathe" can be connected with the previous
verse, as "my life" is not in the Hebrew text. Meaning—"I
despise death more than my pain."[11] Vanity is the same word
translated "vanity of vanities" in Eccl. 1:2.

Verses 17-18—Here we note a parody of Ps. 8:4ff (Hebrews
2:6). We encounter strong irony in Job's words "set thy mind
upon" or pay attention. God, why are you devoting so much
unfriendly attention to man in general, and specifically to
Job? Is this divine providence? Pope describes this "as overbearing inquisitiveness and unrelenting surveillance,"[12] 23:10;
Zech. 13:3; Ps. 17:3—*visit*—*test* parallel (note this is true of
Israel, Jesus, the Suffering Servant, and Christians) in the
temptation narratives.

Verse 19—Job feels that he cannot get away from God's
hostile eye, even for a moment. Compare Job's experience and
David's—Pss. 33:18; 34:15. The idiomatic expression "Let
me swallow my spittle" means "wait, or let me alone for a
moment."

Verse 20—Surely Job is not that important to God that He
should watch over him. Even if Job admits that he has sinned,

---

[11] See Dhorme, *Job*, p. 107.
[12] Pope, *Job*, Anchor, p. 62; also J. Hempel, *Forchungen and Forschritte*, Vol. 35
(Berlin, 1961), p. 123, for analysis of surveillance theme.

he has not hurt God commensurate with the suffering with which Job has been inflicted. The word translated "mark" (only found here in the Old Testament) is not a target, but something which one strikes—I Kings 2:25. Job is weary of being a mark for God's hostile action that life (burden—*massa*) has become an intolerable malaise.

Verse 21—Even inadvertent sin does not deserve all the inflicted pain which was fallen to Job's lot. Even if God forgives, it will be too late. Job will be dead. Again the pessimism that only resurrection can shatter. God—"seek me" (from noun meaning dawn or early)—Prov. 8:17. Jeremiah speaks of God "rising up early" to send the prophets to Israel—Jer. 7:13, 25; 25:4. Job maintains that God will in the end realize His mistake, but it will be too late. Throughout Job maintains belief in a creator-redeemer God of *Justice, Holiness,* and *Love,* while attacking Him for cruelty and inhuman threat.[13]

TODAY'S ENGLISH VERSION

7 Human life is like forced army service,
  like a life of hard manual labor,
  2 like a slave longing for cool shade;
  like a worker waiting for his pay.
  3 Month after month I have nothing to live for;
  night after night brings me grief.
  4 When I lie down to sleep, the hours drag;
  I toss all night and long for dawn.
  5 My body is full of worms;
  it is covered with scabs;
  pus runs out of my sores.

---

[13] The twentieth century has and continues to express deep unbelief regarding the Christian view of God. Without question the fundamental reason is the intensification of injustice, suffering, evil, and general cultural crisis. See my syllabus *Discovering the Christian Mind* (Apologetics-Evidences); and Martin Marty, *Varieties of Unbelief* (New York: Doubleday); Jas. Collins, *God in Modern Philosophy* (Chicago: Regnery, 1967); and S. Schrey, *L'atheisme Contemporain* (Paris, 1964).

[6] My days have passed without hope,
    passed faster than a weaver's shuttle.

[7] Remember, God, my life is only wind;
    my happiness has already ended.
[8] You see me now, but never again.
    If you look for me, I'll be gone.
[9-10] Like a cloud that fades and is gone,
    a man dies and never returns;
    he is forgotten by all who knew him.
[11] No! I can't be quiet!
    I am angry and bitter.
    I have to speak.

[12] Why do you keep me under guard?
    Do you think I am a sea monster?
[13] I lie down and try to rest;
    I look for some help for my pain.
[14] But you—you terrify me with dreams;
    you send me visions and nightmares,
[15]   until I would rather be strangled,
    rather die than live like this.
[16] I give up. I am tired of living.
    Leave me alone. My life makes no sense.

[17] Why is man so important to you?
    Why pay attention to what he does?
[18] You inspect him every morning and test him
    every minute.
[19] Won't you look away long enough
    for me to swallow my spit?
[20] Are you harmed by my sin, you jailer?
    Why use me for your target practice?
    Am I that big a burden to you?
[21] Can't you ever forgive my sin?
    Can't you pardon the wrong I do?
    Soon I will lie down in the dust,
    and I'll be gone when you look for me.

74

QUESTIONS FOR DISCUSSION 7:1-21

136. Job compares life to three states of existence. What are they?
137. What was Nietzsche's remark which relates to Job's problem?
138. What is the difference between the expression "human nature" and "human condition"?
139. What general principle can be drawn from the sufferings of Job that has application to all of life?
140. How does Job compare himself to a slave in verse two?
141. How long did Job's affliction last? Discuss.
142. Verse five was omitted by the LXX. Why?
143. Is Job contradicting himself when first he claims that life passes so slowly, and now complains in verse 6 that it is too brief?
144. How is life like a thread?
145. Does Job in verse seven deny the resurrection? Discuss.
146. What is the meaning of verse eight?
147. Give five characteristics of Sheol.
148. In this book death does seem to be final. Read 7:21; 10:21 and 14:10 and discuss.
149. Job has grown bitter and now for the first time he complains against God. Why?
150. What does Job mean by asking if he is a sea or a sea-monster?
151. Job can find no rest on his bed or in his sleep. Why? Who causes this?
152. Terror is a major word with Job—show why.
153. Job suggests a form of death in verse 15. What is it?
154. ". . . My days are vanity"—what is the meaning of this expression?
155. Job feels God has taken an overbearing inquisitiveness or an unrelenting surveillance in the affairs of man. Is this wrong? Discuss.
156. Job wishes God would leave him alone, but David wanted just the opposite—Ps. 33:18; 34:15. Why?

D. THE GREAT ABSENCE: EMPATHY AND SYMPATHY—BILDAD 8:1-22

1. God is just and has not been unrighteous. (8:1-7)
   (A rebuke of Job.)

TEXT 8:1-7

8 Then answered Bildad the Shuhite, and said,
   2 How long wilt thou speak these things?
And *how long* shall the words of thy mouth be *like* a mighty wind?
   3 Doth God pervert justice?
   Or doth the Almighty pervert righteousness?
   4 If thy children have sinned against him,
   And he hath delivered them into the hand of their transgression;
   5 If thou wouldst seek diligently unto God,
   And make thy supplication to the Almighty;
   6 If thou wert pure and upright:
   Surely now he would awake for thee,
   And make the habitation of thy righteousness prosperous.
   7 And though thy beginning was small,
   Yet thy latter end would greatly increase.

COMMENT 8:1-7

Verse 1—Job concludes that even if God does finally respond to his outcries, it will be too late. Enters Bildad,[1] the younger, less tactful comforter. He is scandalized by Job's familiarity with God. A fundamental assumption in Bildad's thought is that God can do no wrong. Concurring with Eliphaz, Bildad sets forth retributive justice as a solution to our dilemma. His world contains only two groups of people—the wicked

---

[1] V. A. Irwin, "The First Speech of Bildad," *Zeitschrift für die alttestamentliche Wissenschaft*, 51, 1953, 205-16.

and the righteous. Suffering is the evidence of sin; and Job's only escape is repentance.

Verse 2—The verb "say" (A. V. speak) is an Aramaism and means "a great wind" full of sound and fury signifying nothing. Bildad continues to concentrate on God's justice,[2] a question Job has never raised.

Verse 3—God (Shaddai) and injustice are incompatible terms. Does God pervert (Heb. *ye'awwet*—distort) justice? The verb is repeated for strong emphasis (pervert—pervert) on the magnitude of Job's sin. There is no need either to use different words, as does the LXX and Vulgate, etc., or to delete one, as do some commentators.

Verse 4—Bildad does not hesitate to emphasize an obvious conclusion, that Job's children were punished for their sinfulness. They received what they deserved. This verse strongly connects the *Dialogue* with the *Prologue*. The A. V. renders the verse so as to connect verses 4-6 (compare with the R. S. V.). Sin carries its own punishment. This is expressed in the translation "into the hand of their transgression."[3] Bildad's inexcusable cruelty is apparent in his suggestion regarding Job's children, i.e., they brought their deaths on themselves. Even though the Hebrew grammar expresses a conditional form, Bildad's deadly apriori concept of God's justice could only more intensely aggravate Job's troubled spirit. (Eliphaz had already hinted at the same legalistic doctrinaire solution—5:4).

Verse 5—Bildad employs the same word used by Job 7:21, "seek," (Heb. *sihor*). But Job had spoken of God seeking him, Bildad suggests that it is imperative that Job seek God, if he desires healing.

Verse 6—The interrelationship between prosperity and piety is again emphasized (cf. American dream turned to nightmare is based on Bildad's theology). Bildad uses anthro-

---

[2] See Schrenk, art. "Dike," Kittel's *TWNT*, Vol. II, 174-225.

[3] Svi Rin, *Biblische Zeitschrift*, N. F., VII, 1963, 32ff, for suggestions based on Ugaritic evidence.

pomorphism—A. V. "he would awake for thee."[4] Is the creator of the universe asleep or insensitive to Job's tragedy? Bildad promises Job that God will—lit. "restore the habitation of thy righteousness," if he will but follow his advice.

Verse 7—Bildad unconsciously prophesies of Job's future restoration (chp. 42), though not for the reason suggested by Job's comforter. Bildad is correct in asserting that the wisdom of the ancients is in harmony with his claims—15:8; Deut. 4:32; and Eccl. 8:9.[5]

2. The wisdom of the ages teaches that it is the godless who perish. (8:8-19)

TEXT 8:8-19

8 For inquire, I pray thee, of the former age,
  And apply thyself to that which their fathers have searched
    out
9 (For we are but of yesterday, and know nothing,
  Because our days upon earth are a shadow);
10 Shall not they teach thee, and tell thee,
   And utter words out of their heart?
11 Can the rush grow up without mire?
   Can the flag grow without water?
12 Whilst it is yet in its greenness, *and* not cut down,
   It withereth before any *other* herb.
13 So are the paths of all that forget God;
   And the hope of the godless man shall perish:
14 Whose confidence shall break in sunder,
   And whose trust is a spider's web.
15 He shall lean upon his house, but it shall not stand:

---

[4] For discussion of this matter, see H. N. Richardson, *Journal of Biblical Literature,* LXVI, 1947, 322; H. L. Ginsberg, *Bulletin of the American Society of Oriental Research,* 72, 1938, 10; and J. Reider, *Vetus Testamentum,* II, 1952, 126.

[5] W. G. Lambert, *Babylonian Wisdom Literature* (Oxford, 1960), pp. 10-20.

He shall hold fast thereby, but it shall not endure.
16 He is green before the sun,
   And his shoots go forth over his garden.
17 His roots are wrapped about the *stone*-heap,
   He beholdeth the place of stones.
18 If he be destroyed from his place,
   Then it shall deny him, *saying,* I have not seen thee.
19 Behold, this is the joy of his way;
   And out of the earth shall others spring.

COMMENT 8:8-19

Verse 8—"For inquire"[6] of the wisdom of the ancients, see that I am right. The ancients "searched out" lit. "searching out," i.e., the results of investigation. Note that it is deduction based on past experience of human correlation between rich-righteousness, and poverty and the power of sin, not revelation from God.[7]

Verses 9-10—The longest life is but a brief flickering candle, so we need to consider the experience of humanity, not merely that of an individual. The brevity of life is a common theme in Wisdom Literature—14:2; Pss. 90:9-10; 102:3-4; 144:4; Eccl. 6:12; 8:13. Every individual needs recourse to total experience of mankind. Bildad claims that the instruction comes from the depth of their understanding (Heb. heart), and not from their lips as mere verbal advice.

Verse 11—Bildad now recites some proverbial sayings which might have Egyptian background.[8] Could the papyrus and reeds (Heb. *gome* and *'ahu*) grow without a proper environment? Can Job prosper without environmental righteousness?

---

[6] For discussion concerning the reading *bonen* for M. T. *konen,* see M. Dahood, *Biblica,* 46, 1965, 329.

[7] See W. F. Albright, *Yahweh and the Gods of Canaan* (Doubleday, pb.), p. 142, n. 85.

[8] In Ugaritic a cognate word is applied to the marshlands of Lake Samak, revealing that the terms above could have Palestinian origin.

The law of retribution is as sure as physical law. The unrighteous will perish in the midst of their prosperity, just as plants die when they are deprived of water—15:32.

Verse 12—When deprived of its life-sustaining environment, it withers "before all," i.e., quicker than everything else. This symbolizes Job's condition.

Verse 13—The paths (Heb. *orhot*), i.e., the fate[9] of all who forget God is suffering. The word translated "godless" occurs eight times in the book. The verb means "to be profane," irreligious, or worldly person.

Verse 14—Though there are technical problems in this verse, its basic meaning is clear. Job's confidence is not in God's justice, so his life will break like a spider's web.[10]

Verse 15—The confidence of the wicked is no more substantial than the proverbial flimsy spider's web—27:18. "Verily, frailest of all houses is the house of the spider," Qoran, 29:40.

Verse 16—Here we observe a radical shift in imagery, that of a flourishing tree suddenly cut down. The tree thrives (lit. is sappy—see also 24:8) in a garden,[11] 15:30-33; 18:16-19; Eccl. 40:15; Matt. 13:4-9.

Verse 17—The tree even grows in the midst of a stone-heap. Though they may appear secure, the wicked live in the midst of stones. The R. S. V. follows the LXX rather than the M. T. Though there are several problems with the translation of the A. V., the general sense is communicated, i.e., the tree strengthens its hold on the earth (even grows within context of stones).[12]

Verse 18—There is no vestige of the tree left; it must be removed from among the stones, which is the final sign of

---

[9] Dhorme retains the M. T. over the LXX, and adduces support from Prov. 1:19 where paths mean "fate"; see also discussion in B. S. Childe, *Isaiah and the Assyrian Crisis*, 1967, pp. 28ff.

[10] See Dhorme, pp. 120ff, and Pope, pp. 66-7, for discussion; J. Reider, *Vetus Testamentum*, IV, 1954, 288ff.

[11] See Jean Leveque, *Job et Son Dieu*, Tome II, 400-408.

[12] Hebrew text reads *yehezeh*—"he sees," LXX reads *zesetai*—"he lives."

its former state and presence. "He shall deny him" or disown him—31:28; reveals its final uprootedness of the tree—Ps. 103:16.

Verse 19—Here "joy" can only be ironic. The grammar shows incongruity between the singular subject and plural verb, though the sense is that others will soon replace him, and he will not even be remembered.

3. If Job is upright, God will restore him. (8:20-22)

TEXT 8:20-22

20 Behold, God will not cast away a perfect man,
   Neither will he uphold the evil-doers.
21 He will yet fill thy mouth with laughter,
   And thy lips with shouting.
22 They that hate thee shall be clothed with shame;
   And the tent of the wicked shall be no more.

COMMENT 8:20-22

Verse 20—Bildad now uses the very term by which God described Job—1:8; see also 1:1—"blameless." The A. V. has "uphold" and in Hebrew it means to "grasp the hand" or take the hand—Isa. 42:6; 51:18. Bildad's conclusion ends on an optimistic note. He has surely consoled Job.

Verse 21—God will "redeem" you, i.e., cause you to laugh, shout of jubilation, at your pain, once it has departed and wholeness returns.

Verse 22—Shame is conceived as the garment which the wicked wear—Ps. 35:26; 109:29; 132:18. The last word in this verse, *'enennu,* "is no more," echos Job's last word, 7:21 " *'enenni"*—"am no more."

TODAY'S ENGLISH VERSION

8

Bildad

1-2 Are you finally through with your windy speech?
3 God never twists justice;
   he never fails to do what is right.
4 Your children must have sinned against God,
   and so he punished them the way they deserved.
5 But now turn and plead with Almighty God;
6   if you are so pure and honest,
   then God will come and help you
   and restore your household as your reward.
7 All the wealth you lost will be nothing
   compared to what God will give you then.

8 Look for a moment at ancient wisdom;
   consider the truths our fathers learned.
9 Our life is so short we know nothing at all;
   we are only shadows on the face of the earth.
10 But let the ancient wise men teach you;
   listen to what they had to say:
11 "Reeds can't grow where there is no water;
   they are never found outside a swamp.
12 If the water dries up they are the first to wither,
   while still too small to be cut and used.
13 Godless men are like those reeds;
   their hope is gone, once God is forgotten.
14 They trust a thread—a spider web.
15   If they lean on a web, will it hold them up?
   If they grab for a thread, will it help them stand?"

16 Evil men sprout like weeds in the sun,
   like weeds that spread all through the garden.
17 Their roots wrap around the stones
   and hold fast to every rock.

¹⁸ But then pull them up—
   no one will ever know they were there.
¹⁹ Yes, that's all the joy evil men have;
   others now come and take their places.

²⁰ But God will never abandon the faithful,
   or ever give help to evil men.
²¹ He will let you laugh and shout again,
²²   but he will bring disgrace on those who hate you,
   and the homes of the wicked will disappear.

QUESTIONS FOR DISCUSSION 8:1-22

157. Who is Bildad?
158. There are only two kinds of people in Bildad's world. Who are they?
159. Someone is accused of being "a bag of wind." Who is it?
160. Why do some commentators delete words from verse three?
161. Bildad knows why Job lost his children. What was the reason? Wasn't this cruel?
162. Job spoke of God seeking him. Bildad reverses the thought. How so?
163. The American dream turned to a nightmare is based on Bildad's theology. Explain how this is true.
164. Bildad does promise Job restoration, but on what basis?
165. The wisdom of the ancients is in favor of Bildad logic. So what?
166. The longest life is but a brief flickering candle. How does this thought relate to learning from history?
167. How does the proverb in verse 11 apply to Job?
168. Job is withering away. Do we know the reason for it? What do the ancients teach us as a cause? (i.e., according to Bildad)
169. Job is accused of being Godless. Why?

E. NOT GUILTY—THE CRIME OF INNOCENCE—JOB'S
   CRY (9:1—10:22)
   1. Man is no match before the all-powerful, all-wise God.
      (9:1-12)

TEXT 9:1-12

9   Then Job answered and said,
    2 Of a truth I know that it is so:
But how can man be just with God?
 3 If he be pleased to contend with him,
He cannot answer him one of a thousand.
 4 *He is* wise in heart, and mighty in strength:
Who hath hardened himself against him, and prospered?—
 5 *Him* that removeth the mountains, and they know it not,
When he overturneth them in his anger;
 6 That shaketh the earth out of its place,
And the pillars thereof tremble;
 7 That commandeth the sun, and it riseth not,
And sealeth up the stars;
 8 That alone stretcheth out the heavens,
And treadeth upon the waves of the sea;
 9 That maketh the Bear, Orion, and the pleiades,
And the chambers of the south;
10 That doeth great things past finding out,
Yea, marvellous things without number.
11 Lo, he goeth by me, and I see him not:
He passeth on also, but I perceive him not.
12 Behold, he seizeth *the prey,* who can hinder him?
Who will say unto him, What doest thou?

COMMENT 9:1-12

Verses 1-2—Job's second response—chps. 9:1—10:22—
has the same general structure as his first chps. 6—7. (1) He
answers his friends, 9:2-24; (2) Brief soliloquy, 9:25—10:1a;

and (3) A direct address to God, 10:1b-22. It is less personal than the previous speech; in fact, the three counselors are addressed only indirectly. The third section is another impassioned plea which subsides into an agonizing appeal for God to leave him alone.[1] It is important to take note of the fact that Job responds more to the things asserted by Eliphaz than Bildad. His opening words contain a sarcastic recognition of the principle enunciated by the three friends, that no man can be righteous in God's eyes. God's justice is identical with his power, i.e., whatever he does is just—4:12; 8:3; and 25:4.

Verse 3—The verse in A. V. takes God as the subject of the verb. "Contend" is a forensic term meaning "go to court" with God, with the odds of winning "once in a thousand times," literally "one from a thousand"—Deut. 32:30; and Jos. 23:10.

Verse 4—No one can challenge God and survive. One can never harden (object unexpressed) his heart (stands for intelligence) against God and win in the encounter—(Remember Pharaoh[2])—Deut. 2:30; 10:16; II Kings 17:14; Jer. 7:26; Ps. 95:8; Prov. 28:14; and 29:1.

Verse 5—The Hebrew text is to be preferred over LXX, etc., and thus we should take the meaning to be "suddenly," i.e., before anyone realizes it, God has overtaken them.[3] Job thus begins a doxology clearly more powerful than Eliphaz's—5:10-16. Content is limited to God's power, not His love and mercy.

Verse 6—For reference to the pillars, see Pss. 75:3; 104:5; and I Sam. 2:8. The verb translated "tremble" is found only here, and has root idea of "tremble with horror"—Ps. 18:7;

---

[1] K. Fullerton, "On Job, Chapters 9-10," *Journal Biblical Literature,* 53, 1934, 321-49; and his "Job, Chapters 9-10," *American Journal of Semitic Literature,* 55, 1938, 225-69; see P. W. Skehan, "Strophic Pattern in the Book of Job, *Catholic Biblical Quarterly,* XXIII, 1961, 125ff.

[2] See my essay on Romans 9 and "Theology of Promise and Universal History," *Grace Unlimited,* ed. by Dr. Clark Pinnock (Minnesota: Bethany Fellowship Press, 1975), pp. 190-208, and the issue of vocabulary and theology of "hardening Pharaoh's heart."

[3] D. W. Thomas, *Journal of Theological Studies,* N. S., XV, 1964, 54ff, translates as "so that they are no longer still," though here the hardening of human initiative.

Isa. 13:10; Joel 2:10.

Verses 7, 8—God is presented as creator of the universe. Job is concurring with his three friends regarding God's creative work in nature—Isa. 44:24.[4]

Verse 9—The order and identity of these constellations varies in different texts—38:31-32; Amos 5:8: (1) The first constellation 'ash, 'ayish in 38:32, is probably Ursa major; (2) The second is kesil—fool is probably Orion; and (3) The third—kimah—is generally taken to be Pleiades—Ps. 78:26; Song of Songs 4:16.[5]

Verse 10—Job ironically repeats 5:9 from Eliphaz. While he asserts that all of God's works have ethical implications, Job maintains that God's immeasurable power is used for His cosmic chess game of arbitrary play with his creatures.

Verse 11—Job avers that he knows God's presence only by His power, manifested in nature. As a result of God's passing by, Job's life lies in ruins.

Verse 12—God "snatches away" (verb—hatap—found only here), and no one can stop Him. The LXX translation is basis of the A. V.'s "he seizeth the prey." The LXX translator attempted to remove any reference to destructive action by God. But even the Greek of the LXX can also be translated "if he moves," and not necessarily "if he destroys."[6]

---

[4] Some attempt to prove thesis that back of this imagery is a reference to the myth of the victory of Ba-al over the sea god Yamm, but this is highly imaginative correlation—F. W. Albright, *JBL*, LVII, 1938, 227; H. H. Rowley, *Studies in Old Testament Prophecy*, 1950, p. 18. For data on myth of conflict between Baal and Yamm, see O. Kaiser, *Die mythische Bedeutung des Meeres*, 1959, pp. 44ff; F. M. Cross, Jr. and D. N. Freedman, *JBL*, 67, 1948, 196-210, n. 93; also J. B. Pritchard, *Ancient Near Eastern Texts*, p. 67. The above research is basis for R. S. V. marginal reading "the back of the sea dragon."

[5] See article "Astronomy" in *ISBI*, Vol. I (Eerdmans); G. Schiaparelli, *Astronomy in the Old Testament*, 1905, pp. 54ff; S. Mowinckel, *Die Sternnamen in A. T.*, 1928, pp. 52ff; and G. R. Driver, *Journal Theological Studies*, XII, 1956, 1ff.

[6] M. Dahood, *Biblica*, 38, 1957, 310, for analysis of the verb yahtop—despoils in verse 12a, A. V. as "seizeth."

2. Arbitrarily God deals with him, no matter what he may do.
(9:13-24)

TEXT 9:13-24

13 God will not withdraw his anger;
The helpers of Rahab do stoop under him.
14 How much less shall I answer him,
And choose out my words *to reason* with him?
15 Whom, though I were righteous, yet would I not answer;
I would make supplication to my judge.
16 If I had called, and he had answered me,
Yet would I not believe that he hearkened unto my voice.
17 For he breaketh me with a tempest,
And multiplieth my wounds without cause.
18 He will not suffer me to take my breath,
But filleth me with bitterness.
19 If *we speak* of strength, lo, *he is* mighty!
And if of justice, Who, *saith he,* will summon me?
20 Though I be righteous, mine own mouth shall condemn me:
Though I be perfect, it shall prove me perverse.
21 I am perfect; I regard not myself;
I despise my life.
22 It is all one; therefore I say,
He destroyeth the perfect and the wicked.
23 If the scourge slay suddenly,
He will mock at the trial of the innocent.
24 The earth is given into the hand of the wicked;
He covereth the faces of the judges thereof:
If *it be* not *he,* who then is it?

COMMENT 9:13-24

Verse 13—Job's gratitude is now poisoned by more bitterness. God has all along only been preparing Job for torture. He thus denies the idea of strict moral causality, which has been presented by his friends. Man's action—whether good or bad—makes no difference to God. Rahab (root—be excited or agitated) is used in Isa. 30:7; Ps. 87:4 as designation of Egypt. Rahab is one of the sea monsters slain by God—26:12; Ps. 89:11; Isa. 51:9. It is not necessary to identify Rahab with the Babylonian Creation Epic; the Leviathan narrative already appears 7:12.[7] The Source of Imagery (Formgeschichte) is one thing; its meaning is another.

Verse 14—Here Job relates that it is impossible to face God in His cosmic court, because God would refuse Job's summon. He would simply manifest His superior power, and Job would lie destroyed. The Hebrew which is translated as A. V. "how much less" can also mean "how much more," or "how than." How can Job expect to face God, if a sea monster cannot? Job would be so overwhelmed that he would be unable to choose his words in order to challenge God.

Verse 15—Even though he is innocent, he cannot expect justice. The A. V. translates "whom though I were righteous," but the term is forensic and probably should be translated as "in the right" or innocent. Similarly, the A. V. has "my judge," but *mesopeti*—opponent—means "my accuser" or "adversary at law." Job's only recourse, since he cannot force a response from his adversary, is to cast himself on His mercy (first time for His theme to appear). Surely one of the central theological themes in Job is that man is hopelessly lost without God's grace.

Verse 16—Now God does answer Job's summons. But Job does not have confidence in the sense of believing that God is listening, giving an ear, or paying any attention to his cries.[8] Because God cannot be required to testify or justify His actions; He is responsible to no one but His own nature.

Verse 17—God now is charged with "crushing" (A. V. "breaketh") Job. The verb is used only here and in Gen. 3:15 which is often translated as "bruise," but surely the context

---

[7] See A. Heidel, *The Gilgamesh Epic and Old Testament Parallels* (Chicago, pb., 1963); and his *The Babylonian Genesis* (Chicago, pb., 1963), for exhaustive analysis of these supposed parallels; also L. R. Fisher (ed.), *Ras Shamra Parallels* I (Analecta Orientalia, 1973.

[8] See Dhorme, *Job*, p. 136.

calls for crush or destroy. God crushes him without cause (same word as in 2:3) as though he were a mere trifle. God's displeasure (*ka'as* as in 5:2a) is not only reserved for the wicked; it also crushes the just.

Verse 18—The Hound of Heaven has filled Job with bitterness[9]—7:19; and Lam. 3:15. Here we return to the theme of chapter 3.

Verse 19—God's power (*koah*) is here in parallelism with his judgment (*mispat*). God is supreme in power and thus subject to no summoner, Job included. The A. V. has "lo" from *hinneh*—behold. The Hebrew verb has a first person suffix "arraign me" instead "arraign him" (the difference is very slight but import is vast—*yo'ideni*—"arraign or summons me," *yo'idennu*—arraign or summons him." Surely this represents an effort to remove any suggestions that man could call God to account. Whether respecting power or justice, Job futiley confronts God.

Verse 20—Even Job's own speech[10] condemns him. Is he saying that I am innocent; I am forced to assert my own guilt?

Verse 21—He defends his innocence, though it may cost him his life. He would forfeit his life, but not his integrity in claiming his innocence. The intense emotional strain causes Job to cry that "I neither know myself nor care"—7:16; Gen. 39:6; Deut. 33:9.

Verse 22—Is "truth forever on the scaffold and error forever on the throne?" The wicked and unjust triumph. Job shouts that God flouts justice indiscriminately. Job, like the late B. Russell, denies any moral order in the universe. This thesis also follows from contemporary attitudes expressed by Skinner, Crick, Monad, Wilson, Watson, *et. al.* God is indifferent to the human condition. Naturalistic humanism in all of its forms, but especially in its Neo-Marxian form, makes identical claims, while charging all non-naturalistic humanists

---

[9] For discussion of this word, see M. Dahood, *Biblica*, 48, 1967, 427.

[10] For discussion of "my mouth," see M. Dahood, *Biblica*, 38, 1957, 311; also *Biblica*, 1967, p. 543. Whether it is God's or Job's mouth, either or both condemn him.

89

with immoral behavior. If the universe is amoral, then there are different types of behavior, but no moral or immoral human acts. Job contradicts what Bildad has set forth in 8:20.

Verse 23—The "scourge" (*sot*) means calamities in general, war, plague, disease, famine, etc., which take lives regardless of their spiritual condition and relationship to God—Isa. 10:26; 28:15, 18. Eliphaz has said (5:22) that if Job accepted God's discipline, he would ultimately laugh at famine and destruction. Job's response to Eliphaz is that it is God who laughs when calamities (*masas*—melt, despair) come. Job says that God is not testing men by disaster, but rather destroying them.

Verse 24—Job is enunciating a universal law, i.e., the miscarriage of justice. Earth has no definite article, and thus probably refers to more than the land. Shall the pious inherit the earth?—Ps. 37:9; Prov. 2:21; Matt. 5:5. Job asserts just the opposite. He holds God solely responsible for the human condition. There is no Satan, or anyone else to blame. Job is actually challenging his friends to declare who is, if God is not, to blame?

3. He will be held guilty in spite of everything. (9:25-31)

TEXT 9:25-31

25 Now my days are swifter than a post:
   They flee away, they see no good.
26 They are passed away as the swift ships;
   As the eagle that swoopeth on the prey.
27 If I say, I will forget my complaint,
   I will put off my *sad* countenance, and be of good cheer;
28 I am afraid of all my sorrows,
   I know that thou wilt not hold me innocent.
29 I shall be condemned;
   Why then do I labor in vain?
30 If I wash myself with snow water,

And make my hands never so clean;
31 Yet wilt thou plunge me in the ditch,
And mine own clothes shall abhor me.

COMMENT 9:25-31

Verse 25—Complain—Complain. Job returns to a pre-occupation with his own condition. From cosmic disorder to personal disorder, how pathetic. Life is passing so rapidly. It is no longer the weaver's shuttle but the runner who serves as point of contrast—7:6. The "courier" refers to a fast runner with the royal messenger service—II Sam. 18:21-23; Isa. 41:27; 52:7.

Verse 26—Reed means papyrus. (For different word, see 8:11.) Reed boats are very light and fast.[11] Isaiah refers to reed vessels (*kele gome*)—Isa. 18:1-2. The imagery from the second clause speaks of speed. The word "swoop" (TWS) refers in falconry to the swift swoop of the bird on the prey. The falcon can attain a speed in excess of 150 mph in such a swoop (for eagles—39:27-30; Deut. 28:49; Jer. 4:13; Hab. 1:8; and Lam. 4:19.[12] The "prey" (*'okel*) is the general word for food.

Verse 27—Literally, Job says "I will abandon my face,"[13] i.e., I will change my countenance. His entire attitude will be changed. He will "be of good cheer" (Heb. "brighten my face"). Here we see change in two dimensions: (1) psychic, and (2) physical appearance.

Verse 28—He no sooner decided to cheer up than he "became afraid" (same word in 3:25—dread). The dread fear haunted him with such intensity that his agony was only magnified.

---

[11] Pliny, *Natural History*, Loeb Classic XXIII.22 where he discusses the fact that the Egyptians used papyrus for boat construction; also recent experimentation with these craft see T. Heyerdahl's *The Ra Expeditions*, 1971.

[12] For such imagery in Job, see W. L. Michel, *The Ugaritic Texts in the Mythological Expressions in the Book of Job* (Univ. of Wisconsin Ph.D. thesis, 1970).

[13] See G. R. Driver, *Vetus Testamentum* Supplement, III, 1955, 76; M. Dahood, *JBL*, LXXVIII, 1959, 304, for analysis of this verse.

Verse 29—Guilty without trial. (Read Kafka's *The Trial* and compare). All of his efforts are futile.

Verse 30—The Hebrew—*seleg*—means both soap and snow or snow water—Isa. 1:16, 18, "I will make my hands never so clean"—*bor,* lye. In Mal. 3:2 the same word *borit* means the fuller's lye soap. Lye is a vegetable alkali made from the ashes of plants—22:30; Ps. 18:20, 24; Isa. 1:25.[14]

Verse 31—The A. V. has "ditch"—*sahat*—which can mean the netherworld—17:14; 33:22, 28. The context calls for filth;[15] and the root suggests repulsive matter and slime, i.e., a characteristic of the netherworld. Job is saying if I wash my body, God would make it so filthy that my clothes would refuse to cover me.

4. There is no mediator between the man and his creator. (9:32-35)

TEXT 9:32-35

32 For he is not a man, as I am, that I should answer him,
   That we should come together in judgment.
33 There is no umpire betwixt us,
   That might lay his hand upon us both.
34 Let him take his rod away from me,
   And let not his terror make me afraid:
35 Then would I speak, and not fear him;
   For I am not so in myself.

COMMENT 9:32-35

Verse 32—A fair trial before God is an impossibility. "Come

---

[14] On handwriting, see R. Press, *Zeitschrift für die alttestamentliche Wissenschaft,* 51, 1933, 246-7.

[15] Several etymologies are possible, but see M. Pope, *JBL,* 83, 1964, 276; D. Hiller's *Interpretations,* 19, 1965, 468; and M. Dahood, *Psalms,* I-II, on Pss. 13:5; 66:9; and 121:13.

together in judgment" means to go to court or before the law—
Ps. 143:2. Here we see that a theology of commutative justice
between man and God will destroy God's transcendence and
ensnare Him in the immanent trap that enslaves man.[16] Zechariah 3:3-5 provides a beautiful background to the problem,
where the acquitted defendant receives clean clothes. (Note
New Testament reference to white garments, esp. in *The
Revelation*—see my *The Seer, the Saviour, and The Saved*,
1972 ed. in this series of commentaries.)[17]

Verse 33—Since God is prejudiced by His despotic power,
Job calls for an arbiter—*mokiah*—mediator, one who decides
with equity—Gen. 31:37; Isa. 2:4. Job is still searching for a
just reconciliation (II Cor. 5:17ff).

Verse 34—Remove your rod (*sebet*—club) same word as
in Ps. 23:4. To David, God's rod was his defense against his
enemies; for Job, God's rod brings only violence and pain. To
Job, the rod signifies coercion and intimidation.

Verse 35—If there is no mediator, then I will speak for
myself. But what shall I say that has not already been said?

TODAY'S ENGLISH VERSION

9

Job

1-2 Yes, I've heard all that before.

---

[16] The nature of God's transcendence and immanence is one of the major issues
in contemporary theological thought. Since the 17th-18th centuries' Scientific Revolution, the transcendence of God has been suspect. The Newtonian World Machine
conceived Deism and Deism gave birth to scientific positivism. Newton is the basis
of Kant, Kant the basis of Hegel's immanent transcendance, and Hegel is the father
of naturalistic panentheism, which is presently expressed by C. Hartshorne, Whitehead, and Teilhard de Chardin, *et al.*

[17] Compare also with the theology of righteousness in the Qumran Literature, esp.
1QH 5:4; 5:4; 7:12; 9:14ff; 12:30ff; 14:15ff; and the teacher of righteousness see W.
Grundmain "Der Lehrer der gerechtigkeit von Qumran," *Revue de Qumran* 2, 1959-
60, 237-259.

But how can a man win his case against God?
³ How can anyone argue with him?
He can ask a thousand questions
that no one could ever answer.
⁴ God is so wise and powerful
no man can stand up against him.
⁵ Without warning he moves mountains
and destroys them in anger.
⁶ God sends earthquakes and shakes the ground;
he rocks the pillars the earth stands on.
⁷ God can keep the sun from rising,
and the stars from shining at night.
⁸ No one helped God stretch out the heavens
or trample the sea monster back.
⁹ God hung the stars in the sky—the Dipper,
Orion, the Pleiades, and the stars of the south.
¹⁰ We cannot understand the great things he does,
and there is no end to his miracles.

¹¹ God passes by, but I cannot see him.
¹² He takes what he wants, and no one can stop him;
no one can ask him, "What are you doing?"
¹³ God's anger is constant. He crushed his enemies
who helped Rahab, the sea monster, oppose him.
¹⁴ So how can I find words to answer God?
¹⁵ Though I am innocent, all I can do
is beg for mercy from God my judge.
¹⁶ Yet even then, if he lets me speak,
I can't believe he would listen to me.
¹⁷ He sends storms to batter and bruise me,
without any reason at all.
¹⁸ He won't let me get my breath;
all he has done to me makes me bitter.
¹⁹ Should I try force? Try force on God?
Should I take him to court? Who would make
him so?
²⁰ I am innocent and faithful, but my words sound
guilty,

and everything I say seems to condemn me.
²¹⁻²² I am innocent, but I no longer care.
I am sick of living. Nothing matters;
innocent or guilty, God will destroy us.
²³ When an innocent man suddenly dies, God laughs.
²⁴ God gave the world to the wicked.
He made all the judges blind.
And if God didn't do it, who did?

²⁵ My days race by, not one of them good.
²⁶ My life passes like the swiftest boat,
as fast as an eagle swooping down on a rabbit.
²⁷⁻²⁸ If I smile and try to forget my pain,
all my suffering comes back to haunt me;
I know that God holds me guilty.
²⁹ Since God holds me guilty, why should I bother?
³⁰   No soap can wash away my sins.
³¹ God throws me into a pit of filth,
and even my clothes are ashamed of me.
³² If God were human I could answer him back;
we could go to court to decide our quarrel.
³³ But there is no one to step between us—
no one to judge both God and me.
³⁴ Stop punishing me, God! Keep your terrors away!
³⁵ I am not afraid. I am going to talk,
because I know my own heart.

QUESTIONS FOR DISCUSSION 9:1-35

170. How does this second response of Job compare with his first response?
171. Job responds more to one friend than he does the other. Who? Why?
172. God's justice is identical to what?
173. When man goes to court with God what is the result?

174. Do we really believe that no one can harden himself against God and prosper? Discuss.
175. What is the point of verse five?
176. Why would the earth tremble? What would be the result?
177. Job agrees with his friends in verse 8. Show how.
178. Why discuss the constellations of the stars?
179. Job repeats the words of Eliphaz (Cf. 5:9) but for a purpose. What was it?
180. Job says we can not see God, but we can see something concerning God. What is it?
181. What is the meaning of verse 12?
182. Job's gratitude is now poisoned. By what?
183. What is meant by the term "Rahab" in verse 13?
184. Job is discouraged with the power of God. Why?
185. Even if he was innocent, Job cannot expect justice, so he says in verse 15. Why does he say this?
186. Does God hear the cries of Job? Discuss.
187. God is charged with crushing Job. Why would God do this?
188. Somehow the root of bitterness has flourished in Job. Is this always the response to suffering? Discuss.
189. Show how Job's own speech condemns him.
190. Job has many who agree with him, i.e., that wickedness and injustice triumph and there is no moral order in the universe. Who are they?
191. Show how contradictory it is for humanists to accuse non-huminists with immoral behavior.
192. What is meant by the word "scourge" in verse 23?
193. Job answers Eliphaz (5:22) with verse 23. Show how.
194. Job charges God with all the troubles of the world. He is not alone in this attitude. There is another answer. What is it?
195. The brevity of life is compared to what in verse 25.
196. Of what were the swift ships made?
197. Who is the bird and who is the prey in the figure of verse 26?
198. What does Job use to wash himself clean of his guilt?

5. He would ask the Almighty the reason for the change in his treatment of His creature. (10:1-22)

TEXT 10:1-22

10 My soul is weary of my life;
I will give free course to my complaint;
I will speak in the bitterness of my soul.
2 I will say unto God, Do not condemn me;
Show me wherefore thou contendest with me.
3 Is it good unto thee that thou shouldest oppress,
That thou shouldest despise the work of thy hands,
And shine upon the counsel of the wicked?
4 Hast thou eyes of flesh?
Or seest thou as man seeth?
5 Are thy days as man seeth?
Or thy years as man's days,
6 That thou inquirest after mine iniquity,
And searchest after my sin,
7 Although thou knowest that I am not wicked,
And there is none that can deliver out of thy hand?
8 Thy hands have framed me and fashioned me
Together round about; yet thou dost destroy me.
9 Remember, I beseech thee, that thou hast fashioned me
as clay;
And wilt thou bring me into dust again?
10 Hast thou not poured me out as milk,
And curdled me like cheese?
11 Thou hast clothed me with skin and flesh,
And knit me together with bones and sinews.
12 Thou hast granted me life and lovingkindness;
And thy visitation hath preserved my spirit.
13 Yet these things thou didst hide in thy heart;
I know that this is with thee:
14 If I sin, then thou markest me,
And thou wilt not acquit me from mine iniquity.
15 If I be wicked, woe unto me;

And if I be righteous, yet shall I not lift up my head;
Being filled with ignominy,
And looking upon mine affliction.
16 And if *my heart* exalt itself, thou huntest me as a lion;
And again thou showest thyself marvellous upon me.
17 Thou renewest thy witnesses against me,
And increasest thine indignation upon me:
Changes and warfare are with me.
18 Wherefore then hast thou brought me forth out of the womb?
I had given up the ghost, and no eye had seen me.
19 I should have been as though I had not been;
I should have been carried from the womb to the grave.
20 Are not my days few? cease then,
And let me alone, that I may take comfort a little,
21 Before I go whence I shall not return.
Even to the land of darkness and of the shadow of death;
22 The land dark as midnight,
The land of the shadow of death, without any order.

COMMENT 10:1-22

Now Job addresses himself to the "real" God. His three friends misunderstand his case. Job begins to theorize on the motives for his suffering—is God sadistic? Verse 4; is He making a mistake? Verse 5; is He jealous of men's pleasure and happiness? All restraint is removed.

Verse 1—My complaint is that "my soul is sick of life." Job is conversing with himself. Does God have a secret motive for afflicting him?

Verse 2—"Do not condemn me" reveals that Job as well as his friends concluded from his suffering that God holds him guilty.

Verse 3—Dhorme translates "Is it profitable to thee?" Job here charges God with injustice. "Can there be any justification for such a state of affairs? Because God made both the righteous and the unrighteous, Job requests to know why

98

men are not treated with equity.[1]

Verse 4—Job's basic question is not does God have limitations, but can He really understand the human condition? The *Hebrew Epistle* declares that God not only is capable of identification with man but that His incarnation is proof—see also Phil. 2:5ff; I Sam. 16:7.

Verse 5—Are God's days as limited as man's; is that why He is quick to exact punishment, even before Job does evil?

Verse 6—He does not believe that God has found any sin in his life, even though He continually searches for it.

Verse 7—If God knows that Job is innocent, then why does He seek to extract a confession of guilt? He knows that no one can take Job from His hand. Why is He punishing Job, as though he is about to slip through His fingers?

Verses 8-9—You formed me with your hands; why are you destroying your own creation? The potter-clay parallel is found in Gen. 3:19; Ps. 90:3; Isa. 45:9; Jer. 18:4ff; and Rom. 9:20.[2]

Verses 10-11—The imagery alludes to the formation of the embryo in the womb. "Semen poured like milk into the womb, is coagulated like cheese, and finally bones and muscles are formed"—Ps. 139:13-16 and Eccl. 11:5.[3]

Verse 12—By using imagery from the miracle of conception and birth, perhaps Job is affirming his belief in the providential order of God, before the suffering and pain befell him. This verse is of crucial importance for the understanding of chapters 9—10. "It shows that, although Job wrestles with God, he is conscious of his absolute dependence upon him" (Buttenweiser, *Book of Job*). The Hebrew text declares that God's grace

---

[1] For the critical issues in this verse, see G. R. Driver, *Die Welt des Orients*, I, 1947-52, 411; and R. Bergmeier, *Zeitschrift für die alttestamentliche Wissenschaft*, LXXIX, (pp. 229ff.)

[2] See my essay, "Theology of Promise and Universal History," in *Grace Unlimited*, esp. pp. 199ff.

[3] Pope, *Job*, p. 80.

and covenant love, i.e., life and *hesed*[4]—Ps. 63:4a, are gifts for which he could never be adequately grateful. *Hesed* means piety, mercy, love, grace, and expresses relationships within the context of covenant. Another Hebrew word, *hen*, expresses similar connotations with the exception of the covenant relationship. In this verse *hesed* conveys the marks of divine favor. God cares (literally visits) for Job. Care is also used in a negative sense of visit for punishment—Hos. 9:7, but here it means a gracious visitation. Before Job's unbearable punishment came upon him, God graciously, providentially visited his life in constant watch-care.

Verse 13—Job's present condition has convinced him that God concealed His true attitude toward His "servant" Job. Job mournfully contrasts his life when he thought that God truly cared for him in his present state. God was all along preparing a victim for sacrifice.[5] God's calculated cruelty was part of His ultimate purpose.

Verse 14—God was watching every act and thought of Job and had already determined to deal cruelly with Job. The word translated "mark" (same as preserved in verse 12) means guard or protectively watch over. God's gracious (*Hesed*) watch has turned to hostility. God is no longer his protector; He is now his cruel accuser—7:18-20.

Verse 15—Does Job merit all this misfortune? He is sated with ignominy, guilt, shame, and misery—but why? Has God determined that Job suffer whether he is wicked or righteous? Job has no pride left; he cannot lift up his head—Judges 8:28; 11:15; 22:26.[6] Job receives nothing from God but trouble and more trouble.

---

[4] See Kittel article "Dike"; N. H. Snaith, *The Distinctive Ideas in the Old Testament*, 1944, pp. 95ff; see also his *The Book of Job*, 1968; and Nelson Glueck, *Hesed in the Bible* (Ktav Pub. House), an indispensable study.

[5] See Calvin's response in his *Institutes*, III, 23, 7. He admits that Job's condition calls for a response of horror at God's dealings with man. See again *Grace Unlimited* for response to Calvin and his views of the Sovereignty of God, Providence of God, and the human condition.

[6] For problems in this verse, see G. R. Driver, *Ephemerides Theologicae Lovanienses*, XXVI, 1950, 351; and R. de Vaux, *Revue Biblique*, XLVIII, 1939, 594.

Verse 16—If my pride (the sense of R. S. V. is best) causes me to lift up my head (Heb. "he lifts himself up"), God would immediately attack me as though I were unrighteous. God's wonders in creation are now contrasted with His wonders (A. V. marvelous) in torturing Job.

Verse 17—His bitterness now overflows in irony. God's witnesses against Job are his sufferings. God is ever bringing "fresh attacks, hosts, warfare"—*saba*—against him. There is no relief; God is hounding him to his grave—7:1; 14:14.[7]

Verses 18-19—He now returns to his lament over being born—3:11ff. Note the emphatic *"lamah,"* why? This is the same word our Lord cried from the cross, quoting Ps. 22:1; Matt. 27:46. This haunting theme opened the discourse. But since not being born is not a live option for Job, he just suffers. Still we see the supreme value of life. In all his suffering, Job shows no sympathy with the idea of Schopenhauer and Camus, *et. al.*, that the ultimate philosophical problem confronting man is—Why not commit suicide, if we live in a meaningless, amoral universe?

Verse 20—The Hebrew literally states that "my days cease." In this verse as a whole, Job asks God to take His attention (watch-care) away from him, in order that he might find comfort. This verse and verse 21a virtually quote Ps. 39:14 (or vice versa).

Verse 21—Job aspires to go into "deep darkness"—3:5; Ps. 23.

Verse 22—This verse contains an abundance of synonyms for darkness. In Sheol, light is but darkness. He is wearing his shroud of despair as he describes the miserable prospects of death—7:21; 14:20ff; 17:13ff; 21:32ff. Job vainly attempts to harmonize the God of his past and present experience. Chaos[8]

---

[7] For various solutions to critical problems present in this verse, see A. B. Ehrlich, *Randglossen zur hebraischen Bibel,* VI, 1913, 180ff, but esp. on this verse.

[8] God created order; man sinned and disordered the universe—Gen. 1-3. Disorder reigns between: (1) Man and God; (2) Man and himself; (3) Man and others; and (4) Man and nature. These areas of disorder are in Job's life and ours. He is our contemporary. G. R. Driver, *Vetus Testamentum,* Supplement, III, 1955, 76ff.

(literally without order) reigns in Sheol as well as here. This presents bleak prospects indeed; even death will not help his situation. He is not prepared "to pull his cloak about him and lie down to pleasant dreams," but "to be or not to be" that is still the question. Still "No light but darkness visible."[9]

TODAY'S ENGLISH VERSION

10 I am tired of living.
　　Listen to how bitter I am.
2 Don't condemn me, God.
　　Tell me what the charge against me is.
3 Is it right for you to be so cruel?
　　To despise what you yourself have made?
　　And then to smile on the schemes of wicked men?
4 Do you see things as men do?
5 　Is your life as short as ours?
6 Then why do you track down all my sins
　　and hunt down every fault I have?
7 You know that I am not guilty,
　　that no one can save me from you.

8 Your hands formed and shaped me,
　　and now those same hands destroy me.
9 Remember that you made me from clay;
　　are you going to crush me back to dust?
10 You gave my father strength to beget me;
　　you made me grow in my mother's womb.
11 You framed my body with bones and sinews
　　and covered the bones with muscles and skin.

12 You have given me life and constant love,
　　and your care has kept me alive.

---

[9] Milton, *Paradise Lost,* Book I, line 63.

102

¹³ But now I know that all that time
    you had a secret purpose for me.
¹⁴ You were watching to see if I would sin,
    so you could refuse to forgive me.
¹⁵ As soon as I sin, I'm in trouble with you,
    but when I do right, I get no credit.
  I am miserable and covered with shame.
¹⁶ If I have any success at all,
    you hunt me down like a lion;
    you even work miracles to hurt me.
¹⁷ You always have some witness against me;
    your anger toward me grows and grows;
    you always have some new attack.

¹⁸ Why, God, did you let me be born?
    I should have died before anyone saw me.
¹⁹ To go from the womb straight to the grave
    would have been as good as never existing.
²⁰ Isn't my life almost over? Leave me alone!
    Let me enjoy the time I have left.
²¹ I am going soon and will never come back—
    going to a dark, gloomy land,
²²   a land of darkness, shadows, and confusion,
    where even the light is darkness.

QUESTIONS FOR DISCUSSION 10:1-22

199. There is a change of attitude and expression in this chapter. What is it?
200. To whom is Job addressing his words in verse one? Why?
201. The expression from Job "do not condemn me" proves what?
202. Job asks a question in verse three. What is it?
203. Job's question of verse four is answered in the epistle to the Hebrews and in Phil. 2:5ff. What is the question and the answer?

204. Job imagines all sorts of possible reasons for God's action in bringing this suffering upon him. Name two reasons as stated in verses 5-7.
205. How does Job interpret the fact that God as the potter created him? Cf. verses 8, 9.
206. To what is "the milk and cheese" alluding in verses 10, 11?
207. Why does Job use the imagery of conception and birth? This is a crucial question—answer it carefully.
208. Job's present condition has convinced him of something— i.e., according to verse 13—what is it?
209. How is the word "mark" used in verse 14?
210. What "wonders" are under consideration in verse 16?
211. Job and our Lord had something very much in common (Cf. verses 18, 19). What was it?
212. Show how Ps. 39:14 and verse 20 relate.
213. Give two synonyms describing Sheol. Where and what is Sheol?

From **Today's English Version**
of the Old Testament, Copyright,
American Bible Society, 1971

F. PIETY AND PROSPERITY—ZOPHAR'S RECOM-
MENDATION: REPENTANCE (11:1-20)
   1. Job's punishment is less than he deserves. (11:1-6)

TEXT 11:1-6

11 Then answered Zophar the Naamathite, and said,
   2 Should not the multitude of words be answered?
And should a man full of talk be justified?
 3 Should thy boastings make men hold their peace?
And when thou mockest, shall no man make thee ashamed?
 4 For thou sayest, My doctrine is pure,
And I am clean in thine eyes.
 5 But oh that God would speak,
And open his lips against thee,
 6 And that he would show thee the secrets of wisdom!
For he is manifold in understanding.
Know therefore that God exacteth of thee less than thine
   iniquity deserveth.

COMMENT 11:1-6

Verse 1—Zophar, the third of Job's friends, enters. He is
the least original and most vitriolic of Job's counselors. He is
more intense in asserting Job's guilt than Job is his innocence.
In fact, Zophar claims that Job should be thankful that he
does not get all the suffering that he deserves. His speech falls
into three sections: (1) Zophar wishes that God would break
His silence—verses 2-6; (2) God's wisdom is beyond human
comprehension—verses 7-12; and (3) Restoration from Job's
present situation is contingent on repentance—verses 13-20.
He neither appeals to *personal experience*, as does Eliphaz,
nor to the *wisdom of the ancients*, as does Bildad. His authority
is identical with God's authority; and his wisdom is self-
authenticating. Therefore, Job fails to heed his advice at his
own peril. The literary form of his speech is similar to that of

Bildad, esp. 11:2-6 to 8:2; 11:7-12 to 8:3-4; and 11:13-19a to 8:5-7. A thematic difference is that Bildad defended "divine justice," while Zophar defends "divine wisdom" which must be defended against Job's scandalous criticism. But like the other two friends, he, too, suggests that Job's repentance is imperative if restoration to a happy prosperity is to be anticipated. His fundamental heresy, which is shared by contemporary western man, is that happiness will elude all non-prosperous persons.

Verse 2—Zophar is annoyed by Job's long speech.

Verse 3—The word "boasting," which is found in the A. V., comes from a Hebrew word generally meaning "idle talk," i.e., babbling. Job has denied the doctrine of retributive justice—6:28, 30; 9:21; 10:15; and in Zophar's theology this means "mocking at religion" (A. V. "when thou mockest")— Isa. 16:6; Jer. 48:30.

Verse 4—"My doctrine is pure" was understood by his friends to be an attack on their wisdom, by claiming a superior understanding. The phrase "in thine eyes" refers to God's eyes. The problem is—If Job is saying that he is "pure in God's eyes" (the Hebrew says "I am pure in your eyes"), why is he complaining about God's injustice?[1]

Verse 5—Zophar believes that if God would break His silence, then Job would hear his indictment from God Himself.

Verse 6—God's wisdom is beyond the human mind's comprehension. The Hebrew word *hisplayim* means double, not "manifold." A. V. the sense is that God knows both the hidden and non-hidden. The last line declares that God gives Job less than he deserves.[2]

2. The Almighty is not fooled; He recognizes iniquity.
(11:7-12)

---

[1] Some suggest a solution by changing one vowel—*hayiti*—"I am," to *hayita*—"you are."

[2] E. F. Sutcliffe, *Biblica*, XXX, 1949, p. 67—important discussion of the last line of verse six.

TEXT 11:7-12

7 Canst thou by searching find out God?
   Canst thou find out the Almighty unto perfection?
8 It is high as heaven; what canst thou do?
   Deeper than Sheol; what canst thou know?
9 The measure thereof is longer than the earth,
   And broader than the sea.
10 If he pass through, and shut up,
   And call unto judgment, then who can hinder him?
11 For he knoweth false men:
   He seeth iniquity also, even though he consider it not.
12 But vain man is void of understanding,
   Yea, man is born *as* a wild ass's colt.

COMMENT 11:7-12

Verse 7—Driver claims that "by searching" is grammatically impossible. He suggests the translation "Canst thou find out the immensity of God?" The R. S. V. accepts Driver's criticism. Zophar is affirming that God's mind and purpose are beyond human capacity to measure. Job's friends are surely correct in this judgment, though he draws a false conclusion from his premises. Job does the same thing, i.e., draws wrong conclusions from true premises. In all probability, the translation "canst thou find out," should be "can you reach" God from your sinful human vantage point.[3]

Verses 8-9—God has no limits—Isa. 7:11.

Verse 10—Compare this verse with 9:11-12. Job has already declared that God's power is limitless, and that it is futile for man to oppose Him—9:2ff. The meaning here is that God does not need to investigate man's condition in order to understand it; He knows immediately.

---

[3] For this suggestion, see M. Dahood's article in *The Bible in Current Catholic Thought*, ed. by J. L. McKenzie (Herder & Herder, 1962), p. 57.

Verse 11—God knows (men of emptiness—Ps. 26:4). The only ultimate knowledge available in the universe is God's, so men ought not to revolt against God for this reason.

Verse 12—Hollow men or men without hearts will not understand their need and return to God. The A. V. is misleading. The R. S. V. seems most likely.[4] The meaning is probably "a stupid man will get understanding, when a wild ass's colt is born a man"—Rowley.

3. The penitent will prosper; for the wicked there is no hope. (11:13-20)

TEXT 11:13-20

13 If thou set thy heart aright,
  And stretch out thy hands toward him;
14 If iniquity be in thy hand, put it far away,
  And let not unrighteousness dwell in thy tents.
15 Surely then shalt thou lift up thy face without spot;
  Yea, thou shalt be stedfast, and shalt not fear:
16 For thou shalt forget thy misery;
  Thou shalt remember it as waters that are passed away.
17 And *thy* life shall be clearer than the noonday;
  Though there be darkness, it shall be as the morning.
18 And thou shalt be secure, because there is hope;
  Yea, thou shalt search *about thee,* and shalt take thy rest in safety.
19 Also thou shalt lie down, and none shall make thee afraid;
  Yea, many shall make suit unto thee.
20 But the eyes of the wicked shall fail,
  And they shall have no way to flee;
  And their hope shall be the giving up of the ghost.

---

[4] For the technical issues involved, see Dhorme, *Job,* p. 163; Pope, *Job,* p. 86; and M. Dahood, *Catholic Biblical Quarterly,* 25, 1963, 123-4.

COMMENT 11:13-20

Verse 13—The pronoun "you" is emphatic in the text and contrasts Job with the "hollow man" of verse 12. Zophar calls Job to do four things: (1) Get his heart right with God; (2) Pray to God for forgiveness; (3) Reform his life style to conform to God's expectations; and (4) Set his entire household in order.

Verse 14—Put evil far away from you. Do not permit it to exist in your household.

Verse 15—Job's face will no longer bear the marks of the guilty. The word translated "steadfast"—secure—comes from a verb used for describing the pouring of molten metal—28:2; 37:18.

Verse 16—Here the phrase "waters that are passed away" is a metaphor for oblivian; in 6:15 it is a metaphor for treachery. Zophar has also promised Job restoration to his former prosperous state. Ultimately, Job's restoration did not come as a result of following any of the advice of his friends. "You" is emphatic. *You* will certainly forget all your misery.

Verse 17—Hope and security will be Job's once more. "Your life" (*heled*—means durable, vigorous) will last into advanced age. The imagery of noonday is derived from—*sohorayim*—zenith—noon. Compare this with Job's descriptions in 10:22—of the darkness of Sheol as light.

Verse 18—Job's security (Hebrew verb means to search or dig about), Zophar claims, will be based on his removing the guilt. When Job's guilt is removed, "rest"—peace—will result.

Verse 19—God will grant Job confidence. This same phrase "none will make you afraid" is also found in Mic. 4:4. When Job lived in the good graces of God, he was famous—29:7-10, 21:5; compare with 19:18 and 30:1-10. When he is restored to God, his fame and respectability, social influence, will also return—Isa. 17:2 and Zeph. 3:13.

Verse 20—The highest hope of the unrighteous is death. The ultimate goal should be to give up the spirit, i.e., lit. "to breathe out of the soul." This assertion is Zophar's not so subtle final suggestion to Job. In response, Job lashes out at his vehement sarcastic attack in chapters 12—14.

TODAY'S ENGLISH VERSION

11

Zophar

1-2 Will no one answer all this nonsense?
    Does talking so much put a man in the right?
3 Job, do you think we can't answer you?
    That your mocking words will leave us speechless?
4 You claim what you say is true;
    you claim you are pure in God's sight.
5 How I wish God would answer you back!
6 He would tell you there are many sides to wisdom;
    there are things too deep for human knowledge.
God is punishing you less than you deserve.

7 Can you discover the limits and bounds
    of the greatness and power of God?
8 The sky is no limit to God,
    but it lies beyond your reach.
God knows the world of the dead,
    but you do not know it.
9 God's greatness is broader than the earth,
    wider than the sea.
10 If God arrests you and brings you to trial,
    who is there to stop him?
11 God knows which men are worthless;
    he sees all their evil deeds.
12 Stupid men will start being wise
    when wild donkeys are born tame.

13 Put your heart right, Job. Reach out to God.
14 Put away evil and wrong from your home.
15 Then face the world again, firm and couragaeous.

110

¹⁶ Then all your troubles will fade from your memory,
    like floods that are past and remembered
        no more.
¹⁷ Your life will be brighter than sunshine at noon,
    and life's darkest hours will shine like the dawn.
¹⁸ You will live secure and full of hope;
    God will protect you and give you rest.
¹⁹ You won't be afraid of any enemy;
    many people will ask you for help.
²⁰ But the wicked will look around in despair,
    and find that there is no way to escape.
Their only hope is that death will come.

QUESTIONS FOR DISCUSSION 11:1-20

214. Zophar is the least helpful and least original. Why do we say this?
215. This comforter tells Job that he should at least be glad for one thing. What was it?
216. Zophar's speech falls into three sections. What are they?
217. To what authority does Zophar appeal in his advice?
218. Bildad defended "divine justice." Zophar defends what?
219. All of Job's words were wasted on Zophar. Why?
220. Notice and discuss the problems of verse four. If Job is saying he is pure in the eyes of God, why is he complaining about injustice?
221. Zophar believes that if God spoke he would say something Job needed to hear. Zophar knows what it would be. What would it be?
222. How should the first line of verse 7 be translated?
223. Zophar and Job agree on something. Compare 9:11, 12 and verse ten of this chapter.
224. What is the meaning of the reference to a wild ass's colt?
225. The pronoun in verse 13 is emphatic—it is a contrast— with what? Name the four things Zophar calls upon Job to do.

G. COURAGEOUS CONFRONTATION—JOB'S RESPONSE
(12:1—14:22)
1. He ridicules the wisdom and judgment of his friends.
(12:1-6)

TEXT 12:1-6

12 **Then Job answered and said,**
2 No doubt but ye are the people,
And wisdom shall die with you.
3 But I have understanding as well as you;
I am not inferior to you:
Yea, who knoweth not such things as these?
4 I am as one that is a laughing-stock to his neighbor,
I who called upon God, and he answered:
The just, the perfect man is a laughing-stock.
5 In the thought of him that is at ease there is contempt for
misfortune;
It is ready for them whose foot slippeth.
6 The tents of robbers prosper,
And they that provoke God are secure;
Into whose hand God bringeth *abundantly.*

COMMENT 12:1-6

Verse 1—This is Job's longest speech apart from his final soliloquy. Each of his three friends has spoken and has unanimously refused to accept Job's claim to innocence. Now, after his attack on God, he turns with burning sarcasm on his three would-be counselors. In resumé each has strongly asserted that a sovereign creator Lord governs the universe. In another doxology Job describes how God, in His own wisdom, guides the rise and fall of peoples, nations, and civilizations. Each participant in the drama has set forth God's sovereignty as a theological truth but each generated a false deduction. In the concrete world of space-time, it is not often an easy task to decipher the presence of a holy, righteous God in human affairs. The friends reject the "mystery" explanations. But the empirical evidence does not always support the claims of God's three would-be spokesmen. Job could endure this brief pitiful pilgrimage of pain if there could finally be happy reconciliation with God. But death is the end of everything (note this attitude is comparable to the contemporary Buddhist influence in American culture—"Live it up today; today is all you may have"). The speech hurtles us toward the same terminal despair as before in chapters 7 and 10. The speech falls neatly into three themes: (1) Job's resentment of the assumed superiority of his friends and recognition of God's power and wisdom (12:2-25); (2) Rejection of the empty arguments of his friends and his determination to reason with God (13:1-28); and (3) Painful acknowledgement of the brevity of life and the ultimacy of death (14:1-22).

Verse 2—Job addresses his listeners as "people of the land" (*'am*), who represent the upper class male citizenry.[1] Only royalty and the priesthood rank above them. With biting sarcasm, Job suggests that wisdom will pass from the earth at their demise. They really have only a monopoly on ignorance.

Verse 3—In view of Zophar's comparison of Job with a wild ass in 11:20, Job asserts that he has 'a heart,' here in the American Version is translated 'understanding' (or comprehension). "I am not inferior to you" is repeated in 13:2.

Verse 4—Job expected sympathy, but received scorn. Instead of support, his friends make him an object of derision, (8:21; Jer. 20:7). To Job his afflictions are not God's answers, but his despotic response to his cry for help. The just and blameless man is a laughing stock (Gen. 6;9; Ezek. 14:14, 20).[2]

Verse 5—This could represent an adage expressing general attitude toward anyone fallen into difficulties. Job's prosperous

---

[1] See for analysis J. Reider, *Vetus Testamentum* IV, 1954, pp. 289ff.

[2] Pope, *Job*, p. 90 remarks that vss. 4-6 break the train of thought. This judgment is both critically unnecessary and gives no consideration to Job's emotion-charged speech.

friends have nothing but contempt for him in his misfortune. Job is here attacking the theology of the prosperous. The second line means that the friends not only withhold help, they even intensify Job's misfortune.

Verse 6—There are a number of grammatical difficulties[3] in this verse, but the meaning is probably "those who make a god of their own power" (Moffatt) are secure; at least the empirical evidence often suggests this deduction. This is Job's presentation of the anomalies of God's providence.

2. God is responsible for all that is. (12:7-12)

TEXT 12:7-12

7   But ask now the beasts, and they shall teach thee;
   And the birds of the heavens, and they shall tell thee:
8 Or speak to the earth, and it shall teach thee;
   And the fishes of the sea shall declare unto thee.
9 Who knoweth not in all these,
   That the hand of Jehovah hath wrought this,
10 In whose hand is the soul of every living thing,
   And the breath of all mankind?
11 Doth not the ear try words,
   Even as the palate tasteth its food?
12 With aged men is wisdom,
   And in length of days understanding.

COMMENT 12:7-12

Verse 7—Job begins by addressing all three friends. Here the pronoun is in the singular, so he is focusing on one, presumably the last speaker, Zophar.[4] The wisdom which is being

---

³ See Dhorme, *Job,* p. 170-1.

⁴ See the discussion by S. Terrien, *Interpreters Bible, Job,* Volume 3, pp. 999-1000.

exemplified by Job's friends is common wisdom even to the lowest animals in God's creation (9:22-24). Job's irony is resumed and concurs with the judgment of Oscar Wilde, that there is "enough misery in one narrow London lane to disprove the notion that God is love."

Verse 8—Why should Job's friends emphasize God's sovereignty over the universe, even the birds of the air and beasts of the field know it. Nature is "red in tooth and claw," and only by brute predatory power do they prevail within nature.

Verse 9—This is the only verse in the discourse which contains the sacred tetragrammaton (Yahweh). This is strange in that Job's friends are Arabs, and not children of the covenant. But the root significance of Yahweh is probably at the heart of the discussion; i.e., the cause of everything is God. The phrase is a direct quotation of Isaiah 41:20 (or vice versa). See the quotation in 1:21 also. The pronoun "this" is obscure. To what does it refer? Perhaps to all that Zophar has said, or rather, all that Job has asserted in verses 4ff concerning the amoral nature of the universe.

Verse 10—God is Lord of every "human individual"—Jer. 32:27; Num. 16:22; and 17:16. The words translated "life" and "breath" are the same ones rendered "soul" and "spirit" in 7:11.

Verse 11—As the palate tastes food, so the intelligence of man evaluates available ideas. Job suggests that the ideas of his friends are not palatable—Jonah 3:7; Daniel 3:10; Ezekiel 4:21; Proverbs 26:16; I Samuel 21:14.

Verse 12—Taken as an assertion the content does not seem to accord with Job's other words. But taken as a question with a negative implication, it accords with his previous evaluation. The discourse clearly reveals the futility of dialogue between persons whose ultimate presuppositions are mutually exclusive. Fruitful discussion requires a clear definition and the public awareness of the assumptions on which the discussion stands. Job and his friends have different views of God and His transcendence and immanence within nature and history.

115

3. Aribtraily he decrees what will be. (12:13-25)

TEXT 12:13-25

13   With *God* is wisdom and might;
     He hath counsel and understanding.
14 Behold, he breaketh down, and it cannot be built again;
     He shutteth up a man, and there can be no opening.
15 Behold, he withholdeth the waters, and they dry up;
     Again, he sendeth them out, and they overturn the earth.
16 With him is strength and wisdom;
     The deceived and the deceiver are his.
17 He leadeth counsellors away stripped,
     And judges maketh he fools.
18 He looseth the bond of kings,
     And bindeth their loins with a girdle.
19 He leadeth priests away stripped,
     And overthroweth the mighty.
20 He removeth the speech of the trusty,
     And taketh away the understanding of the elders.
21 He poureth contempt upon princes,
     And looseth the belt of the strong.
22 He uncovereth deep things out of darkness,
     And bringeth out to light the shadow of death.
23 He increaseth the nations, and he destroyeth them:
     He enlargeth the nations, and he leadeth them captive.
24 He taketh away understanding from the chiefs of the people
          of the earth,
     And causeth them to wander in a wilderness where there is
     no way.
25 They grope in the dark without light;
     And he maketh them to stagger like a drunken man.

COMMENT 12:13-25

Verse 13—God only has power and wisdom (II Kings 18:20).
Though Job's friends have not asserted that might and wisdom

116

are possessions which only the "old" may receive, neither does Job assert that God keeps all of this wisdom and power to Himself. The universe reveals God's absolute power, but does not expose His cosmic expression of justice. If God is the ultimate source of all things (vss. 13-21), then He is responsible for pain and suffering.[5]

Verse 14—God's sovereignty is cosmic. And man, especially Job, cannot discern any moral dimension in His violence. The victims of God's violence are from both the wicked and the righteous—Psalm 107; Isaiah 54:24-28. Compare the verbatim agreement of Ps. 107 and vss. 21a and 24b. Though God's might may be applied with loving kindness and beneficence, Job sees only destructive violence and human ruin. The imprisonment to which God shuts up the universe is to be taken both figuratively and literally.

Verse 15—Job presents an example of God's amoral behavior by the extremes of flood and drought. God has the power to dominate the water systems of His creation, but He does so with complete disregard for man's needs. God's might is arbitrary and despotic.

Verse 16—God's wisdom is always efficient, i.e., it is always victorious. All of mankind falls into one of the two categories—deceived or deceiver. Thus far God has been scrutinized under three categories: (1) wisdom and power, (2) counsel and understanding, and (3) might and prudence—compare with 11:7-10. But Job denies Zophar's conclusion about evil—11:11.

Verse 17—God makes all human counselors go stripped or barefoot—Micah 1:8. Perhaps the meaning is that God leads all would-be counselors into confusion or error.

Verse 18—Here we encounter imagery of the liberation of prisoners (Isa. 52:2; Ps. 116:16). In 39:5, the words are applied to a wild ass's release from restraint. This verse contrasts former glory with present humiliation. The binding of a king's loins is an image of being reduced to the status of a menial

---

[5] See G. R. Driver, *Die Welt des Orients,* I, 1947-52, pp. 410f for discussion of import of God's counsel.

117

laborer. They are stripped of their royal robes and sandals and made to work with their hands and backs. Theirs have been troubled economic times, too.

Verse 19—Even the established ('*etanim* means perpetual, Jer. 5:14) authorities in the cultural are humiliated. Priests are mentioned only here in Job. Honored and influential persons are as nothing in the face of God's power.

Verse 20—The honored community leaders are baffled by a sudden turn from prosperity to ruin. Compare with persons who lost their fortunes in 1929 or since through bad investments. The spokesmen for the community are reduced to silence (deprived of speech, literally, removes the lip). Their discernment (taste-palate) is also removed.

Verse 21—Psalm 107:40 is identical with the first line of this verse and the second line of verse 24.[6] The belt—Ps. 109:19 referred to here was used to strengthen the back, especially during hard labor. The word *aphik* normally means 'water-channels' but here 'strong.' Streams are called *aphikim* because they follow rapidly or strongly.

Verse 22—God recovers plots and conspiracies out of the deepest darkness. Before Him, there is no hiding place. Nothing designed by men can be hidden from the sovereign Lord of creation. He exposes all secrets. Even Sheol cannot hide its prey from Him.

Verse 23—Another example of the amoral nature of the universe is seen in the rise and fall of nations and civilizations. God's arbitrary exercise of power is visible in the "rise" and "fall" of world powers.[7]

Verse 24—Where there is no intelligence (literally heart-rendered understanding in A. V.) no nation or civilization can long endure. When the organizing principle of any social group is either abandoned or forgotten, it does not have long

---

[6] See A. Cohen, *Psalms,* Soncino, on Ps. 107:40.

[7] A. Toynbee's multiple volumed work, *A Study of History* (Oxford); and the indispensable *Cambridge History* series; and on this verse, see J. Reider, *Vetus Testamentum,* IV, 1954, pp. 290f.

to live. Compare the second part of this verse with Ps. 107:40b, where the Hebrew is identical. The "no way" of A. V. is waste (Heb. *tohu*—Gen. 1:2; Deut. 32:10) or disordered. The "formless" of our translations makes no sense, as matter cannot be formless, but it can be disordered. Job is here setting forth a philosophy of history and culture.

Verse 25—Men grope in unrelieved darkness. They grope as blind men and stagger or wander—vs. 24. When God removes understanding, men continue to move and function, but purposelessly (Ps. 107:27; Isa. 19:14; 24:20; Rom. 1:18ff; Prov. 29:18; and Jn. 1:18; Col. 1:17; Eph. 1:10). Life is meaningless to millions in our present world because nothing and no one organizes their lives meaningfully. But if the universe is purposeless and thus amoral, then what else could either Job or contemporaries expect? H. Thielicke says of our world—that it is the first generation which has "absolutized nothingness."[8]

TODAY'S ENGLISH VERSION

12
Job

1-2 Yes, you are the voice of the people.
   When you die, wisdom will die with you.
3 But I have as much sense as you have;
   I am in no way inferior to you;
   everyone knows all that you have said.
4 Even my friends laugh at me now,
   they laugh, although I am righteous and
     blameless;
   but there was a time when God answered
     my prayers.

---

[8] See my article "Nihilism" in Baker's *Dictionary of Christian Ethics*, ed. by C.F.H. Henry, p. 461-62.

⁵ You have no troubles, and yet you make fun of me;
   you hit a man who is about to fall.
⁶ But thieves and godless men live in peace,
     though their only god is their own strength.
⁷ Even birds and animals have a lot they could
     teach you;
⁸   ask the creatures of earth and sea for
     their wisdom.
⁹ All of them know that the Lord's hand made them.
¹⁰ It is God who directs the lives of his creatures;
     every man's life is in his power.
¹¹ But just as your tongue enjoys tasting food,
     your ears enjoy listening to words.

¹²⁻¹³ Old men have wisdom,
       but God has wisdom and power.
     Old men have insight;
       God has insight and power to act.
¹⁴ When God tears down, who can rebuild,
     and who can free the man God imprisons?
¹⁵ Drought comes when God withholds rain;
     floods come when he turns water loose.

¹⁶ God is strong and always victorious,
     both cheater and cheated are under God's
     control.
¹⁷ He destroys the wisdom of rulers,
     and makes leaders act like fools.
¹⁸ He dethrones kings and makes them prisoners;
¹⁹   he humbles priests and men of power.
²⁰ He silences men who are trusted,
     and takes the wisdom of old men away.
²¹ He disgraces those in power,
     and puts an end to the strength of rulers.
²² He sends light to places dark as death.
²³ He makes nations strong and great,
     but then he defeats and destroys them.

²⁴ He makes their leaders foolish,
   and lets them wander, confused and lost;
²⁵   they grope in the dark and stagger like drunkards.

QUESTIONS FOR DISCUSSION 12:1-25

226. This is Job's longest speech (i.e., 12:1—14:22). What is the purpose of this speech?
227. Job and his friends all agreed on one truth—what is it?
228. The attitude of Job is much like the present day Buddhist influence in America. What is it?
229. Name the three themes covered in this speech.
230. Job is bitingly sarcastic in verse two. Show how.
231. Why does Job assert his ability to understand? Cf. 11:20.
232. Job expected sympathy. What did he get? Why?
233. Job believed he was "a just and blameless man." Wasn't this false pride on his part? Discuss.
234. Do we share the attitude today expressed in verse five?
235. Give your interpretation of verse six.
236. To whom does Job address the words of verses seven through 12?
237. Why does Job refer to the beasts and the birds? What do they teach us?
238. Only in verse nine do we have the name Jehovah. Why is it used?
239. In what sense is the soul or life of every man in the hand of God?
240. How does the reference to the palate and food relate to the words of Job's friends?
241. How does verse 12 relate to the subject at hand?
242. Why does Job assert the absolute power and wisdom of God? Cf. verse 13.
243. Job cannot discern any moral dimension in the violence God manifests in this universe. What is missing in the understanding of Job?

121

4. The friends are self-deceived. (13:1-12)

TEXT 13:1-12

13 Lo, mine eye hath seen all *this,*
Mine ear hath heard and understood it.
2 What ye know, *the same* do I know also:
I am not inferior unto you.
3   Surely I would speak to the Almighty,
And I desire to reason with God.
4 But ye are forgers of lies;
Ye are all physicians of no value.
5 Oh that ye would altogether hold your peace!
And it would be your wisdom.
6 Hear now my reasoning,
And hearken to the pleadings of my lips.
7 Will ye speak unrighteously for God,
And talk deceitfully for him?
8 Will ye show partiality to him?
Will ye contend for God?
9 Is it good that he should search you out?
Or as one deceiveth a man, will ye deceive him?
10 He will surely reprove you,
If ye do secretly show partiality.
11 Shall not his majesty make you afraid,
And his dread fall upon you?
12 Your memorable sayings are proverbs of ashes,
Your defences are defences of clay.

COMMENT 13:1-12

Verse 1—Job warns of defending God dishonestly: by opposing his experience to that of Eliphaz—4:8, 12; 5:3, 27. He turns to face God with his charges regardless of the cost.

Verse 2—This is a repetition of 12:3b.

Verse 3—Job's "but as for me" is possibly a sarcastic response to Eliphaz's use of the same phrase. He told Job "but as for me, I would seek God." Job replies, "but as for me," I will challenge him to defend His behavior. Job desires to "reason" (cf. Isa. 1:18—reflective, reason together) with God. The term is a juridical word which means argue, reprove, reason in the sense of establish a case. Two emphatic words strongly set forth Job's commitment to debate God, rather than his counselors. He denounces them.

Verse 4—He accused his friends with forging a lie ("plasterers of lies"—verb means "to besmear" Ps. 119:69) to cover up the pain and agony which God causes. They are healers of no value (*eli*—may come from the root, not, i.e., worthless). Physicians, heal yourselves!

Verse 5—Even a fool that is silent is counted among the wise—Proverbs 17:28. He implies that if his friends are truly wise they would show it by their silence. It is not their lot to *shatter God's silence.*

Verse 6—Hear (emphatic in Hebrew) my reproof—Proverbs 1:23-25. The noun is from a root to "argue my case" (vs. 3). The R. S. V. is perhaps the best translation of this verse. Now to the impeachment in vss. 7-9.

Verse 7—Literally, you speak injustice (noun "wrong" 6:29; and parallel to deceit in 27:4). For God is in the emphatic position. The meaning is that—For God—you lie or speak deceitfully. Will you defend God by speaking "proverbs of ashes"?

Verse 8—Will you present God your face as His defender? What would God think (and do) if He investigated your actions? If God is a foe of injustice, He would be your foe. God's cause is always the "cause of truth." He is not flattered by your present dishonorable behavior. Why show favoritism with God, if He is just?

Verse 9—Sarcasm continues to flow as mighty waters from Job's mouth. God is the sovereign creator of everything; He cannot be flattered. If God "searched" out the truth (same word used by Eliphaz 5:27) He would condemn you too.

Verse 10—Job's prediction is later fulfilled, 42:7f. The paradox here is seen as Job affirms his own righteous indignation against lying deceivers, and the creator of the universe seems less concerned than he is. This thesis is shared by contemporary naturalistic humanists who build their world-live view on the assumption of the inherent worth of the individual. Yet scientific naturalism's "functional" view of man precludes any defense of such a universal value. There is no way to empirically justify a universal moral value.[1]

Verse 11—There is a magnificent play on words here in the Hebrew text. The parallelism between God's majesty (*se'etho*) or "lifting up" and "show partiality" indicates that God's face (lift up his face) will strike fear or horror not joy in the beholder.

Verse 12—Job accuses his friends of coming to his aid with "proverbs of ashes." (*Zikrom*—maxims or memorials) Their words serve no purpose; they are already dead. Their answers (*gabbim*) are like crumbling clay (4:70), with biting sarcasm he becomes more aggressive. "How long will you rake trifles" or debris (*megabbeb*)? Your words and arguments are useless bits of clay.

5. Job would dare to present his case before God.
(13:13-19)

TEXT 13:13-19

13　Hold your peace, let me alone, that I may speak;
　　And let come on me what will.
14　Wherefore should I take my flesh in my teeth,
　　And put my life in my hand?
15　Behold, he will slay me; I have no hope:

---

[1] For a critique of the relationship of Scientific Theories to Scientific Progress, see my analysis of the epistemological possibility of the scientific method in my doctoral thesis in process on *The Kuhn-Popper Debate concerning the relationship of Presuppositions, Evidence, and the Paradigm Revolution: Two Contemporary Paradigms of Scientific Knowledge.*

Nevertheless I will maintain my ways before him.
16 This also shall be my salvation,
That a godless man shall not come before him.
17 Hear diligently my speech,
And let my declaration be in your ears.
18 Behold now, I have set my cause in order;
I know that I am righteous.
19 Who is he that will contend with me?
For then would I hold my peace and give up the ghost.

COMMENT 13:13-19

Verse 13—The prounoun *I* is emphatic. Once more he is asking that his friends keep silent that he may speak to God.

Verse 14—There is a problem in this verse in that it begins with "why."[2] But the sense is clear enough; since his life may pass away any moment, he will not hesitate to risk his life (Hebrew *nepes*) by confronting God (Judges 12:3; I Samuel 19:5; and 28:21).

Verse 15—With abandoned desperation, Job is prepared to challenge God. Yet (A. V. nevertheless is strong Hebrew adversative) absolutely nothing will cause Job to refrain from defending his innocence. His suffering is not self-entailed, his conscience is clear. He is not a rebel without a cause. Job is not revolting against God; rather he is going to face Him. Evil men inevitably run from the face or presence of God, as Adam did (Genesis 3:8) and Jonah.

Verse 16—Perhaps he can be saved by boldness, as Dostoevsky mistakenly thought, that man could be saved by suffering, to whom all suffering was vicarious. To Job, his readiness to face God is his guarantee of innocence. He believes that if God should speak to him, He would do so favorably. But love alone knows the healing art.

---

[2] See M. Dahood, *Biblica et Orientalia,* XVII, 1965, p. 16.

125

Verse 17—Job calls for his opponents to listen carefully. *Hear* is a plural imperative—13:6.

Verse 18—Job says I will set my things in order (Gen. 22:9; Ps. 23:5; Job 23:4, 5; 27:19) and gain for myself acquittal (11:2).

Verse 19—My things are in order—now "who can contend with me" (Isa. 1:8)? Who can sustain the charge of guilty? If one could reveal to him his guilt, he would gladly become silent and acknowledge his wickedness—through silence.

6. He calls on God for an arraignment. (13:20-28)

TEXT 13:20-28

20 Only do not two things unto me:
   Then will I not hide myself from thy face:
21 Withdraw thy hand far from me;
   And let not thy terror make me afraid.
22 Then call thou, and I will answer;
   Or let me speak, and answer thou me.
23 How many are mine iniquities and sins?
   Make me to know my transgression and my sin.
24 Wherefore hidest thou thy face,
   And holdest me for thine enemy?
25 Wilt thou harass a driven leaf?
   And wilt thou pursue the dry stubble?
26 For thou writest bitter things against me,
   And makest me to inherit the iniquities of my youth:
27 Thou puttest my feet also in the stocks,
   And markest all my paths;
   Thou settest a bound to the soles of my feet:
28 Though I am like a rotten thing that consumeth,
   Like a garment that is moth-eaten.

COMMENT 13:20-28

Verse 20—Spare me two things: (1) one request is negative,

(2) one positive. The substance of Job's present request has been presented before in 9:34; see also Isa. 51:19; Jer. 2:13. God first gives Job peace "in suffering" before relief "from suffering." Job addresses God directly throughout the remainder of his speech.

Verse 21—Job's two-pronged request is here stated: (1) "withdraw your hand" (*yadecha*) used in both positive sense of protection, and negative sense of afflicting pain and suffering (Ex. 33:22; and (2) do not use your sovereign power to terrify me.

Verse 22—The imagery is that of a law court where Job offers to appear as either appellant or repondent—14:15. The call is for either fellowship or indictment.

Verse 23—Job boldly asks for God to list the number and nature of his sins.[3] There are three different Hebrew words for sin used here: (1) root meaning to deviate from prescribed course; (2) root to miss attaining a goal or fulfilling an intentionally chosen goal; and (3) root form to revolt, freely rebel (Ps. 51).

Verse 24—God does not break His silence.

Verse 25—The A. V. harass should be translated something like terrify. Why should God, as sovereign of the universe, assail one so trivial and impotent to meet His challenge—Ps. 1:4?

Verse 26—Has some sin in my youth brought on your bitter punishment? (Ps. 25:7) The word translated "bitter" is used of poison 20;14, and gall bladder in 20:25.

Verse 27—The three images employed here suggest arrest and the impossibility of escape (33:11). God draws a line and no one can step beyond it. Slaves were identified by markings on various parts of the body (Isa. 44:5; 49:16), apparently also on the sole of the slaves' feet, in order to make tracking easier.

Verse 28—His life is rotten and like a pest-eaten vine decaying

---

[3] See G. Quell, G. Bertram, G. Stahlin, and W. Grundmann's article in *TWNT*, Vol. I, E. T. Eerdmans; and K. Menninger, *Whatever Became of Sin?* (Hawthorn, 1973.)

with no hope of recovery. This is despair conceived in the womb of pessimism and fathered by "manacles of the mind."

TODAY'S ENGLISH VERSION

13

¹⁻² Everything you say, I have heard before.
I understand it all. I know as much as you do.
I'm not your inferior.
³ But my dispute is with God, not you;
I want to argue my case with him.
⁴ You cover up your ignorance with lies;
you are like doctors who can't heal anyone.
⁵ Say nothing, and someone may think you are wise!

⁶ Listen to me state my case.
⁷ Why are you lying?
Do you think your lies will help God?
⁸ Are you trying to defend God?
Are you going to argue his case in court?
⁹ If God looks at you closely will he find anything good?
Do you think you can fool God, the way you fool men?
¹⁰ Even though your prejudice is hidden,
he will reprimand you,
¹¹ and his power will fill you with terror.
¹² How stale your proverbs and arguments are!
¹³ Be quiet and give me a chance to speak,
and let the results be what they will.

¹⁴ I am ready to risk my life.
¹⁵ I've lost all hope, so what if God kills me?
I am going to state my case to him.
¹⁶ It may even be that my boldness will save me,
since no wicked man would dare face God.
¹⁷ Now listen to my words of explanation.

128

¹⁸ I am ready to state my case,
because I know I am in the right.

¹⁹ God, are you going to come and accuse me?
If you do, I am ready to be silent and die.
²⁰ Let me ask for two things; agree to them,
and I will not try to hide from you:
²¹ stop punishing me, and don't crush me with
terror.

²² Speak first, God, and I will answer.
Or let me speak and you answer me.
²³ Of how many wrongs and sins am I guilty?
What crimes am I charged with?

²⁴ Why do you avoid me?
Why do you treat me like an enemy?
²⁵ Are you trying to frighten me? I'm nothing but
a leaf;
you are attacking a dry piece of straw.

²⁶ You bring bitter charges against me,
even for what I did when I was young.
²⁷ You bind chains on my feet;
you watch every step and even examine my
footprints.
²⁸ As a result, I crumble like rotten wood,
like a moth-eaten coat.

QUESTIONS FOR DISCUSSION 13:1-28

244. What warning does Job give in verse one?
245. Job could be giving a sarcastic response to Eliphaz in
verse three. How so?
246. Job calls his friends "plasterers of lies." Why? (vs. 4)
247. Job says in verse five that the best way to show wisdom is
not in words. In what then?

248. Job is going to argue his case. In verse seven who is involved in deceit or lying? Discuss.

249. Job's friends are asked in verse eight to allow God to do
for them what they want God to do for Job. What is it?

250. Why is Job so sarcastic? What lesson can we learn from this?

251. In Job's promise of verse ten, what was fulfilled? When?

252. God seems less concerned than Job (or man). Such a
thought has been used by present day humanists. To what
purpose? How answered?

253. What is the play on words in verse eleven?

254. Job's evaluation of his friend's words could be described
in two words. What are they?

255. Who is Job addressing in verses 13-19?

256. Explain verse 14 in your own words.

257. Job is willing to face God in a defense of his innocence.
Was Job right? Discuss.

258. Job has a certain guarantee of innocence. What was it?
Discuss.

259. Job actually believed that if he were called before God
he could set his cause in such a way that he would be
acquitted. Was he right? Discuss.

260. Spare me two things. What are they? This has been discussed before in 9:34. Cf. Isa. 51:9; Jer. 2:13.

261. What were Job's two requests? Why make them? Was
this a reasonable request? Discuss.

262. Job would like to appear in God's law court in one of
two positions. What were they? Cf. vs. 22.

263. There are three different Hebrew words for sin in verse
23. What are they? How do they relate to Job and us?

264. What point is made in verse 25?

265. The suffering of Job is bitter. In what way? Job imagines
another reason for such suffering. What is it? Does God
punish for past sins?

266. Discuss the three images of verse 27.

267. Job's life is "rotten and like a pest-eaten vine decaying
with no hope of recovery." Are there such pessimists in
our world today? Discuss.

7. So brief is man's allotted time he should be left to enjoy it.
   (14:1-6)

TEXT 14:1-6

14 Man, that is born of a woman,
Is of few days, and full of trouble.
2 He cometh forth like a flower, and is cut down:
He fleeth also as a shadow, and continueth not.
3 And dost thou open thine eyes upon such a one,
And bringest me into judgment with thee?
4 Who can bring a clean thing out of an unclean? not one.
5 Seeing his days are determined,
The number of his months is with thee,
And thou hast appointed his bounds that he cannot pass;
6 Look away from him, that he may rest,
Till he shall accomplish, as a hireling, his day.

COMMENT 14:1-6

Verse 1—Job continues to generalize his agonizing cry, returning to the theme expressed in 7:17. Man's[1] frail origin betrays him to the suffering in an amoral universe. Life is so short (7:6ff; 9:25f; Gen. 47:9). Here both pity and contempt are mixed as oil and water. His condition arouses the contrary feelings of *wonder*[2] and despair. The Hebrew text will not

---

[1] For analysis of the Hebrew word *'adham* see Maass, "adham," in *TWOT*, ed. Botterweck and Ringgren, Vol. I, E.T., 1974, Eerdmans, pp. 75-87; A. Gelin, *L'homme selon la Bible* (Paris, 1962); E. Lussier, "Adam in Gen. 1:11—4:24," *CBQ* 18, 1956, pp. 137-39; and Hans W. Wolff, *Anthropology of the O.T.*, E.T., 1973, Fortress Press.

[2] *Wonder* is a powerful human response to reality. Plato correctly claims that all series thinking (Philosophy) begins with wonder. Again in the decade of the '60's wonder appeared in the Dionysian spirit re-dividius. Sam Keen's *Apology for Wonder* can be celebrated only because of God's Wonder, Christ (Isa. 9:1ff) "and His name shall be called *wonder.*" The Hebrew word is a noun-wonder, not an adjective, which is translated by "wonderful."

131

sustain the assumption of some of the Church Fathers that this verse sets forth the doctrine of "original sin." Verses 7-9 and 10-12 are parallel strophes which sharply contrast man's limitations, not just Job's. Here we encounter another paradox; if Job is describing the condition of humanity, why is he preoccupied with his own plight?

Verse 2—In Job's powerful description he uses a verb "comes forth" which is often applied to plants—Isa. 11:1; 40:6f; Ps. 90:6; 103:15f; Job 8:9; Jas. 1:10f. Nothing is more ephemeral than a flower. "Life's but a walking shadow" (Macbeth) Even the longest life is but a brief flickering candle— Ps. 90:9-10 and filled with strife (*rogez*—also 3:17, 26).

Verse 3—Why should God scrutinize one so ephemeral as man? To "open your eyes" means to focus attention on or to pay attention to. "Me" is in the emphatic position which focuses attention on Job.

Verse 4—Pope, et al. suggest that this verse be deleted because the context speaks of the shortness of life and not his wickedness. Job is concerned with his sin and guilt in vss. 16, 17. "Who will give (Hebrew *mi yitten*) cleanness to the unclean?" The text says "not one," but ultimately only God.

Verse 5—Since man's life is so short, why doesn't God just leave him alone? The verse contains a rather fatalistic note. If God has determined (literally cut, perhaps engrave a statute on stone) everything and it is thus under his control, let these conditions suffice Him.

Verse 6—God, stop your cruel surveillance of man. Let him alone—Ps. 39:14. Let him enjoy each day like a laborer who receives his reward each evening at the close of the work day (7:1). Job's attitude was completely at variance with that of Milton who ever lived "under the Great Taskmaster's eye."

8. When man goes to his death, he does not return. (14:7-12)

TEXT 14:7-12

7 For there is hope of a tree,

If it be cut down, that it will sprout again,
And that the tender branch thereof will not cease.
8 Though the root thereof wax old in the earth,
And the stock thereof die in the ground;
9 Yet through the scent of water it will bud,
And put forth boughs like a plant.
10 But man dieth, and is laid low:
Yea, man giveth up the ghost, and where is he?
11 *As* the waters fail from the sea,
And the river wasteth and drieth up;
12 So man lieth down and riseth not:
Till the heavens be no more, they shall not awake,
Nor be roused out of their sleep.

COMMENT 14:7-12

Verse 7—The figures now change to a tree. Trees can be cut down, but some species will sprout again.[3] Even trees have more hope than men (Vss. 7-9 reveal Near Eastern custom of cutting trees off in order to produce new life.)

Verse 8—A tree may not be completely dead, but drought retards its growth. The roots are withering in the ground.

Verse 9—But the scent of water will bring new hope for life (Ps. 92:12f; and Prov. 14:11).

Verse 10—There are two Hebrew roots for man in this verse, one "to be strong" and "to be weak." (The word translated "laid low" in A. V. is *h-l-s*—weakening, defeating, or helpless; the "gibbor" is a strong person, translated in A. V. as "giveth up the ghost.") Even a strong man dies and is no more (Joel 3:10). Job here reflects a very limited view of life after death.

Verse 11—Though the contexts are different, the second line of this verse is identical with Isaiah 19:5b. Dhorme's

---

[3] For this image see F. Delitzsch, *Job,* Vol. I, E.T., Eerdmans, p. 227.

point is well taken regarding the word rendered "sea." The Hebrew term is used in a wider sense than the sea; it can mean a lake (Isa. 19:5). The sea could not dry up; if it did it would not make any difference to the dead.[4]

Verse 12—When man lies down to pleasant dreams, "they shall not wake,"[5] as long as the heavens do not burst.

9. Job longs for an afterlife. (14:13-17)

TEXT 14:13-17

13   Oh that thou wouldest hide me in Sheol,
      That thou wouldest keep me secret, until thy wrath be past,
      That thou wouldest appoint me a set time, and remember me!
14 If a man die, shall he live *again?*
      All the days of my warfare would I wait,
      Till my release should come.
15 Thou wouldest call, and I would answer thee:
      Thou wouldest have a desire to the work of thy hands.
16 But now thou numberest my steps:
      Dost thou not watch over my sin?
17 My transgression is sealed up in a bag,
      And thou fastenest up mine iniquity.

COMMENT 14:13-17

Verse 13—Job passionately longs for life. If there is a positive possibility of life after death, then Job could endure the present affliction. The abode of the dead (Sheol) could be Job's hiding place. (Read Isaiah 26:20 and Amos 9:2.) Perhaps he is acknowledging a belief in life after death, or a strong desire

---

[4] Dhorme, *Job,* p. 199.
[5] G. R. Driver, *Vetus Testamentum,* Supplement, III, 1960, p. 77.

that there might be one.

Verse 14—The LXX omits the interrogative, and makes Job deliver a positive claim—"he shall live again."[6] The image is derived from a military figure of soldiers being relieved after strenuous service—7:1.

Verse 15—Again two views of God are struggling within Job's heart. He "longs for" the former days of fellowship with God, from which his present agony has cut him off. Job so deeply longs for this relationship with God (Hebrew, care, be pale, color of silver) (Gen. 31:30; Ps. 84:3; and Isa. 29:22) that he is sick with care.

Verse 16—This verse probably continues verse 15, so R. S. V., but not A. V. God is graciously watching over Job's every step; then, all of a sudden, God is jealously observing every detail in his life. Job's hope is in the future; perhaps God will change His attitude toward him. The negative particle "not" in verse 16 is inserted in order to smooth out the poetic parallelism. Job has vehemently complained—7:12, 19, of God's tyrannical observation, as a cosmic moral efficiency expert; now he hopes for grace rather than surveillance.

Verse 17—The imagery reflects that of accounting or recording of Job's sins.[7] He seeks to be acknowledged as righteousness. Righteousness is always a correlate of right relations in our daily experiences. Job has come as a Titan hoping to meet God as an equal. There has been no room for "grace" in the relationship. Job desires to meet God face to face but "neither to change nor falter, nor repent."[8] Job has sought justification by seeking righteousness. "Rather than seek help he would prefer to be himself with all the tortures of hell, if so it must be." Job has come before God with a radical over-self estimate of himself; and therein is his "sickness unto death."[9]

---

[6] See D. H. Gard, *J.B.L., LXXIII,* 1954, pp. 137ff.

[7] A. L. Oppenheim, *Journal Near Eastern Studies,* XVIII, 1959, pp. 121ff.

[8] Shelly, *Prometheus Unbound,* Act IV.

[9] Soren Kierkegaard, *Fear and Trembling* and *The Sickness Unto Death* (Double-

10. But hope is destroyed in Sheol. (14:18-22)

TEXT 14:18-22

18 But the mountain falling cometh to nought;
   And the rock is removed out of its place;
19 The waters wear the stones;
   The overflowings thereof wash away the dust of the earth:
   So thou destroyeth the hope of man.
20 Thou prevailest for ever against him, and he passeth;
   Thou changest his countenance, and sendest him away.
21 His sons come to honor, and he knoweth it not;
   And they are brought low, but he perceiveth it not of them.
22 But his flesh upon him hath pain,
   And his soul within him mourneth.

COMMENT 14:18-22

Verse 18—How can man hope to escape destruction, since the greatest mountains can be leveled, and the deepest valleys covered over. *Impermanence* is the central theme.

Verse 19—As water erodes the stones, so God is destroying (eroding) man's hope. Job here dismisses the very possibility of life after death. We can hope—until that ultimate leveler—death smashes our last moment of life.

Verse 20—In man's last moment of struggle against death, he is defeated by the despair of finality.[10] Death is extreme and permanent in its conflict with human hope. The phrase

---

day, Anchor pb., ed. 1954; also Princeton University Press, 1951, p. 114.) On the vital problem of the "distance between" God and man in Biblical data, neo-orthodoxy, egs. Barth-Brunner controversy, and Post-Vatican II Catholicism; but especially since the 19th century paradigm of evolution - Kant, Hegel, Marx, Freud, Kierkegaard, Nietzsche, et. al., see R. Kroner, "Kierkegaard or Hegel?" *Revue Internationale de Philosophie,* 19, 1952, pp. 7-8.

[10] D. W. Thomas, *Journal of Semitic Studies,* 1, 1956, p. 107 - for translation of superlative of *nesah* - "Thou prevailest utterly against him."

"sends them away" is a verb used euphemistically of dying—
"The land from whose borne no traveler has returned"—10:21;
II Sam. 12:23; Ecc. 1:4; 3:20; and Ps. 39:13.

Verse 21—The dead have no knowledge—Eccl. 9:5. This
is the fate of all mankind. Even children, who think only of
life, also share in this fate—1:9. Consciousness in death is
limited only to the dead individual, so claims Job. Those who
"come to honor" are also "brought low." The sense of R. S. V.
is more in line with the text than that of the A. V.

Verse 22—Job now abandons the traditional resolution of
man's troubles, that of leaving a prosperous family behind.
But Job has no family. Whether the source be Job or classical
naturalistic liberals, it is not very exciting to hope only in
the survival of humanity—18:13 and Isaiah 66:24.

The first series of speeches is ended. Job is enslaved more
deeply in despair than in the initial lament. The "slough of
despond" is deeper than his pain. "There he was 'half in love
with easeful death' " here he stands alone before "the grisly
terror" (*Job, Interpreters Bible*, Vol. III, p. 1015). But "Death
Be Not Proud" for *The Shattering of Silence* is yet to come.

TODAY'S ENGLISH VERSION

14 All men lead the same short, troubled life.
² They grow and wither as qucikly as flowers;
they disappear like shadows.
³ Will you even look at me, God,
or bring me before you to be judged?
⁴ Nothing clean can ever come
from anything as unclean as man.
⁵ The length of his life is decided beforehand—
the number of months he will live.
You have settled it, and it can't be changed.
⁶ Look away from him and leave him alone;
let him enjoy his life of hard work.

⁷ There is hope for a tree that has been cut down;
   it can come back to life and sprout.
⁸ Even though its roots grow old,
   and its stump dies in the ground,
⁹   with water it will sprout like a young plant.
¹⁰ But a man dies, and that is the end of him;
   he dies, and where is he then?

¹¹ A time will come when rivers stop running,
   and even the seas go dry.
¹² But dead men will never rise;
   they will never wake up while the skies last;
   they will never stir out of their sleep.
¹³ I wish you would hide me alive in the land of
   of the dead;
   let me be hidden until your anger is over,
   and then set a time to remember me.
¹⁴ If a man dies, can he come back to life?
   But I will wait for better times,
   wait till this time of trouble is over.
¹⁵ Then you will call and I will answer,
   and you will be pleased with me, your creature.
¹⁶ Then you will watch every step I take,
   but you will not keep track of my sins.
¹⁷ You will forgive my sins and put them away;
   you will wipe out all the wrongs I have done.

¹⁸ A time will come when mountains fall,
   and even rock cliffs are moved away.
¹⁹ Water will wear down rocks,
   and hard rain wash away the soil;
   so you destroy man's hope for life.
²⁰ You overpower a man and send him away forever;
   his face is twisted in death.
²¹ His sons win honor, but he never knows it,
   nor is he told when they are disgraced.
²² He feels only the pain of his own body
   and the grief of his own mind.

QUESTIONS FOR DISCUSSION 14:1-22

268. The mixture of pity and contempt arouse the contrary feelings of _____ and _____. Why? Is this right?

269. Is this a proof-text for original sin? Discuss.

270. What is meant by saying, "Nothing is more ephemeral than a flower"?

271. Give three figures of speech which describe the briefness of life.

272. Give in your own words the meaning of verse three.

273. Verse four seems out of place in the context. Explain.

274. There is a fatalistic note in verse five, the thought of which is often repeated today. What is it? Discuss.

275. The omnipresence of God is a real hinderance to man, i.e., according to Job. Why? Cf. vs. 6.

276. Man has less hope than a tree. How so? Why does Job say this?

277. A Near Eastern custom is revealed in verse seven. What is it?

278. What type or condition of a tree is described in verses eight and nine?

279. There are two kinds of man in verse ten. What is the reason for using two Hebrew words?

280. How is man like the water of a sea, lake or river?

281. Job surely has a limited view of man and life, but he had more reason than many who share the same view today. Discuss.

282. Explain in what sense Job wants to be hid in Sheol. Does Job believe in an afterlife after all? Discuss.

283. Life after death is couched in an image of a military figure of soldiers. How so?

284. Two views of God are struggling within Job's heart. What are they? Discuss.

285. Why does God watch or mark our every step? Job has conflicting answers to this question. What are they? What is your answer?

286. Give in your own words the meaning of verse 17. (This is a very important verse. Think well about it.)

II. CRISIS IN COMMUNICATION OR THE MIRACLE OF DIALOGUE? (15:1—21:34).

A. THE GOODNESS OF GOD AND THE FATE OF THE WICKED—ELIPHAZ'S REBUTTAL (15:1-35).

1. Job's speech and conduct are perverted and show that he is guilty. (15:1-16)

TEXT 15:1-16

15 Then answered Eliphaz the Temanite, and said,
2 Should a wise man make answer with vain knowledge,
And fill himself with the east wind?
3 Should he reason with unprofitable talk,
Or with speeches wherewith he can do no good?
4 Yea, thou doest away with fear,
And hinderest devotion before God.
5 For thine iniquity teacheth thy mouth,
And thou choosest the tongue of the crafty.
6 Thine own mouth condemneth thee, and not I;
Yea, thine own lips testify against thee.
7 Art thou the first man that was born?
Or wast thou brought forth before the hills?
8 Hast thou heard the secret counsel of God?
And dost thou limit wisdom to thyself?
9 What knowest thou, that we know not?
What understandest thou, which is not in us?
10 With us are both the grayheaded and the very aged men,
Much elder than thy father.
11 Are the consolations of God too small for thee,
Even the word that is gentle toward thee?
12 Why doth thy heart carry thee away?
And why do thine eyes flash,
13 That against God thou turnest thy spirit,
And lettest words go out of thy mouth?
14 What is man, that he should be clean?
And he that is born of a woman, that he should be righteous?

15 Behold, he putteth no trust in his holy ones;
   Yea, the heavens are not clean in his sight:
16 How much less one that is abominable and corrupt,
   A man that drinketh iniquity like water!

COMMENT 15:1-16

"Every man is a potential adversary, even those whom we love," Reuel L. Howe

In times of crisis people tend to withdraw timidly. "We do not want anything to happen . . . Seven years we've lived quietly, succeeded in avoiding notice, living and partly living . . . but now a great fear is on us," Chorus in T. S. Eliot's *Murder in The Cathedral*

Men are mesmerized by the magic of media in our global village, yet "Thy hand, great Anarch! lets the curtain fall; and Universal Darkness buries All," J. Joyce, *Finnegan's Wake*

"God's implicated in that cruelty if He has the power to control it," Ivan in Dostoevsky's *The Brothers Karamazov*.

Verse 1—The second cycle of speeches now begins. Eliphaz's second speech—15:1-35—has an entirely different ring to it than his first speech—chapters 4—5. In his first speech he looked on Job as a wise, God-fearing man—4:3-6. Now after hearing Job deny his guilt, reject the thesis that his suffering is the inevitable result of his sins, and challenge God to explain his existential situation to him, Eliphaz's deep insecurity finds expression in his attack on the person of Job. The encouraging tone of the first speech—reward to the righteous—has escaped from his consoling heart, and now the negative and menacing one—punishment of the unrighteous—controls the speech. He accuses Job with being a windbag, full of hot air. The word "wise" is emphatic in the text and means "a truly wise man." Job's claim to wisdom, which is in complete opposition to the wisdom of the ancients, is

141

adjudged to be sheer arrogance. Job is now presented as a rebel without a cause; whereas Eliphaz in his first speech asserted Job's essential piety, now he is hardened against the sovereign creator of heaven and earth. God's *moral perfection* has been set forth in Eliphaz's first speech, while Bildad eloquently presents His unchanging justice, and Zophar His omniscience (all knowing). Job's responses have thus far failed to prick either their conscious or God's concern for his suffering. Now in Eliphaz's second speech, the irreligious and impious Job is confronted with his inevitable fate: (1) Job is rebuked for his irreverent rashness—verses 2-6; (2) Denounced for his presumptive confidence in his superior wisdom—verses 7-16; and (3) The doctrine of the fate of the wicked—verses 17-35.

Verse 2—Job has claimed that his wisdom is not inferior to that of his friends—8:2; 11:2; 12:3; and 13:2. This stance receives Eliphaz's blistering denunciation—it's all empty (*ruah* and *hebel*) knowledge. The parallel between Job's words and the dreaded, hot violent searing sirocco winds is self-evident. If Job were truly wise, he would have better arguments.

Verse 3—Eliphaz picks up a Jobian word from 13:3, 6, and deduces that Job's arguments are profitless (lit. "which does not profit," used five times in Job in this sense). The words are useless; they neither convince nor convict.

Verse 4—Job's words bring only pain and spiritual suffocation to man. His speech does away with reverence (*sihah*—meditation—Ps. 119:97-99, fear) of God—4:6. In fact, Job's words, if taken seriously, would destroy his religion, and impair the faith of others. The verb employed here means "to violate" the covenant or vow. This meaning of the first line of the verse is confirmed by the second line, as Eliphaz asserts that Job's words are hindering—lit. "diminishing"—devotions in others. Eliphaz's orthodoxy is both threatened and challenged. But Job remains a seeker after Truth who is still deeply pious. Still we hear their outcry—"What further need have we of witnesses?" Matt. 26:65.

Verse 5—Job's blasphemous utterances are too grounded in his diabolical desire to conceal his own evil heart. Job is, like the "crafty" (used here and 5:12) serpent of Gen. 3:1ff, attempting to misrepresent God. The Hebrew can be translated several ways, but "your guilt teaches your mouth" is, in accordance with the parallelism of verse 5b, to be preferred. Eliphaz, like his many contemporary counterparts, seeks to psychoanalyze Job, rather than answer his arguments.[1] Job's attempts to express his innocence, Eliphaz insinuates, are really efforts to hide his guilt (cf. Freudian rationalization).[2]

Verse 6—Eliphaz is arguing that Job's own protestation of innocence is his own condemnation—9:20. Thus far Job has admitted only of youthful sins—13:26, but he has asserted that God could coerce him into a false confession of guilt—9:20. Is not Job's protest against God tantamount to self-incrimination? Job is convicted out of his own mouth.

Verse 7—Eliphaz here questions Job with a blistering series of interrogations. Though we can often encounter the claims that this verse has reference to the Jewish myth of primeval man (*'adam haq-quadmon*), there is neither need nor proof that this is the case here. Simply, the verse declares that if you were the first man (*'adam*) you might be wise enough to say what you're saying, but you are not. The first man did not steal God's wisdom as Prometheus stole fire from the gods—Prov. 7:25 and Ps. 90:2.

Verse 8—Jeremiah derides the false prophets who talk like they have stood in God's council room and heard Him speak directly to them—Jer. 23:18, 22. Jeremiah chides them by declaring that they have neither divine word nor mission. The word "council" (*sod*—meaning intimate and confidential) is one of the designations of the assembly of the gods. The usage of the council of the gods is at least as old as Mesopotamian and Canaanite antecedents. Eliphaz is asking Job whether or not he has a monopoly on wisdom—Ezek. 28:11-19;

---

[1] Certainly since Herder, Schelling, Dilthey, Nietzsche, and Freud hermeneutics (Literary Criticism) has become psychologized. (Interpreters ask "Why" anyone declares what he does, instead of asking whether "what" anyone declares is true or false.)

[2] M. Dahood, *Biblica*, 44, 1963, 204, for technical analysis of the grammar of this verse.

143

Prov. 8:22, 26.

Verses 9-10—Here we encounter questions which assume that Job is claiming the possession of "superior knowledge." This is minimally odd in that he has never made such claims. He has only criticized "their" claims to "superior knowledge" of God's will and purpose—12:3; 13:3. His friends are actually the ones who are claiming "superior knowledge," not Job. *Wisdom*[3] is a virtue of seniority acclaims Eliphaz's theme. Job has already rejected the thesis that wisdom is a necessary result of "old age"—12:12. Senility and sagacity are not necessarily causally related—*Wisdom of Solomon*, 4:8-9.

Verse 11—Eliphaz is claiming that the consolation of Job's three friends is from God. Yet Job dismisses his friends as "miserable comforters"—16:2. Perhaps the "deals gently" does apply to Eliphaz's initial speech, but certainly not his second. His words (*dabar*—means creative and often relevatory. This is the Hebrew word for the Genesis creation account and the Ten Words or commandments) are scarcely to be termed "consolation," unless his doctrine of "suffering is always merited" is to be understood as consolation. His words are identical with God's, according to Eliphaz.

Verse 12—Why do you allow your heart (feelings) to carry you away.[4] The verb *r-z-m* is here translated "flash" in A. V.[5] The word means to wink or flash, perhaps in rage, not weakness as some suggest. Job is being rebuked for his uncontrolled passion, not his helplessness.

Verse 13—Job is rebuked for his anger against God. Your

---

[3] For exhaustive analysis of the "wisdom" concept, see A. Feuillet, *Le Christ Sagesse de Deus* (Paris: 1966), and articles in both Kittel, *TWNT*, and Botterweck and Ringgren, *TDOT*.

[4] See for technical analysis of grammatical possibilities, G. R. Driver, *Die Welt des Orients* I, 1947-52, 235.

[5] The Jewish scholar Rashi suggests that the verb is the same as *ramaz* (Aramaic root) "to flash" in anger. This is most likely as R.S.V. translates.

spirit refers to Job's anger. In anger you attack God by letting such words out of your mouth.

Verse 14—The theme from 4:17ff reoccurs here—9:2 and 24:4. Eliphaz also quotes Job's phrase—14:1. "A man," not the genus but a particular individual, whom Eliphaz need not name. The image suggests impurity not finitude. The Near Eastern negative attitude toward women is here apparent.

Verse 15—Eliphaz returns to his thoughts expressed in 4:18; 25:5, 6; 38:7; and Isa. 40:25-26. The holy ones, perhaps angels, are not without fault before God—II Pet. 2:4.[6]

Verse 16—The word translated "corrupt" (foul) appears in the Old Testament only in a moral sense—also Pss. 14:3; 53:3. Perhaps a proverbial saying—"a man sins like drinking water" presents Eliphaz's judgment on Job. "One" is abominable,[7] i.e., disgusting, revolting, loathed as R. S. V.—also Pss. 107:15; 119:163.

2. The destiny of the ungodly shows the retributive justice of God. (15:17-35)

TEXT 15:17-35

17 I will show thee, hear thou me;
    And that which I have seen I will declare
18 (Which wise men have told
    From their fathers, and have not hid it;
19 Unto whom alone the land was given,
    And no stranger passed among them):
20 The wicked man travaileth with pain all his days,

---

[6] On heaven and the power of evil, see Calvin R. Schoonhoven, *The Wrath of Heaven* (Eerdmans, pb., 1966). See also eschatology of Isa. 60-66; I Pet. 3; and Rev. 21ff. The imagery of a "new heaven" as well as a "new earth"—why a new heaven? P. Volz, *Die Eschatologie der judischen Gemeinde in neutestanmentliche Zeitalter* (Tubingen, 1934; and D. H. Odendaal, *The Eschatological Expectation of Isaiah 40-66* (Presb. and Reformed Pub. Co., 1970).

[7] For analysis of this word root, see Paul Humbert, *Zeitschrift für die alttestamentliche Wissenschaft*, N. F. XXXI, 1960, 217ff.

Even the number of years that are laid up for the oppressor.
21 A sound of terrors is in his ears;
In prosperity the destroyer shall come upon him.
22 He believeth not that he shall return out of darkness,
And he is waiting for the sword.
23 He wandereth abroad for bread, *saying,* Where is it?
He knoweth that the day of darkness is ready at his hand.
24 Distress and anguish make him afraid;
They prevail against him, as a king ready to the battle.
25 Because he hath stretched out his hand against God,
And behaveth himself proudly against the Almighty;
26 He runneth upon him with a *stiff* neck,
With the thick bosses of his bucklers;
27 Because he hath covered his face with his fatness,
And gathered fat upon his loins;
28 And he hath dwelt in desolate cities,
In houses which no man inhabited,
Which were ready to become heaps;
29 He shall not be rich, neither shall his substance continue,
Neither shall their possessions be extended on the earth.
30 He shall not depart out of darkness;
The flame shall dry up his branches,
And by the breath of *God's* mouth shall he go away.
31 Let him not trust in vanity, deceiving himself;
For vanity shall be his recompense.
32 It shall be accomplished before his time,
And his branch shall not be green.
33 He shall shake off his unripe grape as the vine,
And shall cast off his flower as the olive-tree.
34 For the company of the godless shall be barren,
And fire shall consume the tents of bribery.
35 They conceive mischief, and bring forth iniquity,
And their heart prepareth deceit.

COMMENT 15:17-35

Verse 17—Here again is Eliphaz's favorite theme, the destiny of the wicked. Once more the doctrine is supported by reference to the accumulated wisdom of the ages. (Compare Eliphaz's claim with Ps. 73). Eliphaz's unbridled eloquence is still not very convincing, though he claims revelation (*hazah*—prophetic gazing) as source for his message.

Verse 18—Eliphaz is here claiming that his convictions are confirmed by the observation of past generations. "Tradition" confirms the accuracy of Eliphaz's judgment. Where have we heard that claim before? (Even Tevye, from *Fiddler on the Roof,* knew both the power of tradition and change.) Eliphaz, like his many successors, never learned that tradition is never to be necessarily identified with truth, either human or divine.

Verse 19—The tradition of wisdom has been transmitted pure, uncontaminated by foreign influences.[8] Edom was the proverbial home of wisdom—Jer. 49:7. Eliphaz's provincialism shines forth in his belief that the purest wisdom is that in the possession of his own people. Remember, he is not a member of the covenant nation.

Verse 20—Job has earlier asserted that robbers prosper—12:6. Eliphaz responds to Job that the wicked are in constant agony—Isa. 57:20ff. The prosperity of the unrighteous man is hollow because he is tortured psychologically, by a guilty conscience—"all his days."[9] The Hebrew text has *mispar,* which means "a number," i.e., a few, but the parallelism calls for "all his days"—"all his years." The word translated oppressor in the A. V., in 6:23; 27:13, comes from the root "to terrify," or "to inspire awe" and means here a ruthless person. The verse means that the unrighteous are miserable and short-lived, but the pious are happy and long-lived.

---

[8] The verse might contain a clue to the date of the book of Job. If the land is Canaan, which the text does not claim, Israel had undisputed control up to the fall of Samaria ca 722-1 B.C.; or perhaps the fall of Judah 586-5 B.C. Surely Delitzsch's views are still appropriate—Eliphaz has reference to his own country and tribe—see Joel 3:17.

[9] For analysis of critical problems with the grammar, see M. Dahood, *Biblica,* 48, 1967, 428ff; A. C. M. Blommerde, *Northwest Semitic Grammar and Job, Biblica et Orientalia,* 22, 1969. This indispensable study follows Dahood's analysis.

Verse 21—Eliphaz continues to describe the frightful calamities that come upon the corrupt man. The imagination of the wicked condemns him—Prov. 28:1. Peace is an illusion to the impious. Prosperity is only temporal security to the wicked. There is a constant dread of coming destruction.

Verse 22—Darkness (*hosek*), the figure of misfortune, hovers over the life and possession of the wicked. The condemning conscience of the wicked is haunted by the finality of darkness. The sword is waiting[10] for the wicked. The threat of assassination generates constant dread. An evil conscience creates a constant apprehension of disaster.

Verse 23—The verse means that the wicked-prosperous is always haunted by fears of poverty. This gnawing dread graphically portrays the frustration of the wandering wicked (so LXX). They expect the worst and receive the worst. The LXX attaches the phrase "a day of darkness" to verse 24, so others follow. The unbearable tyranny of a pessimistically conceived "day of darkness" is ever lurking at hand to bring all of existence crashing down.[11]

Verse 24—"A day of darkness" (from Hebrew of verse 23) terrifies him. Anguish and "sickness unto death" prevail against him. Misfortune is pictured as an army of vultures prepared for attack.

Verse 25—A divine assault is imminent. Suddenly, Eliphaz switches to imagery portraying an attack on God. Job is here projected as one attacking God. An outstretched hand is a symbol of a threat—Isa. 5:29; 9:21; 10:4; Prov. 1:24.

Verse 26—The picture of Job's foolish defiance continues. Job stubbornly (stiff neck, insolently; LXX—*hybris*—pride) opposes God "with the thickness of the bosses of his shields," i.e., the bosses (or convex side of shield turned toward the enemy) of his shields are set closely together for more protection against the Almighty.

---

[10] See analysis of grammar by G. R. Driver, *Vetus Testamentum*, Supplement III, 1955, 78, renders this phrase "he is marked down for the sword."

[11] For technical discussion, see Dhorme, *Job*, pp. 217-8.

Verse 27—The image is one of gluttonous fatness, the characteristic of spiritual insensibility—Deut. 32:15; Jer. 5:28; and Pss. 73:7; 119:70. This wicked insensitive person sits around and gets fatter. The Hebrew *pimah* means "blubber" or a superabundance of fat on the man's loins. This imagery stands in marked contrast to Job's present physical condition.

Verse 28—Formerly inhabited cities, now desolate, were considered to be so because of God's judgment. Again the same theology appears—*failure means judgment; success means blessing*—Jos. 6:26; I Kg. 16:34; Isa. 13:20ff; and 34:13ff. The wicked man, according to Eliphaz, is prepared to risk God's curse in his idolatrous confidence in his own prosperity.

Verse 29—Here we return to the theme of the fears of the wicked. Though there are lexical problems in this verse, the sense is clear enough. Dahood[12] yields a relevant meaning. The stretching out of the shadow is a figure of the extent of a person's influence—Ps. 80:8ff. The A. V. makes little sense, and does speak to several important grammatical issues in the verse. The essence of the verse is that a wicked man's influence will not long endure on the earth.

Verse 30—Here the fate of the wicked is described. Darkness is an image of misfortune—verses 22ff. The destiny of the wicked is not an accident, but rather it is set by God. The Hebrew text reads *ruah*—breath or spirit of God—and does not require repointing as some suggest. The verse describes the swift disaster of the unrighteous, whose security through prosperity will vanish like flames that reduce a forest to ashes.

Verse 31—The verse might be incongruous with a series of images based on plant life—verses 29, 30, 32, and 33. He who trusts in emptiness will be rewarded by emptiness. The image of the tree from verse 30 continues into this verse. All of the promised greatness will not reach fulfillment, rather

---

[12] See M. Dahood, "Northwest Semitic Philology and Job," in *The Bible in Current Catholic Thought,* ed. by J. L. McKenzie, 1962, pp. 60ff; also M. Dahood, *Biblica,* 50, 1969, 343.

it will be rewarded with destruction—4:8.[13]

Verse 32—The subject "it" refers to his recompense which will be demanded of him before his number of years is finished, i.e., his end will be premature. If we take the LXX reading, "it will be withered," rather than the Hebrew text, "it will be paid in full," we continue the parallel, which speaks of palm tree and not a trading profit. His "branch"—Isa. 9:13—supports the view that the "palm tree" should be supplied in the first line of the verse; therefore, the A. V. translation is probably not an adequate rendering of the verse. The metaphor becomes more vivid when we recall that the palm tree is the symbol of longevity.

Verse 33—Delitzsch correctly observes that the vine does not cast off (Heb. lit. "treat with violence"—Isa. 18:5) its unripe fruit. What then can be the sense of this verse? The tree will not produce mature fruit—Jer. 31:29ff and Ezek. 18:2. The second line of the verse beautifully symbolizes the point at stake. The Syrian olive tree bears during its first, third, and fifth years, but rests during the second, fourth, and sixth years. It also sheds many of its blossoms like snowflakes.

Verse 34—The word translated "company" of impious in A. V. is the Hebrew term for "congregation" and is here used in a derogatory sense—13:6; 17:8; 20:5; 27:8; 34:30; 36:13. Bribery is frequently condemned in scripture and is here used as a general term for injustice. The word rendered "barren" in A. V. appears also in 3:7 and should be translated "sterile." The phrase "tents of bribery" carries the meaning that the wealth of the wicked has been obtained through deceptive and unjust means by either giving or receiving bribes. How appropriate an image for twentieth century industry and multi-national industrial combines!

Verse 35—At the beginning of his speech, Eliphaz attacked Job for filling his "belly" with the hot east wind—verse 1.

---

[13] See Dhorme, *Job*, p. 223, for tree imagery.

Here, once more, their belly (lit. their belly, though translated "heart" in A. V.) produced only deceit. Eliphaz's conclusion is that misfortune is self-entailed. The penalty of the ungodly is premature death—verses 31-33, and lack of prosperity—verse 34.

TODAY'S ENGLISH VERSION

The Second Dialogue
(15.1—21.34)

15

Eliphaz
¹⁻² Empty words, Job! Empty words!
  ³ No wise man would talk the way you do,
     or defend himself with such meaningless words.
  ⁴ You discourage people from fearing God;
     you keep them from praying to him.
  ⁵ Your guilty conscience is speaking now;
     you are trying to hide behind clever words.
  ⁶ There is no need for me to condemn you;
     you are condemned by every word you speak.

  ⁷ Do you think you were the first man born?
     Were you there when God made the mountains?
  ⁸ Did you overhear the plans God made?
     Does human wisdom belong to you alone?
  ⁹ There is nothing you know that we don't know.
  ¹⁰ We learned our wisdom from gray-headed men—
     men born before your father was.

  ¹¹ God offers you comfort; why still reject it?
     We have spoken for him with calm, even words.
  ¹² But you are excited and glare at us in anger.
  ¹³ You are angry with God and denounce him.

  ¹⁴ Can any man be really pure?

Can anyone be right with God?
15 Why, God does not even trust his angels;
  even they are not pure in his sight.
16 And man drinks evil as if it were water;
  yes, man is corrupt; man is worthless.

17 Now listen, Job, to what I know.
18 Wise men have taught me truths
  which they learned from their fathers,
  and they kept no secrets hidden.
19 Since their land was free from foreigners,
  there was no one to lead them away from God.

20 A wicked man who oppresses others
  will be in trouble as long as he lives.
21 Voices of terror will scream in his ears,
  and robbers attack when he thinks he is safe.
22 He has no hope of escaping from darkness,
  for somewhere a sword is waiting to kill him,
23   and vultures are waiting to eat his body.
  He knows his future is dark;
24   disaster, like a powerful king,
  is waiting to attack him.

25 That is the fate of the man
  who shakes his fist at God,
  and defies the Almighty.
26-27 That man is proud and rebellious;
  he stubbornly holds up his shield
  and rushes to fight against God.

28 That is the man who captured cities
  and seized houses whose owners had fled,
  but war will destroy those cities and houses.
29 He will not be rich long;
  nothing he owns will last.
  Even his shadow will vanish,
30   and he will not escape from darkness.
  He will be like a tree

whose branches are burned by fire,
whose blossoms are blown away by the wind.
³¹ If he is foolish enough to trust in wickedness
then wickedness will be all he gets.
³² Before his time is up he will wither,
wither like a branch and never be green again.
³³ He will be like a vine that loses its grapes before
they are ripe;
like an olive tree that never bears fruit.
³⁴ There will be no descendants for godless men,
and fire will destroy the homes built by bribery.
³⁵ These are the men who plan trouble and do evil;
their hearts are always full of deceit.

QUESTIONS FOR DISCUSSION 15:1-35

287. There is a real difference in the two speeches of Eliphaz. What is the basic difference?
288. Eliphaz calls Job "wise" but it is not a compliment. What does he mean?
289. Job's speeches did not reach the conscience of his friends. Why?
290. Job is irreverent, presumptive, and wicked. How does Eliphaz arrive at this conclusion?
291. Why say Job is full of hot air?
292. Eliphaz tries to condemn Job with Job's own words. How?
293. Job's words if followed could destroy the faith of others. How is this strange conclusion made?
294. Discuss the principle here used and used again in Matt. 26:65 and today.
295. Job's arguments are not answered. What has happened? Is such happening now?
296. In what way is Job supposed to have condemned himself?

297. Verse seven is supposed to contain a reference to a Jewish myth. What is it? How answered? What is the point of the verse?

298. Are the words of Jeremiah relevant here? Cf. Jer. 23:18, 22.

299. Who has claimed "superior knowledge"? Are age and wisdom causally related? Discuss.

300. Who is supposed to have offered "the consolations of God"? Has anyone dealt "gently" with Job?

301. Job's eyes have "flashed" in what way? For what reason?

302. Job is supposed to have attacked God. How?

303. What is the meaning of the term "man" in verse 14? What opinion of woman is inferred?

304. Even the angels are not without fault. How can Job claim to be righteous. Is this a fair argument?

305. Job is characterized as sinning "as a man drinking water." Explain this figure.

306. Eliphaz is very confident of the truthfulness of his advice. To what does he appeal for support?

307. What help is tradition in establishing the truthfulness of any claim?

308. According to Eliphaz what nation was the depository of pure wisdom? Why make this claim?

309. Job had said that robbers prosper (12:6). Eliphaz violently disagrees. Who is right? Discuss.

310. Are the psychological problems of verse 21 really with the wicked or is this only bigoted imagination? Cf. verse 22.

311. Is destruction built in to the life of the wicked man?

312. Much that Eliphaz has to say is very true. What is the basic mistake he has made? Is this mistake repeated today? Where? Why?

313. Job attacks God. What are "the thick bosses of his bucklers"? See verses 25, 26.

314. Job is a fat insensitive glutton. What a figure of speech to apply to a man in Job's condition! How did Eliphaz's image of Job have any meaning?

315. Of what is darkness a symbol. Cf. verse 30.

B. JOB'S TRIAL—VINDICATION OR ? (16:1—17:16).

1. The words of his friends are aimless and unprofitable. (16:1-5)

TEXT 16:1-5

16 Then Job answered and said,

2 I have heard many such things:
Miserable comforters are ye all.

3 Shall vain words have an end?
Or what provoketh thee that thou answerest?

4 I also could speak as ye do;
If your soul were in my soul's stead.
I could join words together against you,
And shake my head at you.

5 *But* I would strengthen you with my mouth,
And the solace of my lips would assuage *your grief.*

COMMENT 16:1-5

Verses 1-2—Job's fourth reply continues the lamentation form and emphasizes the denunciation of enemies, who are his three friends and God. But suddenly in the midst of his response there is a sudden appeal to "a witness in heaven," who will take up Job's defense. But the speech ends, as do his previous responses, with consideration of approaching death and Sheol. He begins with statement of weariness. He has heard all of this unprofitable talk before. The A. V. translates 'amal as miserable, which is a good rendering. Eliphaz has offered "divine consolation"—15:11. Using a cognate word, Job accuses them of being "miserable consolers" (wearisome is not strong enough).

Verse 3—Their comfort only serves to increase his suffering. He turns their talk—8:2; 15:2—upon them by calling them perveyors of "windy words," which only irritate—6:25.

Verse 4—In verses 4-5 the pronouns are plurals, thus Job is speaking to all three friends. Were our positions only reversed, I would have no difficulty playing a pious moralist, "shaking my head in scandalized self-righteousness" (*Job*, Soncino, p. 81). How Job actually conducted himself in the past in similar circumstances is projected in 4:3ff. Job further encroaches on his self-righteous friend by crying out that he too "could join words together" as Eliphaz had done—15:20ff.[1] The imagery of the shaking of the head is associated with mockery and derision—II Kg. 19:21; Isa. 37:22; Pss. 22:8; 109:25; Lam. 2:15; Eccl. 12:18; and Matt. 27:39. As in all cultures, "body language" can have different meanings in different circumstances.

Verse 5—Job continues to heap scornful sarcasm on the heads of his helpers. Mere words have no power to console. The word translated "solace" is a noun from the root used in 2:11. The original meaning of the verb was "to be agitated." (Brown, Driver, Briggs, *Lexicon*, have "quivering motion" for the noun.) Time-honored cliches will not and cannot heal when removed from a sympathetic heart of the utterer.

2. Though innocent, he suffers the hostility of God and man.
(16:6-17)

TEXT 16:6-17

6 Though I speak, my grief is not assuaged;
And though I forbear, what am I eased?
7 But now he hath made me weary:
Thou hast made desolate all my company.
8 And thou hast laid fast hold on me, *which* is a witness *against me*:
And my leanness riseth up against me,

---

[1] For critical analysis of this verse, see J. J. Finkelstein, *JBL*, 75, 1956, 328-31; and O. Loretz, *CBQ*, 23, 1961, 293ff, who suggests the translation "I could also speak to you with mere noise."

It testifieth to my face.
9 He hath torn me in his wrath, and persecuted me;
He hath gnashed upon me with his teeth:
Mine adversary sharpeneth his eyes upon me.
10 They have gaped upon me with their mouth;
They have smitten me upon the cheek reproachfully:
They gather themselves together against me.
11 God delivereth me to the ungodly,
And casteth me into the hands of the wicked.
12 I was at ease, and he brake me asunder;
Yea, he hath taken me by the neck, and dashed me to pieces:
He hath also set me up for his mark.
13 His archers compass me round about;
He cleaveth my reins asunder, and doth not spare;
He poureth out my gall upon the ground.
14 He breaketh me with breach upon breach;
He runneth upon me like a giant.
15 I have sewed sackcloth upon my skin,
And have laid my horn in the dust.
16 My face is red with weeping,
And on my eyelids is the shadow of death;
17 Although there is no violence in my hands,
And my prayer is pure.

COMMENT 16:6-17

Verse 6—In verse 5, "your grief" is unexpressed in the Hebrew text. Here the noun is expressed and also a passive form of the verb. Job here presents his alternatives by forcibly depicting his dilemma. Neither vehement protestation nor silence would bring him healing. Both his physical and mental anguish tenaciously hold his soul in a state of unwelcome torture. Here we have *mah* as a negative rather than interrogative—31:1. Job is not asking "What?" but rather strongly asserts that nothing eases his suffering.

Verse 7—The subject of this verse is probably "my sorrow" rather than God ("he hath made" A. V.) Though the second line does have "thou hast made" (note the change of person and shift to the third person in verse 8), the best sense seems to be "my pain hath made me weary" (the same verb is intransitive in 4:2, verb translated "weary" is used with sense of appall or devastate).[2] Some commentaries emend -'*adati*—my company—to *ra'ati*—my calamity—at least this emendation has the dubious honor of making sense, which is not a characteristic of the Hebrew text as it now stands.

Verse 8—Job's calamity has seized (Heb. *kamat*—seize, grasp tightly) him (A. V. laid fast hold) and is a witness against him. In the eyes of his friends, his suffering was evidence of his sin. The witness of his calamity "has risen against me" (Heb. phrase stands immediately after "witness" and should remain there in translation). "my gauntness or leanness" is evidence to men of my guilt—Ps. 59:12; Nah. 3:1; Hos. 7:3; and 10:13.

Verse 9—Job here pictures God as a ferocious animal tearing him apart with His teeth. The verb *satam* means to bear a grudge or sustain hate against—30:21; Gen. 49:23; 50:15; Ps. 55:3. The hate was so intense that he "gnashed his teeth"—Ps. 37:12—in anger—Matt. 8:12 and Acts 7:54. The imagery of "sharpness" comes from a verb used of sharpening a sword —Ps. 7:12. Here it means looking sharply as does an animal for its prey. God, like an animal pursuing its prey, is concentrating His hostility on Job.[3]

Verse 10—There is no expressed subject in this verse, but these are the people who like jackals follow God's attack by their assaults. All the figures in this verse are human actions "wide mouth"—desire or greed—29:23; Isa. 5:14. They insult or talk openly behind ("struck me"—A. V. has "smitten me")

---

[2] See Dhorme, *Job,* p. 231, though his reconstruction is unnecessary.

[3] For analysis of the phrase "sharpeneth his eyes," see M. Dahood, *Psalms,* Vol. I, Anchor, note on Ps. 7:13; Vol. II third note on Ps. 89:44. His reference to Ugaritic cognate words—"whetted sword their eyes."

his back and mobilize⁴ against him—I Kg. 22:24; Mic. 5:1; Matt. 5:39; Lk. 6:29.

Verse 11—Job says that God has delivered him to the ungodly (Heb. young boys—*'awil*), perhaps a sarcastic denial of their status as wise men and supposed accumulation of wisdom because of their age. Their behavior toward Job is described in 30:9ff. The word translated "casteth" is the verb *ratah* which means to "wring out" (see Brown, Driver, Briggs). He is asserting that God has cast him into the hands of wicked men who "wring" him out.

Verse 12—Suddenly and unexpectedly God attacks him. How? Through whom? This verse makes a couplet with verse 13a, both emphasizing the archer and target—6:4; Ps. 64:7; Lam. 3:12. God is directing the attack on Job, though the volleys come from human archers.⁵ He is the target—I Sam. 20:20.

Verse 13—The word for archers—*rabbim*—is also found in Jer. 50:29. Here we are faced with mixed metaphors. Job is a target; God shoots arrows at him. "His reins" is a metaphor of the most sensitive and vital part of the body, his kidneys. He slashes me open. "He pours out my gall" (used only here and stands for liver, i.e., seat of emotions in Hebrew psychology) upon the ground. In other words, God has dealt him a death blow.

Verse 14—Now Job metaphorically compares his body to that of a fortress which is being repeatedly assailed—30:14. He feels like a stronghold being stormed by warriors, not giants as A. V.

Verse 15—Here appears the same word as in Gen. 3:7 for "sewed." Sackcloth is the symbol of mourning and was worn next to the body—II Kg. 6:30. The sewing of it on his skin was a sign of permanent mourning. Literally the text says

---

⁴ D. W. Thomas, *Journal of Semitic Studies,* III, 1952, 47ff, for defense of military connotation, i.e., mobilize.

⁵ G. R. Driver, *Vetus Testamentum,* III, 1955, 78.

"I have caused my horn to enter," which is a symbol of pride or strength[6]—Pss. 75:5; 89:17; 92:10; and 112:9.

Verse 16—Involuntary weeping is a symptom of leprosy, which could be Job's physical ailment. His face is red, i.e., inflamed (verb *chamar*) from crying. Eyelids stand for his eyes. The word *salmawet* should not be translated as "the shadow of death" as in A. V., but possibly as the blackness around the eyes of a sick person. There is no allusion to death in this verse, so the translation should conform to the basic theme of the verse.

Verse 17—This cruel suffering has come upon me, though I have done no violence—Isa. 53:7. He completely rejects the possibility of his guilt; thus he once more asserts that his suffering is unmerited. When the hands are unclean, prayer is unacceptable to God—Isa. 1:15; Job 11:13ff. In 31:7 he affirms that his hands are clean, and here that his prayer is pure. Job's last possession is the certainty of his integrity before God.

3. He must be vindicated by a heavenly witness. (16:18-22)

TEXT 16:18-22

18   O earth, cover not thou my blood,
       And let my cry have no *resting*-place.
19 Even now, behold, my witness is in heaven,
       And he that voucheth for me is on high.
20 My friends scoff at me:
       But mine eye poureth out tears unto God,
21 That he would maintain the right of a man with God,
       And of a son of man with his neighbor!
22 For when a few years are come,
       I shall go the way whence I shall not return.

---

[6] Svi Rin, *Biblische Zeitschrift*, VII, 1963, 23, for Ugaritic evidence for his translation "I shall lower, or dip my horn in the dust."

COMMENT 16:18-22

Verse 18—Shed blood cries out for vengeance—Gen. 4:10; 37:26; Isa. 26:21; Ezek. 24:8, hence the effort to hide it in the dust. Job desires that his blood remain uncovered as a protest and appeal to God for vindication. Dahood presents strong evidence that the A. V. rendering of "resting place" should be "burial place." Here it is improbable that Job thinks of vindication while still alive. The passage (16:18—17:9) shows a very important development towards 19:24ff.

Verse 19—Exegetically and theologically, it would be very difficult, even impossible, to deny that the witness in heaven is Job's mediator, redeemer (or Vindicator—S. Terrien in *Interpreter's Bible*, Vol. III, 1025-1029), even though God is already Job's Accuser, Judge, and Executioner—9:33; 19:25; and 33:23-24.

Verse 20—"My scorners (*mᵉlisay*) are my friends" (Rowley, p. 150), so as I turn from them, I turn to God with tears streaming down my face. The above word for friend (*re'a*) is used of Eliphaz, Bildad, and Zophar—2:11; 32:3; 42:10; and Jesus in John 15.

Verse 21—The one to whom Job turns is surely the same person as the witness of the preceding verse, and the vindicator of 9:33 and 19:25 (see bibliography on this verse). This is one of the most profound verses in all scripture. Job appeals to God, who had indicted him with cruel agony and as the God of his faith the object of Job's faith is also Lord of justice and righteousness, the one who will "maintain the right" (verb from which the word umpire is derived in 9:33). Now he pleads that God might present the case to himself. (Note the significance of the *Incarnation* in explaining the wonderful things here disclosed.) "A son of man" simply means a person, i.e., Job. Neighbor comes from the same word that is translated "friend" in verse 20. The neighbor is not God, as some suggest, rather a fellow human being.

Verse 22—Job here lapses into the thought of the inevitability and finality of death that has been expressed before—

7:9ff and 10:21. [7]

TODAY'S ENGLISH VERSION

16
Job

¹⁻² I have heard words like that before;
    the comfort you give is only torment.
³ Are you going to keep on talking forever?
    Do you always have to have the last word?

⁴ If you were in my place and I in yours,
    I could say everything you are saying.
I could shake my head wisely
    and drown you with a flood of words.
⁵ I could strengthen you with advice
    and keep talking to comfort you.

⁶ But nothing I say helps,
    and being silent does not calm my pain.
⁷ You have worn me out, God;
    you have let my family be killed.
⁸   You have seized me. You are my enemy.
I am skin and bones,
    and people take that as proof of my guilt.

⁹ In anger, God tears me limb from limb;
    he glares at me with hate.
¹⁰ People sneer at me;
    they crowd around me and slap my face.
¹¹ God has turned me over to evil men.
¹² I was living in peace,
    but God took me by the throat
    and battered me and crushed me.

---

[7] M. Dahood, *Biblica,* 48, 1967, 429.

God uses me for target practice
¹³ and shoots arrows at me from every side—
arrows that pierce and wound me;
and even then he shows no pity.

¹⁴ He wounds me again and again;
he attacks like a soldier gone mad with hate.

¹⁵ I mourn and wear clothes made of sackcloth,
and I sit here in the dust defeated.
¹⁶ I have cried until my face is red,
and my eyes are swollen and circled with shadows,
¹⁷ but I have not committed any violence,
and my prayer to God is sincere.

¹⁸ Earth, don't hide the wrongs done to me!
Don't let my call for justice be silenced!
¹⁹ There is someone in heaven
to stand up for me and take my side.
²⁰ I want God to see my tears and hear my prayer.

²¹ I want someone to plead with God for me,
as a man pleads for his friend.
²² My years are passing now,
and I walk the road of no return.

QUESTIONS FOR DISCUSSION 16:1-22

316. Job has four enemies. Who are they? Why call them enemies?
317. What is the meaning of "my witness in heaven"? Cf. verse 19.
318. Job says, "I have heard it all before." When does repetition have meaning?
319. Job says of his friends that they are miserable, windy enemies. Why don't they leave?
320. The pronouns in verse four are in the plural form. What

does this mean?

321. Job reveals the selfishness and pride of man in verse four. Explain.

322. Explain the scornful sarcasm of verse five.

323. Are there persons in hospitals near us who feel as Job?— i.e., if I speak or am silent yet am I miserable. How can we help them?

324. What is the meaning of verse seven?

325. Job's calamity is a witness against him. How so? Do we believe this principle today? Discuss.

326. Job pictures God as a ferocious animal. How does he expect God to react to all this?

327. There is no expressed subject in verse ten, but Job strongly infers the subject. Who are they? How are they described?

328. The Hebrew word for "ungodly" in verse 11 has an interesting meaning. What is it? Why used?

329. God is attacking Job. How? Through whom?

330. There is a very graphic mixing of the metaphors in verse 13. Explain figures used.

331. Job imagines his body to be like a fortress. What happens to him? Are giants involved? Cf. verse 14.

332. Isn't it extreme to suggest that sackcloth was actually sewn upon the skin? What is meant by reference to "the horn"? Cf. verse 15.

333. We might catch a hint as to the type of sickness from verse 16. What is it? "The shadow of death" is not accurate. Why?

334. Job rejects the possibility of his guilt. He teaches us something in this. What?

335. Why does Job request that his blood be not covered?

336. Who is Job's "witness" as in verse 19? Isn't this a contradiction of previous descriptions? Discuss.

337. There is much comfort for many of us in verse 20. We know more than Job. Discuss.

338. Verse 21 is one of the most profound verses in all the scriptures. Discuss its meaning.

339. To Job death was inevitable and final. What is it to us? Discuss.

4. Yet his condition is such that his hope will soon go
   with him to the grave. (17:1-16)

TEXT 17:1-16

17 My spirit is consumed, my days are extinct,
The grave is *ready* for me.

2 Surely there are mockers with me,
And mine eye dwelleth upon their provocation.

3 Give now a pledge, be surety for me with thy self;
Who is there that will strike hands with me?

4 For thou hast hid their heart from understanding:
Therefore shalt thou not exalt *them.*

5 He that denounceth his friends for a prey,
Even the eyes of his children shall fail.

6 But he hath made me a byword of the people;
And they spit in my face.

7 Mine eye also is dim my reason of sorrow,
And all my members are as a shadow.

8 Upright men shall be astonished at this,
And the innocent shall stir up himself against the godless.

9 Yet shall the righteous hold on his way.
And he that hath clean hands shall wax stronger and stronger.

10 But as for you all, come on now again;
And I shall not find a wise man among you.

11 My days are past, my purposes are broken off,
Even the thoughts of my heart.

12 They change the night into day:
The light, *say they,* is near unto the darkness.

13 If I look for Sheol as my house;
If I have spread my couch in the darkness;

14 If I have said to corruption, Thou art my father;
To the worm, *Thou art* my mother, and my sister;

15 Where then is my hope?
And as for my hope, who shall see it?

16 It shall go down to the bars of Sheol,
When once there is rest in the dust.

COMMENT 17:1-16

Verse 1—Job sees his vindication in heaven, not on earth where his condition is hopeless. To him, death is inevitable, but his estrangement from God is not permanent. Speaking under intense emotional strain, he gasps that my "spirit" (*ruach*) is consumed, my days are extinct (*za'ak*—extinguished, snuffed out). The grave (instead of plural, we take this as singular with enclitic particle -m) is all ready for me.

Verse 2—The verse begins with a formula introducing an oath—"I swear that" (as in 31:36)—there are mockers around me. The noun is abstract, which yields the meaning of "mockery" (Brown, Driver, and Briggs—give "truly mockery surrounded me"). Eliphaz's illusory promises of Job's restoration Job adjudges to be mockeries.

Verse 3—The LXX omits verses 3b to 5a. The giving and taking of pledges was common practice, and the risk was great—Gen. 38:17-20; Ex. 22:26; Deut. 24:6-17; Prov. 6:1; 11:15; 17:18; 22:26; and Eccl. 29:14-20. The striking of the hand ratified the pledge. Job is asking God, not his friends, to ratify a pledge—see Heb. 6:13ff.

Verse 4—The verse answers the question found in the second line of verse 3. The suffix "their" attached to the word translated "heart" means that Job is referring to the three friends. He appeals to God (the "who" of verse 3) since his friends have deprived him of insight. In the great temple hymn book, Pss. 13:3-5; 30:2; 37:19; and 41:11, we read of the common prayer of the innocent sufferer that his foes not be allowed to triumph over him. The friends' hands have not been raised to strike a pledge or guarantee, until Job's innocence can be established. No one will risk providing Job's bail until his trial is arranged. Job is left alone. God is responsible for Job's condition and his friends' lack of understanding.

Verse 5—This is a very cryptic verse. The K. J. V. follows the old Jewish interpreters in taking *heleq* in sense of flattery or smooth. The translation of the A. V. "He that denounceth" connects the root of the Hebrew word to "divide" or "share" and assumes the same meaning as in Jer. 20:10. The imagery of this verse is rather simple, though the grammar is not. It means that Job's friends are represented as turning against him for no higher motive than an informer's share of his property. The second line asserts that their children will suffer for their lack of compassion. In verse 4, Job declares that God would not permit his friends to triumph, and he asserts that their treacherous behavior will negatively affect their offspring—6:27 and 13:7-11.

Verse 6—God is referred to in the third person—"He has made me" an object of scorn of the neighboring people (lit. peoples—'ammim). Culturally, the bitterest insult and expression of contempt is to spit in someone's face—30:10; Isa. 1:6; Matt. 26:6; 27:30. (The K. J. V. follows Rashi, who mistakenly identifies Topheth with top.)[1]

Verse 7—The verb employed here expresses eyesight dimming with age—Gen. 27:1; Deut. 34:7. Here grief causes the dim eyesight—Ps. 6:8. Job's body has deteriorated to a skeleton.[2]

Verse 8—Righteous men are deeply perplexed when they see what is happening to me. The more they observe, the more indignant they become.[3] Righteous men "are appalled," same verb found in Isa. 52:14 as astonished, while the "innocent stirs himself up against (verb means arouse self to excitement— pleasurable in 31:29; here it is negative excitement) the prosperity of the godless," i.e., unrighteous.

Verse 9—Job taunts his friends. He contradicts Eliphaz— 15:4. Though he cannot intellectually resolve the moral anomaly of the universe, the righteous man will hold to that which is right. Neither mystery nor anomaly will cause him to abandon the path of righteousness.[4] Blommerde well sums up the verse

---

[1] See remarks by E. J. Kissane, *The Book of Job* (Dublin: Browne and Nolan, 1939), p. 104.

[2] See the suggested emendation of N. Sarna, *Journal of Jewish Studies,* 6, 1955, 108-110.

[3] Verses 8-10 are removed by some editors, but see Dhorme, *Job,* p. 248-51, for defense of their integrity; note Pope, *Job*—rejection and reasons for so doing, p. 130.

[4] Delitzsch, *Job,* Vol. I, 300, compares these words to a "rocket which shoots above

"because of the misery which has befallen the just Job, the rightous are astonished. This is against all rules; they have to cling to their force, to defend themselves against this trial of their faith."[5]

Verse 10—Job challenges his friends to renew their attack on him. Your unsympathetic words will only expose your unfeeling folly. Repetition of their old words will not convince Job of their validity. Their assaults on him fail once more.

Verse 11—The verse reflects Job's deep emotions. Convulsed with fear, Job acknowledges that death is near. His plans or purposes (Zech. 8:15; Prov. 2:11; 8:12) are thwarted. Plans shattered—now what? The literary form here is problematic, but could very well express Job's heightening of his emotion-charged speech. Prodding ever deeper into his inner self, Job cries out that even his desires (Heb. root *yaras'* or *'aras*—translated as thoughts in A. V.) are destroyed.

Verse 12—This verse does not appear in earliest LXX texts. Job's mockers distress him so that his nights turn into days. Sleepless nights and distress-filled days add up to dark despair. (Pope's comments on this verse that it is incompatible with context is indefensible; compare with Dhorme's defense.) Is light near to brighten Job's darkness before dawn?

Verse 13—His morbid preoccupation with death returns in this verse and continues through verse 16. He is resigned to death without any hope, even in the time of abandonment. Is Sheol the best Job can anticipate?[6]

Verse 14—Job speaks to corruption (Heb. root—act

---

the tragic darkness of the book, lighting it up suddenly, although only for a short time."

[5] See the indispensable, though technical, work of A. C. M. Blommerde, *Northwest Semitic Grammar and Job,* Biblica & Orientalia, 22, 1969, on this verse; also on the parallelism between *derek* and *'omes;* see M. Dahood, *Psalms*, Vol. I, Ps. 1:1; and Vol. II, Ps. 67:3.

[6] See N. J. Tromp, *Primitive Conceptions of Death and the Nether World in the Old Testament* (Rome: Biblica et Orientalia, 21, 1969); and my essay "Death Be Not Proud" in my *Seer, Savior, and the Saved* (College Press, 1972 ed.) for Old Testament data, pp. 366ff.

corruptly) as though it is his origin and destiny.[7] Job feels the closest kinship with "corruption"—Ezek. 19:4, 8; Job 33:18, 22, 28; and Ps. 16:10.

Verse 15—His prospects are poor; thus he predicts the ultimate end of his hopelessness. He has no hope of the future prosperity, which his friends have suggested.

Verse 16—The only ones who will see his hope will go down to Sheol with him. Note that even here Job is not presenting extinction, only a less than noble destiny for the righteous. The bars probably stand for the "gates of Sheol." Job is here asserting that his last hope for a happy and prosperous life will be carried to the grave. Only in Sheol does he have a future. Though the Hebrew noun "rest" is translated so in A. V., probably the meaning of the second line of this verse is best described by R. S. V.—"Shall we descend together into the dust."

TODAY'S ENGLISH VERSION

17 The end of my life is near. I can hardly breathe;
there is nothing left for me but the grave.
[2] I watch how bitterly people mock me.
[3] I am honest, God. Accept my word.
There is no one else to support what I say.
[4] You have closed their minds to reason;
don't let them gloat over me now.
[5] In the old proverb a man betrays his friends for money.
and his children suffer for it.
[6] And now they use this proverb against me;
people hear it and come and spit in my face.

---

[7] See E. F. Sutcliffe, *The Old Testament and the Future Life* (London, 1946), pp. 76ff.

⁷ My grief has almost made me blind;
  my arms and legs are as thin as shadows.
⁸ Those who claim to be honest are shocked,
  and they all condemn me as godless.
⁹ Those who claim to be respectable
  are more and more convinced they are right.
¹⁰ But if all of them came and stood before me,
  I would not find even one of them wise.

¹¹ My days have passed; my plans have failed;
  my hope is gone.
¹² But my friends say night is daylight;
  they say that light is near,
  but I still remain in darkness.
¹³ My only hope is the world of the dead,
  where I will lie down to sleep in the dark.
¹⁴ I will say that the grave is my father,
  and the worms that eat me are my mother
    and sisters.
¹⁵ Where is there any hope for me? Who sees any?
¹⁶ Hope will not go with me
  when I go to the world of the dead.

QUESTIONS FOR DISCUSSION 17:1-16

340. Job really welcomes death and the grave because in heaven
he will be able to solve his problem. Is this the thought
of this chapter? Discuss.

341. What are the "mockers" or "mockeries" of which Job
speaks in verse two?

342. Job wants someone to pledge with him. Who is it? Why?

343. There is a poignant picture in verse four: "No one will
risk providing Job's bail until his trial is arranged."
Discuss.

344. Job's friends are likened to informers. In what way?

Cf. vs. 5.

345. Job has received the bitterest insult from the neighboring people and God is responsible. Explain how this is true (or not).

346. Job has become prematurely old and has lost excessive weight. What was the cause of this? Isn't Job full of exaggeration?

347. Job calls both the righteous and the innocent to his defense. How so?

348. Verse nine is compared to "a rocket which shoots above the tragic darkness of the book." Explain.

349. Job challenges his friends. What is the purpose of his challenge? Cf. vs. 10.

350. Verse 11 reflects Job's deep emotions. What does Job decide? Is it ever right to make a decision when so super-charged with emotion?

351. Job's mockers must have reached Job's conscience or confused his mind to actually turn his nights into days. Cf. vs. 12. Discuss.

352. Job has adapted a morbid preoccupation with death. Is he suggesting this is his extinction?

353. The only ones who will see Job's hope (i.e., according to Job) will be what persons?

354. Discuss the preoccupation with "the death wish" of today.

From **Today's English Version** of the Old Testament, Copyright, American Bible Society, 1971

171

C. THE GRANDEUR AND MISERY OF MAN OR IM-
POSSIBILITY OF SELF-JUSTIFICATION (18:1-21)
1. Sharp rebuke of Job (18:1-4)

TEXT 18:1-4

18   Then answered Bildad the Shuhite, and said,
      2 How long will ye hunt for words?
Consider, and afterwards we will speak.
3 Wherefore are we counted as beasts,
  And are become unclean in your sight?
4 Thou that tearest thyself in thine anger,
  Shall the earth be forsaken for thee?
  Or shall the rock be removed out of its place?

COMMENT 18:1-4

Verse 1—Bildad's second speech (18:1-21) reveals a consciously restrained lack of feeling. He attacks Job for his lack
of appreciation for ancient wisdom, his abusive language, and
also implies that Job cannot expect to be exempted from
the universal law—that suffering is inevitably punishment
for sin—12:6. The content of the speech is largely composed
of a legalistic tirade concerning the fate of those "who know
not God." The tone of the speech is exhausted by a "warning"
and threat syndrome. There is not one word of consolation
to be found in it. Bildad always addresses Job in the plural
(you as plural is obscured in our translations), perhaps as a
member of the class of unrighteous persons. His speech is
divided into two parts: (1) verses 2-4; and (2) verses 5-21.

Verse 2—The first part of his speech seeks an answer to
the question: Why is Job so contemptuous of his friends? He
charges that Job is so egocentric that he expects God to change
the laws of creation for him. Bildad suggests that Job has
spoken long enough and should stop long enough for his friends
to give rebuttal. Dhorme suggests that the Hebrew word

172

translated in A. V. as "consider" is a rhetorical device which is used to ask Job to be intelligent, i.e., if the dialogue is to continue, Job must show some signs of intelligence, thus far absent.

Verse 3—Bildad resents Job's comparison of his friends as "dumb beast"—16:9-10. Line two in A. V. hardly conveys what the text says—"Why are we stupid" from *tamah,* to be "stopped up" intellectually, not unclean as A. V. (so Brown, Driver, and Briggs, *Lexicon*)—Ps. 73:22.[1]

Verse 4—Bildad asserts, without feeling, "that Job is the cause of his own suffering" because he refuses to take the proper means to remove God's judgment from himself and his household. The rock is sometimes an epithet of God, probably so here. The law of retribution is as solid and firm as a rock and is part of the structure of the universe. Bildad alludes to Job's remarks in 16:9—to the effect that God has "torn me in His wrath." He retorts that Job has torn himself. If the established order of the universe dictates that suffering is the empirical proof of sin, does Job think that this order is to be modified for him?[2] The last phrase is a quotation from 14:18b.

2. The certain dreadful doom of the hardened evildoer (18:5-21)

TEXT 18:5-21

5 Yea, the light of the wicked shall be put out,
   And the spark of the fire shall not shine.
6 The light shall be dark in his tent,
   And his lamp above him shall be put out.
7 The steps of his strength shall be straitened,

---

[1] Blommerde,'s *Northwest Semitic Grammar and Job* remarks do not seem to be helpful in understanding this verse.

[2] M. Dahood, *JBL,* 1959, p. 306, for analysis of this theme.

And his own counsel shall cast him down,
8 For he is cast into a net by his own feet,
And he walketh upon the toils.
9 A gin shall take *him* by the heel,
And a snare shall lay hold on him.
10 A noose is hid for him in the ground,
And a trap for him in the way.
11 Terrors shall make him afraid on every side,
And shall chase him at his heels.
12 His strength shall be hunger-bitten,
And calamity shall be ready at his side.
13 The members of his body shall be devoured,
Yea, the first-born of death shall devour his members.
14 He shall be rooted out of his tent wherein he trusteth;
And he shall be brought to the king of terrors.
15 There shall dwell in his tent that which is none of his:
Brimstone shall be scattered upon his habitation.
16 His roots shall be dried up beneath,
And above shall his branch be cut off.
17 His remembrance shall perish from the earth,
And he shall have no name in the street.
18 He shall be driven from light into darkness,
And chased out of the world.
19 He shall have neither son nor son's son among his people,
Nor any remaining where he sojourned.
20 They that come after shall be astonished at his day,
As they that went before were affrighted.
21 Surely such are the dwellings of the unrighteous,
And this is the place of him that knoweth not God.

COMMENT 18:5-21

Verse 5—This verse initiates the second part of Bildad's speech. Job's sole remaining possession is the horrible memory of his past prosperity and present agony. The Hebrew tenses convey the meaning that this is a condition which is continuous.

The light burning in a house is symbolic of continuous prosperity—21:17; I Kg. 11:36; Prov. 13:9; 20:20; and 24:20. The extinction of these symbols of happiness and prosperity is a mark of judgment on the household. Failing light is a sign of disaster. (cf. Jesus said that "I am the light of the world," Jn. 8:12).

Verse 6—The tent implies that the event is occurring in the patriarchal age (see discussion of possible date for authorship)—5:24; 8:22; 12:6; and 15:34. Bildad's speech progresses with the use of proverbial sayings: (1) verses 5-7—sinner's light goes out; (2) verses 8-11—deterioration to downfall; (3) verses 12-14—final condition; (4) 15-17—extinction of his race and names; and (5) verses 18-21—horror of his fate. His home is engulfed by darkness—"his lamp above him shall be put out."

Verse 7—Like the strength of an aging man, the fortunes of the wicked will fail. Metaphorically, "the steps of his strength" expresses the confident stride of a prosperous man—Ps. 18:36. The evil motives of an unrighteous man will ultimately "throw him down," i.e., bring him to calamity and ruin.

Verses 8-9—This verse and the next develop the image of the perils in the path of the wicked. Bildad uses a variety of terms for the traps and snares which the wicked will encounter in life. The steps of the unrighteous man are reduced to a feeble hobble, then ensnared by his own evil motives. The *net* (for catching birds—Prov. 1:17; Ps. 140:5) and *toils* (lit. network, webbing—things interwoven) are means of his own destruction.[3] Probably the latter snare has reference to "webbing" placed over a pit to catch an animal—suddenly and unawares. This is Bildad's description of Job's ensnaring himself. In verse 9 the world of an evil man is full of traps. The "gin" is a fowlers trap—Hos. 9:8. The term "snare" comes from a root meaning veil—Isa. 47:2. Probably it refers to a

---

[3] G. Gerleman, *Journal of Semitic Studies*, 4, 1958, 252-254, for interpretation of *beragloyw*—"with his feet" as an idiomatic phrase meaning "on the spot," or immediately. But this hardly fits the context.

trap made from some kind of mesh.

Verse 10—A rope, or cord, lies hidden in the ground—Isa. 8:14; Jer. 48:44; Pss. 74:7; 140:6; and Prov. 5:22. This type is used to ensnare birds and smaller animals. The term "trap" (root means to capture) in the second line is found only here and probably is a general descriptive word for any catching device.

Verse 11—Bildad is here referring to an actual experience which a wicked person will have, not one caused by a fearful conscience. The verb translated "chase" is usually employed to denote the scattering of a group, but here of an individual. The image suggests bewilderment and almost total emotional and intellectual confusion.[4]

Verse 12—Trouble and calamity, about to seize him, are ravenously hungry. The Hebrew text can be saying "Let his strength be hungry." Dahood's emendations suggest "hungry one" is an epithet of *mot*—death. The second line literally says "to or for his rib" which, as the Targums suggested, can mean wife. But the general sense is that misfortune is always ready and able to bring him to destruction.

Verse 13—Here is a cryptic reference to the lethal disease that is consuming Job's body. The Hebrew texts make no sense—lit. "It shall consume the limbs of his skin." Perhaps the late G. E. Wright's suggestion at least produces a meaningful line—"By disease his skin is consumed." Wright's suggestion, reinforced by the one provided by Sarna, reveals the essence of the meaning of this verse. "The firstborn of *mot* will devour his skin with two hands, yea with his two hands he will devour (him)."[5] The firstborn of death is probably a metaphor for Job's deadly disease. Death is firstborn—*bekor,* i.e., heir with rights of primogeniture—Ps. 89:28. Disease is death's firstborn.

Verse 14—The wicked is marched[6] from the security of his

---

[4] M. Dahood, *Psalms,* Vol. I, Anchor, on Ps. 38:18.

[5] N. Sarna, *JBL,* 1963, p. 317, suggests that *badde* here means "two hands" and *baddayw* in verse 14 means "with his two hands."

[6] W. Moran, *Biblica,* 1964, p. 82, n. 1.

own tent, then conducted into the presence of the "King of Terror." This phrase is a personification of death, as "first-born" is of disease.

Verse 15—The Hebrew literally states "In his tent no trace of him remains. . . ."[7] Perhaps the brimstone or sulphur is to be understood as disinfectant.

Verse 16—Bildad returns to his metaphor based on vegetable life—8:11ff; 14:7ff. Destruction of root and fruit is proverbial—Amos 2:9. Here the image refers to progeny and posterity. Branches is a collective term as in 14:9, and they "shall be cut off." Nothing will remain of Job's household.

Verse 17—Job and his posterity will be completely cut off from the earth. His children are destroyed, and even his name will be erased from memory—Pss. 9:6; 34:16; and 109:15b.

Verse 18—The Hebrew word found here and translated as "world" expressed the finality, totality, and cosmic absence of his name. The verbs are in the indefinite third person and are equivalent to the passive voice, meaning "They shall chase or drive him from light into darkness"—3:20 and 17:13.

Verse 19—The feared fate of the extinction of the family is set before Job. Nothing could be more disastrous than the demise of a man's household. A lack of progeny is a lack of God's blessings.

Verse 20—The "day" is his final day or fate—I Sam. 26:10; Jer. 1:27; Ezek. 21:29; and Ps. 37:13. The words translated before and after are literally "behind" and "before"—meaning followers and predecessors. The A. V. "were affrighted" is literally "they laid hold on horror," 21:6—"laid hold on shuddering." Perhaps the best translation would be "over his end coming generations will be appalled, and his contemporaries will be seized with shuddering."[8]

---

[7] This verse is grammatically corrupt, so see suggestions of M. Dahood, *Biblica,* 37, 1956, 339; and his *Biblica,* 38, 1957, 312ff; and G. R. Driver, *Vetus Testamentum,* 1955, p. 79.

[8] M. Buttenweiser, *The Book of Job,* 1922.

Verse 21—Bildad summarily assures Job of his fate, as a member of the class of the wicked. Job, can you not see the irrefutable proof that you are a godless man? Here again Bildad's truth is half a lie. Severity, not sympathy flows from his lips. Violent indignation, but no mercy, is heaped upon Job's pitiful head. Is there no "grace" in a world of suffering? Surely Job will later cry—"In my hands no price I bring; simply to the cross I cling." But not yet!

TODAY'S ENGLISH VERSION

18

Bildad

¹⁻² Job, can people like you never be quiet?
      If you stopped to listen we could talk to you.
 ³ What makes you think we are as stupid as cattle?
 ⁴ You are only hurting yourself with your anger.
      Will the earth be deserted because of you?
      Will mountains be moved because of you?

 ⁵ The wicked man's light will be put out;
      its flame will never burn again.
 ⁶ The lamp in his tent will be darkened.
 ⁷ His steps were firm, but now he limps;
      he falls—a victim of his own advice.
 ⁸ He walks into a net and his feet are caught;
 ⁹   a trap catches his heels and holds him.
¹⁰ On the ground a snare is hidden for him;
      a trap has been set in his path.

¹¹ All around him terror is waiting;
      it follows him at every step.
¹² He used to be rich, but now he goes hungry;
      disaster stands and waits at his side.
¹³ A deadly disease spreads over his body,
      and causes his arms and legs to rot.

¹⁴ He is torn from the tent where he lived secure,
    and is dragged off to face King Death.
¹⁵ Now anyone may live in his tent—
    after sulfur is sprinkled to disinfect it!
¹⁶ His roots and branches are withered and dry.
¹⁷ His fame is ended at home and abroad;
    no one remembers him any more.
¹⁸ He will be driven out of the land of the living,
    driven from light into darkness.
¹⁹ He has no descendants, no survivors.
²⁰ From east to west, everyone who hears of his fate
    shudders and trembles with fear.
²¹ This is the fate of evil men,
    the fate of those who care nothing for God.

QUESTIONS FOR DISCUSSION 18:1-21

355. Bildad attacks Job for three reasons. What are they?
356. Bildad's speech is "exhausted" by a syndrome. What is it?
357. Why does Bildad call Job egocentric?
358. Does Job call his friends dumb unclean beasts?
359. Job said God tore him (16:9). Bildad says Job tore himself. Who is right?
360. What is the meaning of the figure of a "rock" in verse four?
361. To what circumstance in Job's life does "the light of the wicked" have reference?
362. Notice the objective, impersonal manner in which the words of Bildad are couched. What does this say of the man?
363. What does the use of the light in the tent suggest as to the time of the writing of this book?
364. Bildad's speech is tied together by what literary device?
365. The wicked (Job in particular) are like an aging man.

How so? Cf. vs. 7.

366. The wicked man falls into all manner of traps. He traps himself by his feebleness. Name three other traps that catch the wicked. Cf. vss. 8, 9. What is "the gin"?

367. Bildad describes an actual experience in verse 11. What is it?

368. Trouble and calamity are personified in verse 12. What are they about to do to the wicked man?

369. Verse 13 contains a reference to Job's disease. What is said about it?

370. Who is "the king of terrors"? Why so described?

371. How was brimstone or sulphur used in verse 15?

372. The metaphor of the root and branch and fruit in verse 16 refers to what in the experience of Job?

373. How can Bildad be so positively cruel in the promises he makes concerning Job's family?

374. Job and all like him will be chased out of the world—from light to darkness. Who will do this? When?

375. The lack of progeny is also the lack of what? i.e., according to Bildad.

376. What "day" is discussed in verse 20? What will happen?

377. Bildad's truth is a half-lie. Explain. Why was this man so void of sympathy?

D. HOPE IN TIME OF ABANDONMENT—VINDICATED BY HIS VINDICATOR (*GO'EL*) (19:1-29)
1. He condemns the friends for shameless abuse. (19:1-4)

TEXT 19:1-4

19 **Then Job answered and said,**
   2 How long will ye vex my soul,
 And break me in pieces with words?
 3 These ten times have ye reproached me:
 Ye are not ashamed that ye deal hardly with me.
 4 And be it indeed that I have erred,
 Mine error remaineth with myself.

COMMENT 19:1-4

Verse 1—Job's comforters show no development in their encounter with him. In contrast, Job has analyzed his position as the result of their criticism. Job thus becomes our great paradigm of growth through suffering. We either see our troubles through God, or God through our troubles. What alternatives are available? In this, Job's central discourse, he achieves a profound faith, which enables him to triumph over his destructive despair. He truly attained "hope in time of abandonment." New power and pathos enter Job's literary style. This new power retouches themes which are set forth in his earlier speeches, egs.: (1) validity of a clear conscience, 6:30; 9:29; 10:7; 16:17, which the righteous judge would ratify if only He would hear them—10:2, 7; 13:23; 16:21; (2) knowledge that God must yearn for him as he does for God—7:8, 21; 10:8-9; 14:15; and (3) his hope that God will finally vindicate him—14:13-15; 16:19-20. Job's response to Bildad contains four parts: (1) His impatience with his friends—verses 2-6; (2) God's abandonment and attack—verses 7-12; (3) Laments his forsaken condition and appeals to his friends once more—verses 13-22; and (4) His certainty concerning his vindication—

verses 23-29. Does the speech present God's attitude change toward Job? Is He his enemy? The change is only apparent and temporary. Though Job's friends are uncharitable, and God is silent in the presence of his agonizing cries, Job waits for vindication. But until then!

Verse 2—His friends have grievously wounded (tormented) Job by their insinuations. "Vex" is not strong enough for the Hebrew word; the same verb is used in Isaiah 51:23 of Israel's tormentors. In Lamentations 1:5, 12, the same word is used to describe the suffering which God inflicted on Israel. The verb (*dk'*) translated as "break me in pieces" is used of the penitent in Isaiah 57:15 and Ps. 51:17. It means "crush" and is here employed to describe the effects of the charges from Job's friends. "I am crushed" by your insinuations, not led to repentance.

Verse 3—The figure 10 is to be understood as a round number and not as Rashi took it as referring to the number of speeches—five for Job and five for friends—Gen. 31:7, 41; Num. 14:22. His friends have wronged him. The verb is found only here and does not call for endless proliferation of emendations. Job is enduring God's silence; need they add their inhumane treatment to his already overburdened life?

Verse 4—This is a very difficult verse whose meaning is not self-evident. Perhaps the best understanding is found in the R. S. V. There it is translated as a hypothetical sentence, though there is no hypothetical particle present. This move enables us to understand the verse without it being an admission of guilt of secret sin, which Job has consistently denied. Taking the verse to mean "Even if I have sinned, I have not injured you" (Rowley, *Job*, p. 167).

2. He has been overthrown by God. (9:5-12)

TEXT 19:5-12

5 If indeed ye will magnify yourselves against me,

And plead against me my reproach;
6 Know now that God hath subverted me *in my cause,*
   And hath compassed me with his net.
7   Behold I cry out of wrong, but I am not heard:
   I cry for help, but there is no justice.
8 He hath walled up my way that I cannot pass,
   And hath set darkness in my paths.
9 He hath stripped me of my glory.
   And taken the crown from my head.
10 He hath broken me down on every side, and I am gone;
   And my hope hath he plucked up like a tree.
11 He hath also kindled his wrath against me,
   And he counteth me unto him as *one of* his adversaries.
12 His troops come on together,
   And cast up their way against me,
   And encamp round about my tent.

COMMENT 19:5-12

Verse 5—Job chides his friends for assuming an air of superiority. If taken as a rhetorical question, the answer is clearly positive. The verb translated "magnify" has a negative sense here as in Ps. 35:26; 38:16. The last line contains a verb used in 16:21 and here means "plead my disgrace against me." His humiliation is taken as proof of the accuracy of their charge.

Verse 6—This verse is proof that verse 4 does not contain a confession of guilt. Bildad has asserted that the godless man is caught in his own net in 18:8. The word for net is a different one from any employed by Bildad. Here the image is one of a hunter's large net into which animals are driven.

Verse 7—Job's friends have built their arguments on the doctrines of "divine justice" from the assumption that he is "conscious of his own innocence." The verse begins with emphatic appeal to "injustice"—Hab. 1:2 and Jer. 20:8. The same verb "cry aloud" appears in 24:12; 19:12; 30:28; 35:9; 36:13. Yet, his pitiful cries for help go unheard. God remains *silent.*

Verse 8—Job has been hemmed in; restrictions surround him—Lam. 3:7; Hos. 2:6; Job 3:23; 13:27; 14:5. In 1:10 Satan had asserted that God had placed protective barriers around Job. Perhaps darkness should be amended to "thorn hedge."[1]

Verse 9—The crown of glory (*kabod*—LXX *doxa*)[2] is a metaphor for esteem. Job's crown of righteousness has been removed from him—Ps. 8:5. Shame as a garment is an image used in 8:22. Honor is a garment to be worn by the godly, or removed from—stripped off—the unrighteous—29:14; Isa. 61:3. Job was once a prosperous man who enjoyed an honorable reputation; now he has nothing.

Verse 10—The metaphors are rich and varied. In this verse God has pulled Job down as one wrecks a building. The second metaphor is that of a tree uprooted—Ps. 52:5. The common verb—*halak*—meaning "walk" used metaphorically as a way of life, i.e., life style, here appears as an image of death, death as a way of existence.

Verse 11—The metaphor now shifts to warfare. God will not cease His aggression against Job. God is pictured as a leader directing one attack after another on Job—10:17; 16:12ff. The Hebrew text has the plural, "his adversaries," but here it is God and probably should be in the singular, "his adversary."

Verse 12—The military metaphor is extended. Here the troops are raising a siege ramp. But there is a strong conflict between the image of the siege ramp and a tent. One does not need to besiege a tent with an attack force. Perhaps this tension suggests the inequity of it all.

3. And depised by all people, including his kindred (19:13-19)

---

[1] A. Guillaume, *Promise and Fulfillment*, ed. by F. F. Bruce, 1963, pp. 106ff.
[2] Kittel and von Rad, "Doxa," *TWNT*, Vol. II, 232-255.

TEXT 19:13-19

13 He hath put my brethren far from me,
   And mine acquaintenance are wholly estranged from me.
14 My kinsfolk have failed,
   And my familiar friends have forgotten me.
15 They that dwell in my house, and my maids, count me for
     a stranger:
   I am an alien in their sight.
16 I call unto my servant, and he giveth me no answer,
   Though I entreat him with my mouth.
17 My breath is strange to my wife,
   And my supplication to the children of mine own mother.
18 Even young children despise me;
   If I arise, they speak against me.
19 All my familiar friends abhor me,
   And they whom I loved are turned against me.

COMMENT 19:13-19

Verse 13—God's apparent hostility produces human hostility. Isolation and loneliness are radically contrasted with the sequence of relationships which develop from less to more intimate: (1) "My brethren"—verse 13a; (2) "men of my family"—verse 17b; (3) "my intimate friends"—verse 19. All of the intimate[3] relationships necessary for life have been

---

[3] See cultural crises which are visible in our institutions; see interrelationship and *Systems Analysis,* Sears and Feldman, *The Seven Ages of Man* (Los Altos, Calif.: Wm. Kaufman, 1973 ed.); and Anderson and Carter, *Human Behavior in Social Environment* (Chicago: Aldine Pub. Co., 1974). Note the developments in contemporary interpersonal psychological studies such as Ericson, Maslov, Sullivan, *et al.* and their analysis of "hierarchy of needs," "levels of needs." Man is gregarious by nature. Men are not born into a nation or universe but a family unit. See my *Newness on the Earth,* chp. 7, "Christians come of age in a world come of age," pp. 113-125, for look at the biblical-maturity model.

ripped apart. Total estrangement is Job's pitiful lot.[4]

Verse 14—Job has a right to expect his most intimate friends to stand by him in his great hours of darkness—Ps. 88:19. In his most desperate hours, he is abandoned by all those with whom he has had intimate interpersonal relations. To whom can he turn? Who cares?

Verse 15—Even "the sojourners" of his house rejected him. He even lost the respect of his maidservants and obedience of slaves; this is the depth of humiliation. Job has experienced a totally broken existence, from alienation to humiliation.

Verse 16—He has sunk so low that even his personal servant ignores him. This is the bitterest form of humiliation and proof of the incredible depth into which he has fallen—Ps. 123:2. His social status has been obliterated; even the slaves will not respond when he personally calls them.

Verse 17—Job's skin is ravaged with eruptions and itching— 2:7-8; 2:12; 7:5; 7:14; 16:16; 19:20; 30:17, 30. Now halitosis is added to his other symptoms. His physical appearance is appalling, and has contributed to his social ostracization. The second line in the A. V. does not represent the Hebrew text which literally says "the sons of my womb." This cannot refer to Job's children, as they are already dead. Since there is no mention of concubines, it probably does not refer to their children. The best meaning in this context is Job's mother's womb—3:10. Womb is used for "body" in Mic. 6:7 and Ps. 82:11. The phrase would ordinarily mean Job's children, but this is all but precluded by the present context.

Verse 18—Even the children show disrespect for Job, as he rises and attempts to walk. Such disrespect calls for drastic punishment—II Kg. 2:23. Perhaps the second line means

---

[4] Estrangement or alienation is a fundamental issue in our culture. Since Hegel and Marx, the Christian view of alienation has been under severe attack. Both Existentialism and Neo-Marxism challenge the biblical data. See R. Schacht, *Alienation* (Doubleday Anchor, 1971) for basic survey; *Marxism and Alienation*, ed. by H. Aptheker (New York: Humanities Press); and for the neo-Marxism of Bangkok Conference of WCC, 1973. For critique, see my *The Word of God for a Broken World* (Lincoln, IL: LCC Press, 1977).

that even little children "turn their backs" on Job, rather than "speak against" him.[5]

Verse 19—Literally the first line says "men of my intimate group" or his bosom friends—Gen. 49:6; Jer. 6:11; 15:17; 23:18; Pss. 25:14; 55:15—"have turned against me."[6]

4. He utters a plea for pity. (19:20-22)

TEXT 19:20-22

20 My bone cleaveth to my skin and to my flesh,
   And I am escaped with the skin of my teeth.
21 Have pity upon me, have pity upon me, O ye my friends;
   For the hand of God hath touched me.
22 Why do ye persecute me as God,
   And are not satisfied with my flesh?

COMMENT 19:20-22

Verse 20—Though the general meaning is obvious, the verse has failed to yield up its grammatical secrets to those whose very lives have been spent in studying this language. The essence is—I have nothing but my bones and the skin of my teeth (Brown, Driver, Briggs understand this as "gums"), and I am nothing.[7] Mere survival is the only claim he can make. The verse has a certain proverbial tone about it. At least it is possible that the meaning is that suggested by Pope— "my flesh rots on my bones, my teeth drop from my gums." The LXX suggest that the translators had a different Hebrew text before them "under my skin my flesh is corrupted; my bones are held in (my) teeth."

---

[5] For this suggestion, see I. Eitan, *Jewish Quarterly Review,* 1923-24, pp. 38ff.
[6] T. Penar, *Biblica,* 1967, pp. 293ff, for this last clause.
[7] D. R. Blumenthal, *Vetus Testamentum,* 1966, pp. 497ff.

Verse 21—The repetition of "have pity on me" is a powerful rhetorical device. The hand of God has "stricken" me (same verb used in Isa. 53:4).

Verse 22—His friends are here accused of imitating God by their ceaseless hounding of Job. They are inhuman. Job is their prey. The idiom means "and will not stop calumniating me." How appropriate for our age which is preoccupied with the humanization of man, without the redemptive activity of God in the world.[8]

5. And asserts his hope of a vindicator (*go'el*) (19:23-27)

TEXT 19:23-27

23 Oh that my words were now written!
   Oh that they were inscribed in a book!
24 That with an iron pen and lead
   They were graven in the rock for ever!
25 But as for me I know that my Redeemer liveth,
   And at last he will stand up upon the earth:
26 And after my skin, *even* this *body,* is destroyed,
   Then without my flesh shall I see God;
27 Whom I, even I, shall see, on my side,
   And mine eyes shall behold, and not as a stranger.
   My heart is consumed within me.

COMMENT 19:23-27

Verse 23—Job still holds out hope of the vision of God (verses 23-27). The foregoing appeal has fallen on deaf ears, as is apparent from the following speech. At the conclusion,

---

[8] Most contemporary views of "redemption" are politico-economic in nature, egs. Neo-Marxism, Liberation Theology, Eastern Meditation—techniques of all varieties, etc.

Job is completely alienated from: (1) family; (2) men, i.e., intimate friends; and apparently (3) God. Yet out of his depth of despair, he achieves a heightened faith in God which maintains that He will "Shatter His Silence" in the future. But for the existential moment, Job will endure this cosmic muteness. Note how his traditionalist friends have appealed to the wisdom of the *past*, how Job is enduring the *present*, and that only the *future* holds the solution to his dilemma.[9] If neither the *past* nor the *present* provide clues to the presence of God (i.e., a transcendent creator-redeemer God who is immanent in nature-history-social institutions-individual lives), where, if there are any, are the clues of God's love and mercy? Since the first scientific revolution, western man has been moving in a naturalistic-humanistic direction. This process called for the death of God and the humanization of man. Oh, Job is our contemporary. Has God abandoned us? Job wants the protestation of his innocence to survive after his death in the form of a book or scroll.[10] *Seper* usually means book or scroll. But the verb here means "to engrave." We now have the copper treasure scroll from Qumran; perhaps it is an illustration of what Job had in mind. He surely wanted his record to be permanent.

Verse 24—A lead stylus could not make an impression on even the softest stone; therefore, the lead here must be to fill the incisions made by an iron tool. An ancient example of the use of lead in stone is Darius I's *Behistun Inscription*.[11]

Verse 25—Here is the central verse of the entire book. Job knows that there is no immanent power within man or nature that can meet his needs. If death is the ultimate and absolute

---

[9] Historical theology has progressed along these same lines: (1) Traditionalists depend on the *past;* (2) after Hegel and Kierkegaard, the emphasis was placed on the "existential moment" and leap of faith, and after the first collapse of Neo-orthodoxy (of Revolution-Liberation-Political Theory) influence, we move toward (3) Theology of Hope, egs. E. Block, J. Moltmann with the emphasis on the *future*.

[10] For possibilities of the form of materials implied, see G. R. Driver, *Semitic Writing*, 1954, p. 92; S. H. Gehman, *JBL*, 1944, pp. 303ff; Pope, *Job*, pp. 143-4.

[11] For ancient evidence of this art, see K. Galling, *Die Welt des Orients*, 1954-59, p. 6; and J. J. Stamm, *Zeitschrift fur die alttestamentliche Wissenschaft*, 1953, p. 302.

monarch of all life, then the late Heidegger is correct—all of reality moves toward death—*Sein zum tode.* The ultimate answer to *evil, suffering,* and *death* comes in this peak passage—verses 25-27.[12] Despite the "but," this verse must not be separated from the foregoing; i.e., these words in verse 23 are to be recorded in stone. The word *go'el* (see Book of Ruth, 4:4-6) means next of kin who was obligated to exact justice in a feud—Deut. 19:6-12; II Sam. 14:11; Lev. 25:25, 48. The *go'el* is the defender of both widow and orphan and the enslaved—Prov. 23:10-11. God is Israel's *go'el* or deliverer from Egyptian bondage—Ex. 6:6; 15:13; exile, Jer. 1:34; dispersion—Isa. 43:1; 44:6, 24; 48:20; and 52:9. God also delivers the individual from death—Ps. 103:4; Lam. 3:58. Job's concluding remarks in verse 26b clearly reveal that his redeemer is God.[13] The word *'aharon* is here taken as adverbial "at last." If it is taken as parallel to *go'el,* it should be taken as adjectival in the sense that the "first and last" is guarantor— Isa. 44:6; 48:12. His vindicator is living and will stand on the earth.[14] The Hebrew *hay*—alive or living—is a designation for God—Jos. 3:10; Hos. 1:10. Job's God is a living God. The much discussed Ugaritic example concerning Baal is upon scrutiny no parallel.[15] The Vulgate changes the Hebrew and reads "I shall rise," meaning that Job shall experience resurrection. The phrase "upon the earth" literally reads "upon the dust." Here is an expressed hope in God's victory

---

[12] See the brilliant and indispensable survey of the interpretation of this passage up to the 20th century by H. H. Rowley, *From Moses to Qumran* (New York: Association Press, 1963), pp. 180ff.

[13] M. Dahood, *Biblica,* 1971, p. 346.

[14] For extensive bibliographical survey of "Faith, History, and Resurrection" and references to the Hebrew, Greek, and Latin texts of Job 19:25-27, see my essays in James Orr, *The Resurrection* (College Press reprint, 1972); since the development of the *Religionsgeschichte Schule,* scholars have become preoccupied over the origin of the idea of resurrection. Bousset and Gressmann suggest a Persian source, so also W. Eichrodt, E. Jacob, and G. Von Rad in their respective Old Testament theologies.

[15] See E. G. Kraeling, *The Book of The Ways of God* (New York, 1939), p. 89; also Pritchard, ed., *Ancient Near Eastern Texts Relating to the Old Testament* (Princeton), p. 140.

over Sheol.[16] Job's answer comes by resurrection. Ultimately our Lord's resurrection is not merely an historical event; it is a history-making event—Matt. 22:32. Death in Sheol never means extinction or annihilation, only existence that is less to be desired; as many claim, especially *Jehovah's Witnesses, Seventh Day Adventists* (Soul Sleeping), Armstrongites, *et. al.*[17]

Verse 26—The problems of translation and understanding are great in this verse. Dahood maintains that the expression in this verse sets forth "the doctrine of the creation of a new body for the afterlife"—I Cor. 15. Job expects to "see God," but not until after death. He does not say how he will be conscious of his vindication (compare with Job's earlier words—14:21ff). Here is one of the Old Testament highwater marks in the development of a belief in resurrection, which culminates in the resurrection of Jesus of Nazareth. This fact is the very essence of the Christian faith. It is an objective fact which must be subjectively appropriated, resulting in a Christian world-life style of existence. It must be *more* than a legalistic doctrinal orthodoxy, but not *less* than orthodox. Jesus alone has revealed the true nature of Job's God—Jn. 1:18—The Great Explanation. Job's desire is to see (*hazah*—see a vision, a revelation) God—42:5. He is certain of two things: (1) His Vindicator will vindicate his innocence; and (2) He will see his God.[18]

Verse 27—God will appear on Job's behalf (Heb. "on my side") and break His *silence*. Job will see Him for himself, not through someone else's eyes. When he sees Him, He will appear as a friend, not as an enemy or stranger. Job is overcome with emotion (heart—lit. "my kidneys wear out in my bosom"). In Hebrew psychology, the bowels and kidneys are regarded as

---

[16] M. Dahood, *Biblica,* 1971, p. 346.

[17] See again N. J. Tromp, *Primitive Conceptions of Death* (Rome, 1969), esp. pp. 32-34, 85-91.

[18] See W. A. Irwin, "Job's Redeemer," *JBL,* 1962, pp. 217-229; R. Martin-Achard, *De la mort a resurrection d'apres l'Ancien Testament* (Neuchatel, 1956); C. R. North, "The Redeemer God," *Interpretation,* 1948, pp. 3-16; and J. Lindblom, "Ich weiss, dass mein Erloser lebt," *Studia Theologica,* 1940, pp. 65-77.

the center of emotions, as was the heart of intelligence. It is wonderful, but not too wonderful to be possible.

6. He warns his friends to cease their persecution.
(19:28, 29)

TEXT 19:28, 29

28 If ye say, How we will persecute him!
And that the root of the matter is found in me;
29 Be ye afraid of the sword:
For wrath *bringeth* the punishments of the sword,
That ye may know there is a judgment.

COMMENT 19:28, 29

Verse 28—The verse is another problem text. Job is probably charging his friends with prejudice—6:14-30; 13:7-11; 17:4-5; and 19:1-5—and persistent persecution, though the Hebrew text changes to indirect speech "in him" rather than direct discourse expressed in the A. V.'s "in me." Though the meaning is clear, it is one of the examples of grammatical confusion in the verse.

Verse 29—If you continue persecuting me, you will be judged by the sword (lit. "because the iniquities of the sword are wrath"—Isa. 31:8 and 34:5ff). After Job's great assertion in verses 25-27, he now lapses back into his not so obscure despair. In Babylonian literature, the sword is a symbol of Nergal, the god of war; perhaps the ideograph has Near Eastern application. Contemporary man is troubled over the very existence of God. Here Job adds to our anxiety by declaring that God will manifest objective wrath in the form of judgment—Rom. 1:18ff.

TODAY'S ENGLISH VERSION

19
Job

¹⁻² Why do you keep tormenting me with words?
³ Time after time you insult me,
   and show no shame for the way you abuse me.
⁴ Suppose I have done wrong. How does that hurt
      you?
⁵ You think you are better than I am,
   and regard my trouble as proof of my guilt.
⁶ Can't you see it is God who has done this?
   He has set a trap to catch me.
⁷ I protest his violence, but no one listens;
   I call for justice, but there isn't any.
⁸ God has blocked the way, and I can't get through;
   he has covered my path with darkness.
⁹ He has taken away all my wealth,
   and destroyed my reputation.
¹⁰ He batters me from every side.
He uproots my hope
   and leaves me to wither and die.
¹¹ God is angry and rages against me;
   and treats me like his worst enemy.
¹² He sends his army to attack me;
   they dig trenches and lay siege to my tent.

¹³ God has made my brothers forsake me;
   I am a stranger to those who knew me;
¹⁴ my relatives and friends are gone.
¹⁵ Those who were guests in my house have forgotten
      me;
   my housemaids treat me like a stranger and a
      foreigner.
   ¹⁶ When I call a servant he doesn't answer—
   even when I beg him to help me.

193

¹⁷ My wife can't stand the smell of my breath,
and my own brothers won't come near me.
¹⁸ Children despise me and laugh when they see me.
¹⁹ My closest friends look at me with disgust;
those I loved most have turned against me.
²⁰ My skin hangs loose on my bones;
I have barely escaped with my life.
²¹ You are my friends! Take pity on me!
The hand of God has struck me down.
²² Why must you persecute me the way God does?
Haven't you tormented me enough?

²³ How I wish someone would record what I am
saying,
and write my words in a book!
²⁴ Or with a chisel carve my words in stone,
and write them so they would last forever.
²⁵ But I know there is someone in heaven
who will come at last to my defense.
²⁶ Even after my skin is eaten by disease,
in this body I will see God.
²⁷ I will see him with my own eyes,
and he will not be a stranger.

My courage failed because you men said,
²⁸   "How can we torment him?"
You looked for some excuse to attack me.
²⁹ But now, be afraid of the sword—
the sword that brings God's wrath on sin,
so that you will know there is one who judges.

QUESTIONS FOR DISCUSSION 19:1-29

378. How does Job become "our great paradigm of growth
through suffering"? Discuss.
379. How does Job's new found faith express itself?

380. The word "vex" in verse two is not strong enough. What should it be?

381. Can we count ten times of reproach? How is the figure "ten" to be understood?

382. Verse four is a very difficult verse to interpret. How are we to understand it?

383. How easy it is to assume an air of superiority in the presence of weakness. What does this do for the weak? Cf. vs. 5.

384. How does verse six prove that verse four was not a confession of guilt?

385. Job is constantly conscious of his own innocence. On what subject? Discuss.

386. In what sense has God walled Job in?

387. What was the crown of glory once worn by Job?

388. Job uses two graphic metaphors in verse ten to describe his condition. What are they?

389. In what sense was God Job's adversary?

390. How are we to understand the phrase "cast up their way against me"?

391. God's apparent hostility has produced human hostility. Why? Show the progression.

392. If we believe a man is suffering because of his own sin, can we yet show him that we really care? Discuss.

393. Job has lost the respect of his servants. Why? Cf. vss. 15, 16.

394. Job's physical appearance is a real hindrance to social exchange. Discuss why.

395. Who are "the children" in 17b?

396. In what way is estrangement or alienation a fundamental issue in our culture?

397. Disrespect on the part of children calls for drastic measures. Discuss. Cf. II Kg. 2:23.

398. In your own words give the meaning of verse 20.

399. Job's friends could have had pity for him even if they felt he was guilty. Is this what Job needed? Discuss.

400. Show how verse 22 is appropriate to our age.

E. POWERLESSNESS OF PROSPERITY—NO ULTIMATE SECURITY—ZOPHAR'S WARNING (20:1-29)

TEXT 20:1-29

20 Then answered Zophar the Naamathite, and said,
2 Therefore do my thoughts give answer to me,
Even by reason of my haste that is in me.
3 I have heard the reproof which putteth me to shame;
And the spirit of my understanding answereth me.
4 Knowest thou *not* this of old time,
Since man was placed upon earth,
5 That the triumphing of the wicked is short,
And the joy of the godless but for a moment?
6 Though his height mount up to the heavens,
And his head reach unto the clouds;
7 Yet he shall perish for ever like his own dung:
They that have seen him shall say, Where is he?
8 He shall fly away as a dream, and shall not be found:
Yea, he shall be chased away as a vision of the night.
9 The eye which saw him shall see him no more;
Neither shall his place any more behold him.
10 His children shall seek the favor of the poor,
And his hands shall give back his wealth.
11 His bones are full of his youth,
But it shall lie down with him in the dust.
12 Though wickedness be sweet in his mouth,
Though he hide it under his tongue,
13 Though he spare it, and will not let it go,
But keep it still within his mouth;
14 Yet his food in his bowels is turned,
It is the gall of asps within him.
15 He hath swallowed down riches, and he shall vomit them up
again;
God will cast them out of his belly.
16 He shall suck the poison of asps:
The viper's tongue shall slay him.

17 He shall not look upon the rivers,
   The flowing streams of honey and butter.
18 That which he labored for shall he restore, and shall not
      swallow it down;
   According to the substance that he hath gotten, he shall
      not rejoice.
19 For he hath oppressed and forsaken the poor;
   He hath violently taken away a house, and he shall not
      build it up.
20 Because he knew no quietness within him,
   He shall not save aught of that wherein he delighteth.
21 There was nothing left that he devoured not;
   Therefore his prosperity shall not endure.
22 In the fulness of his sufficiency he shall be in straits:
   The hand of every one that is in misery shall come upon him.
23 When he is about to fill his belly,
   God will cast the fierceness of his wrath upon him,
   And will rain it upon him while he is eating.
24 He shall flee from the iron weapon,
   And the bow of brass shall strike him through.
25 He draweth it forth, and it cometh out of his body;
   Yea, the glittering point cometh out of his gall:
   Terrors are upon him.
26 All darkness is laid up for his treasures:
   A fire not blown *by man* shall devour him;
   It shall consume that which is left in his tent.
27 The heavens shall reveal his iniquity.
   And the earth shall rise up against him.
28 The increase of his house shall depart;
   His goods shall flow away in the day of his wrath.
29 This is the portion of a wicked man from God,
   And the heritage appointed unto him by God.

COMMENT 20:1-29

Verse 1—Zophar explodes with anxiety at Job's charges
and closely parallels Bildad's speech in chapter 18. Both deal

with the destruction of the godless. More heat than light flows from Zophar's speech. In his passionate speech, he once more emphasizes the insecurity of the prosperity of the unrighteous. Every "syllable of his remorseless invective" is irrelevant, even if true. Bildad's tirade in chapter 18 and Zophar's irrelevant speech in chapter 20 together frame Job's marvelous credo in chapter 19. His is a living faith; theirs is a rigid retribution-oriented religion. Two characteristics of Zophar's speech are: (1) greater hostility than before, and (2) use of crude imagery, especially in verses 7 and 15.[1]

Verses 2-3—Zophar has almost choked on his silence; now in exasperation he must speak. The verse begins with *laken*— "therefore"—which suggests something is missing. For the first time one of Job's friends admits to being impressed by his speech. "I hear censure which insults me." (See Isa. 53:5 for same word—censure—as chastisement.) Zophar's thoughts cause him to intervene once more. Perhaps the line means that he is boiling over inside and cannot control his hostility. (Brown, Driver, Briggs gives "thy inner excitement.") He claims to speak out of (Heb. preposition *min*—source from which) knowledge which Job does not. Job has shamed him; he must respond. There is a possibility that the phrase "shameful rebuke" refers to homosexual abuses—31:31. Dhorme very nicely handles the grammatical problems in verse 3b by translating the verb in a causative sense—"a wind (or impulse) arising from my understanding prompts me to reply," *Job*, p. 290.

Verse 4—Zophar is not asking himself if he knows but "Do you not know?"[2] If the wicked prosper, it is only for a brief time. He continues to maintain the invariableness between ungodliness and disaster. The success of the wicked in contrast to the suffering of the righteous plagues the writers of our biblical wisdom literature. Zophar once more expounds his

---

[1] See B. H. Kelly, "Truth in Contradiction: A Study of Job 20 and 21," *Interpretation*, 1961, pp. 147-156.

[2] On this point see R. Gordis, *Harvard Theological Review*, 1940, p. 244.

traditional, standard answer—Ps. 37:73. The answer has always been the same—Deut. 4:32.

Verse 5—The solution to the problem presented by the prosperity of the wicked is that it is only for a short time— Ps. 73. Empirically this is not a happy solution, either for individuals or groups, nations, haves and have nots. It is the kind of talk that revolutions are made of. Ultimately the only consolation of the righteous is in resurrection. The rejection of resurrection possibilities is the basis of twentieth century efforts at the humanization of man, through socio-political means. Central to this naturalistic humanism is a denial of a *vertical* dimension to sin, which leaves only a *horizontal* vision of salvation, which becomes merely better and more factors which generate a positive response to daily existence.[3] Christ, our risen Lord, is our only and ultimate consolation. *Joy* and *grace* co-mingle in His empty tomb and ascension.

Verse 6—His loftiness, i.e., his eminence, is only momentary. But great will be the fall—Matt. 9:24ff. As Strahan has well declared, "It is not Zophar's sermon against pride that makes him a false prophet, but his application of it to Job."[4]

Verse 7—Zophar sinks to a new low in his use of the brutally inelegant metaphor—II Kg. 9:37. His vigorous coarseness is bested only by his boorish brutality.

Verse 8—Job is contrasted to a dream which is gone upon awakening. He will be as unavailable as a night vision; continued chase will only cause future crisis—Ps. 73:20 and Isa. 29:8.

Verse 9—The verb translated "saw"—*sazap*—28:7—means "to catch sight of" and emphasizes the brevity of the appearance. The image has appeared before in 7:8, 10; 8:18; Pss.

---

[3] One of the Christian faith's deadliest foes is contemporary Neo-Marxism which comes in well-tailored sheep's clothing, first to Italy, then to France, on to England, then perhaps the USA with our socialistic democracy as its noblest habitat. When Capitalism lost God as a transcendent moral basis of stewardship, only materialistic hedonism remains. See Bell, *Contradictions of Capitalism,* 1975.

[4] R. H. Strahan, *The Book of Job Interpreted,* 1913, see esp. chapters 18-21.

1:4; 103:16.

Verse 10—The poverty of the wicked will force their children to beg from the poor, so destitute is their condition. Perhaps Zophar is suggesting that the sons of the wicked will be forced to return to those whom he has made impoverished through his illicit gain. It is also possible that "hands" in the second line stands for "offspring."[5]

Verse 11—Here the imagery suggests that the wicked will die prematurely, i.e., "full of youth"—Ps. 55:23.

Verse 12—The riches of the ungodly are like sweet food in the mouth which turns to poison in the stomach. Evil is compared with something tasty. "The sweetness of sin turns into the gall of retribution, and riches wrongfully acquired must be vomited up again" (Rowley, *Job,* p. 178)—Heb. 11:15. Sin is so sweet that it is hidden under the tongue to retain maximum pleasure for as long as possible.

Verse 13—The verb translated spare means have "compassion on," implying that Job loves sin so much that "he has compassion" on it and will not let it go. His secret sins are concealed in his mouth.

Verse 14—The sweet-tasting food has become poison. The enjoyment of sin metamorphizes into tragic bitterness and destroys the imbiber—Prov. 20:17. Pliny expresses the ancient belief that "it is the gall which constitutes the poison of asps."

Verse 15—The figure is in keeping with Zophar's coarse rhetorical devices. The evil greedy man must vomit up all his ill-gotten wealth. Here God does not administer an emetic to cause the unrighteous to disgorge the poison; the evil person is so sick that he self-imposes the vomiting.

Verse 16—The poisonous greed proved the undoing of the ungodly. Greed generates oppression; opression generates alienation. The central problem of western economic man, from Keynes to our gross national product, is that greed is the dynamic which enables unwise and unreasonable men to make

---

[5] For this possibility, see R. Gordis, *JBL*, 1943, p. 343.

decisions as though infinite economic growth is possible. Perhaps we note here the assumption that the darting tongue of the viper is the actual source of poison.

Verse 17—The time of enjoyment for the wicked is passed. The joy of leisure is an unavailable goal for the ungodly. The nature of work and leisure are once more fundamental issues in our culture, and for the same reason as is suggested in our text. The flowing rivers will not be available to evil men.[6] Refreshments for the leisure time of the greedy, which are honey and curds—Judges 5:25 and Isa. 7:14—will also avoid them.

Verse 18—The wicked cannot swallow the profit of labor (one Hebrew word extended in A. V., "that which he labored for"). The metaphor depicts one who is gagging, i.e., one who cannot swallow what is in his mouth. "The profits of his trading" is choking him, therefore, not rejoicing.

Verse 19—The wicked have callously abandoned the poor to their fate, after oppressively mistreating them.[7] The second line declares that the wicked man does not enjoy the fruit of his violence, even though he will not abandon it. He is not satisfied even after violently oppressing the powerless poor. Dahood renders the verse, For he crushed the huts of the poor, "He has sacked a house which he did not build."

Verse 20—The greed of the wicked is insatiable. This verse repeats the same thoughts as found in verse 19. Those with insatiable appetites defeat themselves. How appropriate these thoughts are for 20th century America, in light of the conditions in the Third and Fourth Worlds.[8]

Verse 21—The verse is not emphasizing gluttony for food, but an oppressive aggression which consumes the pitiful powerless poor. It repeats the same thoughts as verses 19-20, but makes emphasis with different metaphors.

---

[6] R. de Vaux, *Revue Biblique,* 1937, p. 533.

[7] For problems in this verse, see M. Dahood, *JBL,* 1959, pp. 306ff; and J. Reider, *Hebrew Union College Annual,* 1952-53, pp. 1-3ff.

[8] See my *The Word of God for a Broken World* (LCC Press, 1977), for a look at missions and the Third and Fourth Worlds; and N. M. Sarna, *JBL,* 1959, pp. 315ff.

Verse 22—The imagery suggests that avarice consumes the wicked. Anguish in the midst of luxury: how can this be? The contradictions continue—"all the blows of misfortune pour upon him," Dhorme. This is an excellent translation of the Hebrew which literally says "every hand or force of one in misery" will fall upon him.

Verse 23—What seems to be self-destructive results of the behavior of the wicked is really God's judgment upon their lives. God, too, sends abundance, abundance of His wrath. While the ungodly person is filling his belly, He (God—not in text but must be the subject) will send His burning anger upon him (Hebrew is *lechum*—bowels—inner feelings, emotions).[9]

Verse 24—The metaphor changes from fiery rain from heaven to that of heavy iron weapons.[10] While trying to elude one death-dealing weapon, another will fall on him. There is no hiding place—Am. 5:19 and Isa. 24:18.

Verse 25—The image is a description of the wicked wounded by an arrow, seeking to withdraw it from his body. Finally, the glittering point (lit. lightning-flashing point of the arrow) is pulled out of the gall—verse 14—Deut. 32:41; Nah. 3:3; Hab. 3:11.

Verse 26—Same image as expressed in 15:22. The consuming fire is not of human origin, and it will destroy everything.

Verse 27—Job has already asked for a heavenly witness, and that the earth not silence the witness of his blood—16:18ff. Here heaven and earth will combine their witness against him.

Verse 28—The word translated "depart" (*yigel*) means "to go into exile." Others will carry away his prosperity into their tents. Nothing remains his own. The flood (torrents for *niggerot*—II Sam. 14:14), like the fire in verse 26, has its origin in the purposes of God. The expression of divine judgment

---

[9] M. Dahood, *Biblica*, 1957, pp. 314ff, for the translation "and he shall rain on him in his flesh."

[10] G. R. Driver, *Vestus Testamentum*, 1960, p. 82.

will result in the total destruction of the wicked.

Verse 29—This is the conclusion of Zophar's speech and repeats what he has already asserted—5:27; 18:21—the end of the wicked is destruction.

TODAY'S ENGLISH VERSION

20

Zophar

¹⁻² Job, you upset me. Now I'm impatient to answer.
³   What you have said is an insult,
    but I know how to reply to you.

⁴ Surely you know that from ancient times,
    when man was first placed on earth,
⁵   no wicked man has been happy for long.
⁶ He may grow great and tower to the sky,
    be so great his head reaches the clouds,
⁷   but he will be blown away like dust.
  Those who used to know him
    will wonder where he has gone.
⁸ He will vanish like a dream, like a vision at night,
    and never be seen again.
⁹ He will disappear from the place where he used
    to live;
¹⁰   and his sons will make good what he stole from
    the poor.
¹¹ His body used to be young and vigorous,
    but soon it will turn to dust.
¹²⁻¹³ Evil tastes so good to him
    he keeps some in his mouth to enjoy the taste.
¹⁴ But in his stomach this food turns bitter,
    as bitter as any poison could be.
¹⁵ The wicked man vomits up the wealth he stole;
    God takes it back, even out of his stomach.
¹⁶ What the evil man swallows is like poison;

it kills him like the bite of a deadly snake.
17 He will not live to see rivers of olive oil,
or streams that flow with milk and honey.
18 He will have to give up all he has worked for;
he will have no chance to enjoy his wealth,
19 because he oppressed and neglected the poor,
and seized houses someone else had built.
20 His greed is never satisfied.
21 When he eats, there is nothing left over,
but now his prosperity comes to an end.
22 At the height of his success,
all the weight of misery will crush him.
23 Let him eat all he wants!
God will punish him in fury and anger.
24 When he tries to escape from an iron sword,
a bronze bow will shoot him down.
25 An arrow sticks through his body;
its shiny point drips with his blood,
and terror grips his heart.
26 Everything he has saved is destroyed;
a fire not lit by human hands
burns him and all his family.
27 Heaven reveals this man's sin,
and the earth gives testimony against him.
28 All his wealth will be destroyed
in the flood of God's anger.

29 This is the fate of wicked men,
the fate that God decrees for them.

QUESTIONS FOR DISCUSSION 20:1-29

401. What prompted Zophar's explosive speech?
402. Chapters 18 and 20 are in strong contrast to the content
of chapter 19. Discuss at least two differences.

403. Give two characteristics of Zophar's speech.
404. The sentence in verse two begins with the word "therefore." Something is missing in the thought. What is it?
405. Job has shamed him—he must answer. Of what has Job accused him?
406. Give in your own words the meaning of verse four.
407. "The prosperity of the wicked is only for a short time" is not a happy solution to the problem of the prosperity of the wicked. It is also a very dangerous concept. Discuss. Why? What is the answer?
408. Zophar sinks to a new low in verse seven. How so?
409. Job is compared to a dream and a vision in the night. Explain. Cf. vs. 8.
410. What is emphasized in verse nine?
411. Whose "children" are involved in verse ten? What is the point of the verse?
412. Why would the wicked die permaturely (see vs. 11)? Does this happen often? Discuss.
413. Sin is both sweet and tasty, but it turns to poison in the stomach. Is it true? Discuss. Why hide it under the tongue?
414. Job actually (according to Zophar) had compassion on sin. In what way?
415. The principle espoused by Zophar is true when properly understood and applied. Discuss. Cf. vs. 14.
416. Zophar's figures of speech are really graphic, if not coarse. Someone is sick. Who? Why?
417. Is America infested with the virus of greed to the extent that verse 16 describes many in our country? Discuss.
418. The use of leisure time is discussed in verse 17. What is it? How does this relate to our society?
419. Someone is gagging. Who is it? Why? Cf. vs. 18.
420. The poor are oppressed without a cause and the oppressor is not satisfied. Does this happen today? Cite examples. Cf. vss. 19, 20, 21.
421. "Anguish in the midst of luxury, how can this be"? Discuss verse 22.

F. INTEGRITY, PROSPERITY, AND THE PRESENCE OF THE HOLY RIGHTEOUS GOD (21:1-34)
1. Job pleads for a sympathetic hearing. (21:1-6)

TEXT 21:1-6

21 Then Job answered and said,
2 Hear diligently my speech;
  And let this be your consolations.
3 Suffer me, and I also will speak;
  And after that I have spoken, mock on.
4 As for me, is my complaint to man?
  And why should I not be impatient?
5 Mark me, and be astonished,
  And lay your hand upon your mouth.
6 Even when I remember I am troubled,
  And horror taketh hold on my flesh.

COMMENT 21:1-6

Verse 1—For the sixth time Job responds to Zophar out of the depths of his realistic experience. Here we vividly see the radical distinction between his experience and the *a priori* theories of his three friends. Job confronts their thesis that the righteous are happy and the wicked are miserable with a counter claim—that the wicked are often prosperous. This Jobian speech falls into five sections: (1) Job appeals for a hearing—verses 2-6; (2) The wicked prosper—verses 7-16; (3) He asks, Do the wicked suffer?—verses 17-22; (4) Death levels everyone and everything—verses 23-26; and (5) Universal experience contradicts the arguments of his three comforters—verses 27-34. It is the only fully polemical speech from Job.

Verse 2—Eliphaz had identified his words with "the consolation of God"—15:11. Now Job asks them to consider real consolation. He has emerged victorious over the temptation

206

presented to him by both his friends and his wife. He has asserted his faith that God knows his innocence and will ultimately testify to it. He still believes in God's goodness and has a basis from which to reject the accusing recommendations of his friends. He passes from mere defensiveness to frontal attack. Theologically, his friends have attacked him from behind the bulwark of the eternal universal principle of retributive justice. Job brilliantly and relentlessly undertakes to falsify the principle from which they continually deduced so many erroneous conclusions. First, it is not universally self-evident that God sends retributive justice in this life (note similar argument in Kant's *Critique of Practical Judgment*). Secondly, God does not destroy the godless in a moment—verses 5, 6; and thirdly, that the impious do not always prosper, but they often do—Jer. 12:1ff; Eccl. 7:15. Job asks only for their discreet silence and attentive ears.

Verse 3—The verbs preceding this verse are all plural, but here this one is in the singular. Job is focusing attention on Zophar's just-ended discourse on the fate of the wicked. After what I have to say, you will no longer mock me.

Verse 4—Job's complaint is against God, not man. He would expect at least sympathy from man. He receives no consolation from either God or man. He is protesting the moral anomalies that God allows in His world. Job has inquired of God, but God remains silent; therefore, Job is impatient (lit. "my spirit is short").

Verses 5, 6—Laying one's hand over the mouth is the gesture of awe and voluntary silence.[1] Job's friends will be silent when they hear and understand his argument concerning the prosperity of the wicked. He shudders at the very thought of an amoral universe.

---

[1] See J. B. Pritchard, ed., *Ancient Near Eastern Pictures Relating to the Old Testament* (Princeton: University Press), p. 333, for picture of Mesopotamian seal cylinder from the third millennium B.C. depicting Etana flying heavenward on eagle's wings while one onlooker has his mouth covered.

2. The wicked enjoy great peace and plenty. (21:7-16)

TEXT 21:7-16

7 Wherefore do the wicked live,
   Become old, yea, wax mighty in power?
8 Their seed is established with them in their sight,
   And their offspring before their eyes.
9 Their houses are safe from fear,
   Neither is the rod of God upon them.
10 Their bull gendereth, and faileth not;
   Their cow calveth, and casteth not her calf.
11 They send forth their little ones like a flock,
   And their children dance.
12 They sing to the timbrel and harp,
   And rejoice at the sound of the pipe.
13 They spend their days in prosperity,
   And in a moment they go down to Sheol.
14 And they say unto God, Depart from us;
   For we desire not the knowledge of thy ways.
15 What is the Almighty, that we should serve him?
   And what profit should we have, if we pray unto him?
16 Lo, their prosperity is not in their hand:
   The counsel of the wicked is far from me.

COMMENT 21:7-16

Verse 7—Zophar (and Plato's *Republic*) had said—20:11—that the wicked die prematurely. Job counters with evidence to the contrary. Job asks "why?" (*maddna*—"from what cause"; *lamah*—3:20; 7:20—"to what purpose?" Jesus on cross—Ps. 22; Matt. 27—how do you explain it?) Zophar's argument is sophistry. If one dies early in life, then he was wicked. The same applies to Bildad's arguments in 18:5-21. One could never refute such an *a priori* position. Not only do many wicked live long lives, but their prosperity continues

208

unbroken—15:20; 18:5; 20:5. Other Old Testament spokes-men were also disturbed about this same phenomena—Jer. 12:1ff; Ps. 73:13; Hab. 1:13; and Mal. 3:15. The evidence does not support Zophar's claim that the prosperous wicked never attain a level of true happiness. The holy pagan, moral atheist, the good-living humanist might be as "happy" as the righteous man, then or now. If *ex hypothesi* happiness is God's gift, is He not encouraging unbelief by such indiscrimi-nate bestowal of prosperity?—Matt. 5:45. The only motives advanced by Job's friends for serving God have been: (1) fear of punishment and (2) hope for reward. This kind of motiva-tion will never produce truly pious people (note arguments against these by Kant and Hannah Arendt).

Verse 8—Job directly contradicts the claims of Bildad con-cerning the fate of the wicked which he stated in 18:5-21. He first attacks Bildad's assertion that Job's ill-fated pros-perity and progeny are proof of ungodliness. The wicked have (lit. *lipnehem*—before them) their offspring.[2]

Verse 9—Here Job sets the security of the ungodly against Eliphaz's claim in 5:24. He had promised Job security in his tent if he would accept his present condition as God's judg-ment and repent. In 9:34 Job complained that there was no "mediator" to remove God's rod of anger from him; here he asserts that the ungodly do not feel the rod of wrath—15:28; 18:14; and 10:28.

Verse 10—Another mark of God's blessing was fertility in herds and flocks—Deut. 28:14; Ps. 144:13ff. If this is a sign of God's blessing, then He is blessing many wicked people with success.[3]

Verse 11—Here we note a beautiful picture of peace, prog-ress, and prosperity as children are playing and singing like

---

[2] Blommerde, *Northwest Semitic Grammar and Job,* follows M. Dahood, *Biblica,* 1966, p. 411—"Their line is stable; their fathers are with them and their offspring are before their eyes."

[3] Compare this argument in a Christian critique of the American Dream, i.e., if you are successful, it is a sign of God's providential presence; if you are a failure, it is a warning to get right with God.

happy little lambs. But the children of the wicked are as numerous as a herd or flock—Ps. 107:41. (Note contemporary preoccupation with leisure and play (see J. Moltmann's *A Theology of Play.* New York: Harper & Row, 1975), Zech. 8:5.[4]

Verse 12—For similar descriptions of revelry of the wicked, see Isa. 5:12 and Amos 6:5, perhaps in their worship of Baal. The same mode, but not motive, is employed in the worship of God.[5] Festivity and celebration are marks of both pious joy as well as sensual revelry.

Verse 13—The wicked often know intense prosperity and come to a peaceful ripe old age. In peace (A. V. has "in a moment") they go down to Sheol (suggesting suddenly, which is not the point here). They have a long and complete life, with little or no suffering and no lingering illnesses.

Verse 14—Radical self-interest is no motive for them to acknowledge God. They already have everything they want. In modern times, from Machiavelli to Mao, radical self-interest has been the basis of totalitarianism.[6] In our own culture it is the basis of hedonistic materialism. What profit is there in knowing God? The happy people have no self-interest to induce them to worship God.

Verse 15—The wicked have no obligation of love or gratitude to worship God. This philosophy of religion says that we will give if we get in return. But the righteous man desires above all else to know God and His ways—Pss. 16:11 and 25:4. The perverse reject God, while they continue to prosper.

Verse 16—The verse is notorious for its grammatical complexities. Perhaps the R. S. V. gets at the meaning better than the A. V., which is: God does not concern Himself with wicked, but leaves their prosperity to themselves; that is their sole

---

[4] For analysis of instruments mentioned in this vivid picture, see essay by M. Dahood, *The Bible in Current Catholic Thought,* p. 65; and for singing, see A. Guillaume, *Journal of Theological Studies,* 1966, pp. 53ff; for biblical music in general, Werner's *The Bridge* (Havard University Press).

[5] See esp. *The Song of Songs* 7:1; and article by R. T. O'Callaghan, *Orientalia,* 21, 1952, 37-46; and M. Dahood, *The Bible in Current Catholic Thought,* p. 65.

[6] See Hannah Arendt, *The Origins of Totalitarianism* (Meridian Books, pb., 1958).

and ultimate award. Job then says that the counsel of the wicked is removed far from him in the sense that despite their success, Job does not wish to be prosperous on their terms.[7]

3. Sometimes they suffer, but not regularly. (21:17-22)

TEXT 21:17-22

17   How oft is it that the lamp of the wicked is put out?
That their calamity cometh upon them?
That *God* distributeth sorrows in his anger?
18 That they are as stubble before the wind.
And as chaff that the storm carrieth away?
19 *Ye say,* God layeth up his iniquity for his children.
Let him recompense it unto himself that he may know:
20 Let his own eyes see his destruction,
And let him drink of the wrath of the Almighty.
21 For what careth he for his house after him,
When the number of his months is cut off?
22 Shall any teach God knowledge,
Seeing he judgeth those that are high?

COMMENT 21:17-22

Verse 17—Job admits that there is some evidence for the claims of his friends, but not enough to claim universal inevitability of the law of retribution. In a moral universe, everyone is responsible for his or her own deeds—18:5-6, 10ff; 20:7, 22, 26-28; 27:20ff; Ps. 1:4. Job asks, Where are the examples which you set forth as universal proof?
Verse 18—The metaphors here also appear in Ps. 1:4; Job

---

[7] For this difficult verse, see A. C. M. Blommerde, *Northwest Semitic Grammar and Job;* one basic problem is: From whom is the prosperity derived? "Is not from his hands their prosperity?" or "Behold, the Mighty One, from his hands is their property."

27:20; Isa. 17:13. The images are figurative for destruction. Compare the claims of David and Job.

Verse 19—"You say" represents nothing from the Hebrew text, but probably is an appropriate addition which suggests a response to a question. Perhaps Job is responding with a proverb or current saying. The verse presents the ancient view that a man's sins are visited upon his children—Ex. 34:7 and Deut. 5:9. He objects that this is unjust. Moses forbids the application of this "law" in Deut. 24:16; Jer. 31:29; Ezek. 18; Jn. 9:1-3; and Matt. 27:25. The vital interrelationship between sin and its consequences must receive careful consideration in light of the biblical view of "corporate personality" and contemporary Systems Analysis Models. There was repercussion throughout all creation when man first sinned, and the empirical evidence sustains the biblical claims regarding the fragmentation of relationships between *God and Man, Man and Self, Man and Others, and Man and Nature.*

Verse 20—The wicked ought to receive the retribution themselves, not their children as "Let his own eyes see his destruction" (punishment)[8] suggests—Isa. 51:17; Jer. 25:15; and Rev. 16:19.

Verse 21—What concern does a dead man have for his house?—Ezek. 18:2; Jer. 31:28ff. The Qumran Targum has what "interest for God in his house" after his death? What difference does God make to a dead ungodly person?

Verse 22—Who can teach God anything? Shall even the "high ones" (Heb., *ramin*, probably angels and not God as claimed by both Blommerde and Dahood) teach Him: It would make little sense of God instructing Himself—4:18; 15:15; 22:13; 15:2; Ps. 73:11. Job is asserting that moral considerations alone do not explain the varieties of human experience, for the intensity of either happiness or despair.

---

[8] For analysis of this verse, see M. Dahood, *Biblica,* 1957, p. 316; and compare with A. F. L. Beeston, *Le muséon,* 1954, pp. 315ff.

4. The only equality is to be found in death. (21:23-26)

TEXT 21:23-26

23 One dieth in his full strength,
   Being wholly at ease and quiet:
24 His pails are full of milk,
   And the marrow of his bones is moistened.
25 And another dieth in bitterness of soul,
   And never tasteth of good.
26 They lie down alike in the dust,
   And the worm covereth them.

COMMENT 21:23-26

Verse 23—One dies "in his perfection," i.e., prime of life. Death levels everyone—verses 23-26. One person dies in prosperity, another in poverty.

Verse 24—The Hebrew hardly says what the A. V. provides in the first line. The first word is *a hapaz* (does not appear elsewhere) but perhaps is a euphemism for "buttocks" which is plump or fat (emend *halab*—milk—to *heleb*—fat). The second line contains figures (moist bones are figures of health) which suggest that the person is well fed or prosperous. Death takes them all, regardless of social status or physical condition.

Verse 25—The verse is Job's description of himself—3:20 and 7:7.

Verse 26—The ungodly and the righteous share the same— death—Eccl. 2:14ff. It is the dissimilarity in the human fate, rather than retribution, which moves Job—17:14; Isa. 14:11b.

5. So, your argument that I am wicked because I suffer is false.
(21:27-34)

TEXT 21:27-34

27 Behold, I know your thoughts,

And the devices wherewith ye would wrong me.
28 For ye say, Where is the house of the prince?
   And where is the tent wherein the wicked dwelt?
29 Have ye not asked wayfaring men?
   And do ye not know their evidences,
30 That the evil man is reserved to the day of calamity?
   That they are led forth to the day of wrath?
31 Who shall declare his way to his face?
   And who shall repay him what he hath done?
32 Yet shall he be borne to the grave,
   And men shall keep watch over the tomb.
33 The clods of the valley shall be sweet unto him,
   And all men shall draw after him,
   As there were innumerable before him.
34 How then comfort ye me in vain,
   Seeing in your answer there remaineth *only* falsehood?

COMMENT 21:27-34

Verse 27—Job has thus far claimed that there is no evident connection between happiness and virtue—21:19-21, 23-26. The friends will simply not face the truth of the blunt realities of life—Eccl. 8:14; Job 21:34b. He knows that his friends meant him while they were claiming that the wicked are destroyed; Job is destroyed; therefore, Job is wicked—4:7. His suffering is the price paid for his sins. He says that they have violently wronged him (word translated wrong is stronger than our English word).

Verse 28—*Nadib* means a rich prince. Here the implication is a wealthy but wicked prince who has exploited the poor— 20:19. God's vengeance has swept his house away—8:15, 22; 18:15, 21; 15:34.

Verse 29—Any wayfarer (those who travel the roads, not necessarily a world traveler) could tell Job's friends that their claims are not universally the case—Lam. 1:12; 2:15; Pss. 80:13; 89:42; Prov. 9:15. The daily experience (signs or monuments)

214

of many will refute their claims. Why do they persist in their *a priori* evaluation of the wicked and the righteous, when the evidence refutes their claims?

Verse 30—Those who travel the roads report that wicked men are delivered (lit. brought away from, A. V. preserved—but the English meaning is not that of the Hebrew) and led to safety on many occasions—20:28; Deut. 32:35; Isa. 26:20; Jer. 18:17; Ezek. 7:19; Zeph. 1:15, 18; and Prov. 11:4.[1]

Verse 31—The reference here is to the successful, powerful despot, not God as some assume. Who would publicly rebuke a tyrant: The way (*halak*—life style; way of life) represents the behavior pattern of the wicked but successful man.

Verse 32—There is abundant evidence that wicked men are honored in both life and death. They are so "respected" that men watch over their tombs. Perhaps there is reference to Near Eastern custom that effigy of important dead persons watch over their own tombs. Whether this be so or not, Job is claiming that often the wicked are buried in pomp and much circumstance. How different from his own situation.

Verse 33—Burial was often in a ravine or valley—Deut. 34:6. After the rains, the clods would become as hard as rocks and so continue to mark the grave. He has no beautiful mausoleum only "clods" to identify the spot where the earth entombs his once strong body. Perhaps the metaphor speaks of a funeral procession. The wicked often have a peaceful death and posthumous fame.

Verse 34—Thus Job's speech completes the second cycle. He dismisses the arguments of his friends as vain in view of the rocks of reality. Their answers are perfidy (Heb. *ma'al*—sacreligious attack on God). The things they have been saying on God's behalf are all lies when tested against experience.

---

[1] F. H. Andersen, *Job*, InterVarsity Press, 1976, p. 201.

TODAY'S ENGLISH VERSION

21
Job

¹⁻² Listen to what I am saying;
   that is all the comfort I ask from you.
³ Give me a chance to speak and then,
   when I am through, sneer if you like.

⁴ My quarrel is not with mortal men;
   I have good reason to be impatient.
⁵ Look at me. Isn't that enough
   to make you stare in shocked silence?
⁶ When I think of what has happened to me,
   I am stunned, and I tremble and shake.
⁷ Why does God let evil men grow old and prosper?
⁸ Their children and grandchildren
   grow up before their very eyes.
⁹ God does not bring disaster on their homes;
   they never have to live in terror.
¹⁰ Yes, all their cattle breed
   and give birth without trouble.
¹¹ Their children run and play like lambs
¹²   and dance to the music of harps and flutes.
¹³ They live out their lives in peace,
   and die quietly without suffering.
¹⁴ The wicked tell God to leave them alone;
   they don't want to know his will for their lives.
¹⁵ They think there is no need to serve God,
   or any advantage in praying to him.
¹⁶ They claim they succeed by their own strength,
   but their way of thinking I can't accept.

¹⁷ Was a wicked man's light ever put out?
   Did one of them ever meet with disaster?
Did God ever punish the wicked in anger

216

¹⁸ and make them like straw blown by the wind
or like dust carried away in a storm?

¹⁹ You claim God punishes a child for the sins of
his father.
No! Let God punish the sinners themselves,
and show he does it because of their sins.
²⁰ Let sinners bear their own punishment;
let them feel the wrath of Almighty God.
²¹ When a man's life is over,
does he really care if his children are happy?
²² Can a man teach God?
Can a man judge Almighty God?

²³⁻²⁴ Some men stay healthy till the day they die;
they die happy and at ease,
and their bodies are well-nourished.
²⁵ Others have no happiness at all;
they live and die with bitter hearts.
²⁶ But all alike die and are buried;
they all are covered with worms.
²⁷ I know what spiteful things you think.
²⁸ You ask, "Where is the house of the great
man now,
the man who practiced evil?"

²⁹ Haven't you talked with people who travel?
Don't you know the reports they bring back?
³⁰ On the day when God is angry and punishes,
it is the wicked man who is always spared.
³¹ There is no one to accuse a wicked man,
or pay him back for all he has done.
³² When he is carried to the graveyard,
to where his tomb is guarded,
³³ thousands join the funeral procession,
and even the earth lies gently on his body.

³⁴ And you! You try to comfort me with nonsense!
Everything you have said is a lie!

QUESTIONS FOR DISCUSSION 21:1-34

422. This speech of Job has some distinctive features. Name three of them. Discuss.
423. How does Job define "real consolation"?
424. Give the three answers of Job to the so-called universal principle of retributive justice.
425. To whom is verse three addressed?
426. Why is Job impatient with God?
427. What is meant by laying one's hand on his mouth? Why does Job shudder?
428. Are only the righteous happy and prosperous? Discuss the contradiction of this in real life.
429. Job really attacks and refutes the arguments of Bildad. Show how.
430. Job sets the security of the wicked against what argument?
431. The American Dream is invalid in verse ten. Discuss.
432. Joy, singing, dancing are all expressions of both the righteous and the wicked. Explain.
433. What is the point of verse 13?
434. What is the basis for totalitarianism? Discuss.
435. Explain in your own words the meaning of verse 16.
436. Job wants to know how often the wicked suffer. Why?
437. What is the proverb considered in verse 19? How answer it? Cf. verse 20.
438. How does the thought that a dead man has no interest in his home relate to the point of these verses?
439. There is dissimilarity, but not according to the definition of Job's friends. What is the real difference among men?
440. How are all men alike? Discuss.
441. Isn't there any evident connection between happiness and virtue?
442. Who is the "prince" of verse 28? How will the wayfarer answer this question? Discuss.
443. The wicked are actually, at times, led to safety instead of wrath. Why?
444. Who is involved in verse 31? What is the point?

III. FALLACIES, FOLLIES, AND LOGOTHERAPY—
THIRD TIME'S A CHARM (22:1—26:14)

A. ELIPHAZ ON THE FUNCTIONAL VALUE OF MAN (22:1-30)
1. God, needing nothing, is not self-seeking in punishing Job; so the punishment must be the result of sin. (22:1-5)

TEXT 22:1-5

22 Then answered Eliphaz the Temanite, and said,
2 Can a man be profitable unto God?
Surely he that is wise is profitable unto himself.
3 Is it any pleasure to the Almighty,
    that thou art righteous?
Or is it gain *to him,* that thou makest thy ways perfect?
4 Is it for thy fear *of him* that he reproveth thee,
That he entereth with thee into judgment?
5 Is not thy wickedness great?
Neither is there any end to thine iniquities.

COMMENT 22:1-5

"I can still hear his cries. It's unbearable. It almost makes you believe in God. . . . Cries like that seem to call God back to life, much more surely than all the happiness in the world, and end-of-the-world silence, more frightening even than instant justice."
—Monteilhet, *Policiers Pour la forme*

Verse 1—The third cycle of speeches now begins. From the very beginning Eliphaz has found Job obstinately perverse. The movement in the content of the speeches has thus far been along three lines of thought: (1) In earlier speeches the three friends have argued from their preconceived notions of God's nature to the conclusion that Job has sinned and that his suffering can be alleviated only through his repentance.

(2) The second cycle develops the thesis of the fate of the wicked and that the universe is governed by moral structures and (3) in the third series to turn with vehemence upon Job and charge him with grave sins. Their assumptions about God, evil, and suffering are once more in evidence; their conclusions follow from their presuppositions, not the evidence in Job's life, as anyone else's. Eliphaz returns to his earlier theme that repentance would lead to Job's restoration. His speech contains four divisions: (1) Since God is disinterested, i.e., silent, Job's suffering is proof of his sins—verses 2-5; (2) Eliphaz's deduction concerning Job's sin—verses 6-11; (3) Eliphaz's envisagement of Job's assumption concerning God's silence—verses 12-20; and (4) Eliphaz's promise and appeal to Job—verses 21-30.

The central issue in this speech is the distance between God and man because of sin.[1] If man suffers, it is a result of his personal sins. Eliphaz here abandons all efforts at gentleness. In his first speech (chps. 4—5) he set forth encouragement; in his second speech (chp. 15) he spoke of Job's irreverence; and now he openly charges Job with hypocrisy and secret sins. The principle from which Eliphaz begins his reasoning is true, i.e., God is just (Rom. 3:21ff), but it is not the entire picture; God is also loving. By isolating God's love and justice, Eliphaz distorts the entire relationship between God and man. Eliphaz still cannot understand how anyone can serve God "for nothing." Somebody must gain from it. Is it man, or is it God?

Verse 2—God can derive no possible advantage from man, but a pious life style can benefit man. God would gain nothing by deviating from strict justice in dealing with human behavior

---

[1] Note the history of this fundamental problem of the relationship between God's immanence and transcendance: (1) There is no separation between God and man— because there is no God, naturalistic atheism; (2) Kierkegaard's total separation, God as "wholly other"; (3) After Hegel's phenomenologically based panentheism the separation is only one of degree. From the Newtonian world Machine Model to 19 "Organiamic Model—Evolutionary naturalism is its 19th dress; (4) Kierkegaard-Buber-Otto-Barth in neo-orthodoxy; (5) God is totally immersed in reality—Death of God, Revolutionary political, Liberation Theologies of all types; and (6) Biblical alternatives.

(Elihu expresses the same theme in 35:7). "God doth not need either man's work or his gifts"—Milton. Job has previously used this argument—7:20. Man cannot harm God; why then should God care what man does? He should just leave man alone.

Verse 3—Is it any advantage (note parallel word in the second line "gain") or pleasure (21:21) to God, if you are righteous? Can a *gebher* (strongest speciman of man) be useful to God? Can a professional wise man give instruction to the Almighty? As a theologian of transcendence, Eliphaz dismisses these ludicrous possibilities—Isa. 62:5; Lk. 15:7; 17:10.

Verse 4—Both Testaments witness to *our unprofitableness* and *God's gracious concern.* Eliphaz has used the word *yirah* (fear, reverence, piety) before (4:6) in the sense of piety. He is assuming that since God is disinterested, His relationship to man must be our advantage and not God's. The A. V. translation "fear" is quite inappropriate in this discussion.

Verse 5—Job will later protest that he is innocent in 31:5ff, which also contains his response to Eliphaz's charges. Job's accuser has no evidence; his accusations are derived from his presuppositions. The two words for sin in this verse are (1) "wickedness"—*resha,* loose, ill-regulated; and (2) *pesha*— deliberate and premeditated; and Job 34:37 speaks of adding *pesha* to *hattah*—miss attaining of goal (see Brown, Driver, Briggs). Eliphaz declares that if God's discipline is not for your piety, then it must be for your sinful rebellion. If your suffering is limitless and God is just, then your sins must also be boundless.

2. Specific sins charged against Job, and their consequences (22:6-11)

TEXT 22:6-11

6 For thou hast taken pledges of thy brother for nought,
   And stripped the naked of their clothing.
7 Thou hast not given water to the weary to drink,

And thou hast withholden bread from the hungry.
8 But as for the mighty man, he had the earth;
And the honorable man, he dwelt in it.
9 Thou hast sent widows away empty,
And the arms of the fatherless have been broken.
10 Therefore snares are round about thee,
And sudden fear troubleth thee,
11 Or darkness, so that thou canst not see,
And abundance of waters cover thee.

COMMENT 22:6-11

Verse 6—Eliphaz begins analysis of specific sins—verses 6-11. Hebrew law required that if a poor man gave his undergarment in pledge for a given transaction, that the creditor must return it by sundown, so the debtor would have at least this covering to protect him against the chill of the night— Ex. 22:26; Deut. 24:10-13; Amos 2:8; Ezek. 18:12. Here Eliphaz charges that Job in his greed has stripped the poor debtors and reduced them to nakedness (strongly denied in 31:19-22). Where is the evidence for this charge? Does he bring some mistreated poor to witness against Job—Gal. 6:1?

Verse 7—Eliphaz continues to confront Job with the violation of the standard list of social crimes which the wealthy and powerful could commit with impunity. The next accusation hurled against Job is that he has neglected basic hospitality to the poor—Isa. 58:7, 10; Job's response is 31:16ff. The charge is more serious than mere neglect; he is charged with calloused indifference to even the minimal needs of the poor— Matt. 25:35, 42. The adjective "weary" is used of the thirsty— Isa. 29:8; Jer. 31:25; and Prov. 25:15. Then, as now, piety demands social expression. There can be *no* private piety.

Verse 8—Job is identified as a "man of arm,"[2] i.e., a person

---

[2] See M. Pope, *JBL,* 1966, p. 529, for analysis of R. Gordis' claim that the verse is a quotation. See R. Gordis, *The Book of God and Man,* "The Use of Quotations in Job," chapter 13, pp. 169-189.

of wealth and rank. Here we read of an oblique reference to Job as a land-grabber—Isa. 5:8. He is also described as the favored man (lit. lifted of face—Isa. 3:3), i.e., on the basis of his wealth.

Verse 9—Supposedly, Job has sent widows away empty handed. He also crushed the arms of orphans. To exploit defenseless orphans or widows was a most heinous crime— Deut. 27:19; Jer. 7:6; 22:3. Job responds to these charges in 29:12ff and 31:16ff.

Verse 10—What Bildad (18:8-11; 19:6) has earlier predicted of the ungodly in general, Eliphaz here specifically applies to Job. In retribution for his sinful acts, God spreads snares or traps all around Job. Terrified with sudden dread, Job falls into the traps with paralyzing fright. The snares are proof of Job's evil deeds, according to Eliphaz.

Verse 11—Job, do you not understand the true cause of your troubles?—in contrast with Isa. 58:10-11. The crushing misfortunes are metaphorically expressed by blinding "darkness" and destructive "floods." The second line in this verse is verbatim found in 38:34b. Water and darkness are figures for the perils of death and Sheol—Ps. 69:2, 3; Job 9:31a.

3. Warning that all evil men have been punished (22:12-20)

TEXT 22:12-20

12 Is not God in the height of heaven?
   And behold the height of the stars, how high they are!
13 And thou sayest, What doth God know?
   Can he judge through the thick darkness?
14 Thick clouds are a covering to him, so that he seeth not;
   And he walketh on the vault of heaven.
15 Wilt thou keep the old way
   Which wicked men have trodden?
16 Who were snatched away before their time.

Whose foundation was poured out as a stream.
17 Who said unto God, Depart from us;
And, What can the Almighty do for us?
18 Yet he filled their houses with good things:
But the counsel of the wicked is far from me.
19 The righteous see it, and are glad;
And the innocent laugh them to scorn,
20 *Saying,* Surely they that did rise up against us are cut off,
And the remnant of them the fire hath consumed.

COMMENT 22:12-20

Verse 12—God's transcendence is understood here in the sense that He is so far off that He is unconcerned with man's condition—Ps. 10:4; 73:11; and Isa. 29:15—or as the Psalmist concludes—Ps. 14:2; 33:13ff, He is so high that He observes every event that transpires in nature-history. Yet, Eliphaz argues in verse 13 that transcendence is understood by Job to mean indifference.[3] Job has actually used this theme to describe the practical atheism of the prosperous who go unpunished in spite of their impiety—21:14-15. Eliphaz deliberately distorts Job's discourse in order to identify him with the ancient wicked—verses 15ff.

Verse 13—Eliphaz intentionally distorts Job's theology as he asks, Does the vast distance create darkness so God cannot discern human deeds? The dark cloud partially hid God from human visibility—Ex. 20:18; I Kg. 8:12; and Ps. 18:10. This verse contains the first overt distortion of Job's position concerning God's transcendence—7:19; 10:6, 14; 14:3, 6.

Verse 14—God is only concerned with the "circle"—Prov. 8:27; Isa. 40:22—of the heavens, not with the events on the earth, so declares Eliphaz, perhaps in response to Job's question in 21:22. God is elsewhere depicted as riding upon the clouds—

---

[3] On this matter, see M. Dahood, *Orientalia,* 1965, p. 171 and his *Psalms,* Vol, I, Ps. 10:4—second note.

Isa. 19:1—and making the clouds his chariots—Ps. 104:3. "Vault" or dome carries a connotation not presented in the creation narratives or here. God is not described as being outside an enclosed world.

Verse 15—Eliphaz next asserts that the attitudes espoused by Job have brought destruction on the ancient wicked. The old way[4]—Jer. 6:16—is best translated "the dark path," or the way of darkness or ignorance (see 42:3—*ma'lin 'esah*— "darkening counsel"; the noun occurs in Eccl. 3:11, darkness or ignorance, Eccl. 2:14 and Prov. 2:3). The wicked walk the path of ignorance of God's presence.

Verse 16—The foundations of their existence collapsed from beneath them, swept away as by a flood—Matt. 7:26. They were snatched away without warning.

Verse 17—Compare with 21:14-16. Eliphaz is commenting on remarks of some of the ancient wicked. He remembers what Job has claimed, in order to assert that his prosperity was only a prelude to his devastation.[5]

Verse 18—Eliphaz again distorts Job's words—21:16—in order to assert that the God he scorns was the source of his prosperity. Any forthcoming disaster was merited. The blessings which the wicked receive will become to them a curse. God's ultimate overthrow of the wicked is proof of His just rule over the affairs of men.

Verse 19—Compare with Pss. 107:41a and 69:33, almost verbatim. For imageries depicting the righteous rejoicing over the destruction of the wicked, see Ps. 52:6ff; 69:32; and see Ps. 107:12 for rejoicing over the victories of the righteous.[6]

Verse 20—Eliphaz argues from remoteness to impartiality— see Zophar's use in 11:7-20. "Our adversaries," i.e., the wicked and their possessions (not as A. V.—remnant) are destroyed.

---

[4] Compare M. Dohood's essay in *Bible in Current Catholic Thought*, 1962, p. 65.

[5] M. Dahood, *Biblica*, 1965, p. 324; also *Biblica*, 1966, p. 409.

[6] See M. Bic, "Le juste et l'impie dans le livre de Job," *Vetus Testamentum*, Supplement, 15, 1966, 33-43; R. B. Y. Scott, "Wise and Foolish, Righteous and Wicked," *Vetus Testamentum*, Supplement, 1972, 146-165; D. S. Shapiro, "Wisdom and Knowledge of God in Biblical and Tamudic Thought," *Tradition*, 1971, 70-89.

4. Repent, and restoration will be certain. (22:21-30)

TEXT 22:21-30

21 Acquaint now thyself with him, and be at peace:
Thereby good shall come unto thee.
22 Receive, I pray thee, the law from his mouth,
And lay up his words in thy heart.
23 If thou return to the Almighty, thou shalt be built up,
If thou put away unrighteousness far from thy tents.
24 And lay thou *thy* treasure in the dust,
And *the gold of* Ophir among the stones of the brooks;
25 And the Almighty will be thy treasure,
And precious silver unto thee.
26 For then shalt thou delight thyself in the Almighty,
And shalt lift up thy face unto God.
27 Thou shalt make thy prayer unto him, and he will hear thee;
And thou shalt pay thy vows.
28 Thou shalt also decree a thing, and it shall be established
unto thee;
And light shall shine upon thy ways.
29 When they cast *thee* down, thou shalt say, *There is* lifting up;
And the humble person he will save.
30 He will deliver *even* him that is not innocent:
Yea, he shall be delivered through the cleanness of thy hands.

COMMENT 22:21-30

Verse 21—Eliphaz entreats Job to reconcile[7] or yield ("agree with God"—verb means be accustomed to—Num. 22:30; Ps. 139:3) himself to God, promising him great material felicity in reward—5:17-27; 11:13-19. This results in Job's submission to God; then he will be at peace."[8] Eliphaz still

---

[7] See W. B. Bishai, *Journal Eastern Studies*, 1961, pp. 258ff, for defense of "acquiesce." Pope concurs and translates "yield to"; see also Blommerde's remarks.
[8] S. N. Kramer, *Harvard Theological Review*, 1956, pp. 59ff.

226

claims that the rewards of the righteous constitute its attraction.

Verse 22—The only occurrence of the word Torah in Job is here. It means instruction or revelation and is one of the most precious words in the Old Testament. (Torah is not to be confused with the legalistic view of *nomos*, esp. see Romans and Galatians, which dominated Rabbinic Judaism in the time of Jesus and Paul.)[9] His "words" is parallel in line two and reflects a scribe taking dictation from God.[10]

Verse 23—If you become reconciled to God, "you will be built up" (reading *te'aneh* for *tibbaneh*). The passive form of the verb build (*b ny*) is used in Jer. 12:16; Mal. 3:15 of persons made prosperous, implying here healing or restoration.

Verse 24—Eliphaz is promising Job the restoration of his wealth if he will but return to God. God will make his gold as common as dirt. The word translated "treasure" in A. V. means ore, or that which is dug out of the earth. The text has only "Ophir" which symbolizes the highly prized gold from that location—Gen. 2:11ff; 10:29. Gold and precious stones will be his in abundance.

Verse 25—Eliphaz exhorts Job to make God, not gold or silver, his treasure. Job vigorously responds to this charge in 31:24ff, though Eliphaz means that God's favor brings wealth. Dhorme is probably correct in claiming that "your gold," which is the plural of the word in verse 24a, is gold as it leaves the crucible, i.e., ingots of gold. The word rendered "precious" probably means "heaps of," i.e., a large amount of silver (see Brown, Driver, and Briggs).[11]

Verse 26—Eliphaz asserts that if Job will make God his treasure, then he will be able to lift up his head in confidence

---

[9] See Kittel "nomos," article, Vol. IV; J. D. Strauss, *Theology of Promise* (New Testament Theology Syllabus); R. N. Longenecker, *Paul, Apostle of Liberty* (Baker reprint, 1976), esp. chapter 4, pp. 86-105; J. Munck, *Paul and Salvation of Mankind* (John Knox Press, E. T., 1959); H. Ridderbos, *Pauline Theology* (Eerdmans, 1976); and W. D. Davies, *Paul and Rabbinic Judaism* (Harper Torch); and H. J. Schoeps, *Paul* (E. T., Westminster, 1961), esp. chapter 5, pp. 168ff.

[10] M. Dahood, *Biblica,* 1966, pp. 108ff.

[11] See this suggestion by W. F. Albright, *JBL*, 1944, p. 215, n. 47.

as in 10:15; 11:15; 27:10; Isa. 58:15; and "delight yourself"[12] in Ps. 37:4 in God alone. The metaphor of "face to face" implies the fact of reconciliation.

Verse 27—God's silence will be broken, and His presence will be restored to Job—Gen. 28:20ff and Ps. 66:13ff. If the prayer was answered, the one making the request would make a vow to sacrifice to God—Isa. 58:8-9.

Verse 28—If Job would return to God, the light of constant success would shine on his way. Instead of darkness, he would walk in light—19:8; 22:11. If Job "will decree a thing and it will stand for you" means that God will fulfill his purpose.

Verse 29—The righteous man (Heb. *saddiq*) has great influence with God—Gen. 18:21-33. Daniel, Noah, and Job were credited with great powers of influence—Ezek. 14:14, 20; but is emphatically rejected by Ezekiel 14:12ff; 18 and Jeremiah 31:29, 30. Here we see an early form of the Rabbinic concept of Zekut Abot, which gradually develops into the Roman Catholic theology of the merits of the saints.[13]

Verse 30—The Hebrew *'i naki* can be rendered as "island of the innocent" or "him that is not innocent"—as A. V. The first line then means that by the cleanness of Job's hands, the wicked shall be delivered—42:8; Gen. 18:27ff; and I Sam. 12:23.[14] The vicarious life and prayer is unquestionably set forth, though many commentaries attempt to remove the vicarious element.[15]

---

[12] G. R. Driver, *Vetus Testamentum,* III, 1955, 84.

[13] See R. Gordis, *Journal Near Eastern Studies,* 1945, pp. 54-55; and Strack-Billerbeck, *Kommentor Zum Neuen Testament,* Vol. I, 1922, 429ff on Matt. 6:19ff. The Rabbinic concept suggested that an ordinary Israelite could draw on the super-erogatory merits of the patriarchs; R. Gordis, "Corporate Personality in Job," *Journal Near Eastern Studies,* 1945, pp. 54ff; N. M. Sarna, "A Crux Interpretum in Job XXII, 30," *JNES,* 1956, pp. 118ff.

[14] M. Dahood, *Biblica,* 1968, p. 363; also J. K. Zink, "Uncleanness and Sin in Job 14:4 and Ps. 51:7," *Vetus Testamentum,* 1967, pp. 354-361.

[15] For how the negative in the first line and the rhetorical question in the second line, are explained, see C. Thexton, *Expository Times,* 1966-1967, pp. 342ff.

TODAY'S ENGLISH VERSION

The Third Dialogue
(22.1—27.23)

22

Eliphaz

[1-2] Is there any man, even the wisest,
   who could ever be of use to God?
[3] Does your doing right benefit God,
   or does your being good help him?
[4] It is not because you fear God
   that he reprimands you and brings you to trial.
[5] No, it's because you have sinned so much,
   and because of all the evil you do.
[6] To make your brother pay you the money he owed,
   you took away his clothes and left him nothing
      to wear.
[7] You refused water to those who were tired,
   and refused to feed those who were hungry.
[8] You used your power and your position
   to take over the whole land.
[9] You not only refused to help widows,
   but you also robbed and mistreated orphans.
[10] So now there are pitfalls all around you,
   and suddenly you are full of fear.
[11] It has grown so dark you cannot see,
   and a flood overwhelms you.

[12] Doesn't God live in the highest heavens
   and look down on the stars, even though they
      are high?
[13] And yet you ask, "What does God know?
   He is covered by clouds—how can he judge us?"
[14] You think the thick clouds keep him from seeing,
   as he walks on the boundary between earth

229

and sky.
15 Is your mind made up to walk in the paths
that evil men have always followed?
16 Even before their time had come,
a flood washed them away.
17 These are the men who rejected God
and believed that he could do nothing to them.
18 And yet it was God who made them prosperous—
I can't understand the thoughts of the wicked.
19 Good men are glad and innocent men laugh
when they see the wicked punished.
20 All that the wicked own is destroyed,
and fire burns up anything that is left.

21 Now, Job, make peace with God
and stop treating him like an enemy;
if you do, then he will bless you.
22 Accept the teaching he gives;
keep his words in your heart.
23 Yes, you must humbly return to God,
and put an end to all the evil
that is done in your house.
24 Throw away your gold;
dump your finest gold in the dry stream bed.
25 Let Almighty God be your gold
and let him be silver, piled high for you.
26 Then you will always trust in God
and find that he is the source of your joy.
27 When you pray, he will answer you,
and you will keep the vows you made.
28 You will succeed in all you do,
and light will shine on your path.
29 God brings down the proud
and saves the humble.
30 He will rescue you if you are innocent,
if what you do is right.

QUESTIONS FOR DISCUSSION 22:1-30

445. The third cycle of speeches begins in this chapter. Give the three lines of thought.
446. What is the essential issue in this speech of Eliphaz?
447. How does Eliphaz distort the entire relationship between God and man?
448. Can God receive anything from man? i.e., that God does not already have?
449. What is the assumption made by Eliphaz in verse four?
450. There are two words used for sin in verse five. What are they and how are they used?
451. How could Eliphaz be so specific with his charges against Job?
452. The list of sins is somewhat standard. Explain. It is also serious.
453. Job is described as a land-grabber and a man of "lifted face." What is meant?
454. Job is in a trap. What does this prove?
455. Explain in your own words the meaning of verse 11.
456. How is the transcendence of God used in verse 12? i.e., by Eliphaz.
457. Job's theology is distorted by Eliphaz. How so?
458. There seems to be a contradiction of who says what in in verse 14. Who is speaking? What is the point?
459. Job is walking in a way that brought destruction—(according to Eliphaz) destruction upon whom? Cf. vss. 15, 16.
460. Show how 21:1b is distorted by Eliphaz.
461. Would it ever be right for the righteous to rejoice over the destruction of the wicked?
462. What is the recommendation in verse 21?
463. The only occurrence of the word Torah is in verse 22. What is meant by its use here?
464. What is Eliphaz saying about gold in verse 24?
465. If Job will make God his gold what will happen?
466. What is meant by the expression "delight thyself in the Almighty"?

B. JOB'S PERSISTENT DESIRE OR VALUE OF ARGU-
   ING WITH GOD? (23:1—24:25)
   1. Job has honored God and obeyed his word, but God
      will not give him a hearing; He intentionally avoids
      him. (23:1-17)

TEXT 23:1-17

23 Then Job answered and said,
  2 Even to-day is my complaint rebellious:
  My stroke is heavier than my groaning.
  3 Oh that I knew where I might find him!
  That I might come even to his seat!
  4 I would set my cause in order before him,
  And fill my mouth with arguments.
  5 I would know the words which he would answer me,
  And understand what he would say unto me.
  6 Would he contend with me in the greatness of his power?
  Nay; but he would give heed unto me.
  7 There the upright might reason with him;
  So should I be delivered for ever from my judge.
  8 Behold, I go forward, but he is not *there;*
  And backward, but I cannot perceive him;
  9 On the left hand, when he doth work, but I cannot behold
  him;
  He hideth himself on the right hand, that I cannot see him.
  10 But he knoweth the way that I take;
  When he hath tried me, I shall come forth as gold.
  11 My foot hath held fast to his steps;
  His way have I kept, and turned not aside.
  12 I have not gone back from the commandment of his lips;
  I have treasured up the words of his mouth more than my
  necessary food.
  13 But he is in one *mind,* and who can turn him?
  And what his soul desireth, even that he doeth.
  14 For he performeth that which is appointed for me:
  And many such things are with him.

15 Therefore am I terrified at his presence;
   When I consider, I am afraid of him.
16 For God hath made my heart faint,
   And the Almighty hath terrified me;
17 Because I was not cut off before the darkness,
   Neither did he cover the thick darkness from my face.

COMMENT 23:1-17

Verse 1—This begins Job's seventh response. As Chapter 21 was entirely polemical, chapter 23 is completely devoted to Job's internal reflections and his search for God. There is no reference, except in verses 11-12, to his consolers or their doctrines. This speech is profoundly mournful. Now, suddenly, Job begins to dwell on God's remoteness and inaccessibility. God still has not broken His silence. Job's dark night of the soul haunts him oppressively, and God's absence is tormenting his soul, as the soul of one who loves and formerly knew God face to face.[1] His reply to Eliphaz falls into four sections: (1) Job's longing to meet God—verses 2-7; (2) The power and inaccessibility of God—verses 8-17; (3) Silence of God in the face of human oppression and injustice—verses 24:1-17; (4) Problem about continuity of verses 18-25. These verses do not appear to come from Job as they rather express the sentiments of his friends concerning the wicked.

The substance of Job's reply to Eliphaz is that his observation of the human situation provides no unchallengeable assurance of the moral structure of the universe.[2] Is it possible that we live in an amoral world? Are moral values nothing more than cultural mores, changing standards of social peer groups?

The friends have charged Job with impious rebellion against God's standards of morality. He responds—"Even or still

---

[1] For discussion of Job's "mystical theology," see *Vie spirituelle,* 1956, pp. 372-391.

[2] Same thesis presented by R. L. Rubenstein, "Job and Auschwitz," *Union Seminary Quarterly,* 1969, pp. 421-437; see also his *After Auschwitz,* Bobbs-Merrill, pb., 1966.

today my complaint is rebellious . . ." So Job declares that he will continue to be a rebel in their eyes. The "even or still" implies that the debate has been going on for some time. "My stroke" should read "his[3] hand is heavy (no justification for "heavier" in A. V.) in spite of my groaning." Job has no scruples against making the charge directly against God.

Verse 3—Even though God suppresses Job, he desires to see Him—9:34ff; 13:3. Strahan correctly observes that a major distinction between Job and his friends is that he desires to see God; they do not. Job aspires to appear before God's dwelling place, His judgment seat.

Verse 4—Once more the courtroom scene is evoked— 9:13-21. But Job is no longer afraid that God would refuse to hear him or continue His agonizing silence—13:18a. He would prepare his case and present it to God.

Verse 5—Job merely wishes to hear God's charges against him. The divine indictment Job would accept, but not the wrathful innuendoes of his three consolers.

Verse 6—He is confident that God would give him a fair hearing and ultimately a vindication. God's power would give way (yasin—give heed to) to His just consolation. Tur Sinai has shown that here koah means legal power and that rab-koah means power of attorney.[4]

Verse 7—The verse is an echo of 13:16. The emphasis is upon "upright." If he could get an audience with God, he would be vindicated (preserve my rights) as a righteous man. There is a powerful image set forth in this verse. The verb here is used in 21:10b of a cow giving birth. The image is that of justice emerging successfully as from a womb. In Hab. 1:4 this idiom is employed to convey the distortion of justice, or

---

[3] The Hebrew suffixes which represent "my" and "his" have only slight variation in form. Following LXX, Dahood, and Bloomerde, we take the text as third masculine suffix.

[4] See his imaginative commentary, Tur Sinai (N. H. Torczyner) *The Book of Job*, rev., ed., 1969, Kirjath Sepher on this verse; see also the excellent analysis in G. Many, *Der Rechtsstreit mit Gott (rib) im Hiobbuch*, (Diss. München, 1970), see *Elenchus bibliographicus*, 1972, p. 144, for full notation.

its unsuccessful delivery.

Verse 8—His hope for encountering God is shattered. He goes forward (Heb. *qedem*—east, west—all directions—Isa. 9:11) seeking God, but He is elusive. In contrast, the Psalmist (139:7ff) declares that God is everywhere.

Verse 9—The Hebrew text says "when he works" as A. V., but this hardly makes sense. Even the grammatical difficulties do not hide the meaning of the verse, which might be rendered "When I turn to the left I do not see Him." This translation would fit the parallelism of the second line very nicely—Pss. 64:14; 73:6; 139:7-10.

Verse 10—There are two possible understandings of the verse: (1) God eludes Job's search because He always knows where Job is going; or (2) In spite of God's unavailability to Job, he knows that God is still watching over him. When God has completely tested Job, He will discover no dross in him, only pure gold—Ps. 139:1-6 and Jer. 11:20. Dahood suggests that the verb translated "come forth" actually means "shine"—with reference to the shining surface of the crucible, after the dross is removed.

Verse 11—Job's assurance is grounded in his conviction that he has always walked in God's way. His integrity is matched only by his loyalty to God—Ps. 17:5. This verse is a denial of 22:6-9.

Verse 12—Eliphaz has exhorted Job—22:22—to receive instruction from his mouth, and lay up His words in his heart. Job responds to this exhortation by asserting that he has always lived in that manner. The A. V. expands the Hebrew text in translating "more than my necessary food," but for this theme see Ps. 119:11. Job's possible Israelite (patriarchal) background is suggested by his use of the word *miswah* for "In my bosom I treasured the words of his mouth."[5]

Verse 13—The first line in the A. V. incorrectly translates the text (adds mind), which literally says "He is in one" meaning

---

[5] For a defense of this translation, see M. Dahood, *Biblica,* 1967, p. 427.

that God freely chooses His own course, and His power is irresistible. The parallelism all but confirms the necessary emendation (change from *b'hd* to *bhr*). In Ps. 132:13 the same two verbs—*wish* and *choose*—occur in parallel structure.

Verse 14—God's decrees are unchangeable—Isa. 45:23; 55:10-11. He will execute "my sentence."[6] This does not imply any Calvinistic fatalism. The last line is ambiguous; it is not certain whether God has more suffering reserved for him or others or both.

Verse 15—When he thinks of God's mysterious ways with men, he is terrified once more—21:6.

Verse 16—The emphatic words in the text are God and Almighty. The verb translated "made . . . faint" means to "be tender." It is used in parallel with fear in Deut. 20:3; Isa. 7:4; Jer. 51:46; in this verse it is in parallel with a strong word meaning "overwhelms." Contemplating all of his misery, Job's "heart" fills him with horror.

Verse 17—There is a difficulty in the verse because of the presence of the negative (*lo*). The Hebrew text reads in part of line one "I was not annihilated because of darkness." The word rendered "cut off" can mean "be silent"; thus Dhorme translates "I was not silent because of darkness."[7] Both make sense and describe how Job actually responded to the darkness of God's silence. In bondage to fear and darkness, Job is reduced to utter despondency. What disturbs Job more than his misery is the thought that God has decreed it.

---

[6] M. Dahood, *Orientalia*, 1963, p. 499; followed by Blommerde, *Northwest Semitic Grammar and Job.*

[7] Dhorme, *Job*, p. 352.

TODAY'S ENGLISH VERSION

23
Job

¹⁻² I still rebel and complain against God;
    I cannot keep from groaning.
³ How I wish I knew where to find him,
    and knew how to go where he is.
⁴ I would state my case before him,
    and present all the arguments in my favor.
⁵ I want to know what he would say,
    and how he would answer me.
⁶ Would God use all his strength against me?
    No, he would listen as I spoke.
⁷ I am honest; I could reason with God;
    he would declare me innocent once and for all.

⁸ I have searched in the East, but God is not there;
    and I have not found him when I searched in
        the West.
⁹ God has been at work in the North,
    and he has traveled to the South,
    but still I have not seen him.
¹⁰ Yet God knows every step I take;
    if he tests me he will find me pure.
¹¹ I follow faithfully the road he chooses,
    and I never wander to either side.
¹² I always do what God commands;
    I follow his will, not my own desires.

¹³ He never changes. No one can oppose him,
    or keep him from doing what he wants to do.
¹⁴ He will fulfill what he has planned for me;
    that plan is only one of the many he has,
¹⁵   and I tremble with fear before him.
¹⁶⁻¹⁷ Almighty God has destroyed my courage.
    It is God, not the darkness, that makes me afraid—
    even though the dark blinds my eyes.

QUESTIONS FOR DISCUSSION 23:1-17

467. This chapter is completely devoted to what subject?
468. Do we live in a moral or amoral world? Prove your answer.
469. Do we, like Job, tend to judge the whole world by the activities of our little world? Discuss.
470. There is a major distinction between Job and his friends, as suggested in verse three. What is it?
471. A courtroom scene is suggested in verse four. Cf. 9:13-21 and 13:18a. What is to be tried?
472. Job is confident of the outcome of a trial before God. What could it be?
473. There is a powerful verb image used in verse seven. What is it?
474. Isn't it a futile effort to look for God in geographical areas? Or is this the meaning of verses eight and nine? Discuss.
475. What are the two possible meanings to verse ten? Which do you prefer? Why?
476. Show how verse 11 is a denial of 22:6-9.
477. Job really loved the words of God. How does he indicate this?
478. Why use the description of God as found in verse 13? What is the point?
479. Is fatalism suggested in verse 14? Discuss the meaning.
480. What kind of fear or terror is right and what kind is wrong. Discuss.
481. What are the emphatic words in verse 16? What is meant?
482. There is darkness. What is it as suggested in verse 17?

2. Many other cases of unequal treatment show
   God's unconcern. (24:1-25)
   a. The wicked and their victims (24:1-12)

TEXT 24:1-12

24 Why are times not laid up by the Almighty?
And why do not they that know him see his days?
2 There are that remove the landmarks;
They violently take away flocks, and feed them.
3 They drive away the ass of the fatherless;
They take the widow's ox for a pledge.
4 They turn the needy out of the way:
The poor of the earth all hide themselves.
5 Behold, as wild asses in the desert
They go forth to their work seeking diligently for food;
The wilderness *yieldeth* them bread for their children.
6 They cut their provender in the field;
And they glean the vintage of the wicked.
7 They lie all night naked without clothing,
And have no covering in the cold.
8 They are wet with the showers of the mountains,
And embrace the rock for want of a shelter.
9 There are that pluck the fatherless from the breast,
And take a pledge of the poor;
10 *So that* they go about naked without clothing,
And being hungry they carry the sheaves.
11 They make oil within the walls of these men;
They tread *their* winepresses, and suffer thirst.
12 From out of the populous city men groan,
And the soul of the wounded crieth out:
Yet God regardeth not the folly.

COMMENT 24:1-12

Verse 1—Job's reply continues. As in chapter 21, he moves
from his specific experience to man's experience in general.

239

He describes the oppression of wicked, unscrupulous princes and the resultant misery of the poor enslaved by the burdens engendered by poverty. This section of Job's speech is a negative parallel to 21:7-17. There God did not punish the impious; here He does not recover the poor from oppression. These two emphases are fundamental in the Old Testament doctrine of God, i.e., that He will judge the wicked and liberate the oppressed. Where is the evidence for God's righteous providence in His dealings with man? Job here reflects upon the cosmic dimensions of human misery. Why are "the times" of judgment (not in the text—added in R. S. V.) for wicked not evident?—18:21; Ps. 36:11.

Verse 2—The LXX adds the subject, "the wicked," to line one and renders as "the wicked remove the landmarks." The Law strictly condemns such action—Deut. 19:14; Prov. 22:28; 23:10; and Hos. 5:10. The powerful wicked not only remove the boundary stones but also seize the flocks of their weaker neighbors, and openly pasture them on stolen land. The images here are crystal clear; the powerful aggressively dispossess the weak, and nothing is done about it. Does God know about this? Does He have any compassion at all?

Verse 3—The defenseless orphans and widows are reduced to abject poverty. Members of these classes had only one animal, and thus they would be rendered without any means of support after their ass or ox was plundered. The wicked publicly flaunt the helpless. Even the Babylonians imposed fines on a person who takes the ox of one in distress (*The Code of Hammurabi,* No. 241)—II Sam. 12:4; Deut. 24:17; and Ex. 22:26. All pledges from the poor were to be returned if they were necessary for livelihood. Job asks God what He does about the behavior of such calloused men. Their heinous crimes against the poor must be judged if we dwell in a moral universe.

Verse 4—The poor are deprived of their rights—Amos 4:1. The poor, once deprived, have no place to turn. This is suggested in the Hebrew text as it has "are hidden together." The normal sense of the reflective form means that they hide themselves, which makes perfectly good sense here.

Verse 5—Hopelessly oppressed, the poor have been destroyed by extortion and diabolical degradation. Even Plato in his *Laws* and *The Republic* held that only the elite minority had a claim to human rights and privileges. Our own American history has its own record of depriving thousands, sometimes millions, of their rights, originally from God as beings in His image.

Verse 6—The poor subsist on the type of food used to feed animals. What "a precious livelihood." They gather their fodder (A. V. provender), and the shift from plural to singular means each one gathers his own. The A. V. renders an uncertain word "glean." Gleaning was an authorized occupation of the poor. If the "reaping" found in line one is that of a hired laborer, then the parallel would necessitate that the gathering of grapes would be done by those being paid for the work. Often, the rich are adjudged to be wicked, and sometimes they are!

Verse 7—The abject poverty of those described in this verse leaves them without clothing in the cold night wind. Misery begets misery—no food, no clothing, no shelter from the cold. Here Job starkly contrasts the poor and the wicked rich—verses 2-4. Job's agonizing description continues; his heartbreaking picture of human privation versus privilege is further enlarged.

Verse 8—The poor embrace the rocks in the mountains since they have no other shelter. They cling (Gen. 29:13) to the security afforded by the rocks. Hardly a more devastating picture could be sketched to reveal their exposure and wretchedness. Their dearest friends are the rocks.

Verse 9—In transition, the imagery takes us from one exploited group to another. The verse presents a problem to many commentators (egs. Kissane, Gray, Dhorme, Pope, *et al*), but does it necessarily interrupt the account of the poor as is alleged? Job has thus far described the meagre possession of the poor, the humiliating circumstances under which scavengers reek out a minimal subsistence. We have toured the

241

cities and the desert places; now we must face those in slavery. Those harsh taskmasters are heartless creditors and take a pledge from off of the poor. The Hebrew means to take something that is on the poor, i.e., their clothing, not merely something from the poor. The first line relates a cruel tyrant removing a baby from his mother's breast while she is being sold at auction. The parallel line suggests taking the clothes from their back (see Brown, Driver, Briggs).

Verse 10—This verse confirms the need to modify the weak A. V. translation and also verifies that their clothes have been removed as pledge, in that they are here described as naked. They are starving and yet must carry the sheaves of their masters.[1] Even animals were not treated like these outcasts—Deut. 25:4. In Israel one could not muzzle an ox when it treads out the grain. Here a laborer is hungry while working in the midst of abundance. How torturing it would be to carry food, which one could not eat, when one is starving. The "haves" and the "have nots" are still with us. Though there are "have nots" in our own midst, the *Third* and *Fourth Worlds* are largely composed of the poor,[2] and with Job our contemporary we must ask why it occurs and how can we do anything about it?

Verse 11—The Hebrew text can be rendered "between their rows"—(as R. S. V.), i.e., "among the olive rows of the wicked they make oil." Dhorme rightly points out that this would be a strange place to press olives, and thus emends the text to read "between the millstones." In sight of mouth-watering succulent grapes, they are panting with thirst.

Verse 12—In verses 12-16 Job focuses attention on violators of the Sixth, Seventh, and Eighth commandments, i.e., murderers, adulterers, and thieves, who compose "the city of men." From the city men cry out because of violence and social

---

[1] E. F. Sutcliffe, *Journal Theological Studies,* 1969, p. 174.

[2] This presents an enormous challenge to our Christian conscience. Neo-Marxism and various species of socialism are presently being set forth with Messianic vengeance, as though the world's problems are all caused by hedonistic capitalism. The problem is human nature, not per se our socio-politico structures. Socialism has one consistency—failure.

anomie.[3] Men cry out, but God pays no attention (same idiom in 23:6) to the moral malaise. The Hebrew term rendered "folly" in A. V. means tastelessness—1:22—or unseasoned and implies a lack of moral savor; yet God remains silent.

b. The lovers of darkness (24:13-17)

TEXT 24:13-17

13 **These are of them that rebel against the light;**
   They know not the ways thereof,
   Nor abide in the paths thereof.
14 **The murderer riseth with the light;**
   He killeth the poor and needy;
   And in the night he is as a thief.

---

[3] All Christian believers must come to an understanding of this phenomenon. Since Hegel, western social theory has had no room for God's purpose as a solution to our concrete problems of violence and social anomie. Nineteenth century social thought developed from Hegel to Marx by way of Weber, Mannheim, and Durkheim, into *The Sociology of Knowledge Thesis* (see the critique in my previous work, *Newness on The Earth,* pp. 44ff) and this socially based theory of knowledge will be critically evaluated in my doctoral thesis: *The Kuhn-Popper Debate - Contemporary Revolution in Knowledge Paradigms: The Relationship of Scientific Theory to Scientific Progress.* From Marx's "creative destruction" to views of contemporary modification of classical Marxism, the neo-Marxist based *Frankfort School of Social Research* utilizes the Freudian psychoanalytic method as a basis of a new epistemology grounded in "Interest." Every creative development in 19th-20th century *Social Theory* makes fundamental contribution to contemporary *Violence and Anomie.* All forms of Politico-Revolutionary-Liberation Theologies (e.g., Frankfort School of Social Research - represented by Horkheimer, Adorno, Marcuse, et. al.) must be understood and confronted in the name of Job's redeemer.

See the following works for initial analysis and confrontation with these issues:

Georges Soul Classic, *Concerning Violence,* many editions.

Hanah Arendt, *On Violence* (Penguin paperback, 1970).

John C. Bennett, ed., *Christian Social Ethics in a Changing World* (NY: Association Press, 1966).

Jacques Ellul, *Violence* (Seabury, E. T., 1969). Also, *Political Illusion,* Knopf, 1967.

Oz Guinness, *The Dust of Death* (Inter-Varsity Press, 1973, chp. 5 "Violence: Crisis or Catharsis?," pp. 151-191.

Karl Popper, *Conjectures and Refutations* (NY: Basic Books, 1963) chp. "Utopia and Violence"; also his *The Open Society and Its Enemies* (2 vols., Harper Torch).

15 The eye also of the adulterer waiteth for the twilight,
   Saying, No eye shall see me:
   And he disguiseth his face.
16 In the dark they dig through houses:
   They shut themselves up in the day-time;
   They know not the light.
17 For the morning is to all of them as thick darkness;
   For they know the terrors of the thick darkness.

COMMENT 24:13-17

Verse 13—Why do these wicked people escape divine retribution? Earlier he describes those who steal because of the circumstances of their poverty; but here Job describes those who are dominated by a wicked heart. The sin described here is more than an act of unrighteousness; it is that the sinner does not abide in the light of God's moral universe.

Verse 14—The first violator of the light is the murderer. The destitute condition of the social structure in which one finds this kind of rebel is clear from the type of persons they prey on. Why the needy and poor; why not more profitable prey? Job is not describing the affluent part of society. The same type of person kills in the daylight and steals in the darkness of the night—verse 16.

Verse 15—As the prostitute seeks the double protection of disguise and darkness—Prov. 7:9—here the adulterer also seeks the hiding power of darkness. These violators of light seek only to perform transgressions in secret—Ruth 3:14.

Verse 16—Generally a thief would gain entrance by digging through the wall of the house (Ex. 22:1), not an adulterer— Matt. 6:19. The first verb "he digs" is in the singular; but the second verb is in the plural, "they shut themselves up." The reference in the plural refers to all three groups who commit their dark deeds hiding from the day. The verb here means "to set a seal upon" night and suggests that the thief had marked the house that he would enter come nightfall. But more probably, the seal identifies the person. The purpose of the seal is to keep unauthorized persons from "opening" or "identifying" something. The image conveys a search for security. Perhaps Job is saying that these criminals are as secure as if they were "sealed." God does nothing about their malignant evil deeds. None (they) of the groups discussed know the light. All wicked people hide from the light because it terrorizes them—Ezek. 8:8; 12:5, 7. In the *Code of Hammurabi,* digging is the thief's mode of entry (No. 21).

Verse 17—Just as ordinary people fear the darkness of the night, the wicked dread the day light. This is every man's long day's journey into night.

c. The unhappy fate of the wicked (24:18-25)

TEXT 24:18-25

18   Swiftly they *pass away* **upon the face of the waters;**
     Their portion is cursed in the earth:
     They turn not into the way of the vineyards.
19 **Drought and heat consume the snow waters:**
     So doth **Sheol** *those that* **have sinned.**
20 **The womb shall forget him;**
     The worm shall feed sweetly on him;
     He shall be no more remembered;
     And unrighteousness shall be broken as a tree.
21 **He devoureth the barren that beareth not,**
     And doeth not good to the widow.
22 **Yet** *God* **preserveth the mighty by his power:**
     He riseth up that hath no assurance of life.
23 *God* **giveth them to be in security, and they rest thereon;**
     And his eyes are upon their ways.
24 **They are exalted; yet a little while, and they are gone;**
     Yea, they are brought low, they are taken out of the way
        as all others.
     And are cut off as the tops of the ears of grain.

245

25 And if it be not so now, who will prove me a liar,
   And make my speech nothing worth?

COMMENT 24:18-25

Verse 18—It must be acknowledged that these verses (18-24) are problematic. They probably express the viewpoint of his friends, rather than Job.[4] After his description in verses 2-17 of the oppressions which are inflicted upon the poor, the question arises: What is the fate of the evil-doers?—8:4. Are they protected in their wicked life style? It is possible to understand verses 18:24, as do Davidson and Driver, as the common attitude introduced by Jobian irony? The singular pronoun "he" represents a member of the class expressed by the plural "their." The wicked person is carried along hopelessly by the flood—20:28; Hos. 10:17. They derive no happiness from their estates (A. V. their portions); because they are cursed, they are also unfruitful. They know that their vineyards are unfruitful and do not visit them, because there are no grapes to tread. It is not self-evident that these images are at variance with Job's theology, as Rowley *et al* contend.

Verse 19—The heat is so intense that snow water is dried up. The verb rendered "consume" means to seize violently or tear away (see Brown, Driver, Briggs); as the snow dissolves in the intense heat, so does the wicked in Sheol. Job uses the same image in 6:15ff of those who have abandoned him.

Verse 20—The wicked man is even forgotten by his own mother's womb (*rehem*). Only the worms who are eating his body find pleasure in him. Wickedness will ultimately be broken to pieces as a tree—19:10.

---

[4] The R.S.V. represents verses 18-21 as Job's citation of the views of his three friends, and verses 22-24 as his reply; but there is no indication of this in the text. Dhorme transfers them to Zophar's third speech, following 27:13, so Terrien in *Interpreter's Bible, Job,* pp. 1088-1089; Pope transposes the verses 18-20, 22-25 to 27:23, *Job,* p. 179.

Verse 21—The images refer to the ungodly who exploit and mercilessly oppress the poor women without sons. Swift retribution shall be his reward—verse 24.

Verse 22—The metaphor used in the A. V. presents a powerful God using His might to destroy the confidence of the wicked. The ambiguity of the grammar raises the question of whether or not it is who rises in condemnation or the ungodly who rises in health (note "he draws," "he rises" probably with God as subject). Either is possible from the Hebrew text—Deut. 28:66.

Verse 23—Job seems to be bitterly claiming that God watches over the wicked so that their path is secure.

Verse 24—The wicked are, in the midst of their exaltation, cut off like flowers or heads of grain before the reaping knife—Ps. 103:15ff; and as all others, they fade and wither. This is his description of the fate of the wicked.

Verse 25—Many critics suggest that it is with this verse that we return to Job's words. The conclusion of Job's speech may refer especially to 24:2-12. This bitter indictment of God's injustice is Job's final words in this speech. Life is pictured in all its ugly anomalies which might be evidence for an amoral universe. He concludes, If I am mistaken about my description of the actual state of affairs, you may call me a liar and my words empty, as you have previously charged. Now to Bildad's third speech.

TODAY'S ENGLISH VERSION

24 Why doesn't God set a time for judging,
a day of justice for those who serve him?

² Men move boundary markers to get more land;
they steal sheep and put them with their own
flocks.
³ They steal donkeys that belong to orphans,
and keep a widow's ox till she pays her debts.

⁴ They keep the poor from getting their rights
and force the needy to run and hide.

⁵ So the poor, like wild donkeys,
search for food in the dry wilderness;
nowhere else can they find food for their children.
⁶ They have to harvest fields they don't own,
and gather grapes in wicked men's vineyards.
⁷ At night they sleep with nothing to cover them,
nothing to keep them from the cold.
⁸ They are drenched by the rain that falls on the
mountains,
and they huddle beside the rocks for shelter.

⁹ Evil men make slaves of fatherless infants,
and take the poor man's children in payment
for debts.
¹⁰ But the poor must go out with no clothes to protect
them;
they must go hungry while harvesting wheat.
¹¹ They press olives for oil, and grapes for wine,
but they themselves are thirsty.
¹² In the city you hear the cries of the wounded and
dying,
but God ignores their prayers.

¹³ There are men who reject the light;
they don't understand it and avoid its paths.
¹⁴ At dawn the murderer goes out to kill the poor,
and at night he robs.
¹⁵ The adulterer waits for twilight to come
and hides his face so no one can see him.
¹⁶ At night thieves break into houses,
but by day they hide and avoid the light.
¹⁷ They fear the light of day,
but darkness holds no terror for them.

[*Zophar*]
¹⁸ The wicked man is swept away by floods,

and the land he owns is under God's curse;
   he no longer goes to work in his vineyards.
¹⁹ As snow vanishes in heat and drought,
   so a sinner vanishes from the land of the living.
²⁰ No one remembers him, not even his mother;
   worms eat him; he is completely destroyed.
²¹ This happens because he mistreated widows
   and showed no kindness to childless women.
²² God, in his strength, destroys the mighty;
   he acts and the wicked man dies.
²³ God may let him live secure,
   but keeps an eye on him all the time.
²⁴ For a while the wicked man succeeds
   but then he withers like a weed,
   like a stalk of grain that has been cut down.
²⁵ Can anyone deny that this is so?
   Can anyone prove that my words are not true?

QUESTIONS FOR DISCUSSION 24:1-25

483. Name and discuss the two emphases fundamental in the O.T. doctrine of God.
484. Does God know or care about the present day oppression of the poor? Discuss.
485. Pure religion (Jas. 1:26, 27) has a real part of the discussion of verse three. Explain.
486. Why do the poor of the earth hide themselves? Cf. vs. 4.
487. How have we in America been guilty of the sin of verse five? Discuss.
488. Some poor live no better than animals. How so? Cf. vs. 6.
489. Why are the poor naked and cold? Who is at fault?
490. What is meant by embracing the rocks as in verse eight?
491. What is the imagery of verse nine; i.e., where does such a cruel act take place?

492. The poor are treated worse than animals in the kind of work given to them. Discuss.
493. What work is discussed in verse 11? What is the point?
494. What commandments are broken as discussed in verses 12-16?
495. Please give your own explanation of the problem of suffering of the poor.
496. Why do wicked people escape divine retribution? What type of stealing is here described?
497. Why steal and kill the poor and needy? Discuss the circumstances.
498. Why are darkness and secret action always associated with wrong doing?
499. Who is digging to get into a house? For what purpose?
500. How does the term "seal" relate?
501. What is "every man's long day's journey into night"?
502. Who speaks in verses 18-24? Discuss.
503. What will happen to the wicked? Discuss.
504. Snow water is compared to whom in verse 19?
505. In what sense will the womb of the wicked forget him?
506. Who is "raised up" in verse 22?
507. Who is speaking in verse 25? For what purpose?

From Today's English Version of the Old Testament, Copyright, American Bible Society, 1971

C. MAN—A LITTLE LOWER THAN THE ANGELS
(25:1-6)
1. Man cannot argue with God. (25:1-4)

TEXT 25:1-4

25 **Then answered Bildad the Shuhite, and said,**
2 Dominion and fear are with him;
He maketh peace in his high places.
3 Is there any number of his armies?
And upon whom doth not his light arise?
4 How then can man be just with God?
Or how can he be clean that is born of a woman?

COMMENT 25:1-4

Verse 1—As with the preceding chapter 24, there are a considerable number of textual problems in the following three chapters.[1] The chapters 25-27 contain the third speech of Bildad, the eighth response of Job, and the third speech of Zophar. One cannot but be struck by the brevity of Bildad's speech. He fails miserably in responding to Job. Let the facts of history stand, but the spirit with which Bildad sets them forth must be forever false.

Verse 2—God alone is Lord, the omnipotent Creator of the universe. His magnificence inspires awe. Perhaps the imagery in line two stems from His reordering the chaos among the heavenly beings—21:22; 40:9ff; and Isa. 24:21. The peace comes in the form of retribution—Dan. 10:13, 20ff and Rev. 12:7-12. The Qumran Targum contains the more specific reference to God in line one—"dominion and grandeur are

---

[1] On the technical matters concerning the section of Job, see P. Dhorme, "Les chapitres XXV-XXVIII du Livre de Job," *Revue Biblique,* 1924, pp. 343-356; and R. Tournay, "L'ordre primitif des chapitres XXIV-XXVIII du Livre de Job," *Revue Biblique*, 1957, pp. 321-334.

with God."[2]

Verse 3—Bildad's thesis is that God's power is His purity—4:17; 15:14. The symbolism here expresses the universal beneficent rule of God. His light emanates and illuminates the entire creation. Nothing is concealed from God's sight.

Verse 4—The argument of Eliphaz in 4:17 and 15:14-16 is repeated in verses 4-6. In comparison to God who can presume to be righteous? No human can be faultless—Eccl. 7:20. The verse has no reference to what classical protestant and Catholic theology has called "original sin."

2. Man is not pure before God. (25:5, 6)

TEXT 25:5, 6

5 Behold, even the moon hath no brightness,
  And the stars are not pure in his sight:
6 How much less man, that is a worm!
  And the son of man, that is a worm!

COMMENT 25:5, 6

Verse 5—Eliphaz had contrasted men and angels—15:15; now Bildad contrasts men and the brightness of the moon and stars. In contrast to God's radiance, all creation pales into darkness. What then is man—a little lower than the angels! In this verse physical light is contrasted with ethical light or righteousness—Ps. 8:3-4 and Eccl. 7:20.
Verse 6—To Bildad, the smallness of man is symbolic of his worthlessness. In the text the first word suggests "decay" and the second "abasement." No man should have the brashness to assert his innocence before God. Certainly no "worm"

---

[2] J. P. M. van der Ploeg and A. S. van Der Woude, trans. and eds., *Targum De Job* (Brill, Leiden, 1971), on this verse.

should argue with God about his integrity or seek self-vindi-
cation. Man is only fit to be compared to a maggot—7:5;
17:14; 21:26—or to a worm—Ps. 22:6; Isa. 14:11; 41:14.
Bildad not only repeats arguments first uttered by his friends;
he introduces a Jobian vocabulary seeking to ensnare Job in
his own words. Bildad, like Eliphaz, is a forerunner of Islamic
Monotheism, which ignores the facts of good and evil, the
nature of God beyond power, and Job's moral integrity before
his holy God.

TODAY'S ENGLISH VERSION

25

Bildad

1-2 God is powerful; all must fear him;
    he keeps his heavenly kingdom in peace.
   3 Can anyone count the angels who serve him?
    Is there any place where God's light does not shine?
   4 Can anyone be righteous or pure in God's eyes?
   5 In his eyes even the moon is not bright,
    or the stars pure.
   6 Then what about man, that worm, that insect?
    What is man worth in God's eyes?

QUESTIONS FOR DISCUSSION 25:1-6

508. What are the textual problems in chapters 25-27?
509. What could be suggested in the imagery of verse two?
     Cf. 21:22; 40:9ff; Isa. 24:21.
510. What is Bildad's thesis? What is wrong with it?
511. Is original sin taught in verse four? Discuss.
512. What is the point of verse five?
513. Is man a worm? Discuss.

D. GREATNESS AND GOODNESS OF GOD (26:1-14)
1. What a giant of comfort Bildad has been! (sarcasm) (26:1-4)

TEXT 26:1-4

26 **Then Job answered and said,**
2 How hast thou helped him that is without power!
How hast thou saved the arm that hath no strength!
3 How hast thou counselled him that hath no wisdom,
And plentifully declared sound knowledge!
4 To whom hast thou uttered words?
And whose spirit came forth from thee?

COMMENT 26:1-4

Verse 1—As the text stands, from chapter 26 to 31, we have Job's final response to his critics. The beautiful symmetry of the cycles of speeches seems to be broken when Zophar does not respond in the final stage of the debate. But that is only a literary consideration. We are left with baffling obscurities when we attempt to follow the continuity between the transitions. Nevertheless, the irony in the speech seems to fit better in Job's response, as he has delivered himself on the theme before—13:12; 16:2; 19:2, 21. His sarcastic self-assurance leaps forth from every word, far from confessing his own moral malaise; he taunts his friends for failing to bring him God's consolation. Despite many textual enigmas, we encounter some of the loftiest insights ever vouched safe to a tortured human spirit concerning the greatness and grandeur of God. Job will eventually cry out in resignation—"Can a man by searching find out God?" He responds with a resounding No!

Verse 2—In an almost violent burst of sarcasm, Job responds to the irrelevance of Bildad's speech. The speech is composed of two parts: (1) Job's confrontation with Bildad, 26:2-4; and (2) Job's unmodifiable protestation of innocence, the extent

254

of which is one of the technical problems which shall be passed in this commentary.[1]

There is no legitimate reason to assume that because "you" is singular this implies that Bildad or Zophar is addressing Job. Job has not been giving them counsel, and counsel before his calamity seems pointless. For the sarcasm in Job's speeches, see 4:3-4; 6:25; 12:2; 13:1ff; and 16:2ff. Elsewhere Job addresses his friends in the plural, except in 12:7ff; 16:3; and 21:3. Since Bildad's speech was dominated by God as all powerful, it is most likely that Job is asking what consolation he has brought to him in his hours of despair. Bildad's cold comfort reveals little concern or compassion in bringing consolation to this cosmic contender.

Verse 3—As short as Bildad's speech was, it was the bearer of abundant (Heb. rendered "plentifully declared" in A. V.) wisdom in only five verses. His speech was packed with superabundant wisdom explaining why one wicked man dies at the peak of his life without disease or despair, who has all along been robbing, murdering, and committing adultery, while another wicked man dies enslaved and embittered of spirit. Explain that, Bildad, if you are so wise.

Verse 4—Though the Hebrew can be translated either as "To whom" (in A. V.) or "with whose help," the latter is perhaps to be preferred. Thus, Job is saying that he is as wise and informed as they are—12:3; 13:2—and who are they to give him instruction on the sovereignty of God and that awe is the only appropriate human response. The word rendered spirit is *neshamah* and is translated as the "lamp of the Lord" in Prov. 20:27. Job is ironically asking, Is the source of your wisdom, revelation, and illumination God? In essence he is saying as Rashi has suggested, "Who does not know this?" Job's friends have often claimed that they were speaking of God—15:11; 20:2; 22:22.

---

[1] Compare analysis in the various critical Old Testament introduction, egs. Young, Harrison, Pfeiffer, and especially Otto Eissfeldt, *The Old Testament, An Introduction* (Harper & Row, E.T., 1965), pp. 454-470. Eissfeldt's introduction is controlled by *Formgeschichte* and*Redactiongeschichte* assumptions.

2. No mysteries are hidden from God. (26:5-14)
   (Some would attribute this section to Bildad.)
   a. There is no close connection between
      it and the preceding verses.

TEXT 26:5-14

5 They that are deceased tremble
  Beneath the waters and the inhabitants thereof.
6 Sheol is naked before *God,*
  And Abaddon hath no covering.
7 He stretcheth out the north over empty space,
  And hangeth the earth upon nothing.
8 He bindeth up the waters in his thick clouds;
  And the cloud is not rent under them.
9 He incloseth the face of his throne,
  And spreadeth his cloud upon it.
10 He hath described a boundary upon the face of the waters,
   Unto the confines of light and darkness.
11 The pillars of heaven tremble
   And are astonished at his rebuke.
12 He stirreth up the sea with his power,
   And by his understanding he smiteth through Rahab.
13 By his Spirit the heavens are garnished;
   His hand hath pierced the swift serpent.
14 Lo, these are but the outskirts of his ways:
   And how small a whisper do we hear of him!
   But the thunder of his power who can understand?

COMMENT 26:5-14

Verse 5—From verses 5-14 we have the theme of God's omnipotence set forth again. He is absolute authority over heaven and earth and Sheol (cf. Matt. 28:19, 20). Bildad has previously declared God's greatness; now Job declares his

256

own faith in the greatness of God. The dead[2] (A. V. renders "deceased"—$r^e pa'im$—Isa. 14:9; 26:14; Ps. 88:10) are still in God's control. They cannot hide from Him, even in Sheol—II Sam. 22:5 and Ps. 18:4. Even the inhabitants of Sheol tremble before God. The reference here, according to the parallelism, is to the inhabitants of Sheol, not fishes, etc.[3]

Verse 6—For this imagery see Ps. 89:8; Prov. 15:11; and Amos 9:2. Abaddon is another name for Sheol and is a perfect parallel in this verse. This parallel description of Sheol is found only in the *Wisdom Literature* Job 28:22; 31:12; Ps. 88:11; Prov. 15:11; and 27:20. Abaddon comes from a root meaning ruin or destruction and is a personal name translated as Apollyon in Rev. 9:11. No one and no place holds secrets from God.

Verse 7—The Hebrew word for north (*Sapon*) originally was the name of the mountain of Hadad or Baal, the Syrian weather-god. The Ras Shamra texts from Ugarit relate how Baal-Hadad constructed his temple on the heights of Mount Sapon. The mountain lay directly north of Palestine; thus we know why Sapon[4] means north in the Old Testament—Isa. 14:13. The parallel is between the "stretched out" heavens—Gen. 1-3—not "firmament" but that which is "stretched out" or pounded outward; Ps. 1—4:2; Isa. 40:22; 44:24; 45:12; Jer. 10:12; 51:15. There is no mythological implication in this description which transcends all primitive concepts of cosmography. Nor need we recall the great advancements made in astronomy among the Babylonians, Egyptians, and Greeks, especially Pythagoras—ca 540-510 B.C.—in order to understand Job's descriptions.[5] The earth stands on nothing

---

[2] For an excellent discussion concerning the *Rephaim*, see A. R. Johnson, *The Vitality of the Individual*, 2nd ed., 1964, pp. 88ff.

[3] See Dhorme and Blommerde on the critical grammatical problems.

[4] Note in Ps. 48:2—Zion is the seat of Yahweh; some translations transcribe this as Zaphon—see Otto Eissfeldt. *Baal Zaphon, Zeus Kasios und der Durchzug der Israeliten durchs Meer,* 1934.

[5] See for details—compare with Jacques Merleau-Ponty, *Cosmologie du XX siecle* (Paris, 1965); *Astronomischer Jahresbericht* (Berlin) 1899 to the present, complete

—verse 11.

Verse 8—Job stands in awe at the clouds pictured as full of water but which do not burst under the weight of their burden—38:37; Prov. 30:4.

Verse 9—The verse presents several problems, specifically as given in the A. V. God hides the face (Heb. *'hz*—grasp, hold—used of barring gates in Neh. 7:3; Matt. 6:6; perhaps we should read *kese*—full moon—instead of *kisse*—throne—as in A. V.) of the full moon by covering it with the clouds. Even the bright light of the moon is under His authority. Though this requires some emendation, it keeps the parallelism and sets forth God's sovereignty which is Job's thesis in this verse.

Verse 10—God "has described a circle," which means that He has set a limit or boundary—Gen. 1:4, 7, 14; Job 22:14; Prov. 8:27. The editors of the Qumran Targum render the Hebrew *"aux bords de la limite"*—reinforcing the limitation of a boundary suggested by the text and the parallel—darkness in line two—II Sam. 22:8; Isa. 13:13; and Joel 2:10. Darkness suggests limitation. God here transcends all pagan mythological dualism; He alone controls chaos.

Verse 11—The earth is here called "the pillars of heaven." The pillars quiver (Heb. *yeropepu*—tremble or shake) at God's rebuke. That which holds up heaven responds when God breaks His silence—Pss. 18:14ff; 29:6; and 104:32.

Verse 12—The verb (*'rg*—disturb or stir up—Isa. 51:15 and Jer. 31:35) suggests that the powerful water supply which the heavens sustain is powerless when He intervenes—Rahab

---

bibliography of astronomical literature; a Koyre, *The Astronomical Revolution* (E. T., Cornell University Press, 1975); P. Duhem, *Le Systeme du Monde; histoires des doctrines cosmologiques de Platon a Copernic* (Paris, 10 Tomes); Rene Taton, *Histoire generale des sciences* (Paris, 4 Tomes); J. L. E. Dreyer, *A History of Astronomy from Thales to Kepeer* (New York: Dover, 1953); all of G. Sarton's works; and F. Russo, *Histoire des sciences et des Techniques bibliographie* (Paris, 1954); also see my essay on *Creation in Job* in this commentary. For biblical data see the excellent work by E. W. Monder, *Astronomy of The Bible* which has been condensed in his article in *International Stanard Bible Encyclopedia* (ISBE), Vol. I, pp. 300-316, Eerdman reprint.

might refer to Egypt—Ps. 87:4—and the experience of the parting of the waters. When God liberates, nothing stands in His way—7:12; 9:13; Jer. 10:12. He is claiming that it is by God's wisdom and understanding, not His power, that He is victorious.

Verse 13—The text probably refers to the clearing of the skies after a storm. The word rendered "garnished" in the A. V. is *siprah*—brightness. The wind referred to is, in all probability, the wind which clears the clouds out of the skies after a storm—3:8; 40:25; Isa. 27:1; and Rev. 12:3. The second line has the same word that appears in Isa. 51:9 for pierced or wounded. If they are present, part of the author's literary style only, the mythological motifs, eg. the fleeing serpent or Leviathon—3:8 and Isa. 27:1—are present only to show the sovereignty of God over nature.[6]

Verse 14—Again the author skillfully evoked imagery portraying God's infinite power. The secret of God's power will forever elude the seeker, and the solution to God's providential control over creation will only baffle and frustrate until in complete faith-trust he rests in His everlasting arms through resignation to God's wisdom and justice. He finally confesses that only God has infinite wisdom and knowledge. Though man has only heard a "soft whisper"—4:12, he stands in "awful dread" at what he has heard. He must wait for *The Shattering of Silence,* but until then, He reveals all that we can manage. God's word, like thunder, cannot be leisurely contemplated and comprehended—37:2, 5.

---

[6] See W. F. Albright, *Bulletin of the American Society of Oriental Research,* 1941, p. 39, for analysis of Ugaritic image of "the primeval serpent."

TODAY'S ENGLISH VERSION

26

Job

¹⁻² What a help you are in rescuing me—
     poor, weak man that I am!
³ You give such good advice
     and share your knowledge with a fool like me!
⁴ Who do you think will hear all your words?
     Who inspired you to speak like this?

[*Bildad*]

⁵ The land of the dead is trembling;
     its inhabitants shake with fear.
⁶ The world of the dead lies open to God;
     no covering shields it from his sight.
⁷ God stretched out the northern sky,
     and hung the earth in empty space.
⁸ It is God who fills the clouds with water,
     and keeps them from bursting with the weight.
⁹ He hides the full moon behind a cloud.
¹⁰ He divided light from darkness
     by a circle drawn on the face of the ocean.
¹¹ When he threatens the pillars that hold up the sky,
     they shake and tremble with fear.
¹² It is his strength that conquered the sea;
     by his skill he destroyed the monster Rahab.
¹³ It is his breath that made the sky clear,
     and his hand that killed the escaping monster.
¹⁴ But these are only hints of his power,
     only the whispers that we have heard.
     Who can know how truly great God is?

QUESTIONS FOR DISCUSSION 26:1-14

514. The first four verses contain what thought?
515. Can a man by searching find out God?
516. To whom is Job addressing himself?
517. Bildad was no help. Why?
518. What question had Bildad failed to answer?
519. How is the word "spirit" used in verse four?
520. Verses 5-14 set forth what theme?
521. Even the dead cannot escape from God. Explain.
522. Discuss verse seven in light of the expression "And hangeth the earth upon nothing."
523. What is a better word than "throne" in verse nine? Why?
524. Verse ten includes a transcendence of all pagan mythological dualism. Please explain.
525. What are "the pillars of heaven"? What happens to them?
526. What is "Rahab" as used in verse 12? What is the thought?
527. How are "Spirit" and "serpent" used in verse 13?
528. We only hear a "soft whisper" of the wisdom and power of God, but it is enough. Explain.

From **Today's English Version**
of the **Old Testament,** Copyright,
American Bible Society, 1971

IV. THE LONELINESS AND ISOLATION OF JOB
(27:1—31:40)
A. THE AFFIRMATION OF INNOCENCE (27:1-6)

TEXT 27:1-6

27 And Job again took up his parable and said,
2 As God liveth, who hath taken away my right,
And the Almighty, who hath vexed my soul
3 (For my life is yet whole in me,
And the spirit of God is in my nostrils);
4 Surely my lips shall not speak unrighteousness,
Neither shall my tongue utter deceit.
5 Far be it from me that I should justify you:
Till I die I will not put away mine integrity from me.
6 My righteousness I hold fast,
   and will not let it go:
My heart shall not reproach *me* so long as I live.

COMMENT 27:1-6

Verse 1—The preceding chapter contains the most powerful cosmological section in the dialogue for insight and scope of expression. All the verbs in verses 5-11 are participles or the imperfect describing God's constant Lordship over nature. Now Job resumes his response to Bildad by his inflexible protestation of innocence—verses 1-6. Job continues his parable (*masal*[1]—not always a parable, *mesalim*—collections in *Book of Proverbs;* brief saying—I Sam. 10:12; longer saying— Isa. 14:4; taunt or mock—Deut. 28:37), preferably discourse, taunt, or mock here. *Masal* is often associated in parallel with *hidah*—riddle or dark saying as in Ps. 49:5; Ezek. 17:2;

---

[1] For examination of the meaning of "masal" and extensive bibliography, see A. R. Johnson, *Vetus Testamentum,* Supplement, 1955, pp. 162ff; also F. Hauck, "Parabole," *TWNT*, Vol. 5, 744-761, esp. 747-751.

Hab. 2:6. It also appears in contexts with words of derision such as Deut. 28:37; I Sam. 10:12; Isa. 14:4; Jer. 24:9; and Hab. 2:6. Clearly *masal* covers a wide variety of literary compositions, thus we should not be alarmed that Job is not uttering a "parable."

Verse 2—The verse is introduced by an oath formula "as God lives"—I Sam. 14:39 and I Sam. 2:27. The tension, still unresolved, is present here as Job swears by the God (*El*—see my theological essay "Is Job's God in Exile?" in this commentary),[2] who has wronged him, i.e., "made my soul bitter"—7:11; 10:1; 21:25. The fact that Job made his vow in God's name suggests that he loved Him. Near Eastern custom would suggest this. From this curious tension the ancient rabbis deduced that Job served God out of love—7:11; 10:1; 21:25; 34:5; 36:6; and Ruth 1:20.

Verse 3—Job is affirming that though he is suffering, he still has control over his mental faculties. The conviction of this battered giant remains unshaken. The use of first person pronoun (12 occurrences) in verses 2-6 is our assurance that Job has introspectively searched out his past and does not remember a single unrighteous act. He will maintain his integrity (*tummah*—2:3) until his death. As long as my life (*nephesh*—derives from God—Gen. 2:7; and returns to God—34:14) is intact and God's *ruah* enlivens me, I will swear loyal allegiance to Him.

Verse 4—He contends that all along he has spoken the truth. This is the content of the oath. He swears in El's name to speak only the truth in defending his innocence. The A. V. rendering of "utter" derives from a verb which means moan—Isa. 38:14; meditate—Ps. 1:2; devise—Ps. 2:1; and here speak—Ps. 71:24; "deceit" is the same word found in 13:7.

Verse 5—As long as Job lives, he will not grant his friends the right to assert his guilt. The formula used, "far be it from

---

[2] See M. Pope, *El in the Ugaritic Texts*, Supplement, *Vetus Testamentum II*, 1955, esp. 12-15, 104; that this is the most solemn oath possible see J. Guillet, *L'homme devant Dieu* (Paris, 1964), pp. 19-20.

me," implies that there is something profane in the idea which he is rejecting—II Sam. 20:20. So long as he lives, he could not deny his own integrity before God. I could never "justify you" (the pronoun is plural), i.e., admit that you are correct regarding my righteousness; the A. V. rendering of "will not put away" comes from a word meaning withhold and also appears in verse two.

Verse 6—The heart is the Hebrew seat of intelligence, reason—2:9; I Sam. 24:6. Job denies any awareness of sins such as his consolers had charged to him—22:6-9. Nothing new is advanced in this speech, but he continues to scorn Bildad's defense of God, and to affirm his own innocence.

B. NO BELIEVERS ANONYMOUS, I.E., NO UNIVERSAL SALVATION (27:7-23)

TEXT 27:7-23

7 Let mine enemy be as the wicked,
  And let him that riseth up against me be as the unrighteous.
8   For what is the hope of the godless, though he get him
      gain,
  When God taketh away his soul?
9 Will God hear his cry,
  When trouble cometh upon him?
10 Will he delight himself in the Almighty,
  And call upon God at all times?
11 I will teach you concerning the hand of God;
  That which is with the Almighty will I not conceal.
12 Behold, all ye yourselves have seen it;
  Why then are ye become altogether vain?
13 This is the portion of a wicked man with God,
  And the heritage of oppressors,
      which they receive from the Almighty:
14 If his children be multiplied, it is for the sword;
  And his offspring shall not be satisfied with bread.

15 Those that remain of him shall be buried in death,
   And his widows shall make no lamentation.
16 Though he heap up silver as the dust,
   And prepare raiment as the clay;
17 He may prepare it, but the just shall put it on,
   And the innocent shall divide the silver.
18 He buildeth his house as the moth,
   And as a booth which the keeper maketh.
19 He lieth down rich, but he shall not be gathered *to his
   fathers;*
   He openeth his eyes, and he is not.
20 Terrors overtake him like waters;
   A tempest stealeth him away in the night.
21 The east wind carrieth him away, and he departeth;
   And it sweepeth him out of his place.
22 For *God* shall hurl at him, and not spare:
   He would fain flee out of his hand.
23 Men shall clap their hands at him,
   And shall hiss him out of his place.

COMMENT 27:7-23

Verse 7—In this present text, Zophar gives no response. Some affirm that verses 7-23 are inappropriate on Job's lips, and ascribe the verses to Zophar. The lot of the wicked, i.e., those without God and hope, is inevitable punishment. Though the words are strong, they are not vindictive but rather express the author's abhorrence of evil.

Verse 8—The verb rendered "get gain" means gain by violence, cut off, break off—Ezek. 22:27. Note that verse 9 speaks of God's deafness to the prayers of the wicked. The verse is relating how lonely and isolated the wicked are, even in this life. The ultimate fate of the wicked is again death. Only the godly man can pray to God; all ears are deaf to the ungodly (Heb. *haneph*—as a class of men). Why do his friends implore him to pray for forgiveness, if God does not hear the

265

prayers of the *haneph*—ungodly?

Verse 9—The verse continues the point from verse 8—If I am unrighteous, God will not hear my prayer for forgiveness. Job presents them with a theological dilemma of their own making. How devastating.

Verse 10—The same verb rendered "delight" himself has already appeared in 22:26. It is useless to pray to God in times of trouble if we have ignored Him in all other circumstances ("at all times").

Verse 11—He here launches on a new theological theme that of God's immoral behavior "in governing the universe." The "you" is again plural. Both Job and his friends claim superior knowledge.

Verse 12—How can you be uninformed concerning the universal phenomenon of God's injustice, if you are so wise? He charges them with intense futility, i.e., lit. "become vain with a vain thing."

Verse 13—These words are almost identical with Zophar's in 20:29. The wicked man is singular, but oppressors is in the plural. The preposition *'im* should be translated *from* and not *with* (as in the A. V.[3]) Shaddai, the almighty. The portion or judgment is from God.

Verse 14—Numerous children were thought to be a great blessing; here they are for destruction—5:4; 18:19; and 21:8, 11. The sword is to break (*pss*—shatter, scatter) his offspring.

Verse 15—His survivors, i.e., children, not destroyed by the sword will be left to the fate of death by pestilence—Jer. 15:2; 18:2. The Hebrew text literally says "His survivors will be buried in death by death," a death which befits the ungodly. Not to be buried—II Kg. 9:10; Jer. 8:2; 14:6; 22:19—or mourned—Ps. 78:64; Jer. 22:10—was a disaster. The strange phrase above could perhaps yield better sense by taking de Vaux's suggestion that *bamot*—rather than—*bammawet*—is a cultic word for tomb.[4] Contrast with 21:32 where Job declares

---

[3] M. Dahood, *Ugaritic—Hebrew Philology* (Rome, 1965), p. 32.

[4] R. de Vaux, *Ancient Israel* (New York: McGraw-Hill, 1 vol. E. T.), p. 287.

that the wicked often have a large funeral.

Verse 16—The image here suggests abundance—Zech. 9:3. After the family is destroyed, their possessions follow the same fate. Silver and elaborate garments are greatly valued, see Gen. 24:53; Jos. 7:21; II Kg. 5:22ff; and Zech. 14:14.

Verse 17—The only ones who will prosper are the righteous. What the ungodly accumulate will be divided by the godly—Ps. 39:6; Prov. 13:22.

Verse 18—The A. V. rendering of "as"—"as moth"—is inappropriate since moths do not build houses. The imagery here comes from the harvest season when a watchman or guard builds temporary shelter from which to watch over unharvested crop. One could hardly derive this since from the A. V. the verbs (*banah*—he builds, *'asah*—he makes) are not parallel. The verb "he makes" refers to the flimsy shelter (*sukkah*) which the watchman constructs.[5]

Verse 19—The rich lie down, but for the last time. The swiftness of the destruction of the wicked is here vividly expressed. The rendering of the A. V., "he shall not be gathered to his fathers," expresses the Hebrew "will do so no more." The second line containing the phrase "and he is not" is an attempt at rendering the Hebrew, which can be either "it is not" or "he is not" and expresses the fact that a dying man is conscious of his own demise.

Verse 20—Dahood renders this verse "terrors will overtake him like a flood, night will kidnap him like a tempest"[6]— 22:11. As in verse 19, calamity calls him from his night chambers. The wicked man is haunted by terrors night and day— Isa. 28:17; Hos. 5:10; and Amos 5:24.

Verse 21—The east wind causes restless and sleepless nights; thus it signifies all that is unpleasant. This sirocco wind is scorching and violent, destroying man's peace—15:2. Even the climatic conditions crash in on the ungodly.

Verse 22—The A. V. makes little sense. There is neither

---

[5] See M. Pope, *Job*, p. 193, for thorough discussion.
[6] M. Dahood, *Biblica*, 1969, p. 342.

subject nor object to "hurl" (word God is not in the text) in the text, but the implication is that of a deadly missile.

Verse 23—The ambiguities of this verse largely stem from the unexpressed subject of the verbs of verses 22-23, which may be God, east wind, or "one man." The metaphors here convey derisive mockery and contemp—Lam. 2:15. The rendering of the A. V. "men shall clap their hands at him," understands the text as an indefinite third person "one claps" or "men clap." When death and destruction come to the wicked, men scornfully clap their hands, while hissing (a gesture of horror) at the very thought of them—Jer. 49:17; Ezek. 27:36; Zeph. 2:15.

TODAY'S ENGLISH VERSION

27
Job

¹⁻² I swear by the living Almighty God,
　　who refuses me justice and makes my life bitter—
　³　as long as God gives me breath
　⁴　my lips will never say anything evil,
　　　and my tongue will never speak a lie.
⁵ I will never say that you men are right;
　　as long as I live I will insist I am innocent.
⁶ I will never give up my claim to be right;
　　my conscience is clear.

⁷ May all who oppose me and fight against me
　　be punished like wicked, unrighteous men.
⁸ What hope is there for godless men
　　in the hour when God demands their life?
⁹ When trouble comes, will God hear their cries?
¹⁰ They should have wanted the joy he gives
　　and should have constantly prayed to him.

¹¹ Let me teach you how great is God's power,
　　and explain what Almighty God has planned.

¹² But no, after all, you have seen for yourselves;
so why do you talk such nonsense?

[Zophar]
¹³ Here is how Almighty God punishes wicked,
violent men.
¹⁴ They may have many sons, but all are killed in war;
their children never have enough to eat.
¹⁵ Those who survive will die from disease,
and their widows will not mourn their death.
¹⁶ The wicked may have too much silver to count,
and more clothes than anyone needs.
¹⁷ But some good man will wear the clothes,
and some honest man will get the silver.
¹⁸ The wicked build houses that will not last;
they are like a spider's web,
or the hut of a slave guarding the fields.
¹⁹ One last time they will lie down rich,
and when they wake up they will find their
wealth gone.
²⁰ Terror will strike like a sudden flood;
a wind in the night will blow them away;
²¹ the east wind will sweep them from their homes;
²² it will blow down on them without pity,
while they try their best to escape.
²³ The wind howls at them as they run,
frightening them with destructive power.

QUESTIONS FOR DISCUSSION 27:1-23

529. Chapter twenty-six contains a powerful section on the
constant Lordship of God over nature. The verbs in verses
5-11 emphasize this. How so?
530. What is meant by the expression "took up his parable"?
531. Job takes the most solemn oath possible. What is it?

What does it suggest?

532. Does Job refer to the fact that he is yet alive? Or is this the thought?

533. Is Job saying that he will speak the truth on all subjects or on just the subject of his innocence? Discuss.

534. Job declares the guilt of his friends in the declaration of his innocence. Why?

535. How is the term "heart" used in the O.T.?

536. Show how we can ascribe verse seven to Job.

537. The term "get gain" in verse eight means more than mere acquiring of possessions. What is added?

538. Job presents his friends with a devastating theological dilemma. Explain.

539. There is a grand lesson of the proper attitude toward God in verse ten. What is it?

540. Job actually charges God with immoral behavior. Discuss. Cf. vss. 11, 12.

541. The "portion of the wicked man" in verses 13-15 is very much like what happened to Job. Is there a relationship? Discuss.

542. Aren't most of these comments idle dreaming about what should happen to the wicked rather than what really happens? Discuss.

543. The "moth" of verse 18 is a man. Explain.

544. What is described in verse 19?

545. The wicked are lonely and haunted by terrors night and day. Why? Is this always true?

546. What was unusual about the east wind?

547. Who is throwing what at whom in verse 22?

548. Men clap their hands at the wicked. When? Why?

C. SOURCE OF TRUE WISDOM (28:1-28)
1. Man finds hidden treasures of the earth, as in mining. (28:1-11)

TEXT 28:1-11

28 Surely there is a mine for silver,
And a place for gold which they refine.
2 Iron is taken out of the earth,
And copper is molten out of the stone.
3 *Man* setteth an end to darkness,
And searcheth out, to the furthest bound,
The stones of obscurity and of thick darkness.
4 He breaketh open a shaft away from where men sojourn;
They are forgotten of the foot;
They hang afar from men, they swing to and fro.
5 As for the earth, out of it cometh bread;
And underneath it is turned up as it were by fire.
6 The stones thereof are the place of sapphires,
And it hath dust of gold.
7 That path no bird of prey knoweth,
Neither hath the falcon's eye seen it:
8 The proud beasts have not trodden it,
Nor hath the fierce lion passed thereby.
9 He putteth forth his hand upon the flinty rock;
He overturneth the mountains by the roots.
10 He cutteth out channels among the rocks;
And his eye seeth every precious thing.
11 He bindeth the streams that they trickle not;
And the thing that is hid bringeth he forth to light.

COMMENT 28:1-11

Verse 1—The theme of this marvelous chapter[1] is the

---

[1] See the doctoral thesis of C. C. Settlemire, "The Meaning, Importance, and Original Position of Job 28," Diss. Drew Univ., 1969, cf. Diss. Abstracts, 1969.

transcendence of divine wisdom and its inaccessibility to man. Man may discover certain dimensions of God's wisdom, but human efforts can never completely fathom the divine purpose.[2] This beautiful portion of Job falls into three divisions: (1) There is no known road to attain wisdom—verses 1-11; (2) No price can purchase it—verses 12-19 (verses 14-19 are missing from the LXX); and (3) God alone possesses it, and only when God makes it available through special revelation can man possess it—verses 20-28.

How appropriate this great poem is to contemporary *homo faber* (man the maker). The Promethian spirit is once more upon us. Technologically dominated man operates on the mythological assumption of his unlimited possibilities. From the Greeks to twentieth century man, optimism has always outrun his concrete performance. This verse clearly means that every valuable thing in creation has a dwelling place. The verse begins with "for" which continues to trouble commentators because it suggests a logical sequence to something which is no longer in our text. The emphasis in Hebrew is on the "there is" a source (Heb. *mosa*—"place of coming forth," i.e., the mining of silver and gold). *Mosa* is used of water in II Kg. 2:21; Isa. 41:18; 58:11; Ps. 107:33; II Chron. 32:30; and of the sunrise in Pss. 65:9; 75:7. In this verse the translation requires "mine," and there are only a few references to mining in the Old Testament—Deut. 8:9; Jer. 10:9; Ezek. 27:12. After the excavations of the late Nelson Glueck, we have confirmation of the presence of a great copper refinery, from the time of Solomon, near Ezion geber. Silver was not mined, to our knowledge, in Palestine but was imported from

---

[2] For analysis of the Near Eastern and biblical doctrine of wisdom (*hokma*), see James Wood, *Wisdom Literature* (London: Duckworth, 1967); H. H. Rowley, *Wisdom in Israel and in the Ancient Near East*, Supplement, V. T., 1955; H. H. Schmid, *Eine Untersuchuung zur altorientalischen und israelitischen Weisheitsliteratur*, 1966; A. Hulsbosch, "Sagesse creatrive et educatrice," *Augustinianum*, 1961, pp. 217-235; G. von Rad, *Wisdom in Israel* (Nashville: Abingdon, E. T., 1972), pp. 144-176; U. Wilckens, *Weisheit und Torheit*, 1959, esp. pp. 174ff; R. B. Y. Scott, "Wisdom in Creation," *Vetus Testamentum*, 1960, pp. 213ff; J. J. van Dipk, *La Sagesse Sumero accadienne* (Brill, 1953).

Tarshish—Jer. 10:9; Ezek. 27:12. (On Tarshish, see Herodotus, IV. 152.) The name Tarshish is probably derived from the Akkadian word meaning "refinery."[3] Gold was imported from Ophir—Isa. 13:12; I Kg. 10:11; I Chron. 29:4; and Sheba—Ps. 72:15 and I Kg. 10:2. The verse is concerned with the source of silver and gold in contrast to wisdom.

Verse 2—The promised land was described as one "whose stones are iron"—Deut. 8:9. In Saul's day the Philistines monopolized the iron deposits—I Sam. 13:19-22; 17:7. In David's time iron became plentiful. Blommerde takes the second line to read "and from stone is the smelting of copper." Copper was smelted very early in Palestine—Deut. 8:9. Major sources being Cyprus, in Edom, and in the Sinai Peninsula.[4]

Verse 3—The metaphors express how the miners penetrate the dark recesses of the earth with their lamps. Miners open up deep shafts and let the sunlight into the hole. The subject is not expressed in this verse; it literally says "one puts an end to darkness," (Hebrew "shadows of death," darkness can mean ignorance or unrighteousness, here physical darkness), i.e., there is a limit to which the laborers will go—3:5 and 26:10.[5]

Verse 4—Perhaps Graetz's suggestion is best. He proposes that the first line means "alien people break shafts," i.e., slave labor is being used to do the mining. The second line suggests that they are deep within the earth and thus the miners are remote from those walking or working above ground. The third line is probably a reference to miners suspended by ropes into the ground and swinging in the dark caverns digging for copper.

Verse 5—As the surface of the earth produces food, so

---

[3] W. F. Albright suggests that the ships of Tarshish means refinery fleet—*Bulletin American Society Oriental Research*, 1941, pp. 21ff.

[4] For details from original excavations, see N. Glueck, *Biblical Archaeologist*, 1938, pp. 13-16; 1939, pp. 37-41; 1940, pp. 51-55; 1965, pp. 70-87.

[5] See R. J. Forbes, *Mining and Geology in Antiquity* (Brill, 1940); and *Bulletin of American Society of Oriental Research*, 1938, pp. 3-17; 1939, pp. 8-22; and 1946, pp. 2-18.

deep below a smelting operation is yielding rich ore—Ps. 104:14; or perhaps more likely, the mining below produces piles of debris similar to that produced by a fire—Ezek. 27:14, where "stones of fire" are precious gems.

Verse 6—The earth yields not only metals but precious stones. It is impossible to identify the specific gem which the text has in mind, but in view of the poetic parallelism, it is not impossible that *lapis lazuli* (as R. S. V. marginal reading) is meant; thus the iron pyrites particles found in *lapis lazuli* which glitters like gold provides a meaning for "dust of gold" which has already been mentioned in the verse.

Verse 7—The paths of miners are remote from most men, as is wisdom. Birds (perhaps falcon, LXX has vulture) of prey live even more remote from men than do the miners. The bird intended by this reference is impossible to identify with certainty, but the reference to its keenness of sight suggests the falcon. The gold mines worked by the Egyptians in Nubia were more than a seven-days' journey into the desert. The emphasis here in verses four and seven is on the remoteness and inaccessibility of the mines, and indirectly also of wisdom.

Verse 8—The "sons of pride"[6] have not even been there, i.e., where wisdom is found. It is imperative that we keep in mind a poetic play on words for origins—*masa*—find and *maqom*—place, source of origin. Man and beast can find many valuable things, but not wisdom. Even the "fierce lion" (Heb. *sahal*—4:10ff; Hos. 5:14; 13:7; Prov. 26:13) has not been there, i.e., where wisdom is found.

Verse 9—The images here—verses 9-11—as in verses 3-4 emphasize man's stubborn insistence in searching for treasure (note Jesus and the Pearl of Great Price). Human achievement emphasizing *homo faber* is the central thrust of the images. Flint, the hardest rock, yields to his persuasive insistence, and the mountains maintain only momentary

---

[6] Only here and 41:26, see Sigmund Mowinckel, *Hebrew and Semitic Studies,* presented to G. R. Driver, eds. D. W. Thomas and W. D. McHardy, 1963, p. 97, for his effort to connect with mythology. It is an unwarranted claim in a context of real birds and beasts.

resistance.

Verse 10—The word rendered channels (*ye'orim*) is the plural of the designation of the Nile, *ye'or*, the one which also describes the Nile. It can refer to mine shafts or drainage ditches—Isa. 33:21. Example of cutting through solid rock is the Siloam tunnel, and the rock city of Petra.

Verse 11—Difficulties in this verse can be overcome by taking the suggestions of some that the meaning is that of a man exploring the sources of rivers by digging down to their underground springs. This also provides a parallel with the next line.[7]

2. But where wisdom is, man cannot discover; only God knows. (28:12-28)

TEXT 28:12-28

12 But where shall wisdom be found?
   And where is the place of understanding?
13 Man knoweth not the price thereof;
   Neither is it found in the land of the living.
14 The deep saith, It is not in me;
   And the sea saith, It is not with me.
15 It cannot be gotten for gold,
   Neither shall silver be weighed for the price thereof.
16 It cannot be valued with the gold of Ophir,
   With the precious onyx, or the sapphire.
17 Gold and glass cannot equal it,
   Neither shall it be exchanged for jewels of fine gold.
18 No mention shall be made of coral or of crystal:
   Yea, the price of wisdom is above rubies.
19 The topaz of Ethiopia shall not equal it,
   Neither shall it be valued with pure gold.

---

[7] For this suggestion, see M. Mansoor, *Revue de Qumran*, 1961-2, pp. 392ff; and G. M. Landes, *Bulletin of American Society of Oriental Research*, 1956, pp. 32ff.

20 Whence then cometh wisdom?
    And where is the place of understanding?
21 Seeing it is hid from the eyes of all living,
    And kept close from the birds of the heavens.
22 Destruction and Death say,
    We have heard a rumor thereof with our ears.
23 God understandeth the way thereof,
    And he knoweth the place thereof.
24 For he looketh to the ends of the earth,
    And seeth under the whole heaven;
25 To make a weight for the wind:
    Yea, he meteth out the waters by measure.
26 When he made a decree for the rain,
    And a way for the lightning of the thunder;
27 Then did he see it, and declare it;
    He established it, yea, and searched it out.
28 And unto man he said,
    Behold, the fear of the Lord, that is wisdom;
    And to depart from evil is understanding.

COMMENT 28:12-28

Verse 12—Man can mine silver, gold, precious gems, but what about "wisdom" and "understanding"?—Prov. 1:2; 4:5, 7; 9:10; 16:16. The wisdom with which God governs creation eludes man's search. ("The fear of the Lord is the beginning of wisdom." Paul calls Jesus the "wisdom of God," I Cor. 1:30ff). This verse is repeated with little modification in verse 20.

Verse 13—Though the Hebrew text has "its price" ('*erkah*) as A. V., this verse is concerned with locating wisdom; verses 15ff treat the value or price of wisdom. Thus it would be appropriate to emend the text to read "the way to it," (*darkah*)[8]

---

[8] Perhaps more support is now available for M. Dahood's suggestion which produces the emendation "house or abode of wisdom"—*Biblica,* 1969, p. 355. Still the emphasis is on the location of wisdom, not its price.

instead of "its price," following the LXX. The thesis here is that man knows the way to find the things discussed in the preceding verses; but he is completely at a loss as to how to locate wisdom. The parallelism strongly favors the emendation, which follows the LXX. The second line suggests that wisdom is not found in the land of the living either, a metaphor for inhabited earth—Pss. 27:13; 52:7—verse 22; Isa. 38:11; 53:8; Jer. 11:19; and Ezek. 26:20.

Verse 14—Tehom, the deep, says wisdom is not there either —Gen. 7:11; 49:25; and Job 3:18. Man may explore the watery abyss as he digs for gold and silver, but he will not find wisdom.

Verse 15—Wisdom cannot be purchased with gold (Heb. *segor*—gold bullion, pure gold). The word is found only here, but a slightly different word is used to describe the gold of Temple ornaments—I Kg. 6:20. The root meaning is "enclose," perhaps prized, or even gold bars—I Kg. 7:49; 10:21; II Chron. 4:20, 22; 9:20. In the ancient world, money was weighed not counted—Gen. 23:16; Zech. 11:12.

Verse 16—Wisdom cannot be obtained for gold (Heb. *keten*—which is a derivation from the Egyptian source of gold—Nubia). The verb rendered "be valued" is found only here and verse 19 and means "to be weighed against"—22:24. The precious gem (Heb. *sohom*) can be given only a precarious and conjectural meaning—Gen. 2:12; Ex. 39:13; and Ezek. 29:13, but the meaning is clear. The things men value most cannot purchase wisdom.

Verse 17—The only direct reference to glass (*gabis*—crystal, used of hail stones in Ezek. 13:11, 13; and 38:22) in the Old Testament is found here. Glass was made in Egypt as early as 4000 B.C. It was used for ornamentation and was very valuable. Because of its value, no one would exchange wisdom for "vessels of fine gold"—Ps. 19:10; Prov. 8:19.

Verse 18—The gems mentioned here cannot be identified with certainty, but Lam. 4:7 gives us a clue to their color as being reddish—Prov. 31:10; Ezek. 27:16.[9]

---

[9] See S. T. Byington, *JBL*, 1945, pp. 340ff.

Verse 19—The price of wisdom continues to be contrasted with topaz ("green pearl" or "yellowish stone") and pure gold—verse 16. Pliny (*Historia Naturalis,* XXXVII, XXXII, 108) indicates that there was an island in the Red Sea called Topazos.

Verse 20—Perhaps this verse is a refrain—verse 12. Both the living and the dead fail to ensnare wisdom. All human searching is futile.

Verse 21—Wisdom is not made available to man through his searching the earth, sea, Sheol, or the heavens—verses 13, 14, 22. No one can locate the hiding place of wisdom. Neither heights nor depths provide a vantage point for observation in order to provide advantage in reconnaissance; wisdom is no place to be "found."

Verse 22—Destruction, Abaddon—26:6b—and death personified have only a rumour; they have no direct concrete knowledge of wisdom. The dread powers have only "heard with their ears"—II Sam. 7:22; Ps. 44:2, i.e., have only second-hand evidence. Man's most dreaded enemy—death—has only a vague rumour as to wisdom's home, source.

Verse 23—God stands in the emphatic position both in the text and in the Universe. He alone knows the nature and source of wisdom.

Verse 24—Heaven and earth were created by wisdom and understanding—Prov. 3:19; Job 37:3; 41:3; Isa. 40:28: 41:5, 9. The Creator surveys His entire creation and knows its every need.

Verse 25—God's providential guidance of the cosmos is illustrated by the fact that He regulates "the force of the wind and measures the waters"—5:10; 36:27-33; 38:26-27; Isa. 40:12; note and contrast with 12:15.

Verse 26—The Hebrew word—*hoq*—should not be translated decree as in the A. V., but in the sense of boundary or limit as in Jer. 5:22; Prov. 8:29; Ps. 148:6. The root significance of *hoq* is "to engrave" (cf. 38:25a uses *te'alah*—trench or groove). God also sets limits on the way (*darek*—path)[10]

---

[10] See E. F. Sutcliffe, "The Clouds as Water Carriers in Hebrew Thoughts," *Vetus Testamentum,* 1953, pp. 99-103.

lightning of the thunder (R. S. V.—thunderbolt, see Zech. 10:1). Probably this means a thunderstorm (*haziz qolot*)—37:4; Zech. 10:1; Ps. 18:13; Isa. 30:30ff; and Jer. 10:13.

Verse 27—The reference here is to the time of creation. Man was not present; therefore, He could not reveal the nature of wisdom to man. The A. V. rendering of declare (verb, *spr*—appraise, evaluate, or count) might suggest that God announced it to man, but this is impossible in that man did not yet exist. The significance of the first two verbs suggests that God perfectly understood the nature of wisdom—14:6; 38:37; Ps. 22:18. God appraised (*spr*) and established (*hekinah*, rather than the emendation *hebinah*—discerned) and tested wisdom. God exhaustively evaluated wisdom in the process of creation. An analogue might be that of a computer evaluating all possible options in a finite system.

Verse 28—After evaluating the process of creation, after man is created, God (*'dnyadonai* is found nowhere else in Job) says to him that there is a practical wisdom available to man, which is the way to ultimate wisdom, that is—"Stand in awe before God." In Proverbs 9:10 and Psalm 111:10 the authors declare that "awe" or "reverence" (not fear as dread or horror) of God is the chief (*rosh*—head) or foundation for wisdom. Reverent submission to the gracious will of God is the only place in the universe where one gains hope of ultimate victory over sin and evil. Evil is irrational in that there is no logical explanation nor technological way of removing evil from the fallen universe. The empirical evidence remains intact; man is separated from *God, self, others,* and *nature* by sinful self-elevation. When pride is destroyed by being born again, the self is crucified, and we accept a new center from which to maintain integrity—that new center is Job's redeemer, Lord of heaven and earth.[11]

---

[11] See statement regarding the problem which chapter 28 presents in F. I. Andersen, *Job*, pp. 222-229.

TODAY'S ENGLISH VERSION

In Praise of Wisdom

28
There are mines where silver is dug;
There are places where gold is refined.
2 Men dig iron out of the ground
And melt copper out of the stones.
3 Men explore the deepest darkness.
They search the depths of the earth
And dig for rocks in the darkness.
4 Far from where anyone lives,
Or human feet ever travel,
Men dig the shafts of mines.
There they work in loneliness,
Clinging to ropes in the pits.

5 Food grows out of the earth,
But underneath the same earth
All is torn up and crushed.
6 The stones of the earth contain sapphires,
And the dust contains gold.
7 No hawk sees the roads to the mines
And no vulture ever flies over them.
8 No lion or other fierce beast
Ever travels those lonely roads.

9 Men dig the hardest rocks,
Dig mountains away at their base.
10 As they tunnel through the rocks
They discover precious stones.
11 They dig to the sources of rivers
And bring to light what is hidden.
12 But where is the source of wisdom?
Where can we learn to understand?

13 Wisdom is not to be found among men;
No one knows its true value.
14 The depths of the oceans and seas

Say that wisdom is not found there.
15 It cannot be bought with silver or gold.
16 The finest gold and jewels
Cannot pay its price.
17 Its value is more than gold,
Than a gold vase or finest glass,
18 The value of wisdom is more
Than coral, or crystal, or rubies.
19 The finest topaz and the purest gold
Cannot compare with the value of wisdom.

20 Where, then, is the source of wisdom?
Where can we learn to understand?
21 No living creature can see it,
Not even a bird in flight.
22 Even death and destruction
Admit they have heard only rumors.

23 God alone knows the way,
Knows the place where wisdom is found,
24 Because he sees the ends of the earth,
Sees everything under the sky.
25 When God gave the wind its power,
And determined the size of the sea;
26 When God decided where the rain would fall,
And the path that the thunderclouds travel;
27 It was then he saw wisdom and tested its value—
He established it and gave his approval.

28 God said to men,
"To be wise, you must fear the Lord.
To understand, you must turn from evil."

QUESTIONS FOR DISCUSSION 28:1-28

549. What is the theme of chapter 28? Show how it is divided.
550. Discuss how important this chapter is to man today.
551. What is the point of verse one?
552. Is there confirmation of the presence of iron and copper in Palestine? Where?
553. What is described in verse three? The methods used for mining have not changed. Discuss.
554. What a graphic picture is found in verse four! What is it?
555. The surface of the earth is compared to what is beneath. What is below the surface? Cf. vs. 5.
556. What gem is possible as being mentioned in verse six?
557. There is a strong comparison being made throughout these verses. What is it? Cf. vs. 7.
558. The "sons of pride" nor the lion have not been to the place described in this chapter. What is it?
559. Verses 3, 4 and 9-11 are alike. How so? Discuss the point being made.
560. Man can mine gold and silver. What is he unable to do? Where shall wisdom be found?
561. Is the price or the location of wisdom the point of verse 13?
562. What is "the deep" of verse 14?
563. The term "gold" of verse 15 is of a particular kind of gold. What is it?
564. What was unusual about the gold from Egypt?
565. How is the only reference to glass used?
566. What of the definite gems of verse 18? i.e., what is said in the Hebrew text?
567. What color is topaz?
568. Perhaps we are reading the verses of a song. Cf. vss. 12 and 20. Discuss.
569. Why is wisdom so elusive? Or is it? Discuss.
570. What is meant by "destruction" in verse 22? What could be meant by "rumor" in verse 22?
571. What is meant by saying that "God stands in the emphatic position."?

D. THE SOLILOQUY OF A SUFFERER (29:1—31:40)
  1. Reminiscence—his former happy life (29:1-25)
    a. The outward aspect (29:1-10)

TEXT 29:1-10

29   And Job again took up his parable, and said,
   2 Oh that I were as in the months of old,
  As in the days when God watched over me;
3 When his lamp shined upon my head,
  And by his light I walked through darkness;
4 As I was in the ripeness of my days,
  When the friendship of God was upon my tent;
5 When the Almighty was yet with me,
  And my children were about me;
6 When my steps were washed with butter,
  And the rock poured me out streams of oil!
7 When I went forth to the gate unto the city,
  When I prepared my seat in the street,
8 The young men saw me and hid themselves,
  And the aged rose up and stood;
9 The princes refrained from talking,
  And laid their hand on their mouth;
10 The voice of the nobles was hushed,
  And their tongue cleaved to the roof of their mouth.

COMMENT 29:1-10

Verse 1—Job's debate with his friends[1] is at an end. Now we will listen to his final soliloquy. The speech is divided into three sections, one chapter each: A: (1) His former happiness— 29:2-10; (2) His past graciousness to the needy—verses 11-17;

---

[1] For *Traditionsgeschichte* analysis of Job's friends, see H. P. Muller, *Hiob und seine Freunde,* Theo. Studien 103, 1970; and P. W. Skehan, "Job's Final Plea (Job 29-31) and The Lord's Reply (Job 38-41)," *Biblica,* 1964, pp. 51-62.

(3) His confidence—verses 18-20; (4) The esteem in which he was held—verses 21-25; B: (1) His present suffering—through the nobodys that despise him—30:1-8; (2) The indignities he is presently enduring—verses 9-15; (3) His present dread—verses 16-23; (4) Contrast between his past and present—verses 24-31; C: His vindication: (1) His integrity sustained—31:1-12; (2) Denial of abuse of power—verses 13-23; (3) Reaffirmation of his piety—verses 24-34; (4) Appeal that specific charges be made against him—verses 35-37; and (5) Invocation of a curse upon himself if he has not been telling the truth—verses 38-40 (compare with 27:1).

Verse 2—His thoughts move back into a happier time in his life. For the moment, the harsh realities of his existential situation[2] are suppressed. Nostalgia enthralls him. He is confronted by thinking of the time when God watched over him—Pss. 91:11; 121:7ff; and Mi. 6:24. The same verb is used of God's hostile surveillance of his life—10:14; 13:27; and 14:16.

Verse 3—The lamp and light are metaphors of God's blessings and presence—Pss. 18:28; 36:9; II Sam. 22:29. There is no word in Hebrew for the "through" of the A. V.; perhaps the reference is to God's glory, the *kobad* (Greek, *doxa*) which later developed into the Shekinah. The sense being if God is not present, there is nothing but spiritual darkness.

Verse 4—The word rendered ripeness in the A. V. symbolizes prosperity and maturity rather than decline. The root meaning of *-hrp* is "be early, young."[3] Earlier in Job's life God's protective hedge was about (not "upon" as A. V.) his household—1:10 and 31:31.[4]

Verse 5—Job places his relationship with God about his most intimate human companionship—Gen. 28:20; 31:5; Pss. 23:4; 44:7. Job poignantly refers to the loss of his own

---

[2] See J. Faur, "Reflections on Job and Situation Morality," *Judaism,* 1970, pp. 219-225.

[3] For analysis of this root, see A. C. M. Blommerde, *Northwest Semitic Grammar and Job,* 1969, p. 109.

[4] D. W. Thomas, *JBL*, 1946, pp. 63ff, for meaning of "protection" rather than "friendship"; also see Dhorme on the preposition, p. 416.

children (Heb. *na'ar* means young men—Gen. 22:3 and II Sam 18:29). Numerous children was a sign of God's favor— Pss. 127:3-5 and 128:3-4.

Verse 6—When Job was prosperous, his herds were fertile; butter flowed like mighty waters. Butter in the A. V. would better be rendered "curds"—21:17. The olive-tree grows profusely in rocky soil,[5] and the olive presses are cut in the rock—Deut. 32:13; 33:24; Ps. 81:16b; and Song of Songs 5:12. The rocks poured out "for me" (rather than lit. "with me" or "poured me out" of the A. V.). The line says in essence, when God watched over my household, blessings came from the most unexpected sources.

Verse 7—The city gate was the central meeting place for the distribution of administrative justice—Deut. 21:19; Ruth 4:1, 11; and II Kg. 7:1, 18. Job's social prestige is clearly emphasized in that he has a prominent seat. The "broad open place" (Heb. *rehob*—is street in A. V.) stood at the entrance of the city gate—I Kg. 22:10. Job's former happiness was based on three relationships: (1) Fellowship with God; (2) Companionship of his own children; and (3) The respect of his community.

Verse 8—Job's public influence is projected by two images in this verse: (1) The young men withdrew (as hid in A. V.); and (2) While the older men remained standing in respect, until Job was settled in a prominent place. In this manner both showed respect for a righteous man.

Verse 9—Another image reveals the overt expression of respect for Job. The princes stopped in the midst of their conversations and waited respectfully to hear this evaluation. The Qumran Targum confirms this reading "[And] nobles became silent of speech, and put hand [to their mouth]."

Verse 10—Their voice became veiled (*nehbau*—hushed and is same as in verse eight for hid), quiet is deferential respect. The image in line two expresses nervousness (tongue cleaved to the

---

[5] See M. Dahood, *Biblica et Orientalia,* suggestion that "rock" should rather be "bakam," 1965, p. 60.

roof of the mouth) in the presence of Job—Lam. 4:4; and Jesus on the cross.

b. The cause of his honored position was benevolence and righteousness (29:11-17)

TEXT 29:11-17

11 For when the ear heard *me*, then it blessed me;
  And when the eye saw *me*, it gave witness unto me:
12 Because I delivered the poor that cried,
  The fatherless also, that had none to help him.
13 The blessing of him that was ready to perish came upon me;
  And I caused the widow's heart to sing for joy.
14 I put on righteousness, and it clothed me:
  My justice was as a robe and a diadem.
15 I was eyes to the blind,
  And feet was I to the lame.
16 I was a father to the needy:
  And the cause of him that I knew not I searched out.
17 And I brake the jaws of the unrighteous,
  And plucked the prey out of his teeth.

COMMENT 29:11-17

Verse 11—Job's righteousness has been vindicated by both his eyes and ears. When his hearers heard of his deeds, they praised him. Their eyes saw his impeccable conduct and also gave witness to his righteousness—Gen. 30:13; Prov. 31:28; Ps. 72:17. The verb "called me blessed" (literally "pronounced me happy") suggests that Job was not only blessed but that he deserved the blessings from God. All of the evidence "bore witness to me," Job declares. Men declared their approval of him.

Verse 12—Job's words stand in radical tension with what Eliphaz had said in 22:6ff. Job had graciously helped the

286

poor[6] and the fatherless as in 24:9.

Verse 13—Ministering to those in despair evokes their blessings upon Job. Here Job speaks of high tribute and rich satisfaction for his benevolence. The verb rendered "to sing for joy" means "to raise a ringing cry" of either grief or joy. Here the context demands joy.

Verse 14—Job wore his righteousness as a robe, which was publicly visible to all—Ps. 132:9; Isa. 59:17. He was so immersed in just acts that "it put on me," i.e., clothed him as a garment. Likewise shame can be worn as a garment—8:22 and Ps. 132:18.

Verse 15—The social significance of Job's piety is here described in a beautiful fashion. He was eyes to the blind and feet to the lame.

Verse 16—As a father who provided for his family, Job expresses his godly nature—Isa. 22:21; I Cor. 4:15. The poor were utterly helpless before the law. Job undertook the task of securing legal justice for the poor. He fed them, protected, and provided in general for their personal and social welfare. Few would even do such a thing for those with whom they were acquainted. Job sought out those who needed help, even when he did not know them personally. He acted selflessly, not as a tyrant, as he was charged—Rom. 3:1ff. So God in Christ sought us out of our darkness. Christ alone is the answer to Job's cries and our needs.

Verse 17—The word rendered "jaws" as in A. V. literally means fangs or gnawing teeth, not jaws. The oppressive wicked are compared to a wild animal; when his "fangs" are broken off, its aggressive power is destroyed. Job rescued the poor from their ruthless oppressors, but he also destroyed the power of the aggressor. He rescued them out of the mouth of ruthless animals.

---

[6] See my analysis of "the poor" in light of world-wide Christian witness today in my *The Word of God for a Broken World*, LCC, 1977.

287

c. The honor that was his (29:18-25)

TEXT 29:18-25

18 Then I said, I shall die in my nest,
   And I shall multiply my days as the sand:
19 My root is spread out to the waters,
   And the dew lieth all night upon my branch:
20 My glory is fresh in me,
   And my bow is renewed in my hand.
21 Unto me men gave ear, and waited,
   And kept silence for my counsel.
22 After my words they spake not again;
   And my speech distilled upon them.
23 And they waited for me as for the rain;
   And they opened their mouth wide *as* for the latter rain.
24 I smiled on them, when they had no confidence;
   And the light of my countenance they cast not down.
25 I chose out their way, and sat *as* chief,
   And dwelt as a king in the army,
   As one that comforteth the mourners.

COMMENT 29:18-25

Verse 18—Praised and honored by both God and man, Job felt secure in the blessings of prosperity. He thought that he would live to a ripe old age and die surrounded by his children ("in my nest")—Deut. 32:11; Isa. 16:2. By a hyperbolic phrase, Job declares that his clan would be "as the sand," i.e., emphasizing longevity and numerous members of the family.[7]

Verse 19—Prosperity is expressed by images of a tree—8:16ff. The tree is green and full of life; water (long root systems,

---

[7] G. R. Driver, *Palestinian Exploration Quarterly*, 1955, pp. 138ff; P. P. Saydon, *Catholic Biblical Quarterly*, 1961, p. 252; and M. Dahood, *Biblica*, 1967, pp. 542ff.

and "dew on the branches") is everywhere abundant—Pss. 1:3; 80:12; Jer. 17:8; Ezek. 31:7.

Verse 20—His respect and social rank (Heb. *kobad*—glory) will continue undiminished.[8] His bow, a symbol of strength, is ever in his hands. A broken bow is a symbol of impotence—Gen. 49:24; Ps. 46:9; Jer. 49:35; and Hos. 1:5. Job never anticipated anything like his present situation.

Verse 21—Beginning with this verse and continuing to verse 25, Job speaks of the response which others afforded him when he spoke (cf. verses 7-10—respect he received when he arrived at the gate). Before his present condition destroyed his prestige, his words brought comfort and hope to those who heard.[9]

Verse 22—His words were accepted as an oracle. After passing his judgment, nothing remained to be said. The image used here with regard to how his words were received is a term describing a refreshing rain (A. V. "dropped"—Deut. 32:12). His words were life-giving drops from heaven—Prov. 16:15; Hos. 6:3; and Deut. 11:14.

Verse 23—His hearers drank up his words as the parched ground absorbed the rain—Ps. 119:131; the word here signifies the spring rain so vital to the crops—Jer. 2:3; Joel 2:23; and Zech. 10:1, cf. "you are my disciples if you abide in my word," Jesus.

Verse 24—Even a smile from Job was considered an undeserved reward. The A. V. rendering of "they had no confidence" should read "they did not believe," which is the common meaning of the verb. The second line means that the despondency of others never destroyed Job's cheerfulness.

Verse 25—Whenever Job gave directions, they were immediately carried out, as a prince (A. V. chief-king) directs his army. If the text is accepted as it stands, then Job's consolation of mourners is emphasized. Dhorme makes a good

---

[8] Though it does yield a parallel with line two, Mansoor's suggestion that glory should be emended to *kidon* or victory is dubious, *Revue de Qumran*, 1961-2, p. 388.

[9] In order to maintain parallelism with the preceding verse, G. R. Driver transposes the verbs "waited" and "kept silence," which is not impossible—see *Vetus Testamentum*, III, 1955, 86.

case for a different sense in the difficult third line as he renders it "where I led them, they were willing to go"[10] (A. V. like one who comforts mourners). Though the text makes sense as it stands, it makes the parallelism more difficult. But now all the nobodys to whom he had been so gracious despise him.

TODAY'S ENGLISH VERSION

Job's Final Statement of His Case

29 Job began speaking again.

Job

2 If only my life could be again
    as it was when God watched over me.
3 God was always with me then,
    and gave me light as I walked through the
      darkness.
4 Those were the days when I was prosperous,
    when God's friendship protected my home.
5 Almighty God was with me then,
    and I was surrounded by all my children.
6 My cows and goats gave plenty of milk,
    and my olive trees grew in the rockiest soil.
7 Whenever the city elders met,
    and I took my place among them,
8   young men stepped aside as soon as they saw me,
    and old men stood up to show me respect.
9 The leaders of the people would stop talking;
10   even the most important men kept silent.

11 Everyone who saw me or heard about me
    had good things to say about what I had done.
12 When the poor cried out, I helped them;

---

[10] For required emendation and justification, see Dhorme, *Job;* and Pope, *Job.*

I helped orphans who had nowhere to turn.
¹³ Men who were in deepest misery praised me,
and I helped widows find security.
¹⁴ I have always acted justly and fairly.
¹⁵ I helped the blind and the lame.
¹⁶ I was like a father to the poor,
and took the side of strangers in trouble.
¹⁷ I destroyed the power of cruel men
and rescued their victims.

¹⁸ I always expected to live a long life,
and to die at home in comfort.
¹⁹ I was like a tree whose roots always have water,
and whose brances are wet with dew.
²⁰ Everyone was always praising me,
and my strength never failed me.
²¹ When I gave advice, people were silent
and listened carefully to what I said;
²² they had nothing to add when I was through.
My words sank in like drops of rain;
²³ everyone listened eagerly,
the way farmers welcome the spring rains.
²⁴ When I smiled on them they could hardly believe it;
their gloom never discouraged me.
²⁵ I took charge and made the decisions;
I led them the way a king leads his troops,
and gave them comfort when they were
discouraged.

QUESTIONS FOR DISCUSSION 29:1-25

572. What is the general content of the next three chapters?
It seems a natural conclusion. Explain.
573. "God will take care of you" seems to be the theme of
Job's life—but just how will this be done? Cf. 10:14;
13:27; 14:16.

574. What is "the lamp" of verse three?
575. "Ripeness" does not mean decline. What does it mean?
576. Children are the gift of God—to lose these gifts should teach us something. What did Job learn? Cf. vs. 5.
577. What is meant by reference to butter and oil in verse six?
578. Job's former happiness was based on three relationships. What were they?
579. How did both the young and the old show respect to Job? Cf. vs. 8.
580. How did princes react to Job?
581. In the presence of Job, men became hushed and nervous. Explain.
582. Isn't Job a bit self-righteous as described in verse 11? Discuss.
583. No wonder Job was so incensed with the words of Eliphaz. Cf. 22:6ff. Explain.
584. Someone shouted for joy because of Job. Who was it? Does this happen today?
585. Americans (as individuals) could hardly be described in the words of verse 14. Why?
586. Were there more blind and lame in Job's day than ours? Was it easier to meet their needs? Discuss.
587. Show how Job acted as a father to the poor. Do they need such care today? Are we obligated?
588. Job not only helped the poor; he did something to the aggressor. What was it? It would seem that much of this describes what our Lord did for us. Discuss.
589. Job contemplated dying in the "nest" and multiplying his days. What is meant?
590. Job is like a tree. Cf. Pss. 1:3 and 80:12.
591. Both Job's respect and social rank would never change. How is this expressed? What a reversal he had!
592. Unless Job is exaggerating he must have been a very wise man. Cf. vs. 22.
593. There seems to be a complete analogical parallel in this chapter to Job and a picture of the blessings we receive from our Lord. Trace them out.

2. Sorrowful description of his present sad estate (30:1-31)
   a. The contempt he has from men of lowest class (30:1-15)

TEXT 30:1-15

30 But now they that are younger than I have me in derision,
Whose fathers I disdained to set with the dogs of my flock.
2 Yea, the strength of their hands, whereto should it profit me?
Men in whom ripe age is perished.
3 They are gaunt with want and famine;
They gnaw the dry ground, in the gloom of wasteness and
desolation.
4 They pluck salt-wort by the bushes;
And the roots of the broom are their food.
5 They are driven forth from the midst *of men;*
They cry after them as after a thief;
6 So that they dwell in frightful valleys,
In holes of the earth and of the rocks.
7 Among the bushes they bray;
Under the nettles they are gathered together.
8 *They are* children of fools, yea, children of base men;
They were scourged out of the land.
9 And now I am become their song,
Yea, I am a byword unto them.
10 They abhor me, they stand aloof from me,
And spare not to spit in my face.
11 For he hath loosed his cord, and afflicted me;
And they have cast off the bridle before me.
12 Upon my right hand rise the rabble;
They thrust aside my feet.
And they cast up against me their ways of destruction.
13 They mar my path,
They set forward my calamity,
Even men that have no helper.
14 As through a wide breach they come:
In the midst of the ruin they roll themselves *upon me.*
15 Terrors are turned upon me;

293

They chase mine honor as the wind;
And my welfare is passed away as a cloud.

COMMENT 30:1-15

Verse 1—Job's irretrievable prestigious past is abruptly contrasted with the present chaos derived from the calamities he is presently enduring. Sharp abruptness is conveyed by the repetition of "But now"—verses 1, 9, 16 ('*k*—surely in verse 24). The prince who has shared his abundance to meet their needs, his compassion to heal their suffering, is now despised; he is beneath them. These miserable outcasts now despised their former benefactor. Their arrogant ingratitude is now one of Job's great burdens. Job pours out his soul in this poem, which contains four divisions: (1) Irreverence of impious men—verses 1-8; (2) Resentment of society—verses 9-15; (3) God's indifference—verses 16-23; and (4) Misery born of destitution—verses 24-31.

The young had formerly treated Job with marked respect—29:8; now "they make sport" of him. The verb translated as "have me in derision" is the same as in 29:24, but the preposition is different. In 29:24 he describes their gracious smile; here their vulgar mockery. The cultural decorum called for the respect of all elders—15:10. But those who watched over his former flocks with their guard dogs publicly expressed disrespect—Isa. 56:10ff; I Sam. 17:43; and Ps. 68:23. The dogs were scavengers and so were those who watched my flocks. Now they think they are better than I am.

Verse 2—Perhaps this verse describes the fathers of the youth in verse one. The fathers are weaklings (*kalah* here, *kelah* in 5:26, where 'firm strength' is conjectured) unfit and unable to do hard work. These men, who are not profitable to anyone, even they despise me.

Verse 3—Through hunger these men are stiff and lifeless. The word "gaunt" as in A. V. is from a word meaning hard or stony and is rendered barren in 3:7. They are so destitute

294

that they gnaw (*'rq*—occurs only here and in verse 17) the roots of the dry ground. The emphasis here is not so much hunger as destitution of diet, diet limited to desert roots. The last line alliterative and literally reads "yesterday desolate and waste," clearly suggesting the ruin and utter desolation of their habitat. Even these "desert rats" hate me.

Verse 4—Their diet is so poor that they eat "saltwort." This is a saline plant with sour leaves, which grows in salt marshes. This is miserable food eaten in miserable circumstances. The broom roots yield charcoal—Ps. 120:4; Isa. 47:14; but they are not edible. Only the destitute would eat this type of plant.

Verse 5—Dahood suggests that the obscure phrase—*min gew*[1]—should be translated "with a shout they are driven forth," i.e., driven away when they approached inhabited places. These are not like the people of 24:5ff who are forced to steal to have subsistence level of food; but they are social outcasts who are chased away from any community.

Verse 6—Since they are not welcome in any community, they live in the dreadful ravines among the rocks. Job bitterly relates how even these people taunt him, now that he is also an outcast living on a dunghill.

Verse 7—The root *-nhq* is used only twice in Job and means "bray." It can mean "bray" suggesting lust, like a stallion in Jer. 5:8; but surely here its meaning is the hoarse cries of hunger. The miserable rabble huddle together under the plant (*harul*) rendered nettle in A. V. They huddle for warmth, not sexual perversion, as Peake suggests. But the meaning is uncertain, though it is related to certain leguminous plants— Prov. 24:31.

Verse 8—These outcasts are "sons of no name." They have no respectable standing in any community; they are nobodys.[2]

---

[1] M. Dahood, *Biblica,* 1957, pp. 318ff.

[2] W. M. W. Roth, *Vetus Testamentum,* 1960, pp. 402ff, suggests "outcasts" for "sons of a senseless person."

These unwelcomed were thrown out of the land (Heb. *naka*—rendered scourged in A. V. should be thrust out or thrown out).

Verse 9—This verse ties the threads together from verse one forward. These nobodys sing taunting songs which make Job the butt of their mockery—Ps. 69:12; and especially Lam. 3:14.

Verse 10—Yesterday kings and princes revered Job. Now the most contemptuous men despise him. His description of this ilk has been rather elaborate—verses 3-8; and Pss. 59; 64; 73. This conglomeration of socially wretched even "spit on the ground in front of me"—the height of insult!

Verse 11—The metaphors are obscure. Line one is in the singular "he has loosed" (following the Kethib reading "his cord" rather than the Qere reading "my cord"); the second line is in the plural, "they have cast off." It is unclear what "cord" is intended, but the removal of the restraint (A. V.—bridle) is an insolent act intended to humiliate Job.

Verse 12—All of the images suggest an assault context. "On my right hand" could suggest a court of law, where the accuser stood at the right hand; but the context is that of a siege or assault. The word rendered "rabble" as in A. V. could mean "chicks" as in Deut. 22:6 and Ps. 83:3, and thus young ones with a deprecatory implication, that is "insolent pups." The verb rendered "cast off" in verse 11 appears here and means to drive out, or forth; thus the line implies that they have driven Job down roads of ruin or destruction (lit. they have cast off my feet).

Verse 13—The verb (*nts*—rendered as A. V. -*mar*) means to "break up" or "pull down." Job continues with the destruction imagery. The outcasts make Job's path impossible. These diabolical persons actively promote (A. V. set forward) his troubles. Those who aggressively attack him have no restraint (A. V. "helper"). G. R. Driver[3] has shown that the word has

---

[3] G. R. Driver, *American Journal of Semitic Literature*, 1935-6; p. 163; see also Blommerde, who renders the line as "there is none to help me against them."

polarized meanings of help or hinder; this context calls for hinder.

Verse 14—The imagery of a besieged city under attack is also maintained in this verse. Here the wall is breached and wave after wave of soldiers pour through the wall like a tempest (*soah*—Prov. 1:27; Ezek. 38:9). "In the midst of the ruin" expresses the fact of falling stones from the breached wall (Heb. "under the crash"). The hordes of soldiers roll through (the verb means roll—Amos 5:24) the wall like billows or waves. As if inexhaustible, Job's enemies roll over him as a storm-tossed sea.

Verse 15—Terrors are overthrown on top of me. The picture is strikingly violent. Job's princely dignity, once so widely acknowledged, is now blowing in the wind—21:18 and Ps. 1:4. His well-being (Heb. *yesu'ah*[4]—prosperity, often rendered salvation) passes swiftly away.

b. His unhappy misery (30:16-23)

TEXT 30:16-23

16 And now my soul is poured out within me;
  Days of affliction have taken hold upon me.
17 In the night season my bones are pierced in me,
  And the *pains* that gnaw me take no rest.
18 By *God's* great force is my garment disfigured;
  It bindeth me about as the collar of my coat.
19 He hath cast me into the mire,
  And I am become like dust and ashes.
20 I cry unto thee, and thou dost not answer me:
  I stand up, and thou gazest at me.
21 Thou art turned to be cruel to me;

---

[4] Material and physical welfare is the dimension of the biblical doctrine of salvation often missed and is presently being strongly emphasized by Neo-Marxist Roman Catholics, especially in Latin America. See my *Seminar Syllabus—Sin and Salvation.*

With the might of thy hand thou persecutest me.
22 Thou liftest me up to the wind,
    thou causest me to ride *upon it;*
    And thou disolvest me in the storm.
23 For I know that thou wilt bring me to death,
    And to the house appointed for all living.

COMMENT 30:16-23

Verse 16—For the third time Job emphasizes the contrast between his past and present existence—"and now"—verses 1, 9, 16; Ps. 42:4. Now he experiences only "days of affliction" —verse 27 and Lam. 1:7. His soul (*nephesh*) can absorb no more emotional strain. His suffering has drained him of all zest for life—I Sam. 1:15; Ps. 42:5; and Lam. 2:19.

Verse 17—The subject of this verse could be either "the night" personified or "He," i.e., God. The night pierces, or God pierces. The A. V. takes "my bones" as subject and renders the verb "are pierced." The night is the time when his suffering is most severe—7:3, 13ff. "My gnawers (lit. Heb.) do not lie down," i.e., sleep.

Verse 18—If God is taken as the subject as in A. V., then God seizes his garment and distorts or disfigures it. The line suggests a tightly fitting collar that binds, but this is problematic in that eastern garments were loose and free flowing. Without extensive emendation, little sense can be made from the text. In spite of this fact, Job is declaring that his diseased body is very uncomfortable.

Verse 19—It is better to supply the unexpressed subject as God (Heb. has "he, or it has cast"), as there is no indication that the subject of this verse is any different from verse 18. It is probable that in both verses Job is reaffirming that God causes his pain and suffering. Perhaps "dust and ashes" are to be understood as symbolizing Job's humiliation.

Verse 20—Job cries to God for respite but God will not break His silence. The verb does not imply that God "stared at"

298

as the A. V. rendering "gazed" might imply—19:7.

Verse 21—The verb rendered "turned" appears in 13:24; 19:11; and Isa. 63:10. The image suggests one falling into enemy hands and being gradually and progressively infected with new and more intense pain.

Verse 22—This difficult verse has caused editors to provide many unconvincing emendations, but the basic sense is clear enough. The image shifts to that of a violent windstorm. He is "tossed about" and can neither control nor resist the wind. God rides the storm, but for Job it represents terror and destruction.

Verse 23—Though the Hebrew has "bring me back" in the sense of return, the context leaves little doubt that it should read "bring" him to death and leave him there. The grave is the house appointed for all the living.

c. The disappointment of all his hopes (30:24-31)

TEXT 30:24-31

24 Howbeit doth not one stretch out the hand in his fall:
   Or in his calamity therefore cry for help?
25 Did not I weep for him that was in trouble?
   Was not my soul grieved for the needy?
26 When I looked for good, then evil came;
   And when I waited for light, there came darkness.
27 My heart is troubled, and resteth not;
   Days of affliction are come upon me.
28 I go mourning without the sun:
   I stand up in the assembly, and cry for help.
29 I am a brother to jackals,
   And a companion to ostriches.
30 My skin is black, *and falleth* from me,
   And my bones are burned with heat.
31 Therefore is my harp *turned* to mourning,
   And my pipe into the voice of them that weep.

299

Verse 24—The idiom, *slh yd b*—"send the hand against" (A. V. as "stretch out the hand")—is to be taken in the hostile sense. In his prosperity Job did not strike the unfortunate; why is he now receiving God's hostile hand? Job declares that I always extended sympathy to anyone in distress, but me, I receive my calamities.

Verse 25—Job continues—Did I not weep for those who experienced—lit. "the hard of day" or the ones grieved. Now no one grieves for me. Will not even God show sympathy to Job?—Rom. 12:15 and I Pet. 3:8. His friends showed no sympathy to him—19:21—but he showed concern for others who suffered—29:12-17. What about God?

Verse 26—He disputes the views of his friends that virtue produces happiness. His prosperity did not continue as a result of his generous sympathy, as they had claimed it would.

Verse 27—His heart (lit. bowels, seat of emotions—Jer. 4:19 and Isa. 16:11) boils (A. V. troubled is not strong enough) within him—Lam. 1:20; 2:11; and Ezek. 24:5. His anxiety rages, yet no respite. God, please break your silence.

Verse 28—The A. V. rendering is defective. In the first line, "without the sun" is derived from the root *qdr*—which has the primary sense of "be or become dark." Job's blackened appearance is not caused by the sun (Heb. *hammah*—means sun, also heat as in Ps. 19:7), but rather his disease. The phrase found in the A. V., "I go mourning without the sun," makes little sense. The same root, i.e., *qdr,* generates the meaning of "sad" or "mourning," but this is probably the less preferred understanding for this context. The sense is that he is "blackened without the sun." He says that I stand in the assembly and cry for help, but no one hears.

Verse 29—Jackals live in the desert, and the only place that Job is welcome is there. The jackals are also known for their plaintive cry, with which he also identifies. The ostrich, too, is known for its hissing, cackling, and doleful moaning—Mic. 1:8; Isa. 13:21; 34:13. The mournful howl of these animals still disturbs the desert nights.

Verse 30—The disease is ravaging Job as his skin peels

off (*me'aloy,* from upon me) his bones. His skin is black (this verse contains a different root than found in verse 28) from the final stages of the disease. Fever penetrates (burns) deeply in his bones. This same verb "burn" is found in Ezekiel 24:10 where it is used of the burning of bones with fire. Here it is used metaphorically, so also Ps. 102:4 and Isa. 24:6.

Verse 31—The harp (*kinnor*) is often used for a joyful religious celebration. Here the celebration has turned to mourning. The glad, happy sounds are no more. The flute (*'ugab*) also expresses the spirit of lamentation. Here is a beautiful but pathetic contrast between Job's past happy experiences and his present "sickness unto death." From the perspective of his own "angst" we turn to hear Job's final oath—the oath of innocence.

TODAY'S ENGLISH VERSION

30 But men younger than I am make fun of me now!
Their fathers have always been so worthless
I wouldn't let them help my dogs guard sheep.

² They were a bunch of worn-out men,
too weak to do any work for me.

³ They were so poor and hungry
they would gnaw dry roots—
at night, in wild, desolate places.

⁴ They pulled up and ate the plants of the desert,
even the tasteless roots of the broom tree!

⁵ Everyone drove them away with shouts,
the way you shout at a thief.

⁶ They had to live in caves,
in holes dug in the sides of cliffs.

⁷ Out in the wilds they howled like animals,
and huddled together under the bushes.

⁸ A worthless bunch of nameless nobodies!
They were driven out of the land.

⁹ Now they come and laugh at me;

301

I am nothing but a joke to them.
¹⁰ They treat me with disgust;
    they think they are too good for me,
    and even come and spit in my face.
¹¹ Because God has made me weak and helpless,
    they turn against me with all their fury.
¹² This mob attacks me head-on;
    they send me running; they prepare their final
      assault.
¹³ They cut off my escape and try to destroy me;
    and there is no one to stop them.
¹⁴ They pour through the holes in my defenses,
    and come crashing down on top of me;
¹⁵   I am overcome with terror.
My dignity is gone like a puff of wind,
    and my prosperity like a cloud.

¹⁶ Now I am about to die;
    there is no relief for my suffering.
¹⁷ At night my bones all ache;
    the pain that gnaws me never stops.
¹⁸ God grabs me by my collar
    and twists my clothes out of shape.
¹⁹ He throws me down in the mud;
    I am no better than dirt.

²⁰ I call to you, God, but you never answer;
    and when I pray, you pay no attention.
²¹ You are treating me cruelly;
    you persecute me with all your power.
²² You let the wind blow me away;
    you toss me about in a raging storm.
²³ I know you are taking me off to my death,
    to the fate in store for everyone.
²⁴ Why do you attack a ruined man
    who can do nothing but beg for pity?
²⁵ Didn't I weep with people in trouble
    and feel sorry for those in need?

> ²⁶ I hoped for happiness and light,
>   but trouble and darkness came instead.
> ²⁷ I am torn apart by worry and pain;
>   there is nothing but suffering ahead.
> ²⁸ I walk in gloom and there is no comfort;
>   I stand up in public and plead for help.
> ²⁹ My voice is as sad and lonely
>   as the cries of a jackal or an ostrich.
> ³⁰ My skin has turned dark; I am burning with fever.
> ³¹ Where once I heard joyful music,
>   there is now only mourning and weeping.

QUESTIONS FOR DISCUSSION 30:1-31

594. There is a great contrast throughout this chapter. What is it?
595. Who are these strange ungrateful men of verses 1-8?
596. What caused these men to show change in their attitude toward Job?
597. What is said of weak old men in verse two?
598. In what sense could these men be called "desert rats"?
599. The diet of these men indicates almost starvation. Why all this emphasis?
600. Are there many men today who live in such a miserable manner? Would they mock? Discuss.
601. The places of living of these miserable men and Job are somewhat alike. How?
602. These men are like braying horses. Explain.
603. "Sons of no name"—What gave them this position?
604. The point of verses one through eight is given in verse nine. What is it?
605. The height of insult is reached in verse ten. What is it?
606. What is meant by the reference to "cord" in verse 11?
607. What is the image created in verse 12?
608. Job is a besieged city under attack. How graphic is the

description! Point out examples.

609. Job is blown away. Explain verse 15.
610. Job's suffering has given him a very despondent view of life. Why?
611. At night pain somehow seems much worse. Is this the thought of verse 17? There is more. Discuss.
612. Explain in your own words the meaning of verse 18.
613. God looks on and sees all but says nothing. Is that the thought of verse 20?
614. In what sense does Job see God as cruel to him?
615. Express in your own words the meaning of verse 22.
616. Is the grave the end as suggested in verse 23?
617. Job says God is not keeping the golden rule. Is this the thought of verse 24. Discuss.
618. Job was grieved for the needy. He wept for those in trouble. What is implied by saying this as in verse 25?
619. Virtue does not always produce happiness. Why?
620. Job is more than worried. Explain verse 27.
621. There is difficulty in translating the first phrase of verse 28. What is meant?
622. How is Job like a jackal or ostrich?
623. The disease affects the skin. How? Discuss.
624. Job used to play harp and a pipe. For what purpose. To whom?

3. Solemn declaration that neither in him nor in his conduct was there justification for the change, and he is ready to face God (31:1-40)
    a. He was not lustful. (31:1-8)

TEXT 31:1-8

31 I made a covenant with mine eyes;
    How then should I look upon a virgin?
2 For what is the portion from God above,
    And the heritage from the Almighty on high?
3 Is it not calamity to the unrighteous,
    And disaster to the workers of iniquity?
4 Doth not he see my ways,
    And number all my steps?
5 If I have walked with falsehood,
    And my foot hath hasted to deceit
6 (Let me be weighed in an even balance,
    That God may know mine integrity);
7 If my step hath turned out of the way,
    And my heart walked after mine eyes,
    And if any spot hath cleaved to my hands:
8 Then let me sow, and let another eat;
    Yea, let the produce of my field be rooted out.

COMMENT 31:1-8

Verse 1—In the ancient Israelite legal procedure the oath of innocence repudiating an accusation was of crucial importance. Where clear evidence was lacking, it was taken as proof of the innocence of the accused. Thus, the swearing of such an oath was a solemn religious celebration, which placed the verdict in God's hands.[1] Job here swears his innocence,

---

[1] For examination of Ps. 139 as an oath denying worship of other gods, see E. Würthwein, *Vetus Testamentum,* 1957, pp. 165-182; R. de Vaux, *Ancient Israel,*

then challenges the creator of the universe to give His verdict, i.e., *acknowledge* that he is innocent.[2] He rests his case on a series of oaths of clearance. Belief in the power of the oath made it the ultimate criterion of probability—Ex. 22:9-10 and I Kg. 8:31-32. Some have compared Job's negative repudiation of evil to the negative confession in the *Egyptian Book of the Dead* where a long list of sins not committed are enumerated.[3] The exact list of Job's disclaimers is difficult to determine because of textual uncertainties. But the oath is no mere formal matter. Job examines both his interior motives and exterior behavior to enumerate what sins or crimes he has been tempted to commit. Only God will impel this oriental aristocrat to virtuous action and self-restraint. His moral standards are perhaps the highest to be found in the Old Testament. He shows sensitive respect for the dignity of his fellow men, even slaves. He also refutes Eliphaz's accusation (chapter 22)—31:16-18, 19-20.[4]

In line one Job declares that he has put a ban (lit. "cut a covenant") on his eyes. The preposition "for" (*le,* not the usual with—'*im* or '*et*) designates a condition imposed by a superior on an inferior party in a covenant or treaty—I Sam. 11:2; II Sam. 5:3; II Kg. 11:4. Job is master of his eyes. If the particle -*mah* is taken as negative rather than as interrogative how, as in A. V., then the line reads "that I would not look

---

1 vol, E. T., 1961, McGraw-Hill, "Hall and Justice," pp. 143-163, esp. pp. 155ff; W. Zimmerli, "Das Gesetz in Alten Testament," *Theologische Literaturzeitung,* 1960, pp. 481-498; D. Daube, *Studies in Biblical Law* (Cambridge, 1947); A. Alt, *Die Ursprunge des Israelitischen/Gesretz* (Leipzig, 1934, Munich, 1953), pp. 278-332; G. E. Mendenhall, *Law and Covenant in Israel and the Ancient Near East* (Pittsburgh, reprinted from *Biblical Archaeologist,* 1954), pp. 26-46, 49-76; see my bibliography on Seminar Syllabus: *Philosophy of Law.*

[2] See S. Blank, "The Curse, Blasphemy, the Spell, and the Oath," *Hebrew Union College Annual,* 1950, pp. 73-95; also his "An Effective Literary Device in Job XXXI, *Journal Semitic Studies,* 1951, pp. 105-107; and F. Horst, "Der Eid im altenteatament," *Evangelische Theologie,* 1957, pp. 366-384.

[3] See J. Murtagh, "The Book of Job and the Book of the Dead," *Irish Theological Quarterly,* 1968, pp. 166-173.

[4] See E. Asswald, "Hiob 31 in Rahmen der alttestamentiche Ethik," *Theologische Versuche,* 1970, pp. 9-26.

upon a virgin." Emending the text is completely unnecessary here. Job here is discussing "sinning by desire," and below the act of adultery. Job is here setting forth his controlled modesty, though as an Eastern prince he could do, with no impropriety or social repercussion, what he has made a covenant not to do. This is religious motive for morals of the highest order—Matt. 5:28 and 18:8. Isaiah contains a beautiful description of a righteous man, "who shakes his hands, lest they hold a bribe, stops his ears against hearing of bloodshed, shuts his eyes against looking at evil"—Isa. 33:5, eg. Joseph's example in Genesis 38.

Verse 2—In the previous verse, Job is clearly thinking of his behavior in the days of his piety, prosperity, and prestige. Job has consistently maintained that piety[5] ought to be rewarded by the blessings of prosperity, and his entire argument is that in practice this is not the case. God has not rewarded his righteousness; rather He has punished him for it.

Verse 3—Job thought that he could depend on the above principle in his own life. "Workers of iniquity" is a common expression for the wicked in the Psalms. Disastrous calamities would be appropriate for the wicked, but not for a righteous man like he is.

Verse 4—God was his friend. He used to graciously watch over his life—14:16. But now God is silent in the presence of his suffering. Do his purity and piety count for nothing? God is viewed here as morally, inwardly, and outwardly available to Job. God "sees" his thoughts and actions and "counts" the steps in his entire existence.

Verse 5—He begins his series of oaths rejecting evil with a general repudiation of any sort of unrighteous conduct. Here

---

[5] In view of our own 20th century crisis in piety and Eastern meditation techniques, eg., T. M., being rushed into the spiritual vacuum, see Brother Lawrence, *The Practice of the Presence of God* (Revell, 1958); the works of both Ritschel and Warfield on *Perfectionism;* Donald G. Bloesch, *The Crisis of Piety* (Eerdmans, 1968); F. E. Stoeffler, *The Rise of Evangelical Pietism* (Brill, Leiden, 1971 ed.); also his *German Pietism During the 18th Century* (Brill: Leiden, 1973); John Bunyan's classic *The Pilgrim's Progress,* many eds.; Augustine's *Confessions* (Oxford, 1958); S. Kierkegaard, *Purity of Heart* (Harper, 1956).

falsehood is personified and presented as a companion. Perhaps Dahood is correct in suggesting that the preposition '*im*, here parallel with -'*al*, has directional significance meaning walking and hastening "toward" falsehood and deceit. He also suggests an emendation which makes the offense specific. He renders, "If I went to an idol, or my foot hastened to a fraud."⁶

Verse 6—The Old Testament condemns false balances consistently—Lev. 19:36; Ezek. 45:10; Amos 8:5; Prov. 11:1; 20:23. For the weighing of a man in the balance for evaluating his character, see Dan. 5:27 and Matt. 7:2. God has previously borne witness to his integrity in 2:3, where the same word as here appears. Job is not a moral fraud; if he were weighed, God's judgment would be positive, as before.⁷

Verse 7—Have I departed from the path of righteousness? His covenant with his eyes in verse one is here extended to a broader sphere. He has not coveted what is another's. Sin is often metaphorically pictured as "staining one's hands"— 11:14; 16:17; and Isa. 1:15. Clean hands are symbolic of one's righteousness—22:30 and Ps. 24:4.

Verse 8—If he has sinned in thought or deed, Job here invokes a curse upon himself—5:5; 27:17; Lev. 26:16; Mic. 6:15; Isa. 45:22. Though it is possible that *se'esa'im* in line two refers to produce of the field, as in A. V., in all probability it means Job's human progeny. As Pope affirms, human beings can be uprooted as well as plants⁸—Ps. 52:5; Job 31:12b. His entire lineage is being removed from the earth, his children are dead, and he is dying.

b. Was upright in his domestic relations (31:9-15)
c. He was kind and neighborly. (31:16-23)

---

⁶ M. Dahood, *Ugaritic Hebrew Philology* (Rome, 1945), p. 32.

⁷ See suggestion by M. Dahood, *Vetus Testamentum*, Supplement, 1967, p. 47, regarding "full weight" instead of "my innocence," but the sense would remain the same regardless.

⁸ M. Pope, *JBL*, 1961, p. 196.

TEXT 31:9-23

9 If my heart hath been enticed unto a woman,
   And I have laid wait at my neighbor's door;
10 Then let my wife grind unto another,
   And let others bow down upon her.
11 For that were a heinous crime;
   Yea, it were an iniquity to be punished by the judges:
12 For it is a fire that consumeth unto Destruction,
   And would root out all mine increase.
13 If I have despised the cause of my man-servant or of my
      maid-servant,
   When they contended with me;
14 What then shall I do when God riseth up?
   And when he visiteth, what shall I answer him?
15 Did not he that made me in the womb make him?
   And did not one fashion us in the womb?
16 If I have withheld the poor from *their* desire,
   Or have caused the eyes of the widow to fail,
17 Or have eaten my morsel alone,
   And the fatherless hath not eaten thereof
18 (Nay, from my youth he grew up with me as with a father,
   And her have I guided from my mother's womb);
19 If I have seen any perish for want of clothing,
   Or that the needy had no covering;
20 If his loins have not blessed me,
   And if he hath not been warmed with the fleece of my sheep;
21 If I have lifted up my hand against the fatherless,
   Because I saw my help in the gate:
22 Then let my shoulder fall from the shoulder-blade,
   And mine arm be broken from the bone.
23 For calamity from God is a terror to me,
   And by reason of his majesty I can do nothing.

COMMENT 31:9-23

Verse 9—The sin of adultery is repudiated by Job. The

"woman" is a married woman, as the parallel makes plain, i.e., "neighbor's door" or house. The picture of laying in wait suggests that of an adulteress—Prov. 7:12; Ex. 20:7; also verse 19; here the thought is of an adulterer who waits for his opportunity, which he might find at dusk—24:15.

Verse 10—The work of a slave is grinding—Ex. 11:5; Isa. 47:2. Samson was reduced to grinding by the Philistines— Judges 16:21. In the second line, Job invokes the principle of the *lex talionis*. His hypothetical adultery would to all Hebrews be an offense against her husband. In Hebrew law, adultery always involved a married woman. Their double standard meant that the marital status of the man was immaterial (compare with Jesus' revolutionary views, His repudiation of the double standard, and His liberation of women).[9] The second line is clearly sexual in connotation, as the verb *kr'* can imply sexual intercourse—Deut. 28:30.

Verse 11—The A. V. rendering "heinous crime" comes from *zimmah* and is consistently used of lewdness, and indecent sexual conduct.[10] The perversion is so lewd that it deserved to receive judicial condemnation.

Verse 12—This verse echoes Deut. 32:22; Prov. 6:27-29. The sure punishment for adultery is compared with deadly fire—Eccl. 9:8b.[11]

Verse 13—In this verse the issue turns to the charge of the abuse of power. If he has abused his servants, permitted the weak to suffer injustice, he again calls a curse down upon himself. The rights of slaves were few in the ancient world. Hebrew laws attempted to mitigate their harsh treatment— Ex. 21:2-11; Lev. 25:39-55; Deut. 5:14; for manumission of slaves, see Jer. 34:8-11.[12] Job had recognized his slaves as

---

[9] This misunderstanding, i.e., thinking that this verse literally means that his wife becomes a slave, is presented in the apocryphal work, *The Testament of Job;* while Job sat on the dunghill, his wife carried water as a slave.

[10] M. Pope, *JBL,* 1966, p. 458.

[11] G. R. Driver, *Vestus Testamentum,* 1955, pp. 88ff.

[12] On the matter of slavery in the Near East and Israel, see R. de Vaux, *Ancient Israel,* pp. 80-90; and J. Mendelsohn, *Slavery in the Ancient Near East,* 1949, for entire picture.

fellow human beings—verse 15—who had rights which were not enforceable by law. He was always ready to listen to their complaints. They often helped Job during his tragedies—19:15ff. These specific social crimes reveal a remarkably advanced moral consciousness for the Near East. Job here maintains that he has not failed in either equity or mercy. Neither virtue was based in law, but in love for his fellow human beings.

Verse 14—Jeremiah says that perfidy in dealing with slaves was a factor in God's condemnation of the southern kingdom to destruction in Babylonian exile—Jer. 34:15-22. Job here feels that he is answerable to God for his social behavior. His personal relationship with God had social significance. Salvation always has public signification and never merely private or personal meaning. The verb "rise" (*yaqum*—arise in vengeance) in line one suggests rising to judgment,[13] i.e., when God visits (verb means to visit 7:18; inspect 5:24; or punish 35:14), Job is conscious that his appeal to God will lead to investigation and consequent vindication or negative judgment. No slave could have made such an appeal legally, but Job can and does.

Verse 15—Job has spoken earlier (10:8ff) of God's merciful care being lavished upon him at his birth. Here he asserts that he has extended this same care upon slaves, who legally had no such rights. We cannot lose sight of the high ethical perspective in this verse. It is remarkable for any age, but in Job's *Sitz im Leben* is all the more remarkable. He declares that men are one because of the creator. The same problem haunts man in the last quarter of the 20th century. Cultural stratification can be overcome only in Job's redeemer, but neither through any proposed classical Liberal Fatherhood of God-Brotherhood of Man thesis, nor neo-Marxian "classless society." The evidence from Asia, Europe, Africa, and Latin America is adequate grounds for suspicion toward the myth that politico-economic conditions can humanize, thus unify,

---

[13] M. Dahood, *Biblica*, 1971, p. 346, suggests the root meaning vengeance.

311

mankind—Mal. 2:10; Prov. 17:5a; Acts 17:16ff; Eph. 6:9. Men's efforts to humanize merely proliferate bureaucracy, and then death by bureaucracy.

Verse 16—Job denies Eliphaz's charges under oath—22:7-9. He has not exploited the weak nor attained unjust victories in the community. It seems strange that one has raised the issue—Why are the poor and unfortunate so important? They do not prosper because they are wicked. If they were not wicked, they would not be the powerless poor. The wicked deserve their fate; so why would Eliphaz ever raise such a charge? It is completely irrational, even on his own assumptions.

Verse 17—Job has invited, or at least permitted, the poor to eat from his own table—Isa. 58:7; Prov. 22:9; and Matt. 25:35. He has fed the destitute; thus, he cared and shared.

Verse 18—He went far beyond heartless charity; he gave them fatherly compassion. That this expresses a behavior pattern and not a single act of charity is revealed in the Hebrew text, which says "he grew up with me" "from my mother's womb." He has always been a righteous man. These images are, of course, hyperbolic—James 1:27.

Verse 19—He even looked around to locate the poor, fatherless, and the widows. Clothing and covering are parallel in 24:7 and Matt. 25:36ff. His behavior was not a mere tax write-off for social prestige, like many of our great foundations in the western world.

Verse 20—The poor, whose loins once ached from the night cold, bless him for supplying a fleece covering. Their warmth praises him, as one's bones might praise God—Ps. 35:10.[14] Job's benevolence is rewarded by praise.

Verse 21—The raised hand (lit. waved or shaken) is symbolic of an overt threat—Isa. 11:15; 19:16; Zech. 2:9. He here denies that he has exploited his power to secure an unjust verdict—29:7. The orphans, widows, and poor had no

---

[14] For analysis of this figure, see G. R. Driver, *American Journal of Semitic Literature*, 1935-36, pp. 164ff.

prospects of justice without the support (Heb. is lit. "saw my help") of a person like Job—39:12; Prov. 22:12.

Verse 22—If what I have just declared is not true, then "may my lower arm be broken off from the upper arm."[15] Perhaps this imagery is derived from the violent mourning rites discussed in the Mosaic Law—Lev. 19:28; 21:5.

Verse 23—God alone, in all His majestic power, restrained Job from exploiting his power over others. He vividly describes his thought about God's presence—lit. "For a terror unto me was calamity from God." Terrien simply states the case: "It was religion which justified, supported, explained, and made possible his morality" (*Interpreter's Bible,* Vol. 4, p. 1121).

d. He did not trust in wealth nor in heavenly bodies.
(31:24-28)

TEXT 31:24-28

24 If I have made gold my hope,
   And have said to the fine gold,
   Thou art my confidence;
25 If I have rejoiced because my wealth was great,
   And because my hand had gotten much;
26 If I have beheld the sun when it shined,
   Or the moon walking in brightness,
27 And my heart hath been secretly enticed,
   And my mouth hath kissed my hand:
28 This also were an iniquity to be punished by the judges;
   For I should have denied the God that is above.

---

[15] Rendering of A. Herdner, *Revue des etudes semitiques,* 1942-43, p. 49.

COMMENT 31:24-28

Verse 24—He denies that he has ever made material wealth his God—22:24ff and 28:16. Deeper and deeper into his own thoughts he penetrates. He exposes two kinds of idolatry: (1) verses 24-25—money, rather than God; and (2) verses 26-28—the secret sin of invoking strange gods—Pss. 49:6ff; 52:7ff; 62:10; Prov. 11:28; Jer. 17:7; Eccl. 31:5-10; Matt. 6:24. His confidence is in God, not gold.

Verse 25—His former good fortune has not made him proud. His great possessions and power have not made him a bigot. He has not abused his wealth.

Verse 26—Here Job denies that he has been an idolator, worshipping the sun and the moon—Gen. 1:16ff. The imagery suggests that the sun was "a precious thing." It is the same word used of gems. Job denies even any secret longing to worship these two beautiful living lords of the eastern skies. The prophets severely condemned the worship of astro-deities by a vast number of covenant persons—Hab. 3:4; Jer. 8:2; Ezek. 8:16.

Verse 27—Job denies that his hand ever touched his mouth in homage to the sun and moon. Ezekiel attacks sun worship in 8:16; and Jeremiah castigates worshippers of the "queen of heaven" in 44:17. Kissing as an act of pagan worship is inveighed against in I Kg. 19:18 and Hosea 13:12. A. Parrot suggests that the gesture is used throughout the Middle East "when one tries to convince another in an argument."[16] The occult practices of the Canaanites are now known from the Ras Shamra literature.[17] Job is here contending for uncompromising monotheism in contrast to the crass, widely disseminated polytheism.

---

[16] See esp. A Goetze, *JNES*, 1945, p. 248, and literature cited, esp. B. Meissner "Der Kuss in alten orient."

[17] For the occult content of this literature, see C. H. Gordon, *Ugaritic Literature* (Rome, 1949); R. DeLanghe, *Le Textes des Ras Shamra—Ugarit* (Paris, 1943); R. Dussaud, *Les decouvertes de Ras Shamra et l' Ancien Testament;* E. Jacob, *Ras Shamra et L'Ancien Testament,* Delachaux et Niestle, 1960.

e. He lived openly and would not hesitate to have the Almighty publish his record. (31:29-40)

TEXT 31:29-40

29 If I have rejoiced at the destruction of him that hated me,
Or lifted up myself when evil found him
30 (Yea, I have not suffered my mouth to sin
By asking his life with a curse);
31 If the men of my tent have not said,
Who can find one that hath not been filled with his meat?
32 (The sojourner hath not lodged in the street;
But I have opened my doors to the traveller);
33 If like Adam I have covered my transgressions,
By hiding mine iniquity in my bosom.
34 Because I feared the great multitude,
And the contempt of families terrified me,
So that I kept silence, and went not out of the door—
35 Oh that I had one to hear me!
(Lo, here is my signature, let the Almighty answer me)
And *that I had* the indictment which mine adversary hath
written!
36 Surely I would carry it upon my shoulder;
I would bind it unto me as a crown:
37 I would declare unto him the number of my steps;
As a prince would I go near unto him.
38 If my land crieth out against me,
And the furrows thereof weep together;
39 If I have eaten the fruits thereof without money,
Or have caused the owners thereof to lose their life:
40 Let thistles grow instead of wheat,
And cockle instead of barley.
The words of Job are ended.

315

COMMENT 31:29-40

Verse 29—Job declares that he has never found pleasure in the destruction of his enemies. We are here presented with a rare treat. "If chapter 31 is the crown of all the ethical development of the Old Testament, verse 29 is the jewel of that crown" (Duhm). Oh, if he could have heard Jesus speak—Matt. 5:43ff. Moses enjoins help to one's enemies—Ex. 23:4ff; Prov. 20:22; 24:17ff; 25:21ff. Though the Psalmists often reveal a spirit of malevolence toward their enemies—58:10; 109:6ff; 118:10ff; 137:8ff—or become exulted over their misfortune—57:7; 59:10; 92:11; 118:7—Job declares against the imprecatory spirit found in some of Israel's hymns.

Verse 30—The contrary-to-fact conditional (*lu*) is not apparent in the A. V. translation; it is stronger than (*lo*—not) a negation. The turn of phrase Job uses, "my palate," suggests a dainty morsel, meaning he never permitted himself to taste such a delicious tid-bit—Eccl. 5:5 and I Kg. 3:11.

Verse 31—Job's hospitality has been shared by his slaves, not only his "social equals." The uncompleted oath "if not" (*'im lo*) has been taken by both Tur Sinai and Pope to imply the reading "to be sated with his flesh," i.e., homosexual abuse, at Job's table or in his house.[18] This is not self-evident from the Hebrew grammar, nor its most likely emendations. Imposing the sexual content of the Ugaritic literature on Job is a precarious pastime, as well as of dubious exegetical value.

Verse 32—His hospitality has been extended to both slaves and strangers (lit. wayfarer)—Gen. 19 and Jud. 19. Extension of hospitality meant the extension of protection from abuses of any kind.

Verse 33—Now Job repudiates the sin of hypocrisy. Job identifies Adam as a person who has sinned and attempted to hide his guilt along with himself from God. The mark of hypocrisy is living a lie. Often men try to hide their sins, but I have not.

---

[18] Pope, *Job,* pp. 236-237.

316

Verse 34—If it refers to guests, then he refused to give up his guest to the aggressive ones outside. Protection both inside and outside the home is the mark of true, i.e., non-hypocritical, hospitality. Or if the verse refers to Job, then had Job actually done the things charged to him by his enemies, he would have been afraid to have gone out of doors. He lived with a pure and unafraid heart—29:7. But if he were guilty, he would be horrified. Hospitality was a sacred trust in Job's world, dominated by God.

Verse 35—What are the specific charges—God? Every accused person has a right to know the charges brought against him. State the charges—God. I will validate my oath by my signature (Heb. *-taw*—last letter of Hebrew alphabet).[19] Job's opponent (lit. "man of my controversy") is God. Divine accuser, specify my charges, write them down, either as a writ of indictment or of acquittal.

Verse 36—What is it that Job would carry on his head or shoulders? The natural antecedent is the "writ" that he has called for in verse 35. To carry or wear something in this manner is to display it proudly—Isa. 9:5; 27:22; Ex. 13:16; Deut. 6:8; 11:18; Prov. 6:21. The exchange of dirty clothes for clean is the symbol of acquittal as in Zech. 3:2-6, 8-9. The mixed images suggest that the display of the "writ" and the symbol of acquittal he would wear as a crown.

Verse 37—There is nothing from his past that he is seeking to hide. He is willing to appear before God as an innocent man, not as an unrighteous one—verse 34. He would appear as a prince with a clear conscience.

Verse 38—Job calls his land to testify. If he has gained the land unjustly, let it cry out—Deut. 15:1ff and Lev. 19:19. Instead the land weeps for joy. The land is personified and identified with its rightful owner, Job.

Verse 39—The imagery is unclear. It is not certain whether

---

[19] For grammatical possibilities, see E. F. Sutcliffe, *Biblica*, 1949, pp. 71ff; P. P. Saydon, *Catholic Biblical Quarterly*, 1961, pp. 252ff.

the reference is to oppressive appropriation[20] of lands which brought death to their owner, such as Naboth—I Kg. 21—or that the owner died from some other cause.

Verse 40—If I have wrongly acquired the land, let it refuse to bear fruit, wheat, etc. Instead, let it bear thorns and putrid smelling plants. Presumably an editorial note adds, "The words of Job are ended." Thus he has delivered his final response to his consolers and his last challenge to God. Job's oath is response to the friends' charges, and it will stand because of default of evidence. His case against them is intact, but he has not won a judicial hearing before his creator. Job has made at least one defective move, i.e., presenting God as an adversary in a lawsuit. He has drawn conclusions from his unblemished life which are inappropriate in the presence of deity. From his suffering he has precariously deduced what God "ought" to do about it. What is the way to mediate between God's transcendence and His immanence? Rilke says that man cried for a ladder of escape, but God sent down a cross! Nonetheless, Job has asserted his rights—9:20; 13:18; 19:7; 23:7; 27:2, 6. He has been what God pronounced him to be—1:8 and 2:3. His presumptiveness face to face with holiness is hybris of the highest order. Prometheus and Iscarus combined had less arrogance than Job. His integrity has become a high wall, separating him from God, while he is searching for Him. He could never find God while walking the path of pride. God must come to Him; he could never come to God—II Cor. 5:17ff.[21]

---

[20] On this point see M. Dahood, *Biblical*, 1960, p. 303; also *Biblica*, 1962, p. 362; and the *Gregorianum*, 1962, p. 75.

[21] For the hermeneutical problems in chapters 29-31, see J. R. Kautz, *A Hermeneutical Study of Job 29-31*. Diss. Southern Baptist Theological Seminary, 1970; see Diss. Abstracts 30, 1970, 5516s.

TODAY'S ENGLISH VERSION

31 I have made a solemn promise
    never to look at a girl with lust.

² What does Almighty God do to us?
    How does he repay human deeds?
³ He sends disaster and ruin
    to those who do wrong.
⁴ God knows everything I do;
    he sees every step I take.

⁵ I swear I have never acted wickedly,
    and never tried to deceive others.
⁶ Let God weigh me on honest scales,
    and he will see how innocent I am.
⁷ If I have turned from the right path,
    or let myself be attracted to evil,
    if my hands are stained with sin,
⁸   then let my crops be destroyed,
    or let others eat the food I grow.

⁹ If I have been attracted to my neighbor's wife,
    and waited, hidden, outside her door,
¹⁰   then let my wife fix another man's food
    and sleep in another man's bed.
[¹¹ Such a sin would be wicked and would be punished
by death. ¹² It would be like a destructive, hellish
fire, destroying everything I have.]

¹³ When one of my servants complained against me,
    I would listen and treat him fairly.
¹⁴ If I did not, how could I then face God?
    What could I say when God came to judge me?
¹⁵ The same God who created me
    created my servants also.
¹⁶ I have never refused to help the poor,
    never let widows live in despair,

¹⁷   or let orphans go hungry while I ate.
¹⁸ All my life I have taken care of them.

¹⁹ When I found someone in need, too poor to buy
        clothes,
²⁰   I would give him clothing made of wool
        that had come from my own flock of sheep.
    And he would praise me with all his heart.

²¹ If I have ever cheated an orphan,
        because I knew I could win in court,
²²   then may my arms be broken;
        may they be torn out of my shoulders.
²³ Because I fear God's punishment,
        I could never do such a thing.

²⁴ I have never trusted in riches,
²⁵   or taken pride in my wealth.
²⁶ I have never worshiped the sun in its brightness,
        or the moon in all its beauty.
²⁷ I have never even been tempted to do it.
²⁸ Such a sin would be punished by death;
        it denies Almighty God.

²⁹ I have never been glad when my enemies suffered,
        or pleased when they met with disaster;
³⁰   I never sinned by praying for their death.
³¹ All the men who work for me know
        that I have always welcomed strangers.
³² I have welcomed travelers into my home,
        and never let them sleep in the streets.
³³ Other men try to hide their sins,
        but I have never concealed mine.
³⁴ I have never feared what people would say;
        I have never kept quiet or stayed indoors
        because I feared their scorn.

³⁵ Will no one listen to what I am saying?
    I swear that every word is true.

Let Almighty God answer me.

If the charges my opponent brings against me
were written down so that I could have them,
36   I would wear them proudly around my neck,
and hold them up for everyone to see.
37 I would tell God everything I have done,
and hold my head high in his presence.

38 If I have stolen the land I farm
and taken it from its rightful owners—
39   if I have eaten the food that grew,
but let the farmers that grew it starve—
40   then instead of wheat and barley
may weeds and thistles grow.

The words of Job are ended.

QUESTIONS FOR DISCUSSION 31:1-40

625. Making a covenant or taking an oath was so very important. Should we do such today?
626. Job is as proud of what he did not do as he is of what he did. Our eyes have a large responsibility in both areas. Explain.
627. Are we indeed "the master of our eyes"? Discuss.
628. Is Job telling the truth in his statement of verse 1b?
629. Was fornication permissible in Job's day? Discuss.
630. What is the connection between verse one and two?
631. Did Job agree with the major premise of his three friends? Cf. vs. 2.
632. How does Job express his friendship with God and God with him? Cf. vs. 4.
633. A series begins in verse five. What series? What is the first of the series?
634. Had Job been weighed in God's balance before? What is

he saying now?

635. The covenant with his eyes in verse one has extended to a broader sphere in verse seven. Discuss.

636. Is Job referring to his children in verse eight. Discuss.

637. There is a vivid picture in verse nine. What is it?

638. Job's wife would suffer for his sin of adultery. Is this fair? Discuss.

639. We have come a long way in America from the moral code of verse 11. Discuss.

640. How is adultery associated with fire?

641. There is revealed in verse 13 a remarkably advanced moral consciousness as related to slaves. Discuss.

642. Job believed that God would make a call upon him. For what purpose? Cf. vs. 14.

643. Job declares that men are one because of what? "Cultural stratification" can be overcome only by what?

644. Job denies the charge of Eliphaz made in 22:7-9, but the charge was irrational. Show how.

645. Job really had a practical and compassionate program for the poor. What was it? Cf. vss. 17, 18.

646. Are some of our acts of charity mere tax write-offs? Discuss.

647. What action is viewed in verse 21?

648. Job calls a drastic result upon himself if what he has said is not true. What was it?

649. How does the greatness of God relate to morality?

650. Job denies that he has had any other gods. Name two he has rejected.

651. The worship of the sun and moon was a real threat to the worship of God. Do we have this problem today?

652. What was involved in "kissing the hand"? Cf. vs. 27.

653. "If chapter 31 is the crown of all the ethical development of the O.T., then verse 29 is the jewel of that crown." Explain.

654. How easy (natural?) it is to rejoice in the destruction of those who hate us. How is such rejoicing done? Job didn't. Cf. vs. 30.

V. RESISTING THE RESTRAINTS—BREAKING OF SILENCE (32:1—37:24)

A. ELIHU CANNOT REMAIN SILENT. (32:1-22)

1. Introduction in prose: Elihu is angry with Job and with the three friends. (32:1-6a)

TEXT 32:1-6a

32 So these three men ceased to answer Job, because he was righteous in his own eyes. (2) Then was kindled the wrath of Elihu the son of Barachel the Buzite, of the family of Ram: against Job was his wrath kindled, because he justified himself rather than God. (3) Also against his three friends was his wrath kindled, because they had found no answer, and yet had condemned Job. (4) Now Elihu had waited to speak unto Job, because they were elder than he. (5) And when Elihu saw that there was no answer in the mouth of these three men, his wrath was kindled.

(6) And Elihu the son of Barachel the Buzite answered and said,

COMMENT 32:1-6a

Verse 1—Job is finished speaking. Enter Elihu, who makes four speeches[1] (32:1—37:24). He is described as a listener who has become too emotionally involved in Job's defense and

---

[1] For good survey of Elihu speeches, see Marvin E. Tate, "The Speeches of Elihu," *Review and Expositor,* The Book of Job, fall, 1971, pp. 487-495; D. N. Freedman, "The Elihu Speeches in the Book of Job," *Harvard Theological Review,* LXI, 1968, 51-59; L. Dennefeld, "Les discours d' Elihou," *Revue Biblique,* 1939, pp. 163-180; G. Fohrer, "Die Weisheit des Elihu," *Archiv für Orientforschung,* 1959-1960, pp. 83-94; H. D. Buby, "Elihu—Job's Mediator?" *S. E. Asia Journal of Theology,* 1965, pp. 33-54; and R. N. Carstensen, "The Persistence of the Elihu Tradition in Later Jewish Writers," *Lexington Theological Quarterly,* 1967, pp. 37-46.

the inadequacies of his friends' arguments that he must break his silence. Theologically, his central theme is not *suffering,* as many assume, but rather the *nature of God.* Elihu disapproves of Job's pride before God and his dogmatic insistence of his righteousness before his holy God.[2] He also rejects the traditional thesis of Job's friends that suffering is exclusively retributory. Rather, he suggests that suffering may be God's way of warning against human hybris. If a person would repent, God would restore him. After all of this is said, Elihu's practical advice is no different from Job's three friends. Elihu's speeches contain approximately 150 lines compared with the ca. 220 lines allotted to all three consolers in the dialogue section of Job. Many critics reject the speeches as integral to the structure of the book. Though his speeches reveal a knowledge of the themes and content of the preceding dialogue, some of the reasons given for rejecting the speeches as an original part of the book are: (1) Elihu is not mentioned in either the Prologue or Epilogue; (2) Job does not respond to his speeches; (3) God's "Shattering of His Silence" in chapter 38 follows naturally from chapter 31, and ignores Elihu's speeches; (4) God's rebuke is addressed only to Job's three friends, completely ignoring Elihu; (5) Perhaps the most crucial and most technically powerful reason is that the Hebrew grammar suggests a later period in the history of the language. The most powerful argument for the presence of this great passage (chapters 32-37) is that it powerfully prepares the way for *The Shattering of Silence,* i.e., Yahweh's speeches. Only the creative relevatory word from "outside" can answer Job's dilemma.

In the first speech (chapters 32-33), we are informed four times that Elihu is angry, and he enters the verbal arena to supply the deficiency, to redeem the failure, and to rebuke Job's three friends. Following his introduction in 32:1-5, the

---

[2] See excellent brief introduction by R. A. F. MacKenzie, "Job," *Jerome Biblical Commentary* (Prentice-Hall, 1968), pp. 528-529; also R. Gordis, "Elihu the Intruder," *Biblical and Other Studies,* ed. by A. Altman, 1963, pp. 60ff; J. H. Kroeze, "Die Elihu—reden in Buche Hiob," *Oudtestamentische Studien,* 1943, pp. 156ff.

speeches divide into six sections: (1) Elihu's youth is wiser than their aged wisdom—verses 6-14; (2) The collapse of Job's friends causes Elihu to intervene—verses 15-22; (3) He invites Job to give attention to his counsel—33:1-7; (4) Elihu declares that Job's contention of innocence and unjust affliction is false—verses 8-13; (5) He maintains that Job's experience refutes his complaint that God is silent—verses 14-18; and (6) Elihu's final appeal to Job—verses 29-33. These three friends in 2:11; 19:21; 42:10 abandon Job. Elihu distributes blame impartially to Job and his three friends by the phrase in "his own eyes" (LXX reads "in their eyes"). The debate was useless and futile because of Job's incorrigible self-righteousness. He is not innocent, and God has not afflicted him without just provocation.

Verse 2—The name Elihu means "he is my God" and appears elsewhere in scripture in I Sam. 1:1; I Chron. 12:21; 26:7; 27:18. He is the son of Barachel, which means "God has blessed." This is a strange inclusion of data in that neither the father of Job nor the fathers of his three friends are mentioned. Barachel is of the clan of Buz (an Aramaen name), the brother of Uz—Gen. 22:21—and so is closely related to Job—1:1. An Arabian Buz is mentioned in Jer. 25:23. Ram (means lofty) has Judahite connections in I Chron. 2:9, 25, 27; Ruth 14:19; Matt. 1:3; Lk. 3:33. Thus, we have genealogical connections all the way to Job's redeemer. But Job not only declared his innocence, he brought an indictment against God.

Verse 3—Elihu is aroused not becaue the friends condemned Job, but because they had not devised effective arguments against him. Rabbinic traditions list this verse as one of the eighteen corrections of the scribes, and the last line of the original text had "declared God" in the wrong, not Job. Yet this seems strange in that no condemnation of God follows from their failure to adequately respond to Job. The text makes perfectly good sense as it stands—"because they had found no answer by which they could prove Job guilty" (as condemned in A. V.)—Blommerde.

Verse 4—Elihu had "waited for Job's words." He gives as reason for his previous reticence his youth. Elihu's youthful modesty is excelled only by his youthful assurance.

Verse 5—The intensity of Elihu's anger is suggested by the fact that the phrase "his wrath was kindled" appears three times in these five verses.

Verse 6—The introductory narrative is finished; now Elihu begins his speech with the omniscience of youth. He initiates his speech with the reasons that compel him to join in the debate.

2. Silent because they are older, yet the spirit of the Almighty has given him understanding. (32:6b-10)

TEXT 32:6b-10

I am young, and ye are very old;
Wherefore I held back, and durst not show you mine
   opinion.
7 I said, Days should speak,
   And multitude of years should teach wisdom.
8 But there is a spirit in man,
   And the breath of the Almighty giveth them understanding,
9 It is not the great that are wise,
   Nor the aged that understand justice.
10 Therefore I said, Heaken to me;
   I also will show mine opinion.

COMMENT 32:6b-10

Verse 6—He denies that wisdom is prerogative of the aged. He has given them adequate time in which to answer Job, if they only had the power of mind and words to do so. He timidly held back—verse 4—"while they spoke" (*bedabberam* rather than *bidbarim*). The rendering of A. V. "opinion" does not

326

express the text which reads "knowledge." Elihu is giving forth with more than his opinion. He is not troubled by timidity. He expresses his position with brashful speech, not bashful silence.

Verse 7—Older men should speak out of their reservoir of experience. Because of his youth, he was silent, but no more.

Verse 8—The spirit (*ruah*) of God gives life, wisdom, intelligence, or any special and significant ability—27:3; 33:4; Ex. 31:3; Isa. 11:2; Dan. 5:12-13. Wisdom does not necessarily flow from old age—12:12 and 15:10. Since wisdom comes from God, piety is a prerequisite—Prov. 1:7; 2:6; 10:31; 15:33; *Wisdom of Solomon* 1:5-7; 7:22-23; I Cor. 2:6. Like the Psalmist—119:99—youthful Elihu believes that he has more understanding than his elders, because God is the origin of all wisdom. Wisdom belongs to God's Spirit rather than age. Elihu is correct in this part of his assertion, but his immodest assertions are inexcusable.

Verse 9—He correctly claims that it is not "the great" (as in A. V. does not mean powerful or influential) in age, as the parallel line shows—cf. Gen. 25:23—that have wisdom. The word means something like seniors, as the use of *zeqenim* in the *Manual of Discipline* suggests, i.e., senior members of the order.

Verse 10—Because wisdom derives from the Spirit of God, not from old age, Elihu said "Heaken to me." The verb hearken or listen is in the singular form and thus addressed to Job. He will declare true knowledge based on real wisdom.

3. Since the friends have no answer, Elihu can no longer restrain himself from speaking. (32:11-22)

TEXT 32:11-22

11 Behold, I waited for your words,
   I listened for your reasonings,
   Whilst ye searched out what to say.

327

12 Yea, I attended unto you,
   And, behold, there was none that convinced Job,
   Or that answered his words, among you.
13 Beware lest ye say, We have found wisdom;
   God may vanquish him, not man:
14 For he hath not directed his words against me;
   Neither will I answer him with your speeches.
15 They are amazed, they answer no more:
   They have not a word to say.
16 And shall I wait, because they speak not,
   Because they stand still, and answer no more?
17 I also will answer my part,
   I also will show mine opinion.
18 For I am full of words;
   The spirit within me constraineth me.
19 Behold, my breast is as wine which hath no vent;
   Like new wine-skins it is ready to burst.
20 I will speak, that I may be refreshed;
   I will open my lips and answer.
21 Let me not, I pray you, respect any man's person;
   Neither will I give flattering titles unto any man.
22 For I know not to give flattering titles;
   Else would my Maker soon take me away.

COMMENT 32:11-22

Verse 11—Elihu now turns to the three friends. He merely repeats in more pompous words what he already has declared.[3] He has listened for their most effective arguments against Job, but he was disappointed. If Job is to be condemned, there must be more cogent reasons than he has heard. I listened until you had finished (Heb. *tblytkm*—your completion—instead of *tbwntykm*—your arguments) your supposed wise

---

[3] See Dhorme, *Job*, pp. 477-478, for analysis of the many complexities of this verse.

words. Though they had "searched out," by laborious efforts, some comforting words, they have been less than effective. In other words, they tried hard, but that was not enough.

Verse 12—He had followed the debate with utmost care, but he failed to find any forceful words which actually convicted Job. Their calloused compassionless consolation lacked enough cogency to convict him of his crime against God.

Verse 13—This verse is made complex by its ambiguity. Perhaps Elihu says Job does not have invincible wisdom. He could be warning the three friends against excusing themselves for not answering Job. He could be suggesting that ultimately there is no human solution to Job's problem, but that does not justify their dropping the argument. Line one might mean that they have found a wisdom that only God can refute. This seems to best fit the structure of the entire book, especially the location of the Yahweh speeches, chapters 38ff. Yet, Elihu is equal to even that occasion; though the line resounds with humility, God will anwer him, not man.

Verse 14—Elihu is saying that when I get finished with him, he will not need God to respond. But these are idle words filled with foolish promises, as his arguments do not go beyond the words of Job's friends, in spite of his claim that he will not answer—lit. "with your words" or arguments.

Verse 15—In his soliloquy, Elihu first sets forth his claim of impartiality. His state of mind is also described. Most of his energy is utilized on rage, rather than effectively responding to Job. Yet, he is actually somewhat ridiculous, wordy, and unoriginal.

Verse 16—Once more Elihu piously emphasizes his patience.[4]

Verse 17—Repetition in order to build up expectation concerning his forthcoming momentous outburst of wisdom—verse 10b.

Verse 18—It would not require God's wisdom to refute

---

[4] For this theme respecting Job, see J. L. Ginsberg, "Job the Patient and Job the Impatient," *Conservative Judaism,* 1967, pp. 12-28; J. K. Zink, "Impatient Job: An Interpretation of Job 19:25ff," *J.B.L.,* 1965, pp. 147-152.

Elihu's claim that he is "full of words." His conceit is insufferable. He claims God as authorizer of his position when he delcares that "the spirit of my belly" is the source of his speech—15:2; Prov. 18:8.

Verse 19—He is as a bursting wineskin—Matt. 9:17; Jer. 20:9. He must speak in order to vent the wineskin, else it will split. The image is much more than a *Taste of New Wine.* What is bubbling inside him is like the force of fermentation which must find an outlet.

Verse 20—The image continues. Relief can come to his troubled spirit only if he finds release. He is so full, all that he needs to do is open his mouth.

Verse 21—His sincerity is bettered only by his candidness. Hypocrisy shall not lead him astray by deference to anyone's title or rank—Isa. 44:5; 45:4. He takes himself too seriously by his proposed impartial vigour (A. V. respect any man—lit. "lift up the fare"—13:8; "flattering title"—verb, *kny* means to give an honorific title).

Verse 22—He would not dare to flatter anyone. If he were so tempted, he would immediately be visited by God's vengeance.

TODAY'S ENGLISH VERSION

The Speeches of Elihu
(32.1—37.24)

32 The three men stopped trying to answer Job, because he was convinced of his own innocence. [2] Then a man named Elihu could not control his anger any longer, because Job justified himself and blamed God. (Elihu was the son of Barakel, a descendant of Buz, and belonged to the clan of Ram.) [3] He was also angry with Job's three friends. They could not find any way to answer Job, and this made it appear that God was in the wrong. [4] Because Elihu was the youngest one there, he had waited until everyone finished speaking.

⁵ But when he saw that the three men could not answer Job, he was angry ⁶ and began to speak.

Elihu

> I am young, and you are old,
>   so I was afraid to tell you what I think.
> ⁷ I told myself that you ought to speak,
>   that you older men should share your wisdom.
> ⁸ But it is the spirit of Almighty God
>   that comes to men and gives them wisdom.
> ⁹ It is not growing old that makes men wise,
>   or helps them know what is right.
> ¹⁰ So now I want you to listen to me;
>   let me tell you what I think.
>
> ¹¹ I listened patiently while you were speaking
>   and waited while you searched for wise comments.
> ¹² I paid close attention and heard you fail;
>   you have not disproved what Job has said.
> ¹³ How can you claim that you have discovered wisdom?
>   God must answer Job, for you have failed.
> ¹⁴ Job was speaking to you, not to me,
>   but I would never answer the way you did.
>
> ¹⁵ Words have failed them, Job;
>   they have no answer for you.
> ¹⁶ Shall I go on waiting, when they are silent?
>   They stand there with nothing more to say.
> ¹⁷ No, I will give my own answer now,
>   and tell you what I think.
> ¹⁸ I can hardly wait to speak.
>   I can't hold back the words.
> ¹⁹ If I don't get a chance to speak,
>   I will burst like a wineskin full of new wine.
> ²⁰ I can't stand it. I have to speak.
> ²¹ I will not take sides in this debate;
>   I am not going to flatter anyone.

331

> ²² I don't know how to flatter,
>   and God would quickly punish me if I did.

QUESTIONS FOR DISCUSSION 32:1-22

655. Discuss the character of Elihu as reflected in this chapter and given in the introduction.
656. Discuss the outline and content of his speeches, i.e., in an overview.
657. Some critics reject the speeches of Elihu as a part of the book of Job. Discuss their reasons and your position.
658. We do not know the father of Job nor of any of his three friends, but we do know the father of Elihu. Who is he? Why included?
659. This man was not angry because the three friends condemned Job—but for what reason?
660. Typical qualities of youth can be observed. What are they?
661. Was Elihu really timid? or humble? Discuss.
662. Elihu believes he has more wisdom than his elders. How so? Was he right? Discuss.
663. To whom is Elihu addressing his words. What is the meaning of the word "opinion" in verse 10?
664. Does Elihu say anything to the three friends he has not already said to Job?
665. Explain in your own words verse 13.
666. This young man is very confident that he has the answer to Job's problem. What does he really offer?
667. Most of his energy is expended on what rather than answering Job?
668. In what way is Elihu's conceit insufferable?
669. He is a bursting wineskin. Explain.
670. If Elihu opened his mouth, new wine would pour out. Is this the figure used? Was it true?
671. He takes himself too seriously. In what respect?
672. Elihu would not dare to flatter anyone. Why?

B. THE WORD FROM OUTSIDE—GOD HAS ALREADY
   SPOKEN. (33:1-33)
   1. A mortal himself, formed by God's spirit, yet he will
      answer Job. (33:1-7)

TEXT 33:1-7

33 Howbeit, Job, I pray thee, hear my speech,
And hearken to all my words.
2 Behold now, I have opened my mouth;
My tongue hath spoken in my mouth.
3 My words *shall utter* the uprightness of my heart;
And that which my lips know they shall speak sincerely.
4 The Spirit of God hath made me,
And the breath of the Almighty giveth me life.
5 If thou canst, answer thou me;
Set thy words in order before me, stand forth.
6 Behold, I am toward God even as thou art:
I also am formed out of the clay.
7 Behold, my terror shall not make thee afraid,
Neither shall my pressure be heavy upon thee.

COMMENT 33:1-7

Verse 1—Elihu has called our attention to his wisdom, impartiality, and competence requisite for his present task of
subduing Job's rebellious spirit. Here for the first time in the
dialogue Job is addressed by name—34:5, 7, 35ff; and 35:16.
This familiarity is more to be attributed to Elihu's tempera-
ment than his close ties with Job, though he could be a blood
relative of Job's—32:2. He summons Job in 33:1-7, and he
sarcastically refers to Job's complaint against God—9:17, 34.
He quotes two of Job's claims: (1) that he is innocent—9:21;
10:7; 16:17; 23:10-12; 27:5, 31; and (2) that God is his enemy—
10:17; 13:24, 27; and 19:11. Elihu deals with each of these

333

in the structure of chapter 33. The banality of his speech is self-evident.

Verse 2—The boundlessness of Elihu's self-evaluation make him a master of banality. His speech is stiltedly redundant.

Verse 3—Job had asked that his friends be sincere; Elihu now declares that Job is going to get the ultimate expression of sincerity, but from him. This first line is without a verb, but the A. V. inserts "shall utter." The meaning of the first line is that Elihu's righteousness is exposed by his words. In the second line Elihu is giving Job assurance of his brilliance—compare 6:25a; Deut. 9:5; Ps. 119:7; and I Chron. 29:17.

Verse 4—He, like Job, is a human being. Both share in God's spirit, which gives life. Verbally, at least, he humbly acknowledges that he has a special endowment from God. He is inspired by God to speak; thus his words are not only sincere, they are of special value. Perhaps he claimed a charismatic gift of wisdom which was lacking in Job's illustrious friends.

Verse 5—Though there is no equivalent to "words" in the text, the verb means "to set in order," i.e., get ready to answer "my" charges—32:14; I Sam. 17:8—"take your stand." Prepare (A. V. in order before me) has no expressed object, but the object may be "words"—32:14; or "case"—13:18; 23:4, or battle as is generally the case. "Take your stand" is used in military sense in I Sam. 17:16; II Sam. 23:12; and in legal sense in 1:6.

Verse 6—In relation to God (A. V. toward God) Elihu, like Job, is human. Elihu's advantage over Job is not in this respect. He is only a mortal whom Job need not fear. The second line is translated by Blommerde as "from clay I too have been pinched off," even as you are (Heb. *kepika*—like your mouth, i.e., like you). The metaphorical use of *peh*-mouth to express relationship is well supported in the Old Testament.[1] Elihu was formed (*qrs*- nipped) from clay, like Job.

---

[1] See E. Dhorme, *L'Emploi Metaphorique des noms de parties du corps en hebreu et en akkadien* (Paris, 1923), p. 85.

334

Verse 7—Elihu here alludes to Job's charges that God intimidated with violence—9:34; 13:21. With clever irony, Elihu assures Job that he need not make this same charge now, because his opponent is also a man. The word rendered "pressure" occurs only here, and need not be emended out of the text because of its *rarity*.

2. He challenges Job's claim that he suffers because God counts him an enemy. (33:8-12)

TEXT 33:8-12

8 Surely thou has spoken in my hearing,
   And I have heard the voice of *thy* words, *saying,*
9 I am clean, without transgression;
   I am innocent, neither is there iniquity in me:
10 Behold, he findeth occasions against me,
   He counteth me for his enemy;
11 He putteth my feet in the stocks,
   He marketh all my paths.
12 Behold, I will answer thee, in this thou art not just;
   For God is greater than man.

COMMENT 33:8-12

Verse 8—God is too great to be guilty of the behavior alluded to in Job's charges. He has never persecuted a righteous man. At this point Elihu gets down to his self-appointed task of effectually responding to Job. After finishing his much-advertized brilliance and competence, Elihu rebukes Job. He has listened to all of the dialogue (A. V. the sound of your words); thus he is prepared to respond.

Verse 9—Job has not claimed sinlessness—7:21; 9:21; 10:7; 13:26; 16:17; 23:7, 10ff; 27:4ff; 31:1ff. Though Elihu's quotation is essentially correct, the twist he places on them distorts the essence of Job's words. Job has consistently claimed that he had never committed sins grave enough to merit the afflictions which he is experiencing. The word rendered as "clean" in A. V. occurs only here, and its root meaning is wash or cleanse.

Verse 10—For line one see 10:13ff; 19:6ff; for line two, 13:24. The word rendered "occasions" (*to'anot*) means opportunities for, expressing hostility as in Judges 14:4; 13:24; 19:6, 11.

Verse 11—Elihu is here quoting Job's words from 13:27. God watches (*yismor*) his every move and hinders him. This very phrase occurs also in 13:27b.

Verse 12—Elihu denies the justness of Job's charges. God is above arbitrary actions such as those that Job has affirmed. But Job has already presented God's power in some of the most magnificent hymns in Scripture—9:1-13; 12:13-25. Job has already declared that man cannot argue with God because he "is greater than man" (so the LXX and the Qumran Targum)—9:14-20, 32; 13:13-16; so Elihu's point is not well taken under any circumstances.

3. God has answered Job in two ways—to discipline him.
(33:13-22)
a. In dreams, to draw him from the fate of an evil course
(33:13-18)

TEXT 33:13-18

13   Why dost thou strive against him,
For that he giveth not account of any of his matters?
14 For God speaketh once,
Yea, twice, *though man* regardeth it not.
15 In a dream, in a vision of the night,
When deep sleep falleth upon men,
In slumberings upon the bed;
16 Then he openeth the ears of men,
And sealeth their instruction,
17 That he may withdraw man *from his* purpose,

And hide pride from man;
18 He keepeth back his soul from the pit,
And his life from perishing by the sword.

COMMENT 33:13-18

Verse 13—Elihu asks Job, "Why are you contentious against Him" because He does not answer? The A. V. includes "saying" which is not in the text and would better be rendered in English as "that." There is a possible reading variation between "my words" and "his words" of the Hebrew text. The reading variation is of no consequence, since Job's complaint that God gives no answer is appropriate for any and all men who ask and receive no answer. All contests with God are futile.

Verse 14—Perhaps the verse implies that God reveals himself in more than one way, and if man does not hear God speak in one place, perhaps he will in another. The sense of this verse is elliptical, though not impossible.[2]

Verse 15—Elihu expresses the classical Near Eastern view of dreams, viz., that they may be a vehicle of divine revelation—Gen. 41:11, 12; Num. 12:6; Judges 7:13, 15; Dan. 2, 4, 7. His specific reference here is to dreams that are warnings about and deterrents from ungodly behavior. Dreams of warnings are found in Gen. 20:3; 31:24; Dan. 4; Matt. 2:13; 27:19; Job 4:12ff; 7:14. The prophets warn us about any uncritical approach to dream interpretation, either before or after Freud—Deut. 13:1-5 and Jer. 23:28.

Verse 16—The Hebrew text has *mosaram* or "their bond," which makes little sense.[3] The dreams may need interpretation. The phrase "open the ears" sometimes inform—Ruth 4:4; I Sam 20:2, 12, 13. When God is the subject, the phrase often

---

[2] See discussion L. Dennefeld, *Revue Biblique,* 1939, p. 175.

[3] For this difficult verse see M. Dahood, *Biblica,* 1968, p. 360; see also Dhorme and Pope.

means revelation—36:10, 15; I Sam. 9:15; II Sam. 7:27. By certain types of dreams, God awakens men to repentance from the error of their ways. The LXX reads "appearances of terrors" (*en eidesin phobou*), which conveys the essence of the meaning.

Verse 17—The Hebrew literally says "to remove man deed," and probably means to remove man from his evil purpose; i.e., warning dreams often cause man to abandon his plans for evil. The second line literally reads "pride from man he covers," which our A. V. interprets to mean "hide pride from man." The sense seems to be that God's warning dreams are also to humble man.

Verse 18—God's purpose is beneficent, i.e., to save man from a worse fate. The parallelism makes it evident that *selah* should not be rendered sword as in the A. V. The reference is to the realm of Sheol and to perishing by the sword. The verb perhaps should be rendered "to pass through," though the noun often means weapon or sword; but the relevancy of this here is suspect.[4]

b. Through affliction God has spoken (33:19-22)
to bring repentance (33:30).

TEXT 33:19-22

19 He is chastened also with pain upon his bed,
   And with continual strife in his bones;
20 So that his life abhorreth bread,
   And his soul dainty food.
21 His flesh is consumed away, that it cannot be seen;
   And his bones that were not seen stick out.
22 Yea, his soul draweth near unto the pit,
   And his life to the destroyers.

---

[4] For the critical considerations, see M. Tsevat, *Vetus Testamentum*, 1954, p. 43; and Svi Rin, *Biblische Zeitschrift*, 1963, p. 25, where *selah* is identified with the "underworld."

COMMENT 33:19-22

Verse 19—Job's afflictions were to humble him; instead by his rebelliousness he reveals his profound pride, which is at the heart of all sin. Eliphaz had earlier said that Job was visited "with pain upon his bed"—Job 5:17; Deut. 8:5; Prov. 3:12; Ps. 38. He has agony (*rib* mean conflict or strife, A. V. continual strife) in his bones. Elihu is saying that God speaks in the discipline of suffering, in the torment of pain.

Verse 20—Here "life" clearly means appetite. It is parallel to soul which also means appetite in the second line—38:39; Ps. 107:17.

Verse 21—His sickness destroys his appetite. The lack of food causes his body to waste away, and his bones stick out—lit. "and his bones which were not seen are laid bare"—Jer. 3:2, 21. His bones protrude because of a lack of flesh to cover them up.

Verse 22—The allusion is perhaps to the destroying angels—II Sam. 24:16; II Kg. 19:35; I Chron. 21:15; Ps. 78:49. The parallelism between pit—*sahat*—and killers—*memitim*—indicates that the reference is to the abode of the dead.[5]

4. A messenger (angel) may interpret to man what is right, that he be led to pray and to confess his guilt. (33:23-28)

TEXT 33:23-28

23 If there be with him an angel,
   An interpreter, one among a thousand,
   To show unto man what is right for him;
24 Then *God* is gracious unto him, and saith,
   Deliver him from going down to the pit,
   I have found a ransom.

---

[5] For Ugaritic enthusiasts, see F. M. Cross, Jr., and D. N. Freedman, *Early Hebrew Orthography*, 1952, as utilized by Pope, *Job*, p. 251, on this verse.

25 His flesh shall be fresher than a child's;
  He returneth to the days of his youth.
26 He prayeth unto God, and he is favorable unto him,
  So that he seeth his face with joy:
  And he restoreth unto man his righteousness.
27 He singeth before men, and saith,
  I have sinned, and perverted that which was right,
  And it profited me not:
28 He hath redeemed my soul from going into the pit,
  And my life shall behold the light.

COMMENT 33:23-28

Verse 23—Mediation by an angel might interpret God's providential meaning of his sickness—Ps. 91:11-13; Matt. 18:10; Acts 12:15; Rev. 8:3. Eliphaz is probably referring to this idea in 5:1—"holy ones." Perhaps the concept is involved in Job's request for a mediator—9:33, a witness-interpreter—16:19-21, and a redeemer—19:25-27. The word rendered interpreter is applied to the prophets—Isa. 43:27. This verse presents the concept of a personal God[6]—I Kg. 22:19; Dan. 7:10; Rev. 5:11. The purpose of the angelic visit is not to justify the sick, but to call to repentance.

Verse 24—The verse implies successful interceding in that "he is gracious." God as in A. V. is not in the text, though the pronoun "he" could refer to God. The imperative form makes little sense in this verse. No man could give a ransom for himself—Ps. 49:7-9; Matt. 16:26; 20:28; I Tim. 2:6; Rev. 5:9. Though the nature of the ransom is not specified, it is clearly vicarious and is the expression of His graciousness. The answer to man's perennial problem lies outside of man's capacity. Only the word from outside can bring the *Shattering*

---

[6] That Yahweh is a personal God there is no doubt, but for general Mesopotamian mythical concept of a "personal god," see S. N. Kramer, *Harvard Theological Review*, 1956, p. 59.

of Silence.

Verse 25—Elihu here describes the recovery of the afflicted person. The A. V. rendering of the first line "fresher than a child" adds nothing to the meaning which is to be "soft" or "tender," probably from the Hebrew *-ratob*. This Hebrew word is found no where else in the scriptures and is of an unusual form. A similar statement is made of Naaman the prophet after his recovery—I Kg. 5:14; Isa. 40:31; Pss. 103:5; 110:3; 144:12; and Eccl. 11:9.

Verse 26—After restoration, the man is admitted into the presence of God—Gen. 32:20; 44:23, 26; II Sam. 3:13; 14:24, 28, 32; Ps. 11:7. Prayer is the seeking of God's presence—Ps. 24:6; 27:8. The joyous shout is a cultic cry—8:21 and 104:4; Prov. 7:15; Hos. 5:15. It can also be a battle cry, which is here inappropriate. The joy bursts forth because—lit. "he restores to his righteousness," i.e., to God's act of acquittal—Pss. 22:22-31; 30; 66; 116. The restoration to righteousness means victory or salvation in a larger sense than "saving his soul."

Verse 27—Public expression of his gratitude for being restored is clearly the thought back of this verse.[7] He sings before men (idiom "sing before"—Prov. 25:20) and acknowledges his sins. The rendering of the final line in A. V. is inadequate. The verb is not found elsewhere in the sense. In other occurrences it means "to be equal," but this yields little sense in this present context, i.e., "it was not equal to me." However we resolve the grammatical difficulties here, it is certain the healed sinner is expressing his gratitude through public thanksgiving and confession.

Verse 28—He has been redeemed from death. Thus darkness has been removed by the glorious light of His presence. The idiom "shall behold" is used for looking with satisfaction on someone or some thing—cf. Ps. 22:17 where enemies "gloat over."

---

[7] For the possibilities in this verse, see J. Reider, *Zeitschrift für alttestamentlische Wissenschaften,* 1953, p. 275.

5. This God does to save man from destruction. (3:29-33)

TEXT 33:29-33

29 Lo, all these things doth God work,
   Twice, *yea* thrice, with a man,
30 To bring back his soul from the pit,
   That he may be enlightened with the light of the living.
31 Mark well, O Job, hearken unto me:
   Hold thy peace, and I will speak.
32 If thou hast anything to say, answer me:
   Speak, for I desire to justify thee.
33 If not, hearken thou unto me:
   Hold thy peace, and I will teach thee wisdom.

COMMENT 33:29-33

Verse 29—Elihu repeats that this is the way God relates to man. Job does not respond, and thus we are left to infer that he was reduced to silence. Elihu, like Job's three friends, fails to come to grips with Job's problem. Perhaps the "twice," "three times" is similar to God's action found in Amos 1:3, 6, etc.

Verse 30—If a man repents, he is restored from pangs of death. Probably the idiom A. V. "that he may be enlightened" means the same as in verse 28—to look upon with great satisfaction. A similar phrase is found in Ps. 56:14, where it beautifully suggests that one's life is illumined by God's presence, in radical contrast to the gloom of the grave.[8]

Verse 31—Since the words have ultimate significance, Elihu once more demands attention. I sat through prolonged debate in silence; now you listen to me. The LXX omits verses 31b-33, thus reducing the length of Elihu's speech.

---

[8] For suggestions from this Psalm, see M. Dahood, *Psalms*, Vol. I, note 3 on Ps. 36:10; and compare with Job 33:30.

342

Verse 32—After telling Job to be silent, he now asks that if he has anything to say that he speak up. But Elihu thinks that his speech if unanswerable, thus not expecting any Jobian response. "I desire to justify you" finds no concrete support in Elihu's speech.

Verse 33—Elihu must believe that his words are final, even if fatal, to Job's need. If you want wisdom, come to me, neither your friends, nor God.

TODAY'S ENGLISH VERSION

33 And now, Job, listen carefully
  to all that I have to say.
² I am going to say what's on my mind.
³ All my words are sincere,
  and I am speaking the truth.
⁴ God's spirit made me and gave me life.

⁵ Answer me, if you can. Prepare your arguments.
⁶ You and I, Job, are the same in God's sight,
  both of us were formed from clay.
⁷ So you have no reason to fear me;
  I will not overpower you.

⁸ Now here is what I heard you say:
⁹ "I am not guilty. I have done nothing wrong.
  I am innocent and free from sin.
¹⁰ But God finds excuses for attacking me
  and treats me like an enemy.
¹¹ He binds chains on my feet;
  he watches every move I make."

¹² But I tell you, Job, you are wrong.
  God is greater than any man.
¹³ Why do you accuse God
  of never answering a man's complaints?
¹⁴ Even though God speaks in many ways,

343

no one pays attention to what he says.
¹⁵ God speaks in dreams and visions
that come at night when men are asleep.
¹⁶ God makes them listen to what he says,
and they are frightened at his warnings.
¹⁷ God speaks to make them stop their sinning
and to keep them from becoming proud.
¹⁸ God will not let them be destroyed;
he saves them from death itself.
¹⁹ God corrects a man by sending sickness
and filling his body with pain.
²⁰ The sick man loses his appetite,
and even the finest food looks revolting.
²¹ His body wastes away; you can see all his bones;
²² he is about to go to the world of the dead.

²³ Perhaps an angel may come to his aid—
one of God's thousands of angels,
who remind men of their duty.
²⁴ The angel, in mercy, will say, "Release him!
He is not to go down to the world of the dead.
Here is the ransom to set him free."
²⁵ His body will grow young and strong again;
²⁶ God will answer him when he prays;
he will worship God with joy;
God will make things right for him again.
²⁷ He will say in public, "I have sinned.
I have not done right, but God spared me.
²⁸ He kept me from going to the land of the dead,
and I am still alive."

²⁹ God does all this again and again;
³⁰ he saves the life of a person,
and gives him the joy of living.

³¹ Now, Job, listen to what I am saying,
be quiet and let me speak.
³² But if you have something to say, let me hear it;

I would gladly admit you are in the right.
³³ But if not, be quiet and listen to me,
and I will teach you how to be wise.

QUESTIONS FOR DISCUSSION 33:1-33

673. Job, for the first time, is addressed by name. What does this mean?
674. Elihu deals with two claims made by Job. What are they?
675. Elihu is a master of *banality*. What is meant by this expression?
676. How many times does this man repeat himself? He keeps emphasizing one point. What is it?
677. In verse 5 Elihu challenges Job to do what?
678. Elihu describes himself as formed out of clay. What does this expression literally mean?
679. Elihu alludes to one of Job's charges against God, i.e., in verse seven. What was it?
680. At last Elihu is down to his self-appointed task. What has preceded?
681. Elihu twists Job's words. Explain.
682. Does he represent Job accurately in verses 10 and 11?
683. His point made in verse 12 is not well taken under any circumstance. Why not?
684. What is the point of verses 13 and 14?
685. God speaks to man in dreams—had Job had any dreams? Does He speak to us today through dreams? Discuss.
686. How does verse 16 relate to dreams?
687. The purpose of dreams is mentioned in verse 17. What is it?
688. God's purpose is beneficent. What is it?
689. God speaks through suffering. What does He say? Was this true of Job?
690. What does the word "life" mean in verse 20?

691. Elihu aptly describes Job's physical condition. To what purpose?
692. God speaks through dreams—through suffering—and now through angels. Was he right? Discuss. What purpose was there in the angel's visit?
693. A very personal God is implied in these verses. How so?
694. There is successful interceding. How was it accomplished?
695. Complete recovery is graphically described in verse 25. Explain.
696. What follows restoration? Does this have any reference or application to the Christian?
697. Elihu is both right and wrong in his expressions in verses 27 and 28. Explain.
698. Something can be inferred from verse 29. What is it?
699. If a man repents, what happens to him? Cf. vs. 30.
700. Elihu claims to be Job's good friend. Was he? Why not?
701. He claims that the true and final source of wisdom is where?
702. Does Elihu have any counterparts today? Who?

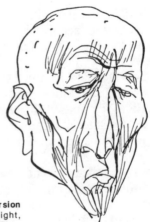

From **Today's English Version** of the **Old Testament**, Copyright, American Bible Society, 1971

346

C. THE SOURCE OF JUSTICE (34:1-37)

1. Job is "walking with wicked men" when he attributes injustice to God. (34:1-9)

TEXT 34:1-9

34 Moreover Elihu answered and said,
2 Hear my words, ye wise men;
And give ear unto me, ye that have knowledge.
3 For the ear trieth words,
As the palate tasteth food.
4 Let us choose for us that which is right;
Let us know among ourselves what is good.
5 For Job hath said, I am righteous,
And God hath taken away my right:
6 Notwithstanding my right I am *accounted* a liar;
My wound is incurable, *though I am* without transgression.
7 What man is like Job,
Who drinketh up scoffing like water,
8 Who goeth in company with the workers of iniquity,
And walketh with wicked men?
9 For he hath said, It profiteth a man nothing
That he should delight himself with God.

COMMENT 34:1-9

Verse 1—Elihu now turns to defend God from the charges of Job, who has argued from his own particular case which is reinforced by evidence of other injustices around him to God's responsibility for his situation. Elihu deals with a general, *a priori* theological assumption, and deduces Job's sin from it. Elihu's second discourse in 34:1-37 divides into four divisions: (1) Job is an impious man—verses 2-9; (2) Response to Job's charges against God—verses 10-15; (3) Defense of omniscience and impartiality of God—verses 16-30; and (4) Exposes Job's rebellion against God—verses 31-37.

Verse 2—Once more he calls on his audience to pay attention. He addresses the bystanders and appeals to their sense of righteousness—verses 10, 34 for support. After 32:11ff, Elihu could hardly be referring to Job's three friends by the phrase "you wise men."

Verse 3—Here we have an almost verbatim quotation from 12:11. The ear is the faculty of man's reason. Hearing is more than listening. In both Old Testament and New Testament, we often find the word rendered "disobedience" to be "to not hear," Isa. 6:1ff; Matt. 13:1ff; Acts 28:16ff; Rom. 9:1ff; and Hebrews 3; 4. The parallelism between the "ears" and the "palate" is crystal clear.

Verse 4—We must determine whether Job has made a just charge against God. We must decide whether Job's or the traditional orthodox view toward the question of theodicy is correct.

Verse 5—Elihu in part quotes Job's words and in part summarizes them—27:2. After a process of discrimination, we will reach a sound conclusion. He proceeds to rip Job's words to shreds.

Verse 6—Job has repeatedly claimed that though he is innocent, he is made to appear impious. Should I lie, i.e., "Should I confess guilt when I am innocent?" The LXX has "he lies," that is, God lies, instead of as in the Hebrew, "I lie." Perhaps the implication is if Job is right, then that is tantamount to making God a liar. Since God cannot be a liar, that necessitates Job's repentance and confession of sin. Job's challenge of God's justice stems from Job's sinfulness, not God's unrighteousness or partiality. The phrase "my wound" is literally "my arrow" or "my dart." "My condition cannot be healed," though I am without sin, so Elihu reports Job's position. Elihu avoids the crude oversimplification of Job's friends by rejecting the thesis that Job's sufferings are sure proof of his evil heart, and that rewards are the infallible results of repentance.

Verse 7—Job had spoken of God scoffing at the sufferings of the innocent—9:23, Zophar of Job's scoffing at traditional doctrinal understanding—11:3, and Eliphaz at the innocent scoffing at the misfortunes of the impious—22:19. Elihu charges that Job is an irreligious man who is a public menace. As with Job's three friends, mercy, grace, love, compassion are not words which Elihu understands.

Verse 8—Psalm one is an excellent commentary on this verse. Who "takes the path" of evil men—11:11; 22:15; 31:5? By expressing his views, Job finds himself in the company of the ungodly.

Verse 9—Elihu correctly attributes to Job the view that piety is not for profit—9:22; 10:3; 21:7; Mal. 3:13-14. Elihu's next discourse—35:5ff—is preoccupied with an effort to refute the thesis. This fundamental assumption is part of the *American Dream,* i.e., piety is to be rewarded by prosperity. As America enters her third century, one of the conditions of spiritual survival will be how production, prosperity, piety, and poverty are correlated, with a biblical world-life viewpoint, as opposed to a humanistic-naturalistic-pragmatic survival-security perspective. Job is our contemporary. The same God who shattered His silence for Job can and will speak to the crises of the last quarter of the twentieth century.

2. God will do no wickedness nor injustice, but imparts to
   every man according to his deeds. (34:10-15)

TEXT 34:10-15

10   **Therefore hearken unto me, ye men of understanding:**
      Far be it from God, that he should do wickedness,
      And from the Almighty, that he should commit iniquity.
11 **For the work of a man will he render unto him,**
      And cause every man to find according to his ways,
12 **Yea, of a surety, God will not do wickedly,**
      Neither will the Almighty pervert justice.
13 **Who gave him a charge over the earth?**
      Or who hath disposed the whole world?

14 If he set his heart upon himself,
  If he gather unto himself his spirit and his breath;
15 All flesh shall perish together,
  And man shall turn again unto dust.

COMMENT 34:10-15

Verse 10—Bildad raised this question in 8:3; Elihu echoes it here in verses 10-12. True wise men, i.e., lit. "men of heart," you know that God can do no evil. Job is not merely in error; he has committed blasphemy—Gen. 18:25.

Verse 11—Whether the man be good or evil, his reward will follow from his character. Elihu, like Job's three friends, is persuaded that God is not unjust. From Genesis to Revelation, the Bible is fully conscious that a person's *desert* and his *fortune* are not often in harmony. The systems of society, history, and nature are so interconnected[1] that negative repercussions do, in fact, come to those who are not personally guilty of any particular heinous crime, egs. famine, earthquake, tornadoes, war, pestilence, etc. Freedom and responsibility are always within structures. There is no such thing as Sartre's "ontological Freedom," which is in reality insanity. But if there is no freedom, neither is there responsibility, i.e., basis for praise or blame for human behavior—4:8; Ps. 62:13; Prov. 24:12; Eccl. 16:14; Matt. 16:27; Rom. 2:6; Gal. 6:7-10. Rowley certainly raises the appropriate question, which is not "Why does God not prevent injustice?" but "why do men perpetrate injustice?" (*Job*, p. 279). In the case of Job, God permitted Satanic injustice as an expression of His confidence in his servant Job. God was prepared to stake His cosmic honor on Job's integrity. The last line as rendered in the A. V. could better read, lit., "will cause it to find him."[2]

---

[1] *Systems Analysis* is the most effective method known to man which can correlate interrelatedness of the systems of the universe, whether natural or societal systems.

[2] See my theological essay on *Evil*—"Silence, Suffering, and Sin: Present Evil and the Presence of God" in this commentary.

Verse 12—Elihu repeats what he has already declared in verse 10. The editors of *The Qumran Targum* render this verse as a rhetorical question—"Eh bien, Dieu fera-T-il vraiment ce qiu est faux?" Well? God will certainly not do that which is false or evil? The Hebrew *'omnom* is rendered by *sd'* which appears in Dan. 3:14 with -*hsd'*, the interrogative particle.[3]

Verse 13—Elihu deduces from the fact that God is all-powerful creator that He can do no wrong. This logically entails that power is moral; whatever God does is by definition moral or just. But Job has already acknowledged that God is answerable to no one—9:12; but he erroneously derived from this premise that God was responsible for all the injustice in the world—9:24. Camus expresses this same viewpoint in his existential literature, specifically *The Plague and The Fall.* Sartre is also a brilliant protagonist of God's justice, eg. *The Devil and The Good Lord, No Exit,* and *The Flies,* etc.

Verse 14—If God only thought of Himself and not of all His creatures, i.e., all of creation, with benevolent mercy, then no one would survive. All flesh would perish from the earth. God gave life to all creatures—Gen. 2:7 and Job 33:4; and when and if He withdraws His spirit, we die—Ps. 104:29 and Eccl. 12:7. We are all alike, dependent on an impartial God.

Verse 15—"All flesh" here indicates that when His spirit is withdrawn, only lifeless "sarx" remains to be ravaged by decay—12:10; 28:21; Isa. 42:5; Ps. 104:29. God is a loving merciful Lord, not a capricious tyrant. We can never gain an adequate perspective on evil until we know God and His cosmic purpose, which is to fulfill His promises in Christ—II Cor. 1:20. It should be all but self-evident that biblical eschatology is the basis for a Christian view of history-nature. the removal of evil is part of the biblical understanding of redemption—Isa. 61—66; Rom. 8; Rev. 21.

---

[3] For analysis of this grammatical possibility, see H. H. Rowley, *The Aramaic of the Old Testament,* 1929, p. 132.

3. God is supreme, sees every hidden thing, and is an impartial
   judge. (34:16-30)

TEXT 34:16-30

16 If now *thou hast* understanding, hear this:
   Hearken to the voice of my words.
17 Shall even one that hateth justice govern?
   And wilt thou condemn him that is righteous *and* mighty?—
18 *Him* that saith to a king, *Thou art* vile,
   Or to nobles, *Ye are* wicked;
19 That respecteth not the persons of princes,
   Nor regardeth the rich more than the poor;
   For they are all the work of his hands.
20 In a moment they die, even at midnight;
   The people are shaken and pass away,
   And the mighty are taken away without hand.
21 For his eyes are upon the ways of a man,
   And he seeth all his goings.
22 There is no darkness, nor thick gloom,
   Where the workers of iniquity may hide themselves.
23 For he needeth not further to consider a man,
   That he should go before God in judgment.
24 He breaketh in pieces mighty men *in ways* past finding out,
   And setteth others in their stead.
25 Therefore he taketh knowledge of their works;
   And he overturneth them in the night, so that they are
      destroyed.
26 He striketh them as wicked men
   In the open sight of others;
27 Because they turned aside from following him,
   And would not have regard to any of his ways:
28 So that they caused the cry of the poor to come unto him,
   And he heard the cry of the afflicted.
29 When he giveth quietness, who then can condemn?
   And when he hideth his face, who then can behold him?
   Alike whether *it be done* unto a nation, or unto a man:

30 That the godless man reign not,
   That there be none to ensnare the people.

COMMENT 34:16-30

Verse 16—If God is truly all powerful, then no one can influence His decisions—Gen. 18:25; Rom. 3:5ff. If God is all knowing, then He must be infallible. When He observes unrighteousness, He punishes. But the dilemma remains, why some *victims* and some *victors?*—33:31, 33. The text has only "if understanding" and is in the singular, and thus invites Job's close attention.

Verse 17—The cogency of Elihu's argument has often been attacked. Cosmic control, i.e., divine government, does not guarantee justice. This is precisely Job's point. Elihu is saying that God can condemn kings and nobles and that this power makes Him righteous. But this is bold assertion, not balanced argument. Omnipotence is neither necessary nor sufficient power of impartiality. The word rendered "govern" in the first line of the A. V. means "bind up"—Hos. 6:1; Isa. 1:6; Ex. 29:9. Only in this verse does it have a sense of governing a kingdom[4]—compare Ps. 31:19 with Job 34:17.

Verse 18—Elihu's argument is crushed against the rocks of reality. A fool may be set in high places—Eccl. 10:5, 20. Present world condition hardly supports the naive but often suggested thesis of "natural leadership," locally, state, nationally, or internationally—Isa. 32:5. Elihu merely continues a theme set forth by Job in 12:17-21, i.e., God's humiliation of the mighty. He also begs the question at hand. The word rendered in the A. V. as vile (*beliyya'al*—worthlessness) is applied to such conduct as greed—Deut. 15:9; I Sam. 25:25; 30:22; and sexual perversion—Judges 19:22; and lying—

---

[4] For possible variation, see E. F. Sutcliffe, *Biblica,* 1949, pp. 73ff. He suggests medical sense here, i.e., God can heal a hater of justice; also see M. Dahood, *Psalms,* Vol. II, p. xxiv.

I Kg. 21:10; Prov. 19:28.

Verse 19—Since all are derived from God's creative power, He is impartial to both the rich and poor.[5] Impartiality does not mean that we are all equal in ability or capacity to produce. The fallacy that we are all "equal" is resident in western thought from the French Revolution (Liberty, Equality, Fraternity) to our canonical national literature, egs. *Declaration of Independence, Constitution,* etc. It should be empirically evident that we are not all equal in the sense of creative intelligence, abilities, etc. This central error is the basis of much "human rights" discussion, at least since 1948 and the *Universal Declaration of Human Rights* of the UN. Rights entail responsibilities just like freedom does. Contemporary man has chosen "security" over "freedom"—Isa. 32:5; Deut. 10:17; Prov. 22:2; Acts 10:34-35; Rom. 2:11; Eph. 6:9; Col 3:25; and I Pet. 1:17.

Verse 20—Proof of God's impartiality is His swift removal, i.e., "at midnight," of the mighty. Unexpectedly God visits all—Lk. 12:20; I Thess. 5:2.[6] The people "all violently agitated" or taken away "by no human hand." This emphasizes the effortlessness of God's removal of the unjust from the world.

Verse 21—God's decisions are made with full awareness of all details. This verse is almost a verbatim citation of 24:23b; 31:4; Eccl. 23:19. When disaster falls, it is evidence of wickedness. Job's thesis is that God knows everything; therefore, He knows that he is innocent—10:7. The Prologue is proof that Job is correct concerning this point. But he is mistaken in inferring that God is indifferent to moral issues.

Verse 22—No human thought or act is concealed from God—Job 31:3; Ps. 139:11ff; Jer. 23:24; Amos 9:2-3; Matt. 6:4.

Verse 23—Job has lamented that he could not bring God to a law court—9:32—even though God would be both adversary and judge—10:2. Here, Elihu declares that God does not need

---

[5] P. Joüon, *Biblica,* 1937, p. 207 regards the "poor" as a social distinction.

[6] E. F. Sutcliffe, *Biblica,* 1949, pp. 75ff.

to go through a legal process to establish guilt. God can summon man any time He chooses. Job has asked God for a
time of hearing—9:32; 14:13; 24:1. The text has *'od*—"yet"—
and the late G. E. Wright proposed "a set time" which would
require *mo'ed*.

Verse 24—God does not need to investigate (A. V. consider—*heqer*—search, inquiry, and inquisition) the human
situation in order to know what is going on. God's will and
power are fused by His loving mercy in all His pronouncements.
Elihu says there is no need for the inquiry which Job has requested.

Verse 25—God knows (*yakhir*) their works and "overthrows
them in the night." Punishment comes with swift certainty to
the tyrannical oppressors.

Verse 26—In spite of the difficulties in this verse, its meaning is that God judges the wicked in public. The A. V. rendering
"in the open sight" means "under" or "among" as Greenfield
has shown.[7]

Verse 27—Whoever turns from God is punished regardless
of who he is. This verse contains only three Hebrew words—
24:13. The parallel line is preserved almost intact in *The
Qumran Targum* and supports the reading of the Hebrew text.

Verse 28—The difficulties in verses 28-33 perhaps caused
the LXX translators to remove them from the text. The verb
is infinitive and could be translated as either singular or plural.
The infinitive "to bring" implies that the cries of the oppressed
brought the oppressor to God's attention. If He is all-knowing,
their cries could bring Him no knowledge which He did not
already possess. The grammar does not necessarily imply
that their cries "caused" God's response, but could also be
understood as "consequential."

Verse 29—This verse is very cryptic. But probably the
meaning is that no man has a right to condemn God, even if
He is silent in the presence of injustice. Job's fundamental

---

[7] See his arguments, J. C. Greenfield, *Zeitschrift für alttestamentlische Wissenschaft*,
1961, p. 227.

question is not "Why does not God punish the wicked?" but rather "Why do the innocent suffer?" The last line reads "upon a nation or upon a man together." The word "together" is our problem in this text. Perhaps the verse means that God is watching over all His creation with unceasing vigilance, though He does often in fact hide His face from our view. His presence returns only after *The Shattering of Silence*. God's visibility returns when He speaks. He has spoken with finality in Job's redeemer, our Lord—Jn. 1:1-18 and Heb. 1:1-4. His silence becomes our ultimate vindication, when His silence is broken by resurrection. Blommerde renders the final line as "upon nation and man he gazes."

Verse 30—The text reads literally "from the ruling of an impious man." The A. V. rendering "godless" is abstract, and the text suggests an existential situation or concrete expression of unrighteousness. The last line reads "from snares of the people," and means God intervenes to remove any and every unrighteous ruler. But the verse does not relate either the method of removal, or the length of time involved in the process of removal. Israel's history is full of such examples.

4. Job is rebellious in multiplying wicked words against God. (34:31-37)

TEXT 34:31-37

31   For hath any said unto God,
    I have borne *chastisement,* I will not offend *any more:*
32 That which I see not teach thou me:
    If I have done iniquity, I will do it no more?
33 Shall his recompense be as thou wilt, that thou refusest it?
    For thou must choose, and not I:
    Therefore speak what thou knowest.
34 Men of understanding will say unto me,
    Yea, every wise man that heareth me:
35 Job speaketh without knowledge,

And his words are without wisdom.
36 Would that Job were tried unto the end,
   Because of his answering like wicked men.
37 For he addeth rebellion unto his sin;
   He clappeth his hands among us,
   And multiplieth his words against God.

COMMENT 34:31-37

Verse 31—"To God" is emphatic in the verse. If one confesses to God, He does not need Job's permission before forgiving. Chastisement of the A. V. is not in the text, which says "I have borne," but what does that mean? Perhaps something like this—"I am not evil, but have been led astray."[8] "I will not offend" suggests a declaration of innocence, rather than confession ("any more" is not in the text).

Verse 32—The verse is a beautiful promise of obedience and a clear confession of sin. He is pleading for God's merciful presence.

Verse 33—"According to your judgment" implies that God is free to pardon; He does not need Job's permission. The first line contains "because you reject it" (in A. V. as "thou refusest it") does not have an expressed object. Elihu is suggesting that if Job does not like the way God rules the universe, does he want to run the cosmos?

Verse 34—With such cogent arguments, how could anyone reply to Elihu? All wise men will condemn Job for arguing with God.

Verse 35—When Job complains against God, he manifests his lack of wisdom and understanding—35:16; 38:2; and 42:3.

Verse 36—Elihu would have pressed Job to the end of his rope—7:18. The first line of this verse expresses wish or entreaty

---

[8] See possibilities in G. R. Driver, *Vetus Testamentum*, Supplement, 1953, pp. 39ff.

(Heb. *'abi*—wish).[9] He wishes that Job would change his attitude toward God, because he responds like all wicked men do.

Verse 37—Elihu, like Eliphaz—22, charges Job with secret sin. He merely intensifies his rebellion against God. Clapping is a gesture of open mockery. ("His hands" is not in the text.) Job is castigated for his contempt toward God and Elihu's impeccable arguments.

TODAY'S ENGLISH VERSION

34

Elihu

1-2 You men are so wise, so smart;
   listen now to what I am saying.

3 You can tell good food when you taste it;
   why can't you tell wise words when you hear
      them?

4 It is up to us to decide the case.

5 Job claims that he is innocent,
   and that God refuses to give him justice.

6 He asks, "How could I lie and say I am wrong?
   I am fatally wounded, but I am sinless."

7 Have you ever seen anyone like this man Job?
   He never shows respect for God.

8 He likes the company of evil men
   and goes around with sinners.

9 He says that it never does any good
   to try to follow God's will.

10 You men understand. Listen to me.
   Will Almighty God do what is wrong?

11 He rewards people for what they do
   and treats them the way they deserve.

---

[9] See thorough analysis in A. M. Honeyman, *Journal of American Oriental Society,* 1944, pp. 81-84, on developments of the root -'*by.*

¹² Almighty God does not do evil;
   he is never unjust to anyone.
¹³ Did God get his power from someone else?
   Did someone put him in charge of the world?
¹⁴ If God took back the breath of life,
¹⁵   then everyone living would die
      and turn into dust again.

¹⁶ Now listen to me, if you are wise.
¹⁷ Do you think the Almighty hates justice?
   Are you condemning the righteous God?
¹⁸ God condemns kings and rulers,
   when they are worthless or wicked.
¹⁹ God created everyone;
   he does not take the side of rulers,
   or favor the rich over the poor.
²⁰ A man may die suddenly at night.
   God strikes men down and they perish;
   he kills the mighty with no effort at âll.
²¹ He watches every step men take.
²² There is no darkness dark enough
   to hide a sinner from God.
²³ God does not need to set a time
   for men to go and be judged by him.
²⁴ He does not need an investigation
   to remove leaders and replace them with others.
²⁵ Because he knows what they do,
   he overthrows them and crushes them by night.
²⁶ He punishes sinners where all can see it,
²⁷   because they have stopped following him
      and ignored all his commands.
²⁸ They forced the poor to cry out to God,
   and he heard their calls for help.
²⁹ If God decided to do nothing at all,
   no one could criticize him.
   If he hid his face. men would be helpless.
³⁰ There would be nothing that nations could do

to keep oppressors from ruling them.

³¹ Job, have you confessed your sins to God,
and promised not to sin again?
³² Have you asked God to show you your faults,
and have you agreed to stop doing evil?
³³ Since you object to what God does,
can you expect him to do what you want?
It is your decision, not mine;
tell us now what you think.

³⁴ Any sensible person will surely agree;
any wise man who hears me will say
³⁵   that Job is speaking from ignorance,
and that nothing he says makes sense.
³⁶ Think through everything that Job says;
you will see that he talks like an evil man.
³⁷ He refuses to stop sinning;
in front of us all he mocks and insults God.

QUESTIONS FOR DISCUSSION 34:1-37

703. Elihu believes he is defending God. How so?
704. Give the fourfold outline of his discourse.
705. To whom does he address his words—surely not to the three friends?
706. What more is involved in hearing than mere listening? Cf. vs. 3.
707. What is "theodicy"? Discuss. Cf. vs. 4.
708. Somebody seems to be a liar. Who is it? Discuss. Does Elihu fairly represent Job's complaint?
709. Job is represented as a monumental scoffer. Explain how. Cf. vs. 7.
710. According to Elihu, Job fulfills Psalm one. In what way?
711. Is piety for profit? How does this question relate to America?

712. Who has accused God of wickedness? Discuss the point of verse ten.

713. The question is *not* "why does God not prevent injustice?". What *is* the basic question? Discuss.

714. Elihu repeats himself in verse 12. What is repeated?

715. Is power itself moral? How is God related to the injustice in the world? Discuss. Cf. vs. 13.

716. We can never gain an adequate perspective on evil until we know something. What is it? Discuss.

717. There is the dilemma of victims and victors in the face of injustice. Explain.

718. Elihu has given a bold assertion, not a balanced argument. How so?

719. Discuss the thesis of "natural leadership."

720. It is fallacy to suggest that we are all created equal. Discuss. Cf. vs. 19.

721. What is emphasized in verse 20?

722. Job is both right and wrong about God as revealed in verse 21. Explain.

723. God does not need to go to court. Why not?

724. Was there a need for the inquiry before God requested by Job?

725. Do we have any examples of the truthfulness of verses 25 and 26? Discuss. Cf. vs. 27.

726. How can we correlate the cries of the oppressed with the response of God? Discuss.

727. Job's fundamental question does not relate to the wicked, but to the innocent. Discuss.

728. Explain the problem and the solution in the word "together" in verse 29.

729. God does not always remove an unrighteous ruler. Explain verse 30.

730. The meaning of verse 31 is not clear. What is its meaning?

731. Elihu is putting words in Job's mouth. Are they the right words?

732. If we do not like the way God runs the cosmos, what can we do?

D. THE ACTS OF GOD AND THE ACTS OF MAN
(35:1-16)
1. Job has said he has seen no profit in righteousness.
(35:1-3)

TEXT 35:1-3

35 Moreover Elihu answered and said,
2 Thinkest thou this to be *thy* **right,**
Or **sayest thou, My righteousness is more than God's,**
3 That thou sayest, What advantage will it be unto thee?
And, **What profit shall I have more than if I had sinned?**

COMMENT 35:1-3

Verse 1—Elihu proceeds to respond to Job's assertion that piety in no way affects God, but that both sin and piety affect only man. This speech is composed of two parts: (1) Elihu seeks to refute Job's claim that the pious person is not rewarded by properity—verses 2-8; and (2) when the cry of the afflicted is not heard by God, they have not responded to the lesson intended by the discipline of suffering—verses 9-16. Elihu first defines the position of Job, then points to the greatness of God, who can neither be positively or negatively affected by anything man does. Man alone is affected by his own behavior.

Verse 2—The antecedent of "this" refers to what follows in verse three. Elihu is quoting Job's claim that he is in the right, or righteous. But Job has never claimed that he is more righteous than God; rather he has consistently asserted that he is innocent in the presence of God—4:17; 13:18; 19:6-7; and 27:2-6.

Verse 3—"How am I profited from my sin?" Job has never denied that he has sinned (Heb. means more than "if I had sinned"), but not serious enough to deserve the unbearable suffering which has fallen upon him—32:2. Elihu could not

362

admit that Job had correctly evaluated his spiritual condition, as that would impugn the justice of God. Job often seems to imply that it would not make any difference whether he had sinned or not, since justice seems to be abortive in the universe; i.e., the universe is amoral—34:9. It is doubtful that the pronoun "thee" in the A. V. refers to God; perhaps it is best taken as a taunt hurled at another one of Job's antagonists.

2. Man's actions, good or bad, do not help nor hurt God; they do affect men. (35:4-8)

TEXT 35:4-8

4 I will answer thee,
And thy companions with thee.
5 Look unto the heavens, and see;
And behold the skies, which are higher than thou.
6 If thou hast sinned, what effectest thou against him?
And if thy transgressions be multiplied, what doest thou
unto him?
7 If thou be righteous, what givest thou him?
Or what receiveth he of thy hand?
8 Thy wickedness *may hurt* a man as thou art;
And thy righteousness *may profit* a son of man.

COMMENT 35:4-8

Verse 4—Elihu here addresses all who have sympathy for Job's position—34:2-4, 10:15, 34-37. The personal pronoun "I" is emphatic, which agrees completely with Elihu's consistent arrogance.

Verse 5—His words here must be contrasted with Job's thoughts on God's transcendance—9:8-11; 11:7-9; 22:12. Job has always maintained that God controlled the heavens—9:8ff. But here the thought is that God is so far removed from us that He is beyond man's reach. God is neither benefitted by our righteousness nor harmed by our sin.

Verse 6—Eliphaz had set forth this same argument in 22:2ff. But Job had already set forth his position in 7:20.

Verse 7—God's self-interest is not the basis of His decisions in distributing His justice—Lk. 17:10; Rom. 11:35.

Verse 8—Eliphaz had said that a man's righteousness only profited himself. Elihu more perceptively exalts God's *greatness* at the expense of His *grace;* His transcendance at the price of His immanence—Prov. 9:12.

3. Pride will keep men from God. (35:9-13)

TEXT 35:9-13

9 By reason of the multitude of oppressions they cry out;
    They cry for help by reason of the arm of the mighty.
10 But none saith, Where is God my Maker,
    Who giveth songs in the night,
11 Who teacheth us more than the beasts of the earth,
    And maketh us wiser than the birds of the heavens?
12 There they cry, but none giveth answer,
    Because of the pride of evil men.
13 Surely God will not hear an empty *cry,*
    Neither will the Almighty regard it.

COMMENT 35:9-13

Verse 9—Job has expressed his attitude toward the magnitude of human misery and injustice in 24:2-17 and there noted that God does not respond to the social injustices caused by unrighteous men in 24:12. Job had already raised the question, "If God's rule is righteous, why the cry of the oppressed?" in 24:12. The phrase "multitude of oppressions" means the excess of oppression and comes from the root for youth or virginity—Amos 3:9; Eccl. 4:1. The "arm" is an image or instrument of oppression.

Verse 10—A righteous God gives "songs in the night" even to the oppressed—Ps. 42:8; Acts 16:25. The scriptures bear witness that God grants songs in the night to the oppressed—Pss. 137; 150:1, 5. The Jews, in *Fiddler on the Roof,* sang Ps. 137 asking, "How does one sing songs in a strange land?" In the birth record of Job's redeemer we are given Mary's song, 1:46-56; Zechariah's song, 1:68-79; the angels' song, 2:14; and Simeon's song, 2:29-35. Each of these were songs from a weary world, as were those of Moses and Hannah in the Old Testament. The word *zemirot* is usually rendered "songs" but can mean "strength."[1]

Verse 11—God teaches us (*mallepenu*) continually because man has a higher intelligence and wisdom than animals. He communicates to man with continuous instruction. The preposition *-min* is usually interpreted as the comparative, i.e., "more than," implying that man derives wisdom from the observation of the natural world. This is a common theme in Wisdom Literature—I Kg. 4:33; Prov. 6:6; 26:2, 11; 30:24-31; Job 38:41. What the content of the instruction is is not clear. *The Qumran Targum* preserves the verb "he makes us wise," as in A. V. as "wiser than." Elihu instructs Job to learn from the animal world how to respond to God—Pss. 104:21; 147:9; and Joel 1:20.

Verse 12—The verse harks back to verse nine but also connects with what follows, so the verse should not be transferred to follow verse nine. Elihu often goes back to something already said. It is not clear whether the verse is discussing the "reason" for their *cry* or the "reason" for not being *heard.* But in Elihu's view, if one is not heard, one is in fact evil. Suffering is for discipline, but evil men do not recognize it.

Verse 13—That God requires pious petitions before His righteousness will prevail on earth but reveals the theological

---

[1] See Pope, *Job,* pp. 263-264; and *The Qumran Targum* rendering of "pour notre plantation dans la nuit," and IQS VIII, 5, 10; Isa. 61:3.

perspective of loquacious Elihu—Hab. 1:13. It is possible that the verse says that the petition is not even addressed to God, but to empty space or void.

4. Job has approached God in the wrong spirit. (35:14-16)

TEXT 35:14-16

14 How much less when thou sayest thou beholdest him not,
   The cause is before him, and thou waitest for him!
15 But now, because he hath not visited in his anger,
   Neither doth he greatly regard arrogance;
16 Therefore doth Job open his mouth in vanity;
   He multiplieth words without knowledge.

COMMENT 35:14-16

Verse 14—If God does not listen to those who do not turn to him, how much less would He listen to Job who relentlessly pursues Him with His complaints. Other men cry out against their oppressors; but Job cries out against God—13:24; 23:8ff; and 30:20. What basis does he have for believing that God will come to his aid and deliver him from disease and death?[2] But Elihu is no more convincing in polemic than in exhortation. Job has argued his case like a lawyer—13:18; 23:4, and Elihu declares that the outcome all depends on the judge. The A. V. rendering of "cause" comes from -din and is best understood as "case" in a legal sense.[3]

Verse 15—In 21:14ff Job has asserted that the wicked go unpunished. Perhaps Elihu is referring to this Jobian claim. God does not regard arrogance, or perhaps with Brown, Driver, and Briggs—folly. The obscurity of this verse is not reduced

[2] See suggestions of G. R. Driver, *Vetus Testamentum,* 1955, p. 89.
[3] G. R. Driver, *Vetus Testamentum,* 1960, p. 89.

by the A. V. rendering of "greatly regard," as the Hebrew has "greatly know," when we would expect—"not know at all."

Verse 16—The verse is addressed to the bystanders, not Job.

TODAY'S ENGLISH VERSION

35 ¹⁻² It is not right, Job, for you to say
        that you are innocent in God's sight,
³ or to ask God, "How does my sin affect you?
        It has done me no good not to sin."
⁴ I am going to answer you and your friends too.
⁵ Look at the sky! See how high the clouds are!
⁶ If you sin, that does no harm to God.
        If you do many wrongs, does that affect him?
⁷ Do you help God by being so righteous?
        There is nothing God needs from you.
⁸ It is your fellow-men who suffer from your sins,
        and the good you do helps them.

⁹ When men are oppressed they groan;
        they cry for someone to save them.
¹⁰   But they don't turn to God, their Creator,
        who gives them strength in their darkest hours.
¹¹ They don't turn to God, who makes us wise,
        wiser than any animal or bird.
¹² They cry for help, but God doesn't answer,
        because they are proud and evil men.
¹³ It is useless for them to cry out;
        Almighty God does not see or hear them.

¹⁴ Job, you say you can't see God,
        but wait patiently—your case is before him.
¹⁵ You think that God does not punish,
        that he pays no attention to sin.
¹⁶ It is useless for you to go on talking;
        it is clear you don't know what you are saying.

QUESTIONS FOR DISCUSSION 35:1-16

733. What assertion of Job is answered by Elihu in this chapter? Is this position of Elihu popular today?
734. Job is supposed to have said that he was more righteous than God. What did he really say?
735. Job never said he had not sinned. What did Job say about his sinning?
736. How does Elihu show a consistent arrogance?
737. How does Elihu interpret God's transcendence? How did Job interpret this quality of God?
738. Job had already answered the argument of verse seven. Cf. 7:20. What was it?
739. What is meant by saying, "God's self-interest is not the basis of His decisions in distributing His justice"?
740. Elihu makes one quality of God's nature contradict another quality. Show how this is so.
741. How do you answer Job's question: "If God's rule is righteous, why the cry of the oppressed"?
742. God does give "songs in the night." Cite three examples.
743. God can and does instruct us above and better than the animals. How? Why?
744. If one is not heard and answered by God, it is because of what? I.e., what is the problem?
745. We must be pious or our cry will not be heard—so says Elihu. Is he right? Discuss.
746. Elihu feels Job has less chance with God than other men. Why?
747. Explain in your own words verse 15.
748. Someone has "multiplied words without knowledge," but it was not Job. Who was so involved?

E. GOD—PERSON, PROMISE, PURPOSE, AND PEOPLE
(36:1-33)
1. God deals with men according to their deeds; the penitent he restores, others perish. (36:1-16)

TEXT 36:1-16

36 Elihu also proceeded, and said,
2 Suffer me a little, and I will show thee;
For I have yet somewhat to say on God's behalf.
3 I will fetch my knowledge from afar,
And will ascribe righteousness to my Maker.
4 For truly my words are not false:
One that is perfect in knowledge is with thee.
5 Behold, God is mighty, and despiseth not any:
He is mighty in strength of understanding.
6 He preserveth not the life of the wicked,
But giveth to the afflicted *their* right.
7 He withdraweth not his eyes from the righteous:
But with kings upon the throne
He setteth them for ever, and they are exalted.
8 And if they be bound in fetters,
And be taken in the cords of affliction;
9 Then he showeth them their work,
And their transgressions, that they have behaved themselves
proudly.
10 He openeth also their ear to instruction,
And commandeth that they return from iniquity.
11 If they hearken and serve *him,*
They shall spend their days in prosperity,
And their years in pleasures.
12 But if they hearken not, they shall perish by the sword,
And they shall die without knowledge.
13 But they that are godless in heart lay up anger:
They cry not for help when he bindeth them.
14 They die in youth,
And their life *perisheth* among the unclean.

15 He delivereth the afflicted by their affliction,
   And openeth their ear in oppression.
16 Yea, he would have allured thee out of distress
   Into a broad place, where there is no straitness;
   And that which is set on thy table would be full of fatness.

COMMENT 36:1-16

Verse 1—Elihu begins his fourth and most impressive speech—chapters 36-37. He will pour out his wisdom on Job concerning God's greatness and the mystery of His unfathomableness. If Job only knew God, he would bow in submissive awe. This speech anticipates Yahweh's speeches in chapters 38-41 in describing the marvels of His creation. The speech is divided into two fundamental issues: (1) The divine discipline of suffering—36:2-25, which deals with the cause and purpose of suffering—verses 2-15, and the application of these points to Job personally—verses 16-25; and (2) The work and wisdom of God—36:26—37:24, God's work in nature—36:26—37:13; and the magnificent transcendance of God—verses 14-24.

Verse 2—The verb -*ktr* here means "wait" or "bear with me," Judges 20:43; Ps. 22:12; and Hab. 1:4. The verb can also mean "surround," and is so interpreted by Blommerde who renders the phrase as "Form a circle around me, . . ." He also suggests that we should understand the preposition as "from," not "on God's behalf." This would reinforce Elihu's judgment that his wisdom is God's wisdom.

Verse 3—Elihu will bring his wisdom from afar and report the truth "from" God, rather than "to my maker" as in the A. V.[1] Elihu is thus God's infallible interpreter; so Job, you fail to listen at your own peril.

Verse 4—Elihu is a total stranger to modesty. He repeatedly

---

[1] For analysis of this preposition, see M. Dahood, *Vetus Testamentum*, 1967, p. 41, note 4.

asserts his own genius. The parallelism precludes that the second line refers to God—37:16, rather than Elihu. The word rendered perfect means complete as God had earlier testified of Job—2:3.

Verse 5—God is all powerful as has been asserted previously by both Job and Elihu. There is no object in the text for "despise" and thus it must be supplied. Of all emendations suggested, Dhorme's is most feasible and enlightening. "God is great in might and He does not despise the pure in heart"[2]— 9:22ff and Isa. 57:15.

Verse 6—Earlier Job had asked why the wicked are allowed to live—21:7. Elihu replies to his query that God does not allow them to live, thus contradicting Job's allegation. God punishes the unrighteous and rights the wrongs which have been inflicted upon the poor. Yes, but when? Why do we still have so many poor?

Verse 7—God does not "withdraw His eyes" from the righteous in watchful concern and compassion. The Masoretic punctuation creates a problem in the middle of this verse. The righteous are left alone, while Elihu refers to a class of rulers, i.e., kings as a separate class. In the Hebrew text it is the righteous who are both protected and exalted to the seats of powerful rulers. This thought is followed in verse eight—Ps. 113:6ff.

Verse 8—"If they" refers to the righteous from verse seven. When the righteous are allowed by God to suffer, it is for the express purpose of purification or refinement. Even Elihu would not adjudge all kings as righteous; he surely means those who are basically good, though not sinless. Here Elihu makes his sole creative contribution to the issue under scrutiny. Affliction is for disciplinary purposes only—5:17.

Verse 9—The purpose of affliction is to humble the sinner in order to destroy the power of pride, the center of sin.

---

[2] Dhorme, *Job*, pp. 539ff; see also for Rabbinic tradition, S. Esh, *Vetus Testamentum*, 1957, pp. 190ff; and M. Dahood, *Psalms*, Vol. II, note 2, on Ps. 75:7 for his defense of rendering the divine description as "the Old One."

Exaltation breeds pride, but humiliation breeds repentance.

Verse 10—God opens "their ear" (*'oznam*); here it stands for their entire mind set. The word *musar* means discipline and is often connected with affliction.[3] When the evil man hears God, he returns, or repents of his rebellion.

Verse 11—Once more the thesis is presented that repentance will gain the restoration of prosperity—Isa. 1:19, 20. If they hear (Heb. has hear), they will obey. Often in both Old Testament and New Testament the vocabulary for obedience is based in the verbal roots for hearing. Their lives will be completed in prosperity, if they will but repent. The Hebrew text describes the way that the righteous will complete their lives as in pleasures (Heb. *banne 'imino*)[4]—Ps. 16:6, 11. Unmistakably this word admits of material pleasure and not some form of mystical bliss like the medieval supreme encounter with God.

Verse 12—If they will not learn from God's discipline, they must perish. Doom is the reward of the ungodly. There is strong evidence that Pope is correct regarding the translation for *'br*—should be "cross over" not "fall" or "perish" as in A. V. The image suggests crossing over into death. The meaning is the same, whether we accept the traditional rendering, as does *The Qumran Targum* on Job, or the more recent lexical data.

Verse 13—The impious of heart nourish anger. The Hebrew has "put anger" for the A. V. "lay up anger." Perhaps this means to nourish anger, rather than contemplating about the justice of the punishment—Rom 2:5; Amos 1:11; and Jer. 3:5. Dhorme takes this to mean that they "keep their anger," reading *yismeru*. This represents the spirit of the verse.

---

[3] See especially J. A. Sanders, *Suffering as Divine Discipline in the Old Testament and Post-Biblical Judaism* (Colgate Rochester Divinity School bulletin, 1955); also E. F. Sutcliffe, *Providence and Suffering in the Old Testament and New Testament;* also W. D. Chamberlain, *The Meaning of Repentance* (Joplin, Mo.: College Press reprint, 1972).

[4] E. A. Speiser, *Genesis*, Vol. I, Anchor Bible, suggests that this word contains unmistakable connotations of sexual pleasure—see his comments on 2:8 and 18:12.

Verse 14—They die an early and shameful death (lit. *qedesim*—"among the male prostitutes" or holy males)—Deut. 23:17; I Kg. 14:24, 15:12, 22:47; II Kg. 23:7. *The Qumran Targum* confirms that *qedesim* here refers to male prostitutes, whose lives both end early and in shame.

Verse 15—Here is the essence of Elihu's first speech—33:16-30. If one accepts affliction as discipline for righteousness, then one may be saved. Discipline can deliver the impious; thus therapy ends in thanksgiving.

Verse 16—Elihu charges that Job's earlier prosperity generated his corruption and injustice, which brought God's judging misfortunes upon him. Yet, in marked contrast, God's speeches —chapters 38ff—inform him that he can have fellowship in suffering, not after he is restored. Technically, this and the following verses are problematic, but the essential meaning is rather clear. Job's great wealth has drawn him away from God. Perhaps it is true that it is difficult for a rich man to enter the kingdom, but it is not impossible.[5] Job returns and God blesses him in a beautiful and marvelous way—42:1ff.

2. Job has had the wrong spirit toward his sufferings.
(36:17-21)

TEXT 36:17-21

17   But thou art full of the judgment of the wicked:
Judgment and justice take hold *on thee.*
18 For let not wrath stir thee up against chastisements;
Neither let the greatness of the ransom turn thee aside.
19 Will thy cry avail, *that thou be* not in distress,
Or all the forces of *thy* strength?
20 Desire not the night,
When peoples are cut off in their place.
21 Take heed, regard not iniquity:
For this hast thou chosen rather than affliction.

------

[5] For the many technical matters, see Pope, *Job,* p. 270, and Dhorme, *Job,* pp. 544-555.

COMMENT 36:17-21

Verse 17—The first verb in the verse is in the perfect tense, "full of judgment," and the second is in the imperfect—judgment and justice "take hold" of him. Job's own attitude toward justice is continually condemning him.

Verse 18—Elihu warns (*hemah*—beware) Job, do not let wrath "entice you evil." The A. V. understands the wrath to be God's, while the R. S. V. understands it to be Job's. The entire issue is concerned with God's judgment on Job's unrighteousness, so surely the wrath (*hemah*) is God's. The parallelism presents a powerful warning against the corruption of justice. Do not let the abundance (*sepeq*) of the reward or ransom pervert you.

Verse 19—Dhorme renders this very difficult verse as "can one compare your crying out to him (Heb. *loe*—to him, not *lo'*) in distress?" "Wealth and bribery cannot influence the divine Judge"—Pope, p. 271. The rendering of the A. V. makes little sense. The essential meaning of the verse is Job's wealth could not save him. The verse, like the previous one, is a warning against corruption.

Verse 20—The most promising of all suggestions as to the meaning of this cryptic verse is that it is condemning the letting of kinship influence his judgments. As usual, night is the symbol of sudden catastrophe—34:20, 25. People, symbol for many, a group, or a clan, are cut off without warning.

Verse 21—Stop rebelling against God because of His chastening hand. Because of your rebellion, you were chosen for testing. Job is being rebuked for choosing rebellion; he certainly did not choose affliction. If one amends the Hebrew text as passive (*bohanta*—"you have been tested"), the sense is precisely Elihu's major assertion—that suffering is for warning and discipline, in order to turn the sufferer from evil.

3. God knows what he is doing and his work should be magnified. (36:22-33)

TEXT 36:22-33

22 Behold, God doeth loftily in his power:
   Who is a teacher like unto him?
23 Who hath enjoined him his way?
   Or who can say, Thou hast wrought unrighteousness?
24 Remember that thou magnify his work,
   Whereof men have sung.
25 All men have looked thereon;
   Man beholdeth it afar off.
26 Behold, God is great, and we know him not;
   The number of his years is unsearchable.
27 For he draweth up the drops of water,
   Which distil in rain from his vapor,
28 Which the skies pour down
   And drop upon man abundantly.
29 Yea, can any understand the spreadings of the clouds,
   The thunderings of his pavilion?
30 Behold, he spreadeth his light around him;
   And he covereth the bottom of the sea.
31 For by these he judgeth the peoples;
   He giveth food in abundance.
32 He covereth his hands with the lightning,
   And giveth it a charge that it strike the mark.
33 The noise thereof telleth concerning him,
   The cattle also concerning *the storm* that cometh up.

COMMENT 36:22-33

Verse 22—The purpose of Job's suffering is here considered by Elihu. God is Job's *moreh* or teacher. The content of the instruction is disciplinary suffering, if Job could only understand. This word (*moreh*) is also applied to God in Isa. 30:20; Job 34:32; 35:11; and Ps. 32:8.

Verse 23—Since God is the almighty, no one can dictate to Him appropriate decisions; therefore, Job should stop criticizing God for his misfortunes. Instead, he should attempt to come to an understanding of what his *moreh*—teacher—is saying to him. God's power and conduct are here under scrutiny. The A. V. "enjoined" is from a verb which means "to prescribe" or determine; i.e., who can determine God's ways for Him? Who can say that His conduct is unrighteous?

Verse 24—Others have sung of God's great handiwork, while you are complaining about it. Praise is at the heart of true righteousness. If you are righteous, praise will break forth from your lips—Ps. 104:33.

Verse 25—All other men have looked upon creation in awe and deep satisfaction. But not you, Job. A man must have perspective (from "afar off") in order to understand the greatness of God's creation. One cannot discern the majestic magnificence of creation close at hand.

Verse 26—God's greatness is here set forth in imagery revealing His control of the universe. He is not bound by time; His years are innumerable (Heb. *mispar*)—16:22a and Ps. 102:28.

Verse 27—The verb *-gr'*, which is rendered "draweth" in the A. V., basically means diminish or deduct—verse 7; Isa. 15:2; Jer. 48:37; and Ex. 21:10. The A. V. rendering of *-'ed* as vapor is defective. The word occurs only here and Gen. 2:6.[6] Albright has argued that this means "the subterranean source of fresh water."[7] The word rendered as distill in the A. V. probably means filter. The image is that God controls the cosmic water system and filters vast amounts of water from a "flood" or giant reservoir. God is Lord of the rain, which is necessary for life and growth.

Verse 28—The late G. E. Wright took *-rab*, abundantly, as equivalent of *rebibim*—showers—Deut. 32:2, and rendered "fall upon man as showers." *Rab* is probably an adjective not an adverb which modifies "upon many men." Perhaps

---

[6] See G. Lisowsky, ed., *Konkordanz zum hebraischen alten Testament*, 2nd ed., 1958; and S. Mandekern, *Veteris Testimenti Concordantiae Hebraicae atque Chaldaicae*, 2 vols., 1955 reprint, for this root.

[7] See W. F. Albright, *J.B.L.*, 1939, pp. 102ff.

adam rab should not be translated "many men" but "man"—
Matt. 5:45. The rain falls upon the just and the unjust. God
is impartial, as even the rain demonstrates.[8]

Verse 29—Who can understand the wonders of a thunderstorm, diffusion of clouds—26:9, thunderings—30:22, all
forming a canopy or pavilion of God—Ps. 18:11?

Verse 30—God spreads His light—*'oro,* i.e., lightning as
in 37:3, 11b, 15b. The second line makes little sense, but
following Ps. 18:16 the passive form of the verb cover (*ksy*—
cover, to *gly*—uncover or reveal) can be uncover; thus God
uncovers or reveals the bottom or roots of the sea by His Lordship. Perhaps the deepest part of the sea is His throne. He is
Lord of both the skies and the seas.

Verse 31—By the thunderstorms and seas He judges (Heb.
yadin) everyone, i.e., blesses them. The imagery is polarized
into judgment and blessing.[9]

Verse 32—Neither the K. J. nor A. V. (1901) make much
sense here. How God covers (Heb. verb *kissah*) His hands with
lightning is our problem—37:3; I Kg. 18:44. Light (Heb.
'or or lightning) is the subject of the verb. Dhorme is probably
correct in rendering the line with the sense that God places
His hands into lightning and directs it to its target.[10] This
imagery must not be identified with that of the Near Eastern
gods hurling lightning bolts. Here we have anthropomorphism,
but in ancient mythology the gods participated in such events.
God is here presented as Lord over nature. If He can providentially control the universe, then He is capable of watching
over Job.

Verse 33—Peake gives a historical survey of over thirty

---

[8] See M. Dahood, *CBQ*, 1963, pp. 123-124.

[9] See M. H. Pope, *El in the Ugaritic Texts,* 1955, where he has demonstrated that
the chief god of the Ugaritic pantheon dwelt at the confluence of the subterranean
seas, pp. 61-81, e.g., Baal as storm god enthroned on a mountain and fused with
features of the *Ugaritic God* El. But *God* is comparable not only in that He is Lord of
these domains, but He is Lord over the entire universe, not merely certain dimensions
of it. See my essay on *Is God in Exile?* in this commentary.

[10] The emendations of G. R. Driver support Dhorme, *Vetus Testamentum,* 1955,
pp. 88ff.

explanations of this verse. Literally the text reads "He declares His purpose concerning it; cattle also concerning what rises."[11] Dhorme presents the least amount of emendation to derive the translation "The flock has warned its shepherd, the flock which sniffs the storm." This is grammatically possible; it makes sense and it emphasizes Elihu's thesis—that God providentially guards all of nature, why not Job, too?

TODAY'S ENGLISH VERSION

36 Elihu went on talking.

Elihu

2 Be patient and listen a little longer
   to what I am saying on God's behalf.
3 My knowledge is wide; I will use what I know
   to show that God, my Creator, is just.
4 Nothing I say to you is false;
   you see before you a truly wise man.

5 How strong God is! He despises no one;
   there is nothing he doesn't understand.
6 He does not let sinners live on,
   and he always treats the poor with justice.
7 He protects those who are righteous;
   he lets them rule like kings,
   and lets them be honored forever.
8 But if people are bound in chains,
   suffering for what they have done,
9   God shows them their sins and their pride.
10 He makes them listen to his warning
   to run away from evil.

---

[11] For some of the more feasible ones, see E. F. Sutcliffe, *Biblica,* 1949, p. 89; and G. R. Driver, *Vetus Testamentum,* Supplement, 1955, pp. 88ff; Pope, *Job,* pp. 276-277.

¹¹ If they obey God and serve him,
    they live out their lives in peace and prosperity.
¹² But if not, they will die in ignorance
    and go to the world of the dead.

¹³ Those who are godless keep on being angry,
    and even when punished, they don't pray for
      help.
¹⁴ They die while they still are young,
    worn out by a life of disgrace.
¹⁵ But God teaches men through suffering
    and uses distress to open their eyes.
¹⁶ God brought you out of trouble,
    and let you enjoy security;
    your table was piled high with food.
¹⁷ But now you are getting the punishment you
      deserve.
¹⁸ Be careful not to let bribes deceive you
    and not to let riches lead you astray.
¹⁹ It will do you no good to cry out for help;
    all your strength can't help you now.
²⁰ Don't wish for night to come,
    the time when nations will perish.
²¹ Be careful not to turn to evil;
    your suffering was sent to keep you from it.

²² Remember how great is his power;
    God is the greatest teacher of all.
²³ No one can tell God what to do
    or accuse him of having done evil.
²⁴ God has always been praised for what he does;
    you also must praise him.
²⁵ Everyone has seen what he has done;
    but no one understands it all.
²⁶ We cannot fully know God's greatness
    or count the number of his years.

²⁷ It is God who takes water from the earth

and turns it into drops of rain.
²⁸ He lets the rain pour from the clouds
    in showers for all mankind.
²⁹ No one knows how the clouds move,
    or how the thunder roars through the sky.
³⁰ He sends lightning through all the sky,
    but the depths of the sea remain dark.
³¹ This is how he feeds the people
    and provides an abundance of food.
³² He seizes the lightning with his hands,
    and commands it to hit the mark.
³³ Thunder announces the approaching storm,
    and the cattle know it is coming.

QUESTIONS FOR DISCUSSION 36:1-33

749. What is the theme of this the final speech of Elihu?
750. What are the two fundamental issues of this speech?
751. This man really has confidence in his message. Why?
752. Is this message for God or from God? Cf. vs. 3.
753. Elihu is a total stranger to modesty. How is this fact shown?
754. There is another way of translating verse five, i.e., other than appears here. How so?
755. Elihu flatly contradicts Job in verse six. Who is right? Discuss.
756. Two grand benefits are promised to the righteous in verse seven. What are they?
757. Elihu makes his sole creative contradiction to the issue under scrutiny in verse eight. What is it?
758. What is the purpose of affliction? Cf. vs. 9.
759. God has a way of opening our inner ear. How does He do it? Cf. vs. 10.
760. The meaning of the Hebrew word for hearing has a lesson in it for all hearers. What is it? Cf. vs. 11.

761. If the ungodly will not learn from discipline, they must "cross over." What does this mean? Cf. vs. 12.
762. The impious of heart nourish anger. Why? With what result? Discuss.
763. Male prostitutes are discussed in verse 14. What is said?
764. The essence of Elihu's speech is in verse 15. What is it?
765. A charge is made against Job in verse 16. What is it? Was it true? Discuss.
766. Elihu charges that Job's attitude toward justice is continually condemning him. In what way? Cf. vs. 17.
767. What is meant by "the greatness of the ransom" in verse 18?
768. What is the meaning of verse 19?
769. Explain in your own words the meaning of verse 20.
770. Elihu knows why Job is suffering—even if Job does not. What reason is given in verse 21?
771. God is Job's teacher, but what is the lesson? Elihu knows. Cf. vs. 22.
772. Has Job been telling God what to do? Is the charge in verse 23 a fair one?
773. Praise is at the heart of true righteousness. Cf. Ps. 102:28. Is this true?
774. A beautiful picture appears in verse 27. What is it?
775. Is Matt. 5:45 involved in verse 28?
776. Does God live in the bottom of the sea, or in the highest heaven? Cf. the meaning of verses 29 and 30.
777. How do thunderstorms and seas judge peoples? Cf. vs. 31.
778. Express in your own words the meaning of the figure of speech in verse 32.
779. There are many possible meanings to verse 33. Which do you prefer? Why?

F. THE CREATOR AND THE CREATION (37:1-24)
1. The marvelous activity of God in nature (37:1-13)

TEXT 37:1-13

37 Yea, at this my heart trembleth,
And is moved out of its place.
2 Hear, oh, hear the noise of his voice,
And the sound that goeth out of his mouth.
3 He sendeth it forth under the whole heaven,
And his lightning unto the ends of the earth.
4 After it a voice roareth;
He thundereth with the voice of his majesty;
And he restraineth not *the lightnings* when his voice is
heard.
5 God thundereth marvellously with his voice;
Great things doeth he, which we cannot comprehend.
6 For he saith to the snow, Fall thou on the earth;
Likewise to the shower of rain,
And to the showers of his mighty rain.
7 He sealeth up the hand of every man,
That all men whom he hath made may know *it.*
8 Then the beasts go into coverts,
And remain in their dens.
9 Out of the chamber *of the south* cometh the storm,
And cold out of the north.
10 By the breath of God ice is given;
And the breadth of the waters is straitened.
11 Yea, he ladeth the thick cloud with moisture;
He spreadeth abroad the cloud of his lightning:
12 And it is turned round about by his guidance,
That they may do whatsoever he commandeth them
Upon the face of the habitable world,
13 Whether it be for correction or for his land,
Or for lovingkindness, that he cause it to come.

COMMENT 37:1-13

Verse 1—In his final speech, Elihu describes his own feelings, and Job is not addressed until verse 14. Elihu's heart leaps (see Brown, Driver, and Briggs—Lev. 11:21; Hab. 3:6) with terror at God's thunderstorm—Pss. 18:13; 77:17-18; Ex. 9:22-35; 19:16; I Sam. 7:10; and Isa. 30:30.[1] The RSV's rendering of "shook" takes the verb as transitive and thus gives insight into the imagery of the second line—A. V. "And is moved out of its place."

Verse 2—Elihu intones a hymn in praise of God who reveals Himself in the winter rains which bring fertility to the earth, and God's gracious presence to men—Pss. 8; 19:2-7; 29; 104; and 147. God's voice is described as thunder in 28:26. The word rendered "sound," or rumbling, appears in verb form in Isa. 31:4 in describing the growling of a lion.

Verse 3—God's sovereignty is expressed in that He sends thunder and lightning throughout the universe. The reference of "it" is to lightning—36:32—in the second line, and the verb has a root meaning of "loosen," i.e., send in the sense of letting it go to the corners (lit. wings) of the earth.

Verse 4—The antecedent of "it" is the lightning in verse 3. God's voice roars—Judges 14:5; Amos 1:2; 3:4, 8; Ps. 104:21; Jer. 25:30; and Joel 3:16; but ". . . He does not restrain the lightning when His voice is heard," R. S. V. The Hebrew word -ye'aqqebem means restrain them. The verb 'aqab means "hold by the heel," as in Hosea 12:3, and thus "hold back" or "restrain." Even though God speaks in the thunder and lightning, He does not restrain everything in the universe merely because He speaks. Job needs to learn this fact, according to Elihu.

Verse 5—Elihu's words echo both Job and Eliphaz—5:9; 9:10. Elihu makes transition to another dimension of God's wonderful creation—snow and frost. God is presented lord

---

[1] This imagery has been much discussed since the discovery of the Ugaritic Myth of Baal-Hadad. The similarities apply to Elihu but not to Job; see F. M. Cross, Jr., *Bulletin American Society of Oriental Research*, 1950, pp. 19-21; and T. H. Gaster, *Jewish Quarterly Review*, 1946-47, pp. 54-67.

of the winter, as He is the lord of the spring and summer in the previous verses. Dhorme provides insight into the verse without any emendation—"God by his voice works (*ya'amol*) wonders." This rendering makes excellent transition from the thunderstorm to the winter snows.

Verse 6—The verb -*hw'*—"to be"—is uniquely used here in the sense of "fall." The Hebrew text has repetition of "downour of rain" and "downpour of rains," perhaps to emphasize the intensity of the rain which would refer to the heavy rain of the Syrian Palestinian winter.

Verse 7—The text says "with the hand of every man he seals"—9:7; Gen. 7:16. The preposition *beyad* probably must be understood as with a similar verb as "shut" or "seal." The meaning is that when it rains men must cease from their agricultural labors while the rain and snow prevail.[2]

Verse 8—The imagery is concerned with the hibernation of animals for the winter. The A. V. renders the noun "coverts," which could better be understood as "lairs." The verb means "to lie in wait." The word translated "dens" is used of God's dwelling place—Ps. 76:2; of man's home—Jer. 21:13; and of the lairs of wild beasts—38:40; Amos 3:4; Nah. 2:12; and Ps. 104:22.

Verse 9—There is also reference to the chambers (Heb. *heder*) of the south in 9:9. But "of the south" is not in the text—Job 38:22 and Ps. 135:7. The unique word -*mezarim* is rendered by "cometh" in A. V., but it probably means to scatter or disperse. It might be a term for storehouse, as Pope suggests. This would make perfectly good sense in our present verse. Likewise the North yields its "cold."

Verse 10—Elihu employs poetic imagery to express that ice and frost are the results of the cold-blast of God's breath. "Straitened" of the A. V. is derived from word meaning "become a solid mass," i.e., frozen solid—Isa. 40:7.

---

[2] D. W. Thomas secures the word "rest" instead of "know" with minimal emendation; see *Journal of Theological Studies*, 1954, pp. 56ff. This makes excellent sense in this verse.

Verse 11—The clouds are loaded or burdened (A. V. ladeth —from root meaning burden or weight—Isa. 1:14) with moisture. Instead of "lightning" as in A. V., this may refer only to "light" as in Hebrew text, i.e., to the sun, thus deriving the meaning that the sunlight dispels the clouds with their moisture (Heb. *beri*). However we understand the grammatical possibilities; the emphasis is on the manifestation of God's power and controls of nature.

Verse 12—Elihu here explains that all of nature obeys the will of God and fulfills His purposes. The antecedent of "it" is the clouds from verse 11. The word -*mithappek* rendered "turned around" in A. V. appears in Gen. 3:24 where it describes the flaming sword turning round and round. The meaning of the entire verse centers on God's control; though lightning appears to act capriciously, it is carrying out His divine directions.

Verse 13—Elihu asserts in conclusion to this section of his that God's control of nature sometimes results in judgment, sometimes in blessing. Both wrath and mercy result from God's control of nature; the same also applies to history. God's universe is balanced between His correction or discipline and His covenant love (*hesed*). Dhorme's emendation provides the verb which is lacking in the first part of the verse. "Whether it be for punishment that He accomplishes His will, whether it be for mercy that He brings it to pass"—I Cor. 4:21.[3]

2. Man should realize his insignificant position and fear God. (37:14-24)

TEXT 37:14-24)

14 Hearken unto this, O Job:
Stand still, and consider the wondrous works of God.

---

[3] For the suggestion that -*le'arso*—rendered as "for his land" in A. V.—should be translated as grace or favor, see M. Dahood, *Psalms*, Vol. II, note 3 on Ps. 58:3. This makes perfectly good sense, while land makes little sense in this verse.

15 Dost thou know how God layeth *his charge* upon them,
   And causeth the lightning of his cloud to shine?
16 Dost thou know the balancings of the clouds,
   The wondrous works of him who is perfect in knowledge?
17 How thy garments are warm,
   When the earth is still by reason of the south *wind?*
18 Canst thou with him spread out the sky,
   Which is strong as a molten mirror?
19 Teach us what we shall say unto him;
   For we cannot set *our speech* in order by reason of darkness.
20 Shall it be told him that I would speak?
   Or should a man wish that he were swallowed up?
21 And now men see not the light which is bright in the skies;
   But the wind passeth, and cleareth them.
22 Out of the north cometh golden splendor:
   God hath upon him terrible majesty.
23 *Touching* the Almighty, we cannot find him out:
   He is excellent in power;
   And in justice and plenteous righteousness he will not afflict.
24 Men do therefore fear him:
   He regardeth not any that are wise of heart.

COMMENT 37:14-24

Verse 14—Elihu turns from his hymn of praise to directly addressing Job once again. Can Job be brought submissively to God? This will be Elihu's last effort. He presents polarized imagery of darkness and light as coming from the North, the traditional source of theophany—Isa. 14:13; Ezek. 1:4. Now, Job, will you consider the wonderful works of God? The ensuing questions are raised in hopes of exposing Job's ignorance of how God works in His creation.

Verse 15—Like Yahweh in chapters 38ff, Elihu asks Job, "Do you know" how God—lit. "puts upon them," i.e., lays charge upon them, probably the clouds? The antecedent is not clear.[4] Lightning is no longer a mystery; it is the direct activity of God, not the inanimate "Laws of Nature."

Verse 16—God's precision in the balancing of the clouds is wonderful testimony of His control of nature. The word "balancing" is from the same root as balance in Prov. 16:11 and Isa. 40:12. In 36:4b Elihu uses the same expression as applied to himself rather than God—*temim de'im*, i.e., "the perfect in knowledge," which Blommerde takes as representing the divine title. He renders this verse "Do you recognize the Most High by His outspread cloud, by his wonderful acts, the Perfect in Knowledge?"

Verse 17—Elihu ironically emphasizes the smallness of man. During the sirocco, i.e., hot east or south winds, clothes feel dry and hot. W. M. Thomson, in his work *The Land and The Book* (Baker reprint, p. 536) gives a most striking description of the type of experience pictured in this verse. All the birds, animals, and men hide from the scorching heat, and wait for the clouds bearing the promise of cooling rain. Elsewhere the sirocco are called east wind.

Verse 18—The verb rendered "spread out" means "beat out"—Gen. 1:6. Can you do that, Job?—Ex. 28:8 and Deut. 28:23. The shimmering heat of the day was compared with burnished copper—Deut. 28:23. Ancient mirrors were made of molten metal. The word rendered "strong" as in A. V. means hard or solid mass—verse 10. The verb means "pour out" or "cast metals."

Verse 19—Job, what will you say in face of all these awesome facts? With biting sarcasm, Elihu challenges him to get his "case" ready, doubtless in reference to Job's desire to encounter God in a court of law—13:8; 23:4; 32:14; and 33:5. How can you prepare or order your case out of such ignorance, i.e., darkness—Eccl. 43:2ff.

Verse 20—Elihu finds it quite incredible that insignificant Job would think of confronting an incomprehensibly great

---

[4] For possibilities, see G. R. Driver, *Vetus Testamentum*, Supplement, 1967, pp. 61ff.

God. Anyone so foolish is merely asking to be destroyed, i.e., "swallowed up." Only an arrogant madman would conceive of such a thing.

Verse 21—Elihu returns to natural phenomena. Man cannot even look at the sun when the wind has drawn away the clouds. How would you imagine that you could possibly look upon the creator in all glory? Looking upon the dazzling majesty of His presence is beyond you, Job.

Verse 22—It is not impossible that this refers to the Aurora Borealis. The text has only "gold," and the A. V. renders it "golden splendor." At least this would make sense in light of the northern phenomena; the mysterious blazing golden beams could suggest the presence of God, so avers Driver.[5] Pope attempts to demonstrate an illusion to mythology associated with the North and gold, but the reference has nothing to do with the metal itself.

Verse 23—Elihu reasserts his conviction that God cannot perpetrate injustice, either directly or indirectly—9:20-24; 11:7; and 23:8-9. God will not violate, afflict, or oppress. We cannot understand God, but He has abundant righteousness (Heb. lit. greatness of righteousness); and in His righteousness He is too inflexible to violate justice. Job completely misunderstands; he has no case against his creator. If he would but acknowledge it, he could be healed and restored to prosperity.

Verse 24—Even the wisest of men cannot see God. Men stand in awe before God because of His greatness and goodness. But all men are beneath God's notice, even the wisest. The Hebrew phrase "the wise in heart" is found in 9:4 with a non-pejorative significance. Here it is clearly pejorative. This conclusion seems to be at variance with Elihu's claim throughout his speeches. If God does not notice anyone, great or small, what does He have to do with punishment of the wicked,

---

[5] See A. Guillaume, *Annual of the Leeds University Oriental Society*, Supplement II, 1968, 129, where he emends and obtains the translation "out of the North comes golden splendour."

or the prosperity of the pious? With these words, Elihu disappears from the drama as abruptly as he first appeared.

TODAY'S ENGLISH VERSION

37 The storm makes my heart beat wildly.
² Listen, all of you, to the voice of God,
to the thunder that comes from his mouth.
³ He sends the lightning across the sky;
from one end of the earth to the other.
⁴ Then the roar of his voice is heard,
the majestic sound of thunder,
and all the while, the lightning flashes.
⁵ At God's command amazing things happen,
wonderful things that we can't understand.
⁶ He commands snow to fall on the earth,
and sends torrents of drenching rain.
⁷ He brings the work of men to a stop;
he made them; he shows them that he is at work.
⁸ The wild animals go to their dens and stay.
⁹ The storm winds come from the south,
and the biting cold from the north.
¹⁰ The breath of God freezes the waters,
and turns them to solid ice.
¹¹ Lightning flashes from the clouds,
¹²   which circle about, obeying God's will.
They do all that God commands,
everywhere throughout the world.
¹³ God sends rain to water the earth;
he may send it to punish men,
or to show them his favor.

¹⁴ Pause a moment and listen, Job;
consider the wonderful things God does.
¹⁵ Do you know how God gives a command
and makes lightning flash from the clouds?

---

¹⁶ Do you know how clouds float in the sky,
  the work of God's amazing skill?
¹⁷ No, you can only suffer in the heat,
  when the south wind oppresses the land.
¹⁸ Can you help God stretch out the sky
  and make it as hard as polished metal?
¹⁹ Teach us what to say to God;
  our minds are blank; we have nothing to say.
²⁰ I won't ask God to let me speak;
  why should I give him a chance to destroy me?

²¹ And now the light in the sky is dazzling,
  too bright for us to look at it;
  and the sky has been swept clean by the wind.
²² A golden glow is seen in the north,
  and the glory of God fills us with fear.
²³ God's power is so great that we cannot come near
  him;
  he is righteous and just in his dealings with men.
²⁴ No wonder, then, that everyone fears him,
  and that he ignores those who claim to be wise.

QUESTIONS FOR DISCUSSION 37:1-24

780. What is the general content of this chapter?
781. Elihu is full of wonder and praise before God. What has thus moved him?
782. How is God's sovereignty expressed? What lesson is there in this for Job—i.e., according to Elihu?
783. It would seem that God is being presented to us as the Lord of all seasons. Show how spring, summer, fall and winter are all represented. Cf. vss. 3-6.
784. What is the meaning of "sealeth up the hand of every man" in verse seven?
785. Discuss the imagery in verses nine and ten.

786. What is the meaning of the word "straitened" in verse ten?
787. The word "lightnings" in verse 11 could refer to something else. What?
788. What is the purpose behind God's control of nature? What else is under the control of God?
789. Elihu turns from his hymn of praise to Job. To what purpose?
790. If lightning is under the direct control of God, what of those persons who are killed by it? Are they all the enemies of God?
791. What is meant by the reference to "the balancing of the clouds"?
792. Is there a title for God in verse 16? Discuss.
793. There is historical and physical confirmation of verse 17. What is it?
794. There is a most meaningful comparison in verse 18; don't miss it.
795. Elihu uses biting sarcasm in verse 19. To what purpose?
796. Elihu thinks it madness to want to even think of confronting God. Has Job been fairly represented by Elihu? Discuss.
797. Explain the point of verse 21.
798. To what does the reference to "golden splendor" refer in verse 22?
799. How does Elihu interpret God's righteousness? Cf. vs. 23.
800. Why assert that "all men are beneath God's notice"? — i.e., why did Elihu make this assertion? Cf. vs. 24.

THE SHATTERING OF SILENCE

VI. THE PRESENCE OF GOD AND THE PENITENCE OF
   JOB (38:1—42:6)
   A. INTEGRITY, CERTAINTY, AND KNOWLEDGE
      (38:1—40:2)
      1. God questions Job about the marvels of the universe.
         (38:1-41)

TEXT 38:1-41

38 Then Jehovah answered Job out of the whirlwind, and said,

2 Who is this that darkeneth counsel
   By words without knowledge?

3 Gird up now thy loins like a man;
   For I will demand of thee, and declare thou unto me.

4 Where wast thou when I laid the foundations of the earth?
   Declare, if thou hast understanding.

5 Who determined the measures thereof, if thou knowest?
   Or who stretcheth the line upon it?

6 Whereupon were the foundations thereof fastened?
   Or who laid the corner-stone thereof,

7 When the morning stars sang together,
   And all the sons of God shouted for joy?

8 Or *who* shut up the sea with doors,
   When it brake forth, *as if* it had issued out of the womb;

9 When I made clouds the garment thereof,
   And thick darkness a swaddling band for it,

10 And marked out for it my bound,
   And set bars and doors,

11 And said, Hitherto shalt thou come, but no further;
   And here shall thy proud waves be stayed?

12 Hast thou commanded the morning since thy days *began,*
   And caused the dayspring to know its place;

13 That it might take hold of the ends of the earth,
   And the wicked be shaken out of it?

14 It is changed as clay under the seal;
   And *all things* stand forth as a garment:
15 And from the wicked their light is withholden,
   And the high arm is broken.
16 Hast thou entered into the springs of the sea?
   Or hast thou walked in the recesses of the deep?
17 Have the gates of death been revealed unto thee?
   Or hast thou seen the gates of the shadow of death?
18 Hast thou comprehended the earth in its breadth?
   Declare, if thou knowest it all.
19   Where is the way to the dwelling of light?
   And as for darkness, where is the place thereof,
20 That thou shouldest take it to the bound thereof,
   And that thou shouldest discern the paths to the house
      thereof?
21 *Doubtless,* thou knowest, for thou wast then born,
   And the number of thy days is great!
22 Hast thou entered the treasuries of the snow,
   Or hast thou seen the treasuries of the hail,
23 Which I have reserved against the time of trouble,
   Against the day of battle and war?
24 By what way is the light parted,
   Or the east wind scattered upon the earth?
25 Who hath cleft a channel for the waterflood,
   Or a way for the lightning of the thunder;
26 To cause it to rain on a land where no man is;
   On the wilderness, wherein there is no man;
27 To satisfy the waste and desolate *ground,*
   And to cause the tender grass to spring forth?
28 Hath the rain a father?
   Or who hath begotten the drops of dew?
29 Out of whose womb came the ice?
   And the hoary frost of heaven, who hath gendered it?
30 The waters hide themselves *and become* like stone,
   And the face of the deep is frozen.
31   Canst thou bind the cluster of the Pleiades,
   Or loose the bands of Orion?

32 Canst thou lead forth the Mazzaroth in their season?
 Or canst thou guide the Bear with her train?
33 Knowest thou the ordinances of the heavens?
 Canst thou establish the dominion thereof in the earth?
34 Canst thou lift up thy voice to the clouds,
 That abundance of waters may cover thee?
35 Canst thou send forth lightnings, that they may go,
 And say unto thee, Here we are?
36 Who hath put wisdom in the inward parts?
 Or who hath given understanding to the mind?
37 Who can number the clouds by wisdom?
 Or who can pour out the bottles of heaven,
38 When the dust runneth into a mass,
 And the clods cleave fast together?
39   Canst thou hunt the prey for the lioness,
 Or satisfy the appetite of the young lions,
40 When they couch in their dens,
 And abide in the covert to lie in wait?
41 Who provideth for the raven his prey,
 When his young ones cry unto God,
 And wander for lack of food?

COMMENT 38:1-41

"Whereof one cannot speak, thereof one must be silent,"
Wittgenstein.

"God, my God, why have you abandoned me?" But there
is only "God's silence, Christ's twisted face, the blood on
the brow and the hands, the soundless shriek behind the
bared teeth" . . . "no, God does not exist anymore,"
                              Bergman from *Winter Light*

"Sir, do you pray?" Tillich replied, "No, I meditate."

Buddhism is parallel to Western atheism's stress on "sheer
silence." Gautama Buddha always answered in terms of
"roaring silence." "Those who know do not speak," Laotse.

Verse 1—We return to the spell of the genius of the weaver of words and the source of the wonders of the world. Yahweh[1] now confronts Job directly. This fact is a direct challenge to the theological assumptions of Job's three friends and Elihu. Job has nowhere renounced God, as Satan predicted. The suffering of Job requires Yahweh's intervention, and in His intervention we all experience *The Shattering of Silence*. In His Word, God declares that Job, as is every saved sinner, is redeemed by grace.[2] The common assumption between Job and his three consolers was that he was alienated from God, and his suffering was concrete proof of this. The speeches of Yahweh are a direct challenge to that thesis. Job can have the presence of God in the midst of suffering. Job is humbled by God. If Job is incapable of the simplest answers, how could he hope to debate Yahweh, creator of the universe? We are told that Yahweh's love and mercy are as fundamental to His nature as are His power and transcendence. Yet, for all their beauty and majesty, the speeches contribute nothing essentially new—5:10-16; 9:4-10; 12:13-25; 22:12-14; 26:5-14. The most striking factor in Yahweh's speeches is that Job's personal problem is completely ignored. Nothing is said about his guilt or innocence, or the cause and meaning of his suffering. Job's response in 42:5 is not that I understand your instructions, but that "I have seen you." In the revelation of His word, God is made known. The theophany, i.e., seeing God, is the solution to the Jobian drama.[3] Ultimately, Jesus, Job's redeemer,

---

[1] The name Yahweh is used here as in the Prologue and Epilogue, and in 40:1, 3, 6; 42:1; but it does not appear in the Dialogue or Elihu's speeches. See my essay, "Is God in Exile?" in this commentary for comments on the descriptive terms for God in the Old Testament and specifically the Book of Job.

[2] See the excellent essay by A. R. Sauer, "Salvation by Grace: The Heart of Job's Theology," *Concordia Theological Monthly,* 1966, pp. 259-270.

[3] For a survey of the theological content and implications of Yahweh's speeches, see J. Leveque, "Et Jahweh repondit a Job"—Job 38:1, *Foi Vivante,* 1966, pp. 72-7; P. W. Skehan, "Job's Final Plea (Job 29-31) and the Lord's Reply (Job 38-41)," *Biblica,* 1964, pp. 51-62; G. Fohrer, "Gottes Antwort aus dem Sturmwind, Hiob 38-41," *Theologische Zeitschrift,* 1962, pp. 1-24; R. A. F. MacKenzie, "The Purpose of the Yahweh Speeches in the Book of Job," *Biblica,* 1959, pp. 435-445; G. von Rad, "Hiob 38 und die altagyptische Weisheit," *Vetus Testamentum,* Supplement, III,

is the great explanation of God's person and purpose—Jn. 1:18. God's answer came from one of the most unexpected places—The Whirlwind. Yahweh ignores Elihu and zeros in on the main figure of the drama, the searching sufferer— 31:35. God's sovereignty over nature was a central thesis of Elihu's speeches—chapters 32-37. We have been prepared for the ensuing thrilling theophany—Ex. 19:16; I Kg. 19:11ff; Isa. 6:4; Ezek. 1:4; Nah. 1:3; Zech. 9:14; Pss. 18:8-16; 68:8-9; Hab. 3:5, 6. Perhaps the storm is anticipated by Elihu—37:2.[4]

Verse 2—The "this" is a plain reference to Job, not Elihu— 40:4ff and 42:2-6. Some take this as literary proof that the Elihu speeches are not integral to the book, but this is purely subjective psychoanalysis of a dead man. The counsel ('esah) referred to is to the purposes of God, not to the dialogical discussion between Job and his friends. The participle -mahsik implies a state of ignorance concerning God's purposes—Ps. 33:10; Prov. 19:21; Isa. 19:17. No one lacking so much knowledge regarding the intricacies of the universe should ever challenge God to a debate. Elihu had earlier charged Job with speaking out of a reservoir of ignorance—34:35. Job has denied that the universe has a moral order, contra Ecclesiastes. All human efforts to search out all the interrelatedness in the universe is doomed to failure.

Verse 3—Girding the loins is a figurative expression of preparation for a difficult undertaking—Ex. 12:11; Isa. 11:5; Jer. 1:17. Job had demanded the opportunity to debate with God—9:32 and 13:3, 15. But God will not submit to questioning. Instead of making specific charges, as Job has requested that He do, God confronts him with unanswerable questions regarding His providential control of the cosmos—13:23 and

---

1955, 293-301; C. Stange, "Das Problem Hiobs und seine Losung," Zeitschrift für systematische Theologie, 1955, pp. 342-355; W. Lillie, "The Religious Significance of the Theophany in the Book of Job," Expository Times, 1957, pp. 355-358.

[4] For information regarding storms in Syria-Palestine, see Y. Levy Tokatly, "Easterly Storms in November 1958," Israel Exploration Journal, 1960, pp. 112-117; and D. Nir, "Whirlwinds in Israel in the Winters 1954-1955 and 1955-1956," Israel Exploration Journal, 1957, pp. 109-117.

31:35. God's design for such interrogation is to bring Job to the awareness of the vastness of his ignorance. Job had claimed earlier that all God would need do was to call him, and he would answer—13:22. This reveals supreme ignorance conceived by pride, which can deliver only darkness. God is only doing what Job asked Him to do. How can he impugn God's wisdom and justice when he knows so little? This is not an arrogant cosmic bully interrogating Job; this is His redeemer preparing him for deliverance. God always extends His merciful forgiveness, but the contingency is that we accept it. Herein lies the defectiveness of universalism in the name of grace. God extends no "cheap grace" despised and rejected. There are no believers anonymous, or holy pagans in God's purpose.

Verse 4—God hurls a series of questions toward Job in order to expose his vast and presumptuous ignorance. By swift ironical interrogation, Job's omniscience is questioned. There cannot be two omniscient persons in the same universe; so, is it Yahweh or Job?—15:7, 8; 37:18. The Hebrew text reads *binah* for understanding or comprehension. There are, of course, levels of understanding: (1) Minimal understanding is exercised in assimilating instruction, memorizing, and returning the content upon request; (2) Maximal understanding requires knowledge of the intricate interrelatedness of all the factors. This knowledge enables one not only to control but to modify various ranges of reality. An example would be that nineteenth century science could control nature; twentieth century science can modify nature through systems analysis of the "gene code," societal, economic, and political structures, etc. *Most* knowledge never changes anything. Most *new ideas* are worthless because they do not expose the intricate interworkings of either nature, history, or society. Twentieth century technologically dominated man is a Jobian counterpart. Both assume that knowledge means salvation. The neo-gnostic heresy is upon us once more in our world where recorded knowledge doubles every three and one-half years. Knowledge is not to be confused with wisdom, which is an integrating force[5]—I Cor. 1:10ff. At least Bunyan's Pilgrim understands God's message. Contemporary astro-physics, microscopic physics, and bio-chemistry reinforce this Jobian imagery which conceives of creation in terms of building or erecting the cosmos. But no atomistic reductionism can remove the intentional, i.e., purposeful, dimension of all reality. We need no longer be hampered by the model of the Newtonian World-Machine Model after Einstein, Planck-Heisenberg, et al. We live in a universe in which we can witness a revolution in cosmic models and knowledge paradigms. (See my doctoral thesis on The Kuhn-Popper Debate and The Knowledge Paradigm Revolution.)

Verse 5—The emphatic -ki strongly sets forth Yahweh's question: "Who sets its measure(s) if you know? Who stretches over it the line"—Qumran Targum—Who does that, Job, answer me, if you know!—26:7; Pss. 24:2; 102:26; 104:5; Prov. 3:19; Isa. 48:13; 51:13, 16; Zech. 12:1; Ezek. 40:3; and 43:17. Who measures it?—Isa. 34:11; Jer. 31:39. Contemporary cosmology sets forth conflicting models of the universe, i.e., "Steady State," "Big Bang." Is the universe finite or infinite? If Einstein's theory of space is scientifically accurate, then the universe is finite. Yahweh's universe is a finite creation, but what or who is the source of its staggeringly intricate design? Measurement means finitude or limitation and imprecision, though accurate to an amazing degree.

Verse 6—Job, who designed and built the universe?—Isa. 28:16; Jer. 51:26; Ps. 118:22. The stone referred to here may be either the initial foundation stone, or the final capstone. These two stones were used for measurement in ancient building procedure—9:6.

Verse 7—When the foundation of the Second Temple was laid, Israel sang—Ezra 3:10, 11; Zech. 4:7. Joyful singing

---

[5] The Qumran Targum on Job reads hkmh—wisdom—for binah—understanding. See M. Dahood's efforts with the personification of wisdom and knowledge in Prov. 8—his Psalms, Vol. III, on Ps. 136:5; and D. S. Shapiro, "Wisdom and Knowledge of God in Biblical and Talmudic Thought," Tradition, 1971, pp. 70-89; see TWNT, VII, "sophia," 465-528—cf. Cross as the integrating power of God's wisdom.

was present when the universe was created—Gen. 1:16; Ps. 148:2ff. In pagan mythology, i.e., the astro-cults, the stars were gods.[6] In contrast, Yahweh was Creator and Lord of the stars, which were subservient to Him and sing His praises, Deut. 4:19; Isa. 40:26; I Kg. 22:19; II Kg. 17:16; 21:3; Pss. 19:2; 29:2; and 148:2, 3. See 1:6 for "sons of God."

Verse 8—Now the origin of the sea is presented. Even Jacque Cousteau has not seen all its marvels. Oceanography is an intriguing science which only serves to illuminate this imagery. Two images are employed in this verse: (1) The sea as an unruly infant bursting forth from the womb; and (2) A flood needing to be controlled. The text says "and he shut" (not as A. V. who, though the grammar calls for a question), i.e.,

---

[6] Astro-deities abound in Ugaritic literature. Occult practices abounded in Canaan, also Egypt and Babylon. The editors of the *Qumran Targum* suggest that certain emendations were motivated by efforts to avoid saying that objects of pagan worship worshipped Yahweh. Historically in western Christian civilization, when occultism, etc., becomes a powerful alternative to the Christian faith, the word of God has been sharply curtailed and spiritual apathy has all but quenched the power of God's Holy Spirit, both in individual Christian lives and the corporate life of the community. Paul clearly declares that "we are not contending against flesh and blood but against principalities, against powers" (Eph. 6:12). But such description is very difficult for technologically oriented 20th century man to appreciate. The 19th century produced the *Comparative Religion school* and the *History of Religions school*, each of which cast serious doubts on the ontological existence of Satan, principalities and powers, and evil spirits, etc. James G. Frazer's *The Golden Bough: A Study in Magic and Experimental Science*, 12 vols., (MacMillan Co., 1935) and Lynn Thorndike's *A History of Magic and Experimental Sciences*, Vols. I-VI (MacMillan and Columbia University Press, 1923-1941) were and are influential in circles which believe that the revolutionary developments in the sciences preclude the validity of the Biblical witness to the existence of supernatural evil beings such as Satan. M. Dibelius, *Die Geisterwelt im Glauben des Paulus* (Gottingen, 1909) was the result of the most radical developments in the history of religion. It is fused with R. Bultmann's radical hermeneutical principle, which relegates the Biblical data concerning Satanology to the category of myth, though to be sure that is the technical connotation of myth which stems from folklore research and comparative religion, Dibelius' work removed the demoniac from serious exegetical consideration until the outbreak of irrational evil forces, especially immediately following World War II. In Heinrich Schlier's inaugural lecture, "Machte und Gewalten in Neuen Testament," (*Theologische Blatter*, 1930), we hear the Marburg of the late Heidegger and Bultmann denounce the objective realities of "principalities and powers." Even the old neo-orthodox exorcist, K. Barth, gives token consideration to the "Powers" in his *Church Dogmatics*, Vol. III/3. Between the 19th and 20th centuries, many in Western Christian civilization rejected the Biblical category of evil

God was both its origin and orderer.[7] *The Qumran Targum* has the interrogative particle before the verbal form—"Did you shut the Sea within doors?" implying, Job, did you do it, or did I do it?

Verse 9—Birth imagery continues in this verse; as an infant is wrapped in swaddling clothes, so the sea is wrapped in clouds.

Verse 10—God "set bounds" for the sea and locked it into its boundaries. Dahood's emendations clarify the verse, "And I traced out its limits, and set bars and two doors."[8] In all probability, the allusion is to the cliffs and rocky shores which mark the coast of the sea—Prov. 8:29.

Verse 11—Upon notification of the death of his son, while still under the guard of Hitler's SS, Martin Niemuller read this majestic verse—"Hitherto shalt thou come, but no further." It fell as a mantle of mercy on Niemuller's soul. The verse clearly describes God's control of the sea.

Verse 12—The succession of light and dark must be controlled if the creation is to be ordered—Ps. 104:19ff. Job, did you ever control the light in the universe? Did you ever assing the dawn (*sahar*) its responsibilities?[9]

Verse 13—In splendid poetic power, Yahweh depicts night

---

powers and replaced the Biblical explanation with the counter-explanation of sociology and psychology, etc. These explanations were satisfactory to many until the most radical outbreak of occult in the history of the world, in the last 25 years. Christian, arm for battle! See Franz Cumont, *Astrology and Religion Among the Greeks and Romans* (Dover, 1960); E. R. Dodds, *The Greeks and the Irrational* (Univ. of Calif. Press, 1951); *Pagan and Christian in an Age of Anxiety* (Cambridge Univ. Press); and Mircea Eliade, *The Forge and the Crucible* (Harper & Row, 1962).

[7] The developments in 17th-18th century science made the classical design argument, as constructed by Aristotle and Aquinas, only a precarious past-time until the Post-Einsteinian developments in the sciences. See R. H. Hurlbutt, *Hume and Newton and the Design Argument* (Lincoln, Neb.: Univ. of Nebraska Press, 1965). The issue is not design versus the absence of design, but whether the origin of the design is transcendent, i.e., God, or immanent, i.e., based on bio-chemical chancism.

[8] See possible emendations by M. Dahood, *Psalms*, Vol. I, note 2 on Ps. 16:6.

[9] Pope continually attempts to give a pan-Ugaritic explanation of all imagery, as Delitzsch sought a pan-Babylonian explanation in the early decades of this century. Often their most creative factor is their high degree of technical imagination.

as a garment covering the earth, which the dawn takes hold of by the fingers and shakes. The wicked who work in the cover of darkness are shaken out of their protection. The garment so essential for protection from the chill of the night here becomes an image of protection for the wicked—22:6. Job, can you do that?[10]

Verse 14—"It changes" refers to the feminine noun earth. Darkness removes all but the shadowed shapes of the landscape. The morning sun returns the beautiful contours to the shapeless surface of the earth. The sun rays give shape to creation's contours, as clay receives the impress of the seal. Dhorme emends the second line to refer to color, i.e., "and it is dyed like a garment." Then the imagery refers to the return of the rich hues to the earth as the creation is bathed in beams of sunlight.

Verse 15—Yahweh repeats what we have already been told, that the light of the wicked is darkness—24:13-17. Light banishes darkness from its kingdom; they are forever incompatible. The "upraised arm" (zero'a ramah) is probably a metaphor signifying powerful wickedness, which Yahweh shatters.

Verse 16—Job shows little knowledge regarding the origins of things visible. Now he is challenged to expose his knowledge concerning the range and extent of things invisible. Matter is reducible to energy. Reality at the miscroscopic level is unavailable to our perceptive field. The nineteenth and twentieth centuries' naturalistic reductionistic positivists gain little comfort from contemporary science[11]—28:11. The word rendered "recesses" (tehom—Gen. 7:11) denotes what is to be sought for or searched out—11:7.

Verse 17—The gates of Sheol hold back the deep darkness— 10:21ff; 26:5ff; Pss. 9:13; 107:18; and Isa. 38:10—which the

---

[10] G. R. Driver, *Journal of Theological Studies,* 1953, pp. 208-212.

[11] See *The Concept of Matter,* edited by Ernan McMullin (Notre Dame: University of Notre Dame Press) for history of the concept of matter from the Greeks to contemporary physics.

parallelism necessitates. The gates restrain the darkness of Sheol—3:5; Ezek. 32:18.

Verse 18—The term rendered as breadth in the A. V. is found only here and 36:16. The plural probably implies the vastness or expansiveness of the earth. If you do not understand creation, Job, how can you pretend to know the creator?

Verse 19—Yahweh separated light and darkness on the first day of creation—Gen. 1:6—and thus they have separate locations in the universe.

Verse 20—The pronouns are both singular, but they must refer to light and dark.

Verse 21—Yahweh's irony and sarcasm increase—"doubtless." You know because you must have been born before creation, if you understand all the intricate balances within nature's systems—15:7; Prov. 8:22ff.

Verse 22—For the use of hail as God's weapon, see Isa. 30:30; for its occurrence in theophanies, see Ps. 18:12ff; Job 37:9; Deut. 28:12, Jer. 10:13. Yahweh has treasuries full of snow and hail.

Verses 23—The imagery continues. God has reserves of snow and hail. Do you, Job?

Verse 24—Light was dealt with in verse 19. The most difficult issue in this verse is the parallel between "light" and "east wind," though Driver argues for a root yielding "parching heat" for the latter.[12]

Verse 25—The time of the rain was more important than the channel (*te'alah*—trench, conduits—I Kg. 18:32, 35; Isa. 7:3; Ezek. 31:4) through which it came. The word rendered waterflood (*setep*—flood waters—Nah. 1:8; Dan. 9:26) is a common Old Testament root for washing and overflowing of streams. The second line is identical with 28:26b, but the parallel is different. In 28:26 the parallelism calls for rain, here flood.

Verse 26—God's providence extends to every factor of

---

[12] G. R. Driver, *American Journal of Semitic Literature,* 1935-1936, p. 166; and *Vetus Testamentum,* 1955, pp. 91ff.

creation, not just man and his societal relationships. Man is repeated in both lines, but they represent two different Hebrew words—*'ys* and *'adam*—12:6-10; 24:4b-5; 30:2-8. Yahweh does not comdemn Job for what he could not possibly know; He condemns for his narrow perspective. If he could see the universe as Yahweh sees it, then he would not complain, but, of course, that is impossible.

Verse 27—God makes the "desolate and waste ground" productive and makes "young grass to grow"—Gen. 1:11. The personification of the ground suggests God's relationship to and control over the productive power of the earth.

Verse 28—Can man cause rain? Can Job explain the nature of rain?

Verse 29—What is the origin and nature of ice?—6:16; 37:10; Gen. 31:40; and in Jer. 36:30 where it means frost.

Verse 30—The rendering "like stone" as in the A. V. confuses the image. Literally the text says "They hide themselves— are hidden," "hardens," i.e., freezes. *The Qumran Targum* translates the Hebrew word *yithabba'u* with the verb *-qrm* which means to cover the surface—Ezek. 37:6, 8, or crust. Freezing water begins with surface layer or crust. This makes perfectly good sense in this verse.

Verse 31—Job, can you chain or bind (*ma'adannot*—only here and I Sam. 15:32; and verb *'nd* is used in 31:36 and Prov. 6:21 with meaning of bind) the cluster[13] of the Pleiades or loose the belt (*mosekot*—bonds) of Orion?"—9:9.

Verse 32—The Hebrew word *mazzarot* appears untranslated in the A. V. because the root occurs only here and its significance is uncertain. But perhaps it is related to *mazzalot,* constellations in II Kg. 23:5. If so, it refers to the southern constellations of the zodiac.[14]

Verse 33—The ordinances (*mistar* is parallel with *huqqot*—

---

[13] For defense of this translation, see G. R. Driver, *Journal of Theological Studies,* 1956, p. 3.

[14] For discussion of these constellations, see G. R. Driver, *JTS,* 1953, pp. 208-212; and *JTS,* 1956, pp. 1-11.

statutes—Ex. 5:6ff; II Chron. 26:11; Num. 11:16; Deut. 1:15; Prov. 6:7) are the laws that govern the movements of the entire universe, but here the sun, moon, and stars in the earth's galaxy.

Verse 34—Compare the first line with 36:29b; 37:2, 4. The image underlying the question is that of God commanding the clouds to release their captive rain. The second line is verbatim with 22:11b, but the contexts are different, thus calling for different parallel analysis. Job, can you interfere with the laws of climatology?

Verse 35—Job, can you direct and control lightning? Will lightning obey you, as it obeys me? It even reports to Yahweh its accomplishments. Lightning is God's servant, not man's— 36:32 and 37:11ff.

Verse 36—The meaning of the two basic words in this verse—"inward parts" and "mind"—is uncertain. These two words are rendered clouds and mists elsewhere. The root meaning of the former is probably "cover over" or hidden, i.e., hidden or inward parts; and the root significance of the latter is perhaps "to look out," i.e., in the sense that men can draw meanings from observing. Regardless of these difficulties, Yahweh is asking Job whether or not he can understand the workings of His wonderful creation.

Verse 37—Who but Yahweh knows the exact number of clouds necessary at any given time?—Isa. 40:26. Who but God knows the precise balance of rain to provide the earth?— 26:8.

Verse 38—When it rains, the dust forms a mass or whole once more. The whole earth is related to His purpose.

Verse 39—The second part of the speech begins in this verse. Eight creatures are described in increasing details. Yahweh calls forth a number of birds and animals and asks Job if he knows the secrets of their habitat and behavior. He begins with the king of the beasts, the lion. Who provides the lion with its prey? It does not require man to obtain its prey. Could man even do it if challenged? God cares for lions and their young—Ps. 104:21.

Verse 40—God provides them with food, even while they are waiting in the "lairs," as rendered in 37:8.

Verse 41—After the king of the beasts, the scavenger Raven is brought to Job's attention. The raven is destructive; it picks out the eyes of its victims—Prov. 30:17. Job, surely this is an example of injustice, at least, to those animals that make up the raven's prey. They have no particular home; they "wander" wherever there is food available. In nature, every living creature has its natural enemies. This, too, is part of God's providential direction of His creation. Will Job learn any lessons from these eight examples from the realm of birds and beasts?

TODAY'S ENGLISH VERSION

The Lord Answers Job

38 Then out of the storm, the Lord spoke to Job.

The Lord
² Who are you to question my wisdom?
  You are only showing your ignorance.
³ Stand up now like a man
  and answer the questions I am going to ask.
⁴ Were you there when I made the world?
  If you know so much, tell me about it.
⁵ Who decided how large it would be?
  Who stretched the measuring line over it?
  You know all this, don't you?
⁶ What holds up the pillars that support the earth?
  Who laid the cornerstone of the world?
⁷ In the dawn of that day the stars sang together,
  and the sons of God shouted for joy.

⁸ Who closed the gates to hold back the sea,
  when it burst from the womb of the earth?
⁹ It was I who covered the sea with clouds
  and wrapped it in darkness.

---

¹⁰ I marked a boundary for the sea
   and kept it behind bolted gates.
¹¹ I told it, "Thus far and no farther!
   Here your powerful waves must stop."
¹² Job, have you ever in all your life
   commanded a day to dawn?
¹³ Have you ordered the dawn to seize the earth
   and shake the wicked from their hiding places:
¹⁴ Daylight makes the hills and valleys stand out
   like the folds of a garment.
¹⁵ The light of day is too bright for the wicked,
   and prevents them from doing violence.

¹⁶ Have you been to the springs in the depths of
      the sea?
   Have you walked on the floor of the ocean?
¹⁷ Has anyone ever showed you the gates
   that guard the dark world of the dead?
¹⁸ Do you have any idea how big the world is?
   Answer me, if you know all this.

¹⁹ Do you know where the light comes from,
   or what the source of darkness is?
²⁰ Can you show them how far to go,
   or send them back again?
²¹ I am sure you can, because you're so old,
   and were already born when the world was
      created.

²² Have you ever visited the storerooms,
   where I keep the snow and the hail?
²³ I keep them ready for times of trouble,
   for days of battle and war.
²⁴ Have you been to where the sun comes up,
   or the place from which the east wind blows?

²⁵ Who dug a channel for the pouring rain,
   and cleared the way for the thunderstorm?
²⁶ Who makes rain fall where no one lives?

406

²⁷ Who waters the dry and thirsty land,
    so that grass springs up?
²⁸ Does either the rain or the dew have a father?
²⁹ Who is the mother of the ice and the frost,
³⁰   which turn the waters to stone
    and freeze the face of the sea?

³¹ Can you tie the Pleiades together,
    or loosen the bonds that hold Orion?
³² Can you guide the stars season by season,
    and direct the Big and the Little Dipper?
³³ Do you know the laws that govern the skies,
    and can you make them apply to the earth?
³⁴ Can you shout orders to the clouds,
    and make them drench you with rain?
³⁵ And if you command the lightning to flash,
    will it come to you and say, "At your service"?
³⁶ Who tells the ibis when the Nile will flood,
    or who tells the rooster that rain will fall?
³⁷ Who is wise enough to count the clouds,
    and tilt them over to send the rain,
³⁸   rain that hardens the dust into lumps?

³⁹ Do you find food for lions to eat,
    and satisfy hungry young lions,
⁴⁰   when they hide in their caves,
    or lie in wait in their dens?
⁴¹ Who is it that feeds the ravens
    when they wander about hungry,
    when their young cry to me for food?

QUESTIONS FOR DISCUSSION 38:1-41

801. When God breaks the silence and speaks to Job, He at
the same time challenges the theological assumptions of
Job's three friends and Elihu. Explain how.

802. Job is like every saved sinner. In what way?
803. Was Job alienated from God? Prove your answer.
804. There are four qualities of the nature of God mentioned—all are essential—what are they?
805. What is the most striking factor in the speeches of Yahweh?
806. What was the ultimate solution to Job's problem?
807. Who is addressed in verse two—Job or Elihu? Job was foolish to challenge God to a debate. Why?
808. Why does God approach Job with the series of questions found in this chapter?
809. "This is not an arrogant cosmic bully interrogating Job"; who is involved? For what reason?
810. What is minimal and what is maximal understanding? Discuss.
811. Man today is trying to "measure" the universe. What has been his conclusions?
812. What is meant by reference to the "cornerstone" in verse six?
813. Do you believe there was real singing at the creation of the earth? Discuss verse seven.
814. What are "Astro-deities"? Discuss the place of the Occult in our world.
815. How does the present science of oceanography relate to verse eight? What two images are used to describe the sea?
816. The sea is compared to an infant. How so?
817. What are "the doors" God has set upon the sea?
818. How did Martin Niemuller respond to verse 11? Why? Discuss its meaning for us.
819. Controlled creation demands what one quality? Cf. vs. 12. How related to Job?
820. A beautiful poetic image is found in verse 13. What is it? How related to Job?
821. The contribution of light and dark to the beauty of the earth is poignantly described in verse 14. Explain in your own words.

2. And of the animal world (39:1—40:2)

TEXT 39:1-30—40:2

39 Knowest thou the time when the wild goats of the rock
bring forth?
Or canst thou mark when the hinds do calve?

2 Canst thou number the months that they fulfil?
Or knowest thou the time when they bring forth?

3 They bow themselves, they bring forth their young,
They cast out their pains.

4 Their young ones become strong,
   they grow up in the open field;
They go forth and return not again.

5 Who hath sent out the wild ass free?
Or who hath loosed the bonds of the swift ass,

6 Whose home I have made the wilderness,
And the salt land his dwelling place?

7 He scorneth the tumult of the city,
Neither heareth he the shoutings of the driver.

8 The range of the mountains is his pasture,
And he searcheth after every green thing.

9 Will the wild-ox be content to serve thee?
Or will he abide by thy crib?

10 Canst thou bind the wild-ox with his band in the furrow?
Or will he harrow the valleys after thee?

11 Wilt thou trust him, because his strength is great?
Or wilt thou leave to him thy labor?

12 Wilt thou confide in him, that he will bring home thy seed,
And gather *the grain* of thy threshing-floor?

13 The wings of the ostrich wave proudly;
But are they the pinions and plumage of love?

14 For she leaveth her eggs on the earth,
And warmeth them in the dust,

15 And forgetteth that the foot may crush them.
Or that the wild beast may trample them.

16 She dealeth hardly with her young ones, as if they were

409

not hers:
Though her labor be in vain, *she is* without fear;

17 Because God hath deprived her of wisdom,
Neither hath he imparted to her understanding.

18 What time she lifteth up herself on high,
She scorneth the horse and his rider.

19 Hast thou given the horse *his* might?
Hast thou clothed his neck with the quivering mane?

20 Hast thou made him to leap as a locust?
The glory of his snorting is terrible.

21 He paweth in the valley, and rejoiceth in his strength:
He goeth out to meet the armed men.

22 He mocketh at fear, and is not dismayed;
Neither turneth he back from the sword.

23 The quiver rattleth against him,
The flashing spear and the javelin.

24 He swalloweth the ground with fierceness and rage;
Neither believeth he that it is the voice of the trumpet.

25 As oft as the trumpet *soundeth* he saith, Aha!
And he smelleth the battle afar off,
The thunder of the captains, and the shouting.

26 Is it by thy wisdom that the hawk soareth,
And stretcheth her wings toward the south?

27 Is it at thy command that the eagle mounteth up,
And maketh her nest on high?

28 On the cliff she dwelleth, and maketh her home,
Upon the point of the cliff, and the stronghold.

29 From thence she spieth out the prey;
Her eyes behold it afar off.

30 Her young ones also suck up blood:
And where the slain are, there is she.

COMMENT 39:1-30

Verse 1—Job, what do you know about ibex[1] or mountain

---

[1] For contemporary efforts to save this specie of goat, see H. Weiner, *The Wild Goat of Ein Gedi,* 1963.

goats and the laws of birth? This specie of wild goat is still found near Khirbet Qumran and En Gedi—Ps. 104:18; I Sam. 24:7. The inaccessible cliffs are their habitat, but God's providence guards over them even there. Hind is a specie of deer that survived in the woodlands of Palestine, before they were denuded in the 20th century—Gen. 49:21; Deut. 12:15; Ps. 18:33; and Prov. 5:19. Job, what do you know about the existence of the hind?

Verse 2—There is duplication between verses one and two. But the first line is concerned with pregnancy and the second with birth. Job, do you or can you "count the months" before the delivery of the young?

Verse 3—The word rendered "bow" as in A. V. themselves is used of human childbirth in I Sam. 4:19. The Hebrew term *hebel* (as in A. V. pain) is the usual word for the pain of childbirth. The line suggests the ease with which they deliver their young—Isa. 13:8.

Verse 4—This verse emphasizes the rapid maturity and parental care of the ibex. The ease with which they are delivered is matched by the quickness with which they develop and become independent. God can provide this marvelous example of His care of the goats even in the open fields.

Verse 5—God guards the wild ass, who roams the steppes. Though he freely surveys the desert, his freedom has been given bounds by God. Even this seemingly untamable creature is under God's sovereignty—6:5; 11:12; 24:5; Gen. 16:12; Hos. 8:9; and Isa. 32:14. The wild ass is described here with two words, one being an Aramaic loan word. The wild ass is so mobile that only the fastest horses can equal its speed.

Verse 6—The steppes and the salt land are the extreme ends of the fertile ground. He lives there in order to be free of man, who lives on or near the fertile land—24:5; Jer. 17:6; Ps. 107:34; and Judges 9:45. *The Qumran Targum* renders the second line as "His dwelling in the salt land."

Verse 7—The wild ass, lit. "laughs at" the restrictions of the city. The freedom of the desert is to his liking. There he fends for himself. Freedom from oppression is derived from

411

the labor of beasts—Isa. 9:3. His yearning for freedom causes him to avoid any place inhabited by man. Man always enslaves him, if he can.

Verse 8—The wild ass pays the price of its freedom. It refuses to be subservient to man. It is often hungry because of sparse food supply in the desert—Jer. 14:6. He must search (Heb. *drs,* but *The Qumran Targum* reads the verb *rdp*— pursue) for his food. But he knows *where* to search. Who informed you of this, Job?

Verse 9—In previous verses a contrast was made between the domesticated and wild ass; here the comparison is between wild and tame buffalo. Hunting this dangerous beast was a sport of royalty—Num. 23:22; 24:8; Pss. 22:21; 29:6; 92:10; and Isa. 34:7. That this animal (*re'em, rem*) had more than a single horn is clear from Deut. 33:17. Tiglathpileser I killed a rimu in Syria. This metaphor in the Old Testament means power—Num. 23:22; 24:8; Ps. 22:21; and Isa. 34:7.[2]

Verse 10—The tame ox was used for plowing, but could man plow with a wild ox?—Prov. 14:4. The first line presents a strange image as rendered in A. V. "canst thou bind the wild ox with band in the furrow?" A slight emendation will yield a more meaningful line, "wilt thou bind him with a cord or rope halter?" This is a more natural image than binding the ox to the furrow, as is implied in the A. V. Clearly the second line pictures harrowing, as opposed to plowing, as the ox was led in the former labor, and man followed the animal in the latter.

Verse 11—Yet, because of the ox's strength, would you allow him to go unguided to the field? He is strong, but man has the plan which can be fulfilled only by thoughtful preparation; this same kind of purposefulness and thoughtful preparation God has given to every dimension of the universe. The ox might be harnessed by *mind* but without intentional guidance, the ox is unreliable.

---

[2] See A. H. Godbey, "The Unicorn in the Old Testament," *American Journal of Semitic Literature,* 1939, pp. 256-296.

Verse 12—The ox has strength but not much intelligence. He could not bring the harvest in from the fields and prepare it for storage, could he? The Hebrew literally has "bring back—and gather your threshing floor." Slight emendation will yield "to your threshing floor," which makes sense.

Verse 13—The A. V. rendering ostrich is derived from the Hebrew word which means "shrill cries" (*renanim*)—Lam. 4:3. The ostrich is cruel to its young, yet is faster than the fleetest horse. The root *'ls*—lit. rejoice, flap wildly—is rendered "wave proudly" in the A. V.[3] The second line has only three Hebrew words in it: (1) *pinion*—Deut. 32:11; and Ps. 91:4; (2) may be either feminine adjective pious or stork derived from noun *hesed*—Lev. 11:19; Ps. 104:17; Jer. 8:7; and (3) plumage—Ezek. 17:3. If the second word is rendered stork, which is known for its affection for the young, then we have a contrast between a bird with affection and one which lacks parental concern. But the comparison may be between the stork's capacity to fly with its wings and the ostrich with beautiful plumage but which cannot fly.

Verse 14—The ostrich places (Heb. *'zb*—put, place)[4] its eggs in the sand. During the day the heat of the sun keeps them warm, but at night the ostrich must sit on them. Generally the hen ostrich hatches only one-third of her eggs. She feeds the other two-thirds to her young at various stages of development.

Verse 15—The eggs are often covered with sand; some might lie unprotected on top of the ground. Though the ostrich egg shells are very hard, there would naturally be some danger of being crushed by jackals and other predators, including man.

Verse 16—The A. V. rendering of "she dealeth hardly" or with cruelty comes from a verb which is used in Isa. 63:17 of the hardening of the heart. The hen often acts unconcerned,

---

[3] For analysis, see D. F. Payne, *Annual of the Swedish Theological Institute,* Vol. V, 1967, 50, 58, 64ff.

[4] For the design in the placing of the eggs rather than merely "leaving" them, see M. Dahood, *JBL,* 1959, pp. 303-309.

i.e., "with no fear." Dahood translated the last line "at the emptiness of her toil with fear."[5]

Verse 17—This judgment of the ostrich's intelligence is reinforced by an Arabian proverbial saying—"more stupid than the ostrich." Both its ignorance and cruelty are proverbial. But in spite of its lack of intelligence, God providentially cares for it.

Verse 18—The acme of speed is the ostrich. Zenaphon, in his *Anabasis,* I, v. 2, provides details of an ostrich who out ran horses. They have been clocked up to 26 miles per hour.

Verse 19—The A. V. is still the most probable rendering, with the exception of the phrase translated "quivering mane."[6] There is consistently a very free rendering throughout Job in the N. E. B., T. E. V., and the Living Bible. Since the word is only found here, it will be impossible to do any more than provide a conjecture, but probably the root implies strength not "quivering." The horse quivers its neck (when it is roused), and this in turn makes the mane stand erect. We must retain the image of the cultural function of each of the animals in the Near East if the parallelism is to be understood. The ass was the beast of burden, the ox was used for plowing, and donkeys or mules were riding animals. The horse was reserved for hunting and warfare, first to draw chariots; later it became a cavalry mount.

Verse 20—Joel 2:4 compares the locust and the horse—Rev. 9:7. The word -*shr* (M. T. *nhr*) means snorting, as the horses prepare for the charge in battle—Jer. 5:29 and 8:16. *The Qumran Targum* reads "with his snorting terror and fear."

Verse 21—The mighty war horse digs (Heb. *yhpr*—much stronger than paws) violently (Heb. *be'emeq*—not as A. V. renders, "in the valley"),[7] the ground. *The Qumran Targum* renders the line "and he paws in the valley and runs and

---

[5] M. Dahood, *The Bible in Catholic Thought,* p. 74.

[6] See M. Dahood, *Biblica,* 1959, p. 58.

[7] That this word here means "power" not "valley," see M. Dahood, *Biblica,* 1959, p. 166; and W. F. Albright, *Wisdom in Israel and in the Ancient Near East,* eds. Noth and Thomas, *Vetus Testamentum,* Supplement, III, 1955, p. 14.

rejoices" revealing the change of the Hebrew text of Job from *b'mq* to *bbq';* the LXX also understands valley instead of power.

Verse 22—This verse makes it crystal clear that the imagery is that of a war horse, rather than a horse in general. Men are afraid of attack in war, but the horse "mocketh fear."

Verse 23—The battle is about to begin. The arrows are rattling (*tirneh*—see Brown, Driver, Briggs) in the quiver. The bright javelin[8] or perhaps sword reflects the flashing sun (lit. flame of).

Verse 24—The two nouns in line one suggest excitement rather than hostility or anger—Ps. 77:18 and Isa. 14:16. The excited horse literally "swallows ground," i.e., races unchecked. The A. V. rendering of the second line is unsatisfactory—"neither believeth he . . ." is all but meaningless. The verb root means "be firm," i.e., the horse "cannot stand still."

Verse 25—The horse hears the trumpet signal for battle—Amos 3:6. There is no verb in the Hebrew text, but -*bede* is probably to be understood adverbially "at the call of the trumpet"—11:3; 41:4. The cry of satisfaction, aha, goes forth as soon as he hears the trumpet—Pss. 35:21; 40:15; Isa. 44:16; Ezek. 25:3; and 36:2. He smells[9] the battle, even at a distance.

Verse 26—This verse alludes to the southward migration of birds in late fall or early winter—Jer. 8:7. Job, you know that it is not your wisdom that performs all of these wonders. Only Yahweh can understand the intricate interworkings of every factor in creation.

Verse 27—In the Old Testament, the word *neser* designates both eagles and vultures—9:26; Prov. 30:18, 19. Either would fit in the context. Eagles often, vultures always, built their nests

---

[8] For a description of this weapon, see G. Molin, *Journal of Semitic Studies,* 1956, pp. 334ff; also Yigal Yadin, *The Scrolls of War of the Sons of Light Against the Sons of Darkness* (Oxford, 1962), p. 284; and his *The Art of Warfare in Biblical Lands,* 2 vols., 1963, p. 172.

[9] P. A. H. de Boer, *Words and Meanings,* eds. Acbroyd and Lindars, 1968, pp. 29ff, suggests that verb means "smells of," "recalls," or "suggests."

in inaccessible locations[10] (Heb. *ki* means falcon). Job, did you provide these birds with their instincts?

Verse 28—Here the great heights of the mountains are vigorously described—Jer. 49:16; I Sam. 14:4. Who told these birds to build their nests at such high elevations?

Verse 29—The imagery signifies the sharp-sightedness of the eagle. Dhorme gives more than adequate testimonies in his brilliant paradigm of writing commentary. The scriptures also bear witness to the swiftness of the eagle in attacking its prey—Deut. 28:49; Jer. 48:40; and 49:16.

Verse 30—Dhorme emends the verb *ye'al le'u* to yield a more appropriate image than eagles "sucking" up blood. His emendation yields the resultant, "shake a thing" from Aramaic. The action of the eagle would then be that of picking at bloody flesh, which is more appropriate for the eagle than "sucking." The New Testament contains a proverbial saying that "where there is a corpse, the eagle/vultures will flock"—Matt. 24:28; Lk. 17:37.

TODAY'S ENGLISH VERSION

39 Do you know when mountain goats are born?
Have you watched wild deer give birth?

2 Do you keep track of the months,
     and know the time when their young will be born?

3 Do you know when they will crouch down
     and bring their young into the world?

4 In the wilds their young grow strong;
     they go away and don't come back.

5 Who gave the wild donkeys their freedom?
     Who turned them loose and let them roam?

6 I gave them the desert to be their home,

---

[10] See J. Reider, *Vetus Testamentum,* 1954, p. 294.

and let them live on the salt plains.
⁷ They keep away from the noisy cities
   and no one can tame them and make them work.
⁸ The mountains are the pastures where they feed,
   where they search for anything green to eat.

⁹ Will a wild buffalo work for you?
   Is he willing to spend the night in your stable?
¹⁰ Can you hold one with a rope and make him plow?
   Or make him pull a harrow in your fields?
¹¹ Can you rely on his great strength
   and expect him to do your heavy work?
¹² Do you expect him to bring in your harvest,
   and gather the grain from your threshing floor?

¹³ How fast the wings of an ostrich beat!
   But no ostrich can fly like a stork.
¹⁴ The ostrich leaves her eggs on the ground
   for the heat in the soil to warm them.
¹⁵ She is unaware that a foot may crush them
   or a wild animal break them.
¹⁶ She acts as if the eggs were not hers,
   and is unconcerned that her efforts are wasted.
¹⁷ It was I who made her foolish
   and did not give her wisdom.
¹⁸ But when she begins to run,
   she can laugh at any horse and rider.

¹⁹ Was it you, Job, who made horses so strong,
   and gave them their flowing manes?
²⁰ Did you make them leap like locusts
   and frighten men with their snorting?
²¹ They eagerly paw the ground in the valley;
   they rush into battle with all their strength.
²² They do not know the meaning of fear,
   and no sword can turn them back.
²³ The weapons which their riders carry
   rattle and flash in the sun.

²⁴ Trembling with excitement, the horses race ahead;
    when the trumpet blows they can't stand still.
²⁵ At each blast of the trumpet they snort;
    they can smell a battle before they get near,
    and they hear the officers shouting commands.

²⁶ Does a hawk learn from you how to fly
    when it spreads its wings toward the south?
²⁷ Does an eagle wait for your command
    to build its nest high in the mountains?
²⁸ It makes its home on the highest rocks
    and makes the sharp peaks its fortress.
²⁹ From there it watches near and far
    for something to kill and eat.
³⁰ Around dead bodies the vultures gather,
    and the young vultures drink the blood.

QUESTIONS FOR DISCUSSION 39:1-30

822. What is the general content of this chapter?
823. What do you know about ibex? Give at least two facts.
824. Job is so very ignorant about so many subjects—such as the pregnancy and birth of hind. What is this fact intended to prove?
825. What is the thought of verse three?
826. What can be inferred from the marvelous care God provides for the ibex? Cf. vs. 4.
827. If the wild ass is under God's sovereignty, what about man? Is this the point of verse five?
828. What is said of "the salt land"?
829. The wild ass laughs. At what? For what reason?
830. What is the price of freedom for the wild ass? How does this relate to Job?
831. Do we have a reference to the unicorn in verse nine? What is discussed?

832. Please point out the distinction between plowing and har-rowing in the possible use of the wild ox as in verse ten.
833. There is an important principle given in verse 11. It is discussed with the ox but it relates to man. What is it?
834. What is the comparison made in verse 13?
835. Several facts are made concerning the behavior of the ostrich. Name at least two. What is the prominent impression given concerning this bird? Cf. vss. 14-18.
836. What is the point of verse 19?
837. The horse is compared to a locust. How?
838. Give at least two characteristics of the horse described in verses 21 and 22.
839. The war horse enjoys the conflict. Point out the indications of his satisfaction. Why all this description? i.e., what is the point of it?
840. God raises the subject of the migrating instincts of birds. Why?
841. What two birds are discussed in verses 27 and 30?
842. God has placed marvelous capacities in these birds. Name two of them? How is this related to Job?

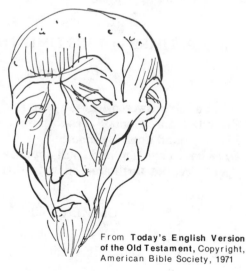

From **Today's English Version**
of the **Old Testament**, Copyright,
American Bible Society, 1971

TEXT 40:1-2

40 Moreover Jehovah answered Job, and said,
2 Shall he that cavilleth contend with the Almighty?
He that argueth with God, let him answer it.

COMMENT 40:1, 2

Verse 1—Yahweh calls on Job to respond to His speech. Job confesses that he is reduced to silence.

Verse 2—The participal form *rab* is the subject and yields something like that which is suggested by Pope—"Will he who argues with Shaddai yield?" Dhorme reads *yasur* with the meaning of "yield." The significance is either Job must sustain his competence to criticize Yahweh by answering all the queries from the first part of the speech of God, or forfeit his right to criticize. This section of the text suffers from a defective division of the chapters which was established in the 13th century, and a confusing variation of verse separation established since the 16th century.

B. JOB LEARNS OF HIS LIMITATIONS. (40:3-5)

TEXT 40:3-5

3 Then Job answered Jehovah, and said,
4 Behold, I am of small account; what shall I answer thee?
I lay my hand upon my mouth.
5 Once have I spoken, and I will not answer;
Yea, twice, but I will proceed no further.

COMMENT 40:3-5

Verse 3—Job breaks his silence by confession.
Verse 4—He acknowledges that Yahweh's challenges are

420

beyond his ability and that he is contemptible (A. V. small account)—Gen. 16:4ff; Nah. 1:14. The hand over the mouth was a Near Eastern gesture of awed silence—21:5; 29:9. Job is no longer hostile, but humble. When Yahweh broke His silence, He also broke Job's pride.

Verse 5—This entire verse is repeated in 42:4, 5. This fact enables us to recover the verb *'wsp*, which is almost totally lacking in *The Qumran Targum*. Job declines to answer Yahweh; he has already said more than he knows—9:22; 13:20. Twice before Job poured forth his rhetorical wisdom, but now he sits in speechless wonder before the mystery of Yahweh's providential might. The majesty of creation now silences this small scoffer. But Yahweh will once and for all speak in *The Shattering of Silence*.

C. NOW UNDERSTANDING (40:6—41:34)
1. Job is not qualified to answer. (40:6-14)

TEXT 40:6-14

6   Then Jehovah answered Job out of the whirlwind, and said,
7 Gird up thy loins now like a man:
  I will demand of thee, and declare thou unto me.
8 Wilt thou even annul my judgment?
  Wilt thou condemn me, that thou mayest be justified?
9 Or hast thou an arm like God?
  And canst thou thunder with a voice like him?
10 Deck thyself now with excellency and dignity;
  And array thyself with honor and majesty.
11 Pour forth the overflowings of thine anger;
  And look upon every one that is proud, and abase him.
12 Look on every one that is proud *and* bring him low;
  And tread down the wicked where they stand.
13 Hide them in the dust together;
  Bind their faces in the hidden *place*.
14 Then will I also confess of thee
  That thine own right hand can save thee.

COMMENT 40:6-14

Verse 6—Then out of the violent whirlwind comes the victorious word which assures Job that the source of the cosmos has vindicated him. Neither Satan nor his friends have captured Yahweh's "servant Job." Job is pious because His God is righteous, and thus answers Satan's original queries.

Verse 7—After Job's submissive confession, Yahweh's second speech is delivered. This final word divides into three parts: (1) Job is invited to stand in God's presence—verses 7-14; (2) Yahweh's description of Behemoth—verses 15-24; and (3) The description of Leviathan—41:1-34. Compare verses 6, 7 and 38:1, 3, which are here repeated except for the conjunction *waw*, for. Yahweh challenges Job to assume control over the universe. If his criticism is valid, then he ought to know how to govern the creation. The great invitation, which is also extended to contemporary technological man, is do you have the power, wisdom, knowledge, and moral integrity to be in charge of the universe? Modern man, do *you* who have violated the dominion mandate in your personal lives, cities, and have raped the earth, have the audacity to claim that you could express a superior providential control over all the systems of creation? Can you, Job, our contemporary, administer divine justice? Job has accused Yahweh of twisting justice—9:24; 19:6; and 27:6. Job has brought a lawsuit against God. Is God, or Job guilty? One must be just, the other unjust, if Job's assumptions about a lawsuit are correct. Job's lethal error is that no such relationship can exist between creator and creature.

Verse 8—Job had denied divine justice in his own case and the world at large—9:22. Job has rendered ineffectual God's judgment in defending his own integrity. The prologue makes clear that Job would have been wholly justified in defending his own integrity, except that in so doing he impugned the justice of Yahweh. Thus, Job had confronted God as to His moral right to govern creation.

Verse 9—Even if Job has the integrity and wisdom, does

he have the power to rule the world? Such dominion requires not only skill but resources of inexhaustible power. His criticism is idle chatter, until he can show that he possesses these attributes. The arm is symbol of power, both human and divine— 22:8; Ex. 15:16; Ps. 77:15; Isa. 40:10; 51:5; and 59:16. Elihu had utilized similar logic—37:2-5. Only if man has God's power does he have a moral right to question God's justice— 33:12; 36:22, 23. Job's rhetorical criticism requires no power to hold the universe in awe—37:2ff. Universal rule requires the power to implement that control. Do you have this necessary sway over the kingdoms of this world, Job? If not, be silent until you know whereof you speak.

Verse 10—Adorn yourself with the symbols of power—Ps. 104:1. Clothe yourself in glory and splendor. These symbols recur in Ps. 21:5 and 96:6 as attributes of God. Show us your credentials, if you are God!

Verse 11—Make your power visible, not merely verbal. "Pour forth" is the word used in 37:11 of "scattering" the lightning. If moral government requires swift retaliation on the wicked, retaliate, Job. He declines the invitation for the obvious reason.

Verse 12—Line one is identical with verse 11b, except that the verb "bring him low," i.e., humble, is a synonym of "abase him." Pride is broken after God has spoken. Judge the wicked immediately, Job, if you have the power.

Verse 13—Obliterate the wicked. Remove them from the sight of men—10:9; 34:15; Isa. 2:10; 29:4; and Ps. 22:29. The A. V.'s rendering of the second line is unnecessarily ambiguous, "Bind their faces in the hidden places" means to hide the wicked persons in literally "the hidden" place or the graves. "The hidden" is a circumlocution for the burial.[1]

Verse 14—When you can obliterate the unrighteous in the grave, then you can govern the universe. Job, you must have power commensurate with the purpose or design of creation,

---

[1] For analysis of the grammatical possibilities, see M. Dahood, *Biblica,* 1968, pp. 509-510; also his *Psalms* III, p. xxix, note 15.

if you are to rule. Do you possess the credentials?—Ps. 98:1; Isa. 59:16; 63:5. Yahweh grants that if Job can govern the vast complex creation he has the right to criticize, but only under the above conditions. If he can do what he has charged that Yahweh has neglected to do, then he could save himself from suffering and death.

2. Jehovah relates more marvels of his creation.
(40:15—41:34)

TEXT 40:15-24

15 Behold now, behemoth, which I made as well as thee;
He eateth grass as an ox.
16 Lo now, his strength is in his loins,
And his force is in the muscles of his belly.
17 He moveth his tail like a cedar:
The sinews of his thighs are knit together.
18 His bones are *as* tubes of brass;
His limbs are like bars of iron.
19 He is the chief of the ways of God:
He *only* that made him giveth him his sword.
20 Surely the mountains bring him forth food,
Where all the beasts of the field do play.
21 He lieth under the lotus-trees,
In the covert of the reed, and the fen.
22 The lotus-trees cover him with their shade;
The willows of the brook compass him about.
23 Behold, if a river overflow, he trembleth not;
He is confident, though a Jordan swell even to his mouth.
24 Shall any take him when he is on the watch,
Or pierce through his nose with a snare?

COMMENT 40:15-24

Verse 15—All of the previous animals and birds which appeared in the first speech are Palestinian. Behemoth has been identified as the hippopotamus, whose habitat is the Nile Valley. Behemoth is probably a loan word from the Egyptian for "water horse," but there is no example of this claim from either Coptic or Egyptian. The Hebrew plural form perhaps expresses the "plural of majesty" meaning large animal. The root of the word is the common noun for cattle or beast—Pss. 8:8; 73:22; Joel 1:20; and Hab. 2:17.[2] The powerful giant is a creature like Job. In many ways he is more powerful than Job, but he does not criticize Yahweh for His unjust governing of the universe.

Verse 16—This description clearly stresses the sexual vigor of this enormous beast. For both man and beast, the loins were image of strength of potency—Deut. 33:11; Ps. 69:23; Nah. 2:1. The dual form of "thighs" is a euphemism which is rendered as "strength is in his loins" in A. V.—Prov. 31:17. The muscles of the belly are particularly strong in the hippopotamus.

Verse 17—The A. V. rendering of part of the first line makes little sense, i.e., "He moves his tail like a cedar." The tail of this animal is very small, hardly appropriate for the express purposes of this image. The verb translated as "moveth" in the A. V. means to "make stiff." There is no reason to miss the point that this is a phallic symbol, with absolutely no necessary Freudian implications. The thighs (Heb. 'esek) also have sexual connotation. The imagery projects the strong virility of the animal.

Verse 18—His bones or limbs are like tubes or bars. The parallelism contains the synonym "bones" which is Hebrew and "limb" which is Aramaic—39:5.

---

[2] These verses sustain no mythological interpretation, though it has long been claimed that both Behemoth and Leviathan have mythological implications, especially since H. Günkel's *Schöpfung und Chaos*, pp. 57, 61ff, and especially since the availability of the Ugaritic literature. In *Intertestamental Literature* the beasts appear in eschatalogical imagery—Enoch 40:7-9; IV Ezra 6:49-52; and *The Apocalypse of Baruch*, XXIV, 4; see D. W. Thomas, *Vetus Testamentum*, 1953, pp. 209-224; P. Volz, *Die Eschatologie der judischen Gemeinde im neutestamentlichen Zeitalter*, 1934; and my New Testament Theology syllabus, *The Theology of Promise* on eschatology.

Verse 19—Perhaps the first line refers to Gen. 1:24 where the first animal created is said to be the *behemah*, i.e., cattle or beast. The word rendered "chief" in the A. V. is *rosh* and also appears in Prov. 8:22, with regard to wisdom. In the Intertestamental Literature, Enoch 40:7-9; Apocalypse of Baruch 24:4; and IV Ezra 6:49-52, Behemoth is a special creation of God, but not so in this Jobian passage. The last line of the verse makes little sense, either in Hebrew or as rendered in the A. V. Perhaps the sword refers to his chisel-edged tusks which the hippopotamus uses to attack its enemies.

Verse 20—But the habitat of the Behemoth is marshland and water, not the mountains. Perhaps the reference is to the vegetables produced in the mountainous areas, which is the understanding of the R. S. V. In the upper valley of the Nile, vegetation is abundant on the hillsides.

Verse 21—The animal rests under the water lily. The Egyptian specie is stronger and taller than the one found in Syria. Perhaps this is the thorny shrub which flourishes from Syria to North Africa in the damp hot areas. The word rendered "lotus tree" is used only here and verse 22.[3] The imagery might suggest an Egyptian habitat—Ps. 68:31 and Isa. 19:6.

Verse 22—The word *wadi* (*nahal*)[4] more strongly suggests Palestine than Egypt, but Behemoth has a wide range of movement—Lev. 23:40; Isa. 15:7; 44:4; and Ps. 137:2.

Verse 23—When the flash flood comes to the wadi, he is in complete control—"he trembleth not." Dhorme mentions the buffalo, though he accepts the hippopotamus, who can be observed on the banks of Lake Huleh with only his muzzle above the surface of the water. Some find difficulty in that this verse mentions the Jordan, some distance from Egypt, and attempts to amend to *ye'or,* the Nile. This is as unnecessary as it is impossible. See footnote below for evidence of the

---

[3] For discussion of this specie, see P. Humbert, *Zeitschrift für alttestamentischen Wissenschaft,* 1949-1950, p. 206.

[4] G. Haas, *Bulletin of the American Society of Oriental Research,* 1953, pp. 30ff, offers evidence that the hippopotamus was found in certain coastal areas in Palestine during the Iron Age.

presence of the hippopotamus in Palestine during the Iron Age.

Verse 24—Who can capture Behemoth when he is on the alert? Though there is no interrogative in the verse, this seems to be its meaning. Dhorme provides insight into the imagery from a reference in Herodotus, II.70, who mentions a process of controlling crocodiles by covering their eyes with mud. The word (*moqesim*) rendered pierce in A. V. usually means snare or trap. But "pierce" is inappropriate for either one. Slight emendation yields barbs or thorns, which is followed by both Pope and Dhorme.

TODAY'S ENGLISH VERSION

40

The Lord
    ¹⁻² Job, you challenged Almighty God;
        will you give up now, or will you answer?

Job
    ³⁻⁴ I spoke foolishly, Lord. What can I answer?
        I will not try to say anything else.
    ⁵ I have already said more than I should.

    ⁶ Then out of the storm the Lord spoke to Job again.

The Lord.
    ⁷ Stand up now like a man,
        and answer my questions.
    ⁸ Are you trying to prove that I am unjust—
        to condemn me and put yourself in the right?
    ⁹ Are you as strong as I am?
        Can your voice thunder as loud as mine?
    ¹⁰ If so stand up in your honor and pride;
        clothe yourself with majesty and glory.
    ¹¹ Look at those who are proud;
        pour out your anger and humble them.
    ¹² Yes, look at them and bring them down;
        crush the wicked where they stand.

¹³ Bury them all in the ground;
      bind them in the world of the dead.
¹⁴ Then I will be the first to praise you,
      and admit that you won the victory yourself.

¹⁵ Look at the monster Behemoth;
      I created him and I created you.
      He eats grass like an ox,
¹⁶   but what strength there is in his body,
      and what power there is in his muscles!
¹⁷ His tail stands up like a cedar,
      and the muscles in his legs are strong.
¹⁸ His bones are as strong as bronze,
      and his legs are like iron bars.

¹⁹ The most amazing of all my creatures!
      Only his Creator can defeat him.
²⁰ From the mountains where the wild beasts play,
      grass is brought to feed him.
²¹ He lies down under the thorn trees,
      and hides among the reeds in the swamp.
²² The thorn trees and the willows by the stream
      give him shelter in their shadows.
²³ He is not afraid of a rushing river,
      he is calm and when the water dashes in his face.
²⁴ Who can blind his eyes and capture him?
      Or who can catch his snout in a trap?

QUESTIONS FOR DISCUSSION 40:1-24

843. God now challenges Job to answer or forfeit his right
      to do what? From what does this section of the text suffer?
844. What is the content of the admission of Job?
845. What is the meaning of the expression: "I lay my hand
      upon my mouth"?
846. Job speaks no more. Why?

847. Does the mere fact that God answered Job indicate that Job is righteous? Explain.

848. Why does God ask Job to assume control over the universe?

849. Modern man stands much in the same place as Job. Show how.

850. What was Job's "lethal error"?

851. Even if Job had established his own integrity and wisdom he would yet lack one essential quality for ruling the world. What was it?

852. For what is God making request in verse ten? Why?

853. Since you know what is wrong, go ahead and correct it—is this the thought of verse 11? Cf. vs. 12. Discuss.

854. Verse 13 is obscure in meaning. Make its meaning clear.

855. God seemed to have neglected some areas of His creation. What does God say to Job about this? Cf. vs. 14.

856. How shall we identify the "behemouth"? Why does God use this fearsome beast in His speech to Job?

857. What is said of the loins and belly of the behemouth?

858. Since the hippopotamus has a very small tail, verse 17 has reference to something else. This is a description of what capacity of the animal?

859. What is the sword of the hippopotamus? In what way could he be called "the chief of the ways of God"?

860. The marshland is the habitat of the hippopotamus. Why the reference to the mountains in verse 20?

861. The setting of verse 21 is Egyptian. Show how this is true.

862. How could we be discussing a hippopotamus and yet locate him in the Jordan?

863. How does blinding his eyes relate to capturing him?

TEXT 41:1-34

41 Canst thou draw out leviathan with a fishhook?
Or press down his tongue with a cord?

2 Canst thou put a rope into his nose?
Or pierce his jaw through with a hook?

3 Will he make many supplications unto thee?
Or will he speak soft words unto thee?

4 Will he make a covenant with thee,
That thou shouldest take him for a servant for ever?

5 Wilt thou play with him as with a bird?
Or wilt thou bind him for thy maidens?

6 Will the bands *of fishermen* make traffic of him?
Will they part him among the merchants?

7 Canst thou fill his skin with barbed irons,
Or his head with fish-spears?

8 Lay thy hand upon him;
Remember the battle, and do so no more.

9 Behold, the hope of him is in vain:
Will not one be cast down even at the sight of him?

10 None is so fierce that he dare stir him up;
Who then is he that can stand before me?

11 Who hath first given unto me, that I should repay him?
Whatsoever is under the whole heaven is mine.

12 I will not keep silence concerning his limbs,
Nor his mighty strength, nor his goodly frame.

13 Who can strip off his outer garment?
Who shall come within his jaws?

14 Who can open the doors of his face?
Round about his teeth is terror.

15 *His* strong scales are *his* pride,
Shut up together *as with* a close seal.

16 One is so near to another,
That no air can come between them.

17 They are joined one to another;
They stick together, so that they cannot be sundered.

18 His sneezings flash forth light,

430

And his eyes are like the eyelids of the morning.
19 Out of his mouth go burning torches,
And sparks of fire leap forth.
20 Out of his nostrils a smoke goeth,
As of a boiling pot and *burning* rushes.
21 His breath kindleth coals,
And a flame goeth forth from his mouth.
22 In his neck abideth strength,
And terror danceth before him.
23 The flakes of his flesh are joined together:
They are firm upon him; they cannot be moved.
24 His heart is as firm as a stone;
Yea, firm as the nether millstone.
25 When he raiseth himself up, the mighty are afraid:
By reason of consternation they are beside themselves.
26 If one lay at him with the sword, it cannot avail;
Nor the spear, the dart, nor the pointed shaft.
27 He counteth iron as straw,
And brass as rotten wood.
28 The arrow cannot make him flee;
Sling-stones are turned with him into stubble.
29 Clubs are counted as stubble:
He laugheth at the rushing of the javelin.
30 His underparts are *like* sharp potsherds:
He spreadeth *as it were* a threshing-wain upon the mire.
31 He maketh the deep to boil like a pot:
He maketh the sea like a pot of ointment.
32 He maketh a path to shine after him;
One would think the deep to be hoary.
33 Upon earth there is not his like,
That is made without fear.
34 He beholdeth everything that is high:
He is king over all the sons of pride.

COMMENT 41:1-34

Verse 1—The belligerence of the Leviathan, or crocodile, is described. His thick hide cannot be penetrated by a fishhook. Can anyone take him captive? Would anyone entertain the vain hope of subduing the Leviathan? All of mankind is impotent before this monster. But Yahweh can control this beast with all but serene detachment. Each interrogation leads to the great question, "Who then is he that can stand before me?"—verse 10. Whether Leviathan is or is not a mythological creature (3:8) as Pope, *et al*, insist is not of ultimate significance. The claim that we have here mythological details was not first discovered with the Ras Shamra texts. Egypt is called Rahab in Isa. 30:7; thus a real nation is called by a mythological name. Discourse analysis, transformational grammar, contemporary cultural and linguistic studies all support the valid use of mythological data for real or historically accurate descriptions. The theological conclusion is not vitiated even if we have mythological elements present in the literary structure. The author believes that the crocodile cannot be captured by a "fish hook"; the word is found only here and in Isa. 19:8; Hab. 1:15. The crocodile has an immobile tongue attached to the lower jaw, and the imagery suggests efforts at capturing the beast with a rope.

Verse 2—Can you place a rope (*'agmon*—rush, reed—Isa. 9:13; 19:15; 58:5—or as *Qumran Targum, zeman*—nose ring) made of reeds through his nose? Both animals and men were held captive or led about with hooks drawn through the nose or jaws—II Kg. 19:28; Isa. 37:29; Ezek. 29:4; 38:4. The stela of Esarheddon depicts him holding the biblical tirhakah of Egypt and Balu of Tyre by ropes attached to clips in their lips.[1] Ea of the Mesopotamian Creation Epic says that "He laid hold on Mummu, holding him by the nose-rope."[2]

---

[1] Pritchard, ed. *Ancient Near Eastern Pictures Relating to the Old Testament* (Princeton), pp. 296, 447.

[2] Pritchard, ed. *Ancient Near Eastern Texts* (Princeton), p. 61, line 72.

We also have inscriptions from the Near East (Asurbanipal's inscriptions) which describe ropes through human jaws— Isa. 37:29.

Verse 3—Leviathan appears here as a human prisoner. Will he plead for mercy as would a human prisoner?

Verse 4—Will he cut a covenant[3] with you? Could you induce him, as a vassal, to enter service forever?—Ex. 21:5; Deut. 15:17; and I Sam. 27:12.[4] *The Qumran Targum* renders the second line "will you take him as eternal slave?"

Verse 5—In the East, doves and sparrows are still a favorite live playmate of children. In view of this fact, Yahweh asks Job if he wants to make Leviathan a playmate.[5]

Verse 6—Fishermen work together, then divide the catch after it is landed, and this procedure entails bargaining with one another. This social institution is the basis for this imagery.[6] Do you want to catch Leviathan and then bargain with one another over how he is to be divided?

Verse 7—The words (*sukkot* and *silsal*) rendered as "barbed irons" in A. V. mean harpoons and "fish-spears" respectively and are unique. But the context makes plain that they are instruments for catching fish, neither of which could ensnare the hard skin of Leviathan.

Verse 8—Effective advice is given to Job by use of powerful imperatives. Before you attempt to take Leviathan, realize what you are trying to do. No one lives to tell of his efforts, because there is no vulnerable spot on Leviathan.

Verse 9—In the Hebrew text, chapter 41 begins with this

---

[3] The covenant envisioned is that of a vassal with the suzerain, i.e., vanquished with the victor—see G. E. Mendenhall, *Law and Covenant in Israel and in the Ancient Near East,* Biblical Colloquim, Pittsburgh, 1955.

[4] See *Ancient Near Eastern Texts,* pp. 138b, 145, for same expression in Ugaritic Texts.

[5] See suggestions of D. W. Thomas, *Vetus Testamentum,* 1964, pp. 115-116, though *The Qumran Targum* contains "your daughters," i.e., young girls, against Thomas' emendation to sparrows.

[6] The word rendered merchant in the A. V. is literally Canaanites or hucksters— Isa. 23:8; Zech. 14:21; Prov. 31:24. See W. F. Albright, "Role of the Canaanites," *The Bible in the Ancient Near East,* ed. by G. E. Wright, 1961, pp. 328-362.

verse. His hope is in vain if he aspires to effectively assail this monster. As there is no antecedent for the pronoun "his," it not only refers to Job, it refers to anyone who attempts it. The A. V. renders the interrogative particle by "will not." Most translators omit the particle. The second line provides an enormous amount of possibility for applying the creative imagination of "motif" research specialists, such as Pope and his pan-Ugaritic hermeneutic. This is another form of contemporary hermeneutical psychoanalysis, which stems from the works of Dilthey, Schleiermacher, Heidegger, Gadamer, *et al.* Here is a warning—not to attempt to capture Leviathan, because the pursuer will collapse by even looking at him.

Verse 10—Who is cruel or fierce enough to awaken Leviathan from sleep? i.e., "stir him up." Arousing Leviathan is sheer folly. It is madness to arouse the monster; it is pure foolishness to criticize Yahweh. Some emend the "before me" to "before him" which keeps the thought on Leviathan. Dahood is followed by Blommerde. See his bibliographical notes.

Verse 11—The text literally says "who has confronted me?" By retaining verse 10, this text would mean that it is more dangerous to criticize Yahweh than to arouse Leviathan. Paul quotes the Hebrew text (not LXX as meaning is slightly different) version of this line in Rom. 11:35. Since God owns everything, no claims can be made against Him. The emphasis is not on the legal aspects but the inequality of power. No one could face Leviathan and survive. Why do you think that you can face me and survive, Job? You cannot even stand before one of my creatures. Why do you suppose that you can encounter your creator and come out of the conflict victoriously?

Verse 12—We now begin to encounter a detailed description of Leviathan. The first line means that Yahweh has broken His silence concerning His strength or physical structure.

Verse 13—Perhaps the imagery here refers to the scales of the crocodile. Dhorme understands "the face of his garment" to be the tough outer layer of protection as opposed to the back. The second line says literally "his double bridle," which

434

is understood to mean "come within his jaws" as in the A. V.

Verse 14—The crocodile's teeth inspire terror. This formidable enemy has thirty-six sharp teeth in his upper jaw and thirty in his lower jaw. In our context, Yahweh is saying that Job cannot even encounter this creature let alone the one who inspires awesome terror, God. If Leviathan is invincible, what of Yahweh?

Verse 15—Literally his pride (*ga'awah*) refers to the hard scales which cover the crocodile. "Close seal" renders the Hebrew *-sar*[7] but emendation yields *-sor*, stone or flint, which gives the thought of hardness of the seals with which the scales are compared.

Verse 16—The scales are so tightly packed that not even air (Heb. *ruah*—wind) can get between them. That the scales are firm and close is confirmed by the presence of the verb *'el*, enter, which means nothing can enter between.

Verse 17—This verse reinforces the imagery from verse 16.

Verse 18—The spray from the sneezing of the crocodile flashes in the sunlight. Pope imagines that he sees a mythological dragon in this verse. Actually it is only in his highly imaginative but brilliant mind. The dawn is symbolized by the crocodile in Egyptian hieroglyphs. The reddish eyes of the crocodile sparkle "like the eyelids of the dawn."

Verse 19—This verse is not describing a "fire-breathing dragon" as Pope suggests. The actual state of affairs makes the imagery perfectly understandable. When the crocodile arises up out of the water, after a sustained period beneath the surface, it propels water in a hot stream from its mouth. The sparkling steam looks like fire in the sunlight. No mythology is required to properly understand the verse.

Verse 20—Yahweh's theophany is described in Ps. 18:9 and II Sam. 22:9. Smoke or steam hurtle heavenward, as a boiling pot (Heb. *kedud*, verse 19—*kidod*, flame, as comparative particle, like, or as a boiling pot) and burning (not in Hebrew

---

[7] For emendation, see M. Dahood, *Biblica*, 1964, p. 399.

text but implied) rushes. Each image is of steam or vapor moving upwards. The word rendered "rushes" is found in verse two and is translated "rage."

Verse 21—This imagery is understandable as hyberbolical language, not necessarily mythological as Gunkel, Pope, *et al.* *The Qumran Targum* renders the second line "Sparks issue from his mouth."

Verse 22—The strength (Heb. *d'bh* is rendered *'lymw* in *The Qumran Targum* and contains connotations of sexual vigor) of the crocodile's neck is very apparent. The neck is often thought of as the place of strength—15:26 and Ps. 75:5. Dismay[8] goes before him. The dancing surely refers to the movement of the panic-striken victims attempting to evade his charge.

Verse 23—The A. V. rendering makes little sense, particularly in the first line. Literally the word rendered as flakes in A. V. is "falling parts," i.e., the flabby parts of his skin. The various possibilities all yield the same basic results, i.e., the hardness of the crocodile is indicated.

Verse 24—The attitude of Leviathan is described by the image of a millstone. In Ezek. 11:19 and 36:26, this same word is used to describe a heart of stone in contrast to a heart of flesh. The bottom or stationary stone received the harder wear.

Verse 25—Leviathan produces only the sensations and manifestations of fear, but he knows no fear.

Verse 26—No human weapons avail (Heb. lit. "does not stand") against his mighty armour. He is impervious to human power. Think, Job, if he can generate fear, what about me?

Verses 27-30—No weapon, not even strong metal, avails against his defenses, which in verse 30 are compared with his scales. When he lies on the ground, he leaves marks resembling the marks of the "threshing sledge."

Verse 31—Leviathan's motion in the water is described

---

[8] For this reading, see F. M. Cross, *Vetus Testamentum,* 1952, p. 163, for dismay rather than terror, but Hebrew also yields an acceptable meaning.

as churning up foam. He churns the water into a "boil"—
30:27. The word for pot describes an ordinary household
utensil—Jer. 1:13. The references to ointment is problematic.
Perhaps it refers to the boiling foam like unguent rising to the
surface during the rigorous underwater activity of Leviathan.

Verse 32—The white foam which Leviathan leaves behind
as "he lights a path"[9] is the basis of the imagery in the first
line. The deep (*tehom*) is his habitat.

Verse 33—Leviathan is peerless and fearless—4:19; 7:21;
10:9; 14:8; 17:16; 19:25; 20:11; and 34:15. Blommerde renders
the first line "on earth is not his equal."[10]

Verse 34—Leviathan is king of the "sons of pride"—28:8.
Surely this suggests a creature from the natural world perhaps
like a crocodile.

TODAY'S ENGLISH VERSION

41 Can you catch Leviathan with a fishhook,
or tie his tongue down with a rope?
² Can you put a rope through his snout,
or put a hook through his jaws?
³ Will he beg you to let him go?
Will he plead with you for mercy?
⁴ Will he make an agreement with you
and promise to serve you forever?
⁵ Will you treat him like a pet bird,
like something to amuse your servant girls?
⁶ Will fishermen bargain over him?
Will merchants cut him up to sell?
⁷ Can you fill his hide with fishing spears,

---

[9] M. Dahood, *Ephermerides Theologicae Lovanienses*, 1968, p. 36.

[10] He follows M. Dahood, *Biblica*, 1964, p. 410. Pope, following Günkel, insists
that the passage is not about the crocodile but a mythological monster, which stems
from his assumption that Ugaritic employment of the "mythological motif" necessitates
the presence of the motif in Job, though Ugaritic evidence does support the antiquity
of the Book of Job.

or pierce his head with a harpoon?
⁸ Touch him once and you'll never try it again;
you'll never forget the fight!

⁹ Anyone who sees Leviathan
loses courage and falls to the ground.
¹⁰ When he is aroused, he is fierce;
no one would dare to stand before him.
¹¹ Who can attack him and still be safe?
No one in all the world can do it.
¹² Let me tell you about Leviathan's legs,
and describe how great and strong he is.
¹³ No one can tear off his outer coat,
or pierce the armor he wears.
¹⁴ Who can make him open his jaws,
ringed with those terrifying teeth?
¹⁵ His back is made of rows of shields,
fastened together and hard as stone.
¹⁶ Each one is fastened so tight to the next,
not even a breath can come between.
¹⁷ They are all fastened so well together
that nothing can ever pull them apart.
¹⁸ Light flashes when he sneezes,
and his eyes glow like the rising sun.
¹⁹ Flames blaze from his mouth,
and streams of sparks fly out.
²⁰ Smoke comes pouring out of his nose,
like smoke from weeds burning under a pot.
²¹ His breath starts fires burning;
flames leap out of his mouth.
²² His neck is so powerful
that everyone who meets him is terrified.
²³ There is not a weak spot in his skin;
it is as hard and unyielding as iron.
²⁴ His stony heart is without fear,
as unyielding and hard as a millstone.
²⁵ When he rises up, even the gods are frightened;

they are helpless with fear.
²⁶ There is no sword that can wound him;
    no spear, or arrow, or lance that can harm him.
²⁷ For him, iron is as weak as straw,
    and bronze as weak as rotten wood.
²⁸ There is no arrow that can make him run;
    rocks thrown at him are like bits of straw.
²⁹ To him a club is a piece of straw,
    and he laughs when men throw spears.
³⁰ His claws are like jagged pieces of pottery;
    they tear up the muddy ground as he walks.
³¹ He churns up the sea like a boiling pot,
    and makes it bubble like a kettle of oil.
³² He leaves a shining path behind him
    and turns the sea to white foam.
³³ There is nothing on earth to compare with him;
    he is a creature that has no fear.
³⁴ He looks down on even the proudest animals;
    he is king of all wild beasts.

QUESTIONS FOR DISCUSSION 41:1-34

864. Is leviathan a real or mythological creature? Discuss.
865. Show how the crocodile perfectly fits the description given in verse one of the leviathan.
866. Ropes were used in the same way for both men and animals. What was the purpose? Give examples.
867. What is the point of the description given in verse two and three?
868. What a playmate a crocodile would be! How easy would it be to tame him and expect his service?
869. What imagery is found in verse six?
870. The barbed irons and fishing spears are of no value with the leviathan. Why?
871. What advice is given to Job in verse eight?

872. The point of verses one through nine is stated in verse ten. What is it?

873. If no one can face a crocodile; who is he who can face the creator of the crocodile? Is this the thought of verse 11?

874. What subject begins in verse 12?

875. What is the "outer garment" of the crocodile?

876. No one can open the doors of the face of leviathan. Why not? What is the point being made?

877. The pride of this creature is in its scales. Explain why. Cf. vss. 15-17.

878. Express in your own words the meaning of verse 18. In what sense are the eyelids of the crocodile "the eyelids of the morning"?

879. Is there a fire-breathing dragon described in verse 19? If not, please explain what is described.

880. The "smoke" is not smoke in verse 20, nor are the "coals" and "flame" what they seem to be in verse 21. Please explain.

881. What is said about his neck? How do we explain the dance of terror or dismay before him? Cf. vs. 22.

882. What are "the flakes of the flesh" of the crocodile?

883. He is as hard as the lowly millstone. In what way? Cf. vs. 24.

884. Why all the detail in the futile attempts of men to injure the crocodile? Cf. vss. 26-30.

885. The leviathan's motion in the water is described in verses 31 and 32. Paraphrase verses 31 and 32.

886. The crocodile is king. Over whom? Cf. vss. 33, 34.

D. MAN IN GOD'S IMAGE VS. GOD IN MAN'S IMAGE
(42:1-6)

TEXT 42:1-6

42 Then Job answered Jehovah and said,
2 I know that thou canst do all things,
And that no purpose of thine can be restrained.
3 Who is this that hideth counsel without knowledge?
Therefore have I uttered that which I understood not,
Things too wonderful for me, which I knew not.
4 Hear, I beseech thee, and I will speak;
I will demand of thee, and declare thou unto me.
5 I had heard of thee by the hearing of the ear;
But now mine eye seeth thee:
6 Wherefore I abhor *myself,*
And repent in dust and ashes.

COMMENT 42:1-6

Verse 1—Job responds to Yahweh in complete submission. The following verses can connect also with 40:4ff.

Verse 2—No purpose of Yahweh can be withheld from Him—Gen. 17:11. God's will and power are co-terminus. Job's complaint had never been against God's power, only His will. Job had lodged his confrontation with God concerning His indifference to moral matters, not His inability to execute justice. His wisdom and omnipotence have been acknowledged from the very beginning. Now Job affirms in faith not only God's wisdom and power but also His goodness and graciousness. He cares for all His creation. His brief excursion throughout the system and societies of nature has provided perspective from which preview His purpose. Now he has a personal knowledge by acquaintance of his vindicator. God's purpose is not a segment but a circle. In order to understand God's ways with man, we must not absolutize any single degree of the cosmic circle, because ignorance of the meaning of the whole will ensue. There are no "value free" decisions, the assertions of many social and behavioral scientists to the contrary. All decisions entail value presuppositions. Now Job knows this fact of reality.

Verse 3—This verse is almost identical with 38:2. Job here repeats the complaint previously lodged against him for the express purpose of admitting its validity. God's rebuke is here acknowledged to have been justified. Only those in ignorance (Heb. verb *'lm*—darkness) of God's complete purpose would speak out against Him.

Verse 4—Again this verse repeats, with only slight modifications, 33:31; 38:3; and 40:7. The marvel of memory is here set before us as Job reminisces on what Yahweh has said to him—13:22.

Verse 5—Here is the heart of Job's restoration. In times past, Job knew God only by hearsay, literally "report of ear"—Ps. 18:45 and Job 28:22. Job is now convinced of that which he formally doubted, i.e., of God's providential care. He had asked for assurance that God was on his side—19:23-27, and Yahweh has once and for all spoken by *The Shattering of Silence*. Job's demand has been met.

Verse 6—Repentance removes himself from the center of the world. Job is truly a crucified self. After all the only alternatives are either a "divided self" or a "crucified self." Job accepts God's evaluation of himself. We are OK only when God says we are OK! Even in 9:21 Job does not loath (Heb. verb *m's*) himself, but his condition.[1] Job's habitat has been ashes for some time—2:8; Isa. 58:5; Jer. 6:26; Jonah 3:6; and Micah 1:10. Like the Phoenix, Job arises up out of the bitter ashes of suffering and stands whole again. But this time Yahweh is his organizing center, and neither his family nor prosperity nor their cultural advantages. To the Christian believer, Job's redeemer, the Christ, is the orderer of all existence—Col. 1:17 and Eph. 1:10. He is truly *Christ the Center*.

---

[1] See the examination of L. J. Kuyper, *Vetus Testamentum*, 1959, pp. 91-94.

VII. RECONCILIATION AND RENEWAL (42:7-17)
A. ELIPHAZ MAKES A GREAT BURNT-OFFERING AND JOB INTERCEDES FOR HIS FRIENDS. (42:7-9)

TEXT 42:7-9

7 And it was so, that, after Jehovah had spoken these words unto Job, Jehovah said to Eliphaz the Temanite, My wrath is kindled against thee, and against thy two friends; for ye have not spoken of me the thing that is right, as my servant Job hath. 8 Now therefore, take unto you seven bullocks and seven rams, and go to my servant Job, and offer up for yourselves a burnt-offering; and my servant Job shall pray for you; for him will I accept, that I deal not with you after your folly; for ye have not spoken of me the thing that is right, as my servant Job hath. 9 So Eliphaz the Temanite and Bildad the Shuhite and Zophar the Naamathite went, and did according as Jehovah commanded them: and Jehovah accepted Job.

COMMENT 42:7-9

Verse 7—Now Yahweh turns to Eliphaz and declares that He is disturbed that they have all along misrepresented Him.[2] They have distorted the will of God in their counsel to Job. Yet they uttered each word as though it had been directly authorized by Him—I Sam. 23:23. Job himself had accused them of lying in order to defend God—13:4, 7-11. Job is surely vindicated now. God has not only broken His silence; He has condemned Job's adversaries. The integrity of God's impatient protester has now been rewarded. He has also judged pious hypocrites, even those who pretend to speak for Him. What a lesson we must all learn! Twentieth century man needs as

---

[2] See J. G. Williams, "You Have Not Spoken Truth of Me, Mystery and Irony in Job," *Zeitschrift für alttestamentliche Wissenschaft*, 1971, pp. 231-255.

never before to know Job's creator-redeemer. God in His mercy has bathed this tormented soul in the healing oils of love and forgiveness. My servant, so acclaimed in the beginning and in the end, has survived the temptations of suffering and pain. He has indeed been in the "furnace of affliction."

Verse 8—This is an enormous sacrifice—Num. 23:1ff, indicating a grave matter. Vicarious atonement is imperative for wholeness—Lev. 4:1ff. Intercessory prayer is a mighty force throughout the scriptures—Gen. 18:23ff; Ex. 8:30; 32:11ff; Deut. 9:20; Isa. 53:12; Jer. 37:3; and Amos 7:2ff. Yahweh tells them to go to Job because, literally, "his face I will lift up," i.e., accept—13:8. As Job is the offended party, he must intercede—22:30. The intercession is for their folly (Heb. *nebalah*)—Gen. 34:7; Deut. 22:21; Jos. 7:15; and Jer. 29:23.

Verse 9—Note that Elihu is not mentioned, in spite of the extensive materials in the Elihu speeches—chapters 32-37. Yahweh forgave them because of Job's sacrifice and intercessory prayer on their behalf. His vicarious suffering approaches our Lord's redemptive suffering as the *Suffering Servant*—Isa. 52:13—53:12; Phil. 2:5ff. But suffering alone is not redemptive, as Dostoevsky assumed; only the suffering of our incarnate Lord and Master can redeem the fallen universe—Rom. 8; Rev. 21.

B. JOB IS RESTORED TO PROSPERITY AND BLESSED WITH CHILDREN. (42:10-17)

TEXT 42:10-17

10 And Jehovah turned the captivity of Job, when he prayed for his friends: and Jehovah gave Job twice as much as he had before. 11 Then came there unto him all his brethren, and all his sisters, and all they that had been of his acquaintance before, and did eat bread with him in his house: and they bemoaned him and comforted him concerning all the evil that

444

Jehovah had brought upon him: every man also gave him a piece of money, and every one a ring of gold. 12 So Jehovah blessed the latter end of Job more than his beginning: and he had fourteen thousand sheep, and six thousand camels, and a thousand yoke of oxen, and a thousand she-asses. 13 He had also seven sons and three daughters. 14 And he called the name of the first, Jemimah; and the name of the second, Keziah; and the name of the third, Keren-happuch. 15 And in all the land were no women found so fair as the daughters of Job: and their father gave them inheritance among their brethren. 16 And after this Job lived a hundred and forty years, and saw his sons, and his sons' sons, *even* four generations. 17 So Job died, being old and full of days.

COMMENT 42:10-17

Verse 10—Job's prosperity is restored, but not as a reward. Being *successful* is not proof of being *saved.* Surely we have learned this much from Job, our contemporary. His fortune has returned (Heb. verb -*sub*)[3]—Jer. 29:14; 30:3; Ezek. 16:53; 39:25. This is the only occurrence of the word fortune, which is applied to an individual and not to the corporate prosperity of a nation.

Verse 11—His wealth and its prestige attracted his relatives and friends once more—19:13. Where were these fair-weather friends when he needed their consolation? *The Qumran Targum* ends with this verse suggesting an early literary ending of the Book of Job.

Verse 12—The numbers are double the amount which Job had before—1:3.

Verse 13—The number of children remain the same. Job's daughters figure more prominently than his sons, who are not even mentioned by name.

---

[3] See R. Borger, *Zeitschrift für alttestamentlische Wissenschaft,* 1955, pp. 315ff.

445

Verse 14—The name of the first, Yemimah, means turtle-dove, which is a symbol of fertility and devotion—Hos. 7:11; Matt. 10:16. Qeziah is the second and means a variety of cinnamon used as perfume—Ex. 30:24; Ezek. 27:19; Ps. 45:9; and Prov. 7:17. The third daughter's name is Keren—*happuch* (*Kohl*) and means powdered paint for the eyelashes and lids—Jer. 4:30; Eccl. 26:9; II Kg. 9:30; and Ezek. 23:40.[4]

Verse 15—The names of Job's daughters represent the natural, physical, and spiritual qualities engendered by the beautician's creative touch. In the cultural context of the ancient Near East, daughters inherited only when there were no sons—Num. 26:33; 27:1-8; and 36:1-12. Here is an example of women's liberation in the ancient world, as women did not receive an inheritance when there were sons, and is unique in the Old Testament.

Verse 16—After his affliction, Job lived 140 years, just about double his former years. Job saw four generations, as compared to Joseph's three—Gen. 50:23. Grandchildren are the crown of life—Ps. 128:6 and Prov. 17:6.

Verse 17—So ends the life of one of God's great servants. The LXX adds a notation after this verse asserting that Job will share in the resurrection of the dead and further traditional details of his life. In the *Shattering of Silence* God vindicated Job's integrity. Suffering men can be righteous. Our Suffering Savior is ultimate proof of this possibility. Life begins as a problem, continues as a promise, and is the fulfillment of a purpose. The dawn of God's new day broke over the destructive darkness that all but destroyed Job, our contemporary. Vindicated Job was no longer enslaved to himself, or his former preoccupation with happiness,[5] or enjoyment of prosperity,

---

[4] For vital sociological parallels between the status of women between the patriarchal age (2000-1800 B.C.) and the period of Homer (ca 1000-900 B.C.), see Cyrus H. Gordon's *Homer and The Bible*, 1955, pp. 43-108, offset from *Hebrew Union College Annual*.

[5] See *Psychology Today*, August, 1976, on our cultural preoccupation with happiness, which comes from "outside"; joy comes from inside a crucified self, a gift from our vindicator, through the presence of His Spirit—Gal. 5:19ff.

family, health, or prestige in the community, for he now knows that before he "had heard of thee by the hearing of the ear; but now mine eye seeth thee," verse 5.

TODAY'S ENGLISH VERSION

42
Job

Then Job answered the Lord.

² I know, Lord, that you are all-powerful;
   that you can do everything you want.
³ You ask how I dare question your wisdom
   when I am so very ignorant.
   I talked about things I did not understand,
   about marvels too great for me to know.
⁴ You told me to listen while you spoke
   and to try to answer your questions.
⁵ Then I knew only what others had told me,
   but now I have seen you with my own eyes;
⁶   so I am ashamed of all I have said
   and repent in dust and ashes.

CONCLUSION

⁷ After the Lord has said all this to Job, he told Eliphaz, "I am angry with you and your two friends, because you did not speak the truth about me, the way my servant Job did. ⁸ Now take seven bulls and seven rams to Job and offer them as a sacrifice for yourselves. Job will pray for you, and I will answer his prayer and not disgrace you the way you deserve. You did not speak the truth about me as he did."

⁹ Eliphaz, Bildad, and Zophar did what the Lord had told them to do, and the Lord answered Job's prayer.

> [10] Then, after Job had prayed for his three friends, the Lord made him prosperous again and gave him twice as much as he had had before. [11] All Job's brothers and sisters and former friends came to visit him and feasted with him in his house. They expressed their sympathy and comforted him for all the troubles the Lord had brought on him. Each of them gave him some money and a gold ring.
>
> [12] The Lord blessed the last part of Job's life even more than he had blessed the first. Job owned 14,000 sheep, 6,000 camels, 2,000 head of cattle, and 1,000 donkeys. [13] He was the father of seven sons and three daughters. [14] He called the oldest daughter Jemimah, the second Keziah, and the youngest Keren-Happuch. [15] There were no other women in the whole world as beautiful as Job's daughters. Their father gave them a share of the inheritance along with their brothers.
>
> [16] Job lived 140 years after this, long enough to see his grandchildren and great-grandchildren. [17] And then he died at a very great age.

QUESTIONS FOR DISCUSSION 42:1-17

887. What is meant by saying "God's will and power are co-terminus"?
888. Job's complaint has never been against God's power, but rather against what?
889. What is meant by saying "there are no 'value free' decisions"? Discuss.
890. The only ones who speak out against God are those who are ignorant of what? Cf. vs. 3.
891. Please explain in detail how verse five becomes the heart of Job's restoration.
892. We are OK only when?
893. Show how Job's experience and understanding, and

commitment can become ours. Cf. vs. 6.

894. There is a very important principle to learn from the fact that Job's friends were so very confident that they were speaking on behalf of God. Discuss.

895. Notice carefully the factors involved in the sacrifice of verse eight. What are the lessons taught by it?

896. What are we to make of the fact that Elihu is not mentioned by God? In what way does Job become like our Lord? Is all suffering redemptive?

897. Job's prosperity was restored, but not as a reward. Discuss.

898. Job's friends (like many today) were really not friends at all. Discuss why.

899. Why make his daughters so prominent?

900. It would seem from the names given to these girls they were but representative of a social condition that prevailed in Job's day. Discuss.

901. How do the scriptures consider grandchildren? Cf. Ps. 128:6; Prov. 17:6.

902. Notice the very meaningful statement about life under the comment on verse 17. Discuss.

903. In what way can we see God and be satisfied today?

904. What part of this grand book has appealed to you the most? Please be specific.

905. If you were going to add something to this book as a text, what would it be?

906. Please refer to the further questions for discussion in the section immediately following.

Fifteen Jobian Themes

for Discussion

GOD AND GOLEM[1]

And Moses said to God, "If I come, I come to the people of Israel, and say unto them, 'The God of your fathers has sent me to you; and they shall ask me, What is his name? What shall I say to them?' " God said to Moses, "I am who I am." Ex. 3:13, 14.

Blessed be the God and Father of our Lord Jesus Christ, the Father of mercies and God of all comfort, who comforts us in all our afflictions, so that we may be able to comfort those who are in any affliction, with the comfort with which we ourselves are comforted by God. II Cor. 1:3, 4.

Have you considered my servant Job, that there is none like him on the earth, a blameless and upright man, who fears God and turns away from evil? . . . Behold, all that he has is in your power; only upon himself do not put forth your hand. Job 1:8, 12.

Freedom and Finitude

If God is good, why do the righteous suffer? If God is all-powerful, why doesn't He do something about human heartache and hurt? If man is only a machine, i.e., a golem, then suffering is an illusion. If he is as the scriptures say—"in the image of God," then his freedom permits decision making which has negative effects on both the individual and his social environment.

God and Justice

Not once did Job deny the existence of God. But he did deny God's justice. What does our view of the nature of God have to do with our attitudes toward *sin* and *suffering?*

---

[1] In Jewish legend, golem is an embryo adam, shapeless and not fully created, hence a monster, an automation.

Discussion Questions

1. What was Job's view of God? How does this compare with your own? (See the essay—"Is Job's God in Exile?" beginning on page 487.)

   Discuss the following descriptions of God:

   Yahweh-jireh—Yahweh will *see to it,* or *provide*

   Yahweh-nissi—Yahweh—my *Banner*

   Yahweh-Shalom—Yahweh—our *Peace*

   Yahweh-Tsidkenu—Yahweh—our *Righteousness*

   Yahweh-Shammah—*Yahweh is there,* i.e., present

2. If God is all-powerful and holy, should He permit sin and evil in His creation? Give reasons for your answer.

3. What is the relationship of your view of God to *creation, self, history, society,* and all the suffering which man experiences? Give at least two reasons why "anyone" should share your belief?

4. How do you relate your belief in God with the fact of disease and suffering? Discuss concrete examples of self-inflicted suffering and non self-inflicted suffering such as accidents, famines, earthquakes, fires, wars, etc.

Freedom and Responsibility

1. Discuss how man's freedom creates sin and suffering. Discuss the moral evil that man creates, then compare with the larger problem of "surd evil," i.e., earthquakes, famines, etc., which human action does not necessarily create. Some suffering is caused by sinful men, but some is caused by fallen nature.

2. To whom is man responsible for his actions? God and/or society? Discuss crime and punishment. Discuss the moral

implications of human law. (See J. W. Montgomery's *The Law Above the Law.* Minneapolis, Minn.: Bethany Fellowship Press, 1976.)
3. Can sinful man create the "good society"?

Bibliography on God

K. Hamilton, *To Turn from Idols,* Eerdmans, 1973, pb.
H. W. Smith, *The God of All Comfort*, Moody Press, 1956, pb.

MEANING OF PERSONS: SUFFERING AND BECOMING

What is man that thou art mindful of him? Ps. 8:4.
Naked I came from my mother's womb, and naked shall I return: the Lord gave, and the Lord has taken away; blessed be the name of the Lord. Job 1:20, 21.
Man is what he eats. Feuerbach
No man is an island. Johnn Donne
None of us lives to himself, and none of us dies to himself. Rom. 14:7

Masks and Roles

As a person, Job played many roles, as do we all. The rich variety of interpersonal relationships with children, wife and friends made Job a very complex person. He was related to nature, as land owner, the community, as an influential wealthy Sheikh to his possessions, and ultimately to his God. As disaster struck, the security grounded in each of the relationships deteriorated, except his relationship to his personal God. Job's personal identity was organized around four types of relationships: (1) God, (2) self, (3) others, and (4) nature. He repeatedly declared that he was alive and suffering and that is an experience that cannot be reduced to a causal explanation. Discuss the above four relationships in your life.

Man the Contradictory Being

In spite of the fact that introspection has failed as a method of discovering the person, contemporary man is once more on the Eastern road inward. Job was conscious of his own inner feelings and attitudes and was unaware of the cause of the cruelty that fell his lot.

The Person and Dialogue

1. Discuss the issues which were stressed in the dialogues between Job and his three friends.
2. Discuss the relationship between *holiness* and *wholeness* in our psychological processes.
3. Does Job have a bad conscience concerning his past behavior? Discuss the implication of your answer.
4. Discuss Job's dialogue with his three friends, then compare with his *monologue* with God. What were some of the results of each respecting Job's *feelings* and *frustrations*. Read Martin Buber's, *I-Thou* and compare with Job.
5. Identify five of Job's anxieties and their resolution or lack of same. Compare with your own.
6. List five obstacles to Job's well-being and discuss them.
7. Discuss how Job becomes what God wants him to be through his grace and encounter with the *Living God.* Is your God living? Is your church relationship based on a personal relationship with Christ, or are there merely social and psychological reasons for your church affiliations?

Becoming and Commitment

1. Trusting God and His purposes are of vital importance for Christian personhood.
2. Job's commitment to the living God enlarges the dilemma of uniqueness. Our personalities are less a finished product

than a transitive process. Compare Job and yourself with respect to trust, commitment, and the processes of maturity. Are we becoming more like God's "servant, Job"? If so, how?

Bibliography on Man

M. J. Adler, *The Difference of Man and the Difference It Makes,* World Pub. Meridian, 1967, pb.

Gordon W. Allport, *Becoming,* Yale, 1968, pb.

Leslie Stevenson, *Seven Theories of Human Nature,* Oxford University Press, 1975, pb.

J. D. Strauss, "Christians Come of Age in a World Come of Age," *Newness on The Earth,* 1969, pp. 113-125.

Paul Tournier, *The Meaning of Persons,* Harper, 1957.

TOUCHED BY EVIL: JOY IN THE MORNING

Shall a faultfinder contend with the Almighty? He who argues with God, let him answer it. Job 40:1, 2

Behold, the man has become like one of us, knowing good and evil . . . Gen. 3:22

If you become a Christian then you will have on your plate a first-class philosophical problem. Hugh Silvester

Dr. Zhivago is a mirror of modern man. The bitter and cruel winter in the Ural mountains, the ruthlessness of the revolution, inhumaneness of the class war, Victor's unbridled lust, and Zhivago's unfaithfulness reveal the "facts of life" in a world which has revolted against God. Human ruin is everywhere visible. What and who causes this decadence on the human scene?

Evils of Man's Inhumanity

We are barraged with the twin claims of genetic and environmental determinism. Contemporary criminology insists that "criminals" are only persons with the misfortune of being born and reared in a completely negative environment. But why should the Jews have suffered such excruciating agony in Hitler's Germany because they bore a certain name? Where was God when they constructed the "Gas Ovens"? Why should individuals suffer for something over which they have no control? Why should evil men prosper? Why should some punishment be out of all proportion to the offense? e.g. Job's charges against God. Why does God allow the loss of life and limb in an auto accident, while he allows the oppression and exploitation by some exploiters?

Disease—Death Milieu

While man is searching for life on Mars, death and disease go unchecked on earth. Overwhelming sorrow results from the loss of a loved one. In C. S. Lewis', *A Grief Observed* he lays bare his broken heart and personal anguish. He describes sorrow, "Grief is like a long valley, a winding valley where any bend may reveal a totally new landscape . . . you wonder whether the valley isn't a circular trench." (Read this beautiful work and discuss death and dying, sorrow and healing and wholeness.)

Nature Red in Tooth and Claw

Animals and insects balance nature's systems by the survival of the fittest. Every animal, fish and insect feeds on some form of life. Everywhere we find either the *prey* or the *plunderer*. Nature is one big slaughter house. Back to nature mentality means back to "tooth and claw." Is this the best of all possible worlds? Should God resign? Should we believe in the existence of a God who cannot control His kingdom with any more benevolent mercy than seems evident as millions of live specimens are daily consumed to perpetrate nature's life systems? Is dualism, i.e., eternal good and eternal evil a feasible solution to our dilemma, if not, why not?

1. Is evil real? What is the ultimate cause of natural and moral evil?
2. If there were no God, would evil exist?
3. Discuss *morals* and the problem of *evil.*
4. Is evil merely caused by environment, economic conditions, psychological conditions, etc.?
5. Discuss the biblical doctrine of judgment and hell in the context of evil.
6. If man is not free as Crick, Wilson, Monad, Skinner, et al., assert then who is responsible for human behavior?

Bibliography on Evil

J. Hick, *Evil and the God of Love,* Macmillan, 1966, pb.
C. S. Lewis, *The Problem of Pain,* Macmillan, pb.
C. S. Lewis, *Surprised by Joy,* Macmillan, pb.
High Silvester, *Arguing with God,* Inter-Varsity Press, 1972, pb.

CARING IN AN AGE OF CRISIS

Be not anxious. Matt. 6:25

Martha, Martha, you are anxious and troubled about many things; one thing is needful. Lk. 10:41

Cast all your anxieties on him, for he cares for you. I Pet. 5:7

Let the day perish wherein I was born, and the night which said, a man-child is conceived. Job 3:3

Why did I not die at birth. Job 3:11

I am not at ease, nor am I quiet; I have no rest; but trouble comes. Job 3:16

Anxieties: Constructive and Destructive

Job's life was filled with anxieties. He was surrounded by death, destruction, heartache, and calloused counselors. Doesn't anyone really *care* for Job? How do you *identify* with Job's needs? Is there any healing for his and our hurt? Can anything creatively good come out of our anxieties? Freud's fallacy concerning the negative nature of our anxieties still haunts modern man. Anything that reduces our anxious hours is adjudged to be good, according to Freud. But creative use of anxiety has been at the heart of every major advancement of man. Imagine a Moses, Isaiah, or Paul without anxiety. These men were anxious about *ultimate issues* not trivial human values. What are some of the areas that cause our deepest frustrations? Locate these crises in Job's life and compare with your own.

Nature of Contemporary Crises

1. *There are economically grounded anxieties:* egs. taxes, inflation, recession, hostility to the work ethic, local congregation, Bible Colleges in the free church tradition, counter cultures and Marxist attacks on our economic institutions and the entire evangelistic outreach of the church.
2. *Death and Dying:* egs. Face death definitely, and thanatology since Elizabeth Kuber-Ross; high school mini courses on death.
3. *Grief and Guilt:* egs. Anxieties grounded in grief and bereavement, are we *guilty* or are we merely culturally caused to *feel guilty?*
4. *Freedom and Security:* We desire to be free, yet need security more. How can we be both free and secure? How do we

458

relate our freedom and security to others? Can freedom and security be only a private matter? How is our individual freedom and security related to others by caring?

5. *Sin and Salvation*: The contemporary behavioral sciences maintain that man is dominated by the twin forces of *genetic* and *environmental* determinism. If true, we could hardly sin against God. If these theses are scientifically definable, then *sin* and *salvation* in the *biblical sense* is false. (If available read the works of Menninger, Crick, Monad, Wilson, and Skinner and discuss in light of the biblical doctrines of sin and salvation.)

Ingredients of Caring

Some of the conditions for caring are:

1. *Knowledge and Caring:* Caring requires knowledge and preparation.
2. *Patience and Caring:* Patience is not passivity, rather a mediation between extremes.
3. *Trusting and Caring:* Trusting in a loving Lord entails *risk* in our relationship with others. Risk entails the possibility of *failure* and *frustration*.
4. *Honesty and Caring:* Honesty implies truth; truth implies responsibility to both God, self, and others.
5. *Hope and Caring:* As Christians we are begotten again unto a *new* and *living* hope; therefore, we must care for God's view of creation, the home, the church, etc.

These ingredients, when well-mixed with love and compassion, will heal lives in our times of crises. So, right on with Christ and caring in an age of crises. Maranatha.

Bibliography on Caring and Crisis

Jay E. Adams, *Your Place in the Counseling Revolution*,

Baker, 1975, pb.

Willard Gaylin, "Caring," A. A. Knopf, 1976 (See excerpt from *Psychology Today,* Aug., 1976).

Seward Hiltner, *The Christian Shepherd,* Abingdon, 1959.

Wayne E. Oates, *Anxiety in Christian Experience,* Westminster, 1955, reprinted by Baker in pb.

Lillian Rubin, *Worlds of Pain,* New York: Basic Books, 1976.

(See the Journals in the bibliography for technical clinical data.)

THE GREAT MYTH: PIETY PRODUCES PROSPERITY

Behold my servant shall prosper. (The word means to attain a goal, not get rich.) Isa. 52:13

Thou hast blessed the work of his hands, and his possessions have increased in the land. Job 1:10

So the poor have hope, and injustice shuts her mouth. Job 5:16

Is not the Lord in the midst of us? No evil shall come upon us. Micah 3:11

Your rich men are full of violence; . . . Micah 6:12

The issue can no longer be evaded. It is becoming clearer every day that the most urgent problem besetting our church is this: How can we live the Christian life in the modern world? D. Bonhoeffer, *Letters and Papers from Prison*

Presence and Piety

We are living in a Jobian world without his piety. Job's integrity was contingent on his awareness of God's presence. Not since the great influence of Lutheran and Reformed pietism has western man shown so much aversion to the devotional life. There is not only a "crisis of piety," there is a "loss of piety" in western civilization. Wayne Oates refers to a "conspiracy of silence about personal religion" that prevails in our

460

churches and theological seminaries.

The post-Reformation spiritual movements known as Pietism, Puritanism, and Evangelicalism sought to recover the centrality of the devotional life. The Reformers place the accent on *Christ for us,* and the pietiestic movements emphasized *Christ with us* and *Christ in us* as well. Francke, Zinzendorf, Spittler, Kierkegaard, Blumhardts, Spener, et al., each in his own way emphasized the Christian life as centering in the devotional life. As contemporary man attempts to deliteralize the demonic, Satan's powers increase as Eastern meditation techniques are utilized to fill the void.

As America enters her third century, perhaps Jobian piety in the face of his loss of prosperity and with it—its security, can rekindle our concern for "Christ in us." We did not learn the *American myth* that prosperity is proof of our piety from Job.

The Gospel of Wealth in America's Third Century

A fundamental driving force in our past two hundred years has been, if you are "successful" it is necessarily a blessing from God. If you are a "failure" it is God's judgment on your entire life-style. But what of Job? What of the world's hungry, destitute, poor? What of the *Third and Fourth Worlds* in the last quarter of the 20th century? Below the thirtieth parallel lies almost eighty percent of the world's population and most of the world's poverty. Above the thirtieth parallel is twenty percent of the world's population and most of its wealth and productive power.

Piety in Spite of Prosperity

Discuss the arguments employed by Job's three friends in light of the following questions:

1. Is poverty proof of God's judgment on your life style?

461

2. Is prosperity proof of His blessings?
3. Was Job not pious without the security of things?
4. Did Job have integrity before God? Was Job's faith (and ours) contingent on God's blessings, i.e., things which his culture valued which in turn produced psychological and sociological security?
5. Discuss the relationship of piety, devotion and prosperity.
6. Discuss Satan's first attack on Job—"Does Job fear God for naught?" Job 1:9. What is the relationship of reward, punishment and piety? Compare Job and yourself.

Bibliography on Piety and Devotion

D. G. Bloesch, *The Christian Life and Salvation,* Eerdmans, 1967.

Donald G. Bloesch, *The Crisis of Piety,* Eerdmans, 1968.

D. Bonhoeffer, *The Cost of Discipleship,* Macmillan, pb.

John Bunyan, *The Pilgrim's Progress,* pb.

Soren Kierkegaard, *Journals of S. Kierkegaard,* Oxford University Press, 1951.

Soren Kierkegaard, *The Purity of Heart,* New York: Harper, 1956.

Bro. Lawrence, *The Practice of the Presence of God,* Revell, pb., 1958.

T. Merton, *Seeds of Contemplation,* Norfolk, Conn., 1949, pb.

HORRORS OF ESTRANGEMENT: RELIEVED BY RECONCILIATION

Naked I came from my mother's womb, and naked shall I return; . . . Job 1:21

And they sat with him on the ground seven days and seven nights, and no one spoke a word to him, . . . Job 2:13

They meet with darkness in the daytime, and grope at

462

noonday as in the night. Job 5:14

He was oppressed, and he was afflicted, yet he opened not his mouth; . . . Isa. 53:7

God was in Christ reconciling the world to himself . . . I Cor. 5:19

The Lonely Crowd

Biblically, alienation is always a consequence of sin. Pablo, in Hemingway's *For Whom the Bell Tolls,* expresses human estrangement after an act of calculated treachery and betrayal—"Having done such a thing there is loneliness which cannot be borne" (p. 367). Restless and rootless Joe Christmas is described in Faulkner's *Light in August*—"there was something rootless about him, as though no town or city was his, no street, no walls, no square of earth his home." Man's contemporary identity crisis is rooted and grounded in alienation. Many live in a *Lonely Crowd* where there is *No Exit.* Lewis Mumford's *The Culture of Cities* contains a brilliant chapter entitled, "A Brief Outline of Hell." In hell no community is possible, no meaningful fellowship, no personal relationships. Sartre magnificently displays his powers of penetration in *No Exit.* The one-act play is structured around three characters: (1) Garcin, a military coward who has been wounded; (2) Inez, a lesbian; and (3) Estelle, a nymphomaniac, who has murdered her own child. In this mirror of modern man, we learn that "hell" is other people.

The Principle of Hell

George Macdonald says—"The one principle of hell is— 'I am my own' " (G. Macdonald, *An Anthology,* London, 1946, p. 85). Radical individualism, whether 19th century or Ayn Rand type is an ultimate expression of alienation. The Church with its 20th century expression has failed to produce an alternative to isolation. Fellowship is a catch-all word for those who seek reduction of the anxiety caused by alienation through activities, all-be-it church activities. American pragmatic activism has all but paralyzed the American Church. Men have been programed to become islands of egocentricity, an island of tormenting loneliness and guilt.

1. Discuss Job's alienation from God, creation, others, and self.
2. Compare your own life with that of Job and list ranges of your most profound alienation.
3. Discuss the neo-Marxian Post-Bangkok W.C.C. attitudes toward economic and political causes of alienation.
4. Compare the biblical doctrines of sin and salvation with the most successful alternative in the history of the church—neo-Marxian theory that all alienation is economically caused; and therefore salvation becomes available only after the socio-politico-economic removal of the conditions which cause the *Horrors of Estrangement.*
5. For advanced students—compare the views of estrangement in *The Scriptures* Hegel, Marx, and contemporary neo-Marxists, e.g. Adorno, Horkheimer, Marcuse, et al.
6. Discuss major characteristics of *The Secular City*—anonymity—e.g. "I'll never forget what's his name."
7. Discuss present Eastern response to the problem of technologically led group alienation, e.g. TM, Hinduism, Zen Buddhism, and I Ching.

Bibliography on Estrangement

Istvan Meszaros, *Marx's Theory of Alienation*, Harper Torch, 1972, pb.

Leon Morris, *The Apostolic Preaching of the Cross,* Eerdmans, 1956, pb.

Richard Schacht, *Alienation,* Doubleday, 1971, pb.

Vincent Taylor, *Forgiveness and Reconciliation,* London, 1946.

DIALOGUE IN DESPAIR:
CONFRONTATION AND INTEGRITY

The word of the Lord came to me saying—Jer. 1:4

In the beginning was the word, and the word became flesh—Jn. 1:1, 14

Man that is born of a woman is of few days and full of trouble. Job 14:1

The Almighty has terrified me; for I am hemmed in by darkness. Job 23:17

How long will you say these things, and words of your mouth be a great wind? Job 8:1

His name will be called Wonderful, Counselor, . . . Isa. 9:6

Authoritative Word vs. Dialogue in Despair

Every time the church abandons God's authoritative Word, she enters dialogue with the world. There is a communication crisis both in and out of the church. Prior to the coming of media specialists, i.e., communication specialists, is the inevitable crisis in communication. We certainly live in McLuhan's "Global Village" which requires a word from outside our cultural malaise, if healing is to be affected.

Changing People's Lives

The purpose of dialogue is for effecting change; it is not for the mere sake of transferring information, or for mutual expression of feelings. If dialogue is to move us beyond despair, then correct diagnostic evaluation is imperative. Contemporary specialists in dialogue know the works and results of Mowrer, Glasser, Perls, Rogers, Harris, Lazarus, Erickson, or Skinner and these men are often known more thoroughly than Paul and Jesus. Often we meet an eclectic accommodation of the gospel in books entitled *Freud and Christ* or *Psychiatry and*

465

the Church, etc. Christ is often only syncretistically added to the clinical works of a Freud or Erickson, et al. But added to what? We must baptize Skinnerian Behaviorism, Piaget's Developmentalism, Rogerian Human Potential Movement or the Berne-Harris-Steiner views of transactional analysis into the body of Christ with utmost care. We must not approach the human need for healing with a "God-as-additive" approach. Pagan naturalism is gummed over by common grace in superficial works like Marian Nelson, *Why Christians Crack Up,* Moody, 1960; or Gary Collins', *Effective Counseling,* Creation House, 1972.

Crisis in Communication: Content and Relationships

Daniel Moynihan recently expressed a widely held opinion regarding the loss of an authoritative word from God in American preaching—"In some fifteen years of listening seriously I do not believe I have more than once or twice heard an interesting idea delivered from the pulpit of an American Church." (*Commonwealth,* July 1, 1966) No wonder we have entered a day of dialogue. Martin Buber's *Between Man and Man* and *I-Thou* present the most defensible approach to an existential viewpoint. Read Reuel L. Howe's *The Miracle of Dialogue* and discuss the following questions in light of Job's experience in contrast to your own.

1. Discuss five purposes of dialogue.
2. Discuss five fruits of dialogue.
3. Discuss five barriers to dialogue.
4. Discuss roles and masks in dialogue.
5. Discuss "contentless encounter" or the new relationalism.
6. Discuss how commitment to either truth or ideology might jeopardize dialogue.
7. Are all or most of our personal and social problems caused by a crisis in communication?
8. Discuss organization and development in the life of a mature, growing church.

Bibliography on Dialogue

Believers need to understand the implications of the loss of an *authoritative* word from God in the last quarter of the 20th century. In Homiletics, based on the new hermeneutics, see D. J. Randolph, *The Renewal of Preaching*, Philadelphia: Fortress Press, 1969, we encounter neo-personalism as the only effective method for communication. For a therapeutic theory of preaching and teaching see Clement Welsh, *Preaching in a New Key,* Philadelphia: Pilgrim Press, 1974, and Karl Menninger, *Whatever Became of Sin,* New York: Hawthorne Books, 1973; Reuel L. Howe, *The Miracle of Dialogue,* New York: Seabury Press, 1963; Walter Wink, *The Bible in Human Transformation,* Philadelphia: Fortress, 1973.

TRUSTING IN THE TRUTH:
INTEGRITY VS. HYPOCRICY

You shall know the truth, and the truth shall make you free. Jn. 3:31

Miserable comforters are you all—shall windy words have an end. Job 16:2, 3

They refused to love the truth and so be saved. II Thess. 1:10

I had heard of thee by the hearing of the ear, but now my eye sees thee. Job 42:6

Though he slay, yet will I trust him. Job 13:15

To Tell the Truth

Ernie Fitzgerald was a cost analyst for the Secretary of the Air Force. He told the truth about wasted billions on weapons systems, etc., and the government fired him. Can one man make a difference against the establishment in our society? Who can survive bucking the system? Ernie Fitzgerald and

Ralph Nader et al. are in the Jobian tradition of trusting in the truth. Yet in our age of *Sentio Ergo Sum* (I feel therefore I am) "truth" is doing your thing. For the philosopher, truth has its logical and ontological dimensions; for the historian, an historical truth, for the lawyer, the truth based in evidence. In our post-positivistic scientific era, science stands only at the edge of objectivity. Since the brilliant analysis of the late Michael Polanyi, science has been chastised for its earlier arrogance based on its unchallengable objectivity, after the collapse of the Unity of Science Movement and the development of Kurt Goedel's theorem which "proves" that even elementary numbers do not contain their own completeness or sufficiency proofs. The developments between Galileo and Newton removed God from the "truth" arena. Now even scientific method and number theories are adjudged to be dependent on presuppositions. If truth will set us free, it becomes imperative that we have some understanding of this freeing agent. Job did.

Trusting Beyond Evidence

The Hebrew word for truth (Heb. *emeth;* Greek *aletheia*) also means trust. Though we must challenge Martin Buber's analysis in his *Two Types of Faith*, we acknowledge that the biblical doctrine of truth entails more than facts and evidence. It means to trust the person of God, but never without some sign of His presence. Trust will not always demand proof, though this must not be carried as far as the late R. Bultmann does, when he asserts that a request for proof is a sign of unbelief. There is a biblical difference between blind gullibility and faithful trust.

Integrity vs. Hypocrisy

The word integrity comes from a root system meaning

468

integration or wholistic perspective. Hypocrisy does not necessarily imply conscious deception. Jesus said that "the Pharisees say and do not," meaning that they have no conscious correlation between theory and practice, saying and doing. Both Job and Jesus call for the unity of word and deed. The Greek word *kalos* means honest in the Latin sense of honest, i.e., winsome, attractive behavior—Matt. 5:16; Rom. 7:16; II Cor. 13:7; Gal. 6:9; I Thess. 5:21. Christian truth is more than telling the truth; it is making the truth attractive—Eph. 4:15. Paul tells us to do the truth (no Greek word for "speak" in the Greek text of Eph. 4:15). Job maintained his integrity in spite of everything. Jesus maintained His integrity all the way to the cross, and He is "the Way, the Truth, and the Life."

Truth, Health, and Wholeness

The Freudian "Ethic of Honesty" demands that we understand the inseparable relationship between truth, honesty, and our psychological well-being. Job and Jesus raise some very crucial questions.

1. Discuss "intellectual integrity" in a world of propaganda, power of manipulation, media, advertisement.
2. Discuss the alienating power of truth in light of Job and his three friends.
3. Discuss emotional health in view of truth, honesty, and wholeness.
4. Discuss Christ's attitude towards hypocrisy, e.g., role playing, etc.—Mk. 6:14; 2:27; 13:25-28.
5. Discuss the relationship between trust, evidence, proof, and faith.
6. Discuss—Can contemporary man "live" with his assumption that there is no truth, only pluralism? Can the world survive if this is true?

469

Bibliography on Truth

Paul S. Minear, "Yes or No: The Demand for Honesty in the Early Church," *Novum Testamentum,* 1971, pp. 1ff.

Rudolf Schnackenburg, *The Truth Will Make You Free,* New York: Herder and Herder, 1966.

James D. Strauss, article on "Honesty," *Baker's Dictionary of Christian Ethics,* ed. by C. F. H. Henry, Baker Book House, p. 297.

TETHERED TO TERROR: DESPAIR AND ANXIETY

There is none to deliver out of thy hand. Job 10:7

When I think of it I am dismayed, and shuddering seizes my flesh. Job 21:6

Today also my complaint is bitter, his hand is heavy in spite of my groaning, oh, that I knew where I might find him . . . Job 23:2, 3

The Almighty, who has made my soul bitter; . . . Job 27:2

We commend ourselves in every way; through great imprisonment, tumults, labors, watching, hunger; . . . II Cor. 6:4, 5

All flesh is like grass and all its glory like the flower of grass. "The grass withers, and the flower falls, but the word of the Lord abides forever." I Pet. 1:24-5; Isa. 40:6-9

Technology and our Global Odyssey

As our knowledge increases (recorded knowledge doubles every three and a half years) and technological prowess causes us to stand in awe, we find man *Tethered to Terror.* There seems to be no healing for our anxieties though the search has turned Eastward for its final failure. The post-World War II generation was the "Lost Generation" who lived between the turbulent forties and the gray-flanneled fifties.

470

Camelot appeared in the early 60's, only to die attempting to deliver the brave new world of the counter culture. The 60's was the generation of Woody Allen's *Sleeper* who believed only in *freedom* and *sex* and not *God* or *government*. (See Kenneth E. Boulding, *The Meaning of the 20th Century*, New York: Harper, 1965, and J. Ellul's, *Technological Society*, Doubleday, 1966, pb.).

Modern man is so frightened by his own potential powers of destruction that all mass-behavior is geared to the survival syndrome. The grim possibilities facing our global village necessitates that "We . . . choose now for survival through population control and global cooperation, or for destruction through short-sighted policies of waste and hatred." (Isaac Asimov) Spaceship Earth is rapidly moving to a condition of Red Alert. The curve of exponential growth—in population, agriculture, industry, and consumption of natural resources is leading western Jobian man on to cataclysm. Doomsday is to be warded off by bioengineering and vast international governmental combines. But man's environment (earth, air, water) is being contaminated faster than his technology can remove the metabolic poisons and pollutants that now befoul our air and water. All informed persons will respond with a high level of anxiety. Man is indeed Tethered to Terror. Is there hope in time of abandonment? Yes, for "He therefore who has learned rightly to be anxious has learned the most important thing" (Kierkegaard).

Fear and Trembling

In our highly complex world, discord causes an anxious dread of an unknown something. We dwell in disquietude. If our abundant life is to enjoy the health and vigor of the presence of the Holy Spirit we must sever the tether of terror. "One thing is certain, that the problem of anxiety is a nodal point, . . ." —Freud.

The Meaning of Anxiety

1. Discuss the relationship of freedom, defiance, and rebellion.
2. Discuss how anxiety destroys our freedom, i.e., reduces our possibilities for growth.
3. Discuss how sin, anxiety, and failure to grow in Kingdom matters are related.
4. Discuss how anxiety and inferiority feelings are related.
5. How might anxiety be related to non-rational dimensions of reality, e.g. occult?
6. How is anxiety related to interpersonal relations both individual and group?
7. Discuss anxiety and the present increase in psychosomatic illnesses, i.e., non-physical illnesses?
8. Discuss anxiety and competitive-aggressive cultures.

Bibliography on Anxiety/Dread

Rollo May, *The Meaning of Anxiety* (Ronald Press, NY, 1950).
Soren Kierkegaard, *The Concept of Dread; The Sickness Unto Death* (Doubleday, pb., 1954).
(See Kittel article, *merimna* words, i.e., rendered by anxiety and care roots; and the works of the late Tillich and Heidegger for analysis of "angst" or dread, especially Tillich's, *The Courage to Be* (Yale, 1953).

THE END OF INNOCENCE

"Think now, who that was innocent ever perished?" Job 4:7
"Move upward, working out the beast, and let the ape and tiger die." Tennyson's 19th century evolutionary naturalism.
"We make men without chests and expect of them virtue and enterprise. We laugh at honor and are shocked to find traitors in our midst." C. S. Lewis, *The Abolition of Man,* p. 14.

"For from within, out of the heart of man, come evil thoughts, fornication, theft, murder, adultery, coveting, wickedness, deceit, licentiousness, envy, slander, pride, foolishness. All these things come from within, and they defile a man" Mark 7:21-23.

Revenge and Irreverent Audacity

We know from our Jobian experience that evil is irrational; therefore no mere rational process will remove it from East of Eden. We live on Spaceship Earth at the end of innocence. Dostoevsky brilliantly relates how man will often, without any discoverable reason, do things completely absurd. He will upbraid the shortsighted fool who talks with excitement and passion about the significance of virtue by revenge and irreverent audacity. (See notes from *The Underground;* also John Steinbeck's novel, *East of Eden.*)

Freed from the Victorians

In the name of freedom what prophet could tell of the totalitarian tyrannies which would arise dedicated to the destruction of the very freedom which gave them birth? We live in a world of shattered illusions. The optimism of our brave new world has been repeatedly revisited. The sanctities of the past have been violated by the audacity of the *Counter Culture* which was conceived in the *Secular City.* Freedom at all costs—but absolute freedom is insanity. One thing that freedom cannot rid us of—is our guilt, or our guilt feelings. We are not innocent and cannot pronounce atonement for our sins. The atonement must be vicarious and commensurate with our guilt (see Romans and Galatians).

473

The Origin of Our Defect?

What is the origin of our social anomie? Is it environment, education, a defect in human nature? After the 19th century Marxian-Darwinian-Freudian revolution, men began to talk of the *human condition* rather than *human nature*. The powers of the scientific method could be applied to our "condition" and thus create new men, or so it was assumed. Job our contemporary knew, as we know, that our problem is a problem fit for God. "Things are now soul size, this time for exploration into God." Contemporary man agonizingly repeats Job's ancient lament—"Oh, that I knew where I might find him, . . ." Job 23:3. The omen of guilt hangs heavy over humanity; it is our cultural albatross.

Questions about Guilt and Innocence

1. Discuss how Job found relief from his guilt.
2. How are faith and repentance related to innocence?
3. Discuss God's gracious forgiveness in your own life.
4. Discuss the differences between Job and his three friends regarding the grounds of his innocence.
5. Discuss the contemporary behavioral science perspective that guilt is a myth.
6. How are love and mercy related to our innocence in Christ?
7. Discuss the conditions for our innocence in light of contemporary universalism and the ecumenical doctrine of *Christians anonymous*.
8. Do you think that man can heal himself? Discuss your reasons.

Bibliography on Innocence/Forgiveness

Woody Allen - (Cinema) - *The Sleeper*
F. Dostoevsky, *Notes from The Underground* (pb., many

474

editions).

James G. Emerson, *The Dynamics of Forgiveness* (Westminster, 1964).

William Klassen, *The Forgiving Community* (Westminster, 1966).

C. S. Lewis, *The Abolition of Man* (Oxford University Press, 1944) also MacMillan pb.

Wm. Golding, *The Lord of The Flies* (pb., 1960).

THE ENIGMA OF FREEDOM: RISK, SECURITY AND FREEDOM

"For freedom did Christ set you free." Galatians 5:1

"For he who has died is freed from sin . . . and having been set free from sin, have become slaves of righteousness." Romans 6:7, 18

"I have spoken once and I will not answer; twice, but I will proceed no further" Job 40:5—Job finds freedom in the will of God.

Search for Security

Job lived a prestigious life style until the "things" that make most men feel secure were removed. His family, prosperity and prestige are also our security blankets. Wealth provides a freedom from certain dimensions of reality. Once these are removed, we begin our Jobian journey, searching for our lost security. Freedom is essential for this pilgrimage, and freedom entails risk, and risk entails anxiety. How are we to break this endless cycle? Freud is correct in his analysis of Self-Investment. We invest ourselves in *others, things, self,* or some creative balance. In an effort to maintain this constructive balance, man meets the enigma of freedom. But contemporary man has an ambivalent feeling toward freedom, because he values security more than freedom.

Beyond Freedom

Paradoxically, B. F. Skinner "reasons" with man to abandon his myths of freedom and dignity. If these are mere illusions, they are the most constructive illusions in the history of human thought.

Faith and Risk

Job's faith in God enabled him to engage his freedom at a high risk level. His faith in God alone survived the onslaught of his suffering and heartache. Only when God Shattered His Silence out of the whirlwind did Job know in whom he had believed through all the hours of lonely darkness. Job reveals to modern man the powerful import of *the enigma of freedom.*

Discuss Our Jobian Freedom

1. Discuss how risk is related to being free.
2. Discuss how freedom can be the cause of anxiety.
3. Discuss how faith and freedom are related.
4. Discuss our American view of legal freedom, i.e., through *The Constitution, Bill of Rights,* etc., in the view of Christ.
5. Discuss the four basic freedoms in our American Heritage.
6. Discuss the view of freedom in Romans (1) *Freedom from wrath*—Chp. 5; (2) *From Sin*—chp. 6; (3) *From the Law*—chp. 7; and (4) *From death*—chp. 8; (5) Freedom *to serve* in the realization of God's purpose in history—chps. 12-16.

Bibliography on Freedom

M. Adler, ed., *Idea of Freedom,* 2 vols. reprint of original (Doubleday).

Jacques Ellul, *The Ethics of Freedom* (Eerdmans, 1976); *The Politics of God and The Politics of Man* (Eerdmans, pb.).

D. Nestle, *Eleutheria: Freiheit bei den Griechen und im Neuen Testament,* 1967/2 Bd.

G. Niederwimmer, *Der Begriff der Freiheit im Neuen Testament* (Berlin, 1966).

Clark Pinnock, ed., *Grace Unlimited* (Bethany Fellowship Press, 1975).

MIND-FORGED MANACLES: GRACE AND GUILT

"In all this Job did not sin or charge God with wrong" Job 1:22

"O that my vexation were weighed, and all my calamity laid in the balances!" Job 6:2

"I had heard of thee by the hearing of the ear, but now my eye sees thee; therefore I despise myself, and repent in dust and ashes." Job 42:6

"Have mercy on me, O God, according to thy steadfast love; according to thy abundant mercy blot out my transgressions." Ps. 51:1

Struggle for Reign

Goethe makes Faust say, "Two souls, alas! are log'd within my breast, which struggle there for undivided reign" Eichmann declared at his Jerusalem trial—"I am not guilty." Who then was guilty? Job, our contemporary, also struggled between guilt and grace (see Paul Tournier's, *Guilt and Grace*). Which shall it be?—Menninger's *Man Against Himself,* or Jung's *Man In Search of a Soul.*

Fact and Feeling

There are certain extreme conditions in which the sense of guilt appears to be completely lacking. The "psychopathic personality" is well known in psychiatric practice and in our law courts. This type of person is emotionally immature and generally accepts no responsibility for his or her own acts. The paranoid also locates all faults, sins, and problems outside of himself. Whatever happens, it is always someone elses fault. It is true that some overly-sensitive people have a disproportionate sense of guilt arising from trivial behavior, but there is objective guilt. All guilt cannot be reduced to guilt feeling and thus removed by depth psychology. Guilt often creates a feeling of helplessness mingled with dread. The resultant disaster can open the door for the healing grace of God.

Symptoms of Guilt

Some of the symptoms of guilt are: (1) *self-rehabilitation* through appeasement; (2) *self-righteousness* or super-religious goodness; (3) *self-concealment* or withdrawal; (4) *self-contraction* because internal forces are unmanageable; (5) *self-expansion* which magnifies the guilt of others; (6) *self-punishment;* and (7) *self-disintegration,* e.g. Judas in John 13. Another large group of disorders fall under the category of psychoses. Carl Whitaker compares neuroses and psychoses to two different conditions of a camel. *Neuroses* nearly broke the camel's back, but by rearrangement of the straws the camel is able to function. In *psychoses,* the camel's back is broken, and thus cannot function. In Job's life, God speaks and reveals His healing grace which frees him of his mind-forged manacles.

Questions

1. Discuss Job's mental health at various stages of his suffering.
2. Discuss any behavioral symptoms of guilt found in Job's life.
3. Discuss the conditions under which Job accepted God's forgiveness.
4. Discuss the relationship of righteousness, wholeness, and suffering.
5. Discuss the characteristics of "real guilt" and "guilt feelings."
6. Discuss the place of grace in the healing processes of life.

Bibliography

Samuel J. Mikolaski, *The Grace of God* (Eerdmans, pb., 1966).

James Moffatt, *Grace in the New Testament* (London, 1932).

Henri Rondet, *The Grace of Christ* (Newman Press, E.T., 1967).

Lewis J. Sherrill, *Guilt and Redemption* (Richmond: John Knox Press, revised edition, 1957).

THE MORTAL NO: DEATH AND DYING

"If a man die, shall he live again?" Job 14:14

"For I know that my vindicator lives, and at last he will stand upon the earth." Job 19:25

"And Job died, an old man, and full of days." Job 42:17

"I am the resurrection and the life." John 11:25

"Why is it thought incredible by any of you that God raises the dead?" Acts 26:8

"By his great mercy we have been born anew to a living hope through the resurrection of Jesus Christ from the dead, . . ." I Peter 1:3

479

Resurrection - The Heart of Hope

Job was resigned to the grave. His only ultimate hope was in a vindicator. This is the very condition in which we all find ourselves. The heart of the gospel is the resurrection of Jesus from the grave. One of the creative architects of contemporary theology and denier of the historical resurrection of Jesus, R. Bultmann, at 92 has now been called into His presence to test the ultimate power of his theology. Without resurrection man only hopes against hope.

God's Eucatastrophe

Tolkien has brilliantly employed the ancient myths of resurrection as an apologetic tool. Though others aspired to resurrection in myth, only in Jesus is the resurrection a historical reality. "There was never a myth that men would rather have true than the resurrection from the dead." It is only in the Christian gospel that hope now has historical justification. All the recent emphasis by the *Theologians of Hope* is futile, if God has not raised Jesus from the dead.

Resurrection and the Recovery of Wholeness

The hope of Job our contemporary was vindicated by the word of God, which broke His Silence and His Absence from Job's human situation. Yet it is in such a world that has witnessed the resurrection that contemporary man is neurotically preoccupied with death. Since the publication of E. Kuber-Ross' *Death and Dying* there has been an epidemic of literature on the ultimate barrier to man's self-conquest—Death. Stoic resignation cannot quench man's desire for life after the grave. Humanity's survival does not satisfy the lure of life.

480

Challenging the Mortal No

1. Discuss how hope comforts the terminally ill Christian.
2. What reasons can you give for believing in the resurrection?
3. How and why is Christ's resurrection the basis of our hope?
4. What are your attitudes toward death? What or who is the origin of your attitude?
5. Discuss hope, resurrection, and artificial life support systems.
6. Discuss suffering, evil, hope, and resurrection.

Bibliography on Death/Dying

D. Culter, ed., *Updating Life and Death* (Beacon Press, pb.).

F. J. Hoffman, *The Mortal No: Death and Modern Imagination* (Princeton, 1964).

E. Kuber-Ross, *Death and Dying, and Questions and Answers on Death and Dying* (MacMillan Collier Books, 1974).

Jean Laplanche, *Life and Death in Psychoanalysis* (John Hopkins University Press, 1976).

J. D. Strauss, *The Seer, the Savior, and the Saved* (Joplin, Mo.: College Press, 1972 edition) Extensive bibliography; see also full bibliography on *Death,* Concordia Press.

FACES OF FRIENDSHIP: HEALING PRESENCE

"If one ventures a word with you, will you be offended?" Eliphaz (Job 4:2)

"How long will you say these things, and the words of your mouth be a great wind?" Bildad (Job 8:2)

"Should a multitude of words go unanswered, and a man full of talk be vindicated?" Zophar (Job 11:2)

"Hear my words, you wise men, and give ear to me, you who know; for the ear tests words as the palate tastes food."

Elihu (Job 34:2, 3)

"Who is this that darkens counsel by words without knowledge?" Yahweh (Job 38:2)

"And Jonathan made David swear again by his love for him; for he loved him as he loved his own soul." I Samuel 20:17

"You are my friends if you do what I command you. . . . I have called you friends, . . ." John 15:15

A Warm Word

Job's three counselors hardly revealed compassion to a friend in need. Their identification with him was through a paralyzingly legalistic tradition-bound response. They located all of Job's woes in some unconfessed secret sin. If he would but recognize this fact and repent, God would restore His blessings. Of all the words used in the scriptures to express human relations—friend is one of the warmest. The most affectionate regard for another is expressed by the Greek noun philia and the verb philein. Our English word cherish is perhaps the closest to its meaning—Matt. 10:37; Jn. 11:3, 20:2. Jesus, Job's vindicator, elevated friendship to its highest form.

The marvelous friendship of David and Jonathan endures trials and heartbreak—I Samuel 18:1-4; 19; 20; II Samuel 1:25ff. Their relationship was so powerful and vivid that it could not be erased from the memory of the heart—II Samuel 9:1; 21:7.

Birds of a Feather

Why do the rich seem to have so many friends, and the poor, the sick, and the persecuted have so few—Prov. 14:20; Pss. 38:12; 55:13f; 88:19; 109:4f; Job 19:19? Many friendships produce only sad experiences. The choice of friends will reveal our ultimate values. Friendship may be sincere—Job 2:12f, but deceiving—Job 6:15-30. Some friendships are even able to draw one into the devil's snare—Deut. 13:7; II Sam. 13:3-15. Friendship with this present world is enmity against God. When God is removed new demons take up residence—J. Ellul, *The New Demons* (Seabury, 1976).

True Faces of Real Friends

God's model of true friendship is always relevant. Abraham was a friend of God—Gen. 18:17ff; Isa. 41:8, so was Moses— Ex. 33:11, and the prophets—Amos 3:7. Jesus has given friendship a face of flesh—Mk. 10:21; Jn. 11:3, 35f. He has many companions (*hetairos*)—Mk. 3:14, but a few friends (*philos*)—Matt. 26:50; Jn. 15:15. His friends share His trials, heartaches, and joys. They are also prepared to face the night of His passion. Jesus created a perfect friendship, something completely lacking in Job's circle of friends. What of you and your friends?

Questions on Friendship/Presence

1. Describe five characteristics of Job's friends.
2. Describe five characteristics of Jesus' friends.
3. Describe five characteristics of your friends.
4. Discuss five differences between Christian and non-Christian friendships.

Bibliography on Friendship

Yves Congar, *The Mystery of The Temple* (London: Burns & Oates, 1962).
Kittel article on "philia" or friend-friendship.
J. D. Strauss, "Is Job's God in Exile?" *The Shattering of Silence* (College Press), for the "presence of God."

CELEBRATION OF WONDER

"His name is *wonder*." Isaiah 9:6

"And the Lord restored the fortunes of Job when he had prayed for his friends; and the Lord gave Job twice as much as he had before." Job 42:10

"The sense of wonder that is our sixth sense." D. H. Lawrence

"Count it all joy, my brethren." "Rejoice, again I say, rejoice." "The fruit of the spirit is . . . joy . . ."

The Great Celebration

What did Job have to celebrate? What do we have to celebrate in a world filled with hate and hunger? Our Jobian cries have been heard and God has broken His Silence. Yet we live in an age of unprecedented human need and search for significance. But only if Job's God is not in exile can there be ultimate meaning to life. "God does not die on the day when we cease to believe in a personal deity, but we die on the day when our lives cease to be illuminated by the steady radiance, renewed daily, of a wonder, the source of which is beyond all reason" (Dag Hammarskjold, *Markings,* p. 56). As believers in Job's vindicator, we ask "what power is it that draws man's mind up through wonder into joy" (Henry Van Dyke). Our joy is based in Him who is the "wonder" of wonders. Believers in the one who Shattered Silence out of the whirlwind have reason to celebrate, but Zorba the Greek only celebrates to a mute Dionysius.

Job's Vindicator and a Dionysian Manifesto

The Apollian way maintains that man is the molder of his environment. His will and intellect are dominant forces. His authentic life is gained by aggression, and his values are created by his action. The Dionysian manifesto forces man to *dance*

484

rather than *think.* His central preoccupation is the gratification of his sensual urges. His values are "created" through his passive encounter of the world in wonder. God's Wonder is the third way. His name is wonder—Isaiah 9:6! In Job's redeemer we have the power which excites to celebration which meets our need for joy, is our source of joy, and object of our expression of joy. Jesus is our joy. He is the cause of our celebration—The celebration of wonder. Yes, Plato was right, all real learning begins in wonder.

Questions on Wonder

1. Discuss Job's rediscovered sense of wonder.
2. List three reasons that you have to celebrate God's precious promises.
3. Discuss the relationship of *hope* and *wonder.*
4. Have you lost the sense of awe? Discuss how our culture has moved from awe to awwww!
5. How is suffering related to celebration?
6. How are wonder, grace, and gratitude related?
7. Discuss the relationship of gratitude and the mystery of God's grace.
8. Discuss the rhetoric of gratitude—worship and praise.
9. How does repentance open the door of appreciation for God's redeeming mercy expressed in Job's vindicator?

Bibliography of Wonder

Dag Hammarskjold, *Markings* (NY: A. A. Knopf, 1964).
Sam Keen, *Apology for Wonder* (NY: Harper, p. 69).
Maurice Merleau-Ponty, *In Praise of Philosophy* (Evanston: Northwestern University Press, 1963).
Psychology Today, "The Pursuit of Happiness," pp. 26ff. Compare and discuss the similarities and dissimilarities of "happiness" and "joy."

Theological Essays:
Theology and Therapy
in
Job

IX. *THE GOD WHO SHATTERED THE SILENCE: THEOLOGY OF THE BOOK OF JOB.*

IS GOD IN EXILE?: JOB'S GOD IS THE CREATOR AND REDEEMER OF THE UNIVERSE.

God
Creation (Nature-History)

IS JOB'S GOD IN EXILE?

"In the book of Jeremiah, the king Zedekiah asks the prophet, 'Is there any word from the Lord?' Our times are haunted and disturbed by a more basic question, 'Is there a Lord?' "[1] During the past three centuries, there has ingressed into western thought five species of atheism. Job, our contemporary, was a monotheist in the Abrahamic and Mosaic tradition. Even in the furnace of affliction he held to his faith and never questioned God's existence, only His justice. But the 20th century Christian belief in God has been confronted with the most sustained attack in the history of the church. The

---

[1] Georg Siegmun, *God on Trial* (Desclee, E.T., 1967 on *Der Kampf um Gott.*). See Bavinck, Herman. *The Doctrine of God.* Eerdmans, 1951.
Burkle, Howard R. *The Non-Existence of God.* New York: Herder and Herder, 1969.
Collins, James. *God im Modern Philosophy.* Chicago: Henry Regnery Co., 1967.
Cottier, G. M. M. *Horizons de L'Atheisme.* Paris: Les Editions du Cerf, 1969.
Dewart, Leslie. *The Future of Belief.* New York: Herder and Herder, 1968.
Fabro, Cornelio. *God in Exile.* New York: Newman Press, 1968.
Luijpen, William A. *Phenomenology and Atheism.* Pittsburgh: Duquesne University Press, 1964.
Marty, Martin E. *The Infidel.* New York: Meridian Books, pb., 1961.
_____. *Varieties of Unbelief.* New York: Doubeday, pb., 1964.
Mascall, E. L. *The Secularization of Christianity.* Holt, Rinehart, Winston, 1965.
Matha, Ved. *Les Theologians de la Mort de Dieu.* Paris: Mame, 1965.
Mooney, S. J. Christopher F., eds. *The Presence and Absence of God.* New York: Fordham University Press, 1969.
Novak, Michael. *Belief and Unbelief.* New York: Mentor-Omega, pb., 1965.
Reid, J. P. *Man Without God.* New York: Corpus, 1971.
Schrey, Simon, etc. *L-Atheisme Contemporain.* Paris: Editions Labor et Fides Geneve, 1964, III Tomes.
Hamilton, Kenneth. *To Turn From Idols.* Grand Rapids: Eerdmans, 1973.
Encyclopedia of Philosophy, Paul Edwards, ed. New York: MacMillan Pub., 4 volumes.

confrontation has been sustained since the 17th century. Contemporary unbelief cannot be evaluated without knowing the five major species of modern atheism. These five forms of atheism must be evaluated before its Promethean spirit can be effectively challenged. They are: (1) *Scientific Atheism* had its origins in the intellectual revolution from Galileo, Kepler, Newton, and Comte (Sociological Positivism). As the social sciences developed, God became absent as a necessary condition for "explanation." (2) *Psychological Atheism* is grounded in Freud's theory of projection, i.e., religion and belief in a personal transcendent creator-redeemer is "caused" by illusion. (3) *Social Atheism* finds expression in Marx's social, economic, and political explanation of the origins of the dehumanization of man, i.e., the fact of human alienation. (4) *Moral Atheism* actually begins with Kant and finds its highest form in Nietzsche. If man is to be moral, he must be free; if he is to be free, he must be free from God; therefore, man's morality is contingent on the Death of God. (5) *Anthropological Atheism* is expressed by Sartre and Merleau-Ponty and Levi Strauss, *et al.* They maintain that if man is to become truly human, he must be free from God once and for all. This search for the fountain of humanization sends out seekers as diverse as Sartre and the Marcuse, and all the contemporary Neo-Marxists from the *Frankfurt School of Social Research,* Frankfurt, Germany.[2]

"That men may know that thou, whose name alone is Yahweh, art the most high over all the earth." Ps. 83:18.

Crisis in Communication

But another nominalistic crisis is upon western man.[3]

---

[2] See my Seminar syllabus, *The Biblical Doctrine of God,* for extensive analysis and bibliography, which compares the biblical heritage with each step in the development of contemporary unbelief.

[3] There has been a basic cultural crisis five times in western civilization, and each time there has been a communication crisis caused by nominalism: (1) During

Nominalism maintains that there is no necessary connection between "words" and "things," i.e., reality. Two very crucial implications of nominalistic assumptions for the Christian belief in God are (1) Man can never receive any final, propositional, personal, rational, and authoritative revelation in linguistic form from God, even if He exists; and (2) God cannot possess a name which communicates His true nature. But the history of western philosophical thought confirms the fact that God has not been without a name. The deity nomenclature in the great creative philosophical literature abounds with names for God., e.g. Socrates' *"Daimon,"* Plato's *"Idea of the good,"* Aristotle's *"Prime Mover,"* Plotinus' *"One,"* Spinoza's *"Causa Sui,"* Hegel's *"absolute geist,"* Nietzsche's *"Ubermensch,"* and Sartre's *transcendental Ego,* though his is a purely human god. These names are often contradictory, and in contrast to the biblical names they are purely of human origin. One need not be Harvard Phi Beta Kappa to understand that when cultures have "communication specialists," crisis has already dawned upon that civilization. Australian Bushmen have no "communication specialists" because they have no communication crisis, and our crisis is more profound than a mere accumulation of data. Recorded knowledge doubles every three and one-half years. The crisis is not merely one of ignorance. We are living in the McLuhan's global village, where there are two communication options, either *hot* or *cold.* Successful media penetration requires "cold," i.e., contentless communication. Prime time TV is almost always entertainment, not information oriented. (Prime time TV costs ca. $18,000 per minute.) Few prophets of "hot" communication

---

Greek culture, 4th and 3rd centuries B.C.; (2) During Roman Empire, 4th to 5th centuries A.D.; (3) During the Medieval Nominalist Controversy, 12th to 13th centuries; (4) In the 17th century after the assent of empirically based epistemology and semantics; and (5) During the 20th century when science and relativistic linguistics generated the world of Wittgenstein, *et al.* The language game acknowledges that we use language according to rules, and there can be contradictory sets of rules. We are banished to the world of Alice in Blunder Land where words mean what the user wants them to mean. Pluralism is the basis of cultural chaos, and nominalism is necessary for pluralism.

have popular audiences; in fact, so few do that they exemplify an empty class. Our culture knows what one means by "Coke," Johnny Carson, the Yankees, but not God. Yet, if God exists, knowing Him and having information *about* His will and purpose would constitute the most significant knowledge available to man. It is no accident that *God* is a cultural unmentionable. Some of us are most grateful that to Job the nature of God is of utmost significance for daily life, and not as a theoretical theistic dialogue with a world of unbelievers.

Job's God was not "named" by progressive speculative insight, but by progressive divine disclosure. As Vos asserts, there is a history in the revelation of God's names. "Certain divine names belong to certain stages of revelation. They serve to sum up the significance of a period."[4] In the same vein, Brunner declares that "The hidden center of the revelation of the Old Testament is the name of God." The name means: God Himself is the One who makes Himself known.[5] In scripture, a name is a description of the person bearing it. The Hebrew word *-shem* probably means sign or signum (cf. Greek *onoma* and Latin *nomen;* Abraham—Gen. 17:5; Israel—32:38; Joshua—Num. 13:16). He broke His silence in creation, then again as He reveals His name. Contemporary man interprets God's *silence* as being synonymous with His *absence.* But in another age of injustice, Amos declares that God's silence is His judgment on His disobedient people. "Behold the days are coming," says the Lord God, "when I will send a famine on the land; not a famine of bread, nor a thirst for water, but of hearing the words of the Lord. They shall wander from sea to sea, and from north to east; they shall run to and fro, to seek the word of the Lord, but they shall not find it," Amos 8:11ff (A. V.) He had withdrawn His presence, not because *He was dead* but because *His people were.* Another prophet

---

[4] G. Vos, *Old and New Testament Biblical Theology* (Eerdmans, 1948), p. 40.

[5] E. Brunner, *Revelation and Reason* (Westminster, 1946), pp. 88ff; see also Karl Barth's first edition of his classic *Kirkliche Dogmatik,* Vol. I, *The Doctrine of the Word of God,* p. 347.

to the spiritually deaf was Hosea. He fearlessly rebuked the apostate people of Israel, but to no avail. Then God reveals to Israel that His most serious judgment upon them will be when they cannot find him. "For I will be like a lion to Ephraim, and like a young lion to the house of Judah. I, even I, will rend and go away, I will carry off, and none shall rescue. I will return to my place, until they acknowledge their guilt and seek my face, and in their distress they seek me saying 'Come, let us return to the Lord,' " Hosea 5:14—6:1. Jesus of Nazareth, God's ultimate shattering of silence, encountered a Canaanite woman. Three times she begged Him to help her. At last he breaks His silence in her healing—"O woman great is your faith!" Matt. 15:21-28. But His loudest silence was before Pilate. The ultimate Word was silent—Matt. 27:14.[6] God's name signifies His presence. Briefly we will discuss two issues: (1) How does the Old Testament describe God? and (2) What names for God are specifically employed in *The Book of Job?*[7] God was present in a special way wherever the "name of Yahweh" was. The last development of this theology came when Judaism evolved the notion of the *Shekinah*, "the dwelling," which is an attempt to express the gracious presence of God amid Israel without taking anything away from his transcendence. The sovereignty of God is what gives the Old Testament its unifying power. There can be no defensible claim concerning an evolutionary development of the person of God in the Old Testament. To speak of Israel is to speak of a people who are called and covenanted to Yahweh creator-redeemer of the universe. The existence of God is never questioned in the Old Testament, only His sovereignty. Fools say "there is no God"—Ps. 14:1; 53:2; Job 2:10. Jeremiah also speaks to unfaithful Israelites who deny God's sovereignty

---

[6] In my following essay, *Silence, Suffering and Sin: Present Evil in His Presence,* we will discuss the biblical doctrine of the *presence* of God, in relationship to both His *absence* and His *silence.*

[7] See the great work of Jean Leveque, *Job et Son Dieu* (Tome I, Paris, 1970), pp. 146-179.

by saying "It is not he," 5:12. But even apostate Israel was not atheistic, only rebellious. He is a "living God" (el hay, elohim hayyim)[8] which differentiates Yahweh from all other gods in Israel's *Sitz im Leben*. The faith of Israel is a full monotheism. Because God is a "living God," we can express in anthropomorphic terms true but non-exhaustive dimensions of the nature of God. F. Michaeli correctly asserts that "the idea of a living God gives to the anthropomorphism of the Bible a significance quite other than that which applies to similar expressions about pagan idols . . . it is because God is living that one can speak of him as of a living man, but also in speaking of him as of a human being one recalls continually that he is living."[9] The names of God can reveal His true nature, but cannot exhaust His transcendent nature. One does not need total knowledge to have correct knowledge about either God or man.[10]

---

[8] For examination of the most extensively used names for God, see Ludwig Koehler, *Old Testament Theology* (Westminster, E.T., 1957), pp. 30-58; H. H. Rowley, *The Faith of Israel* (Westminster, 1956), pp. 50-73; Edmond Jacob, *Theology of the Old Testament* (Harper, E.T., 1958), pp. 43-67; Paul Heinisch, *Theology of the Old Testament* (Liturgical Press, 1955), pp. 36ff; G. von Rad, *Theology of the Old Testament,* 2 vols., 1965; Paul van Imschoot, *Theology of the Old Testament,* Vol. I; God, 1965; W. Eichrodt, *The Theology of the Old Testament,* 2 vols., Vol. I, 1961, Vol. II, 1967. For the relationship between the "name" of God, "human language," and the hermeneutical problem raised by anthropomorphis, see H. M. Kuitert, *Gott in Menchengestalt Eine dogmatisch-hermeneutische Studie uber die anthropomorphismen der Bibel,* 1967; F. Michaeli, *Dieu a l'image de l'homme etude sur la notion anthropomorphique de dieu dans l'ancien Testament,* 1950; W. Vischer, "Words and the Word, The Anthropomorphisms of the biblical revelation," *Interpretation,* 1949, pp. 1ff; J. Hempel, *Die Grenzen des Anthropomorphismus Jahwes in alten Testament Zeitschrift für alttestamentlischen Wissenschaften,* 1939, p. 75; Charles T. Fritsch, *The Anti-Anthropomorphisms of the Greek Pentateuch* (Princeton, 1943).

[9] F. Michaeli, *Dieu a l'image de l'homme,* p. 147; see also O. Grether, *Name und Wort Gottes in A. T.,* 1933.

[10] This is a fundamental error in Barth. His view of God's sovereignty is apriori. If God is actually sovereign, then let Him define His sovereignty, i.e., the nature and extent of His transcendence in relationship to His immanence.

Job's Redeemer[11]

The four names used for God in the Book of Job are: (1) *El,* (2) *Elohim,* (3) *Shaddai,* and (4) *Yahweh. El* is used in the Book of Job by Elihu 19 times, by Eliphaz 8, Bildad 6, and Zophar 2 (a total of 55 times). It is the most common and certainly the earliest description for God among all Semitic peoples except the Ethiopians, and means *might* or *power.* It appears in many compound forms in the Old Testament. *El* is the usual word for God in the Ugaritic texts from Ras Shamra. But Israel's *El* and the Canaanite El are simlar in name only,[12] Gen. 14:18; 16:13; 21:33; 35:3; 49:25; Ex. 20:5; Jos. 24:19; Deut. 7:9, 21; 32:4. But when the term is applied to God, the article occurs—46:3; Ps. 68:20; or some modifier, eg. *el'olam*—Gen. 21:33, *el hay*—Jer. 3:10, *el beth el*—Gen. 35:7. The appearance of *El* in the materials from Job's three friends merely sustains the widespread appearance of the description.

Elohim is probably a plural form of *El,* and thus has the meaning of force or power. The name appears in the Tell-el-Amarna and Ras Shamra documents. When Elohim designates the true God, generally the modifiers and following verbs are in the singular—Jos. 24:19; I Sam. 17:26; Gen. 20:13; also the Creation narrative; Ex. 32:4, 8. Yahweh alone is the *ha-elohim*—Deut. 4:35, 39. Idols, too, are called elohim—Ex. 20:23. And the pagan gods are also Elohim—Ex. 12:12; I Sam. 5:7. Judges, too, are called Elohim (note Jesus' quotation of the Psalm, "I called you gods; this matter has nothing to do with the often disseminated nonsense that God is a family, e.g. Mormonism and Armstrongism). An especially powerful description of God is *-elohey ha elohim*—God of

---

[11] Elohim is used 41 times, Shaddai 31 times, which only occurs 17 other times in the Old Testament, and 55 times El, El-Elohim only once—12:8; and Yahweh in chapters 1, 2, 38:13; 40; 42, 31 times.

[12] See M. H. Pope, *El in the Ugaritic Texts* (Leiden, 1955); compare with A.S. Kapelrud, *Baal in the Ras Shamra Texts* (Copenhagen, 1952).

gods—Deut. 10:17.[13]

The third name which appears in Job is *Shaddai*. This name appears most frequently in the patriarchal narratives and Job—Gen. 43:14; 49:25. In Ex. 6:3 God says that "I appeared unto Abraham, unto Isaac, and unto Jacob as el shaddai," and in Gen. 17:1 "The Lord appeared to Abraham, and said unto him, I am el-shaddai; walk before me and be thou perfect." (See the play on words in Isa. 13:6 and Joel 1:15.) In Gen. 49:24, 25 *shaddai*[14] is parallel to *'abbir*, the Mighty one, so probably the root means the all-powerful one, the Almighty (Latin trans. as omnipotence, and LXX as pantocrator).

The fourth and final name to appear in Job is *Yahweh*.[15] God is called Yahweh over 6700 times in the Old Testament. Yahweh is not both designation and name as Baal is. Baal can mean a possessor, but Yahweh is only a name; technically it is God's only name, the others are designations. We find many appendages to the name: Yahweh God of Israel, Yahweh Sabaoth, etc. The name Yahweh or the tetragrammaton (from its four consonants) is never used of false gods as are the names El, Elohim, Eloah—Isa. 42:8. In Ex. 3:14, 15 the name is derived from -*hawah*, thus the meaning of Yahweh is probably "to be," i.e., the one who is. In this classic passage of scripture we are told that God was known as El Shaddai in the past, but now by His name Yahweh. It was through Mosaic revelation that God became known as Yahweh. The root analysis

---

[13] Though it is an "establishment assumption" that the various names for God actually reflect different documents, redactors and theologies, in reality this type of subjective analysis belongs to the area of Creative Literature rather than scientific exegesis.

[14] W. F. Albright, "The Names Shaddai and Abram," *JBL*, 1935, p. 173; and A. Alt, *Der Gott der Vater*, 1929.

[15] E. Dhorme, "Le nom du dieu d'Israel," *Revue de l'histoire des religions*, 1952, p. 5; A. Murtonen, "The Appearance of the name YHWH outside Israel," *Studia Orient Society* (Helsinki, 1951); J. Obermann, "The Divine name YHWH in Light of Recent Discoveries," *JBL*, 1949, p. 301; G. Lambert, "Que signifie le nom divin YHWH?" *Nouvelli revue theologique* (Louvain), 1952, p. 897; R. de Langhe, "Un dieu Yahweh a Ras Shamra," *Bulletin d'histoire et d'exegese de l'A. T.* (Louvain, 1942), p. 91; A. M. Dubarle, "La signification du nom de Yahweh," *Revue des sciences philosophiques et theologiques*, 1951, p. 3.

of the name Yahweh of Driver, Albright, Buber, *et al.,* is technically not unimportant but adds little more than can be expected of speculative linguistics. Though Albright's position is the more probable, he maintains that Yahweh could be a hiphil form of the verb *hawa,* so Abermann, but up until now they know of no example of *hawah* in the hiphil, though there is no necessary linguistic reason why we need more than the one before us in Ex. 3:14, 15.[16] In the *Book of Job,* only Job employs the name Yahweh, which is consistent with the assumption that he is a son of the covenant. His three friends use *El, Eloah,* and *Shaddai* interchangeably in the dialogues. God is described by many other terms in the scriptures, some of which are (1) the God of the Father[17]—Gen. 26:24; 28:13; Ex. 3:6 and throughout Deuteronomy; (2) *Jahweh Sabaoth*[18] does not appear from Genesis to Judges, nor Isaiah 56-66, Ezekiel, Ezra, Nehemiah, Joel, Obadiah, Jonah, Proverbs, Job, Song of Solomon, Ruth, Lamentations, Ecclesiastes, Esther, Daniel, and II Chronicles. It appears 77 times in Jeremiah, 14 times in Haggai, 44 times in Zechariah 1-8, 9 times in Zechariah 9-14, and 24 times in Malachi. Sabaoth (occurs 279 times in the Old Testament) probably means a leader who summons armies; (3) He is the *Holy God* of Israel— Num. 6:8; Neh. 8:9; Lev. 21:6; Hos. 12:6; Amos 3:13; Jer. 5:14; Ps. 89:9. Holy is at once exalted, supreme, and fearful. It reveals God's attitude toward sin and His demand for a holy life; (4) Yahweh is the *Living God*—I Sam. 17:26, 36; Isa. 37:4, 17; esp. Deut. 5:26; Jos. 3:10; and Ps. 42:2; (5) He is the *Terrible God*—Isa. 10:33; Jer. 20:11; Ps. 89:8; (6) God is also called *Baal,* a very common name among the Semites— Hos. 2:10, 15, 19. Names compounded with Baal disappear after the time of David. Hosea requested that Israel no longer

---

[16] See his *From the Stone Age to Christianity,* p. 198; also *JBL,* 1924, p. 370; and his *Yahweh and the Gods of Canaan,* pb. (Doubleday, Anchor).

[17] A. Alt, *Der Gott der Vater,* 1929; and G. van Rad, *Der heilige Krieg im alten Israel.*

[18] B. N. Wambacq, *L'epithete divine Yahweh sabaoth* (Paris, 1947).

use the word Baal to designate Yahweh as her husband—Hos. 2:18, 19;[19] (7) *God of the Heavens* was used often during and after the Persian period, but note also Gen. 24:3; Dan. 4:23. He is also referred to as the *Mighty One of Jacob, Rock of Israel, Fear of Isaac*—Gen. 31:42, 53; (8) *King* is another common name among the Semites. In Israel Melek[20] was applied to God as early as the time of Moses—Num. 23:21; 24:7, 8. Gideon rejected the concept of kingship for himself, because "Yahweh is your king"—Judges 8:22, 23; I Sam. 8:6ff. After the establishment of the Kingdom, the ruler was Yahweh's representative. The later prophets battled with the Canaanite Melekh, who later reappeared—Isa. 43:15; Zech. 14:16; Mal. 1:14. Even in slavery, Israel believed that Yahweh remained her king. This is a very important insight of Israel's suffering and God's sovereignty.

We will conclude this brief study by returning to the name Yahweh, because He was Job's God. The name occurs in several compound forms in the concrete context of Israel's historic experience (1) *Yahweh-Jireh* (verb to see) appears in Gen. 22:8 where the verb is translated Yahweh shall provide, or see to it; (2) In Ex. 15:22-26 *Yahweh-Rophe* (verb "heals") describes the triumph which is the origin of the victory song; (3) In Ex. 17:15 *Yahweh-Nissi* describes the presence of Yahweh in times of crisis. The compound means Yahweh my banner; (4) Yahweh sanctifies His people, and in Lev. 20:8 He is called

---

[19] Names compounded with Baal inscribed on the ostraca of Samaria from the time of Jeroboam are certainly from Baal worshippers; see Prichard, ed., *Ancient Near Eastern Texts* (Princeton), p. 321; compare also with A. S. Kapelrud, *Baal in the Ras Shamra Texts* (Copenhagen, 1952). Some of Baal's names were Baal-Hadad, Baal-Zebul, Baal-peor, Baal-Sidon, Baalbek, *et al.*

[20] There is no "necessary proof" that Israel borrowed the Enthronement concept from her neighbors, but see on Near Eastern parallels I. Engnell, *Studies in the Divine Kingship in the Ancient Near East* (Upsala, 1943); H. Frankfort, *Kingship and the Gods* (Chicago, 1948); J. Gray, "Canaanite Kingship in Theory and Practice," *Vetus Testamentum* 1952, pp. 193-220; S. Mowinckel, *Studies in the Psalms*, 2 vols, (E.T., Abingdon) contains his thesis on the Enthronement Psalms; A. R. Johnson, *Sacral Kingship in Ancient Israel* (Cardiff, 1955); *The Sacral Kingship*, Supplement IV to *Numen* (Leiden, 1955), pp. 285-293; and esp. J. Coppen's "Les apports du Psaume CX a l'ideologie royale israelite," pp. 338-348 in above *The Sacral Kingship.*

Yahweh-M'kaddesh, II Cor. 5:21; Heb. 7:26; 10:14; (5) He is the righteousness of His people. In Jer. 23:5, 6 He is called *Yahweh-tsidkenu*, Yahweh our righteousness; Acts 3:14; Heb. 11:8, 9; I Cor. 1:30; I Pet. 3:18; Eph. 4:24; Rom. 6:18; (6) In the great Psalm 23, He is Yahweh my Shepherd, *Yahweh-Rohi;* II Sam. 5:2, 12; Ex. 33:11; Jn. 10:11; Heb. 13:20; Rev. 7:15-17; (7) During the great national crisis (cf. National Condition Red), Ezekiel describes God as *Yahweh-Shammah*—Yahweh is there—48:35. His presence is both audible and visible where His people are lovingly obedient. He is silent and absent—only as His final acts of judgment; see Col. 1:19; Isa. 7:14; Jn. 1:14; Matt. 28:19, 20; II Cor. 6:16; and Rev. 21:1-3. Job's God, though Lord of heaven and earth, is both *silent* and *absent* for millions once more as we hurtle toward the 21st century. What follows is a brief sketch of the cultural, though not ontological, demise of Yahweh our creator-redeemer in Western civilization. An historical perspective might provide *awareness* for some; challenge others who are intellectually discouraged, as well as spiritually empty; and provide, hopefully, enough insight to challenge contemporary unbelievers to come to know both the intellectual and spiritual satisfaction of personally knowing the presence of Yahweh in His living Word. Lord, give us this generation of your church to equip them, while the

Shattering of Silence
is still

possible for millions who wait in enslaving muteness for the excitement of the sound of the Word which can empower us to call God from His Exile into the daily lives of billions.

Is Job's God in Exile?

It is true that Job's God shattered His silence and in speaking revealed Himself to Job, but to contemporary western man

He has become silent once more. To most of the world's four billion people (over two billion have never heard of Christ), God is in exile, that is if He even exists. Evil, moral and surd, is everywhere evident. Injustice is the order of the day in every social structure known to man. Every major cultural category— art, literature, law, the physical, biological and behavioral sciences, economics, politics—express His absence from creation. The only remaining "place" for God to dwell is deep within man, in his "heart"! Here He is unavailable for public scrutiny. His abode within this radically "subjective"[21] dimension of man precludes any exposure of His presence in either *nature, history,* or *society.* This is the basis of both the

---

[21] All those informed concerning the intellectual developments of the past three centuries are aware of two powerful but divergent mental streams which control the flow of the western mind. One of these creative forces finds its headwaters in the *methodology* and *epistemology* of *Descartes.* The other is in the methodology and epistemology of *Science.* See Carl F. H. Henry's *Remaking the Modern Man,* College Press, reprint, 1972 with my extensive bibliography. The former spawned phenomenology, existentialism, and the contemporary aberrations of various "mindless" sorts. The later has generated a secularistic, naturalistic basis for protection of the "status quo." Against this implication much of our recent hostility to the industrial, educational, military complex expressed itself. Scientific empiricism does not often generate *paradigm revolutions* (one of the issues which I am presently considering in a doctoral thesis). Suspension of anything resembling newness, i.e., challenge to the assumptions of the establishment, religious or scientific, will not be well or pleasantly received. Generally, derision or concrete repudiation will be the results. This was also one of Job's dilemmas; he rejected the traditional views of God, and how He related to justice within the world. His integrity stood or fell on whether or not he received the advice of those who both held and transmitted the ancient traditional "answers" to his suffering. For an excellent initiation into Cartesian Subjectivism, see T. A. Burkill, "Une Critique de la tendance subjectiviste de Descartes a Sartre," *Dialogue,* 1967, pp. 346-354; also Hiram Caton, *The Origin of Subjectivity,* New Haven, Yale University Press, 1973; see the indispensable bibliography by Gregor Sebba, *Bibliographia Cartesiana:* A Critical Guide to the Descartes Literature 1800-1960, *Archives internationales d'histoire des idees,* The Hague: Hijhof, 1964, pp. 1-510. The second powerful force is that of the methodology of physical sciences. For an excellent survey of *Scientific Theories,* see *Theories of Scientific Method: The Renaissance through the Nineteenth Century,* Blake, Ducasse, and Madden, eds., Seattle: University of Washington Press, 1960; and Gerd Buchdahl, *Metaphysics and the Philosophy of Science, the Classical Origin: Descartes to Kant,* Oxford: Blackwell, 1969; further see the Journals—*British Journal for the Philosophy of Science: Archives internationales d'histoire des sciences; Journal of the History of Ideas; Isis; Archive for the History of Exact Sciences.* For further resources, see my seminar syllabus on *The Philosophy of Science* with extensive bibliographical tools.

Death of God thesis and *New Humanism*. The depth of being is resident in each human being and is His last opportunity for residence within creation. This possibility opens up our present pluralistic universalism. God is everywhere and in everyone. Kierkegaard's "Scandal of Particularity" has been forever removed. Experience-oriented culture welcomed the Beatles, the Drug Scene, Eastern Gurus with their meditation technique, because the West had become mindless in the 17th century, with the ingression of an epistemology based "within" the human psyche, which provided only a pluralistic constitutive activity of the ego, from which reality could be erected. This thesis is based in Kant's epistemology, rather than Descartes'. With the 19th century developments of the social and behavioral sciences, western man attains to his most destructive form of relativism ever conceived by man, i.e., the *Sociology of Knowledge Thesis* (cf. my critique in my *Newness on The Earth*). This was soon reinforced with the Darwinian Model of development throughout all of nature-history. God was soon to be attacked by the application of the scientific method in the History and Comparative Religion schools. Soon the biblical God found welcome residence only within pietistic groups or those who were *anti-intellectual*, because they assumed that all human contributions to reality are evil, as man's nature and reason are fallen. Here is the basis for most *anti-cultural* positions found in the religious groups from the counter-culture perspective. The implications of this mental stance for eschatology are all but self-evident. Since this is supposedly a terminal generation, witnessing is that which calls to people to get off the sinking ship of human culture and society. Yet those who call to this spiritually destitute generation hold that the faith to which they call men is the *True faith*. But it is surely self-evident that they have removed the faith from any arena in which its *Truth Claims* can be *verified* or *falsified*. Who should believe them? Why? This neo-gnosticism is not an adequate ground for calling sinners to repentance. If God has shattered silence by speaking His word, where and when has He done so? Now how did western man come full circle to be once more faced with the Jobian dilemma of the silence of God in a world filled with malignant suffering? A brief survey must be adequate for our present purposes. The Renaissance emphasis on man's indeterminateness or freedom surfaces in the Faustian interpretation of Pico. His *Oration on the Dignity of Man* (composed 1486, pub. 1495-1496) argues for man's special rank in the universe, which is grounded in his creative freedom and strikes at the scholastics, as does Erasmus' *The Praise of Folly.* [22]

God on Trial: What? How Can That Be?

With this emphasis in Renaissance thought we are on the way toward realization of the actual conditions which constitute the polemity between freedom and necessity or fortune, which appears in Machiavelli. Here is our challenge: We are living at a time of the most extensive unbelief in the history of the church. If this is true, how can such a phenomena develop in Western Christian Civilization where millions are waiting for Beckett's Godot? Though it oversimplifies the actual development of contemporary unbelief, it does not distort the facts to say the lack of awareness of the influences which were present in our world, from Descartes to the decline of the unity of science movement, are largely responsible for our present condition. Freud is correct, most "decisions" are not rationally made; they are subliminally accepted. But "the real, the deepest, the sole theme of the world and of history, to which all other themes are subordinate, remains the conflict of belief and unbelief" (Goethe).

The Resurgence of Promethean Spirit

Goethe is symbolic of resurgence of the Promethean spirit

---

[22] See the *Renaissance Philosophy of Man,* edited by Cassirer, Kristeller, and Randall; and H. Jantz, *Goethe's Faust As a Renaissance Man* (Princeton, 1961).

in the western world. The great western revolt against Job's God has its origins in a misunderstanding of the "nature of faith" in God which permeated medieval Christian Europe. Believers misplaced faith in God—in an institution which could not possibly justify their allegiance. Then the great metaphysical revolt shook most of the intellectual *au courant*. But grass-roots believers were still intact.

Spiritual Transformation of Europe

Then the Reformation powerfully altered the social and political structures of Europe. But by the end of the 19th century, it had spent its force, and a new messianic movement developed rapidly in its efforts to save civilization. That movement was authorized by the staggering success of the scientific enterprise turned practical in technology (cf. J. Ellul's *The Technological Society,* 1964). The developments in scientific method brought the demise of Aristotle as the reigning philosophic monarch. The new *Grand Inquisitor* was science.[23]

Banishment of God by the Absolutization of Finitude

The scientific power to modify reality, and not merely to control it, soon reinforced man's Promethean spirit. If man is to freely apply his new-found strength, God's domination of the world of nature-history must be challenged. Now western man, schooled in the natural sciences, espouses an atheistic world-view. God is an unnecessary explanatory hypothesis whose term of heuristic authority has expired; no longer scientifically feasible, God has become an obstacle to free thought. Belief and unbelief are the ultimate poles around which reality revolves. The revolt of Titans expressed the

---

[23] Cf. A Koyré, *From a Closed to Open Cosmos,* John Hopkins, Press, pb.; and A. O. Lovejoy, *The Great Chain of Being,* Harper Torch, pb.

atheism of their age. God was dethroned and forgotten. Contemporary Titans believe that the time has come for the last god, the god of the Christians (cf. Tillich's *God Above Gods*), to abdicate. Ernst Juenger and others corroborate the message of Nietzsche's assertion that "God is Dead."

Paradox of Pluralism

Paradoxically, this is the basic fact of our present pluralistic chaos, and the premise for the unfolding of man's immanent power to redeem the universe. Heidegger interprets the nihilism of Nietzsche as the message of the fate of man, a fate which he must shoulder resolutely. If the fact and significance of atheism is an event of radical ramification, then there is "no virtue in belief or sin in unbelief." Man is "condemned to freedom." The last quarter of the 20th century is the final act in the drama of western man's valiant struggle for emancipation from God.[24] The East has always exemplified an atheistic stance within their monastic perspective, but this western brand of atheistic scepticism keeps man tethered to terror. He is terrified by death and dying. No longer is atheism merely voiced from Russia or China. Marx and Engels are now involved in necessary dialogue with western Christians; I believe the reason that is given for such dialogue is called survival. Post-Vatican II Catholics, especially in Europe and Latin America, are busy removing the classical stigmas of materialism and atheism from what is now adjudged to be the real Marxist humanism. Will the real Marx please stand up. After we have put away God, then we must utilize our cosmic "brain tanks" to bring about the humanization of man and redemption

---

[24] For excellent survey, F. Mauthner, *Der Atheismus und seine Geschichte im Abendland*, reprinted 1963; Kant's second critique held that *God, Freedom*, and *Immortality* were practical decisions, but were not amenable to verification or falsification; then followed A. Vailhinger's *Philosophy as If*, we act as if there is a God that we are free, and that there is immortality, but none of the three claims are open to evidence or justification. The next generation asked, then why act as if?

from exploitation and injustice. Few neo-Marxists would concur with Eduard Humann, though he is absolutely correct in his evaluation, "Atheism is integral to all Marxist thought and is, in a way, its climax and the test of its perfection."[25]

Coming of Contemporary Titans

The Titans are moving among us once more. Once Aeschylus had observed Etan's volcano while on a voyage to western Greece. Then men believed that the Titan Typhon, brother of the rebel Prometheus,[26] lay imprisoned under Etna, and from time to time expressed his freedom from the chains that bound him, in helpless rage. For Typhon too had rebelled against the gods. The rebellion against God as creator-redeemer and origin of True Belief necessitated a counter-explanation which became the Pan applicability of Darwinian Model of the development from primitivism to civilization.[27] Richard Mohr, the ethnologist, presents 20th century technologically dominated man this curious bit of truth. We find particularly among peoples with few technological interests a highly developed religion, ritual, and art, which leads us to suspect that "these people display little interest in the development of technical accomplishments because their physical attention is absorbed by other things."[28] Western man now finds fulfillment in things. Things and more and more things make us happy; the key word is happy. The word is present, but the experience is not. When Hegel's geist evolved, for all his dialectical shuttling, he is utilizing what is really a pre-intellectual and subpersonal category that has no connection with spirit. Hegel's geist, under Freudian psychoanalysis, becomes the

---

[25] *Reason and Faith in Modern Society* (Middletown, Connecticut, 1961).

[26] Aeschylus' *Prometheus Bound;* Edith Hamilton, *Three Greek Plays* (Norton, 1937); C. Kerenyi, Prometheus, *Archetypal Image of Human Existence* (Pantheon Books, 1963).

[27] Cf. contra see R. Mohr, *Die Christliche Ethik im Lichte der Ethnologie,* 1954.

[28] R. Mohr, *Die Christliche,* p. 3.

driving force of the irrational and non-rational in our present chaos, because chaos begets chaos. Monad, *et al.*, are wrong; the feasibility is zero for a chance origin of the universe and man. Yet since God's demise, man has been living in a universe that is actually a colossal Las Vegas where change and chance prevail. Man's low level of toleration drove him to Camelot where magic and mysticism continue to multiply his misery. One group of modern western man's cohorts, in a rampant raging world, are the pygmy races which show no interest in religious ideas or God in their daily lives. *Egotism* is a flagrant characteristic of such tribes (cf. Mohr above). Altruism is not a characteristic of egocentric western individuals either. Naturalistic humanism's effort to defend rational self-interest cannot survive the blistering attack of the Freudian rationalization category.

Contemporary man has been tamed by technology. Technology and specialization are imperative for production; production is imperative for our well being, but our well being becomes enslaved to the security of things. "But for freedom did Christ set us free," Gal. 5:1. Contemporary atheism was conceived in a free enquiring atmosphere similar to that expressed in Genesis. Satan was not an atheist; his first attack on God was not his existence but His word—"Did God say that?"— Gen. 1—3. The old Egyptian Kingdom collapsed when more and more gods were included in the celestial ranks.[29] What is the difference between Egyptian pluralism and our present western pluralism? Modern unbelievers are impotent in a creation that is out of joint; man is inclined to make the creator responsible for an original flaw in creation, thereby freeing man of responsibility. But if God is dead, who is to blame? Once more Homer's Titans have invaded the world of man.[30] Even in chains Prometheus boasts of his accomplishments, as does our contemporary Prometheus who is enslaved to

---

[29] M. Eliade, *The Sacred and The Profane* (New York, 1959).

[30] See H. Schrade, *Gotter und Menschen Homers*, 1952; B. Snell, *The Discovery of The Mind*, The Greek Origins of European Thought (Oxford: Blackwell, 1953); and W. Jaeger, *The Theology of the Early Greek Philosophers* (Oxford, 1947).

technological efficiency, which reduces man to mere functional value. "Enough of that. I speak to you who know. Hear rather all that mortal suffered. Once they were fools, I gave them power to think. Through me they won their minds . . . Seeing they did not see, nor hearing hear. Like dreams they led a random life."[31] But "all human skill and science was Prometheus' gift." Even Hesiod's theogony cannot give a coherent account of a free Prometheus, because freedom means the lack of coherence, which smacks of rational determination. But man will be free, but at the expense of God's existence and man's mind. Certainly Olympian Zeus can conjure up a transcendent God.

Two more creative actors in our drama are Socrates and Plato. Surely once and for all a personal transcendent God will be removed from the human scene. Neither Plato's "one," nor Aristotle's "unmoved mover" will be able to save fallen man in his or from his demoniac environment. The state will redeem man (cf. *The Laws*) and unbelief can be corrected by dialectical arguments. Erroneous opinions can be irradicated by education and improved logic. Yet, the first word in the book of *The Laws* is God, written large—GOD. God is necessary for a stable world and justice, according to Plato. Yet, the Neo-Hegelians revived an ancient error—that God did not create the world, rather man created gods.

A Contemporary Prototype

A classical precursor of Feuerbachian atheism is Lucretius, "the father of western atheism." In his *De Rerum Natura* he dared to relieve man of his religiously oppressive load.

Then into the dark chaotic world of Graeco-Roman religion came the revolutionary word of God, Jesus Christ. This powerful force saved and sustained both sinners and society, until

---

[31] Edith Hamilton, ed. and trans., *Prometheus Bound,* p. 115.

505

the disintegration of the medieval world-view, which was not Christian but pagan, Aristotelian. The "order" of the world was no longer grounded in God or His structures. Order was to be placed in man's hands.

Ecology of The Nietzschean Revolt

From the Renaissance to the French Revolution man was being encouraged to rebel against God. From the 18th century forward western man was in metaphysical revolt against God as Lord of heaven and earth. Fichte, Kant, and Rousseau were the prophets of autonomous man. *The Enlightenment*[32] or the Age of Reason conceived the cultural basis of contemporary unbelief and the *Age of Reason* (1680-1715) paved the way for the *Age of Revolution*. One of the belligerent voices of the era was D'Holback who put God on trial in the modern world, as Job did in his world. Faith in God was an illusion, according to D'Holback, (cf. *System of Nature*), thus paving the way for Freud's psychological atheism.

Onto the stage of this great drama came some of the most creative minds in the history of the world. Copernicus, Galileo, Kepler, and Newton were among them. When the intellectual revolution was complete, the Newtonian World-Machine model dominated the western scientific enterprise. Fast on the heels of this vast cosmic machine, based in total Newtonian quantification of reality, came Deism. God was ruled out of the universe by science. Meanwhile back on earth, Locke's essay on *Toleration* and Rousseau's *Social Contract* removed God from the social institutions of man. Their naturalistic functional approach to the origins of all social structures is in direct conflict with the scriptural witness. Rousseau's world-view was based in man as the center of self-legislation. Camus' *Rebel* is a self-legislator, who was born in another revolutionary era, our own.

---

[32] See indispensable work of Peter Gay *The Age of The Enlightenment*, 2 vols. (New), A. A. Knopf, Vol. I, 1967, Vol. II, 1969.

Revolt Against Heaven

As though revolt against God's Lordship was not enough, Kant's *First Critique;* his *The Only Possible Evidence for a Demonstration of the Existence of God,* 1763; and his *Religion Without the Limits of Reason* produced a dichotomy between *volition* and *act* (cf. theory and practice are fractured, i.e., *thinking* and *acting* are unrelated). Man is just now realizing the tragic consequences of Kantian philosophy for the Christian enterprise. Kant's upper and lower storied universe places *faith* outside of the world of causation and scientific analysis, and evidential justification, or rejection. Even Fichte refers to Kant's "skeptical atheism," and Schelling triumphantly shouts that "Kant has cleared the decks completely." Marx called the classical proofs for God's existence "empty tautologies," clearly not worth close analysis. His conclusion was the terminal results of Kant's epistemological revolution.

Creative Nothingness and the Exiled Living God

Next came Fichte's loud cry for human freedom. Now with the death of God, man can be free! Fichte marks the culmination of the *Age of Reason.* Prometheus redivivus! Goethe had written in 1793 that the Titan was conscious of his good and just deed—laughs, unafraid, to see the ruins of the world crash down upon him. While the world laughs, God returns to Tübingen by way of Hegel's influence. Kant removed God from the universe; Hegel reinstated him, but as totally immanent. There is thereafter a rumor of angels, but it is only an immanent rumor. Hegel preached the gospel of self-liberation from the fear of sin. Hegel's drive to freedom as self-liberation was from an ominous burden.[33]

After Kant and Hegel, it is a cultural presupposition that

---

[33] Cf. for the relationship of revolution to Hegel see J. Ritter, *Hegel und die Franzoesische Revolution,* 1957.

man's reason is autonomous and his will is autonomous. Both claims are in direct confrontation with biblical assertions. Fate or destiny replaces deity. In the wake of this fate, a young Hegelian, Bruno Bauer's path moves from that of theologian to that of atheist. His circle of influence intensified greatly the power of unbelief.

The waves of unbelief swept over Ludwig Feuerbach and His mind shifted from idealism to atheism.[34] Feuerbach's anthropological atheism is discernable in his claim that "Der Mensch ist dem Menschen Gott," man is the supreme being for man. Following in Feuerbach's atheistic footsteps came Marx's powerfully articulated hostility to Job's redeemer. Marx's naturalistic atheism maintains that man's world-view is the "perfect construct of the consciousness." The Hegel-Marx consciousness is not necessarily materialistic, but it is a naturalistic expression of human creativity. From now on it will be God in man's image, whereas in classic Christian thought it was man in God's image. The new atheistic world-view now only requires a prophet to popularize its tenets and implications. Nietzsche is that prophet. His message is man's "will to power." His authorization is man's creative and autonomous reason. Scientific Method and man's will to power became the foundations for the coming totalitarian systems of western Europe. This phenomena occurred just one generation ago, and we have forgotten what a group of elite tyrants can do to man, even when it is in the name of man's betterment. *Zarathustra* declares that God is only a projection, and Freud psychoanalyzes that projection into an illusion. Kant's incurable dichotomy generated unprecedented human hybris, and our cultural sickness unto death.

---

[34] Cf. L. Feuerbach, *Das Wesen des Christentums,* 1956.

Hybris and Our Present Crisis:
The Cogito of Atheistic Nihilism

How did we arrive at western man's postulatory atheism today? The brilliant work of Elimar von Fuerstenberg[35] correctly asserts that the death of God has created the death of man. God's death causes man to misconstrue his own essence, resulting in self-contradiction. He says that "a philosophy that must contradict itself in order to trace being back to nothingness is basically a futile philosophy which can only rivet man to despair." Atheists are opponents of the establishment, from Dostoevsky's Dmitri Karamazov to Camus' hero.

Intoxication of Pride: The True Adversary of God

Arrogance is always the true adversary of faith. *Pride* is always the pyramid to rise against God, as it is the basis of unsupportably exaggerated self-estimate. A new fall will be required, but this time a fall from pride, as did Job our contemporary. For the "fear of the Lord is always the beginning of wisdom." This thesis is in dramatic opposition to Fichte's *The Vocation of Man.* As believers, we must rebel against unbelief—Ps. 2:2.

From Indictment to Imprisonment: Banishment of God

Atheism is a fact of life in the contemporary world, but what is the fundamental relationship between *unbelief, freedom,* and resurgent *naturalistic humanism?* How does God's nature and existence relate to man's nature and existence? It is a fundamental mistake and ultimately will seriously impoverish and disfigure human existence. The mute gloom

---

[35] Elimar von Fuerstenberg, *Der Sebstwidespruch der philosophischen atheismus,* 1960, p. 8.

which man's newly found freedom from God has created requires that we retrace the tragic steps of western man's journey into oblivion. From Descartes to Sartre we can discern the fatal flaws which follow man's Promethean rejection of God. Where are the focii of freedom, and what of their fate in the last quarter of the 20th century, as America enters her third century? We have excellent resources by which we can trace our path to oblivion. Interdisciplinary methodology will certainly be concerned with the correlation between man's rejection of God and his search for "freedom,"[36] especially from the 17th century to the present. "The fact remains that a mighty power of affirmation both of the human and of the divine permeates and sustains Descartes' world. Two centuries of crises—religious as well as scientific—had to pass before man could win back that creative freedom which Descartes attributed to God, before at last truth, the essential foundation of humanism, understood: Man is the being whose appearance causes the world to exist. . . . Let us admire him for insisting on the demands of the idea of autonomy and for understanding long before Heidegger . . . that the only foundation of being is freedom,"[37] freedom from God.

God As a Cultural Unmentionable

Today one does not discuss God in public. The Death of God is a cultural unmentionable, often in the most conservative groups. But for Job's contemporaries, this can be no norm of behavior. Naturalistic humanism has fabricated a freedom that enslaves. Security, not freedom, is the fate of our

---

[36] On the nature of freedom, see M. Adler, *Idea of Freedom* (Doubleday), 2 vols, reprint; the article Eleutheria in *TWNT*; the *Syntoptican;* D. Nestle, *Eleutheria, Freiheit bei den Griechen und im Neuen Testament*, 1967; Niederwimmer, *Der Begriff der Freitheit im Neuen Testament*, 1966; also my extended bibliography in my two essays in Clark Pennock, ed., *Grace Unlimited* (Bethany Fellowship Press, 1975).

[37] Jean Paul Sartre, *Rene Descartes, Discours de la Methode*, 1948, pp. 203ff.

civilization. One must taste the fruit to be able to evaluate the tree that bears it. The fruit of the fear of the Lord will be freedom, His freedom for our fulfillment. This is true humanism. As long as Kierkegaard's parable of the barnyard is an appropriate evaluation of many churches, men will not expect any word from the Lord from that quarter. In order to recover God's authentic voice in His church and His creation. Fichte's arrogant ape must be replaced, but man's creative imagination has produced gods in his own image and in every stage of progress they think of him ". . . as a greater man, and still a greater; but never as [Job's] God—the Infinite whom no measure can mete. I have only this discursive, progressive thought, and I can conceive of no other."[38] Only Job's vindicator can challenge the powerful human pride present in Fichte's proclamation. If the church is to *Shatter the Silence* again, it must avoid repeating the triple fall of Christendom: (1) The first temptation was to seize earthly power by autonomous human reason,[39] which completely disregarded the prophetic word in times of crisis. This attitude reached its apogee in Hegel and the late Heidegger. (2) The second temptation was to assert the power of speculative abstract reason, which collapsed under the intolerable burden of objective truth as it emerged from scientific investigation. (3) The last and worst deviation is the arrogance of the flesh. Western technology, which recognizes only man's earthly needs, was tempted to turn stones into bread, but man cannot live by bread alone.

God in Exile?

Finally fell the sentence of banishment in the stormy sea of conflict of interests, "the name of him who was accused of

---

[38] J. G. Fichte, *The Vocation of Man* (New York: Liberal Arts Press, 1956), p. 140.

[39] For excellent history of *The Enlightenment*, see F. Valjavec, *Geschichte der abendlendischen Aufklärung* (Munich, 1961).

THE SHATTERING OF SILENCE

aspirations to tyranny, illicit circumscription of man's rights, connivance at or imbecility in consent to evil, inaccessibility to man's reason or defiance of that reason, logical inconsistency and mythical monstrosity." Who is able to respond? Only Job's Vindicator who invaded the fallen earth to redirect the systems of nature-history toward redemptive fulfillment. II Cor. 5:17f.

Change is imperative, and change of heart always begins in the quiet privacy of contemplation. We must contemplate the Word from God which *Shatters His Silence,* and also the intellectual developments of the past three centuries in order to understand why millions in western civilization believe that God is in Exile. *Is God in Exile?* Job knew better, but what of his contemporaries[40] Renegade theoretical theists are no match for roused atheists, roused by man's inhumanity to man. Only those who hear Him say, "As you have done it unto the least of these my brethren, you have done it unto me," will be able to respond in the name of Job's Jesus. God still pursues all who fluctuate between *anxiety* and *pride.*

APPENDIX TO *IS GOD IN EXILE?*

Salvation by Humanization

"Take care, Brethren, lest there be in any of you an evil unbelieving heart leading you to fall away from the living God." Heb. 3:12, 4:1

Subject: Contemporary idolatry and the youth culture: by

---

[40] Utilize the excellent film series depicting and documenting *How Should We Then Live? The Rise and Decline of Western Thought and Culture* written by and featuring Dr. Francis Schaeffer (Gospel Films, Inc., P.O. Box 455, Muskegon, MI, 49443); for the book version, Fleming H. Revell Co., 184 Central Ave., Old Tappan, NJ, 07675. If possible, examine the BBC series on *The Ascent of Man* and critically compare the assumptions and their implications for witnessing in the 20th century.

1980—75% of the world's population will be 21 years old and under; and 50% of the population in the USA will be 25 years old and under. Problem: What does this group believe? What are some of the ideologies which are competing for this age group?

I. *With Heart and Head: The Whole Person and Christian Faith*
   A. What does it mean to be a Christian believer in the 20th century?
   B. What does the O.T. mean by faith? Person, promise, content, purpose, response, i.e., root significance is reply or answer to question/challenge.
   C. What does the N.T. mean by faith? (Believing that something is true and believing in a person, apistia, apeitheia)
   D. What does it mean to hear the Word of God?
   E. Faith after Freud
   F. Hearing God's Word in a visibility culture (audibility and visibility of Word of God)
   G. Proclaiming the Word of God in an entertainment culture: Listening for "ego" satisfaction rather than decision—life changing, behaviour modification decision.
   H. Word of God, Decision, and Integrity (wholeness of person, integration, i.e., lifestyle from new life—we need both integrity of mind and emotion, i.e., feelings).

II. *Social and Psychological* (personal and group) *Reasons for Unbelief*
   A. European cultures—from revival to revolution (e.g. French Revolution and Russian.)
   B. American culture—200 years in the Promised Land. The Spirit in "76" Restoration principle—from the Frontier to Watergate—A study in influence.
   C. Social and Psychological reasons for belief: Alternatives unknown or unavailable.

    D. Ignatius Lepp—with Christ on the psychiatrist couch (converted communist propaganda expert—now Roman Catholic priest.)

    E. Third times charm—Resurgent concern in counseling (3rd time in 20th Century) and for meaning—belonging—caring—sharing.

III. *American Forms of Unbelief—18th and 19th Centuries*

    A. The Great Intrusion: Tom Paine's form of Infidelity—1784-1809.

    B. The Great Definition: Coming of New England Liberalism—1749-1805.

    C. The Great Foil to Orthodoxy—1759-1818 (e.g. Timothy Dwight, President of Yale, most effective vanquisher of infidelity in American history).

    D. The Great Alliance—Syncretism and the Established Church 1776-1818.

    E. The Great Adjustment—Modification of attitudes of religious institutions.

    F. Robert Owens (A. Campbell's debate) Image Maker—after 1824—churches as Virtuosi of Exploitation.

    G. From Liberalism and Unitarianism to the Frontier—"Muscular Christianity"

    H. Infidelity Incarnate—Robert Ingersol to 1899.

    I. The Great Decline after 1899.

    J. The Great Absence

    K. The Great Silent Majority—The Sin of Silence European forms Kant, Hegel, Marx, Darwin, Freud, Nietzsche.

IV. *Characteristics of Our World and Forms of Unbelief in the 20th Century*

    A. Originality of Modern unbelief (not merely ignorance, faithlessness, apathy or rebellion because they were present in age of Faith)—secularism, humanism, and scientism.

    B. Characteristics are worldwide: Penetration into every

area of life, dispensable, processes of secularization.
C. Pluralism, i.e., contradictory claims have equal standing in universe of discourse.
D. Loss of truth as basis of community.
E. Community based on symbolic order (communication) has disintegrated (e.g. McLuhan's Hot and Cold Communication)

V. *Secular Varieties of Unbelief*
A. Anomie (no norm, i.e., lawlessness) and Accidie (paralysis of action, listlessness).
B. Rejection of possibility of positive belief, i.e., Nihilism or absolutization of nothingness (see my article on Nihilism in *Dictionary of Christian Ethics,* edited by Carl F. H. Henry, Baker, Grand Rapids).
C. Atheism (see Ephesians 2:12) and anti-theism touches every individual and structure of the new humanity.
D. Pantheisms (Panentheisms, e.g. Spinoza, Hegel, Whitehead and Teilhard de Chardin) and Paganism of history and power.
E. Syncretistic unbelief, e.g., combines elements of Christian beliefs and contradictory cultural features.
F. Syncretistic unbelief and contradictory political features, eg. Nazism, Communism, Americanism (we cannot have two absolutes: Only God and His Word is absolute and sets in judgement on every facet of this world's experience).

VI. *Religious Varieties of Unbelief: Integral Unbelief—of the Grand Inquistor*
(O.T. and N.T. examples of unbelief—Baalism, Gnosticism, Judaistic Legalism, etc.)
A. Private and public faith
B. Private lives and public morals (Nixon, Mills, et al.)
C. Individual faith and institutional unbelief (Part is faithful; whole is visibly unfaithful, e.g. Niebuhr's *Moral Man and Immoral Society*).

    D. Social functionalism, institutionalism (free association since Hegel and modern democracy), specialization and commitment to organizational development and the cult of efficiency, i.e., heresy of success orientation.

    E. Reasons for affiliation and cultural stratification, egs. Poor and store front, rich and elaborate edifice complex. Christ and cultural basis of being successful.

    F. Church and acculturation—Christ and culture—(against, parallel assimilated, critical interaction or confrontation).

VII. *Positive Approach to Problem: Education for a Christian World Life Style*

    A. Being Christian is representing God in this world.

    B. Being Christian is committing one's life to ultimate vindication of God's promise and purpose for His creation.

    C. Let us not witness throughout the remainder of the 20th Century, or until He comes, with—not much, not yet, or not enough.

Conclusion:

We are living once more in a Dionsysian age where we exist—Sentio Ergo Sum: Therefore, unbelief is a problem fit for God. It cannot be effectively responded to by the church in its present spiritual and educational condition. Revival is imperative; and equipping every saint in every congregation for service in a sine-qua-non for a Christian response to contemporary unbelief.

Toward a Bibliographical Delimitation of the Notion of Atheism:

(A) *Principal Works:*

Adolfs, Robert. *The Church Is Different.* London: Compass Books, 1966.

———. *The Grave of God.* translated by N. D. Smith, New York: Harper and Row, 1967.

Barth, Karl. *Church Dogmatics* III/1, translated by G. T. Thomson. Edinburgh: T. & T. Clark, 1952.

Bartley, William Warren. *The Retreat to Commitment.* New York: Knopf, 1962.

Baumer, Franklin L. *Religion and the Rise of Scepticism.* New York: Harcourt, Brace, 1960.

Bayle, P. *Dictionnaire historique et critique,* 5th edition, Basle, 1738.

Blackman, H. J., editor. *Objections to Humanism.* London: Constable, 1963.

Borne, Etienne. *Atheism,* translated by S. J. Tester. New York: Hawthorn Books, 1961.

Burke, T., editor. *The World in History.* New York: Sheed & Ward, 1966.

Collins, James. *The Emergence of Philosophy of Religion.* New Haven: Yale University Press, 1967.

Descartes, R. *Correspondence. Oeuvres de Descartes,* Vol. V. Edited by C. Adam and P. Tannery. Paris, 1909.

Denzinger, Henricus. *Enchiridion Symbolorum,* edited by J. B. Umber. 25th edition. Barcelona: Herder, 1948.

Dewart, Lesie. *The Future of Belief.* New York: Herder & Herder, 1966.

Diderot, D. and dAlembert. *Encyclopedie ou Dictionnaire raisonne'des sciences, des artes et des métiers.* Paris, 1751; 2nd ed. Lucca, 1758.

Dondeyne, Albert. *Contemporary Christian Faith and European Thought,* translated by John Burnheim and Ernan McMullin. Pittsburgh: Duquesne University Press, 1958.

———. *Faith and the World,* translated by Walter van de Putte. Pittsburgh: Duquesne University Press, 1958.

Duquoc, Christian, editor. *Opportunities for Belief and Behavior* (Concilium Vol. 29). Glen Rock, N.J.: Paulist, 1966.

Etcheverry, A. *Le Conflit actual des humanismes.* Rome: Gregorian University Press, 1964.

Fabro, Cornelio. *God in Exile,* translated by Arthur Gibson.

Westminster, Md.: Newman, 1968.
Feuerbach, L. *Grundsatze der Philosophie der Zukunft.* Werke, Vol. II. Stuttgart, 1904. Ed. by M. G. Lange. Leipzig, 1950. English translation by Manfred H. Vogel, *Principles of the Philosophy of the Future.* Indianapolis-New York-Kansas City: The Library of Liberal Arts, Bobbs-Merrill, 1966.
Hartshorne, Charles, and Reese, William L., editors. *Philosophers Speak of God.* Chicago: University of Chicago Press, 1953.
Hebblethwaite, Peter. *The Council Fathers and Atheism.* Glen Rock, N.J.: Paulist, 1967.
Hegel, G. W. *Enzyklopaidie der philosophischen Wissenschaften,* Ed. by J. Hoffmeister. Leipzig, 1959.
_____. *Philosophie der Weltgeschichte.* Werke, Vol. 1. Ed. by Lason, Leipzig, 1925.
Hofmans, Flor. *Jesus: Who Is He?* Glen Rock, N.J.: Paulist, 1968.
Johann, Robert. *The Pragmatic Meaning of God.* Milwaukee: Marquette University Press, 1966.
Küng, Hans. *The Unknown God?* translated by W. W. White. New York: Sheed & Ward, 1966.
Lacroix, Jean. *The Meaning of Modern Atheism,* translated by Garret Barden. Dublin: Gill & Son, 1965.
Lepp, Ignace. *Atheism in Our Time,* translated by Bernard Murchland. NY: Macmillan, 1963.
Marx, K. *Kritik der Hegelschen Dialektik und Philosophie uberhaupt. Oekonomisch-philosophische Manuskripte aus dem Jahre* 1844, M.E.G.A. (Marx-Engels Gesamtausgabe) Abt. I, Vol. 3. Ed. by D. Ryazanov and V. Adoratsky. Moscow and Berlin, 1926ff.
Metz, Johannes. *Poverty of Spirit,* translated by John Drury. Glen Rock, N.J.: Paulist, 1968.
_____. editor. *The Church and the World* (Concilium, Vol. 6). Glen Rock, N.J.: Paulist, 1965.
Novak, Michael. *Belief and Unbelief.* New York: Mentor-Omega, 1965.
Ogden, Schubert M. *The Reality of God.* New York: Harper &

Row, 1966.

Rahner, Karl. *Belief Today,* translated by M. H. Heelan. New York: Sheed & Ward, 1967.

_____. *On Heresy,* translated by W. J. O'Hara. London: Burns & Oates, 1964.

_____. editor. *The Pastoral Approach to Atheism* (Concilium, Vol. 23). Glen Rock, N.J.: Paulist, 1967.

_____, editor. *The Renewal of Preaching* (Concilium, Vol. 33) Glen Rock, N.J.: Paulist, 1967.

Reid, John P. *The Anatomy of Atheism.* Washington, D.C.: Thomist Press, 1965.

Röper, Anita. *The Anonymous Christian,* translated by Joseph Donceel. New York: Sheed & Ward, 1966.

Schleiermacher, F. *Der christliche Glaube.* Gesammelte Werke, Vol. I. 7th edition by M. Redeker, Berlin, 1960.

_____. *Zur Theologie.* Gesammelte Werke, Vol. I. 7th ed. of M. Redeker, Berlin, 1960.

Schlette, Heinze Robert. *Toward a Theology of Religions,* translated by W. J. O'Hara. New York: Herder & Herder, 1966.

van de Pol, W. H. *The End of Conventional Christianity,* translated by Theodore Zuydwijk. New York: Newman, 1967.

Verneaux, Roger. *Lecons su l'Atheisme Contemporain.* Paris: P. Tequi, 1964.

Veuillot, Mgr., et al. *L'Atheisme: tentation du monde, reveil des chretiens?* Paris: Editions du Cerf, 1963.

Yvon, Abbé. article "Athée," *Encyclopédie of Diderot and d'Alembert,* Vol. I. fol. 798b ff. (1751 edition), fol. 692a ff. (1758 edition).

Periodical Articles:

Barthelemy, D. 'Les idoles et l'image.' *La Vie spirituelle,* March, 1962, 288-294.

Fabro, Cornelio. 'The Positive Character of Modern Atheism.' *Concurrence* 1 (1966): 66-76.

Krejci, Jaroslav. 'A New Model of Scientific Atheism.' *Concurrence* 1 (1969): 82-96.

519

Murray, John C. 'On the Structure of the Problem of God.' *Theological Studies* 23 (1962): 1-26.

Rahner, Karl. 'Atheism and Implicit Christianity.' *Theology Digest*, February, 1968, pp. 43-56.

(B) *Secondary Works:*

L'Atheisme contemporain. Geneva: Edition Labor et Fies, 1956.

Bacon, F. *De augmentatione scientiarum. The Works of Francis Bacon*, Vol. I, Edited by J. Spedding, R. L. Ellis and D. D. Heath. London, 1879.

Brunschvicg, L. *Héritage de mots, héritage d'idées.* Paris, 1945.

_____. "La querelle de l'atheisme," *De la vraie et de la fausse converions.* Paris, 1950.

_____. *La raison et le religion.* Paris, 1939.

Dilthey, W. *Einleitung in die Geisteswissenschaften.* Werke, Vol. I. Leipzig, 1933.

Flint, R. *Agnosticism.* Edinburgh and London, 1903.

Hazard, P. *La pensee europeene au XVIII siecle.* Paris, 1946. English translated *European Thought in the Eighteenth Century.* Cleveland: World, 1964.

Jacoby, F. "Diagoras, d' AOeos," *Abhandlungen der deutschen Akademie der Wissenschaften Klasse fur Sprachen*, Literatur und Kunst, Jahrgang 1959, Nr. 3.

Kant, I. *Kritik der reinen Vernunft. Kants gesammelte Schriften*, Abot. I, Vol. 3. Berlin: Reimer, 1911. English translation by F. Max Muller, *Critique of Pure Reason.* Garden City, NY: Dophin Books, Doubleday & Co., Inc. 1961.

Kierkegaards, S. Edited by Walter Lowrie, *Concluding Unscientific Postscript to the "Philosophical Fragments,"* Oxford-Princeton, 1941.

Lacrois, J. "Sens et valeur de l'atheisme contemporain," *Monde moderne et sens de Dieu.* Paris, 1954.

Lange, F. A. *Geschichte des Materialismus.* Leipzig: Reclam, 1905.

Leibniz, G. W. *Confessio naturae contra Atheistas. Gesammelte Werke*, Vol. IV. Edited by Gerhardt. Hildesheim, 1961.

Marcel, G. *Le sens de l'atheisme moderne*. Paris-Tournai, 1958.

Merleau-Ponty, M. *Eloge de la philosophie*. Paris: Gallimard, 1953. English trans. by John Wild and James W. Edie, *In Praise of Philosophy*. Evanston, IL: Northwestern University Press, 1963.

Schlegel, D. B. *Shaftesbury and the French Deists*. Chapel Hill, N.C.: University of North Carolina Studies, 1956.

Voltaire, *Questions sur les miracles*. Geneva, 1765. *Oeuvres completes de Voltaire*, Vol. XXV. Edited by Moland, Paris, 1883.

The Atheism of Rationalism

A. Principal Works:

Bayle, P. *Pensees philosophiques*. Edited by P. Verniere. Paris, 1961.

Descartes, R. *Epistola ad G. Voetium*. *Oeuvres de Descartes*, Vol. VIII. Ed. by Adam and Tannery. Paris, 1909.

d'Holbach, D. *Systeme de la nature*. 2nd ed. London, 1774.

Montesquieu, C. *Del'Esprit des Lois*. Paris, An IV de la Republique; first edition, 1748.

Rousseau, J. J. *Emile*. *Oeuvres Completes*, Vol. II. Paris: Hachette, 1856.

Spinoza, B. *Ethica*. *Opera*, Vol. II Ed. by C. Gebhardt, Heidelberg, 1924.

B. Secondary Works:

Blondel, M. *L'action*. Paris, 1936.

Brunschwicg, L. *Descartes et Pascal lecteurs de Montaigne*. 2nd ed. NY-Paris, 1944.

Busson, H. *Le Rationalisme dans la litterature francaise de la Renaissance*. 2nd ed. Paris, 1957.

Deborin, A.M. "Spinoza's World-View," Kline et al., *Spinoza in Soviet Philosophy*. London, 1952.

Desautels, A. R. *Les Memoires de Trevoux et le mouveme nt des idees au XVII siecle*. Rome, 1956.

Feuerbach, L. *Pierre Bayle, Ein Beitrag zur Geschichte der*

Philosophie und Menschheit. Werke, Vol. V. Stuttgart, 1905.

_____. *Geschichte der neueren Philosophie von Bacon von Verulam bis Benedikt Spinoza. Werke,* Vol. III. Stuttgart, 1906.

_____. *Vorlaufige Thesen zur Reform der Philosophie. Werke,* Vol. II. Stuttgart, 1904.

_____. *The Essence of Religion,* NY: Harper and Row, 1967.

Hazard, P. *La crise de conscience europeenne.* Paris, 1935.

Hegel, G. W. *Geschichte der Philosophie.* Ed. by Michelet. Berlin, 1844; reprinted as Vols. 17-18 of the Jubilaumsausgabe of Hegel's *Samtliche Werke.* Stuttgart, 1959. Ed. by J. Hoffmeister. Leipzig, 1944.

Jaquelot, I. *Dissertations sur l'existence de Dieu, ou l'on demontre cette verite par l'histoire universelle, par la refutation du systemme d'Epicure et de Spinoza par les caracteres de divinite qui se remarquent dans la religion des Juifs.* The Hague, 1697.

Kline, G. et al. *Spinoza in Soviet Philosophy.* London, 1952.

Labrousse, E. *Pierre Bayle.* The Hague, 1964.

Lachieze-Roy, P. *Les origines cartesiennes du Dieu de Spinoza.* Paris, 1932.

Marx, L. and F. Engels. *Die Heilige Familie. K. Marx-F. Engels Werke,* Vol. II Berlin, 1958.

Mason, H. T. *Pierre Bayle and Voltaire.* Oxford, 1965.

Mauthner, F. *Der Atheismus und seine Geschichte im Abendlande.* Stuttgart and Berlin, 1921.

Plechanov. G. W. *Die Grundprobleme des Marxismus.* Berlin, 1958.

Randall, J. H. *The Career of Philosophy, From the Middle Ages to the Enlightenment.* NY: Columbia University Press, 1962.

Rex. W. *Essays on Pierre Bayle.* The Hague: Nijhoff, 1965.

Sartre, J. P. *Descartes. Collection Les classiques de la liberte.* Paris, 1946.

Soviet tem of historians of philosophy. *Geschichte der Philosophie.* Berlin: VEB Deutscher Verlag der Wissenschaften, 1959.

Strauss, L. *Die Religion skritik Spinozas als Grundlage seiner Bibelwissenschaft.* Berlin, 1930.

Verniere, P. *Spinoza et la pensee francaise avant la revolution.* Paris, 1954.

Wolfson, H. A. *The Philosophy of Spinoza.* New York, 1958.

Deism and Atheism in English Empiricism

(A) *Principal Works:*

Berkeley, G. *Alcyphron, or the minute Philosopher.* Berkeley's Works, Vol. II. Ed. by A. C. Fraser. Oxford, 1901.

_____. *Dialogues between Hylas and Philonous.* Berkeley's Works, Vol. I. Oxford, 1901.

_____. *A Treatise concerning the Principles of Human Knowledge.* Berkeley's Works, Vol. I. Oxford, 1901.

Butler, J. *The Analogy of Relgion natural and revealed to the Constitution and Course of Nature.* Originally published in 1736; reprinted Glasgow-London, 1827.

Hobbes, T. *The Question concerning Liberty, Necessity and Change.* English Works, Vol. V. Aalen, 1962.

Hume, D. *Dialogues concerning Natural Religion.* Ed. by Norman K. Smith. 2nd ed. Toronto-NY, 1947. German trans. by Paulsen, Berlin, 1904.

Jacobi, F. H. *Idealismus und Realismus,* Ein Gesprach. *Werke,* Vol. II. Leipzig, 1816.

Lenin, V. I. *Materialism and Empiriocriticism.* Moscow: Foreign Languages Pub. House, no date. German trans. Berlin: Dietz Verlag, 1949.

Locke, J. *An Essay concerning Human Understanding.* The Works of John Locke, Vol. VII. London, 1823; Aalen, 1963.

_____. *A Second Vindication.* The Works of John Locke, Vol. VII. Friends. London, 1708.

Marx, K. and F. Engels. *Die Heilige Familie.* K. Marx-F. Engels Werke, Vol. II. Berlin, 1958. Marx Engels, Historisch-kritische Gesamtausgabe: Werke, Schriften, Briefe (M.E.G.A.), Abt. I, Vol. 2. Ed. by D. Rjazanov and V. Adoratsky. Moscow and Berlin, 1926ff; English Trans. *The Holy Family.*

(B) *Secondary Works:*

Benn, A. W. *The History of English Rationalism in the Nine-teenth Century.* New York-London, 1906.

Cassirer, E. *Die Philosophie der Aufklarung.* Tubingen, 1932.

Crous, E. *Die Religionsphilosophischen Lehren Lockes und ihre Stellung zu dem Deismus seiner Zeit.* Abhandlungen zur Philosophie und ihre Geschichte. Leipzig, 1910.

Dilthey, W. *Aus der Zeit der Spinozastudien Goethes.* Gesammelte Schriften, Vol. II 4th ed. Leipzig and Berlin, 1940.

Fabro, C. "Foi et raison dans l'oeuvre de Kierkegaard," *Revue de sciences philosophiques et theologiques,* 1948, pp. 169ff.

Gibson, J. *Locke's Theory of Knowledge and its Historical Relations.* Cambridge, 1917.

Heinemann, F. H. "Toland und Leibniz," *Beitrage zur Leibniz-Forschung,* ed. by G. Schichkoff. Reutlingen, 1947.

Helfbower, S. G. *The Relation of John Locke to English Deism.* Chicago, 1918.

Hildebrandt, K. *Leibniz und das Reich der Gnade.* The Hague, 1953.

Lempp, O. *Das Problem der Theodicee in der Philosophie und Literatur des 18. Jahrhunderts bis auf Kant und Schiller.* Leipzig, 1910.

Leroy, A. *La critique de la religion de David Hume.* Paris, 1930.

Meinecke, F. *Die Entstehung des Historismus.* 2nd ed. Munich, 1964.

Mintz, S. *The Hunting of Leviathan,* 17th Century Reactions to the Materialism and Moral Philosophy of Th. Hobbes. Cambridge, 1962.

Mossner, E. C. *The Forgotten Hume, Le bon David.* NY: Columbia, 1943.

_____. *The Life of David Hume.* Austin: University of Texas Press, 1954.

Smith, N. K. *The Philosophy of David Hume.* London, 1941.

Söderblom, N. *Naturliche Theologie und allgemeine Religiongeschichte.* Stockholm and Leipzig, 1913.

Sorley, W. R. *A History of English Philosophy.* Cambridge,

1920.

_____. *Moral Values and the Idea of God.* 3rd ed. Cambridge, 1935.

Staudlin, C. F. *Geschichte des Rationalismus und Supernaturalismus.* Gottingen, 1826.

Troeltsch, E. "Deismus," *Realencyklopedie fur protestantische Theologie und Kirche,* Vol. IV. Leipzig, 1898. Abridged version in *Augsatze zur Geistesgeschichte und Religionssoziologie.* Werke, Vol. IV. Tubingen, 1925.

Wild, J. *George Berkeley, A Study of his Life and Philosophy.* Cambridge, 1936.

Enlightenment Atheism

(A) *Principal Works:*

Bergier, Abbe J. *Examen du materialisme ou refutation du Systeme de la Nature.* Tournai: J. Casterman, 1838.

d'Holbach, D. *Systeme de la nature.* 2nd ed. London, 1774.

La Mettrie, J. O. de. *L'Homme machine.* Ed. by M. Solovine. Paris: Boissard, 1921.

_____. *L'Homme Plante.* Leyden, 1748. Ed. Francis Rougier. Columbia University Press, 1936.

Vartanian, A. *La Mettrie's L'Homme Machine, A Study in the Origin of an Idea,* Critical Edition with an Introductory Monograph and Notes. Princeton: Princeton University Press, 1960.

Voltaire. *Dictionnaire Philosophique.* Ed. by J. Benda and R. Naves. Paris: Garnier, 1954.

(B) *Secondary Works* in addition to those already listed:

Belaval, Y. Preface to the 1966 reprint of the Paris 1821 edition of d'Holbach's *Systeme de la nature.* Hildesheim, 1966.

Lenin, V. I. *Ueber die Religion.* Berlin: Dietz Verlag, 1956.

Plechanov, G. W. *Beitrage Zur Geschichte des Materialismus.* Berlin, 1957.

Soviet author team. *Grundlagen der marxistischen Philosophie.* Berlin, 1959.

Vartanian, A. *Diderot and Descartes,* A Study of Scientific

Naturalism in the Enlightenment. Princeton: Princeton University Press, 1953.

_____. "From Deist to Atheist," *Diderot Studies,* Vol. I. Syracuse: 1949.

Wartofsky, M. W. "Diderot and the Development of Materialist Monism," *Diderot Studies,* Vol. II. Syracuse: University Press, 1952.

Zebenko, M. D. *Der Atheismus der franzosischen Materialisten des 18. Jahrhunderts.* Berlin: Dietz Verlag, 1956.

Disintegration of Idealism into Atheism

(A) Principal Works:

Fichte, J. G. *Angewandte Philosophie.* Werke, Vol. VI. Ed. by F. Medicus. Leipzig, 1912.

Hegel, G. W. *Berliner Schriften.* Ed. by J. Hoffmeister. Hamburg, 1956.

_____. *Glaube und Wissen. Werke,* Vol. I. Ed. by Lasson. Leipzig, 1930.

_____. *Phänomenologie des Geistes.* Ed. by Hoffmeister. Leipzig, 1937.

_____. Philosophie der Geschichte. Ed. by Gans. Stuttgart, 1961.

Hegel, G. W. *Philosophie der Religion.* Reprinted Vols. 15-16 of the Jubilaumsausgabe of the Samtliche Werke. Stuttgart, 1959. Ed. Lasson. Leipzig, 1930.

_____. *Die Positivitat der christlichen Religion.* In *Hegels Theologische Jugendschriften.* Ed. by H. Nohl. Tubingen, 1907.

Schlegel, F. *Die Entwicklung der Philosophie.* Werke, Vol. XIII. Ed. by J. J. Anstett. Munich, 1964.

Schleiermacher, F. *Der christliche Glaube. Werke,* Vol. I. 7th ed. by M. Redeker, Berlin, 1960.

_____. *Dialektik.* Ed. by R. Odebrecht. Leipzig, 1942.

(B) Secondary Works:

Brunner, E. *Die Mystik und das Wort.* Tubingen, 1924.

Erdmann, J. E. *Die Entwicklung der deutschen Spekulation*

526

seit Kant. Stuttgart, '31.

Fabro, C. *Hegel, La dialettica.* Brescia, 1960, 2nd ed., 1966.

Levy-Bruhl, L. *La philosophie de Jacobi.* Paris, 1894.

Rohmer, F. *Gott und seine Schopfung.* Nordlichen, 1857.

Vaihinger, A. *Die Philosophie des "Als ob."* 7th-8th ed. Leipzig, 1913.

Wahl, J. "A propos de l'Introduction a la Phenomenologie de Hegel par A. Kojeve," *Etudes Hegeliennes,* Deucalion 5. Neuchatel, 1955.

Explicit and Constructive Post-Hegelian Atheism

(A) Principal Works:

Engels, F. *Die Lage der arbeitenden Klasse in England.* Leipzig, 1845. Berlin, '58.

Feuerbach, L. *Principles of the Philosophy of the Future.* Bobbs-Merrill, 1966.

Lowith, K., ed. *Die Hegelsche Linke.* Stuttgart, 1962.

Reding, M. *Der politische Atheismus.* Graz-Vienna-Cologne, 1957.

(B) Secondary Works:

Arvon, H. *Ludwig Feuerbach ou la transormation due sacre.* Paris: P.U.F., '57.

Cornu, A. "L'idee d'alienation chez Hegel, Feuerbach et K. Marx," *La Pensee* 17, 1928.

Cottier, M. M. *L'atheisme du jeune Marx, see origines hegeliennes.* Paris, 1959.

Dicke, G. *Der Identitatsgedanke bei Feuerbach und Marx.* Cologne and Opladen, '60.

Ehlen, P. *Der Atheismus im dialektischen Materialiamus.* Munich, 1961.

Garaudy, R. *Dieu est mort, Etude sur Hegel.* Paris, 1962.

Gollwitzer, H. *Die marxistische Religionskritik und christlicher Glaube.* Tubingen, '62.

Hyppolite, J. *Genese et structure de la Phenomenologie de l'esprit de Hegel.* Paris, 1946.

Landgrege, L. "Das Problem der Dialektik," Marxismus-

527

Studien III, 1960.

Nudling, G. *L. Feuerbachs Religionsphilosophie.* Die Auflo-sung der Theologie in Anthropologie. Paderborn, 1936; 2nd ed., 1961.

Rohr, H. *Pseudoreligiose Motive in den Fruhschriften von K. Marx.* Tubingen, '62.

Vuillemin, J. "L'humanisme athee chez Feuerbach," Deucalion IV. Neuchayel and Paris, 1952.

Religious Atheism of Anglo-American Empiricism

(A) *Principal Works:*

Alexander, S. Space, Time and Deity. Gifford Lectures, Glasgow, 1916-18. London, 1920; 2nd ed., 1934.

Bradley, F. H. *Appearances and Reality.* London, 1893; 9th ed., 1930.

Dewey, J. A. "The Philosophy of Whitehead," *The Philosophy of A. N. Whitehead,* Ed. by P. A. Schilpp. NY: Tudor, 1951.

Hartshorne, C. Philosophers Speak of God. Chicago. University of Chicago Press, '53.

_____. "Whitehead's Idea of God," Schilpp, Tudor, '51.

James, W. *A Pluralistic Universe.* NY: Longmans, Green, 1909.

McTaggart, E. *The Nature of Existence.* Ed. C. D. Broad. Cambridge, 1927.

Morgan, L. *Emergent Evolution.* NY: H. Holt & Co., 1923.

Schilpp, P. A. *The Philosophy of George Santayana.* NY: Tudor Pub. Co., '51.

(B) *Secondary Works:*

Bixler, J. S. "Whitehead's Philosophy of Religion," Ed. Schilpp, NY, 1951.

Christian, W. A. "The Concept of God as Derivation Notion," The Hartshorne Festschrift, *Process and Divinity,* Ed. by W. L. Reese and E. Freeman, LaSalle, IL. 1964.

_____. "Whitehead's Explanation of the Past," *A. N. Whitehead, Essays on his Philosophy.* Prentice-Hall, 1963.

Reck, A. J. "The Philosophy of Charles Hartshorne," *Studies in Whitehead's Philosophy.* The Hague, 1961.

Reese, W. L. and E. Freeman, eds. The Hartshorne Festschrift, *Process and Divinity,* LaSalle, IL, 1964.

Stokes, W. E. "Whitehead's Challenge to Theistic Realism," The New Scholasticism 38, 1964.

Williams, D. W. "How does God Act?" An Essay in Whitehead's Metaphysics, *The Hartshorne Festschrift, Process and Divinity,* ed. by W. Reese and E. Freeman, LaSalle, 1964.

Freedom as an Active Denial of God in Existentialism

(A) *Principal Works:*

Camus, A. *L'homme revolte.* Paris: The Rebel, NY: Vintage Books, Random House, 1956.

Heidegger, M. *Identitat und Differenz.* Pfullingen: Neske, 1956. English translation by Kurt F. Leidecker, *Essays in Metaphysics: Identity and Difference.* NY: Philosophical Library, Inc., 1960.

Jaspers, K. "Antwort," in Karl Jaspers, Philosophen des 20. Jahrhunderts. Stuttgart, 1957.

_____. *Nietzsche and Christianity.* Chicago: Gateway, 1961.

Merleau-Ponty, M. *In Praise of Philosophy.* Evanston: Northwestern University Press, 1963.

Nietzsche, F. Thus Spoke Zarathustra. London, 1961.

(B) *Secondary Works:*

Birault, H. "De l'etre, du divin, des dieux chez Heidegger," *L'existence de Dieu.* Tournai, 1961.

Lowith, K. *Heidegger Denker in durftiger Zeit.* Frankfurt a. M., 1953.

Ricoeur, P. Phenomenologie existentielle in "Philosophie-Religion," *Encyclopedie Francaise,* Vol. XIX. Paris, 1957.

Schofer, E. *Die Sprache Heideggers.* Pfullingen, 1962.

Welte, B. *Nietzsches Atheismus und das Christentum.* Darmstadt, 1958.

Dialectical Theology and Death-of-God Theology

(A) Principal Works:

Altizer, T. J. J. *The Gospel of Christian Atheism.* Phil: Westminster Press, 1966.

Barth, K. *Die christliche Dogma tik.* Zurich, 1927.

Bonhoeffer, D. "Concerning the Christian Idea of God," The Journal of Religion, 1932. *Gesammelte Schriften,* Vol. III. Ed. E. Bethge. Munich: C. Kaiser Verlag, 1966.

Ogden, S. M. "The Christian Proclamation of God to Men of the So-Called 'Atheistic Age,' " Concilium, Vol. 16. NY: Paulist Press, 1966.

"The Temporality of God," *Zeit und Geschichte.* Dankesgabe an Rudolf Bultmann zum 80. Geburtstag. Tubingen, 1964.

Tillich, P. *Biblical Religion and the Search for Ultimate Reality.* University of Chicago Press, 1953.

Tillich, P. *The Shaking of the Foundations.* NY: Chas. Scribner's Sons, 1948.

Vahanian, G. *The Death of God.* NY: George Braziller, 1961.

Van Buren, P. M. *The Secular Meaning of the Gospel.* New York: MacMillan, 1966.

(B) Secondary Works:

Hamilton, W. *The New Essence of Christianity.* New York: Association Press, 1961.

Hartnack, J. *Wittgenstein und die moderne Philosophie.* Stuttgart, 1962.

Kasch, W. F. "Die Lehre von der Inkarnation in der Theologie Paul Tillichs," *Zeitschrift fur Theologie und Kirche 58,* 1, 1961.

Krause, G. "Dietrich Bonhoeffer und Rudolf Bultmann," *Zeit und Geschichte,* Dankesgabe an R Bultmann zum 80. Geburtstag. Tubingen, 1964.

Krech, W. "Analogia fidei oder analogia entis?" *Antwort,* Festschrift zum 70. Geburtstag von K. Barth. Zollikon Zurich: Evangelischer Verlag, '56.

Schmithals, W. *Die Theologie Rudolf Bultmanns*. Tubingen, 1966.

Schnubbe, O. *Der Existenzbergriff in der Theologie Rudolf Bultmanns*. Gottingen, 1959.

Thomas, J. H. "Some Comments on Tillich's Doctrine of Creation," *Scottish Journal of Theology* 14, 2, 1961.

The Inner Nucleus of Modern Atheism

(A) *Principal Works:*

Great Soviet Encyclopedia (Bol'shaya Sovetskaya Entsiklo-pediya). German translation, Grosse Sowjet-Enzyklopedie. Berlin: Dietz Verlag, 1950.

Hegel, G. W. *Die Beweise vom Dasein Gottes*. Ed. by Lasson. Leipzig, 1930.

(B) *Secondary Works:*

Alexandrov, G. Introduction to the Russian and German translations of M. Cornforth, *Science versus Idealism*, Berlin, 1955.

Bultmann, R. "Der Gottesgedanke und der moderne Mensch," *Glauben und Verstehen*, Vol. IV. Tubingen, 1965.

Chatelet, F. *Logos et Praxis*, Recherches sur le signification theorique du marxisme. Paris, 1962.

Horkheimer, M. "Theismus-Atheismus," *Zeugnisse*, Theodor W. Adorno zum 60. Geburtstag. Frankfurt a M., 1965.

Jordan, P. *Der Naturwissenschaftler vor der religiosen Frage*. Oldenburg-Hamburg. 1963.

Titius, A. *Natur und Gott*, Ein Versuch zur Verstandigung zwischen Naturwissenschaft und Theologie. Gottingen, 1926.

Ueber die formale Logik und Dialektik. Berlin: Verlag Kultur und Fortschritt 1952.

Vorret, M. *Les marxistes et la religion*. Paris, 1961.

SILENCE, SUFFERING, AND SIN:
PRESENT EVIL IN HIS PRESENCE

I have done no harm. But I remember now
I am in this earthly world; where to do harm
Is often laudable, to do good sometime
Accounted dangerous folly. — Lady Macduff —
in *Macbeth,* IV, IX, 74-77.

A knavish speech sleeps in a foolish ear. — Hamlet

The rest is silence — Good-night, sweet prince, and flights
of angels sing thee to thy rest. — Horatio

Is there any cause in nature that makes these hard hearts
— King Lear

It will come, humanity must perforce prey on itself, like
monsters of the deep. — Albany's prediction in *King Lear*
of our Nuclear Age

To thine own self be true
And it must follow, as the night the day,
Thou canst not then be false to any man. — Charles Lamb

I shouldn't be surprised if in this world
It were the force that would at last prevail. — Robert Frost

It was Brutus who stabbed Caesar with "the most un-
kindest cut of all" — "Et tu, Brute? Then fall, Caesar!"
Cinna cries — "Liberty! Freedom! Tyranny is dead!"

"A cruel sensuality" is close to the fountainhead of all
human evil whatsoever.—Dostoevsky

(Our culture has moved from *Crime* and *Punishment* to
the *Crime* of *Punishment.*)

Evil and Symbolic Duel

The duel is the solution in Shakespeare's *Romeo and Juliet;*
Turgenov's *Fathers and Sons;* Tolstoy's *War and Peace;* Dostoev-

sky's *The Brothers Karamazov;* and Chekhov's *The Duel.*

Our chief concern in the following essay is to allow the scriptures to speak their mind on the *nature of the presence of God* in a fallen universe. The *Silence* of God in a world of suffering does not make our Christian witness any easier. The biblical doctrine of the fall has since the 19th century developments in the genetic and comparative sciences been interpreted according to the Darwinian model. Two features of this model are: (1) the fall was not an historical event, and (2) the fall is a "myth" which seeks to interpret man's loss of innocence. The presuppositions of naturalistic evolution cannot be harmonized with the biblical claims. Man cannot "fall" upwards. Though the evidence does not support the four basic assumptions of *Classical Liberation* their influence persists unabated in the intellectual life of the last quarter of the 20th century. The four assumptions are: (1) the complete animality of man; (2) the inevitibility of progress; (3) the inherent goodness of man; and that (4) reality is exhausted by nature.[1]

The Four Horsemen

Suffering is a fact in our world. Death, disease, war and rumor of wars, famine, social unrest, political intrigue, deception and intimidation as characteristic of multinational industrial complex, Lockheed pay-offs, Washington scandal, crime in the streets are marks of our present condition. The four horsemen of the apocalypse are running rampant through the third and fourth worlds. The 30th parallel divides the *haves* and the *have nots.*

In order to respond to the contemporary epidemic of alternatives to the biblical view of newness, we must take note that according to the scriptures, nature is not autonomous.

---

[1] See C. F. H. Henry's *Remaking of The Modern Mind,* College Press reprint, 1972, with my extended bibliographical essay.

Neither is man who applies the scientific method to correct all of nature's alterations. The biblical witness is plain, and the evidence overwhelmingly supports its consistent judgment that neither man, nor nature, nor man's methods are autonomous. The ecological crisis was caused by man's failure to acknowledge the wholeness of nature. The ectosystemic imbalance was created by a lack of wholistic perspective on man's part of nature and her interconnected systems.

The collapse of the unity of science movement is "proof" that scientific method is not autonomous; and K. Godel's theorem demonstrates that even elementary mathematics contain no eminent consistency proof; i.e., metamathematics is imperative for both completeness and consistency proofs. Pluralism is the price paid for the loss of any universally valid organizing principle. Biblically, God is the solely autonomous being in the universe, as well as man's universe of discourse. Chancism, i.e., probability theory, is the basis for modern man's effort to explain the negative factors in a finite universe (cf. evil in a finite universe, Whitehead's, Hortshorne's, and Teilhard's statistical views of evil). Man sinned and disorder entered the universe. The first Hebrew word for sin (ra') in the book of Genesis has a root significant of violent rebellion against order. The fall narrative reveals three important matters: (1) how sin happens, (2) what it is, and (3) what consequences it produces. The disordering power of sinful rebellion extended into four areas of reality: (1) the relationship between God and man, (2) the intersubject relationship of man's wholeness, (3) the societal dimensions, and (4) the interrelation between man's dominion mandate—Gen. 1:26 and God's purpose for nature—history, resulting in fragmentation, i.e., the ecological crisis.[2]

Salvation in the biblical sense is the recovery of God's fallen universe and the consummation of God's purposes for His

---

[2] See my analysis in my doctoral thesis—*Theology of Creation and The Ecological Crisis*—Eden Theological Seminary, 1974, under Dr. M. Douglas Meeds, translator and friend of Jürgen Moltmann.

creation. In both creation and re-creation God's creature and relevatory Word and His organizing *Spirit* are inseparably involved. If we are to be representatives of Job's Creator-Redeemer God in the last quarter of the 20th century, then we must be (or become) aware of the presence of non-Christian and revolutionary concepts of salvation which dominate most contemporary international discussions (cf. Conference on *Salvation Today* at Bangkok, WCC, 1973, compare and contrast with The Chicago Declaration on the relationship of Evangelism and Social action).[3] No informed person is satisfied with the present human condition. Man as he is cannot create the good society, let alone the great society. Creative architects of contemporary thought from Kant to Hegel sought to remake man in their own image. Nietzsche's *Ubermensch* is his Frankenstein monster created to replace Christian man in 19th century Europe. The 19th-20th received many new models of newness: Darwin's biological man, Freud's indivisible man, Monod's genetic man, Crick's "coded man," Skinner's "conditioned man," Zen's and TM's inward true self, but what of Christ and the new man?—Rom. 8:19ff; 12:1ff; Gal. 6:15; II Cor. 5:17ff; Eph. 2:15; Rev. 21:5.

The Christian view of salvation in no way dismissed as irrelevant many of the creative insights of our late great mental giants, but for the most part the *vertical dimension* of both sin and salvation have been abandoned and replaced by a totally immanent *horizontal dimension* of sin and salvation. If Job's God is in exile or perhaps ever died, then neither sin nor salvation have anything to do with a fragmented relationship between God and man. Therefore, we must not forget the state of the God question, as discussed in the previous essay—*Is Job's God in Exile?*, if we are to have proper perspective in our considerations of salvation from sin. What is the nature of sin? Our answer to that question will largely determine our answer to the question, what does one mean

---

[3] For my analysis of the relationship between Evangelism and Social action see my *The Word of God for a Broken World,* LCC, 1977.

by *salvation?*

The Bible is consistent and clear that sin has both *personal* and *social* dimensions; therefore, an emphasis on only "personal salvation," which is certainly biblical, pays no heed to the *social significance* of either sin or salvation.[4] Sin is more than economic exploitation and alienation by poverty, but it is not less than these social results. Salvation is more than acceptable living standards, the recovery of just social and political structures, and the happiness attained from the possession of things, which gives to us a sense of psychological well-being and personal security. But salvation must become *publicly visible,* fulfilling David's admonition "Let the redeemed say so," if millions in our present world will ever come to believe that God is working out His purpose within the context of nature-history. The Biblical Theology of sin includes: (1) fractured relationship with God, (2) negative results throughout the structures of nature-history—Gen. 1-3; (3) fragmentation and alienation of man's essential nature, (4) the Fall as an event which disorganized created order at every level of reality, (5) the distinction between the principle of *sin* and *sins,* e.g., I John, (6) recognition of the socio-psychological dimensions of sin, (7) redemption in Christ as victory over the powers of sin and guilt, through the loving merciful forgiveness of our Creator-Redeemer God, and (8) redemption has an eschatological dimension which is empowered by hope (see next essay—*Hope in Time of Abandonment*) to live the abundant life (see John for the present reality of *Abundant Life*) now, even in a context of pain, suffering, and death.

Sin in the Secular City

How does the Bible describe sin? The irony of sin is seen in the biblical semantics. Sin is both personal and social.

---

[4] The classical prolonged debate between Billy Graham and Reinhold Niebuhr, the late neo-orthodox Social Ethicist, was doomed at the start as each was emphasizing only one dimension of the problem of "Sin" and "Salvation" to the exclusion of the other.

Man is both individual and corporately responsible for the consequences of sin. A systems analysis of the effect of sin and sins reveals the interrelatedness of human acts to the social drama. All evil is not accountable from personal sins. Many suffer (Jn. 9) and their personal sins are not the cause. As with Job, and our Suffering Servant, often the righteous suffer and the wicked prosper. Surd evil, e.g. tornado, famine, war, disease, etc., is a larger category of cosmic disorder than mere moral anomie on man's part. The large picture reveals both macro and micro disorder in the universe. Before turning to the biblical semantics of sin we must briefly confront alternative explanatory systems to our own biblical base. Biblical presuppositions regarding the nature and significance of sin were challenged in the very century in which the totally secularization of man was initiated, the century of Rousseau, et al. The naturalistic counter explanation to the biblical position maintains that *evil* originates in man's *environment* (cf. contemporary thesis of the Behavioral Sciences that man is totally genetically and environmentally determined). Man is neither naturally good nor naturally neutral. He learns to do evil in the contexts of his environment institutions. J. J. Rousseau says that "man is naturally good and that our social institutions alone have rendered him evil." Marx's creative destruction thesis is derived from this naturalistic assumption. Contemporary anti-institutionalism also stems from this position. Man's vested interests, i.e., his values cause him to create institutions to protect his vested interest. If the status quo is to be effectively challenged, then destruction of his social institutions is imperative. One of the men with whom A. Campbell debated, R. Owen, about whom Marx remarked that he was the only intelligent socialist that he knew, claimed that man is essentially good and that evil arises from ignorance and harsh living conditions (cf. plot of *The Republic* and *The Laws*). In those characters which now exhibit crime, the fault is obviously not in the individual but the defect proceeds from the system in which the individual has been trained. Evil comes from governments and institutions.[5] (Cf. contemporary naturalistic functionalistic theory of the origins of *all* human institutions, e.g. marriage, home, church, etc. The thesis asserts that institutions exist merely to meet needs, when they no longer meet the needs, then one abandons the institution to oblivion.) Karl Marx claims that the origin of evil is outside of man, i.e., the capitalistic economic system and the deprivations spawned by it. When economic needs are met, harmony will result. But empirical evidence from Neo-Marxists states, even Cuba and China, hardly justifies this optimism. B. F. Skinner believed that the current malaise could be redeemed in one giant Skinner Box. But a funny thing happened on the way to the Skinner Box, man lost his freedom and dignity. Man "is indeed controlled by his environment. Practices in which a person is held responsible for his conduct and given credit for his achievements; a scientific analysis shifts both the responsibility and the achievement to the environment." These four classic examples of the naturalistic theory of the origin of evil have at least two factors in common with our immediate concern: (1) for these men, God is dead; and (2) only a scientific study of the social interrelationship can modify man's environment which ultimately will make new man. The central problem which they all share is: If we are all *totally* environmentally determined, how could the scientific method have broken the power of nature, and where does the scientist *stand* in a determined universe to set us free from nature's claims? If God is not allowed to be transcendent over the systems of the universe, why and how could the scientific method achieve saving transcendence? This sounds like the myth of value free, "i.e., objective science." At least it is possible to demonstrate that "value free" decision making is not the case, but

---

[5] Consider the brilliant survey on *World Economy* in the 1976 edition of *The Great Ideas Today* and a concrete evaluation of the expropriation of our health by the famous Roman Catholic priest, Ivan Illich, *Medical Nemesis*, New York: Pantheon, 1976, as men have been "programmed" to think that economic security and physical and mental well-being are our supreme values since man has become terrified by death and dying.

the same cannot be substantiated regarding the existence of a Creator-Redeemer God. God is still the most viable option available.

Other naturalistic cohorts of the above famed prophets of environmental determinism are those who claim against the Christian understanding, that evil originates in man himself. Naturalistic evolutionary presuppositions maintain that "human nature," now known as the "human condition," has evolved from lower to higher forms of life—and certain innate tendencies, which may have been functional at one time in man's development ceased to be functional, yet continued to exist, thus plaguing man's attempt to build a good society. Since these assumptions control contemporary *social, legal, penal* theories, it is imperative that Christians understand their significances. For a naturalistic reading of our problem, see the thesis of the anthropologists, Lionel Tiger and Robin Fox. *The Imperial Animal,* New York, Dell, 1971, and Morris', *The Naked Ape.* For a slightly more advanced defense, see the work of the Austrian naturalist, Konrad Lorenz, *On Aggression,* Harcourt, Brace, and World, E.T., 1966. Lorenz sees aggression in man as a part of his innate, inherited nature and as a drive which is presently malfunctioning to the point of being a disease: aggression and technological competence to destroy. Darwin's "survival of the fittest," is not surviving. "Natural selection" (cf. When God is dead, men must speak anthropomorphically of nature.) has failed to eliminate the aggressive drive. The American dream has been built on conflict, competition, disruption, tragedy and in that order. Koren Horney's *The Neurotic Personality of Our Time* originally published in 1937 had already warned of the destructive tendencies in a society whose very dynamic for progress was nothing more than a friendly competitive spirit that would become demonic in power and fragment its users. Her prophecy had been fulfilled long before America entered her third century.

From the naturalistic assumptions regarding the origins of evil follow the contemporary socio-politico-economic theory

539

of salvation.[6] But the biblical witness sees evil as a much more radical phenomenon than mere privation of good, as did the Rationalists, or as something that progressive development in biological and social evolution will eliminate as did the participants in the Enlightenment,[7] "nature is red in tooth and claw" and man continues to inflict pain on his fellow pilgrim.

Pilgrims with Cold Feet in the Promised Land

What are the prospects of the promised land of faith? What evil do the believers experience as they travel through existence? Evil is an irrational and malignant force in the fallen universe. Since Hume's classical argument in *Dialogues Concerning Natural Religion,* it has been philosophically acceptable to

---

[6]   I. *Sociological Views of Salvation* (corporate versus individual)
    a. Auguste Comte - Positivism
    b. Herbert Spencer - Evolution and society
    c. Marx - Economic determinism
    d. Schools of Sociological Theory: Social Darwinism, Psychological Evolution, Early Analytical Sociology, Russian Sociological Theory, Decline of Evolutionism and rise of neo-Positivism, Sociology of Knowledge thesis, Interdisciplinary approach.
   II. *Political and Economic Views of Salvation:* From Marx to the Theology of Revolution
  III. *Psychological Views* (Sin, Sickness, Psychosomatic medicine, etc.) and Psychological Theories of Explanation of Individual Disorders
    a. *Areas of Psycho-Pathology*
      1. Ethics, guilt, responsibility
      2. Psychosomatic concept of disease
      3. Psychoneuroses
      4. Narcotics
      5. Physiochemical methods of therapy
      6. Mental deficiency - the exceptional child
      7. Psychopathic personalities
      8. Sex deviation and immediate need for sex education within Christian context.
    b. Subliminal research in the age of technique: Manipulation via Brain washing, Madison Avenue Hard sell.
   IV. *The Concept of Conversion and/or Salvation in Non-Christian Religions*

[7] For Kant's view of evil see *Kant et Le Probleme du Mal,* Presses de L'Universite de Montreal, 1971; see also Jean Nabent, *Essai sur le Mal,* reprinted 1966.

assert that the fact of evil is "proof" against the very existence of the Christian God.[8] Though it is not our intention here to deal technically with this crucial challenge to the Christian reading of reality, we must briefly state the fundamental issues. Often the opponent of the Christian view of reality poses the question—Why does God allow it: Perhaps there is an equally appropriate interrogation—Why does man perpetrate it? Does evil vanish from the human scene upon the arrival of Nietzsche's madman announcing the cultural demise of the deity? Hardly!

A Metaphysic of Evil[9]

Though an attack on the existence of the Christian God from the penomenon of evil is not a recent insight, or lack

[8] See the brilliant but technical response by Alvin Plantinga, *God and Other Minds,* Ithaca: Cornell University Press, 1967; and his *God, Freedom, and Evil,* New York: Harper Torch, 1974; for non-technical discussion see C. S. Lewis, *The Problem of Pain,* pb. 1940; and *A Grief Observed,* New York: Seabury Press, 1961; for some excellent but futile efforts to formulate the problem of evil against the Christian perspective see N. Pike, *God and Evil,* Englewood Cliffs: Prentice Hall, 1964; for confrontation with Plantinga—Robert Pargetter, "Evil as Evidence Against the Existence of God," *Mind,* Apr. 1976.

[9] Metaphysics of Evil:

Altizer, Thomas J. J., and Hamilton, William. *Radical Theology and The Death of God.*
Barth, John. *The End of the Road.*
_____. *The Floating Opera.*
Buber, Martin. *Eclipse of God.*
Camus, Albert. *The Myth of Sisyphus.*
_____. *The Plague.*
_____. *The Rebel.*
Dewart, Leslie. *The Future of Belief.*
Dostoevsky, F. *The Brothers Karamazov.*
Eliade, Mircea. *Cosmos and History.*
Fabry, Joseph P. *The Pursuit of Meaning* (read with Frankl, Victor, *Man's Search for Meaning*)
Gilkey, Langdon. *Naming the Whirlwind.*
Hamilton, William. *The New Essence of Christianity.*
Hartshorne, Charles. *The Divine Relativity.*
Hick, John. *Evil and the God of Love.*

of it, we will take David Hume's (cf. *Dialogues*) questions as the classical formulation of our dilemma: (1) what is the origin, i.e., cause of evil; (2) what is the purpose of evil, i.e., its justification; and (3) what is the purpose for allowing evil to continue to function, if there does in fact exist a God both holy and all-powerful?

Suppose that these are fundamental questions but that they cannot be answered with our present level of information. If these questions are unanswerable, what *philosophical* consequences follow? We must not confuse biographical, socio-psychological questions with theological or philosophical ones.

Hume, David. *Dialogues Concerning Natural Religion.*
Jung, Carl. *Psychology and Religion.*
Kaufman, Gordon. *Relativism, Knowledge, and Faith.*
_____. *Critique of Religion and Philosophy.*
Kazantzakis, N. *Report to Greco.*
_____. *Spiritual Exercises.*
Keen, Sam. *Apology for Wonder.*
_____. *To a Dancing God.*
Kierkegaard, Soren. *Fear and Trembling.*
_____. *The Concept of Dread.*
_____. *Sickness Unto Death.*
Lamont, Corliss. *The Philosophy of Humanism.*
Lewis, C. S. *The Problem of Pain.*
Macquarrie, John. *An Existentialist Theology.*
Marcel, Gabriel. *The Philosophy of Existence.*
Meland, Bernard E. *The Secularization of Modern Cultures.*
Munitz. *The Mystery of Existence.*
Nietzsche, F. *Thus Spake Zarathustra.*
Novak, Michael. *Belief and Unbelief.*
_____. *The Experience of Nothingness.*
Robinson, John A. T. *Honest to God* (read also in connection with this, Edwards, D. L., ed., *The Honest to God Debate*).
Rosen, Nathan. *Nihilism.*
Rubenstein, Richard. *After Auschwitz* (for studies in socio-pathology of evil see Sanford N. and Comstock, C. *Sanctions for Evil,* San Francisco, Jessey-Bass, Inc., 1971).
Siwek, Paul. *The Philosophy of Evil.*
Smith, Huston. *Condemned to Meaning.*
Sontag, F. *The Existentialist Prolegomena.*
Tannant, F. R. *Philosophical Theology,* Vol. II.
Tillich, Paul. *The Courage to Be.*
_____. *Dynamics of Faith.*
Vahanian, Gabriel. *The Death of God.*
_____. *Wait Without Idols.*

This warning is appropriate because it has been assumed that Hume's arguments are "necessary proofs"[10] against the existence of the Christian God.

The epistemic consequences of Hume's questions center around the justification for believing that God is both *omnipotent* and *benevolent*. What reasons can we give for believing that He possesses both of the above characteristics yet allows evil to continue? Before we become too troubled with this dilemma, let us ask ourselves a fundamental question. Why does man need to know why God permits evil? Epistemologically the argument is not effective. But psychologically it has a more telling effect on the seeker. Yet our concern is for "necessary reasons" for rejecting either *God's existence* or His *omnipotence* and *benevolence*. Even from a human viewpoint we should not be disturbed, at least logically, by our ignorance of God's ways because we do not very often understand man's ways. An example might be that we do not understand a given behavior pattern found in a non-western culture. In order to understand the given behavior we would need to comprehend the cultural configuration of that particular group. Missionaries have made the mistake of putting clothes on girls in cultures where such garments are not used. The people begin to think that the missionaries have made their daughters into prostitutes because only prostitutes can afford clothes in that particular culture. Another example might be the behavior of a CIA agent. Without knowing the *overall* plan which dictated a given behavior, we cannot understand the interrelationship of each given behavior as it relates to the overall plan. In God's case, we would need to know the interrelatedness of the systems of the entire universe, which is not an appropriate aspiration

---

[10] The nature of "proof," evidence, argument in relation to world-views must be considered, but for our basic purposes their consideration will be postponed. For an analysis of the "nature of necessity" see Alvin Plantanga, *The Nature of Necessity,* Oxford University Press, 1974; also John Machie "Evil and Omnipotence," in *The Philosophy of Religion,* ed. B. Mitchell, Oxford University Press, 1971; and A. Flew, "Divine Omnipotence and Human Freedom," in *New Philosophical Theology,* eds., A. Flew and A. MacIntyre, London: SCM, 1955, pp. 150-3.

even for our contemporary Prometheus. This approach is an effective response only for those who believe that the Human arguments "necessarily" prove the non-existence of God.

But the second argument which is concerned with the justification for God's allowing evil to continue, depends on a conceptual connection among the notions of *evil, power,* and *goodness.* If God is *omnipotent,* then He is surely justified in allowing evil. But if He is *benevolent,* why does He: But the "why" does not provide any "necessary" argument against either His *benevolence* or *omnipotence.* Yet the dilemma as an epistemic problem continues. It is strange that those who are often most hostile to "truth" and "logic" are the most certain that evil is "necessary proof" against God's existence. What effect would an epistemic solution have on belief? Belief must be kept distinct from truth, because one may believe that which is either demonstrably false, or has no verification whatsoever. Anyone can believe what he wishes, but if he wishes others to share that belief, then justification must be forthcoming, via logic, evidence and arguments. Why should *anyone* believe *anything* about anything? We do not believe that our brief statement has resolved the haunting hurt caused by the fact of evil, but we do maintain that technical arguments can be structured to "prove" that evil is not a "necessary" proof either against God's *omnipotence* or His *benevolence.* Since Hume's classic statements it has been "assumed" that his arguments "necessarily" generate a dilemma for any informed person, that either *God's existence* or His *benevolence* must be rejected.[11]

For millions, God is still *silent* and their suffering unbearable. Denying the existence of evil or postulating an eternal dualism is neither philosophically defensible, nor existentially encouraging. Stoic resignation does not remove the broken heart of the rivulets of tears, but what of man's participation in the cosmic malignancy?

---

[11] See the excellent survey of views of the nature and reality of evil—R. P. Sertillanges, *Le Probleme du Mal,* Paris: Ambier, 1948, for statement of the positions espoused by Eastern religions, Graeco-Rome religions, Gnosticism, Neo-Platonism, Christianity on into the Enlightenment and present world.

A Problem Fit for God[12]

Evil is a larger problem than sin, but man is no match for sin, let alone evil. What does the Word say regarding *sin* and *sins?* How does human sin perpetrate the disordering effect on life and man's environmental structures?

Design and Disorder

God has a design for His creation; and man's sin disorders it. Redemption is the ultimate eschatological recovery of that order through Christ, our Savior from sin and its consequences. How do the scriptures address themselves to the fact of sin?

Old Testament Vocabulary for Sin: (1) Early vocabulary— (a) *hattah,* miss the mark (Judges 26:16), (b) *awon,* iniquity, crookedness (Genesis 4:13, 15:16), and (c) *ra,* evil (earliest root), physical calamity or violent breaking of God's orders (Genesis 2:9); (2) Patriarchial Period—two new words—(a) *resha,* wickedness (Genesis 18:23—root, loose, ill-regulated), and (b) *pesha*—transgression (Genesis 50:17—root rebel, I Kings 12:19, deliberate and premeditated—Job 34:37 speaks of adding pesha to hattah); (3) Moses period—2 new words— (a) *ma-al,* trespass (Leviticus 5:15, Numbers 5:12, marital faithlessness, root—treachery or faithlessness to covenant (I Chron. 9:1); (b) *awel* (or awal), perversity (Leviticus 19:15— root, to deviate, man's deviation from right course; and (4) Moses-David—*awen,* wickedness—root, to be tried.

---

[12] On the Biblical doctrine of *sin* see J. Pedersen, *Israel, its Life and Culture,* pp. 411ff; C. H. Dodd, *The Bible and the Greeks,* pp. 76-81; G. F. Moore, *Judaism,* 3 vols., Harvard University Press; H. Büchler, *Studies in Sin,* 1928; E. Brunner, *Man in Revolt,* especially chapters 6-7; R. Niebuhr, *The Nature and Destiny of Man,* chapters 7-10; F. R. Tennant, *The Concept of Sin;* N. P. Williams, *The Ideas of the Fall and of Original Sin,* 1927; Quell, Bertram, Stahlin, and Grundmann, art "harmatia" *TWNT,* Vol. I; A. Gelin, *Sin in the Bible,* New York: Desclee, 1965; S. Porubean, *Sin in the Old Testament,* 1963; P. Schoonenberg, *Man's Sin,* Notre Dame, 1965; S. Kierkegaard, *The Sickness Unto Death,* especially "Despair is Sin," and G. C. Berkouwer, *Sin,* Grand Rapids: Eerdmans.

New Testament Vocabulary for Sin: Sin in the New Testament is regarded as the missing of the mark or aim (*hamartia* or *hamartema*); the overpassing or transgressing of a line (*parabasis*); the inattentiveness or disobedience to a voice (*parakoe*); the falling alongside where one should have stood upright (*paraptoma*); the doing through ignorance of something wrong which one should have known about (*agnoema*); the coming short of one's duty (*hettema*); and the non-observance of a law (*anomia*); *adikia,* unrighteousness. The Biblical Theology of Sin includes: (1) God, (2) Created Cosmos; (3) Man; (4) the Fall; (5) Sin and Sins; (6) Social and Psychological Dimensions of Sin; (7) Redemption through the victory of Christ, love, guilt, forgiveness, etc.

The sound of His *silence* continues to deafen man in his cauldron of pretentious piety. *Suffering,* both physical and spiritual, is an everywhere event. Who is to blame? Who can do anything about it? The biblical witness, for which we are responsible, calls us once more to bear witness to His presence, even in a fallen universe. He "is in Christ reconciling this world unto Himself."

The Manner of His Presence [13]

The only hope man has in his time of abandonment is the presence of our redeemer God. Evil and silence raise the issue of His presence, not His existence. God manifested His presence by His creative word. He said "let be" and there was creation.

---

[13] For the Biblical theology of His presence see J. Danielou, *Le Signe du Temple ou de la Presence de Dieu,* Paris: Gallimard, 1942; M. Foeyman, "La spiritualisation de l' idee du temple dons les epitres Pauliniennes," *Ephemerides Theologicae Lovanienses,* 1947, pp. 378-412; W. J. Phythian-Adams, *The People and The Presence,* London, 1942; E. C. Dweick, *The Indwelling God, Historical Study of the Christian Conception of Immanence and Incarnation,* London, 1938; On the glory—Kabod see Kittel, *TWNT,* Vol. II, pp. 237-41; G. R. Berry, "The Glory of Yahweh and the Temple," *JBL,* 1937, pp. 115-7; for Shekinah concept see M. J. Lagrance, *Le judaisme avant Jesus Christ,* p. 446ff, and Yves Congar, *The Mystery of the Temple,* London: Burnst Oates, E.T., 1962.

Creation was good, very good, but sin disordered that purpose for which God had created. Neither man nor nature can find fulfillment when God's presence is not only acknowledged but publicly visible. At the time of the Exodus, God's presence was visible in confrontation with the gods of Egypt. His presence always liberates for fulfillment of His purpose, not necessarily ours. As Israel marched in the desert the pillar of clouds was the visibility of His presence, then Moses acted in unbelief. The result was that God withdrew His public visibility and chose to be available only in the "holy of holies" (Hebrew is root for "word" or that which supports or holds up everything else in the universe) and available to a special mediator, the high priest. God came closer to creation in the words of the prophets, then one dark night—the Word came to enlighten the fallen world. His redemptive presence engaged the forces of evil, sin, and suffering. The majesty and mystery of His presence again becomes silent before Pilate, and Pilate marvels. God manifested His redemptive grace in His presence.[14]

God's supreme identification with the fallen universe and sinful man was in the incarnation of Jesus, Job's vindicator. As in the Old Testament, so in the New Testament, only a faithful remnant will hear and obey the living word, who was silent, who suffered, and bore the sting of sin and evil in Himself. His resurrection is the shattering of silence, a permanent clue in nature-history for man that God's purpose will prevail.

The return of God's silence to 20th century man is, as it was in the Old Testament, a sign of His judging presence, but the history making resurrection is the source of power to live between the times until all creation fulfills its original purpose. There is hope in times of abandonment, but that hope must not be based in man's Promethean pride, but in the power of His presence.

---

[14] G. Philips, "La grace des justes de l'Ancien testament," *Ephem. Theo-Lovan,* 1947, pp. 521-56; 1948, pp. 23-58.

APPENDIX: ORIGINS OF THE SECULAR CITY

I. *A. Comte: Presuppositions, Scientific Method, and Quantifiability of Total Reality.*

A. Fundamental Theories—"the law of the three stages," history of human thought can be divided into three stages: (1) Theological, (2) Metaphysical, and (3) Positive.

1. In the first stage man attempts to explain everything in terms of supernatural causes, progressing from animism to polytheism to monotheism. This stage extends from the most primitive times down through the Middle Ages.

2. The second stage is characterized by the substitution of abstractions for a personal God or gods. Nature is frequently substituted for God, and fictions such as the "social contract," natural rights, and the sovereignty of the people appear in the social philosophy of this stage, e.g. 18th century.

3. The third stage is the age of science when man discards all abstractions and metaphysical concepts and confines himself to the empirical observation of successive events from which he induces Natural Laws—all other stages have been progressing toward the Goal: Establishment, with and of scientific methods, of perfect order and social harmony. New Science of Society necessary—Social Physics, later renamed *Sociology*—to replace *Theology*.

Comte's order—from Simple to Complex: (1) Math, (2) Astrology, (3) Physics, (4) Chemistry, (5) Biology, (6) Sociology—social statics, i.e., categories, ideas, customs, institutions; social dynamics—describing development of society in terms of the three stages—progress. Social Statics and Social Dynamics emphasize both *order* and *progress*. Positivism consists in substituting study of "invariable laws of phenomena" for "causes," i.e., studying *How* instead of *Why*.

A religion necessary to harmonize man's *Intelligence*

548

and heart—by surrendering himself to something outside himself and to which he is necessarily related. Comte proposes *Religion of Humanity* (on the Way to *Secular City Secularism*).

B. *From Comte to John Stuart Mill:* Logic of the Moral Sciences
Scientific Method to Human and Social Phenomena. Sect. "On the logic of the Moral Sciences," in his *System of Logic,* 1843.

1. Mill's presuppositions: establishment of natural science of man and of society.

2. All phenomena of Society are phenomena of Human Nature generated by action of outward circumstances upon masses of human beings, and if, therefore, phenomena of human thought, feeling, and action are subject to fixed laws, the phenomena of society cannot but conform to fixed laws.

3. The Great Obstacle: Obstacle to establishment of Natural Social Science is lack of sufficient data. (Prediction of history of society?) Difference of certainty is not laws per se but data to which laws are applied; amount of knowledge quite insufficient for prediction, may be most valuable for guidance.

4. New Science of the Formation of Character Mill called "Ethology." This science will discover "what makes one person, in a given position, feel or act in one way, another in another." Deductive Science. Mill concludes: Good man—typical 19th century gentlemen.

C. *From Mill to Darwin: Origin and Significance of the Darwinian Model*
Evolution—Progressive development in nature of plants and animals from lower stages to higher ones. Modern theories of evolution seek to explain progressive change in purely naturalistic terms—causes of change immanent in the process itself rather than outside the process. (See *Newness on the Earth,* Strauss)

Theories:
1. Simple to Complex—Greeks
2. Ceaseless flux and change—Lucretius and Heracletus
3. Recent Theories—From Darwinian model to Big Bang, Steady State Models, and DNA, etc., of Watson, Crick, Monad, Wilson, et al. and the Genetic and Environmental determinism.

APPENDIX: COSMIC DISORDER AND THE ECOLOGICAL CRISES:

Scripture: Psalm 24—The Whole Earth Is The Lord's
Introduction: The O.T. begins by asserting that God *created* the heavens and the earth. The N.T. ends with the *consummation* of God's purpose for His universe. All in between reveals that God is the God of both *creation* and *redemption.*

  a. Man's relationship to God   *The Fall*
  b. Man's relationship with himself   (Genesis 3)
  c. Man's relationship with his fellowmen affected the
  d. Man's relationship with nature   four areas.

The biblical doctrine of reconciliation includes all four categories and not just fallen man, as is often popularly supposed.

A. *God, Creation (Nature), Man and the Dominion Mandate* (Genesis 1—3)
  1. Nature of God
  2. Purpose of nature
  3. The image of God and creation freedom to participate in God's purpose in nature and history (Genesis 1:26).
  4. Biblical account vs. creation myths from the Near East

B. *Place of Creation in Israel's Worship*—i.e., in the Psalms
  1. Psalm 3   3. Psalm 24
  2. Psalm 19   4. Psalm 104

C. *Doctrine of Creation in Job*—especially chapters 33—41
  1. Creation and evil   3. Creation and righteousness
  2. Creation and justice   4. Creation and suffering

D. *Theology of Creation in Isaiah*—chapters 40—55
  1. The relationship of creation and redemption

550

2. The relationship of creation and history
3. The relationship of nature, history, and God's final purpose for activity
4. The relationship of God's act and man's scientific technological activity

E. *Christ as Lord of Nature*
   1. Miracles—nature   2. Miracles—seeing, hearing, etc.

F. *Christ and Cosmology*
   1. Christ and the Cosmos—Ephesians 1:10; Colossians 1:17
   2. Christ, Redemption and Creation—Romans 8:19ff
   3. Christ and the New Heaven and New Earth—Isaiah 60—66; II Peter 3:13; Revelation 21:5
   4. Man as creature and new creation—Revelation 21:5; "Behold, I am making all things new." Maranatha

G. *Christ, the New Creation, the Dominion Mandate, and Fragmented Nature*—Our Present Ecological Crisis
   1. Schaeffer's, *Pollution and the Death of Man* (Inter-Varsity Press).
   2. Commoner, Barry. *The Closing Circle* (Knopf Press).
   3. My doctoral thesis. *Theology of Creation and The Ecological Crisis* with bibliography.

APPENDIX: SOCIAL THEORY AND THE
SIGNIFICANCE OF SIN AND SALVATION:
CHRIST, MARX, AND CRITICAL SOCIAL THEORY:

Theologies of Hope, Revolution, and Liberation:
(Neo-Marxism of The Frankfort School of Social Research)

(Spokesmen - G. Lukas, E. Bloch, H. Marcuse, J. Habermas,
M. Horkheimer, Mao-Tse-Tung, E. Fromm. et al.)

I. *Critical Questions:*
   A. Nature of Critical Knowledge, i.e., Dialectical Logic.
   B. Relationship of Theory and Practice
   C. Control and Liberation of Critical Consciousness (i.e., necessary condition for revolutionary social/cultural

change
D. Labor and its relationship to man's Essence
E. Industrial Technological Society and its impact on Liberation (Basis for non-aggressive, non-repressive society); Vested Interests, Values, and Repression, Domination and Aggression.

II. *Methods and Consequences:*
   A. Kant's Epistemology
   B. Hegel's Dialectical Method (and Dialectical theory of Society).
   C. Phenomenology, critique of certain types of scientific models, and emphasis of primacy of life-world.
   D. Hermeneutics and Historical interpretation of meaning (Heidegger-Bultmann; Dilthey - Gadamer - Hirsch and the Post-Bultmannians.)
   E. M. Weber's theory of rationalization and its contribution to the development of one-dimensional society.
   F. Adaptation of Freud's psychoanalytic theory as the basis of a radical social theory (esp. Marcuse and Habermas— and their philosophy of history and theory of knowledge).

III. *Critical Theory, The Individual as agent of liberation, Structure of Communication, and the Nature of Technological Rationality*
   A. Habermas' three types of knowledge: Natural science, cultural science, and critical science.
   B. The great failure in theories of knowledge and science— taking account of Interests guiding modes of knowledge.
   C. Theory is not merely intellectual contemplation; it is also practice.
   D. The Party of Eros: Post World War II—Radical Social Theorists—Marcuse, Goodman, Brown, and the new R. C. Left, e.g., Joseph Petulla. Basic assumptions: (1) Common "on look" on the question of man's *alienation* and *liberation.* (2) Nature-history is the arena of

552

man's *self-creation* and *self-redemption.*

IV. *The Word in a World of Dissident Voices* (John 1:1-18)
   A. Data of Doom
   B. Spiritual Renewal or Marx's Creative Destruction
   C. Jesus the Revolutionary
   D. The Enemy of the People (Ebsen)—The Truth
   E. New Life—New Life Style—Pursuit of the Good Life;
   Life—Death—The Resurrection (Romans 6:1ff; John's
   Gospel)

SATAN IN A SCIENTIFIC WORLD:
RISE AND FALL OF SATAN IN WESTERN CULTURE

"For now the devil, that told me I did well, says that this deed is chronicled in hell." Exton in *Hamlet.*

"The idea of Satan and demons is finished. Finished is the theory of the Virgin Birth. Finished is the question of whether Jesus of Nazareth is God's Son or not. Finished is the teaching of the substitutionary atonement, the resurrection, and the ascension. Finished is the belief in the Second Coming. Finished are the miracles and answers to prayer." R. Bultmann, *Kerygma and Myth.*

"There are two equal and opposite errors into which our race can fall about the devils. One is to disbelieve in their existence. The other is to believe, and to feel an excessive and unhealthy interest in them." C. S. Lewis, *The Screwtape Letters.*

"Satan is the absolute anti-model." Denis de Rougement in *The Devil's Snare.*

"The demonic is the elevation of something conditional to unconditional significance." Paul Tillich *Systematic Theology,* Vol. I, p. 140.

"To set himself in glory above his peers, He trusted to have equalled the most high." Milton, *Paradise Lost,* I, pp. 39-40.

"Look to your feet, for you shall presently be among the snares." Bunyan, *Pilgrim's Progress,* p. 256.

"Resist the devil, and he will flee from you." James 4:7

Satan and The Jobian Drama

The third major participant in the Jobian drama is Satan.[15] But since the scientific revolution in the 17th century and the behavioral-cultural studies revolution in the 19th century, more and more people find belief in a personal evil being difficult to accept. After the developments in the history and comparative religious areas the case against the existence of an ontological Satan grew more secure. Paul clearly declares that "we are not contending against flesh and blood but against principalities, against powers." (Ephesians 6:12) But such description is very difficult for technologically oriented 20th century man to appreciate. The 19th century produced the Comparative Religion School and the History of Religions school, each of which cast serious doubts on the ontological existence of Satan, principalities and powers, and evil spirits, etc. James G. Frazer's, *The Golden Bough: A Study in Magic and Experimental Science,* 12 volumes, MacMillan Co., 1935, and Lynn Thorndike's *A History of Magic and Experimental Sciences* Volumes, I-VI, MacMillan and Columbia University Press, 1923-41 were and are influential in circles which believe that the revolutionary developments in the sciences preclude the validity of the biblical witness to the existence of supernatural

---

[1] For a thorough analysis of the person and role of Satan in Yahweh's adversary see Roland Villeneuve, *Bibliographie demoniaque,* pp. 647-664; A. Lefevre, *Ange ou bete,* pp. 13-27; A. Frank-Duquesne, *Reflections sur Satan en marge de la tradition Judeo-Chretienne,* pp. 179-315; C. G. Jung, *Symbolik des Geites,* 1948, pp. 151-319; A. Lods "Les origines de la figure de Satan, ses fonctions a la cour celeste," in *Melanges Syriens,* for R. Dussaud, Vol. II, Paris, 1939, pp. 649-660; Kittel article, "Diabolos," *TWNT,* Vol. II; pp. 71; and R. S. Kluger, *Satan in The Old Testament* (Evanston: Northwestern University Press, 1967.

evil beings such as Satan. M. Dibelius, *Die Geisterwelt im Glauben des Paulus,* Gottingen, 1909 was the result of the most radical developments in the history of religion. Fused with R. Bultmann's radical hermeneutical principle, which relegates the biblical data concerning Satanology to the category of myth, though to be sure that is the technical connotation of myth which stems from folklore research and comparative religion, Dibelius' word removed the demoniac from serious exegetical consideration until the outbreak of irrational evil forces, especially immediately following the II World War. In Heinrich Schlier's inaugural lecture, "Machte und Getwalten im Neuen Testament," *Theologische Blatter,* 1930, we hear the Marburg of Heidegger and Bultmann denounce the objective realities of "principalities and powers." Even the old neo-orthodox exorcist, K. Barth, gives token consideration to the "Powers" in his *Church Dogmatics,* Vol. III/3.

Between the 19th and 20th century, many in Western Christian civilization rejected the biblical category of evil powers and replaced the biblical explanation with the counter explanation of sociology and psychology, etc. These explanations were satisfactory to many until the most radical outbreak of occult in the history of the world, in the last 25 years. Christian—arm for battle!

The near Eastern parallels hardly prove that Satan is unreal, i.e., only a mythological projection of man in his search for a solution to his experience of evil and suffering. The existence of counterfeit ten dollar bills do not prove that there are no genuine bills, but rather that there are also some spurious ones. Note the implications of the following statements concerning shifts in assumptions.

There are three great configurations of basic assumptions in the revolution in Western thought and education: 1) The Graeco-Roman or classical outlook flourished to the 4th century; 2) The triumph of Christianity; the post 4th century replaced the classical outlook by a Christian world-view; 3) A Christian Weltanschauung dominated western European education and civilization until the 17th century rise of modern science inaugurated a third way—the modern mind.

Three basic assumptions of the Christian Weltanschauung are: 1) Ultimate reality focuses in a person; i.e., God; 2) The mechanics of the physical world exceed our comprehension (mechanics and explanatory hypotheses vs. God); 3) The way to salvation lies not in conquering nature but in following the will of God (secular salvation: educational, political and economic messianism). The Renaissance interest revived Hellenistic interest in nature. The second of the above assumptions was challenged by 16th-17th century science. For the first time in 2000 years western man began to look intently at his environment instead of beyond it. Newton caught the excitement perfectly—"God, I think thy thought after thee" (quip—God said "Let Newton Be and there was light.") Needed: One contemporary Christian Newton!

Three basic assumptions of the scientific outlook are: 1) Reality may be personal—but is less certain and less important than that it is ordered; 2) Man's reason is capable of discerning this order as it manifests itself in the laws of nature; 3) The path to human fulfillment, i.e., redemption or salvation, consists primarily in discovering these laws, utilizing them where this is possible and complying with them where it is not. (Salvation through the Behavioral Sciences and Social Engineering). One of the contemporary problems is the failure of the unity of science movement and the fragmentation of knowledge (cf. C. P. Snow, *The Two Cultures*—The Humanities and the Sciences.)

Some controlling assumptions of Western secularistic education are: 1) The death of God—a culture coming of age from Nietzsche to Bonhoeffer. The age of secularization and religionless Christianity (see T. S. Eliot, *The Idea of a Christian Society,* pb; Ernest Koenker, *Secular Salvation;* E. L. Mascall, *The Secularization of Christianity* criticism of Robinson's *Honest to God;* Paul van Buren, *The Secular Meaning of the Gospel;* Bonhoeffer, *Prisoner for God*); 2) Ethics after Kant: Morality without God; 3) The secularist reduction of the sacred to a complex of pre-scientific cosmologies, outmoded metaphysical projections, or merely psychological cultural economic phenomena, has been plausible to an increasing number of persons in the contemporary world. The new unbelief, the new Jesuit order to analyze and answer resurgent atheism in its multiple forms, the new cultural status of the unbeliever—all stem from the above assumptions. (See Martin Marty, *The Infidel,* pb. and his *Varieties of Unbelief* for introductions to this phenomena of the age of secularization.); 4) Witnessing to Christ and His Word: Christian thinking and witnessing is grounded in propositional revelation; 5) Hegel and Historicism: The results of this culminated in the Sociology of Knowledge thesis of Mannheim, et al. Historical, religious, ethical, relativism follows logically from this thesis; 6) Thinking and witnessing in an age which is materialistically oriented. From Science to technology, from technology to cultural materialism—theism and things—Man and matter, etc. The cutlural captivity of the Church! As man finds himself at the end of his 20th century technological tether, he adjudges Satan to be no more than a cultural myth. But . . .!

Aninism: Biblical and Contemporary

One-half of the contemporary world live in fear of demons. This is very similar to the pre-Mosaic period, as well as later times in Israel. During Israel's wilderness journey, they sacrificed to the Se'irim (Lev. 17:1-7), a practice continued in the reign of Jeroboam I in the North (II Chron. 11:15), and in the South during Menasses time of rule. The demons might have been symbolized as having a goat's body as is suggested by the Hebrew word—sa'ir (Isa. 34:14). On the day of atonement Israel sacrificed to Yahweh and to Azazel (Lev. 16). He stands opposed to Yahweh as Satan does in Job 1—2, and the serpent does in Genesis 3. In Deuteronomy 32:17, we are told that the Israelites sacrificed to the-Shedim (root sud—meaning mighty one)—Psalm 106:37. Deut. 18:9ff is the classical Old Testament passage against Canaanite occult

557

practices. The LXX was influenced by Greek, i.e., Intertestamental Hellenistic demonology. The Hebrew 'elilim—things of nought, or no gods was rendered by demon in the LXX—Isaiah 13:21; 34:141; 43:20; Jeremiah 50:39; Micah 1:8; and Job 30:29.

The Coming of The Accuser

The word Satan means to accuse, to attack or manifest hostility toward a person or thing—Gen. 17:41; 49:23; 50:15; Ps. 55:4; Job 16:9; 30:21; and Hos. 9:7 contains mastema-hostility or animosity. In Israel there is a more advanced notion than among the Mesopotamian religions, which maintained that Satan was responsible for evil, especially disease. Following Persian influences, A-Lods and Torczyner declare that Satan is a type of secret police. R. Scharf, following the Jungian theory of the origin and nature of symbol, maintains that Satan was originally identified with the angel of Yahweh. But there is no concrete evidence for any of the above notions. Von Rad more accurately describes Satan as an antagonist of Yahweh throughout the scriptures.[16] Yet in classical Hebrew, Satan is not a proper name, but the name of a function. It designates: (1) an adversary in I Sam. 29:4; II Sam. 19:23; I Kgs. 5:18; 11:14, 23, 25; Ps. 109:6; (2) angel of Yahweh in Mi. 22:22, 32 as adversary confronting Balaam; (3) the person of Satan the adversary—Job 1—2; Zech. 3:1; (4) In a single place it is employed as a proper name without the article—I Chron. 21:1. Satan incites David to number the Israelites—II Sam. 24:1, thus he is both an accuser and one who initiates to sin. The Philistines called David Satan in I Chron. 5:18; 11:14, 23, 25. In Job, chapters 1—2, the name Satan with the article indicates an individual already known to the readers. Satan seeks to cause Job to despair and thus destroy his

---

[2] G. Von Rad, *Theo. of O.T.*, Vol. I, p. 353.

relationship with God. Satan is not only man's enemy, but God's as well. He sought to falsify God's judgment concerning Job. He is the diabolus (source of Devil), "the slanderer par excellence."[17]

In Zechariah's fourth vision, 3:1-5, Satan appears as the accuser at the right hand of the high priest, Joshua. Here it is not a case of personal sin, but a national one. If the high priest can no longer absolve the people, then the judgment of God's wrath will abide destructively on the nation. Yahweh commanded that Satan be silent and forgave the high priest's guilt. In Job, Satan confronted an individual, in Zechariah he confronted an entire nation endeavoring to destroy God's plan of redemption. Satan is presented as an intelligent creature from Genesis to Revelation.

Belial at Qumran

Satan is generally called Belial in the Qumran literature, especially IQS 3:13—4:26. God has set two spirits for man, one light, one darkness. The sons of righteousness walk in the light; the sons of wickedness walk in the darkness. Demons or evil spirits are associated with fallen angels and are understood as seducers of men. They are so understood in *Pseudepigraphic Literature,* but in Rabbinic Literature they are understood primarily as beings who are morally neutral, but cause sickness. The spirit of error, Belial, is the root of all evil in the world of men. In IQH 4:6 Belial is called Satan, in the *War Scroll* 13:11 and *Damascus Document* 16:5 Satan is called

---

[3] For advanced study see E. Langton, *Essentials of Demonology,* 1949; Foerster and Schaferdiek, *TWNT,* article "satanas," pp. 151-165; also the articles in *TWNT* "daimon," II, 1ff; "echthros," II, pp. 814ff; "kategoros," III, pp. 636ff; "peira," VI, pp. 24ff; and "poneros," VI, pp. 558; H. W. Huppenbauer, "Belial in dem Qumrantexten," *Theo. Zeitzchrift,* 1959, p. 819; L. Bouyer, "Le probleme du mal dens le christianisme antique," *Dieu Vivant,* 1, 1947, pp. 17-42; for Dead Sea Scrolls see P. Wernberg Moller, *The Manual of Discipline,* p. 70ff, E.T., 1957; see E. Schweizer's essay in *The Background of the New Testament and Its Eschatology,* Cambridge University Press, 1956, pp. 482-508.

an angel of enmity (Mal'ak mastemah), he is called *mastema,* prince of evil spirits in *The Book of Jubilee* 17:15-18; 48:2; 48:17; 49:2. In both the Qumran Literature and the *Testaments of the Twelve Patriarchs* Satan is called Belial. In the *War Scroll* Satan is spoken of in reference to "angels of the dominion" of Beliah 1:15 and of "spirits of his lot"—15:11ff. "Angels of destructions" (malake hebel) are mentioned in IQS 4:12 and they carry out punishment of evil men.

Gnostic Demiurge

No specie of Gnosticism fails to manifest the Demiurge as a distored image of Yahweh. The Gnostic concept of Satan shows interaction with Judaism and current popular philosophy, though ultimately deriving its demonology from Persia, Satan being modeled on Ahriman.[18] But the Persian model exemplified an eternal dualism. There is no redemption from that form of dualism, as in the New Testament, e.g. I John.

Christ and the Principalities and Powers

Once the supernatural, i.e., paranormal, was removed from western man's interpretative schema, it was apparent that Satan and demons, as well as angels must be removed from objective existence, of course, in the name of the scientific method. Classical Liberal Christology of the 19th century confronted the Gospel records and their detailed description of the influence of demons on human behavior with scepticism. This central issue became immediately apparent, if Jesus is God in human flesh, why does He believe in the objective nature of demons? Mere survey level of awareness makes the

---

[4] See Dupont, *Gnosis,* entire; H. Wolfson, *Philosophy of the Church Fathers,* Harvard, Vol. I, p. 538ff; R. Mc L. Wilson, *The Gnostic Problem,* London: Mowbray, 1958; B. Reicke, *The Disobedient Spirits and Christian Baptism,* 1946.

"theology of the frog in beaker" crystal clear. In the laboratory a frog can be made comfortable in a beaker filled with warm water, by turning up the heat gradually, the frog's system adjusts to the heat until the terminal point of death. He thinks that he is comfortable and thus he adjusts to the new increased heat influence until his body systems collapse. This is a paradigm of 19th, 20th century theological adjustment to the "necessary rigors of scientific hermeneutics." When supernatural evil beings are removed, supernatural good beings will be removed shortly thereafter. The issue is not one of evidence but of the radical shift in controlling presuppositions. Cultural and psychological, i.e., subjective, explanations were given for the belief in such beings as Satan, demons, and angels.[19]

A complete rewriting of the Gospel records would be necessary if the category of demoniac is removed as primitive superstition. As long ago as the work of A. B. Bruce, *The Miraculous Element of the Gospel,* it was clear that a rejection of demons entailed a rejection of the picture of Christ presented in the Gospels. The Synoptic Gospels do not discuss Satan's origin nor do they set forth the solution as the problem of evil as in IQS 3:13. Satan is the great seducer from the temptation narratives to the cross. As the cross comes closer, Satan intensifies his efforts to destroy Jesus of Nazareth—Matt. 4:7ff; 12:34; 23:23; Jn. 8:44; Rom. 7:11; Rev. 12:9; Lk. 4:13; 22:53; I Jn. 3:8; 20:8-10. Satan comes as in the Prologue of Job to test God's Son. Christ defeats the "prince of this world"— (Jn. 7:31; 16:11; Rev. 12:9-13), tells us to witness to His victory over sin, Satan, and death. Satan is always seeking to destroy both individual and corporate witness through the New Testament records—Mk. 4:15; Matt. 13:39; II Cor. 12:7-10;

---

[5] It is very strange that in our crisis-filled world of the decade of the 70's that Billy Graham's work on *Angels* was the best seller in the general field of evangelical religious books, perhaps challenging the documentation of works on Occult and demonology. It is not necessary here to discuss the bene elohim which the LXX renders as the "angels of God." Cf. Gen. 6:2-4; Ps. 29:1; 82:1, 6; 89:6; Dan. 3:25; I Kgs. 22:19; Zech. 6:5.

I Thess. 2:18; I Thess. 3:5; Gal. 5:7; I Pet. 5:8; and Ps. 22:14. The entire biblical theology[20] of the anti-Christ—Acts 5:3; I Thess. 3:5; I Cor. 7:5; Jas. 4:7; I Jn. 3:18; Eph. 6:12; II Thess. 2:7ff; Rom. 5:12; 7:7; Heb. 7:25—reveals the presence of an evil person, not merely an abstract evil force, which symbolizes forms of social economic, and political injustice. Again the issue is Christ or Belial? II Cor. 6:15.

In the New Testament Epistles Satan is mentioned predominantly in connection with his confrontation with the Christian community—Rev. 2:10; 12:17; 13:7; I Pet. 5:8; I Thess. 1—3; II Cor. 2:11. The climax in the work of the anti-Christ is his seducing activity—II Thess. 2:3-12; Rev. 13, 17. Victory over his temptations is grounded in the blood of Christ—Rev. 12:11, by putting on the whole armour of God—Eph. 6:11; I Cor. 7:5; I Tim. 3:6ff; 5:14ff; Eph. 4:27; Rom. 16:17, 20. God's victory is through the community. Satan prevents the community from carrying out its purpose— I Thess. 2:18; II Cor. 12:7. For rejection of traditional Rabbinaic interpretation of Satan's works see Phil. 2:25-30 and Romans 1:13; I Cor. 5:5; I Tim. 1:20. Biblical references to the final destruction of Satan are only two in number—Matt. 25:47 and Rev. 20:10. Paul also speaks of the end of every *arche, exousia,* and death in the great resurrection narrative— I Cor. 15:24-6.

The Kingdom of God and the Prince of This World

John uses the designation—diabolos seven times in I Jn. 3:10; Satan occurs only once in Jn. 13:27 in reference to Judas

---

[6] Paul employs *ho satanas* most frequently, but also *ho diabolos, ho pierazon, ho poneros;* see Foerster, *TWNT* 7, especially pp. 156ff. All major commentaries reject the biblical category of paranormal evil beings as mythology, e.g. Bultmann, et al. The ultimate issue is the nature of science and the "Critical Scientific Historical Method" which is my doctorate thesis category at St. Louis University—cf. a critique of the scientific historical method. The nature of Scientific Epistemology I am examining in another doctoral thesis.

Iscariot. *Ho proneros* occurs in Jn. 17:15 and six times in I John. This description cannot always be distinguished from the neuter *to poneros*. John's final name for Satan is the archon toy kosmou toutou—and appears in Jn. 12:31; 14:30; and 16:11. The crucial passage occurs in Jn. 8:44 where Satan's power to determine man's whole being is discussed—Jn. 6:70; Mk. 8:33; Jn. 13:27; and Lk. 22:3. The imperative is enclosed in the ontic sayings of John—Jn. 17:15; I Jn. 2:13ff; I Jn. 3:8; 3:12; 5:18. Christ is the bearer of God's presence, *The Kingdom of God* and our salvation, according to the scriptures. One of the central challenges to Christian thought, since science supposedly removed the supernatural category and reduced it to a mythical hermeneutical limbo, is the place and significance of *The Powers*[21] which certainly have a dominant place in New Testament theology.

The Challenge of the Powers

Paul repeatedly refers to cosmic powers which play a definite role in the cosmic conflict between good and evil—Rom. 8:38f; I Cor. 2:8; I Cor. 15:24-6; Eph. 1:20f; 2:1f; 6:12; Col. 1:16; 2:15. What is the significance of this biblical category after the first and second scientific revolutions, and especially since the work of the comparative religion school?

---

[7] See H. Berkhoff, *Christ and the Powers*. Herald Press, E.T., 1962; A. J. Badstra, *The Law and the Elements of the World*, Grand Rapids, Eerdmans; P. Benoit, "La loi et la croix d'apres Saint Paul"—Rom. 7:7—8:4) *Revue Biblique*, 1938, pp. 481-509; H. Bietenhard, *Die himmlische Welt im Urchristentum und Spatjudentum*, 1951; G. B. Caird, *Principalities and Powers*, Oxford, 1956; J. Huby, "Stoicheia dous Bardesane et dons Saint Paul," *Biblica*, 1934, pp. 365-368; H. Koller, "Stoicheion," *Glotta*, 1955; pp. 161-174; H. B. Kuhn, "The Angelology of the Non-canonical Jewish Apocalypses," *JBL*, 1948, pp. 217-232; E. Langton, *The Angel Teaching of the New Testament*; S. Lyonnet, "L'histoire du salut selon la chapitre vii de le'epitre aux Romains," *Biblica*, 1962, pp. 117-151; "L'epitre aux Colossians (Col. 2:18) et les mysteres d'apollon Clorien." *Biblica*, 1962, pp. 417-435; G. H. C. Macgregor, "Principalities and Powers," *NTS*, 1954-5, pp. 17-28; C. D. Morrison, *The Powers that Be*, Naperville, 1960; and J. S. Steward, "On a Neglected Emphasis in the New Testament Theology," *SJT*, 1951, pp. 292-301.

Culturally we have witnessed the rise and fall of Satan in our scientific age. But the empirical evidence does not destroy the place of the powers (exousia, *TWNT*) in interpreting personal and international anomia, which clearly has irrational dimensions which cannot be forced into any *a priori* model, even in the name of science. After the Einsteinian revolution, nothing can be rejected on *a priori* grounds, not even the existence of Satan and his demonological cohorts. Paradoxically, our generation has witnessed the most radical occultic outbreak in the history of the world. Yet recorded knowledge doubles every three and one-half years in the technological categories.

Biblically, the powers are structures of fallen creation—"He is before all things and in Him all things have their being" (Greek synesteken relates to our word system and means to order for fulfilling a purpose) Col. 1:15-17. The disordering power of sin can be overcome only in Christ, not in the organizing strength of the powers or scientific enterprise. The organizing center of Rome was *The Law;* the organizing center of the medieval world was the Church; after the scientific revolution in the 17th-18th centuries, the organizing center of western civilization became the scientific method. But after the collapse of the *Unity of Science Movement,* the western mind had no organizing center, thus cultural pluralism precipitated, of course in the name of freedom. If Christ is the undying center of God's cosmic purpose, what forces unify the state, politics, class social struggles, national interest, public opinion, accepted morality, ideas of decency, humanity, democracy, exploitation, capitalism, socialism, Communism? Fragmentation is everywhere empirically evident, perhaps the organizing powers vs. Christ's organizing power is not an irrelevant mythological category from an ancient and prescientific age when men were guided by irrational superstition. Our cosmic Humpty-Dumpty cannot be restored by any known human contemporary power. Paul is so relevant to our age. He needs to be voiced in our present crisis. He reminded the Galatians (4:1-11) that they formerly lived under world powers, before they learned of Christ and His organizing presence—Eph. 1:10. Redemption in Christ frees us from bondage to the organizing power of the stoicheia. God's preserving mercy still holds life together where men do not know Christ's liberation.

In His resurrection Christ broke the power of the organizing forces which refuse to order life and live around Christ the center, Col. 2:13-15. The cosmic Christ is the cosmic orderer and re-orderer; He is not merely my personal Savior, though He is that, too. He alone triumphed over the power to give every man and all men regulations for ultimate joy. In Galatians 4:20, Paul employs the verb dogmatizein, rendered "to impose regulations." The dogmata in question is expressed in verse 22. No law can organize life, only the living, risen Lord. Contemporary man finds life to be meaningless.

Loss of Center

All powers but His power can only organize for frustration and despair. Death was dethroned (katergein means "to make ineffective, to disconnect") by Him—I Cor. 15:28, yet only E. Kuber Ross' *Death and Dying* seems to stimulate concern for life after death. Why not Him, because of His resurrection? Christ alone reveals the cosmic purpose of God—Eph. 1:10. We live between the "already" and the "not yet" in this organizing power. Demons ask Jesus if He had come to torture them before their time?—Matt. 8:29. Since Christ's resurrection their time is fulfilled.

Powers, Cultural Crisis, and Christ

Christ not only limited the influence of the powers, He destroyed it. Yet in secularized western civilization the powers have reappeared. But Christ's desacralization of the fallen universe canot be undone. Yet the powers of a humanistic ideal or personality, of a decent human existence, of public morality, or mammon, eros, and technology, limit and presuppose one another, maintaining a range of tolerable equilibrium. But the balance, as is everywhere evident, is extremely unstable. Nihilistic pragmatism hardly engenders optimism of human solution. Anti-Christian usurpers, propaganda, terror, and the artificial ideologizing of every dimension of life are inseparable concomitants of the rule of the powers since Christ. World view is no longer a word in good repute but neutrality is epistemically impossible. World-views are expressed either implicitly or explicitly. Total scientific objectivity is a myth which can no longer be tolerated either scientifically or theologically. We must recover the organizing center of Christ in our lives, churches, school or continue to be dominated by fragmentations. One of the fundamental factors of Christ's power to fulfill God's purpose is His destruction of the "principalities and powers," which since Martin Dibelius' *Die Geisterwelt in Glauben des Paulus*—a mature product of the "history of religions" school has been relegated to a nostalgic museum of myth. Schier's effort to voice the marburg of the late Heidegger and Bultmann his *Machte und Gewalten un Neuen Testament,* which sees no objective reality in the powers, but projections of what some call, with Bultmann, man's self-understanding, must not go under-challenged by followers of Job's vindicator from the powers of sin, evil, suffering, and death.

HOPE IN TIME OF ABANDONMENT: JOB'S JESUS IS LORD OF THE FUTURE

What have you done? Gen. 4:10
I shall be a fugitive and a wanderer on the earth. Gen. 4:14

I fled Him, down the nights and down the days;
  I fled Him, down the arches of the years; . . .
Adown Titanic glooms of chasmed fear,
  From those strong Feet that followed, followed after.
Hound of Heaven

That night, in Magdalen College, Oxford, C. S. Lewis says that he was conscious "of the steady, unrelenting approach of Him who I so earnestly desired not to meet. . . ."

The hardness of God is kinder than the softness of men, and His compulsion is our liberation. *Surprised by Joy,* p. 215.

Hell is oneself—Hell is alone, the other figures in it merely projections. There is nothing to escape from and nothing to escape to. One is always alone. T. S. Eliot, *The Cocktail Party,* p. 342.

There was something rootless about him, as though no town or city was his, no street, no walls, no square of earth his home. William Faulkner, *Light in August.*

Can contemporary man maintain hope in the time of abandonment, like Job our contemporary? Is there any hope for "the trousered ape" (C. S. Lewis) in an age of *The Abolition of Man?* Can we hope in a salvation from elite specialists as the decision makers in Orwell's *1984,* especially in light of Marshall McLuhan's definition of a specialist as "one who never makes small mistakes while moving towards the grand fallacy"? Our whole world is out of joint. The anti-civilizing trend in art, cinema, and literature is all but ubiquitous. We live in a world of *Juliet of the Spirits,* i.e., there is no discernible difference between *illusion* and *reality.* If you are insane then you are a member of the secure establishment; if you are healthy you are an archist. Men as diverse as the German philosopher Ernst Junger, Norman Mailer, and Jean Paul Sartre canonize the criminal and pervert because they both lead an existence outside of "normal society." Social anomie abandons a permissive world. Permissiveness is here identified as freedom, but this form of freedom is actually—insanity. George Santayana insightfully presents an analysis of our world which expresses, instead of freedom, "a many-sided insurrection of the unregenerate natural man . . . against the regimen of Christendom." The resurgent interest in the manifold mysticism of William Blake is also proof of our value vertigo. Many hold that Blake's nonsense has salvic potentiality—

"active evil is better than passive good." Golding's *Lord of Flies* provides no hope for a naval officer to rescue us from the onslaught of savagery. This savagery is empirically available in Ireland, the Middle East, or at the Olympics as a Russian participant attempts to use a specially equipped sword to score without touching the opponent.

Tragic Consequences of Awareness

The words of Burke are truer today than when first uttered, "the age of chivalry is gone—that of sophisters, economists, and calculators has succeeded; and the glory of Europe is extinguished forever." Only the truth of heart's imagination prevails. The evil nightmarish symbolism of Wordsworth and Blake prevail, as in *Christabel* and *The Ancient Mariner*. The "reasoning power in a man" is the negation of energy and therefore the source of *all* evil, according to Blake. His strategy was "to cast aside from poetry all that is not inspiration." James Joyce brilliantly and accurately describes the romantic dimension of the 18th revolutionary spirit by contrasting the classical and romantic tempers; the classical frame of reference displayed "security and satisfaction and patience," and the romantic temper as being "insecure, unsatisfied, impatient." These emotional responses to harsh reality required the coming of Napoleon to reintroduce into France even the vestiges of discipline and control which had been destroyed because all Europe had been following the advise of Blake that "the road of excess leads to the palace wisdom." These conditions are exemplified by 20th century culture. The romantic temper always produces a revolutionary milieu. Voltaire, Diderot, Rousseau, Blake, Coleridge, Wordsworth based the arguments against injustice on reason. Yet the revolutionary action came when the power passed from the moderates to the extremists and finally to the mob. The literary trends during the revolutionary 18th century are once more exemplified in the literary trends between 1900-1960. The psychological theories of Freud and

Jung dominate Camus, Genet, Gide, Proust, Sartre, Valery in France, and Albee, Eliot, Ginsberg, Miller, Hemingway, Pound in America, and Ireland's Joyce, Beckett, Shaw, and Yeats, to say nothing of the ubiquitious Brecht, Kafka, and Lawrence. The possibilities for political justice as envisioned in William Godwin's *Political Justice* are strangely present in contemporary neo-Marxian politico-Liberation theology. Since reason and technology have enslaved man, we are told that we must return to the concept of *Noble Savage,* i.e., back to nature (cf. hippie and various 20th century subcultures). This contempt for rationality is always a symptom of decline, as was recognized by Spengler in his classic the *Decline of the West.* When culture looks back nostalgically to childhood and becomes preoccupied with the darkness of proto-mysticism, it is in its death-throws. Western culture is certainly past its gleaming autumn and rapidly moving into its winter of discontent. When virtue is sacrificed to convenience, we are always moving in a down hill, self-destructive direction. "Now there are times when a whole generation is caught . . . between two ages, between two modes of life and thus loses the feeling for itself, for the self-evident, for all morals, for being safe and innocent." (Hermann Hesse, *Steppenwolf,* 1929)

The Reasons Why

Once more Matthew Arnold's words cause us to sit in wonder at his powers to deduce the results of the temper of his age, as he mourns the fact that "rigorous teachers seized his youth and purged its faith, and trimmed its fire." Little wonder that his age, like ours, is "wandering between two worlds, one dead, the other powerless to be born." Do we have any hope in our 20th century time of abandonment? Ultimately there are two sources of hope—God or technological man. There is no empirical ground for optimism that man possesses Promethean powers. Yet our age has generally abandoned the only God who can save to the uttermost. The scientific secularistic stance of our age maintains that anyone who believes in Job's Creator-Redeemer is either an escapist, e.g. a moral coward or clown, or else lacks the mental apparatus to challenge those that know. Will we rise up to witness to the viable alternative to atheism, despair, situation ethics, the theatre of the absurd and the conditions rampant in our age of unbelief, i.e., unbelief in a supernatural creator-redeemer in whom we place our trust. Ortega Y. Gasset draws the ultimate conclusion regarding the fatal flaw in relativism, which dominates our age of pluralism, when he says, "if truth does not exist, relativism cannot take itself seriously . . . belief in truth is a deeply-rooted foundation of human life; if we move it, life is converted into an illusion and an absurdity" (his *Modern Theme*).

Believers in the living God do have hope in a time of abandonment; we are not victims of a hostile cosmos. Because George Santayana's insight into our plight is truly appropriate to man in his long day's journey into night, "spiritual anguish . . . cannot be banished by spiritual anarchy." Men have abandoned mimesis, i.e., imitation in the name of freedom, but this merely becomes the mimesis of chaos and anarchy, which inevitably generates social anomie. As believers in the living God revealed in Christ, we must provide a concrete alternative to a cosmic *Animal Farm* or *1984*. Almost sixty years ago, Yeats (1919) expressed our nihilistic potentiality in *The Second Coming*.

Things fall apart, the centre cannot hold: mere anarchy is loosed upon the world. The blood-dimmed tide is loosed, and everywhere the ceremony of innocence is drowned.

Greece was organized by a world-view, Rome by law, Christendom by Catholicism, modern Europe by science, but by the 20th century the organizing center collapsed with the demise of the unity of science movement. After the Second World War, the results were plain. By the 60's, riots and revolution shook the last vestiges of the unifying power of the establishment's control of education, industry, and of life style it was visibly at an end. But for God we might actually be the "terminal generation." Dostoevsky's Rasholnikov is the prototype of our age, as "Rashol" means dissent. Dissent is never more viable than in an age of widespread dissatisfaction. Man's craving for security causes a vast muteness to hover over his deep despair. But the sin of silence has now been set aside.

Job and Our Present World Weariness

This world weariness is caused by the silence and absence of Job's vindicator. "Contemporary disbelief no longer relies on science as it did at the end of the last century. It denies both science and religion. It is no longer a sceptical reaction to miracles. It is passionate unbelief."[22] Man's technological competence reached its zenith July 20, 1976, when the invader from earth set down on the surface of the planet Mars. Yet science cannot still man's longing for a greater hope. The sum of man's "negligible atrocities" has reached astronomical proportions. Norman Mailer's prototype of a pathological person who murders his wife can hardly save this present age. Murder as a positive act in the development of his personality, as a liberating catharsis can hardly recover man's lost innocence. The moral should be apparent; when man attempts to be God, he descends to the level of the brute. Violence is a mark of Cain. "When the environment tolerates violence, violent behavior is apt to happen."[23] Western man seems to be dwelling in "a self-annihilating moment-to-moment continuum." Who wants to live in a world shaped by John Osborne, or plunged into lunacy by Harold Pinter or peopled by the hideous strength of a Beckett or Genet?

How can man still hope in the future of a world where the absurd perveyors of avant garde can verbalize with "Newspeak"

---

[1] Albert Comus, *La Vie Intellectuelle*, 1949.

[2] At a recent meeting of the American Psychiatric Association, 80% of those present concurred with this judgment. Our cultural anomie is adequate evidence.

in response to Duncan Williams sane advice. At a university lectureship where he was exposing the fact that an extreme ideology is in process of seizing power over our minds, a young student of very avant garde views of moral and literary license responded, "Your're advocating censorship; you shouldn't be allowed to publish it." This is an extreme representation of the myth of a liberal mind and *The Crisis of Our Age,* the age of the sensate culture.[24] If we do not provide a living alternative to this despair, then "we are all guilty of ignorance, frivolity and blindness and the accusing fingers of billions of the unborn are pointed angrily towards us" (Kenneth Boulding, Economist, Ecologist). If this sounds a bit reactionary, let us be reminded that we are counseling a blind culture to remain immobile as it stands tottering precariously on the edge of a cosmic cliff, until it gains an organizing perspective. Not just any perspective, but the perspective of the one for whom all reality exists. Job's hope is once more relevant!

An Erroneous Diagnosis

Man has committed an enormous diagnostic error in announcing the premature demise of God. In a world where 1,000 new Christian congregations are started every week, there are also signs of abandonment in some local situations. Death by mediocrity and institutional paralysis caused by the virus known as identifying God's purpose with local vision and aspirations, or lack of same, is generally visible. Dryness and derision are widespread. Those who are both informed concerning the world conditions and without hope in the living God are conjuring up their own form of humanistic aspiration[25]

---

[3] Read Pitirim Sorokin's *The Crisis of Our Age;* and Talcott Parsons and E. A. Shils, eds., *Toward a General Theory of Action* and weep, then after tearful catharsis rise up and witness to our Hope. See my Seminar-syllabus for *Philosophy of Culture* and its extended bibliographical references.

[4] Since the rise of the *Theologies of Hope* and Neo-Marxian *Liberation Theology* there has been an epidemic of literature on hope. J. Moltmann's *Theology of Hope;* P. Schutz, *Parusie Hoffnung und Prophetie,* 1960; E. Block, *Das Prinzip Hoffnung;* E. Gleg, *Nous de l'esperance;* A. Moillot, *L'Epitre de L'Esperance,* 1970; and the absolutely indispensable study of A. Neher's *L'exile de la parole,* 1970.

based in magic and mysticism. But the cultural magicians cannot turn stones into bread. Human initiative is encouraged as we are called to "rise up oh men of God and be done with lesser things" to create the Kingdom of God. This social gospel admonition is futile inducement to service.

Contemporary theology has grossly overstated the silence of God thesis. God has not chosen impotence in order to give man freedom, a freedom to transform himself and his environment into a paradisical utopia.[26] It does not follow that God is powerless because there is widespread institutional impotence. God's word will not return unto Him in vain. His word is always both *creative* and *revelatory,* from Genesis (dabar) to Jesus (logos) the scriptures bear witness to His powerful word. But what are the signs of His presence to 20th century man? Western man can only faintly hear "the fading murmur of silence" or "the subtle voice of silence"—I Kgs. 19:12. Much artificial importance is pressed into the fact that Hebrew has no thematic word for God. There is only the proper name for the purpose of calling upon God. God's name is pronounceable only in dialogue[27] with a view to mutual covenant commitment. The entire group of *Death of God* theologians have "refuted" God's existence by the cultural myth that He does not exist, only Vahanian sees this fact clearly. If God does not exist, then it is much ado about nothing. "Nothing" has ever before in human history generated so many heated debates. Even in Tillich the absence of God has a positive value. He asks for the *cause* of *His* absence? Is it our apathy, indifference, callousness, cynicism, our advanced knowledge? The final answer to the question as to whom and what makes God absent is God himself![28]

---

[5] This fatal plan is visible in all progressive post-Vatican II theology, but especially see I. Mancini, *Alayse du language theologique,* Paris, 1969, for analysis of the incarnation as God's instrument of *silence, absence,* and *impotence.*

[6] So Martin Buber's *I-Thou* thesis, see my critique in my Seminar-syllabus in *Contemporary Continental Theology,* also for critique of his reduction of *faith* to the single category of "trust," it is trust but not only trust.

[7] P. Tillich, *The Eternal Now,* Scribner, 1963, especially pp. 87-9.

Clues of His Absence

No longer does man attribute his catastrophic injustices, misfortunes, famines, and wars to God's *wrath;* they are attributed to his *abandonment*—Ps. 30:8; 104:29; 143:7. Few there are who interpret the present human condition as resulting from God's judging silence, as Amos and Hosea. The Old Testament reverberates with the anxiety that God might turn away His face. This panic inducing experience is more than psychological angst caused by the "hidden face of God," it is a theological problem, stemming from the silence of the Creator-Redeemer when it is interpreted as His abandonment. This is the brilliant and biblical thesis of Neher which he expresses in his *L'exil de la parole*. This thesis is corrective to the errors of Harvey Cox, who thinks that God's absence is His granting the power of triumph to man. God triumphed over the fallen universe in our risen, regnant reigning Lord, as God was silent on the cross (Ps. 22:69; Mk. 15:34; Matt. 27:1), but verbal in the resurrection event. God speaks under His own conditions, not those imposed by His creature-man. Neither Robinson's "Depth" nor Tillich's "Ultimate Concern" can provide clues of His presence.

Much contemporary preaching causes us to remember what the *First Book of Samuel* declares "the word of the Lord was rare in those days." In the history of preaching, every time God's people abandon an *authoritative word* from God they enter *dialogue* with those who can neither save nor heal. If God is eclipsed[29] it is not as Sartre asserts in his *Being and Nothingness,* that God's silence is proof of His non-existence.

Some of the real reasons for the eclipse of God are (1) the *mediocrity of the church,* i.e., being satisfied with being average in the name of the Creator of heaven and earth. Every church that has no higher vision than average brings the average down. Though in this mediocre church there are

---

[8] M. Buber's critique of the Death of God mentality—*The Eclipse of God.* New York: Harper, Torch, 1957.

many who tasted new wine and are God's becomers. Mediocrity manifests itself in the cultural death of God's influence in this world. Churches do not reflect the image of mediocrity from the "face of God," but from the face of the archangel of confusion and personal impotence in daily lives. Kierkegaard is surely correct in claiming that "mediocrity is the constituent principle of the compact mass of humanity." Personal power has often been relegated to the bureaucratic machine called the Ecumenical council. The crushing dominance of this dead demagog is visible from Africa to Asia. It attacks one specie of sociological and theological conformity as demoniac, while imposing its own "value conformity" on all who would espouse the laurels of the world's theological au courant. (2) Another sign of God's absence is the lack of excitement and joy in the assembly of the saints. Worship has often become a spectator sport for those who aspire to leave their heads in the vestibule and be fed theological pablum or psychological aspirins which is supposed to provide them a "fleeting high"![30] (3) Another sign of this absence is in the western pulpit. On the right, we note legalistic belligerants who often destroy the power of the redeeming mercy of God by their constant projection of God as an angry cosmic tyrant. On the left, we find the hermeneutical rehabilitation of Prometheus who probes deeper and deeper into the meaning of the text, but in the marvelous moment of discovery, he finds that God is both silent and absent. This generation of hermeneutical Prometheuses find God's voice is actually a verbal reflection of their own profound wisdom and learning, which is available only to those with

---

[9] The hermeneutical presuppositions of both C. Levi Strauss' *Structuralism* and *Redaktionsgeschichte* contribute to the evaporation of even the possibility of trans-cultural meaning. These are major factors for the *Silence* and *Absence* of God in major theological seminaries in the western world. Contemporary *Homiletical* theories and *Hermeneutical* theories (e.g. Gadamer) both reinforce the unintentional expression of the silence of God. I suspect that it would do us all good to compare the sophistic rhetoricians in Plato's *Gorgias* with Jeremiah, Isaiah, and Paul on speaking in behalf of the Lord of the universe. Today these great bearers of the Word would be judged as "authoritarian personalities."

THE SHATTERING OF SILENCE

the correct academic credentials. (4) Another sign of God's absence from any institutional churches is (We must not forget that Christ's Church is an empirical institution, but not all empirical religious institutions reflect His Church.) *conformity to culture.* Historically the church related to culture one of four ways: (1) *Parallel* to culture, which forever precluded witness; Kierkegaard's parable of *The Barn Yard* is so appropriate for this lack of response. (2) by being *immersed in culture,* which meant the loss of identity of the unique purpose of the people of God. (3) It has *withdrawal* from contact, which stems from the assumption that everything that fallen man has made is per se evil. This monastey mentality has done untold harm in the history of Christian existence. (4) The only possible response to human culture in the context of Christ's Commission—Matt. 28:19-20 is creative confrontation. Every thought and act must be consciously brought under the Lordship of Christ. There are no "value free" decisions; there is no neutrality. Luther's misunderstanding of the "two kingdoms" has done irreparable damage to man's awareness of the presence of God in His creation through His Church. By conformity to its cultural context, the church has often come to identify the culture's patterns and norms with God's presence—only His *Word* is autonomous in human culture. It sits in judgment on all things human. His Church is God's revolutionary force in a troubled world. To identify a certain dress code, physical appearance, types of music, worship services, songbooks, etc. with God in all probability is a futile identification of God with our cultural values, whether in America, Europe, or the Third World. Only God's autonomous word is transcultural. Only if it is a universal word can it have ultimate authority for all cultural contexts. As long as we continue to listen with "our" cultural filters, or evaluate with "our" cultural norms, millions will continue to experience the deafening silence of God and the terrible loneliness produced by His absence.

"When the light of the world becomes a darkened light, when the rainbow is reduced to the physical phenomenon, when the Ark of the Covenant is eaten by termites, when the empty tomb is filled with our hermeneutics, when the Kingdom of God is a political product, when the dethroned King takes refuge in speeches, then the dead of night has won the heart and darkened the eyes. That dead of night is now."[31]

I Believed, and So I Spoke—I Cor. 4:13

Pessimism is rationally imperative for those who believe that there is no God and are informed of the present human condition. No less a person than our Secretary of State, H. Kissinger, recently, non-officially, announced that there is no human salvation to the multiplicity of international crises. But believers in Job's Redeemer have hope in this time of abandonment. Job's entire response becomes a paradigm for his contemporaries. The very essence of Job's hope is also expressed by Isaiah—"Truly, thou art a God who hidest thyself, O God of Israel, the Saviour," Isa. 45:15 and "I will wait for the Lord who is hiding his face from the house of Jacob, and I will hope in him" Isa. 8:17. Neher marvelously meditates on the ramification of God's absence and silence. Hope is the shield against defeat, against God's rejection— "freedom's shield against death." Hope is alive and well in the face of His silence. Our brother in hope, Daniel, brings great comfort to those of us who wait hope. Before Nebuchadnezzar he affirms that "Our God . . . is able to deliver us . . . and he will deliver us." Then the most awful of all falls on the ears of that tyrant, "But if not," in spite of everything, "be it known to you, O King, that we will not serve your gods or worship the golden image which you have set up"—Dan. 3:17-18.

---

[10] See the brilliant critique of Jacque Ellul, *Hope in Time of Abandonment*, Seabury Press, E.T., 1973, p. 155; and the indispensable work A. Neher, *L'exile de la parole*, Paris, 1970.

Hope in the Face of Failure

This hope is the very opposite of stoic resignation as of human revolution. The central issue is—who must change—God or man? Even God said that He "repented that He made man." Many stand troubled before such a declaration. But here is hope. The Hebrew word rendered "repent" is *nehoma* which means regret, weariness, miscarriage of his expectations, but also consolation, recovery in the face of failure. Likewise, the Hebrew word *azav* means both "abandonment" and "gathering in." Abandonment and ingathering do not necessitate change in God, or His silence and absence, but the unbreakable relationship grounded in His promises.[32] We live from promise to promise; hope is inseparably linked to abandonment. If we thought that we were not abandoned, would we hope? Yes, hope is imperative for powerful daily existence. When His promise is fulfilled, His presence will be complete and Ezekiel's last word will be actualized, *Yahweh Shammah,* i.e., Yahweh shall be there—Rev. 21—22. We must never confuse "hope" and the thing "hoped for," as many theologians of hope and liberation have done.

Hope for Saints Without God

Contemporary man aspires to the status of self-imposed sainthood. But to Job's contemporaries creation was God's act of hope. God's creative word must be the only basis for an ethic of freedom, which is actually an ethic of hope.[33] The only hope for saints without God is the absent God who has *Shattered His Silence* in His ultimate word. When He speaks, He breaks His silence, displays His absence, provides our

---

[11] See *The Theology of Promise* theme worked out in my forthcoming biblical theology study—II Cor. 1:20, "All the Promises of God are Yes in Jesus"—see the appendix after this present essay.

[12] See J. Ellul's *The Ethics of Freedom,* Eerdmans, E.T., 1976.

freedom, which is freedom to please Him, not ourselves. His freedom is His gift to man. This gift enables us to *please* Him, *praise* Him, and *wait* for Him, because in the beginning and the end is hope, His hope in Himself. Prometheus must be bound once more, but not by chains of intolerance or censorship, but by His Presence. The pride of Prometheus can never "inherit the promises"—Heb. 6:12.

—S.O.S. - Maranatha—[34]

APPENDIX: HOPE IN TIME OF ABANDONMENT OR THE CHRISTIAN FAITH AND THE HISTORIOGRAPHICAL REVOLUTION

ANTECEDENTS and CONSEQUENCES: Lk. 1:1-4; Acts 1:1ff
Before the 18th and 19th century Historiographical Revolution it was considered a supreme advantage of the Christian faith to be historically grounded against the myth structures of non-Judaeo Christian religion. After Kant's *First Critique,* which maintained that all of reality was reducible to thinking and acting, western thought progressively grew more hostile to the classical Christian faith. The *Scientific Revolution* from Galileo-Newton-Maxwell removed God from the explanatory hypothesis and reduced the Judaeo-Christian God to a "God of the gaps." Two of Kant's students, Lessing and Herder, played fundamental roles in the new historiography. Hegel leads directly to Heidegger and the historization of *all* reality.
  A. Kant's *First Critique; Critique of Practical Reason*
  B. Lessing's *Theological Writings:* The Leibnitzian Epistemology of the "broad ugly ditch"

[13] *His Presence in His Kingdom*—see Bright, *The Kingdom of God,* pb.; J. Ellul's *The Presence of the Kingdom,* Seabury Press, and *False Presence of the Kingdom,* Seabury Press; H. Ridderbos, *The Coming Kingdom,* Presbyterian Reformed Publishing Co., E.T., 1962; also the eschatology section in his *Paul,* Eerdmans, E.T., 1976; G. C. Berkouwer, *The Return of Christ,* Eerdmans, 1972; and James D. Strauss, "Apocalyptic Literature," *The Seer, The Saviour, and The Saved,* College Press, 1972 ed., extensive bibliography on apocalyptic and prophetic literature, pp. 438-457.

C. Herder's Naturalistic Pantheism, Natural Religion, and Immanent god
D. Hegel's *geist* as the orderer of all matter; Marx invented "geist" into natural laws controlling matter, directing it to higher forms of expression.
E. Marx and Hegel's dialectical view of reality—contra
  1. *Law of Identity*, i.e., $1=1$
  2. *Law of Excluded Middle*, i.e., A cannot be both A and non A at the same time. From absolute Time and Space to Space-Time
  3. *Law of Contradiction*, i.e., A cannot be both *true* and *false* at the same time under the same circumstances.
F. Theory and Practice from Aristotle to Marx: Priority to Theory or Practice?
G. From Dilthey to Darwin: *Erlebnis* and the meaning of history
  1. Dilthey to Troeltsch: Analogy of expression and recovery of the past
  2. Overcoming polarity of Subject/Object Logic and Epistemology in 19th century Existentialism and Penomenology, e.g. Husserl Ebner and Buber
  3. Encounter Epistemology and historically mediated data about *truth* (from Realism to Existential view of Truth)
  4. History, Truth and Encounter
  5. God, Mediated Knowledge and Man
H. Nietzsche and Freud: Death of God and rejection of objective status of God's existence
I. From death of God and death of absolutes to death of man Keat's "All things are falling apart . . . the center cannot hold."

Conclusion: The Historiographical Revolution and the Christian Faith in the 20th Century Mad, Mod World

APPENDIX: CHRISTIAN FAITH AND THE FUTURE
CHRIST—LORD OF THE FUTURE

I. Eschatological Perspectives in the O.T.: Theology of Promise (I Pet. 1:10ff)
   A. Genesis 3:15
   B. Genesis 12:1ff. (Promise to Abraham and N.T. interpretation—Lk. 24:44f; Acts 26:6, 7; Heb. 6:13-17; Heb. 11:9f; 39—40; Rom. 4:13-14, 20; (pl) Rom. 9:4; 15:8, 9; Heb. 7:6; 8:6; Acts 7:2, 17; Acts 13:22, 23; 32—33; Lk. 1:69-72-73; Gal. 3:15-18, 22, 29; 4:23, 28.
   C. Promise and the Patriarchs
      1. "Seed" is promised to Abraham, Sarah, Isaac, Jacob (Gen. 13:14ff; 15, 17:6, 7; 15-16; 26:3, 4; 28:3, 4; 35:11, 12; 48:3, 4.
      2. Persons
      3. A Great Nation—18:18; 35:11; 46:3;
      4. Gathered Nations—28:3; 35:11; 48:4; 17:6, 16;
      5. Kings from Abraham, et al.—17:6, 16; 35:11;
      6. Promised Land—18:18; 22:17, 18; 26:3, 4; 17:4, 5. Paul correctly cites this passage in proof that the Gentile Christians are children of Abraham—Rom. 4:11, 12, 16-18.
   D. Covenant is promise in different form "Seed"—Gal. 3:16-19.
   E. Promise renewed to Israel and David.
      1. Israel—Ex. 6:7; Deut. 29:12, 13; Ex. 31:16, 17; Lev. 26:44, 45; Deut. 4:30, 31; Deut. 28:9, 10; Ex. 19:5, 6 (see I Pet. 2:5-10); (Rev. 1:6; 5:9, 10); Ex. 3:13; 2:24; 6:3-5; 4:31.
      2. House of David—II Sam. 7; I Chron. 22:9. Promise to David parallels that to the patriarchs and to Israel of the exodus. Is the promise to David for all mankind like the promise to Abraham and Israel?
   F. Promise of the Prophets and Psalms
      1. Ps. 89 (Identity of promise made to David, Israel and Abraham).

2. The nations, the Temple and the Promise—Isa. 55:1, 3; 56:3-7; Matt. 21:13; Mk. 11:17; Lk. 19:46; Zech. 14:16-21. Nations going up to Jerusalem to worship at feast of tabernacles.

G. Promise and the Messiah—Isa. 40—55; Isa. 55:3; I Kings 2:4; 8:25; 9:5; Isa. 41:8; 43:5; 44:3; 45:19-25. Promise is for the nations—Isa. 39—66; Servant as Israel—41:8-10; 42:18, 19; 43:9, 10; 44:1-3; 44:21; 45:4; 48:20; 49:3; Rom. 9:6-8.

1. Isa. 42:1-4—Matt. 12:18-21.
2. Isa. 52:13-53—Acts 8:32, 33; "Light to the nations" —Isa. 49:6.

H. Promise—Kingdom of God (Kingdom and the Messiah)
1. Isa. 9:7; 11:6-9; Ez. 34:24-31; Isa. 4:2-6; Dan. 2:44-45; 7:27;
2. Messiah as coming person—Matt. 11:3; 21:9; 23:39; Lk. 7:19, 20; 19:38; Jn. 6:14; 11:27; 12:13; Acts 19:4; Joel 3:12; 2:28-32; Acts 2:14ff; Obadiah 3:14-16; Amos 3:14;
3. "Day of Yahweh"—Matt. 24:31; I Thess. 4:16; Acts 2:17; II Tim. 3:1; Heb. 1:2; II Pet. 3:10-12; I Thess. 5:2-4; Matt. 9:22; 11:22-24 (See Ladd's, *Jesus and the Kingdom*).

I. Eschatology in Intertestamental Literature.
J. Eschatology of the Book of Enoch.
K. Eschatology of the Similitudes
L. Jewish Eschatology in time of Jesus Christ (see Voltz' *Eschatology*).
M. Parousia in Teaching of our Lord.
1. Reply to Caiaphas.
2. Prophecies of Jerusalem's Fall.
3. Parables.
4. New Israel.
5. Goyyim.

II. N.T. Eschatology Since the 19th Century.
   Eschatology:

A. Derived from eschaton, "the last things." Used only since 19th century.

B. God's definitive intervention in history through Christ Jesus.

C. N.T. generally regards as being deployed in two distinct phases delineated by Christ's first and second coming.

D. Biblical eschatology may be subdivided into *personal* (ultimate destiny of the individual), *collective* (national in O.T., Body, i.e. Church in N.T.), and *cosmic* (final status of the universe).

E. Biblical understanding is far more comprehensive in its concern than with judgment, heaven and hell.

F. be'aharit hayyamim, "at the end of days," i.e., at the conclusion of history, or simply "the last times"? The question is—what is the relationship of history to eschatology. (B. Wawter, "Apocalyptic: Its Relation to Prophecy," *CBQ*, 1960, Vol. 22; J. Barr, *Biblical Words for Time*. London, 1962; O. Cullmann, *Christ and Time*. Phil. Westminster.

G. Biblical view of time as linear in sense of implying teleological conception of history, i.e., history of Israel, Church, and the universe, is a history with definable beginning, moving toward a purposeful goal, determined by God's power and providence.

H. On the other hand, the biblical view of time is not linear if that term implies an evolutionary process.

I. The End is based upon set of occurrences in the past by which salvation has been essentially accomplished in the death and resurrection of Jesus Christ.

J. The Future is determined by crucial events of N.T. history involved in the person of Christ. Eschatology is inseparable from Christ and His mission of redemption.

K. A. Ritschl eliminated the eschatological element from Jesus' teaching. A. R. claimed that Jesus had preached a purely spiritual invisible Kingdom of God existing in the souls of men. See P. Hefner, *Faith and Vitalities of History* (NY: Harper, 1966).

L. J. Weiss, A. R.'s son-in-law, and A. Schweitzer "rediscovered" the significance of the eschatological features of the Gospel.

M. A. Schweitzer maintained that Jesus thought himself to be the Messiah (wrongly) and that the Kingdom was imminent. Jesus forced the issue of Kingdom and was crucified (Schweitzer's "thoroughgoing eschatology").

N. C. H. Dodd's reaction comes to be known as "realized eschatology." Eschatology has been realized in history in the person of the historical Jesus. Paul and John introduced realized eschatology into N.T. theology, according to Dodd, et al.

O. Eschatology of Synoptics and in Apostolic preaching.

P. Pauline Eschatology—Two characteristics which differentiate it from Jewish eschatology and apocalyptic:
   1. He who comes at the end of history is not some unknown but the glorified historical Jesus (Kummel, *Promise and Fulfillment*).
   2. N.T. eschatology is consistent with and dependent upon O.T. thought for most of its conceptions and imagery. The tension between "the already" and "the not yet." e.g., II Peter 3:4. Where now is the promise of his coming? Our fathers have been laid to rest, but yet everything continues exactly as it has always been since the world began.

Q. Conversion of Israel—difficulty in converting Diaspora Jewry.

R. Apocalyptic Imagery (ref. Synoptic imagery) egs. I Thess. 1:10; 4:13-18; II Thess. 2:1-10; I Cor. 2:6; 15:23-28; II Cor. 4:4; Col. 2:14; Eph. 1:22.

S. Salvation "the redemption of our body"—Rom. 8:23; I Thess. 5:8; II Thess. 2:18; Phil. 2:12; II Cor. 6:2 (Isa. 49:8; II Cor. 6:2); Rom. 13:11; Eph. 2:5-8; II Tim. 1:9; 4:18; Titus 3:5.

T. *Parousia, apocalypsis, epiphaneia*—I Thess. 2:19, 3:13, 4:15, 5:23; II Thess. 2:1, 8, 9; I Cor. 15:23; II Thess. 1:7; I Cor. 1:7.

U. Judgment—I Thess. 5:2; II Thess. 2:2; I Cor. 1:8; 5:5; II Cor. 1:14; Phil. 1:23; II Cor. 5:8-10. For excellent bibliography on Pauline Eschatology see B. Rigaux, *Les Epitres aux Thessaloniciens* (Paris, 1956), pp. xxiii - xxix; and H. A. A. Kennedy, *St. Paul's Conception of the Last Things* (London, 1905), and G. Voss, *Pauline Eschatology* (Grand Rapids: Eerdmans, pb).

V. Jesus and the Future (Eschatology of the Synoptics)
   1. John the Baptist's eschatology—Matt. 3:10f; Lk. 3:10-14.
   2. Matt. 4:14-16; 10:23; 13:24-30, 37-40; 25:1-13; 27:51-53 (Matt. 24 considered elsewhere).
   3. Lk. "Gospel of Salvation" 1:69, 71, 77; 2:30; 3:6; 19:9 - savior - 1:47, 2:11.
   4. Mk. 1:21-27; 2:1—3:6; 3:11, 12; 5:1-17; 7:24-30; 9:14-29. J. M. Robinson, *The Problem of History in Mark* (London, 1957); E. Best, *The Temptation and the Passion.* (Cambridge, 1965); Gr. Beasley Murray, *Jesus and the Future* (NY: MacMillan).
   5. Johannine Eschatology—12:31—krisis aspects of Jesus' ministry. See J. Blank, *Krisis:* Freiburg, 1964; P. Ricca, *Die Eschatologie des Vierten Evangeliums,* (Zurich, 1966). The Apocalypse is only prophetic book in N.T. Central theme is eschatological Lordship of the Risen Lord (see my *The Seer, Saviour, and the Saved*).

The Significance of the Future has been created and revealed to us by Jesus Christ.

III. Maranatha: The King Is Coming!
"And this gospel of the kingdom will be preached throughout the whole earth as a testimony to all nations; and then the end will come." Matthew 24:14

"Come, Lord Jesus" Revelation 22:20

Christ is coming! The time between His first and last

coming (second coming is not a biblical term) is the "last days." (Read Matt. 24—25; Mk. 13; Lk. 21; I-II Thess.; and the Revelation). Ours is the day of insecurity and prophets on every hand, from every spectrum, from occult practitioners to Edgar Cayce and Jean Dixon, reveal the secrets of the future. What does the Word say regarding these signs?

The Coming Again of Jesus Christ
A. New Testament terms for the Second Coming.
1. Personal Presence (Gk. *Parousia*)—denotes both an arrival and consequent presence—I Thess. 4:15; Matt. 24:27; II Thess. 2:8; Matt. 24:38, 39; II Pet. 3:12, 13.
2. Come (Gk. *Erchomai*)—to come from one place to another—Matt. 24:30; Matt. 25:6-13; 24:37, 44; I Thess. 5:2; II Thess. 1:8-10; Rev. 22:7, 12, 20. Be waiting and watchful.
3. Arrive (Gk. *Heko*)—in contrast to *erchomai* it stresses the point of arrival—Matt. 24:14; II Peter 3:10; Heb. 10:37; Rev. 2:15. Hope for Christians and warning to the lost.
4. Revelation (Gk. *Apokalupsis*)—a manifestation, uncovering and unveiling—Rom. 2:5; Rom. 8:19; I Cor. 1:7; II Thess. 1:7, 8; I Pet. 1:7, 13; I Pet. 4:13; Lk. 17:26-30; I Pet. 1:5. Revelation brings final judgment to the lost and final peace and joy to the saints.
5. Appearing (Gk. *Epiphania*)—an appearance or a shining forth—II Thess. 2:8; I Tim. 6:13, 14; II Tim. 4:1; II Tim. 4:8; Titus 2:12, 13.
B. The Day of Christ: "In these last days"—Joel 2:28-32; Acts 2:16-21; Heb. 1:1, 2; I Cor. 10:11; I Pet. 1:20; I Jn. 2:18.
1. Day of the Son of Man—Luke 17:24, 30.
2. Day of Judgment—Matthew 10:15.
3. Day of Wrath—Romans 2:15.
4. Day of Our Lord Jesus Christ—I Cor. 1:8; 5:5; Phil. 1:6.

5. Day of Christ—Phil. 1:6, 10; 2:16.
6. Day of the Lord—I Thess.
7. Day of Visitation—I Peter 2:12.
8. Day of God—II Peter 3:12.
9. Great Day—Jude 6.
10. Day of Redemption—Eph. 4:30.
11. Day of Vengeance—Isa. 61:2.
12. The Day—I Cor. 3:13; Heb. 10:25; Matt. 24:36.
C. Old Age and World Order.
D. New Age and New World Order.
  Believers live in "last days" upon which "the end of ages
  are come" but the "last day," the consummation of the
  age still lies in the future. (Matt. 13:39, 40, 49; 24:3;
  28:20; Jn. 6:39, 44, 54; 12:48; I Cor. 10:11; II Tim.
  3:1; Heb. 1:2; 9:26; I Peter 1:5, 20; II Pet. 3:3; I Jn.
  2:18; Jude vs. 18.)
E. Two Ages: (1) This age (*Houtos ho aion; ho nun aion*);
  (2) the Present Age (*ho enestos aion*) Matt. 12:32; 13:22;
  Lk. 16:8; Rom. 12:2; I Cor. 1:20; 2:6, 8; 3:18; II Cor.
  4:4; Gal. 1:4; Eph. 1:21; 2:2; 6:12; I Tim. 6:17; II Tim.
  4:10; Titus 2:12.
F. That Age (*ho aion ekeinos*); The Future Age (*ho aion
  mellon; ho aion erchomenos*) Matt. 12:32; Lk. 18:30;
  20:35; Eph. 2:7; Heb. 6:5. (Dalman, *Die Worte Jesu*, I,
  pp. 132-46—*Kosmos* never used of future world.)

Christ-centered character of N.T. Eschatology: (1)
Resurrection; (2) Judgment. Consequent upon the
Parousia of Christ.

The realities of the future life are so vividly and intensely
felt to be existent in heaven and from there operative in
the believer's life.

Anticipation—Eph. 1:3, 20-22; 2:6; 3:9, 10; 6:12.

Realization—Phil. 2:5-11; 3:20; Col. 1:15-17; 3:2;
Heb. 1:2, 3; 2:5; 3:4; 6:5-11; 7:13-16; 9:14; 11:10-16;
12:22, 23.

The Coming King (Parousia)—never applied to Incarnation—II Thess. 2:8; II Tim. 1:10; 4:1; Titus 2:11-13; I Thess. 6:14—only to coming again, i.e., final culmination (First advent/Second advent appears only in Test. of 12 Patriarchs, "Test. of Abraham" 92:16).

G. Signs Preceding His Coming
  1. Characteristics
     a. Sudden—Rev. 22:29; Lk. 17:24.
     b. Unexpected—Matt. 24:39; Lk. 12:40; I Thess. 5:2; Rev. 16:15.
     c. Visible by all—Rev. 1:7.
     d. Heard by all—Matt. 16:27; Mk. 13:26; II Thess. 1:7.
     e. Accompanied by angels and clouds—Matt. 16:27; 24:30, 31; 25:31, 32.
     f. Calamities and afflictions.
  2. Results
     a. Complete work of first coming—Heb. 9:28.
     b. Complete salvation—Heb. 9:28.
     c. Complete and final separation—Matt. 24:37-39.
     d. Kingdom consummated—I Cor. 15:24; Rom. 8:20, 21; II Pet. 3:7.
     e. Defeat of Satan—Rev. 12:10-12; 20:3; II Thess. 2:8.
     f. Purpose of God worked out in history—Matt. 12:32; Mk. 10:30; Lk. 20:34.
  3. Millennium and Signs of the Times: Rev. 20:4; Ps. 56:8; Acts 1:7; Matt. 12:38; 16:4; Lk. 11:29; Mk. 8:12; Matt. 24; Mk. 13; Lk. 21.
     a. A-millennial
     b. Premillennial (Dispensational, e.g. *Scofield Reference Bible* and *Late Great Planet Earth,* etc.).
     c. *Post-millennial* pp. 438-457; and Boettner's *Millennium.* (See Strauss, *Seer, Saviour, and the Saved.*)

H. Prophets—Isaiah, Zechariah, Ezekiel, Daniel, et al.
  1. Kingdom and Church (use of Kingdom and Matt.

16:16f; Isa. 40—66.)

2. Covenant (Heb. 8—9; Jer. 31:31f).
3. Israel and the Church (Rom. 8, 9, 10; Gal.)
4. Meaning of Everlasting
5. Tribulation
6. Anti-Christ and Man of Sin
7. Judgment
8. Resurrection (First and Second)
9. Heaven and Hell (See Strauss study, esp. pp. 455-457).

I. Conflict (1) Parousia will come suddenly and unexpectedly; (2) Come heralded by these signs; (3) This generation—2 references to 2 different issues. Vs. 30—"these things (a. dem. pron. "that"); Vs. 32—"that day or that hour" (b. dem. pron. "but") Mark 13:28, 29 preceding parable. These things and parousia are distinguished.

Question: How much—"these things" (vs. 20: Lk. 21:31) "all these things" (Matt. 24:33, 34; Mk. 13:30), "all things" (Lk. 21:32) is intended to cover up what is described in the preceding discourse.

Answer: depends on—Is Jesus referring to 2 crises or 1? a. Zahn—Signs cover only Matt. 24:4-14. What is related afterwards. viz. "the abomination of desolation," great tribulation, false prophets and christs, commotions in the heavens, the sign of the Son of man, all this belongs to "the end."

Prediction fulfilled in Jesus' World or Ours?

1. Mark 13:15-29 subsume under "The End"? Compare with vs. 4-14—Signs.
2. Problem of existence of Temple and Temple worship as presupposed in last days immediately before the parousia.
3. The "abomination of desolation" taken from Deu. 8:13; 9:27; 11:31; 12:11.
   destruction of city—Temple
   desecration of temple—site by setting up idolatry

flight from Judaea

4. Recurrence of difficulty—II Thess. 2:3, 4 where "the man of sin" is represented as sitting in "the Temple of God" and in Rev. 11:12 where "temple of God," and "altar" and the court which is without the temple and "the holy city" (between sixth and seventh trumpet).

5. It is not easy to conceive of preaching the Gospel to all nations as falling within the lifetime of that generation (Matt. 24:13; Rom. 1:13; 10:18; 15:19-24; Col. 1:6; I Tim. 3:16; II Tim. 4:17.)
   a. Preaching to all nations
   b. Preaching to Gentiles

6. Jesus' discourse relates to 2 things:
   a. Destruction of Jerusalem and Temple
   b. End of the world

7. Signs (negative Mk. 13:5-8; Positive vss. 9-13).
   a. Signs of destruction of Jerusalem and the Temple —vss. 14-20.
   b. Abomination of Desolation in period preceding the national catastrophe.
   c. Signs of parousia—vss. 24-27.
   d. Attitude toward national crisis is defined in parable of fig tree.
   e. Attitude toward the parousia—vss. 32-37.

J. Events Preceding Coming Again:
   1. Uniform teaching of Jesus, Peter, Paul—Israel— Matt. 23:39; Lk. 13:35; Acts 1:6, 7; 3:19-21. "Seasons of refreshing" and "Times of restoration of all things" dependent on eschatological sending of Christ to Israel and dependent on Israel's repentence, conversion and blotting out of the sins of Israel— Rom. 11—Israel's unbelief: (1) Now in Israel an election according to grace; (2) Future extensive conversion of Israel—vss. 5, 25-32.
   2. Coming Anti-Christ
      a. I Jn. 2:18-22; 4:3; II Jn. 7 (also in Synoptics, Paul,

and Revelation).

b. Synoptics—coming of false Christs and false prophets (Mk. 13:6, 22).

c. Paul's view of Counter Christ: II Thess. 2:6-8 (vss. 9-12) e.g. Gunkel, Bousset whose works have been reprinted, claim the origin of concept of final struggle between God and great enemy—found in myth of chaos conquered by Marduk, i.e., what had happened at the beginning of the world is transferred to the end (compare with O.T. eg. Ez., Dan., and Zech.) Note also conception of a single enemy in Apoc. Baro. 40:1, 2 which charges conception of 4 Esdras Plurals "false Christs" and "false prophets," and instigator of "the abomination of desolation." (I Jn. 2:18-22; II Jn. 7— spirit of anti-Christ and the "mystery of lawlessness is already at work.") Same expectation in Rev. 13:3, 12-14; 17:8, 10-17; II Thess. 2:9-12.

d. Working of Satan: Supernatural character of Satan's activity in the world ("the lawless one," "the man of sin" "power" "signs" and "wonders" —to accredit a lie. (gen. pseudous).

e. Who is the "hinderer" in II Thess. 2:7?

f. "The abomination of desolation" connected with apostasy via false teaching (Mk. 13:22, 23; "the lawless one" and destructive effects of error II Thess. 2:9-12).

g. Evangelion, anti-Christ and Apostasy, Forces of evil gather strength toward the "end" (Matt. 24:27ff; Lk. 17:24ff; I Thess. 5:2, 3; II Thess. 1:7.

Resurrection and the Coming Again of Christ.

History Making Power of the Resurrection:
1. Resurrection and Coming Again—Lk. 20:35; Jn. 6:40; I Thess. 4:16; 3:13.
2. Resurrection of the Word—*Egeirein*—to awake; *Anistanai*—to raise (Resurrection and the Spirit—

Isa. 26:19; Deu. 12:2).

3. Resurrection a single event. N.T. nowhere teaches, as chiliasm (Millennium) assumes, a resurrection in two stages, one at the coming again of Christians living and dead, and a second one at close of the millennium. Passages supposedly teaching a double resurrection are: Acts 3:19-21; I Cor. 15:23-28; Phil. 3:9-11; I Thess. 4:13-18; II Thess. 1:5-12; Rev. 20:1-6 (Acts 3:21—"must receive"—a present, not future tense; "times of restoration of all things"; and "seasons of refreshing.")

4. Two Orders: Two "tagmata"—I Cor. 15:23-28.
   a. Two orders not "believers" and "unbelievers"
   b. Two orders are "Christ" and "Christians"

5. Possible exclusion and provisional reign? I Thess. 4:13-18 (vs. 14—resurrection is guaranteed); II Thess. 1:5-12.

6. Resurrection for all believers—Phil. 3:9-11.

7. Millennial Reign of Christ—Rev. 20:1-6.
   a. First resurrection—Rev. 19.
   b. Second resurrection—spiritual, physical (compare resurrection in I Thess. and I Cor.) (See Straus bibliography on Resurrection in Orr's *Resurrection*, College Press reprint and my paper "The Resurrection as a History-Making Event.")
   c. Nature of the Resurrection Body—I Cor. 15:35-58 vs. 35 "with what manner of body do they come" —answer from vs. 50ff.

An Appointed Time: Judgment

Day of Judgment—Matt. 7:22; 10:15; 24:36; Lk. 10:12; 21:34; I Cor. 1:8; 3:13; II Tim. 4:8; Rev. 6:17 (e.g. O.T. "The Day of Yahweh").

1. N.T. does not speak of judgment after death, not even Heb. 9:27, 28.

2. Recognize two groups—condemned and saved (Matt. 25:33, 34; Jn. 5:29).

592

3. Degree of guilt—based on knowledge of Divine will possessed in life (Matt. 10:15; 11:20-24; Lk. 10:12-15; 12:47, 48; Jn. 15:22-24; Rom. 2:12; II Pet. 2:20-22.)

4. Descriptions of destruction—eternal fire—Matt. 18:8; 25:41; Jude vs. 7; eternal punishment—Matt. 25:36; eternal destruction—II Thess. 1:9; eternal judgment—Mk. 3:29; Heb. 6:2; unquenchable fire—Matt. 3:12; never-dying worm—Mk. 9:43-48; the smoke of their torment goes up for ever and ever—Rev. 14:11; tormented day and night forever and forever—Rev. 20:10.

5. Conditional immortality urged via terms—*apoleia*, perdition; *phtora*, corruption; *olethros*, destruction; *thanatos*, death. Both testaments use these terms in sense of undesirable state of existence, not non-existence.

6. Restoration of All Things—fulfillment of promises to Israel. *Apokatastasis panton* only Acts 3:21—never used in sense of absolute universalism, but rather to fulfillment. Universalism as cosmic not "every individual," e.g. Rom. 5:18; I Cor. 15:22; 28; Eph. 1:10; Col. 1:20.

7. *Kingdom, Life* and *Glory*—New Heaven and New Earth—Isa. 61—66; Rev. 19—21; II Peter 3:6; Rom. 8:18-22.

8. Second chancism and intermediate state between death and the consummation of the Kingdom of God. (I Peter 3:19-21; 4:6).

a. Punishment, Person and Place—(*Gehenna*—Matt. 5:22, 29, 30; Jas. 3:6; *Abussos*—Lk. 8:31; Rom. 10:7; Rev. 9:1, 2; *Tartaroun*—II Peter 2:4; Hades, Sheol—Matt. 11:23; 16:18; Acts 2:27-31; I Cor. 15:55; Rev. 1:18; 6:8; 13:14; Lk. 16:23—only passage where concept is localized.

b. *Maranatha*

593

BIBLIOGRAPHY

Eschatology and Apocalyptic in General

The Background of the New Testament and its Eschatology, In honor of C. H. Dodd, Ed. by W. D. Davies and D. Daube, 1956.

Bietenhard, H., *Die himmlische Welt im Urchristentum und Spatjudentum,* 1951.

Block, J., *On the Apocalyptic in Judaism,* 1953.

Bousset, Wilhelm, *Der Antichrist in der Ueberlieferung des Judentums,* des Neuen Testaments und der Alten Kirche, 1895.

_____. *Die Religion des Judentums in Spathellenistischen Zeitalter,* 3rd edition by H. Gressmann, 1926.

Bultmann, Rudolf, "Die Bedeutung der Eschatologie für die Religion des Neuen Testament," in *Zeitschrift für Theologie u. Kirche,* Bd. 27, (1917), p. 76ff.

Bultmann, Rudolf, "The Bible Today und die Eschatologie," in *The Background of the New Testament* (Dodd-Festschrift), 1956, p. 402-408.

Bultmann, Rudolf, "History and Eschatology in the New Testament," in *New Testament Studies* I (1954-55) p. 5-16.

Burkitt, F. C., "Life, Zoe, Hayyim," in ZNW, 12 (1911), p. 228-230.

Charles, R. H., *A Critical History of the Doctrine of Future Life in Israel, in Judaism, and in Christianity,* 1899. (2nd ed. 1913).

Conzelmann, Hans, "Auferstehung V. Im N.T." in RGG I^3, p. 695-696.

_____. "Eschatologie IV. Im Urchristentum" in RGG II^3, (1958), pp. 665-672.

Cullmann, Oskar, *Le retour de Christ,* 1943.

_____. "Unsterblichkeit der Seele und Auferstehung der Toten," in *Theol. Zeitschrift* 12 (1956), pp. 126-156.

Dodd, C. H., *The Apostolic Preaching and its Developments,*

1936.

Fascher, E., "Anastasis-Resurrectio-Auferstehg," in ZNW 40 (1941), p. 166-229.

Glasson, F. G., *The Second Advent,* 1947.

Goguel, M., "Eschatologie et apocalyptique dans le Christianisme primitif," in *Revue de l'Histoire des Religions* 106 (1932) p. 381-434, 489-524.

──────. "Eschatologie et apocalyptique dans le Christianisme primitif," in *Revue de l'Histoire et de Philos. Religion,* 1937, p. 337-356.

Gunkel, Hermann, *Schöpfung und Chaos in Urzeit und Endzeit.,* 1895.

Guy, H. A., *The New Testament Doctrine of the Last Things,* 1948.

Käsemann, Ernst, "Eine Apologie der urchristlichen Eschatologie," in *Zeitschrift für Theologie u. Kirche* 49 (1952) p. 272-296.

Körner, J., "Endgeschichtliche Parusieerwartung und Heilsgegenwart im N.T.," in *Evang. Theologie* 14 (1954), p. 177-192.

Kümmel, Werner George, *Promise and Fulfillment,* 1957.

Lohse, Eduard, "Auferstehung IV. Im Judentum" in RGG I3, p. 694-695.

Manson, William, *Eschatology in the New Testament.*

Meyer, R., "Eschatologie III, Im Judentum," in RGG II3, 1958, p. 662-665.

Minear, P., *The Christian Hope and the Second Coming,* 1954.

Nikolainen, A. T., *Der Auferstehungsglauben in der Bibel und ihrer Umwelt.* Bd. II, 1946.

Ringgren, H., "Apokalyptik II, Jüdische A." in RGG3 Bd. I (1957), p. 464-466.

Rowley, H. H., *The Revelance of Apocalyptic,* 1947.

Schütz, R., "Apokalyptik III., Altchrisliche Apokalyptik" in RGG I3 (1957), p. 467-469.

Schweizer, Eduard, "Die Gegenwart des Geistes und die Eschatologische Hoffnung . . .," in *The Background of the*

New Testament (Dodd-Festschrift), 1956, p. 482-508.

Torge, P., *Seelenglaube und Unsterblichkeitshoffnung im A.T.,* 1909.

Volz, P., *Die Eschatologie der jüdischen Gemeinde im neutestamentlichen Zeitalter,* 1934.

Wilder, A. N., "Kerygma, Eschatology and Social Ethics," in *The Background of the New Testament* (Dodd-Festschrift), 1956, p. 509-536.

Eschatology of Paul

Braun, Herbert, *Gerichtsgedanke und Rechtfertigungslehre bei Paulus,* 1930.

Bonnard, P., "mourir et vivre avec Jesus-Christ selon St. Paul" in *Revue d'Histoire et de Philos. Relig.* 36 (1956), p. 101-112.

Clavier, H., "Breves remarques sur la notion de *soma pneumatikon,"* in *The Background of the New Testament* (Dodd-Festschrift), 1956, p. 342-362.

Deissner, K., *Auferstehung und Pneumagedanke bei Paulus,* 1912.

Dibelius, Martin, *Die Geisterwelt im Glauben des Paulus,* 1907.

Faw, C. E., "Death and Resurrection in Paul's Letters," *Journal Bibl. Rel.* 27 (1959), p. 291-298.

Goquel, M., *Le caractere a la fois actuel et future, du salut dans la theologie Paulinienne,"* in *The Background of the New Testament* (Dodd-Festschrift), 1956, p. 322-341.

Guntermann, F., *Die Eschatologie des heiligen Paulus,* 1932.

Hamilton, Neill Q., "The Holy Spirit and Eschatology in Paul," *Scottish Journal of Theology* Occasional Papers No. 6, 1957.

Kabisch, Richard, *Die Eschatologie des Paulus inIhren Zusammenhängen mit dem Gesamtbegriff des Paulinismus,* 1893.

Macgregor, G. H. C., "Principalities and Powers, The

Cosmic Background of St. Paul's Thought," in *New Testament Studies* I (1954), p. 17-28.

Molitor, H., *Die Auferstehung der Christen und Nichtchristen nach dem Apostel Paulus,* 1932.

Porter, Frank C., "The Place of Apocalyptical Conceptions in the Thought of Paul," in JBL 1922 (Vol. XLI), reprinted in Kepler, *Contemporary Thinking,* 1950, p. 283-292.

Teichmann, E., *Die Paul. Vorstellungen von Auferstehung und Gericht und ihre Beziehungen zur jüdischen Apocalyptik,* 1896.

Vos., G., "The Pauline Doctrine of the Resurrection," in *Princeton Theological Review* 27 (1929) p. 1-35, 193-226.

Vos., G., *The Pauline Eschatology,* 1930.

BIBLIOGRAPHY

I. HEBREW TEXT AND ANCIENT VERSIONS

A. The Hebrew Text

Jeffrey, J. *The Massoretic Text and the Septuaginta Compared, with Special Reference to the Book of Job,* ET 36, 1924/ 25, 70-73.

Jouon, P. "Notes philologiques sur le texte hebreu de Job," *Bibl* 11, 1930, 322-4.

Sarna, N. M. "Some Instances of the Enclitic -m in Job," *JJS* 6, 1955, 108-110.

Stevenson, W. B. *Critical Notes on the Hebrew Text of the Poem of Job.* Aberdeen: University Press, 1951.

Sutcliffe, E. F. "Notes on Job, Textual and Exegetical," *Bibl* 30, 1949, 66-90.

_____. "Further Notes on Job, Textual and Exegetical," *Bibl* 31, 1950, 365-378.

B. Greek Versions (LXX)

Brock, S. *The Testament of Job, Edited with an Introduction and Critical Notes* (in Greek). Dans *Pseudepigrapha Veteris Testamenti Graece,* II. Leiden E. J. Brill, 1966.

Gard, D. H. *The Exegetical Method of the Greek Translator of the Book of Job. JBL Monograph Series,* Vol. VIII. Philadelphia, Sec. of Biblical Literature, 1952.

_____. *The Concept of Job's Character According to the Greek Translator of the Hebrew Text. JBL* 1953, 182-186.

_____. *The Concept of the Future Life According to the Greek Translator of the Book of Job. JBL* 1954, 137-143.

Gehman, H. S. *The Theological Approach of the Greek Translator of Job 1-15. JBL* 1949, 231-240.

Orlinsky, H. M. *Job 5, 8, a Problem in Greek-Hebrew Methodology, JQR* 25, 1935, 271-278.

_____. *Some Corruptions in the Greek Text of Job, JQR* 26, 1935-36, 133-145.

_____. *apozaion and epizaion in the Septuagint of Job, JBL*

56, 1937, 361-367.

_____. *The Hebrew and Greek Text of Job 14, 12, JQR* 28, 1937-38, 57-68.

_____. *Studies in the Septuagint of the Book of Job, HUCA* 28, 1957, 53-74; 29, 1958, 229-271; 30, 1959, 153-167; 32, 1961, 239-268; 33, 1962, 119-151; 35, 1964, 56-68.

Zimmermann, L. *The Septuagint Appendix to Job,* The Scotist (Teutopolis), 1960, pp. 48-59.

C. Latin Versions

Barret, L. *Job selon la Vulgate,* Toulon Imprimerie J. d'Arc, 1925.

D. The Syrian Text

E. The Arabian Text

Ulback, E. *An Arabic Version of the Book of Job,* The Open Court 46, 1932, pp. 782-786.

F. Coptic, Ethiopian, and Georgian Versions

G. The Targum

Fohrer, G. *400rNab, 11QTgJob und die Hioblegende, ZATW* 75, 1963, 93-97.

Van der Ploeg, J. P. M. *Een Targum van het boek Job: een nieuwe vondst in de woestijn van Juda,* MAA XXV, 9, 1962; and *Le Targum de Job de la grotte 11 de Qumran* (11QTgJob). *Premiere communication,* MAA, Nieuwe reeks, Deel 25, No. 9, Amsterdam, 1962.

Van der Woude, A. S. *Das Hiobtargum aus Qumran Hohle XI,* Congress Volume, Bonn, 1962-3, 322-331.

II. THE BOOK OF JOB IN DIFFERENT TRADITIONS

A. Jewish Tradition

B. Greek Tradition

C. Latin Tradition

Wasselynck, R. *L'influence des Moralia in Job de S. Gregoire le Grand sur la theologie morale entre le VII et le XII siecle,* These Lille, 1956.

D. Syrian Tradition

III. COMMENTARIES

Bourke, M. M. *The Book of Job,* Pamphlet Bible Series, 35 and 36, New York: Paulist Press, 1963.

Buttenwieser, M. *The Book of Job,* London: Hedder & Stoughton, 1922.

Catmull. *An Interpretation of the Book of Job,* Diss. Univ. of Utah, 1960.

Cranfield, C. E. B. *An Interpretation of the Book of Job,* ET 54, 1943, 295-8.

Davidson, A. B. *A Commentary on the Book of Job,* 1862.

_____. *Job (Book of),* in *Hasting's Dictionary of the Bible.*

_____. *The Book of Job, with Notes, Introduction and Appendix,* adapted to the Text of the Revised Version with some supplementary Notes by H. C. O. Lanchester, in *The Cambridge Bible for Schools and Colleges,* Old Testament, edited by A. F. Kirkpatrick. Cambridge: University Press, 1951, 1960.

Delitzsch, F. & Wetzstein. *Das Buch Hiob,* BC IV, 2, Leipzig, Dorffling & Franke, 1864, 2nd ed., 1876.

Dhorme, P. *Le livre de Job* (Etudes bibliques). Paris: Gabalda, 1926.

Driver, S. R. & Gray, G. B. *A Critical and Exegetical Commentary on the Book of Job* together with a New Translation, ICC, 3rd ed., 1964.

Ellison, H. L. *From Tragedy to Triumph,* The Message of the Book of Job. Grand Rapids: Eerdmans, 1958.

Freehof, S. B. *Book of Job, A Commentary,* New York: Union of American Hebrew Congregations, XV, 1958.

Guillaume, A. *Job,* in *A New Commentary on Holy Scripture,* edited by Charles Gore, Henry Leighton Goudge, Alfred Guillaume. London: S.P.C.K., 1951.

Hanson, A. & M. *The Book of Job,* Torch BC. London: SCM Press, 1953, 1962.

Jastrow, M., Jr. *The Book of Job. It's Origin, Growth and Interpretations.* Philadelphia, London: Lippincott Company, 1920.

Kissane, E. J. *The Book of Job* translated from a critically revised Hebrew text with commentary. Dublin, Browne & Nolan, 1939; New York: Sheed & Ward, 1946.

Lods, A., and Randon, L. *Job,* in *La Bible du Centenaire,* t. III. Paris, 1947.

Lofthouse, W. F. *Book of Job,* in *Abingdon Bible Commentary.* New York and Nashville: Abingdon-Cokesbury Press, 1929, 483-508.

MacBeath, A. *The Book of Job.* Glasgow: Pickering & I., 1967.

Minn, H. R. *The Book of Job.* A Translation with Introduction and Short Notes. Auckland (N. Zealand). The University of Auckland Press, 1965.

Nairne, A. *The Book of Job,* edited with an Introduction. Cambridge: University Press, 1935.

Pope, N. H. *Job.* in *The Anchor Bible,* 15, New York: 1965.

Reichert, V. E. *Job with Hebrew Text and English Translation,* Commentary in *Soncino Books of the Bible,* ed. A. Cohen. Hindhead, Surrey, The Soncino Press, 1946.

Schweitzer, R. *Job* (coll. *La Bible et la vie,* 6). Paris: Ligel, 1966.

Snaith, N. H. *The Book of Job.* London: The Epworth Press, 1945.

Stier, F. *Ijjob. Das Buch Ijjob hebraisch und deutsch.* Munchen: Kosel, 1954.

Terrien, S. "Job," in *Commentaire de l'AT,* XII. Neuchatel-Paris, Delachaux & Niestle, 1963.

Torczyner, N. H. *The Book of Job Interpreted.* Jerusalem: Hebrew University Press, 1941 (See Tur-Sinai).

Tur-Sinai, N. H. (=Torczyner). *The Book of Job;* a New Commentary. Jerusalem:

IV. STUDIES AND ARTICLES

Albright, W. F. "The Name of Bildad the Shuhite," *ASJL* 44, 1927-8, 31-36.

———. *Archaeology and the Religion of Israel.* Baltimore: John Hopkins Press, XII, 1946.

———. "A Catalogue of Early Hebrew Lyric Poems," *HUCA* 23, 1950-1, 1-39.

———. "Some Canaanite-Phoenician Sources of Hebrew Wisdom," in M. Noth & D. Winton Thomas. *Wisdom in Israel and in the Ancient Near East, VTS,* Vol. III, Leiden, 1961, 1-15.

Anderson, H. "Another Perspective on the Book of Job," in *Transactions publiees par la Societe Orientale de l'Universite de Glasgow.* Leiden: E. J. Brill, 18, 1961, 43-46.

Baab, O. J. *The Book of Job.* Int 5, 1951, 329-343.

Baker, A. "The Strange Case of Job's Chisel," in *CBQ* 11, 1969, 370-379.

Barrett, W. "The Hebraic Man of Faith, Hebraism and Hellenism," in *Irrational Man, A Study of Existential Philosophy.* Garden City: 1958, p. 64.

Barton, G. A. "Some Textoritical Notes on the Elihu Speeches, Job 32-37," in *JBL* 43, 1924, 228.

Barton, G. A. "The Composition of Job 24-30." *JBL* 30, 1911, pp. 66.

———. "Some Textcritical Notes on Job." *JBL* 42, 1923, 29-32.

Barucq, A. "Prophetisme et eschatologie individuelle," *VS* 100,

1956, 407-420.

Baumgartner, W. "The Wisdom Literature, III, Job"; in *The Old Testament and Modern Study,* ed. H. H. Rowley. Oxford: Clarendon Press, 1951, 216-221.

Beaucamp, E. *Sous la main de Dieu,* 11. *La Sagesse et le destin des elus.* Paris: Fleurus, 1957, 80-126.

_____. "Justice 'divine et pardon; ut justificeris in sermonibus tuis" (Ps. 51, 6b), in *Memorial A. Gelin.* Le Puy—Paris, X. Mappus, 1961, 1929-144.

Bentzen, A. *Introduction to the Old Testament.* Kopenhagen: C. Gads Forlag, 1952.

Berry, D. L. "Scripture and Imaginative Literature Focus on Job," in *Journal of General Education,* 19/2. Pennsylvania, 1967, 119-131.

Blackwood, A. W. *Devotional Introduction to Job.* Grand Rapids, Michigan: Baker Book House, 1959.

Blank, S. H. "The Curse, the Blasphemy, the Spell, and the Oath," *HUCA* 23, Part I, 83 et 85, note 44.

_____. "An Effective Literary Device in Job" 31, *JJS* 2, 1951, 1-5-7.

_____. "Men Against God. The Promethean Element in Biblical Prayer," *JBL* 72, 1953, 1-13.

Blommerde, A. C. M. *Northwest Semitic Grammar and Job,* Diss. Pont. Biblical Institute. Rome: 1968, dactyl. (==Biblica et Orientalia, no. 22, in preparation.

Blumenthal, D. R. "A Play of Words in the Nineteenth Chapter of Job," *VT* 16, 1966, 497-501.

Bottero, J. "Le 'dialogue pessimiste' et la transcendance," in *RThPh* XCIX, 1, 1966, 7-24.

Breakstone, R. "Job. A Case Study," New York: Bookman Associates, Inc., 1964.

Burrows, M. "The Voice from the Whirlwind." *JBL* 47, 1928, 117-132.

Cambier, J. "Justice de Dieu, salut de tous les hommes et foi," *RB* 71, 1964, 537-583.

Carstensen, R. M. *Job, Defense of Honor.* New York/Nashville: The Abingdon Press, 1963.

_____. "The Persistence of the 'Elihu' Tradition in Later Jewish Writers," in *Lexington Theological Quarterly* II/2, 1967, 27-46.

Cazelles, H. "A propos de quelques textes difficiles relatifs a la justice de Dieu," in *l'Ancien Testament*. RB 58, 1951, 169ss.

Condon, K. "The Biblical Doctrine of Original Sin," IThQ 34, 1967, 20-36.

Cosser, W. *The Meaning of "Life" (hayyim) in Proverbs, Job, Qoheleth*. Glasgow: University Oriental Society Transactions 15, 1955, 48-53.

Coste, J. "Notion grecque et Notion biblique de la 'Souffrance educatrice.' " *RSR* 43, 1955, 481-523.

Cross, F. M., Jr. "The Council of Yahweh in Second Isaiah," *JNES* 12, 1953, 274ss.

_____. *The Ancient Library of Qumran and Modern Biblical Studies*. London: 1958, pp. 120-145.

_____. "Yahweh and the God of the Patriarchs," HThR 55, 1962, 225-259.

Dahood, M. "Some North-west—Semitic Words in Job," *Bibl* 38, 1957, 306-320.

_____. "Hebrew-Ugaritic Lexicography," I. *Bibl* 44, 1963, 289-303; II. 45, 1964, 393-412; III. 46, 1965, 311-332; IV. 47, 1966, 403-419; V. 48, 1967, 412-438.

_____. "Mismar, 'muzzle,' in Job 7, 12." *JBL* 80, 1961, 270s.

_____. "Northwest Semitic Philology and Job," in J. L. MacKenzie: *The Bible in Current Catholic Thought*. Gruenthaner Memorial Volume. New York: 1962, pp. 55-74.

_____. "Ugaritic usn, Job 12, 10 and 11QPs" Plea 3-4. *Bibl* 47, 1966, 107s.

_____. "The Metaphor in Job 22, 22." *Bibl* 47, 1966, 108-109.

_____. "S'RT 'Storm' in Job 4, 15." *Bibl* 48, 1967, 544s.

_____. "HDK in Job 40, 12," in *Bibl* 40, 1968, 509-510.

David, M. "Travaux et service dans l'Epopee de Gilamesh et le livre de Job." *Revue Philosophique* 147, 1957, 341-349.

Davison, W. T. "Art. Job (Book of)," in *Hasting's Dictionary of the Bible*, II, 1889, 660ff.

Dhorme, P. "Le pays de Job." *RB* 20, 1911, 104ss.

_____. "Ecclesiaste ou Job?" *RB* 32, 1923, 5-27.

_____. "Les c. 25-28 du livre de Job." *RB* 33, 1924, 343-356.

Donald, T. "The Semantic Field of 'Folly' in Proverbs, Job, Psalms, and Ecclesiastes." *VT* 13, 1963, 285-292.

Driver, G. R. "Studies in the Vocabulary of the OT." *JThS* 36, 1935, 293-301.

_____. "Problems in the Hebrew Text of Job." *VTS* 3, 1955, 72-93.

_____. "Two Astronomical Passages in the OT (Job 9, 9; 39, 31s)," *JThS*, 7, 1956, 1611.

Dussaud, R. "La nephesh et la rouah dans le livre de Job." *RHR* 129, 1945, 17-30.

Eerdmans, B. D. *Studies in Job,* 2 vol. Leiden: Burgerdijk & Niermans, 1939.

Esh, S. "Job 36, 5a in Tannaitic Tradition," *VT* 7, 1957, 190s.

Feuillet, A. "L'enigme de la souffrance et la response de Dieu," in *Dieu Vivant* 17, 1950, 77-91.

Fine, H. A. "The Patient Job." *JBL* 72, 1953, pp. vi and vii.

_____. "The Tradition of a Patient Job." *JBL* 74, 1955, 28-32.

Fohrer, G. *Glaube und Welt in Alten Testament.* Frankfurt a.M.J. Knecht, 1948.

_____. "Vorgeschichte und Komposition des Buches Hiob." *TLZ* 81, 1956, 333-336.

_____. "Art. 'Sophia' " in *TWNT*, VII, 1962, B: Ales Testament, pp. 476-496 (see Wilckens).

Freedman, D. N. "The Elihu Speeches in the Book of Job," in *Harv. Theol. Rev.* 61, 1968, 51-59.

_____. "The Structure of Job 3," in *Bibl* 49, 1968, 503-508.

Friedman, M. "The Modern Job: On Melville, Dostoevsky and Kafka" in *Judaism* 12/4, 1963, 436-355.

Fullerton, K. "The Original Conclusion to the Book of Job." *ZATW* 42, 1924, 116-145.

_____. "Double Entendre in the First Speech of Eliphaz." *JBL* 49, 1930, 320-74.

_____. "On the Text and Significance of Job 40, 2." *AJSL* 49, 1932-3, 197-211.

_____. "On Job 9 and 10." *JBL* 53, 1934, 321-349.

_____. "Job, Chapters 9 and 10." *AJSL* 55, 1938, 225-269.

Gehman, H. S. "Job II" in *The Westminster Dictionary of the Bible*. Philadelphia: The Westminster Press, 1944.

Gemser, B.: "The Rib-or Controversy Pattern in Hebrew Mentality," in M. Noth & D. W. Thomas: *Wisdom in Israel and in the Ancient Near East, VTS,* III, 1961, 135.

Gerber, I. J. *A Psychological Approach to the Book of Job.* Diss. Boston: 1949.

_____. *The Psychology of the Suffering Mind.* New York: The Jonathan David Company, XVI, 1951.

Ginsberg, H. L. "The Ugaritic Texts and Textual Criticism." *JBL* 62, 1943, 109-115.

_____. "Job the Patient and Job the Impatient"; in *Conservative Judaism*. New York 21, 1966/67, 12-28.

Goldsmith, R. H. *The Healing Scourge.* Int. 17, 1963, 271-279.

Good, E. M. *Irony in the Old Testament.* Philadelphia: 1965, 196-240.

Goodheart, E. *Job and Romanticism* (Reconstructionist 24, n. 5, 1958, 7-12).

_____. "Job and the Modern World." in *Judaism* 10, 1961, 21-28.

Gordis, R. " 'All Men's Book.' A New Introduction to Job." *Menorah Journal,* XXXVII, 1949, 329ss.

_____. "The Lord out of the Whirlwind. The Climax and Meaning of 'Job.' " *Judaism* 13/1, 1964, 48-63.

_____. *The Book of God and Man. A Study of Job.* Chicago-London: The University of Chicago Press, 1965.

Guglielmo, A. "De: Job 12, 7-9 and the Knowability of God." *CBQ* 6, 1944, 476-482.

Guillaume, A. "The use of *h-l-sh* in Exod. XVII, 13, Isa. XIV, 12, and Job XIV, 10," in *JTS* 14 (1963), 91-92.

_____. "The Arabic Background of the Book of Job," in *Promise and Fulfillment,* Edinburgh: 1963, 106-127.

_____. "The Unity of the Book of Job," in *The Annual of*

Leeds University Oriental Society, IV, 1962-63, released 1965, 26-46.

_____. "A Root *s-'h* in Hebrew," *JTS, NS,* 17, 1966, 53s.

_____. *Studies in the Book of Job, with a New Translation,* ed. by John MacDonald (Supplement II to the Annual of Leeds University Oriental Society). Leiden: E. J. Brill, 1968.

Hanson, R. P. C. "St. Paul's Quotations of the Book of Job." *Theology* 53, 1950, 250-253.

Hastoupis, A. P. "The Problem of Theodicy in the Book of Job." *Theologia* (Athenes), 1951, 657-668.

Heras. "The Standard of Job's Immorality." *CBQ* 11, 1949, 263-279.

Holladay, W. L. "Jeremiah's Lawsuit with God." *Int.* 17, 1963, 280-287.

Irwin, W. A. "An Examination of the Progress of Thought in the Dialogue of Job." *JR* 13, 1933, 150-164.

_____. "The First Speech of Bildad." *ZATW* 51, 1933, 205-216.

_____. "The Elihu Speeches in the Criticism of the Book of Job," *JR* 17, 1937, 37-47.

_____. "Poetic Structure in the Dialogue of Job." *JNES* 5, 1946, 26-39.

_____. "Job and Prometheus." *JR* 30, 1950, 90-108.

Irwin, W. A. *The Old Testament: Keystone of Human Culture,* 1952, (pp. 72, 99ss).

_____. "Job's Redeemer." *JBL* 81, 1962, 217-229.

Jeffre, C. J. *La Providence, mystere de silence.* Lumiere et Vie, no. 66, 55-77.

Johnson, A. R. "The Primary Meaning of *g-'-l."* *VTS,* 1, 1953, 67-77.

Jung, C. B. *Antwort auf Hiob.* Zurich, Raschen, 1952.

_____. *Response a Job, traduction de R. Cahen.* Postface de Henri Corbin. Paris.

King, A. R. *The Problem of Evil. Christian Concepts and the Book of Job.* New York: Ronald, X, 1952.

Knight, H. "Job (Considered as a Contribution to Hebrew Theology)." *SJTh* 9, 1956, 63-76.

Kraeling, E. G. H. *The Book of the Ways of God.* London: S.P.C.K., 1938.

_____. *Recension du livre de J. Lindblom.* "La composition du livre de Job," in *JBL* 65, 1946, 224-228.

_____. "Man and His God. A Sumerian variation on the 'Job' Motive." *VTS,* 111, 1953, 170-182.

Kuyper, L. J. "The Repentance of Job." *VT* 9, 1959, 91-94.

Langdon, S. *Babylonian Wisdom.* Paris-Londres, Geuthner, Luzac & Co., 1923.

Legrand, L. "La creation, triomphe cosmique de Yahwe." *NRT* 83, 1961, 449-470.

Leveque, J. " 'Et Yahweh repondit a Job' "; in *Foi Vivante.* Bruxelles-Paris, 7, 1966, No. 28, 72-77.

Lillie, W. "The Religious Significance of the Theophany in the Book of Job." *ET* 68, 1956, 355-8.

Lindblom, C. J. "Die Vergeltung Gottes im Buche Hiob. Eine ideenkritische Skizze," in *Blumerincq-Gedenkschrift, Abhandlungen der Herder-Gesellschaft und der Herder-Instituts zu Riga,* VI, No. 3, 1938, 80-97.

_____. "Vedergallningsporblemet i Jobs bok." *SvTK* 14, 1938, 209-228.

_____. *Job and Prometheus, a Comparative Study.* Acta Instituti Romani Regni Sueciae, II/1. Lund, 1939, 280-287.

_____. "Joblegenden traditionshistoriskt undersokt." *SEA* 5, 1940, 29-42.

_____. *Boken om Job och hans Lidende.* Lund, C. W. K. Gleerup Forlag, 1940.

Lods, A. *La croyance a la vie future dans l'antiquite israelite.* Paris, 1906.

_____. "Recherches recentes sur le livre de Job." *RHPR* 14, 1934, 501-533.

_____. *Les origines de la figure de Satan, ses fonctions a la cour celeste;* dans: Melanges Syriens, offerts a R. Dussaud, II, Paris, 1939, 649-660.

Lods, A. *Histoire de la litterature hebraique et juive.* Paris, Payot, 1950.

Lusseau, H. "Job," in *Introduction a la Bible,* under the

direction of A. Robert and A. Feuillet, t. I, 2 ed., 1959, 642-654.

Macdonald, D. B. "Some External Evidence on the Original Form of the Legend of Job." *AJSL* 14, 1898, 137-164; cf. *JBL* 14, 63-71.

_____. *The Hebrew Literary Genius.* Princeton: University Press, 1933.

MacKenzie, R. A. F. "The Purpose of the Yahweh Speeches in the Book of Job." *Bibl* 40, 1959, 435-445.

Martin-Achard, R. *De la mort a la resurrection d'apres l'Ancien Testament.* Neuchatel, 1956, 133-134.

May, H. G. "Prometheus and Job: the Problem of the God of Power and the Man of Worth," *AThR* 34, 1952, 240-246.

Michael, J. H. "Paul and Job. A Neglected Analogy." *ET* 36, 1924/25, 67-70.

Morgan, G. C. *The Answer of Jesus to Job.* London: Marshall, Morgan & Scott, s.d.

North, C. R. "The Redeemer God." *Int.* 2, 1948, 3-16.

Obermann, J. "Sentence Negation in Ugaritic." *JBL* 65, 1946, 233-248.

O'Neill, G. *The World's Classic: Job.* Milwaukee: 1938.

Onimus, J. *Face au monde actuel.* Paris: 1963, 249-260.

Parente, P. P. "The Book of Job. Reflections on the Mystic Value of Human Suffering." *CBQ* 8, 1946, 213-219.

Paton, L. B. "The Problem of Suffering in the pre-exilic Prophets." *JBL* 46, 1927, 111-131.

Peake, A. S. *The Problem of Suffering in the Old Testament,* 1887; reprinted at London, the Epworth Press, 1946; 73-91.

Pfeiffer, R. H. "Wisdom and Vision in the OT." *ZATW* 52, 1934, 93-101.

_____. "The History, Religion and Literature of Israel. Research in the OT 1914-1925," *HThR* 27, 1934, 241-325, surtout pp. 286 and 319-321.

_____. *Introduction to the Old Testament.* London, New York: 1948.

Philonenko. M. "Le Testament de Job et les Therapeutes." *Semitica* 8, 1958, 51-53. "Le Testament de Job," in *Semitica*

18 (1968), 1-77.

Philp. H. L. *Jung and the Problem of Evil.* London: 1958, 133-171.

Pope, M. H. "The Word *s-h-th* in Job 9, 31." *JBL* 83, 1964, 269-278.

Pury, R. De. *Job ou l'homme revolte.* Geneve (Caheris du Renouveau), 1955.

Rankin, O. S. *Israel's Wisdom Literature, its bearing on the Theology and the History of Religion.* Edinburgh: T. & T. Clark, 1954.

Rendtorff, R. "El, Ba'al and Yahwe. Erwagungen zum Verhaltnis von kanaanaischer und israelitischer Religion." *ZATW* 78, 1966, 272-292.

Robertson, St. "The Nature of Religious Truth (Job 19, 26)." *ET* 39, 1927/28, 181-183.

Rohr Sauer, A. von. "Salvation by Grace: The Heart of Job's Theology," in Concordia Theological Monthly XXXVII/5, 1966, 259-270.

Rowley, H. H. "The Book of Job and its Meaning." *BJRL* 41, 1958, 167-207; reprinted in *From Moses to Qumran. Studies in the Old Testament.* London: Lutterworth Press, 1963, pp. 139-183.

Sanders, J. A. *Suffering as Divine Discipline in the Old Testament and Post-Biblical Judaism.* Colgate Rochester Divinity School Bulletin 28, 1955, 28-33.

Sanders, P. S. *Twentieth Century Interpretations of the Book of Job. A Collection of Critical Essays.* Englewood Cliffs, NJ: Prentice-Hall, 1968; abbreviation: TCI.

Sekine, M. "Theodicee dans l'Ancien Testament." *Orient* (Tokio), 1960, 23-24.

_____. "Schopfung und Erlosung im Buche Hiob; dans Von Ugari nach Qumran." *BZAW* 77, 1958, Berlin: A. Topelmann, pp. 213-223.

Sewall, R. B. *The Vision of Tragedy.* New Haven, 1959, Yale U. P. IX, 9-24.

Shapiro, D. S. "The Problem of Evil and the Book of Job." *Judaism* 5, 1956, 46-52.

610

Skehan, P. W. "Job 36, 16." *CBQ* 16, 1954, 295-301.

_____. "Job's Final Plea (Job 29-31) and the Lord's Reply." *Bibl* 45, 1964, 51-62.

_____. "Second Thoughts on Job 6, 16 and 6, 25," in *CBQ* 30, 1969, 210-212.

_____. " 'I Will Speak Up!' (Job 32); The Pit (Job 33)," in *CBQ* 30, 1969, 380-382.

Smid, T. D. "Some Bibliographical Observations on Calvin's Sermons sur le livre de Job." *Free University Quarterly* 1960, 51-56.

Snaith, N. H. *Notes on the Hebrew Text of Job 1-6.* London: The Epworth Press, 1945.

_____. *The Book of Job. Its Origin and Purpose.* Studies in Biblical Theology, Second Series, 11, SCM Press, London: 1969.

Steinmuller, J. E. *A Companion to Scriptures Studies,* II. New York, 1944, p. 167.

Stockhammer, M. *Das buch Hiob.* Versuch einer Theodizee. Wien, Europaischer Verlag, 1963.

_____. "The Righteousness of Job," in *Judaism* 7/1, 1958, 64-71.

Sutcliffe, E. F. "Notes on Job, Textual and Exegetical." *Bibl* 30, 1949, 66-90.

_____. "Further Notes on Job, Textual and Exegetical," *ib.* 31, 1950, 365-78.

Sutcliffe, E. F. *The Old Testament and the Future Life.* 2 ed., 1947.

_____. *Providence and Suffering in the Old and New Testament.* Oxford: 1955.

Taylor, W. S. "Theology and Therapy in Job." *Theology Today* (Princeton) 12, 1955/56, 451-463.

Terrien, S. T. "The Babylonian Dialogue on Theodicy and the Book of Job." *JBL* 63, 1944, p. vi.

_____. *Job: Poet of Existence.* Indianapolis: Bobbs Merrill Co., 1958.

_____. "Quelques remarques sur les affinites de Job avec le Deutero-Isaie." *VTS,* XV, 1965, 295-310.

Thomas, D. W. (See M. Noth). "Job XXXVII, 22" *JJS* 1, 1948, 116-7.

_____. "The Root '-d-' in Hebrew." *JTS* 36, 1935, 409-412.

_____. "The Interpretation of *bsod* in Job 29, 4." *JBL* 65, 1946, 63-66.

_____. "Note on lada'at in Job 37, 7." *JTS* (NS) 5, 1954, 56-57.

_____. "Job XL, 29b. Text and Translation." *VT* 14, 1964, 114-116.

Thompson, K. Jr. "Out of the Whirlwind. The Sense of Alienation in the Book of Job." *Interpreter* 14, 1960, 51-63.

Tillich, P. *The Courage to Be.* New Haven, 1952, 171ss.

Tsevat, M. "The Meaning of the Book of Job." *HUCA* 37, 1966, 73-106; see also, under the same title, an article in Fourth World Congress of Jewish Studies, Vol. I, Jerusalem, 1967, 177-180.

_____. "Hiob XI und die Sprache der Amarna-Briefe," *BiOr* 9, 1952, 162ss.

_____. *Job* 30, 17ss, Sefer Jobel S. K. Mirsky, New York, 1958.

Ulanov, B. *Job and His Comforters.* The Bridge 3, 1958, 234-268.

Vischer, W. *Hiob ein Zeuge Jesu Christi,* ZZ 11, 1933, 386-414 (6th edition: Zurich, Ev. Verlag Zollikon, 1947).

_____. *Valeur de l'Ancien Testament. Commentaire des livres de Job, Esther, Ecclesiaste, Second Isaie.* Geneve, Labor et Fies, 1958.

_____. *God's Truth and Man's Lie. A Study of the Message of the Book of Job.* Interpreter 15, 1961, 131-146.

Ward, W. B. *Out of the Whirlwind. Answers to the Problems of Suffering from the Book of Job.* Richmond: J. Knox Press, 1958.

Waterman, L. "Note on Job 19, 23-27: Job's Triumph of Faith." *JBL* 69, 1950, 379-380.

_____. "Note on Job 28, 4." *JBL* 71, 1952, 167-170.

Wedel, Th. O. "I Hate Myself." A Sermon, Job 7, 20, in *Interpretation* 5, 1951, 427-431.

Wilckens, U. Art. "Sophia, sophos, sophizo," in *TWNT* VII, 1962, 465-528 (except B, consecrated to the OT, and which is owing to George Fohrer, 476-496).

Williams, R. J. *Theodicy in the Ancient Near East.* Bulletin of the Canadian Society of Biblical Studies, tire a part, 1954 (20 p), or Canadian Journal of Theology, 1956, 14-26.

Wood, J. *Job and the Human Situation.* London: G. Bles, 1966.

_____. *The Idea of Life in the Book of Job.* "Transactions" published by the Oriental Society of the University of Glasgow, 18, 1959-60, 29-37. Leiden: Brill, 1961.

Zhitlowsky, C. *Job and Faust.* Translated with Introduction and Notes by P. Matenko. Leiden: Brill, 1966.

Zimmerli, W. "Zur Struktur der ATlichen Weisheit." *ZATW* 51, 1933, 177-204.

_____. *Der Mensch und seine Hoffnung in Alten Testament.* Gottingen, Vandenhoeck & Ruprecht, 1968.

Zink, J. K. "Impatient Job," *JBL* 84, 1965, 147-152; Uncleanness and Sin. a Study of Job XIV, 4 and Psalm LI, 7, in *VT*, 17 (1967), 354-361.

Goodheart, E. "Job and the Modern World," in *TCI* (cf. P. S. Sanders), 98-106.

Kissane, E. J. "The Metrical Structure of Job," in *TCI* (cf. P. S. Sanders), 78-85.

Lipinski, E. "Le juste souffrant," in *La Foi et le Temps* 1 (1968), 329-342.

MacKenzie, R. A. F. "Job," in *The Jerome Biblical Commentary,* ed. by R. E. Brown, J. A. Fitzmyer and R. E. Murphy. London: Geoffrey Chapman, 1968, I, 511-533.

Murray, G. "Prometheus and Job," in *TCI* (cf. P. S. Sanders), 56-65.

Toynbee, A. J. "Challenge and Response; The Mythological Clue," in *TCI* (cf. P. S. Sanders), 86-97.

INDEX OF NAMES

INDEX OF SUBJECTS

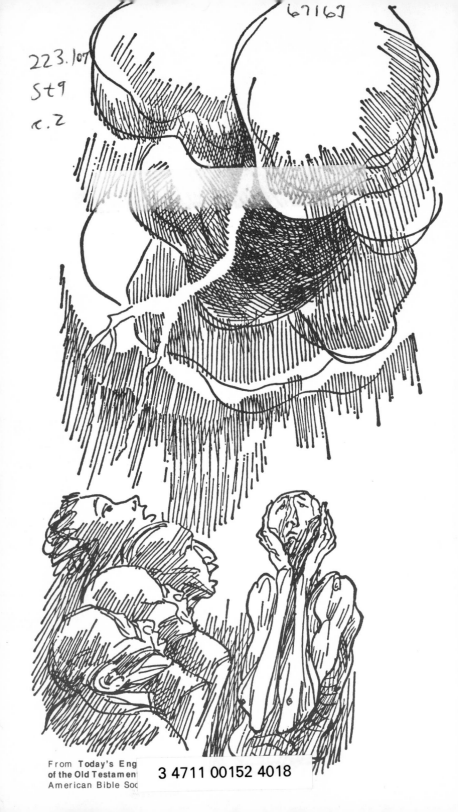

From **Today's Eng**
of the **Old Testam**en
American Bible Soc